NORTH AMERICA:
THE HISTORICAL GEOGRAPHY OF A CHANGING CONTINENT

NORTH AMERICA

The Historical Geography of

a Changing Continent

EDITED BY

ROBERT D. MITCHELL & PAUL A. GROVES

ROWMAN & LITTLEFIELD

PUBLISHERS

ROWMAN & LITTLEFIELD

Published in the United States of America in 1987
by Rowman & Littlefield, Publishers
(a division of Littlefield, Adams & Company)
81 Adams Drive, Totowa, New Jersey 07512

Library of Congress Cataloging-in-Publication Data

North America : the historical geography of a
  changing continent.

  Includes bibliographies and index.
  1. North America—Historical geography.
I. Mitchell, Robert D., 1940–   . II. Groves,
Paul A.
E41.N68 1987   911'.7   86-13918
ISBN 0-8476-7347-2
ISBN 0-8476-7549-1 (pbk.)

90 89 88 87
6 5 4 3 2 1
Printed in the United States of America

Contents

Tables

Figures

Preface

This volume is a response to a felt need in the discipline for an up-to-date, comprehensive treatment of the evolving geography of North America during the past four centuries. Americans have had no sequel to Ralph Brown's *Historical Geography of the United States* (1948), and the series of reprinted essays entitled *Geographic Perspectives on America's Past* (1979), edited by David Ward, is now out of print. Canadians have been served somewhat better by R. Cole Harris and John Warkentin's *Canada Before Confederation* (1974) and the historical sections in *Heartland and Hinterland: A Geography of Canada* (1982), edited by L.D. McCann. The need remains for a new synthesis of the entire continent that will reflect the research findings of the past forty years, which gap this book will fill.

This volume can be viewed as serving two purposes. First, the book can be used as a college text on the historical geography of North America. These essays have been designed for an upper division or beginning graduate student level and also for an interested lay audience. It seemed important to address not only students and professional colleagues, but also those outside the academic world who are equally fascinated with the landscapes and changes that have been wrought on this great continent. Therefore the essays contain neither elaborate, scholarly footnotes nor totally comprehensive reading lists. The readings were designed to provide basic materials that are reasonably accessible as well as informative. Second, and perhaps of more enduring significance, the volume can be viewed as a series of original, interpretive essays of broad spatial and temporal sweep that have no direct counterparts in the current literature. Not only have some topics and periods received no previous synthesis, but the interpretations and the illustrations (many of which are also original) present new ways of thinking about the North American past. Indeed, many of the contributors have discovered new research questions and uncovered significant research gaps in the process of writing their chapters.

North America here is defined as comprising the United States and Canada, but the definition is sufficiently flexible to accommodate the changing geography of the continent over time. Thus, Mexico and the Caribbean-West Indies region, and their changing relationships with the United States and Canada, are particularly noted. Indeed, the current political boundaries between the United States and both Canada and Mexico remain fluid and solid at the same time, depending on one's perspective.

The book is organized chronologically, although not according to strict conventional periodicity. After a brief introduction to the development of historical geography in North America and to the themes around which the entire volume has been written, the individual presentations are arranged under four headings. Part II, Colonization, discusses the initial phases of European intervention and regional division on the continent prior to American independence. Part III, Expansion, is concerned with the dramatic interior penetrations of the 19th century and the regional consequences of the resultant settlement prior to the tumultuous 1860s, which ultimately reunified America after a civil war and finally unified Canada through confederation. Part IV, Consolidation, addresses the processes of territorial and economic integration within the two nations between the 1860s and approximately 1920, particularly those associated with European immigration, urbanization, industrialization, and transport innovations. The final section, Part V, Reorganization, deals with the continent in the 20th century and particularly since the 1920s, as a new geography of redistribution and balance has emerged both within and between the two nations of North America.

This volume has been a truly concerted effort. The many authors, each a specialist in his field, helped contribute to the unusual synergism produced by so many stimulating people working toward the same goal. Donald Meinig, to our misfortune, was too far along with his own grand interpretation of America to participate. Coordinating the efforts of 17 scholars was a complex task, but one that has been facilitated by the tremendous support of the Geography Department at the University of Maryland, College Park. We extend our thanks to Ken Corey, Chairman of the Department of Geography, who coordinated relief efforts on our behalf when we most needed them, and to Doris Olds, who arranged for special staff support during an extremely busy summer. We also acknowledge the help of Ron Linton, Director of Cartographic Services, and Joel Miller, former acting director, in mustering the cartographic forces required for our own chapters and for perpetual last-minute emergencies. Our greatest departmental thanks must go, however, to Pat Leedham, whose efforts to put 18 chapters on the word processor in such a short time were truly extraordinary, to Dorie Taylor, who carefully corrected the final manuscript, and to Guinn Cooper, who responded to our seemingly endless demands for illustrations with beautifully crafted maps. Indeed, we thank all the cartographers who participated, in particular Wayne Banon, for their contributions to the book.

We would also like to extend special thanks to our editors, Paul Lee, who has nurtured this project since its inception and whose immense patience and constructive criticism helped to bring it to final fruition, and to Janet Johnston, who gave the final manuscript a careful and sensitive reading. And, finally, we extend our most heartful thanks, in ways that only they will understand, to our wives, Nava and Phyllis, who can now rest assured that their husbands have returned to the land of the living.

Robert D. Mitchell
Paul A. Groves

PART I

INTRODUCTION

The Muses care so little for geography.

Oscar Wilde, *Sententiae*

We shall not get far if we limit ourselves in any way as to human time in our studies. Either we must admit the whole span of man's existence or abandon the expectation of major results from human geography. Either we must produce or warm over what others have prepared. I see no alternative. From all the earth in all the time of human existence, we build a retrospective science, which out of this experience acquires an ability to look ahead.

Carl O. Sauer, "Foreword to Historical Geography"

The old past is dying, its force weakening, and so it should. Indeed [we] should speed it on its way, for it was compounded by bigotry, of national vanity, of class domination . . . May history step into its shoes, help to sustain man's confidence in his destiny, and create for us a new past, as exact as we can make it, that will help us achieve our identity.

J.H. Plumb, *The Death of the Past*

The North American Past:
Retrospect and Prospect

ROBERT D. MITCHELL

University of Maryland, College Park

This book is about a place that was not sup-posed to exist. Fifteenth-century European views of the world had inherited from Ptolemy and the ancient geographers the idea that the earth as the home of mankind comprised the three continents of Europe, Africa, and Asia; that the world was latitudinally symmetrical (comprising a torrid zone bordered succes-sively by temperate and frigid zones); and that it was occupied by many strange peoples (mostly uncivilized because they lacked Chris-tianity and urban life). The landscapes and societies Columbus encountered in the Carib-bean in October 1492 hardly matched previ-ously recorded descriptions of Japan and east-ern China. Yet it is doubtful that Columbus fully appreciated his discovery of a world that was not simply another appendage of Asia.

It did become clear, however, as the delinea-tion of a new continental mass took shape during the 16th century, that the Spaniards who followed Columbus had identified the central and southern parts of their newly claimed territory as being of most interest to them. The area that has become known as North America was considered to be of little consequence. It presented the appearance of a sparsely populated territory occupied by native societies that had created none of the grandeur and offered none of the resource potential of the Aztec-Maya and the Incas. Yet during the last 400 years this least promising part of the New World has been transformed, in the cul-ture-bound terms of the development special-ist, from one of the world's most backward areas into its most advanced: a dynamic world comprising two vast political units, Canada and the United States, that have created the earth's most materially successful post-industrial soci-eties of some 265 million inhabitants. The task of the historical geographers in this book is to explore and to understand this remarkable cre-ation.

THE NORTH AMERICAN PAST:
RETROSPECT

"Past" and "present" are simplified notions of our conceptions of time. If the past is indeed prologue to the present, the present is contin-ually reshaping the past as new ideas, ap-proaches, and information allow us to produce an improved retrieval of previous human con-ditions. Time, therefore, is the exclusive do-main of no single set of practitioners, although in the Western world historians generally have been viewed as the special guardians of the human past. Earth-space, similarly, is a con-cept fundamental to many organized branches of endeavor. The geographer's principal claim to this domain rests on elucidating the relation-ships that exist between people and place as they are reflected in locational, environmental, distributional, and regional expressions. The primary concern of the historical geographer is to study how and why these expressions per-sist and change in place and over space through time. The hope is to create a more historically informed human geography, a more accurate context against which to gauge the complex content of the present.

Retrieving the past, however, is an exceed-ingly difficult task and one that, even in its most detailed form, can hope to reconstruct only a small fraction of human actions and events. Retrieving the past geographically has been the task of a mere handful of geographers at any given time, and they have always been greatly outnumbered by historians. Historical geography until very recently, therefore, was influenced enormously by a few unusually creative individuals who have had distinctive ideas about the uses of the past.

Early Uses of the Past

The professionalization of knowledge in a North American context began during the last third of the 19th century as the academic world reorganized its structure and its curricula. This reorganization occurred within the framework of a post-Darwinian world dominated by the perspective of the natural sciences and by the presumed closing of the American settlement frontier. In history, the first generation of American professional historians began to replace 19th-century views of the past as the exemplification of Western ideas of progress with approaches that rested on more empirical and systematic foundations. Shortly thereafter, a group of Canadian historians, known as the Laurentian School because of their interests in the impact of land and landscape on human settlement, began to redefine the Canadian past.

Geographers, trained almost exclusively in the natural sciences, had a different use for the past. Their principal concern was to elucidate what they believed to be the immutable relationship that existed between humanity and the biophysical environment. The relationship for them was primarily one of the direct, or almost direct, control of this environment on human actions and on human distributions, and the limitations thus placed upon human behavior. It seemed logical to them to look for these environmental forces in the past as well as in the present. The American past became the vehicle for testing their ideas rather than a subject of study in its own right. Despite some common concerns in the everyday affairs of society, the association between geographers and historians remained superficial. Such ideas as the presumed causal connection between the siting of major Atlantic seaboard cities (Philadelphia, Baltimore, Washington, and Richmond, for example) and the location of falls and rapids on major eastward-flowing rivers, and the seemingly impenetrable barrier of the Appalachians that "forced" late-colonial settlements to remain east of the mountains, were promulgated in works, like Ellen C. Semple's *American History and Its Geographic Conditions* (1903), that were influenced by current geographical thought in Europe. Not only were the assumptions of such so-called "environmental determinists" highly questionable from a scientific point of view, they also approached the past in terms of the physical setting to human activities, rather than from the viewpoint of the human participants themselves, and they used

as evidence the secondary sources of historians and others, rather than the primary sources generated by past societies. It is understandable, therefore, that most historians dismissed their conclusions as being simplistic, extreme, and ultimately ahistorical.

Neither Semple (1863–1932) nor her contemporaries were determinists in the strictest sense. That such a label can prove somewhat misleading over time may be observed in the research and teaching of Harlan H. Barrows at the University of Chicago, in one of the first geography departments in North America. Barrows (1877–1960) began in the early Semple mold, gradually toned down environmental "controls" to "influences," and was advocating geography as human ecology by the early 1920s. Nevertheless, the basic assumptions of such an approach increasingly were called into question by the first generation of geographers not trained solely in the natural sciences.

Alternative Uses of the Past

The most direct challenge to the deterministic perspective came from the young Carl Sauer at the University of California at Berkeley during the early 1920s. He excited his colleagues with the suggestion that human geography should focus not on the presumed effects of the natural setting, but on the processes whereby human beings had altered patterns of land use and distributions of living forms on the earth's surface (an approach he had been introduced to in Germany). Sauer's particular contribution was to present the subject as the impact of culture on nature and to examine how "natural landscapes" were transformed into "cultural landscapes." Culture, in Sauer's view, was as much a genetic or historical concept as a functional one. Human geography was thus historical geography writ large, because one needed to understand how societies had created different cultural patterns from place to place in terms of their origins, evolution, and spread.

Sauer (1889–1975) influenced many of his 37 doctoral students as well as other contemporaries, during a period of more than fifty years of teaching and research, to approach the past as a fertile field for studying culture history. New concepts were introduced to the geographer's repertoire—culture traits and complexes, diffusion, cultural landscape, and culture area, for example—and many studies were undertaken of tracing genetic themes (such as the origins and spread of cultures, plant and animal introductions to new environments, and the destruction of natural habitats) over long periods of time. Studies grounded in field-work and in prehistory were encouraged: fire as a tool in landscape change, the origins of agriculture in the New World, and the diffusion of American Indian traits. The breadth of Sauer's own interests can be appreciated in two collections of essays, *Land and Life* (1963) and *Selected Essays 1963–1975* (1981). Some of his hypotheses were almost impossible to verify, and he and his students often had more in common with the anthropologist and the ar-cheologist than with the historian. Their work was distinctively genetic, empirical, diffusion-ist, materialist (tangible culture traits), and dia-chronic (time viewed "vertically" rather than as "horizontal" cross-sections), and in many re-spects ran counter to what was later to become a more accepted historical geography firmly based on the written historical record.

Despite Sauer's enormous influence, and in-deed the modifications he made in his own interests and ideas during the last 15 years of his life, the culture history approach came in for increasing criticism after the 1950s. It was based on historicism (phenomena to be com-prehended only through tracing their origins and development); it was non-theoretical and non-comparative; it was overly diffusionist (to the relative exclusion of other processes); and it was focused on pre-industrial societies (to the neglect of urban-industrial processes and phe-nomena). But the most penetrating criticsm has been that it was overly materialist and ne-glected "the inner workings of culture," the formation of the habits, beliefs, attitudes, val-ues, and institutions that existed behind the practices, the actions, and the phenomena themselves. The concept of the cultural land-scape, for example, was ambiguous because it involved not only the content in the landscape, but also the perception of that content. In the past few years, however, as historians in partic-ular have penetrated deeper into the North American past, there has been renewed inter-est in Sauer's ideas about European exploration and colonization, culture contact, and habitat modification, as he articulated them in his later studies.

At least three other approaches to the past that were contemporaneous with Sauer's views also influenced how geographers dealt with time and place: Derwent Whittlesey's refine-ment of the concept of sequent occupance; John K. Wright's mapping interests and advocacy of historical geosophy; and Ralph H. Brown's concern with reconstructing past geographies.

The notion of occupance or settlement of an area has been a long-standing theme in human geography. Derwent Whittlesey (1890–1956), trained in history and geography, who taught for most of his career at Harvard University, had interests in regional and political geogra-phy as well as in historical studies. What in-trigued him most by the late 1920s and early 1930s was the study of "chronology in place" rather than the geography of past times; that is, the idea of the sequential stages of occupance that he believed had occurred in all places over time. American geography had entered a pe-riod dominated by economic and regional stud-ies, and Whittlesey's refinement of the sequent occupance concept by emphasizing place, land use, and economic activities made it acceptable to many geographers interested in regional description and classification. Geographers added an "historical" dimension to what were primarily regional studies. Every settled area in North America, it was assumed, had under-gone a series of sequential landscape changes as different groups of people at progressively more complex stages of development had occu-pied it. The geographer's task was to identify, describe, and reconstruct these stages by the landscape features that typified each stage at particular cross-sections in time. California, for example, could be examined in terms of its Indian, Spanish-Mexican, or early and later American stages of occupance, each with its own distinctive human patterns.

When such general ideas were put into prac-tice, however, several problems arose. Most damaging was the fact that neither the concept of areal or regional variation nor that of change through time was dealt with adequately. It became apparent that the sequent occupance concept was best suited to areas where the basic settlement features had persisted over substantial periods of time. Where change was rapid, problems of transition between, and overlapping of, stages occurred, and little al-lowance was made for differential rates of change of specific phenomena such as population, land use, and settlement. Few studies, moreover, paid much attention to making connections between stages; process was believed to be implicit in stage; and factors producing change between each cross-sectional reconstruction were generally inferred rather than analyzed. Internal regional differences were also slighted because the concept emphasized the dominant landscape elements that gave character to an area, rather than how phenomena varied from place to place within the area. Each area delimited was viewed discretely without reference to other areas, and changes induced from outside the area tended to be regarded as aberrations.

Despite further experimentation and modification during the 1930s and early 1940s, the concept proved to be an oversimplification of both temporal change and areal variation. Yet it continued to appear in unpublished theses well into the 1960s. One modification that did have short-term significance was the idea of "relict features" of previous occupance stages surviving in later landscapes. The method employed here was retrospective; that is, working backward in time and tracing these elements to their historical contexts. It was seldom easy to identify specific phenomena with specific contexts, and it was also clear that the past influenced its future in more important ways than by leaving material residues. Further experimentation with the whole idea ended in the 1950s.

John K. Wright's contributions were of a more diffuse character. Trained in both geography and history, Wright (1891–1969) spent most of his career on the staff of the American Geographical Society in New York and thus had few opportunities to train students. He made three enduring contributions to the understanding of the North American past. First, he became involved in editing the society's publications, one of which was the historian C.O. Paullin's massive *Atlas of the Historical Geography of the United States* (1932), a collection of maps depicting the history of the United States and arranged in episodic cross-sections. Although the work is now much dated, the sections dealing with the 19th century have yet to be superseded. Wright's three-year involvement with this project has been acknowledged in the profession by the work being referred to simply as "the Paullin and Wright" atlas. Sec-

ond, Wright was one of the first geographers to advocate the importance of studying the perceptions and worldviews that societies entertained about peoples and places in the past— "human nature in geography," as it came to be identified. His views of geography as a subjective, humanistic discipline were not much heeded at the time and were overshadowed by the views of Sauer and his students. Not until the more sympathetic environment of the 1960s was the prescience of Wright's suggestions appreciated. Third, Wright made a plea for a fusion of historical geography and the history of geography, a kind of historical "geosophy," as he termed it. For Wright the link between the two endeavors was exploration and the growth of geographical knowledge and ideas through time, because they again involved "terrae incognitae: the place of imagination in geography"—the context within which all geographical study should be undertaken.

Between the early 1930s and the 1950s geography in North America became identified increasingly with regional, functional, and morphological studies that had a distinct predilection for field-oriented and applied techniques grounded firmly in the present. The distinction between geography and history was clear. Geography was a discipline concerned with identifying the areal association and differentiation of phenomena distributed over the earth's surface (chorology). History was a discipline that dealt exclusively with the past (chronology). Studying a past period as geography was a permissible if rather odd practice, despite the historical tradition within the discipline, but one that had little substantive contribution to make to geography as a whole. It was in this atmosphere that Ralph H. Brown worked to put the study of the North American past on a sounder historiographic basis.

Trained as an economic and regional geographer, Brown (1898–1948) began his historical research at the University of Minnesota where, because of the absence of an organized graduate program during his tenure, he had no students to continue his work directly. His early studies during the late 1920s and early 1930s were characterized by the use of the sequent occupance concept and the employment of historical maps in conducting regional studies of Colorado and adjacent areas of the Great Plains. By the mid-1930s, however, he had shifted his interests to the eastern seaboard and to the use of early maps in clarifying the area's settlement history. Yet a visit to a variety of libraries and repositories along the east coast convinced him that insufficient primary data were available to reconstruct the geography of early America until after 1790 (Herman Friis was to prove him wrong by publishing his meticulously constructed monograph, *A Series of Population Maps of the Colonies and the United States, 1625–1790*, in 1940). Instead, Brown examined the materials available for the 1790–1810 period and decided to write a geographical description of the seaboard as it might have appeared to a Philadelphia geographer in 1810. He published the study in 1943 as *Mirror for Americans: Likeness of the Eastern Seaboard, 1810*. Methodologically, the work represented something of a dead end: it dealt with only a brief cross-section in time; it was highly imaginary; and it used only sources available before 1810. Literally, however, it has become a geographical classic: independently Brown had taken Wright's suggestion for the use of imagination in geography to its logical conclusion; he had made extensive use of primary source materials; and he has given us a vivid portrait of a place in time.

The problem remained, however, for geographers to deal adequately with examining, in a dynamic manner, changes within and between places through time. Brown addressed this issue directly in his last major work, *Historical Geography of the United States*, published in 1948 shortly after his death. It was the first attempt to provide a comprehensive reconstruction of the geography of the United States in past times using both secondary and primary sources. Brown divided his text into six parts: the colonization period; the Atlantic seaboard at the opening of the 19th century; the Ohio River and the lower Great Lakes region to 1830; the new Northwest, 1820–1870; the Great Plains and bordering regions to 1870; and the area from the Rocky Mountains to the Pacific Coast to 1870. He began by reminding the reader, as he had done in *Mirror for Americans*, that people have always been "influenced as much by beliefs as by facts." By using contemporary eyewitness accounts and early maps within the context of more general narrative description, Brown believed that such past perceptions could be identified. He created an elaborate series of regional geographies, paying close attention to diversity within and between areas as he progressed westward across the country. The work was clearly more selective than comprehensive; more than one-third of the space is devoted to the early eastern seaboard, and there is little reference to the seaboard, the South, or the Middle West after the early 19th century. The study, moreover, ends in the last quarter of that century, perhaps reflecting less the possibility that Brown ran out of time than his apparent conviction that there were two "pasts": past geographies that could be reconstructed by the methods of historical geography and a more recent antecedent past that could be incorporated in the geography of the present.

Revised Uses of the Past

Ralph Brown's contributions to the understanding of the North American past on its own terms might have been pushed aside eventually by the increasing ahistorical bias of the discipline if one of his younger contemporaries, a Canadian named Andrew H. Clark, had not taken the reins and proceeded aggressively during the 1950s and 1960s to make a powerful case for historical studies in geography. Exposed to training in mathematics, economic history, and geography at the University of Toronto before completing his doctorate under Sauer at Berkeley in 1944, Clark (1911–75) established at the University of Wisconsin the foundations of an historical geography in North America not only as a perspective in geography, but as a recognizable subfield with its own distinctive procedures and scholarly contributions.

In 1954, Clark authored a committee report on historical geography as part of a larger inventory of geography during the first half of the 20th century. The report was more of a plea for an historical geography to be than a survey of a proud lineage of past achievements. Clark could point only to the work of Brown, Wright, himself, a few others and, with some ambivalence, that of Sauer and his students as elements on which to build a revised and improved use of the past. Fifteen years later, in 1969, Cole Harris, one of Clark's students, made a similar plea for Canada. Asked to survey the Canadian scene, Harris bemoaned the fact that little substantive research had been done since the 1930s and that most of it was hidden in unpublished theses. With few achievements to discuss, he suggested the outlines of a research program that could rejuvenate historical geography in the future. When Clark again reviewed the progress in historical geography throughout North America three years later in 1972, the tone of his presentation was more confident. Not only could he point to a proliferation of new studies of the past, but he could also present the published achievements of many of his 19 doctoral students.

The transformation that occurred in the renewed interest in the North American past between the early 1950s and the early 1970s in part can be attributed to Clark's leadership in teaching and research. His enduring contribution was to build upon Brown's historiographic predilections and to impart an appreciation of high-quality scholarship, of thorough empirical research, of the importance of both archival and field methods, of current historiographic issues and, above all, of the value of geography. Clark had already been well trained in historical methods before going to Berkeley and was thus less influenced by some of Sauer's cultural history ideas than were his contemporaries. He proceeded to create one of the first coherent programs of publishable work in historical geography. He was to devote most of his own research to elucidating the geographical outcomes of European colonization in maritime Canada. In 1960 he argued before an audience of economic historians for greater cooperation between the two subdisciplines and for historians to recognize the importance of "geographical change through time," a concept he defined generally as the study of continually changing geographies revealed through changing patterns and relationships between phenomena in and through areas. He made a more explicit statement on how this was to be achieved than had been done earlier: by examining the locational aspects of change itself (the mapping of change); by measuring rates of change; by identifying the distribution of individually significant phenomenon; by appreciating the multiple functions of phenomena; and by identifying the important interactive processes involved. This statement of his approach to the past was designed to go beyond previously stated views of historical geography as the reconstruction of past geographies, whether as the tracing of genetic cultural themes, temporal cross-sections, or the geography of a past period. The emphasis needed to be placed on a more analytical approach to geographical change itself.

This was an ambitious program indeed and one that Clark himself could not always live up to, because it forced him out of the regional historical-geographical framework that continued to be his basic approach to the past. This can be seen in his two books on Canada. In *Three Centuries and the Island* (1959), Prince Edward Island was the laboratory for a very intensive study of geographical change, one that traced patterns of rural settlement and land use through five successive eras by means of a series of temporal cross-sections and the use of 155 maps of distributions and areal characteristics. He thus had addressed already his suggestions of identifying the locational aspects of change, the distribution of individual phenomena, and trying to measure change. His *Acadia: The Geography of Nova Scotia to 1760* (1968) also was an intensive case study, but its intent was to provide a sequential presentation of development over a 125-year period and to integrate a systematic treatment of relevant topics into the time frame. The focus was again on colonization and on the formation of rural localities in new environments, with considerable attention devoted to the statistical presentation of change, but with much less attention this time to measuring change through the comparative mapping of distributions at selected time periods. In a concluding section Clark attempted to view Nova Scotia within the larger historiography of Canada by evaluating the region with reference to the well-established frontier and metropolitan-dominance interpretations of Canadian development. The published result was recognized as a prize-winning performance by Canadian historians.

Yet major changes had occurred in geography in North America during the 1960s to make the *Acadia* study quite controversial. The basically empiricist world of pre-1960 geography had come under mounting criticism as the discipline was influenced increasingly by the emerging social sciences. A distinct shift was in progress toward the formation of a more analytical and systematic geography more concerned with hypothesis formulation, generalization, and theory testing. Historical geography was not immune to such changes, and Clark's work came in for criticism because it did not demonstrate these desired qualities. A younger generation of geographers, less exposed to the regional and cultural traditions of human geography but interested in historical problems, argued that Clark's work had avoided explicit generalization and had remained essentially inductive. For Clark, generalization was an end in itself and not to be indulged in lightly; rather, synthesis was the highest goal to which a geographer could aspire after careful compilation of conclusions derived from a number of case studies. More pointed was the argument that Clark had been unable to fill his prescription for confronting geographical change. What he had done was to quantify changes and modifications in certain features through maps and, by means of sequential comparisons, to identify the periodic results of change. But he had not really addressed the dynamics of change through time, because he had placed little emphasis on the processes themselves. As Donald Meinig has put it, Clark tended to be more interested in area than in process, in changing geographies than in geographical change. But he had helped to create a vigorous historical geography in North America and to provide a framework for the debate that was to ensue among young historical geographers, many of whom were of Canadian or British origin.

THE NORTH AMERICAN PAST: PROSPECT

The magnitude of change that has occurred in historical geography in North America during the last 10 to 15 years has been such that one might have difficulty relating its genealogy to its current status and practice. Some observers have labeled the results as a "new" historical geography fundamentally different in philosophy and practice from previous efforts. The trends, however, are often unclear, frequently contradictory, and subject to various interpretations. The aggregate changes, for example, are confusing. The number of professional geographers with avowed interests in the subject has increased substantially, especially in Canada; the number of publications continues to proliferate; and in 1975 the first international journal devoted solely to the subject, the *Journal of Historical Geography*, appeared as a forum for scholarly communication. Yet the broader

context within which geographical studies of the past are now undertaken has begun to challenge this progress. Geography and history have experienced considerable philosophical and methodological changes in recent years and have emerged in the 1980s as more analytical and pluralistic disciplines. Current trends in geography, for example, are toward increasing specialization, increased cross-disciplinary communication, and greater emphasis on technical applications and policy implications.

Historical geographers have derived much from these trends: trading ideas, concepts, and comparative themes with other disciplines; making wider use of statistical methods; developing, applying, and testing generalizations; and exploiting more explicit behavioral approaches to the past. But, at the same time, they have acquired a status that is marginal to the contemporary scientific and ahistorical character of geography, and they have been confronted with a larger cadre of historians who have assimilated geographical ideas and techniques and applied them to a broad range of problems, such as man-environment relations and landscape interpretation, long assumed to be the geographer's domain.

APPROACHES AND OBJECTIVES

Historical geographers in North America rarely have devoted as much time as their western European (especially British) counterparts to philosophical discourse. Assumptions about objectives generally have been implicit rather than explicit, and most of the "founding fathers" avoided making overt philosophical or methodological statements. But recent trends in history and the social sciences have forced a greater awareness of the need to examine basic assumptions underlying historical research in geography. Philosophy is important because it guides inquiry. How we approach the past will help us to determine whether and how we choose significant topics, frame insightful questions, identify current research problems or issues, formulate sound methodological procedures, identify relevant sources, and choose appropriate techniques. In general, most historical geographers would agree that the history of a place or of a population is embedded in its geography; that spatial structures and patterns are both a condition of and a result of social and biophysical situations; and that the geography of change needs to be viewed in terms of both processes and effects. These assumptions underly the geographical synthesis of North America that the essays in this book represent.

Yet the debate that ensued in North America during the 1970s over alternative approaches to the past originally was framed within the context of the opposing goals of synthesis and theory. Concepts rather than specific personnel became the driving force for progress in the discipline. Synthesis involved a humanistic, even particularistic, perspective that focused on comprehending the special character of places, regions, and landscapes as they persisted and changed in past periods. Theory involved the application of deductive models of geographical patterns to the past to identify process laws that provided explanations of the changing distribution of phenomena that were still present in the contemporary world. Regional historical geography, with its long lineage, seemed to contrast with a retrospective, theoretical geography that used the past for more current objectives. Later participants tended to exaggerate these distinctions and to identify a dichotomy between the particular interests of more "traditional" historical geographers, which contained references to the distinctiveness and differentiation of places that were not capable of scientific testing, and the insights to be gained from "new" generic approaches, which involved the application of current principles and generalizations to examining everything from past geographical regularities to the perceptions of past landscapes. In this latter view, a genealogy of geographical uses of the past as traced earlier in this chapter was irrelevant or, if addressed, was employed as a purgative to indicate a habit of mind that should no longer exist.

The intellectual tension created was tempered by two factors that resulted in a reframing of positions by the early 1980s. First, it had become clear that geographical theory could not be separated from social theory. Attempts to comprehend spatial patterns as attributes of place proved inadequate because spatial arrangement and areal variation were not independent variables; they could not be explained in terms of their own formation independent of a cultural and social context. Second, contemporary theories of social behavior produced far from satisfactory explanations of current societies, thus making moot their wholesale application to past circumstances. If there were indeed historical regularities in patterns of behavior, there had also been fundamental changes. Defining the specific locational and environmental dimensions of this behavior and explaining long-term, secular changes in society and economy remained in their infancy. Distinctions between the range of perspectives on the past tended to be overdrawn, even while generalization had become a widely accepted goal throughout all branches of the discipline. Geographers interested in the past tend to generate historiographic generalities that are associated with interpreting and comparing studies within an increasing pool of knowledge about related places. Geographers more concerned with the contemporary world use concepts and principles from modern human geography and apply them to past situations to determine their general applicability. And those who profess interest in long-run, developmental perspectives often employ reconstructions of past geographies as part of their analysis. The distinctions between "old" and "new" approaches to the past appeared less and less clear; all studies that involved an historical dimension could benefit from these philosophical and methodological exchanges.

Nevertheless, a contrast does remain between studies that use the past as the distinctive focus to be examined on its own terms, and those that use the past selectively to explore the historical validity of current theories of human behavior. The former position maintains that one cannot comprehend the present without comprehending the past, and that the applicability of current ideas needs to be evaluated for particular historical contexts. The latter position is more concerned with evaluating the universality of current processes in the past without necessary reference to the contextual framework within which the processes operate. The "historical" position is likely to produce a discussion of urban growth, for example, that takes note of current social and economic theory and adapts it discriminately to illuminate and explain the growth of a place or set of places during a particular period. The more "contemporary" approach to urban growth in the past would be to view it as a general process fully comprehensible in terms of current social and economic theory and needing few adjustments for particular places or periods.

METHODOLOGICAL TRENDS

Philosophy and methodology scarcely can be separated. The debates of the last fifteen years have both created and been shaped by the increasing range and variety of our questions about the past. Among historical geographers in North America, methodological issues continue to generate more discussion than ideological issues. We operate differently today than we did before the early 1970s. First, we pay more attention to measuring and generalizing the geography of change itself. Second, we have humanized the past by incorporating social processes of behavior more firmly into our work. And third, we have redressed the topical imbalance in earlier studies by paying more attention to urban and industrial patterns. These trends, in turn, have forced us to rethink our ideas of time and periodicity, the scales at which we operate, the techniques we can use, and the sources we deem important.

Analyzing the Geography of Change

The fact that we can now approach the past more systematically and more analytically is the result primarily of expanding and reframing the line of questioning about change that Sauer and Clark began over a quarter of a century ago. First, we need to ask about origins—when and where a particular process or set of events began. We can then define the start of an occurrence and locate the appearance of phenomena. Second, we ask about sequence—what followed what in time and how this is related to the distribution of the phenomena. Third is the question of temporal and spatial structure—the order of the occurrence and distribution, and why the change happened in the sequence that it did. Fourth is the matter of timing—why things happened when and where they did and not in some other fashion. The last is a particularly important question because it helps us not only to identify the factors producing change (the necessary conditions), but also to determine the minimum combination of these factors that might account for change (the sufficient conditions). Fifth, we must ask about duration and

rate—how long the sequence lasted, how extensive the distribution became, and whether different elements changed at different rates. And, finally, we may need to address the question of magnitude or scope—whether the change occurred within a temporal and spatial system as a matter of degree (evolutionary or developmental), or instead involved a change in the entire system as a matter of kind (transformational or revolutionary). The initial colonization of North America by Europeans fits into the latter category, while later changes generally are interpreted within the former.

Historical geographers prior to the late 1960s, insofar as they studied processes in the past, largely focused on what they regarded as factors that would account for spatial patterns or regional distinctiveness without direct reference to behavioral considerations. We saw earlier how cultural geographers were being taken to task by the mid-1960s for failing to incorporate the deeper, mental aspects of culturally informed behavior into their studies. But when the change came in historical geography, it was less influenced by culture theory, which remains weakly developed, than by social and economic theory. We can demonstrate this with two examples: the revised synthesis of American cultural and social origins, and the rise of urban historical geography.

American Origins

The study of American origins and American regionalism is epitomized by the research contributions of Donald Meinig. Although Meinig, who received his graduate training at the University of Washington and who has spent most of his career at Syracuse University, has cut an independent path through the North American past, his approach effectively integrates the traditions of Sauer, Brown, and Clark. Meinig's interest in origins began, after a brief examination of the colonial era thirty years ago, with a study of the trans-Mississippi West. His research focused on processes of settlement and regional formation on a broad scale. His interpretations are characterized by a special interest in the creation of cultural regions and cultural landscapes, portrayed with a felicity of style and cartographic exposition seldom matched by his peers.

His study of the Mormon cultural region (1965) attempted to elucidate the origins and spread of one of America's most distinctive cultural groups from their hearth area of the Great Salt Lake basin in Utah. This was followed by *The Great Columbia Plain* (1968), an historical regional geography of the Palouse area of the Pacific Northwest between 1805 and 1910, which remains thus far his most substantive contribution to understanding the shaping of North America. This rich and massive study of the settlement and resource development of what was to become one of the continent's principal wheat-producing areas combined Sauer's emphasis on cultural origins and diffusion with the regional historical concerns of both Brown and Clark, the field orientation of Sauer, and the primary source concerns of Clark. "The distinguishing mark of historical geography," Meinig wrote, "is its emphasis upon places rather than persons"—a position that he has maintained ever since. Meinig also turned his attention to the Southwest, which resulted in *Imperial Texas* (1969), an extended essay on the evolution of the state's cultural distinctiveness, and *Southwest: Three Peoples in Geographical Change 1600–1970* (1971), which he described as "a coherent picture of regional change" from the beginning of Spanish contact until the present. He later synthesized his ideas on the geographical emergence of the trans-Mississippi West in an essay entitled "American Wests: Preface to a Geographical Interpretation" (1972). Employing themes of population, culture, political organization, and interregional integration, Meinig considered his perspective and methodology applicable, with modification, to other areas of colonization.

When other geographers applied this approach to the origins and development of the American East, however, they found, as Wilbur Zelinsky did, that "the cultural gradients tend to be much steeper and the boundaries between regions more distinct than is true for the remainder of the continent. There is greater variety within a narrower range of space." Meinig himself was no stranger to America's colonial origins. He had contributed a sketch of the early American colonies in 1958 and chapters on the historical geography of New York State in a book on regional geography in 1966. And, in 1978, he restated his research philosophy before the American Historical Association. Geographers needed to focus on two issues: culture hearths, which deal with why and where major cultural patterns and movements

originate, and spatial diffusion, which is concerned with how these patterns and movements spread to other peoples and places. Some scholars have continued the tradition of viewing American colonial origins in terms of culture hearths, spatial diffusion, and enduring cultural pluralism. But this approach has come under increasing criticism in recent years on the grounds that the scale of analysis is too broad, the attention to primary documentation too limited, the evidence from surviving cultural traits and landscape relics too inconclusive, and the treatment of economic processes too simplistic.

When migration and dispersion are viewed in a more analytical fashion as a series of "creative interactions" in which settlers were faced with a number of functional alternatives, an alternative approach can be followed. The point of departure for exploring colonial origins need not be western Europe, but rather along the Atlantic seaboard, where the initial encounters with a new world took place. What settlement and social characteristics actually emerged there can then provide clues for further enquiry. Who actually came, and precisely how and where did they settle?

Evidence from shipping records, as well as from county and parish records, has revealed that transatlantic migration was a more selective process than formerly recognized. Many emigrants had been mobile geographically in their home territories prior to emigration to America, making it difficult to determine their local cultural "source areas." Cultural transfer was associated also with the social context of settlement. The distinctiveness of early New England, for example, derived not only from the fact that most early settlers were "Puritans," but also because it was settled predominantly by families who had been formed long before emigration. Thus the creation of new, cohesive communities was more regular and continuous in New England than in the Chesapeake tidewater, where settlement and societal characteristics were dominated by commercial interests, high immigration rates of single, male indentured servants, and a slower process of societal formation. Moreover, the institution of slavery was not integrated into this Chesapeake system until 70 years after initial settlement, which contradicts the notion of some simultaneously forming "hearth" process.

An examination of the pioneering process at

local county and township levels has revealed a more drastic cultural simplification than previous scholars had imagined. Institutional settings were pared initially to their bare essentials in the New World. Land was abundant and relatively easily acquired, resulting in widespread landownership, regardless of regional location. Both labor and capital were in short supply. While fixed capital emerged from the creation of productive farms, and liquid capital appeared (theoretically) as surplus commodities were sold, labor shortages were endemic. The high costs of labor helped to create a variety of labor institutions to complement family labor: indentured servitude, periodic contractual wage labor, and eventual hereditary slavery. The complex interdigitation of free and slave labor revealed intricate patterns of internal differentiation within the so-called "hearth regions" as well as between them. Rather than three initial regional divisions, basically there were two, a "northern" region of free labor with minor slave concentrations, and a "southern" region of substantial slave populations with significant proportions of alternative labor systems.

It has been suggested that the thesis of liberal individualism seems to fit best the particular actions of the early colonists. Settlers, regardless of cultural heritage, were almost everywhere motivated by values of property ownership, the overwhelming importance of individual and family interests, participation in a market-oriented economy, and social stability guaranteed by limited but benevolent governmental intrusions into private life. The most dramatic landscape effect was the virtual ubiquity of dispersed settlement based on the individual family farm. Moreover, an examination of land records to determine where and how settlers actually took up land has demonstrated that, although there was some group settlement, the dominant pattern was one of great intermixing of national and cultural groups. This provided a social environment within which a widespread sharing of commonly held goals and values led to a distinctive American "worldview" probably by the early 18th century.

Urban Historical Geography

Historical geographers prior to about 1970 operated within a narrow range of topical interests. Most studies dealt with three major topics: rural settlement and agriculture; regional disinctiveness and identity; and cultural origins and diffusion. The most dramatic growth in research and publication, however, has been in urban and industrial topics and especially in exploring the relationships between large-scale immigration, urbanization, and industrialization during the 19th and early 20th centuries. The focus on such topics remains somewhat uneven, but urban historical geographers have developed two principal orientations: the evolution of cities in terms of internal spatial and social structure, and the emergence of city systems and the external relations of cities. These topical concerns have also presented new methodological problems, because the processes of urban change and their spatial consequences seem less explicit and less enduring than those associated with rural and pre-industrial North America. Change has been more rapid, more massive, and thus more dramatic.

Internal evolution. The study of the internal geography of the city has proceeded within the context of understanding the urban past from empirical studies, especially by social historians, and from the application of spatial concepts from contemporary human geography. Studies of population turnover in large northeastern cities during the second half of the 19th century have revealed rates of geographical mobility that were higher than those experienced during the 20th century. If this was indeed true, how had the formation of European immigrant and black ghettos been made possible? Linked with this theme of transiency, therefore, has been the theme of inequality, as revealed in evolving urban class structures, the residential movements of the upper classes, and the residential persistence of the poor. The framework for analyzing this pattern-process relationship is still the subject of debate. Older environmentalist perspectives that were common until the 1940s have been replaced with a model of laissez-faire "privatism." Urban development occurred under the decision-making conditions associated with mercantile and, later, industrial capitalism that reversed the social and spatial gradients of the early 19th-century city. European immigrants and southern blacks moved into the central areas of cities after 1850, and intra-urban transport innovations after 1870 allowed the upper classes and, later, the skilled and professional middle classes, to move to the suburbs.

Much of the early work done on American mobility was based on record linkages of individuals at ten-year census dates and at the level of census enumeration districts and city blocks. But as the exploration of residential patterning proceeded, scholars faced scale problems of how best to organize the manuscript census data in terms of units of analysis (single blocks, block faces, and household addresses) and of appropriate sampling techniques for handling the sheer mass of material. A second problem was how to interpolate information between census-year data. The available censuses between 1850 and 1910 provided detailed information only at ten-year intervals. Thus a major concern has been to construct computerized files on individuals and families between census years from sources ranging from tax and occupational records to church records and family papers. This data collection has revealed considerable discrepancies in the availability of source materials from one city to another (the Philadelphia social history project is a rare case of an exceptionally rich data base). Hence it has proven difficult to make interurban comparisons of residential and occupational patterns at similar levels of discrimination.

Another research thrust has been to try to delineate the functional and spatial links between urbanization and industrialization. This has been explored in two ways: the distinctive characteristics of mercantile cities, and the processes of urban growth during periods of industrialization. Research into urban evolution has led scholars to conclude that the appropriate model of early American urbanism is the mercantile city, rather than the classical pre-industrial city. American post-colonial cities—in the Northeast in particular—were dominated not by landed elites, but by business elites who organized factors of production not only in wholesale and overseas trade, but also in manufacturing. The onset of large-scale industrialization during the third quarter of the 19th century, therefore, was more of an elaboration of existing trends than a revolution in economic activities, even though the scale and pace of industrial change were unprecedented. But there has been little empirical underpinning to this research so far. The study of the larger cities has focused on three elements: expansion of the Central Business District, the emergence of factories and large-scale industrial employment, and intra-urban transportation. There has been little discussion yet on what happened with these elements in smaller cities and towns.

City systems. The study of the emergence of city systems, on the other hand, has been of much more interest to historical geographers than to urban historians. Consequently, geographers have monopolized research into the evolution of urban networks, using theoretical constructs from modern human geography. The use of descriptive models has been especially noteworthy.

What appears to fit best the evolution of a North American urban system is an imperial model of the colonial cities along the Atlantic seaboard. They created their own internal hinterlands and were linked with a mercantilist transatlantic trading world dominated by London and the demand and supply needs of the mother country. A mercantile model of wholesale trading patterns suggests that these colonial cities became the key unraveling points of trade with the expanding interior—that is, the final destination of a sufficient number of supply lines—to assure the profitability of long-distance trade to the traders. As settlement and trade spread farther westward, new cities emerged along major trade routes at highly accessible localities, where frontier merchants concentrated to organize and conduct wholesale trade. These cities became interior unraveling points with forward linkages to the seaboard metropolises and backward linkages into the expanding settlement frontier, thus pulling the entire system together into a functioning whole. These wholesaling cities also became the points of origin for the creation of more regional and localized retailing trading systems. The application of central-place theory is more appropriate for this level of activity. The arrangement of retailing at this scale was more hierarchical and the spacing of towns more regular. The larger the urban center, the greater was its array of central functions (the number and kind of retail and service businesses), the more extensive was its hinterland, and the farther apart it was located from other cities of equal size.

Mercantile and central-place theories provide some valuable clues to the emergence of national patterns of city systems, but they create demand-generated models that fail to account for differential rates of development of regional urban systems, for the unusual size and regional concentration of the largest cities, and for the impact of industrial localization, among others. The first problem has been addressed by regional growth theory, which seeks to address the core-periphery dynamics that occur within urban regions. This combines examining the selective results of interregional trade impacts (between the Northeast, the Middle West, and the South) and their varying control, in particular by the northeastern cities. It also involves examining interregional growth through the intensification of commercial activities in the largest cities, which influences the growth and distribution of agricultural and processing activities in local hinterlands. The concept of metropolitan dominance has been refined to help resolve the second problem. In a continent that has undergone such recent settlement, it is an easier matter to unravel the processes of urban evolution than it would be in a longer-settled continent such as Europe. Thus, areas in proximity to or easily accessible to newly emerging towns will have their economies influenced by these towns. The towns, in turn, achieve an "initial advantage" in influencing economic development over later-founded centers, which explains the initial and continued importance of the northeastern seaport cities (especially New York) and of Montreal and Toronto.

The onset of industrialization during the second quarter of the 19th century superimposed industrial factors of location on the preexisting pattern of commercial city systems. This has forced researchers to focus on two issues: the concentration of high manufacturing capacity in the major cities of the Northeast, and the emergence of specialized regional-industrial systems. A model of circular and cumulative growth has been used to explain how the mercantile city benefits from establishing industries by means of a "multiplier effect." The growing urban workforce creates a demand for consumer goods and industrial raw materials that, through time, produces new local or regional demand thresholds, which then stimulate further industrial expansion and, through encouraging innovations, may also create new industries. This model says little, however, about the forces that encouraged industrial activities in medium and small-sized towns and, conse-quently, about the timing, regional arrangement, and interregional spread of entire urban-industrial complexes. Only recently has there been an attempt to explain the coalescing of these complexes into the world's greatest industrial region during the late 19th century. This research has focused on the expansion of demand for processed and consumer goods in the major cities and their hinterlands and the critical importance of producer durable goods (for example, machinery, iron foundries, and transport equipment) to supply not only local and regional demand but, ultimately, interregional and national markets for such products. This, in turn, led to the emergence of specialized regional manufacturing districts which, through regional spread, had coalesced and consolidated in the Northeast and eastern Middle West before the end of the 19th century to form the American Manufacturing Belt.

ENDURING THEMES

From this survey of interpreting the past, a number of principal themes can be identified around which this synthesis of the North American experience can be organized. The choice of themes must necessarily be arbitrary, but the seven chosen here appear to capture much of the dynamic element of change that has shaped the geography of the continent during the past 400 years and continues to shape it today.

Acquisition of Geographical Knowledge

As a "new world," what came to be known as North America had to be discovered and eventually uncovered through exploration, description, mapping, and subsequent place-naming in a continuous process of growth, repetition, and revelation. This was a complex process involving mental as well as physical negotiation of a vast new continent. To the educated European a direct relationship existed between the appearance of the landscape and the cultural quality of its inhabitants. The wild landscapes of North America suggested a need for taming and transformation into semblances of the subdued landscapes of western Europe; the seeming wildness of the natives suggested a lowly status for them in the great chain of civilization and cast doubts on their capacity to become Christians.

Geographic knowledge of the continent continued to increase during the interior penetrations of the 18th and 19th centuries, largely following major river courses, and built up a vast storehouse of information about a seemingly inexhaustible territory. This information was collected and described by a variety of observers—explorers, traders, missionaries, travelers, naturalists, and occasionally artists (who were indispensable before the beginnings of photography in the 1840s). It was not until the great railroad and scientific surveys of the trans-Mississippi West after 1860 that we began systematically to record the continent as a whole. Vast areas of northern and western Canada remained only partially explored at the beginning of the 20th century.

The accumulation of geographic knowledge had important effects on later settlement. Prior discovery was used by England, France, and the Netherlands to justify territorial acquisition and colonization. Early maps and descriptions of particular areas therefore need to be viewed with caution, because they were often designed to please royal patrons or investors and to promote settlement. As well as accurate information, the cartographic record is replete with exaggeration, misconception, and geographical fantasies. If sound geographical knowledge could guide the direction of pioneer settlers to new agricultural lands, geographical misinformation could retard settlement in other areas. Early visitors to the western High Plains reported the area as barren and unsuitable for farming. The image of a "Great American Desert" portrayed in eastern newspapers and in official government reports probably retarded large-scale settlement of the area until the last quarter of the 19th century.

Cultural Transfer and Acculturation

No other land mass, except perhaps Australia, has undergone such a dramatic cultural replacement and transformation in such a short time as North America. The "Europeanization" of the continent in the later 16th and in the 17th centuries, though rapid, was a highly selective process. Only a few western European countries controlled colonization, and settlers who came (except for African slaves) were more geographically and socially mobile than those who remained in Europe. They brought with them only a sample of their national cultures

which, through hybridization with native and imported traits, eventually created distinct colonial cultures and societies.

A process of "Americanization" set in during the 18th century as colonial-born generations had increasingly weaker ties with the mother country. The ethos of this American society lay in liberal individualism, capitalism, and geographical expansion. The dramatic break with Britain left the continent with a robust new nation, dominated by Anglo-American institutions and the presence of slavery, and a Canadian colony in which both French- and English-speaking settlers remained under direct British control.

The principal cultural configurations of the two territories were well established by the time of the massive European immigration that occurred after 1830. The 50 million immigrants who arrived in the United States before 1920 had to adjust to an already existing framework of the English language and other American institutions. They, in turn, enriched the continent's cultural heritage. Instead of a continental "melting pot," a widespread sharing of common values occurred while ethnic diversity increased. These processes of cultural and social intermixing have left a distinctive imprint on modern North America. The persistence of older cultural forms remains evident, for example, among French-Canadians, among Hispanics in the Southwest, and on some Indian reservations. The more varied cultural heritage of the United States is reflected in the presence of large black and Hispanic populations that do not exist in Canada. Both countries continue to be, in reduced ways, "nations of immigrants," and the 19th- and early 20th-century urban concentrations of European and Asian immigrant groups has given way to massive 20th-century suburbanization and renewed migration, the long-term cultural results of which are as yet uncertain.

Frontier Expansion

There is little need to dwell here on the historiographic and symbolic importance of an interior-moving settlement frontier in North America. Both Frederick Jackson Turner in the United States and the Laurentian school in Canada have etched in the national psyche the significance of settling the land. In the United States this was especially significant because of the continuity of the frontier experience across a vast, mid-latitude territory that encountered few obstacles to settlement until the Great Plains was reached in the middle of the 19th century. In Canada, on the other hand, westward settlement expansion was interrupted in the 19th century by the immense extent of the heavily glaciated, generally infertile, and extensively forested Canadian Shield that separated Ontario from the prairies. Thus many immigrants to Canada during the 19th century who wished to acquire farmland did so in the northern Middle West.

Frontier expansion was a process of both continual reappraisal and increasing geographical divergence. The so-called "westward movement" was a process of sustained geographical mobility that has always characterized American life, an experience that was cumulative and undertaken under different temporal and locational contexts. Successive pioneer generations swept across the country with knowledge accumulated through earlier encounters with modifying new areas for settlement. The pace of this development was speeded up further by the federal government's desire, after 1790, to dispose of the public domain to the private sector as rapidly as possible, and by the impact, after 1850, of the railroads that reoriented both the direction and the pace of frontier expansion and reduced the traditional isolation of pioneering. In the Far West a slight reversal of this westward process occurred as settlement expanded discontinuously eastward from the Pacific coast or from isolated interior centers. The end result of this frontier process was the creation of an elaborate system of rural-agrarian regions and subregions latitudinally across the continent (until the Rockies), each defined by its own settlement experiences and regional economic development.

In 1890, the director of the U.S. census declared, somewhat inaccurately, that the American frontier was officially "closed": no new agricultural areas remained to be occupied; the filling of the vast national ecumene was complete. American was now a "closed space" entity of finite resources that would have to be used more carefully; further dynamism for American life would have to be sought in urban and industrial opportunities. Such ideas influenced the New Deal measures employed by Franklin Roosevelt's administrations to alleviate the stresses of national economic depression and the Dust Bowl disaster. The opening up of Alaska since 1945 has, in a small way, kept open the idea of the American frontier, while for some Canadians settlement of "the North" remains an unfulfilled dream.

Spatial Organization of Society

The processes whereby a society arranges its members, its institutions, and its materials on the ground provide a fundamental geographical expression of its goals and achievements. What is remarkable about the social initiation of the new continent was the way in which the diversity of pioneer societies was integrated by the early 18th century within a social framework characterized by liberalism, individualism, Protestantism, and capitalism. The overwhelming concern for material well-being, social stability, and continuity within the vast spaces of North America provided ample opportunities for the acquisition of land and the pursuit of commercial interest or, conversely, for the right to be left alone on the social or geographic margins of society. Most settlers saw little conflict between religious and material ends; the "work ethic" was believed to provide access to the spiritual world through success in the material world. North American society soon deviated from its European counterparts: it was less hierarchical and more egalitarian; there was no hereditary aristocracy and, at least in the American system, no imposed state church. The options for creating a new life were greater than in Europe, although this was often at the expense of the native Indian or the imported African.

In the new American nation two forms of society emerged: a largely free-labor, mixed-farming system in the North and a more stratified, slave-labor, and staple-farming system in the South. The reduction of differences between the two societies was to remain unresolved until the Civil War, and the continued social distinctiveness and economic dependency of the South remained well into the 20th century. But the expression of these two early societies on the ground was broadly similar in the form of dispersed farmsteads. Attempts to recreate European-style settlements failed almost everywhere, even in French Canada where the social nexus was tighter, and the ubiquity of dispersed settlement was guaranteed by the reassignment of the public domain under the design of cheap land policies and rectangular survey systems initiated in the United States and in Canada during the 1790s.

Early North American urban life had demonstrated a more complex differentiation of wealth and social status than in the countryside. While rural tenancy was present, in the burgeoning 18th-century cities were collected those who had found or made few opportunities in the new land, the urban poor and the unskilled laborer. Problems of residential congestion, traffic, sanitation, and crime were apparent long before the large-scale immigration, urbanization, and industrialization of the mid-19th century. If the expression of social segregation in rural life became symbolized in southern slave quarters and in western Indian reservations, it was represented in the urban centers of the Northeast and Middle West by the inner city immigrant ghettos and slum quarters that formed in the late 19th century. This segregation was enhanced enormously by the transportation developments of the late 19th and early 20th centuries that allowed the wealthy to move to emerging suburbs. The most dominant social expression of the past sixty years has been the increasing suburbanization of skilled and professional middle classes that now comprise more than half the total population of North America.

Resource Exploitation

The concept of resources, like that of hazards, involves continuous reappraisal of nature and of society. The future of North American economic development was founded on European ideas about natural resource exploitation played out on a vast 7.5 million square-mile canvas. After initial searches for gold, silver, and quick riches, the continent settled down to gradual extraction of its immense animal, agricultural, forest, and mineral wealth with few concerns for the rate and magnitude of exploiting finite resources. The process was to be also distinctly territorially unbalanced. The more southerly, mid-latitude United States was to prove far more amenable to resource development than its northern neighbor; more than 65 percent of the total area of the United States, for example, has been used for agricultural

purposes, while only 16 percent has been so used in Canada.

Early Americans were thus a people of plenty. Their successful transformation of nature was predicated on a rich resource base, a liberal, free-market economy, overseas trade, and a growing internal demand that led to increasing regional specialization. Eastern Canada was to remain largely a raw material supplier of fish and furs, and later of timber and wheat; the northern colonies produced small grains, livestock products, and small crafts; and the southern settlements focused on tobacco, rice, indigo and, after, 1790, on cotton. The urbanization and industrialization of the northeastern United States during the mid-19th century oriented economic development in new directions: the cities produced the manufactured goods and the financial and marketing organization, while their peripheries produced the food supply and the industrial raw materials. The settlement of the western periphery presented new problems and possibilities: the near extinction of the buffalo; competition for the Plains grasslands; problems of water supply in the Southwest; the timber resources of the Pacific Northwest; and the oil discoveries of the turn of the century. By the end of the 19th century the United States had surpassed Germany and Britain as the world's most productive industrial nation. At the same time, this immense growth fostered increasing sensitivity toward the conservation of resources and the creation of preserved natural places in the 20th century.

The resource legacy has been staggering. Probably between one-quarter and one-third of all the wheat, coal, iron ore, and petroleum extraction from the earth's surface during the past 200 years has occurred in North America. But continued change remains uneven. Regionally, maritime Canada and Appalachia prove the effects of differential resource fortunes. On a continental scale, the economic dependency of Canada on American investment and markets remains high. And Americans continue to generate a 30 percent greater demand for electrical energy than their Canadian neighbors. On a global scale, the increasing decline of older "smoke-stack" industries within the Manufacturing Belt, and the global competition from both advanced economies, such as Japan, and low-cost, developing economies guarantees new challenges to North American resource strategies into the 21st century.

Regional and National Integration

One of the most remarkable characteristics of North America is that it came to be divided not into a series of little Europes but into only two national-political units of approximately equal size. To be sure, the northern territory proved to be less attractive for settlement, so that Americans continue to outnumber Canadians by almost ten to one. But the sheer challenge to conquer the vast spaces and distances of the continent by technological means and within similar cultural traditions meant that both countries had much to share.

In the American colonies, a range of institutional units was created to organize local affairs: counties, townships, and parishes. Patterns of political behavior varied enormously within a colonial system that, nevertheless, allowed for a relatively wide participation in the political process. The provision for a new nation was a remarkable experience: a democratic republic formed as a federal union, with a central government of limited power, and its idealism patently recorded in a series of written documents. Threats to the unity of the nation might have come from the settlement of the West, where factors of distance and isolation, sparsely settled populations, and discrete urban cores created a potentially fragmented situation (as in Mormon Utah) until the development of the railroads and the telegraph. The greatest threat was to come during the Civil War which, if its outcome had been different, might have resulted in an American experience that paralleled rather than diverged from that in South Africa. Since the 1920s, however, the increasing redistribution of population to the West and South and the increasing movement of blacks from the South have created a regional balance of economic and political power throughout the United States. Today, the integration of unwieldy metropolitan regions, where deep political and social cleavages exist between inner city and suburban populations, remains a major problem.

Canada's political evolution and efforts at national integration have taken a somewhat different direction. The late acquisition of independence from Britain (in 1867), the deep geographical divisions between French and Anglo Canada, and the slow growth of population relative to the United States left Canadians with a less unified legacy. The division between French and English Canada had been institutionalized first in the recognition of Lower (French Québec) and Upper (English Ontario) Canada in 1791 and then into the provinces of Québec and Ontario in 1867. The Canadian provincial system was thus well established before independence so that the allocation of powers between governing units resulted in a relatively weak central government, strong provinces, and continued constitutional ties with Britain. A confident American nation negotiated the boundary between the two territories west of the Great Lakes in its favor, thus leaving Canada as the "true country of the North." The delayed westward movement in Canada produced an additional problem of integrating the Prairies and British Columbia into a seemingly distant eastern Canada by means of a transcontinental railroad. The American presence exerts considerable impact on Canadian affairs, although the reverse is less true, and this continues to raise questions both about Canadian identity and about North American unity in the late 20th century.

Landscape Change

Landscape has been an unending theme in the geography of the North American past. But it is not simply a collection of observable objects on the continent's surface, nor does it reflect equally all the forces and processes that have occurred during the past 400 years. It is a receptacle for continuity and change, a palimpsest that can be "read" for what it contains as well as for what it represents symbolically.

The most important attribute of landscape is its capacity to synthesize the formative ideas that have shaped the continent. Control over nature is expressed dramatically in the selective removal of much of the forested wilderness to create more familiar, more domesticated environments; these have come to be identified with the rural and small town "middle" landscapes between the less desired forested and urban wildernesses at the extremes. The idea of individualism is reflected in a range of landscape expressions from the colonial dispersed farmstead to the modern low-density, residential suburb. Private property meant a multitude of fragmented, small private territories that continue to dominate most of the settlement landscapes of North America.

The emergence of a new nation encouraged regularity and symmetry that resulted in perhaps the most extensive geographical expression of values on the landscape. The creation of national rectangular survey systems produced a sequence of designed rural landscapes of grid-pattern roads, fields, and settlements that stretch almost uninterrupted from southern Ontario and the Alleghenies westward to the Pacific. In urban North America, the rectangular street and block patterns and regular naming and numbering of streets are a more widespread expression of urbanism than the late-appearing skyscraper. Design can also be observed in the continued pattern of regionally diverse folk housing styles, as well as in a myriad of borrowed urban architectural styles. Regional landscapes, therefore, continue to survive despite the homogenizing influences of historic national survey systems and contemporary urban life, as any trip to Québec, the Appalachians, or Louisiana, or New Mexico will attest.

Ideas of separation and segregation are also well expressed in the landscape. We can observe the dismal results of Indian removal to western reservations, while we appreciate their potential for fostering cultural survival. If the slave plantation is a thing of the past, we can interpret the continued segregation of blacks in inner cities and whites in the suburbs as a reflection of the enduring racial divisions of American society that compound the urban-suburban tensions of modern metropolitan life. We can appreciate also the idea of conservation on a continent that has experienced more rapid and extensive resource exploitation than any other. The creation of wilderness and recreation areas, national parks, national forests, national seashores, and wildlife management areas reflects abiding concern in the management, if not always the preservation, of landscape and nature. And ultimately, on a continent that is seemingly notorious for lack of a sense of place or a sense of past, we can acknowledge the survival of landscape relicts from previous settlement eras, from historic structures to "living farms," from factories and foundries to sanitized colonial townscapes, that still reflect on the landscape the forces of change, paradox, and contradiction that continue to reshape North America.

ADDITIONAL READING

Books

Baker, A.R.H. *Progress in Historical Geography.* New York: John Wiley, 1972.

Baker, A.R.H., and Billinge, M., eds. *Period and Place: Research Methods in Historical Geography.* Cambridge: Cambridge University Press, 1982.

Baker, A.R.H., and Gregory, D., eds. *Explorations in Historical Geography: Interpretive Essays.* Cambridge: Cambridge University Press, 1984.

Barrows, H.H. *Lectures on the Historical Geography of the United States as Given in 1933.* Edited by W.A. Koelsch. Chicago: University of Chicago Department of Geography, 1962.

Brown, R.H. *Mirror for Americans: Likeness of the Eastern Seaboard 1810.* New York: American Geographical Society, 1943.

———. *Historical Geography of the United States.* New York: Harcourt, Brace & World, 1948.

Clark, A.H. *Three Centuries and the Island: A Historical Geography of Settlement and Agriculture in Prince Edward Island, Canada.* Toronto: University of Toronto Press, 1959.

———. *Acadia: The Geography of Early Nova Scotia to 1760.* Madison: University of Wisconsin Press, 1968.

Ehrenberg, R.E., ed. *Pattern and Process: Research in Historical Geography.* Washington, D.C.: Howard University Press, 1975.

Friis, H.R. *A Series of Population Maps of the Colonies and the United States 1625–1790.* New York: American Geographical Society, revised edition, 1968.

Gibson, J.R., ed. *European Settlement and Development in North America: Essays on Geographical Change in Honour and Memory of Andrew Hill Clark.* Toronto: University of Toronto Press, 1978. See chapters by Meinig, Mitchell, Ward, and Lemon.

Guelke, L. *Historical Understanding in Geography: An Idealist Approach.* Cambridge: Cambridge University Press, 1982.

Harris, R.C. *Reflections on the Fertility of the Historical Geographic Mule.* Toronto: University of Toronto Department of Geography, 1970.

Herbert, D.T., and Johnston, R.J., eds. *Geography and the Urban Environment: Progress in Research and Applications*, Volume 4. New York: John Wiley, 1981. See chapters by Conzen and Radford.

Lowenthal, D., and Bowden, M.J. eds. *Geographies of the Mind: Essays in Historical Geosophy in Honor of John Kirtland Wright*. New York: Oxford University Press, 1976.

Meinig, D.W. *The Great Columbia Plain: A Historical Geography, 1805–1910*. Seattle and London: University of Washington Press, 1968.

———. *Imperial Texas: An Interpretive Essay in Cultural Geography*. Austin and London: University of Texas Press, 1969.

———. *Southwest: Three Peoples in Geographical Change 1600–1970*. New York: Oxford University Press, 1971.

Norton, W. *Historical Analysis in Geography*. London and New York: Longman, 1984.

Sauer, C.O. *Land and Life: A Selection from the Writings of Carl Ortwin Sauer*. Edited by J. Leighly. Berkeley and Los Angeles: University of California Press, 1963.

———. *The Early Spanish Main*. Berkeley and Los Angeles: University of California Press, 1966.

———. *Sixteenth Century North America: The Land and the People as Seen by the Europeans*. Berkeley and Los Angeles: University of California Press, 1971.

———. *Selected Essays 1963–1975*. Berkeley: Turtle Island Foundation, 1981.

Semple, E.C. *American History and Its Geographic Conditions*. Boston and New York: Houghton, Mifflin, 1903.

Thompson, J.H., ed. *A Geography of New York State*. Syracuse: Syracuse University Press, 1966; 2nd edition 1977. See chapters by Meinig.

Vance, J.E., Jr. *The Merchant's World: The Geography of Wholesaling*. Englewood Cliffs: Prentice-Hall, 1970.

———. *This Scene of Man: The Role and Structure of the City in the Geography of Western Civilization*. New York: Harper & Row, 1977.

Ward, D. *Cities and Immigrants: A Geography of Change in Nineteenth Century America*. New York: Oxford University Press, 1971.

———, ed. *Geographic Perspectives on America's Past: Readings on the Historical Geography of the United States*. New York: Oxford University Press, 1979.

Warkentin, J., ed. *Canada: A Geographical Interpretation*. Toronto: Methuen, 1968.

Wright, J.K. *Human Nature in Geography: Fourteen Papers, 1925–1965*. Cambridge: Harvard University Press, 1966.

Zelinsky, W. *The Cultural Geography of the United States*. Englewood Cliffs: Prentice-Hall, 1973.

Bibliographies

America: History and Life.

Geo-Abstracts. D: Social and historical geography.

Grim, R.E. *Historical Geography of the United States: A Guide to Information Sources*. Detroit: Gale Research Company, 1982.

Periodicals

American Behavioral Scientist (Harris, 1978; Zelinsky, 1978).

American Historical Review, journal of the American Historical Association (Meinig, 1978).

Annals, Association of American Geographers (Whittlesey, 1919; Meinig, 1965 and 1972; Harris, 1977; Mitchell, 1983).

Canadian Geographer, journal of the Canadian Association of Geographers (Harris, 1969 and 1971).

Journal of Economic History (Clark, 1960).

Journal of Historical Geography (Lemon, 1980; Meyer, 1983).

Proceedings, Royal Geographical Society, South Australian Branch (Meinig, 1957–58).

PART II

COLONIZATION

1490s–1770s

If the soil were as good as the harbours, it would be a blessing; but the land should not be called the New Land, being composed of stones and horrible rugged rocks; for along the whole of the north shore [of the Gulf of St. Lawrence], I did not see one cart-load of earth and yet I landed in many places . . . In fine, I am rather inclined to believe that this is the land God gave to Cain.

Jacques Cartier, *Journal*, 1535

Thus I have given a succinct account of the Indians; happy, I think, in their simple State of Nature, and in their enjoyment of Plenty, without the Curse of Labour. They have on several accounts reason to lament the arrival of the Europeans, by whose means they seem to have lost their Felicity, as well as their Innocence. The English have taken away great part of their Country, and consequently made every thing less plenty amongst them. They have introduc'd Drunkenness and Luxury amongst them, which have multiply'd their Wants, and put them upon desiring a thousand things, they never dreamt of before.

Robert Beverley, *The History and
Present State of Virginia*, 1705

Why should we, in the Sight of Superior Beings, darken its People? Why increase the sons of Africa, by planting them in America, where we have so fair an Opportunity, by excluding all Blacks and Tawneys, of increasing the lovely White and Red? But perhaps I am partial to the Complexion of my Country, for such kind of Partiality is natural to Mankind.

Benjamin Franklin, *Observations Concerning
the Increase of Mankind*, 1751

2

The New Land: The Discovery and Exploration of Eastern North America

LOUIS DE VORSEY
University of Georgia

One of the most colorful and exciting stories in the literature of mankind's history describes the discovery and exploration of North America by Europeans. The Age of Discovery and Exploration is almost universally acknowledged as a major temporal division or period employed to help organize and focus understanding of humanity's march through time. A large measure of the events forming that period involve North America. This, in itself, does not explain why study of the discovery and exploration of North America should be a part of this book. What are the relationships between discovery and exploration and historical geography? Like most apparently simple questions, it can be answered in a variety of ways.

In the main, the significance of the history of discovery and exploration to historical geography derives from what it can reveal about areas discovered and the cultural groups responsible for the modification of those areas. Seen in this light, the history of discovery and exploration can contribute to what the geographer Carl Sauer saw as the special concern of historical geography:

Historical geography may be considered as the series of changes which the cultural landscapes have undergone and therefore involves the reconstruction of past cultural landscapes. Of special concern is the catalytic relation of civilized man to area and the effects of the replacement of cultures. From this difficult and little-touched field alone may be gained a full realization of the development of the present cultural landscape out of earlier cultures and the natural landscape [*Land and Life*, 343].

The North American cultural landscape, in all its incredible richness of diverse forms and patterns, comprises a document. The reading of this "landscape document" is challenging because it is not like a modern printed document that reveals its message easily. Rather, the landscape of today is similar to ancient parchments called palimpsests. Because parchments (ordinarily goat or sheepskins) were expensive and durable, they were seldom thrown away and were used over and over again. More often than not, the scholars and monks of old merely scraped the ink off portions of a palimpsest where they wanted to change an idea or passage. In other instances they crossed out errors or old ideas and introduced their changes and corrections between the lines of written text. The word "palimpsest" is derived from the Greek term which meant "scraped again." In modern speech, the phrase "to read between the lines" is commonly used to indicate the search for hidden or deeper meaning.

Because the scraped erasures and corrections on the palimpsests were seldom complete, "It became the fascinating task of scholars not only to translate the later records, but also to reconstruct the original writings by deciphering the dim fragments of letters partly erased and partly covered by subsequent texts." The patterns of trails, streets, powerline grids, railways, highways, fields, and farmsteads contributing to today's urban and rural landscapes can be viewed as modern interlinings and glosses on a centuries-old landscape palimpsest.

CREATION OF THE ABORIGINAL LANDSCAPE

The first bands of Old World hunters spreading across the broad low-lying belt of tundra, sometimes inadequately described as the Bering Land Bridge, found North America in a truly natural state. As they moved south to exploit the continent about 30,000 years ago, they began to alter their surroundings and permanently change ecological relationships. Their numbers were small, but they possessed and made wide use of fire for major landscape modification.

The people who erroneously came to be called Indians by the Europeans continued to add their cultural signatures and messages to North America's landscape palimpsest during the centuries that followed. Majestic earthworks, massive effigies, and mounds were raised; palisaded villages were built; fields and trails were hewn from the forest; fish traps were constructed in rivers, lakes, and coastal lagoons; and everywhere fire was deliberately loosed on the land to drive game, clear undergrowth, and achieve other desired alterations. Giovanni da Verrazano, whose first landing near Cape Fear, North Carolina, was guided by Indian fires, was only one of scores of early 16th-century visitors to North America who drew attention to the Indians' recurrent use of fire as a tool in landscape modification and management.

As their cultures evolved and their numbers grew over much of North America, the Indians altered their habitat in major ways. The sum total of these alterations to the natural state of the continent by the time of the first European contacts is still to be determined accurately. One thing is clear, however: eastern North America was far from being a "forest primeval" when Europeans reached it in the 15th century. On the contrary, what the European explorers found and reported is best described as an aboriginal landscape—a landscape palimpsest already inscribed with patterns and forms reflecting the cultural use of Indian occupants for whom it had been a home for centuries. As North America's first culturally modified environment, it was a new land only to the Europeans (Table 2.1). In the words of John Collier, longtime U.S. Commissioner of Indian Affairs, "At the time of white arrival there was no square mile unoccupied or unused. . . . The million Indians of the United States and Alaska were formed within more than six hundred distinct societies, in geographical situations ranging from temperate oceansides to arctic ice, from humid swamps to frozen tundras, from eastern woodlands to western deserts [Collier, 101–2]."

AMERICAN INDIAN CULTURAL REGIONS

The concept of a cultural region—a geographical area occupied by a large number of people

Table 2.1 Selected Phases in Landscape Evolution

A. Natural or Pre-Human
B. Aboriginal
   1. Pre-Agrarian—Hunting, Gathering, and Fishing
   2. Agrarian + Hunting, Gathering, and Fishing
   3. Sedentary Agriculture
C. European/American
   1. Agrarian/Pre-Industrial—Aboriginal Acculturated Agriculture
   2. Agrarian/Proto-Industrial
   3. Commercial Agrarian/Industrial
   4. Commercial Agrarian/Modern Post-Industrial

whose culture shows a significant degree of dissimilarity with the cultures of the people of adjacent areas—is a useful one to consider when attempting to gain some idea of the geographical conditions encountered by early European voyagers to the New World. "Culture" in this context refers to the entire way of life and thought of a people. The cultural region provides a convenient framework for describing, in general terms, the ways of life of the hundreds of different peoples who were inhabiting and energetically modifying North America's landscapes before they were acquired by Europeans in the post-exploratory period. The difference in their cultures, especially their technological attainments in the area of subsistence, resulted in differing impacts on their biophysical environments which, in turn, were revealed by distinctive patterns on the landscapes they inhabited.

In his attempt to arrive at a set of meaningful Indian cultural regions, the anthropologist Harold E. Driver prepared an impressive set of 37 maps to illustrate the wide range of trait distributions. Not all these distributions are of equal help in gaining an appreciation of the aboriginal landscapes that the first Europeans encountered as they began to explore and form impressions of the geography of North America. Nevertheless, a few must have played a significant role as those impressions were being formed and reinforced in a system of information flows that eventually led to decision-making on the part of European leaders and entrepreneurs. These were the decisions that, in time, changed North America from a realm of aboriginal landscapes to a mosaic of Europeanized landscapes.

Figure 2.1 is a composite showing a sample of these distributions for the eastern portion of North America. It gives some idea of the diversity of Indian culture groups before the arrival of Europeans. As one of the earliest and most serious explorers of the middle Atlantic seaboard, Giovanni da Verrazano provided excellent commentary on the Indian diversity he observed. In the vicinity of modern Newport, Rhode Island, where his expedition remained for more than two weeks in 1524, Verrazano recorded the following observations:

Many times we were from five to six leagues [15 to 18 miles] inland, which we found as pleasing as it can be to narrate, adapted to every kind of cultivation—grain, wine, oil. Because in that place the fields are from 25 to 30 leagues [75 to 90 miles] wide, open and devoid of every impediment of trees, of such fertility that any seed in them would produce the best crops. Entering then into the woods, all of which are penetrable by any numerous army in any way whatsoever, and where trees, oaks, cypresses, and others are unknown in our Europe. . . . Animals there are in very great number, stags, deer, lynx, and other species, which . . . [the Indians] capture with snares and bows which are their principal arms. The arrows of whom are worked with great beauty, placing at the end, instead of iron, emery, jasper, hard marble, and other sharp stones, by which they themselves use instead of iron in cutting trees, making their barges from a single trunk of a tree, hollowed with wonderful skill, in which from 14 to 15 men will go comfortably. . . . We saw their habitations, circular in form, of 14 to 15 paces compass, made from semi-circles of wood separated one from the other . . . covered with mats of straw ingeniously worked, which protect them from rain and wind. . . . They change said houses from one place to another according to the season in which they live. . . . There live in each a father and family to a very large number, so that we saw 25 and 30 souls. Their food is like the others; of pulse [succotash?] (which they produce with more system of culture than the others, observing the full moon, the rising of the Pleiades, and many customs derived from the ancients), also of the chase and fish [Hoffman, 111].

After their almost idyllic sojourn in "the Country of Refugio," as they termed it, Verrazano and his expedition sailed northward, skirting the hazards of Nantucket Shoals, to make a landfall near Casco Bay in present-day southern Maine. While, by his reckoning, he covered only 50 leagues (150 miles), Verrazano noted striking contrasts in both the biophysical and human landscape he encountered:

We found a high land and full of very thick forests, the trees of which were pines, cypresses [red cedar] and such as grow in cold regions. The people all different from the others, and as much as those passed were of cultivated manners, these were full of uncuthness and vices, so barbarous that we were never able, with howsoever many signs we made them, to have any intercourse with them. They dress with the skins of bear, lynxes, seawolves, and other animals. The food, according to that which we were able to learn through going many times to their habitations, we think is of the chase, fish and some products which are of a species of roots which the ground yields by its own self. They do not have pulse, nor did we see any signs of cultivation, nor would the ground, on account of its sterility, be adapted to produce fruit or any grain. If, trading at any time with them, we desired their things, they came to the shore of the sea upon some rock where it was very steep and— we remaining in the small boat—with a cord let down to us what they wished to give, continually crying on land that we should not approach, giving quickly the barter, nor taking in exchange for it except knives, hooks for fishing, and sharp metal. They had no regard for courtesy, and when they had nothing more to exchange, at their departing the men made at us all the signs of contempt and shame which any brute creature could make [Hoffman, 111].

Doubtless smarting from the rude gestures and unintelligible, abusive catcalls hurled by the wary Indian inhabitants of the rock-ribbed coast of Maine, Verrazano named the area "Land of the Bad People" when he wrote his report to the king of France.

These brief extracts from Verrazano's report of his first-hand experiences and observations suggest a number of hypotheses concerning the true nature of the geography of aboriginal North America. Instead of an impenetrable "forest primeval," the writings of Verrazano and early explorers reveal a landscape mosaic comprised of a biophysical environment greatly altered by its American Indian occupants armed with fire. Certainly the "fields . . . from 25 to 30 leagues [75 to 90 miles] wide, open and devoid of every impediment of trees, and woods . . . penetrable by any numerous army,"

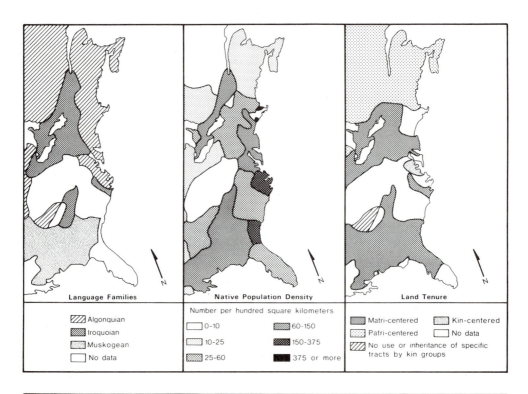

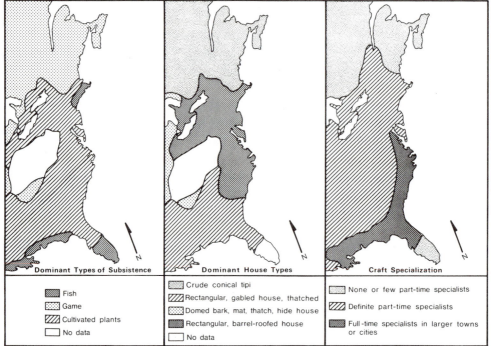

Figure 2.1 Indian Culture Traits That Contributed to Aboriginal Landscape Diversity

described by Verrazano, are proof of the efficacy of the Indians' use of fire in what is now southern New England. It is probable, therefore, that many areas of Indian activity exhibited a relatively open, parklike appearance, although forested areas still constituted the dominant landcover of much of the Atlantic seaboard encountered by later Europeans.

The disturbing behavior of the Indians Verrazano called "bad people" provides evidence for further hypothesis building. Could it be, for example, that these hunter-gatherers of the Maine coast were wary because they had some good reason to fear Europeans? Perhaps their proximity to the fishing grounds off the northern New England–Canadian coasts had provided early and continuing barter opportunities with European fishermen. Although not universally accepted, there is evidence that points to the presence of European vessels on the fishing banks off northeasternmost North America as much as a century before Verrazano's voyage. If and when new evidence is found to substantiate such a hypothesis, historians of discovery may begin shifting from the position currently identifying John Cabot as the first modern European to accomplish a landfall on these northern coasts in 1497.

THE TRAGEDY OF THE COLUMBIAN EXCHANGE

One of the great tragedies of human history is that few, if any, of the early European explorers possessed either the time or training that would have permitted them to discover and record the subtle cultural differences and non-material nuances of Indian social and political life. As a consequence, we must view the period of original contact between the people of the Old and New Worlds through a dark and often distorted lens. By the time that more careful and complete records of their beliefs, lifestyles, and landscapes were being compiled, the Indians had already begun to suffer the catastrophic fatal shocks introduced by Old World epidemic diseases such as smallpox, measles, and influenza.

Thomas Hariot, a member of Sir Walter Raleigh's abortive Virginia settlement in the 1580s, described his visits to the Indian villages on the coastal plain of North Carolina. He mentioned that he and his English companions "sought by all means possible to win them by gentleness," but that "within the few days after our departure from every such town, the people began to die very fast, and many in short space, in some towns about twenty, in some forty, and in one six score, which in truth was very many in respect of their numbers [Corbett, 97]." Any doubt that this post-contact decimation of the Indians was caused by some infectious disease being carried by members of Hariot's party is dispelled by his further observation that "this happened in no place that we could learn, but where we had been. . . . The disease also was so strange, that they neither knew what it was, nor how to cure it, the like by report of the oldest men in the country never happened before, time out of mind [Corbett, 97]."

This example of the impact of some infectious disease, for which Hariot and his fellows were the carriers, typifies an important aspect of what historian Alfred Crosby investigated in his study *The Columbian Exchange*. Thanks to the widespread acceptance of Crosby's work, the term "Columbian Exchange" is now used to describe the complex and many-faceted chain of ecological exchanges and impacts that began when Columbus spearheaded the current age of continuous contacts and reciprocal flows that tie the New and the Old Worlds. As Crosby points out in writing of Columbus's 1492 landfall, "The two worlds which God had cast asunder, were reunited, and the two worlds which were so very different, began on that day to become alike. That trend toward biological homogeneity is one of the most important aspects of the history of life on this planet since the retreat of the continental glaciers [Crosby, 3]."

The American Indians, like the aborigines of Australia, had enjoyed the ultimately perilous, long-term isolation from the people inhabiting the Old World of Afro-Eurasia and its fringing islands. As a consequence, they had inherited none of the resistance to disease that had evolved in Old World populations. Even commonplace diseases, such as whooping cough, scarlet fever, and chicken pox, proved to be devastating scourges when introduced to vulnerable Indian populations for the first time.

It is tempting to hypothesize that the "bad people" of Verrazano's account were aware of the doleful consequences of hand-to-hand exchange with Europeans. Perhaps they possessed the sort of awareness described by French Jesuits almost a century later. The Jesuits wrote that the Indians

are astonished and often complain that, since the French mingle with and carry on trade with them, they are dying fast and the population is thinning out. For they assert that, before this association and intercourse, all their countries were very populous and they tell how one by one, the different coasts according as they have begun to traffic with us, have been more reduced by disease [Crosby, 41].

Once begun, the Columbian Exchange could not be reversed; the New World and the Old World were launched on an inexorable course that ultimately led to what Alvin Toffler has described as the interdependent "world village" of the present.

PRE-COLUMBIAN CONTACTS BETWEEN THE OLD AND THE NEW WORLDS

Hardly a month goes by when the news media do not report some new evidence or theory concerning a pre-Columbian "discovery" of the New World. Many verge on the bizarre and fail to bear up under even mild scientific scrutiny. Some, however, spawn fascinating and often long-lived debates that add spice to the history of discovery. The Kensington Rune Stone debate, for example, waxed and waned for a half-century and can still enliven discussions and stir Nordic pride among many upper-middle westerners.

The Kensington stone was found in the small central Minnesota farming community of that name in 1898. Inscribed in the stone were markings that were recognized to be Scandinavian runes. Rendered into modern English, the runic message was reported as follows:

8 Swedes and 22 Norwegians on an exploration journey from Vinland westward. We had our camp by 2 rocky islets one day's journey north of this stone. We were out fishing one day. When we came home we found 10 men red with blood and dead. AVM save us from evil. We have 10 men by the sea to look after our ships, 14 day's journey from this island. Year 1362 [Morison, *Northern Voyages*, 76].

With its tale of a Viking exploration in Minnesota a full 130 years prior to Columbus's first landfall in the Bahamas, it is little wonder that the Kensington Rune Stone was a featured artifact unveiled in St. Paul on March 15, 1949, on Minnesota Day, the occasion of the state's centennial celebration. The authenticity of the Kensington stone is not generally accepted. Erik Wahlgren's careful linguistic analysis showed that it was very probably "inscribed" with its pattern of runic characters in 1898, the year of its alleged discovery. Exactly why this elaborate hoax was prepared and perpetrated remains unclear.

Another more current cause for similar debate is the map now owned by Yale University and widely known as the "Vinland Map." Amid fanfare and the widest possible news media attention, the Yale University Press chose Columbus's birthday in 1965 to present publicly their scholarly study entitled *The Vinland Map and the Tartar Relation*. In this handsome and well-illustrated volume, three internationally respected scholars discussed the map that was being presented to the world as "the earliest known and indisputable cartographic representation of any part of the Americas." A photographic facsimile of the Vinland Map revealed it to be an elliptically shaped world map that included the western ocean (Atlantic) with delineations of Iceland, Greenland, and a large island or landmass identified as "Island of Vinland, discovered by Bjarni and Leif in company." The apparently definitive scholarly analysis of the Vinland Map and the document with which it had once been bound, the "Tartar Relation," led to the conclusion that both map and its accompanying document had been copied in about 1440 from earlier originals.

That Norsemen had visited North America as much as 500 years before Columbus's voyage was not a new idea. The Icelandic sagas and the archeological finds by the Norwegian Helge Ingstad at L'Anse aux Meadows on the north coast of Newfoundland had provided convincing evidence of Viking contacts in the period around A.D. 1000. What was new and exceedingly newsworthy was the fact that a map dating from before 1492 clearly and unequivocally showed a land called Vinland in the position of North America. In the words of Yale University Press releases, the Vinland Map was "the most important cartographic discovery of the century."

Not all who read the book and studied the map were convinced of its authenticity, however, and critical voices were soon raised. The provenance of the map was shadowy, if not suspect. It had been bought from an unidentified owner in Europe, then resold to an anonymous buyer, who gave it to Yale. The timing of the release of the book on Columbus Day was interpreted by some as an attack on Italians and Italian-Americans. It became a date which Yale administrators later came to regret.

More than embarrassment for Yale resulted from the interest and debate the map stimulated. School textbooks, for example, came under revision and increasingly reflected the Norse New World contacts. In an effort to convert some of the heat into scholarly light, the Smithsonian Institution's Department of American Studies organized a conference to facilitate the exchange of the views and insights the Vinland Map had stirred among scholars and experts in a number of diverse disciplines. The *Proceedings* of this conference were published as a book that should be consulted when the original Yale University Press volume is read.

The Norse Discovery of Vinland and North America

What can be determined and generally accepted with respect to the Norse contacts with North America in the period around A.D. 1000? First, the historical record makes clear that the peoples of northern Europe in the early Middle Ages were an extremely energetic and venturesome group. The progenitors of the peoples we now know as Swedes, Norwegians, and Danes appear to have poured forth from their northern homelands in a number of waves from the 8th to the 11th centuries. What triggered these movements is not entirely clear. Some suggest that overpopulation may have been the stimulus for sea roving and migration; others hold that political unrest, triggered by unpopular and repressive rulers, provided the impetus.

The western wing of this Norse expansion surged beyond continental Europe to reach and colonize the remote shores of Iceland in the 9th century. From Iceland, the next step was to the island that the outlawed Eric the Red named Greenland to encourage others to follow and join in the settlement he pioneered. In time, two large Norse settlements were founded on the coast of southern Greenland. The most southerly colony came to be known as the East Settlement, and the other, centered in the area of modern Godthaab about 160 miles to the north, was called the West Settlement (Fig. 2.2).

Like their relatives in northern Europe, the settlers of Iceland and Greenland were pagans who worshipped the old Norse gods Odin, Freya, and Thor. According to many experts, Leif Ericson brought Christianity to Greenland from Norway in the same year he is believed to have sighted Vinland. According to interpretations of the Icelandic sagas, Norway's King Olaf converted Leif and sent him to spread Christianity to Greenland. In the words of the saga:

The king provided him with a priest and various other holy men to baptize folk there and instruct them in the true faith. Leif set sail for Greenland that summer [A.D. 1000], and while at sea picked up a ship's crew of men who lay helpless there on a wreck. On this same journey he found Vinland the Good. He reached Greenland at the end of the summer and went to the lodge of Brattahild with Eric his father. From this time forward men called him Leif the Lucky, but his father contended that one thing cancelled out the other, in that Leif has rescued a ship's company and saved the men's lives, but had also introduced a man of mischief [as Eric styled the priest] into Greenland [Quinn, *New American World*, v. 1, 33].

In spite of reactionaries like Eric, the pagan status quo gave way to the zeal of the early Christian missionaries. Churches were built and, by 1126, an ecclesiastical see was established in the East Settlement to provide for the spiritual needs of the almost 10,000 Greenland colonists.

A Latin inscription on Yale's Vinland Map, located on the north of the land area named Vinland, may relate to the activities of one of the early bishops of Greenland, as well as the discovery credited to Leif Ericson. The text states:

By God's will after a long voyage from Greenland to the south toward the most distant remaining parts of the western ocean sea, sailing southward amidst the ice, the companions Bjarni and Leif Erickson discovered a new land, extremely fertile and even having vines, the which island they named Vinland. Eric, legate of the Apostolic See

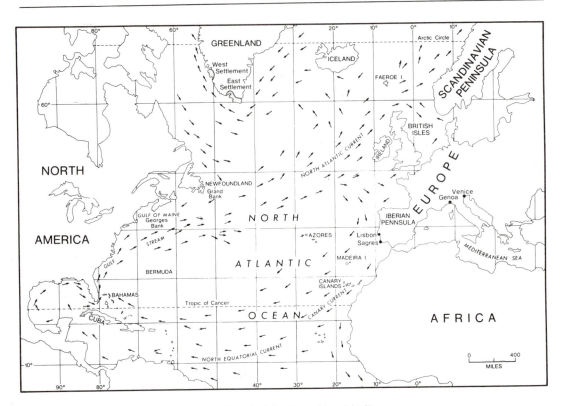

Figure 2.2 The North Atlantic, a New Mediterranean

and Bishop of Greenland and the neighboring regions, arrived in this truly vast and very rich land, in the name of Almighty God, in the last year of our most blessed father Pascal, remained a long time in both summer and winter, and later returned northeastward toward Greenland and then proceeded [home to Europe?] in most humble obedience to the will of his superiors [Skelton, 140].

Whatever are the specific dates and details concerned with the Norse discovery of North America, one thing appears reasonably clear: the Greenland colonists, and not the Viking kingdoms in Europe, provided the manpower and equipment that made such contacts a reality. Further, the small numbers of Greenlanders and their limited resource base soon came under stress, which eventually led to their loss of contact with Europe and ultimate extinction. Carl Sauer is only one of many scholars who have speculated on the reasons for the decline of the Greenland colonies. It is appropriate to conclude that the mystery of Vinland and its Norse colonists will be understood only when

the larger mystery of the decline and extinction of the Greenland settlements is solved.

The debates concerning the authenticity of the Vinland Map are not finished, nor is the historical record of Norse contacts with North America, five centuries before those by Columbus, a completed one. It is probably best to keep an open mind on the whole subject of pre-Columbian contacts. That such contacts took place seems certain. Exactly who made them, and when and where they occurred, represent research challenges to workers in a number of disciplines concerned with mankind's past. Most scholars would agree that impacts of those early contacts were probably very limited in scope compared with the revolutionary character of the impacts that flowed from the European rediscovery of the New World spearheaded by Columbus.

A THEORY OF EXPLORATION

J.D. Overton, writing in the *Journal of Historical Geography*, correctly criticized the traditional narrative approach that has characterized most writing on the history of exploration. He urged that geographical exploration be studied in its widest context with greater emphasis placed on its causes and effects, rather than simply on the colorful personalities and dramatic events that have dominated most literature in the field.

In developing a theoretical model of a process-oriented approach to exploration, Overton was careful to distinguish between geographical discovery and exploration. Discoverers, he argued, merely find or uncover places; it remains for explorers to begin the continuing assessment and evaluation. He wrote, "whether an area is 'known' or 'unknown' depends on how much knowledge and what type of knowledge is required." Reassessments and reevaluations of areas for newly determined purposes or needs are thus just as legitimate for study as are the reports of the first explorers or surveyors who provided the earliest descriptions or maps of those areas. Exploration, in Overton's scheme, implies an intention that results in "a conscious search for knowledge within and about imperfectly known areas." Thus, Columbus should be considered as an explorer consciously searching for

a western sea route to Asia, who unwittingly discovered two continents that were absent from the worldview of the Europeans and the Old World to which they belonged.

Exploration seen as a process involves six main elements (Fig. 2.3). The first represents "push" or demand factors that suggest or encourage a society or individual to extend interest to unexplored or little-known areas. Overton suggests economic factors, such as land shortage, shortages of natural resources, restricted fields of trade, or isolation from markets, as typical factors that have prompted exploration. Such factors as religious zeal and scientific curiosity have also operated to create demand. At the individual level, factors such as the desire for wealth and status have been potent forces leading many to leave the security of homelands to blaze new trails in distant areas. The second element in the exploration process involves the choice of area to be explored. Just *when* journeys of exploration occur is largely determined by demand factors, but the choice of *where* is related to the assessment and evaluation of prospective unexplored or underexplored areas before the act of exploration is undertaken.

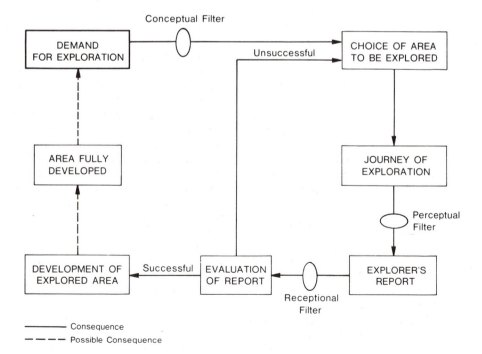

Figure 2.3 Main Elements of the Process of Exploration

A third element is the actual journey of exploration. Overton notes that this is the stage on which writers on exploration concentrate. The product of the journey, the explorer's report, forms the next element in the process. This vital component, written or orally related, official or private, includes the descriptions and assessments of the newly explored area. Next in the process is the evaluation of the explorer's report by decision-makers. Based on their evaluation, the exploratory adventure is judged to be successful or unsuccessful. A verdict of less than successful will result in demand factors remaining unfulfilled, and the process may be repeated in a newly selected area. A judgment of success, whether partial or full, could trigger development such as fisheries, trading posts, mines, plantations, missions, or permanent settlements in the newly explored territory. The development of the new area could become complete in time and the pioneer occupants themselves enter into the exploration process.

A further important component of Overton's theoretical process of exploration model is the concept of perception. He emphasized the fact that, as Ralph Brown wrote, "men at all times have been influenced quite as much by beliefs as by facts." Explorers, like most humans, view, assess, and describe environments they encounter from the perspective of the culture group and age to which they belong, as well as from their personal backgrounds, beliefs, aspirations, and values. These can be thought of as forming selective filters or lenses through which passes the information gleaned from the exploratory process. Overton's model forms, he wrote, "a more holistic perspective, stressing the links between the different facets of the exploration process and placing exploration in its broader economic and social context."

EUROPE'S ATLANTIC OUTLOOK BEGINS

The many original impulses leading Europeans to the discovery and exploration of North America can be compared with the roots of a large tree, which can be followed in any number of directions. The Age of Discovery had complex and interlocking origins that touched almost every facet of European life and existence. Only a few of the many rich themes elucidating the causes and effects of the European New World exploration can be considered

here. Important among these themes is the emergence of the Atlantic outlook and orientation that came to characterize and eventually dominate the lives of western Europeans. By the middle of the 17th century, the Atlantic Ocean ceased to be the limit of the known world and became another Mediterranean—a sea within the lands—to those Europeans now occupying or exploiting practically its whole littoral (Fig. 2.2).

To understand how this came about, it is necessary to appreciate that the orientation of Europe toward the Mediterranean Sea and the East did not end with the decline of Roman control and the onset of the so-called Dark Ages. Crusaders from the far corners of Christian Europe and merchant travelers, such as Marco Polo, were familiar with Middle Eastern caravanseries, where luxuries and indispensable spices from the "Indies" and Cathay were traded. European demand for these commodities grew, if for no other reason than because of increasing population. It is estimated that, between the beginning of the Christian era and A.D. 1500, the world's population doubled from 250 million to 500 million. The increases appear to have been greatest in the areas of the old Roman Empire, with western and central Europe showing the largest gains.

Shortly after Marco Polo's return from China in 1295, the power balance in the Mediterranean basin tipped sharply against the interests of the Europeans and Christendom. The capture of Acre in northern Palestine by the sultan of Egypt eliminated the last of the many Christian strongholds won during the Crusades. An awareness of the strength of Islam was thrust on the Europeans, as first Egypt, and then the Ottoman Empire, gained control of the trade routes to sources of the commodities, particularly spices, on which the Europeans had come to rely. Food preservation and preparation in that unrefrigerated age demanded spices as essentials, not luxuries for the favored few. Italian merchant republics, dominated by Venice and Genoa, entered into trading alliances with the Moslem powers and became profiteering middlemen in commercial links with the East.

As these pressures developed in the Europe–Mediterranean–Middle East trading system, important events were transpiring on the Atlantic front of Europe. Technological advances pioneered by Mediterranean navigators made safe oceanic sailing a reality. The compass, astrolabe, and portolan sea charts aboard ships that could sail almost into the wind were the basic tools needed for exploring the far reaches of the globe. All had been perfected in the Mediterranean and were at hand when the Spanish and Portuguese led the way into the Atlantic.

Portugal and Henry the Navigator

Portugal was particularly well suited to adopt programs of Atlantic exploration. A long Atlantic coastline provided numerous ports vital in the sea link between northwestern Europe and the Mediterranean. Genoese merchants and navigators formed important and influential communities in those ports and contributed to the growth of the Portuguese merchant fleet. Aided by their Genoese guests, the Portuguese began to probe the Atlantic off their shores and northern Africa. Prince Henry, immortalized with the title "Navigator," played a truly extraordinary role in these developments. As the third son of his royal father, Henry had little hope of ever assuming the throne and seemed destined for an army career. He led the military campaign that drove the Moors from Cueta in north Africa in 1415, and planted the first seed of what was to become a vast Portuguese empire in Africa.

His encounters with the Moors probably gave him good opportunities to absorb their geographical lore and add it to his own body of European knowledge. He was instrumental in mounting expeditions that discovered and colonized the islands of the Madeiras and the Azores (Fig. 2.2). Oceanic discovery and exploration were not hit-or-miss undertakings to Henry. On the contrary, he set up a highly organized center at Sagres in southern Portugal for gathering geographical intelligence and training navigators. From this "think tank" command center at Europe's southwestern tip, he conducted a national program of discovery and exploration that culminated, after his death, in the rounding of Africa and regular trade between Portugal and India and beyond. Reflecting on the Portuguese accomplishment, Carl Sauer argued that Portugal could have gained control of the Atlantic had not wars with Castile, which invaded Portugal repeatedly, and the Black Death impeded her.

By the time Columbus sailed under the banner of Portugal's enemy-neighbor Spain, Ma-deira had become integrated into the economies of Europe and Africa. T. Bently Duncan wrote, "The island was the prototype of that momentous and tragic social and economic system of sugar and slavery that was to be repeated, on a far larger scale, in the West Indies and Brazil." Only 75 years after first settlement, Madeira was the world's greatest sugar producer and an important center of commerce and navigation.

Spain Supports Columbus's Western Sea Route Hypothesis

Christopher Columbus was one of the many Genoese navigators familiar with the Iberian coast and Atlantic sea routes to northern Europe. Experts believe that he voyaged aboard ships bound as far as Iceland, an important source of salt fish for Iberia's Roman Catholics. If this is true, he may well have gained a knowledge of the lore surrounding the early Norse voyages west of Greenland. It is certain that he shipped aboard Portuguese vessels to the coast of western Africa, where trading contacts followed Prince Henry's exploratory expeditions.

Columbus married the daughter of a wealthy Madeira landowner but, after her death, he and his brother took up residence in Lisbon and entered the nautical chart and instrument trade. There he put his experiences and acquired knowledge to work in formulating a well-thought-out hypothesis and proposal concerning a western sea route across the Atlantic to the islands and coasts of easternmost Asia. When one considers his background, it is not difficult to imagine that he was able to structure a convincing and persuasive proposal.

The widespread European belief in legends of islands and lands in the Atlantic to the west doubtlessly aided such a scheme. The legend of Antilia, a rich, luxurious island peopled by Christians who had migrated there from Europe, was typical of these legends (Fig. 2.4). Some scholars believe that Antilia may have been based on misunderstood or garbled reports of the early Greenland settlements. Whatever its inspiration Antilia, in one form or another a fixture on pre-Columbian maps, did nothing to detract from Columbus's hypothesis and bold scheme for discovery.

Columbus petitioned the king of Portugal in 1484 to send him on a voyage of discovery to the west. Portugal, deeply committed to a

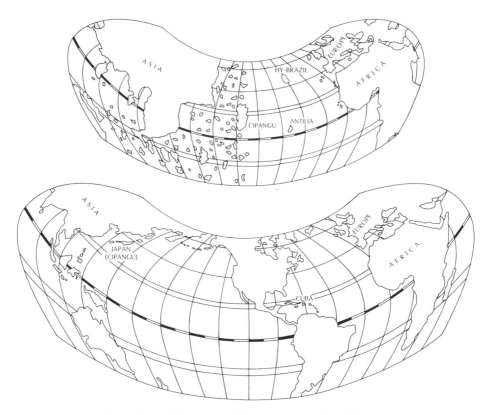

Figure 2.4   Worldview of Columbus and Real World

southern approach to the Orient, refused. Columbus tried vainly for six years to receive royal backing for his westward discovery scheme from both the Spanish and Portuguese monarchs. Finally, in 1492, following the Spanish expulsion of the Moors from Granada, their last Iberian stronghold, Columbus was granted his long-sought support. Spain, eager to enter the exploratory race with its often hostile neighbor on the Atlantic coast, decided that Columbus's scheme was worth a modest investment.

COLUMBUS'S WORLDVIEW AND THE BEHAVIORAL ENVIRONMENT

Columbus knew that the world was a sphere, as did every educated European of his day. What he did not share was the prevailing estimate of the earth's circumference and the width of the Atlantic Ocean. He was convinced that the value of a degree of longitude at the equator was about 45 miles in length, rather than 60 nautical miles. In other words, he underestimated the earth's size by 25 percent! On this small world, the three continents of Europe, Asia, and Africa were surrounded by an all-embracing ocean (Fig. 2.4). Asia, in his mind, stretched far beyond its true east-west width to face Europe across a sailable Atlantic. The Canary Islands, by his calculations, were only 2,400 nautical miles from Japan (in fact this distance is 10,600 nautical miles). Columbus assiduously gathered sources and authorities to support his small earth–wide Asia hypothesis.

Columbus's worldview was largely in keeping with what geographer William Kirk would recognize as the "behavioral environment" of his day, a view generally shared by his informed western European contempories in the late 15th century. Kirk urges that we try to put ourselves into the minds of people like Columbus and other past decision-makers to understand why and how they undertook actions that profoundly affected world history and geography. In the view of Spanish royal advisors, Columbus was promoting a reasonable scheme worth a modest gamble in terms of then-current demand factors.

Columbus's accomplishment, termed "the most spectacular and most far-reaching geographical discovery in recorded human history" by his biographer Samuel Eliot Morison, was not immediately perceived as such. Many experts believe that Columbus probably never realized the true nature of his great discovery and died still assuming that the Caribbean islands and shores were parts of eastern Asia, rather than portions of two continents comprising a "New World." He reported Cuba as the easternmost cape of Asia and Honduras, Nicaragua, and Costa Rica as provinces of Cathay. This did not prevent Spain from beginning to colonize the new discoveries almost as soon as he had found them.

King Ferdinand and Queen Isabella endorsed Columbus's proposal to return to the "Indies" and establish a trading colony on Hispaniola. In their instructions, issued on May 29, 1493, they set the conversion of the natives to Christianity as the first object for Columbus's second expedition. Six priests were assigned to the fleet, and Columbus was ordered to see that the Indians were "treated very well and lovingly." Despite the pride of place given these lofty religious aims, the expedition's commercial motive is amply revealed in the fact that most of the 1500 other people recruited were aboard for the second declared motive—the creation of a trading colony. A third charge to Columbus, now an admiral, was the exploration of Cuba to discover whether it was a part of the Asian mainland and a potential route to the riches of Cathay.

THE EMERGENCE OF A NEW WORLD

John Cabot, like Columbus, appears to have been born in or near Genoa. Some time after assuming Venetian citizenship, he found his way to Bristol, England's second-largest port. In the early 1490s, Bristol was a large fishing port as well as an important center in the trading network that linked Iceland, northwestern Europe, the Iberian Peninsula, and the Mediterranean.

Leaders in both the merchant and fishing communities of Bristol were responding to demand factors and sponsoring occasional exploratory voyages during the 1480s and 1490s. In a report forwarded by the Spanish ambassador in London, the ambassador wrote that Bristol was in the habit of sending from two to four ships a year "in search of the island of Brazil and the Seven Cities." In Bristol, exploration for new fisheries and trade routes was a recognized undertaking.

Cabot's scheme of discovery, in its broad outlines, shared much with the one Columbus had promoted successfully. Cabot proposed sailing west to the Indies by a route farther poleward and thus shorter than the admiral's. On his route, the legendary island of Hy-Brazil took the place of Antilia as a way station. King Henry of England would not invest directly in the expedition, but did issue a patent allowing Cabot to sail to any part of the world unknown to Christians. This device by which England did not appear to be in direct competition with the Iberians asserted England's right to sail in search of unknown lands. This assertion meant little then, but later served as a significant argument when England actively began to compete for overseas trade and possessions. Prior discovery was frequently used to justify colonization.

Cabot first undertook a single-ship reconnaissance voyage in 1497 to test his thesis. His navigation was good, and wind conditions allowed him to make a swift crossing from Bristol to Newfoundland in just over a month. If Morison's reconstruction of that voyage is correct, Cabot made his first North American landing only a few miles from the L'Anse aux Meadows site that is believed to be the location of Leif Ericson's Norse settlement—a rare coincidence! Cabot's first voyage appears to have caused a brief sensation when he rushed to London to inform the king. King Henry rewarded the discoverer with a gift of £ 10 "to hym that founde the new Isle." Unfortunately, little is known of where he explored and what he reported. What evidence exists must be inferred from the letters and reports of others. Unlike Columbus, no journals or reports by Cabot have survived.

In February 1498, Henry VII issued letters patent giving John Cabot permisison to organize a large expedition to explore the coast he had discovered. According to one contemporary report, Cabot planned to sail along the coast to the island of Cipangu, where he felt the jewels and spices of the world originated (Fig. 2.5). Once there he intended, it was reported, to set up a trading factory and make London "a more important mart than Alexandria."

In the late spring of 1498 four ships sailed past Ireland on a westward course and they were never heard from again. What befell Cabot's second expedition is unknown. His son, Sebastian, was not with the flotilla. He continued in his father's footsteps with a later expedition to find a northwest passage to Asia. After his voyage in Arctic waters, Sebastian shifted his service to Spain and became the Pilot Major in that country.

Transatlantic probes like those of Columbus and Cabot were contributing to a growing fund of still-disconnected geographical intelligence bearing on the western Atlantic rim (Fig. 2.5). Coasts and islands forming that rim were being reported and described in terms that failed to accord with what was known to exist in eastern Asia. Where were the rich and teeming cities and fabulously wealthy potentates and their

palaces? Nothing found in these "Indies" of the explorers even began to approach the reality that formed the behavioral environment of the Europeans with respect to Asia.

Many innovative geographical hypotheses were formulated to accommodate the new discoveries. Several involved the concept of a projection or peninsula of Asia that jutted far to the east in one form or another. Other hypotheses were based on the belief that the explorations being reported were on islands off the Asian coasts. It was these remote peninsulas and islands and not the "known" lands of Cathay, Japan, and India that were being encountered. Figure 2.6 presents a few of these hypotheses in graphic form. As the maps drawn during the Age of Exploration are studied, it is a good idea to think of them in this light. What may appear to our eyes to be bizarre distortions of the continents and oceans were actually graphic statements of what were, at the time they were drawn, perfectly reasonable geographical ideas.

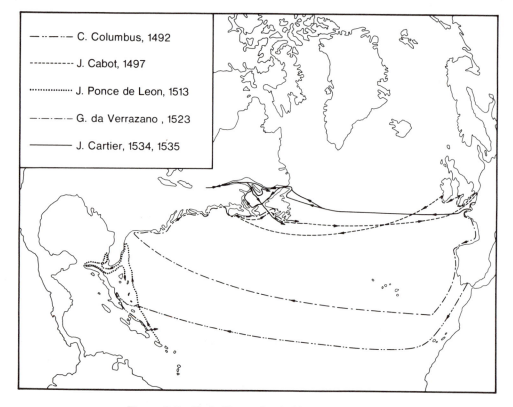

— ·· — ·· —   C. Columbus, 1492

----------   J. Cabot, 1497

··············   J. Ponce de Leon, 1513

— · — · —   G. da Verrazano , 1523

——————   J. Cartier, 1534, 1535

Figure 2.5   Early Transatlantic Voyages to 1535

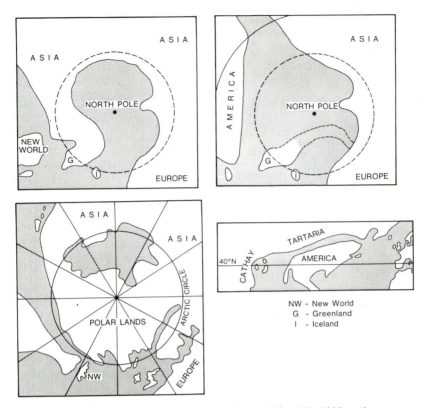

Figure 2.6   Diagrammatic Models of Several New World Hypotheses

THE NAMING OF AMERICA

In the early 1500s, a circle of scholars in the small Vosges mountain town of St. Die, in what is today Alsace-Lorraine, were working on an atlas publishing project that would incorporate the new discoveries gradually being reported. One member of the small group was a German-born priest named Martin Waldseemuller who, in addition to his knowledge of geography, was a skilled draftsman and cartographer. The "Gymnase Vosgien," as the group was known, was equipped with a printing press on which their material could be copied rapidly.

When word of Amerigo Vespucci's discoveries along the South American coast reached the St. Die scholars, they were quick to realize that he had been skirting more than a mere peninsula of Asia. In their printed treatise entitled *Cosmographiae Introductio*, the St. Die scholars explained that he had in truth found "another fourth part of the world." The paragraph, which gave the rationale for a name to

be applied to this new fourth part of the world, is worthy of quotation:

Now, really these [three] parts [Europe, Africa, and Asia] were more widely travelled, and another fourth part was discovered by Americus Vesputius . . . for which reason I do not see why anyone would rightly forbid calling it (after the discoverer Americus, a man of wisdom and ingenuity) "Amerige," that is land of Americus, or "America," since both "Europe" and "Asia" are names derived from women. Its location and the customs of its people will be easily discerned from the four voyages of Americus which follow [Smithsonian Institution, exhibit brochure, *The Naming of America*, Oct., 1983].

The *Cosmographiae* was accompanied by Waldseemuller's maps, showing a separate landmass in the sea between Europe and Asia. They are the first maps to use the name "America" to designate a major portion of the New World. The fundamental concept of a tripartite world, tracing its roots back to the ancient Greeks and emerging as a theological truism when Christianity flowered, was extremely hard for the Europeans to abandon. The accumulating evidence of the existence of a New World became overwhelming in time, however, and they were forced to wrestle with the countless spiritual and material ramifications that realization brought to their lives.

EXPLORATION OF THE
EASTERN SEABOARD

Probably the most surprising aspect of the exploration of North America is how slow the process was in getting underway. For most of the century following its discovery by the Europeans, North America represented a hazily defined barrier more than a field for exploration. Only slowly did the New World enter the minds of European leaders and decision makers as an arena in which exploratory effort should be expended. This accounts for the unusually long period during which, Ralph H. Brown found, "beliefs about America were dominant over facts." As Brown noted, "the long years intervening between the arrival of the adventurous explorers and the no less courageous colonists had been curiously unproductive of new geographical knowledge." The remainder of this chapter will be a brief review of those "long years" to illustrate the process by which the European colonial powers followed initial discovery with exploration, territorial acquisition, and resource appraisal along the eastern seaboard of North America.

The 15th century closed with the discoveries of Christopher Columbus in the south and John Cabot in the north, still considered essentially disconnected events. Both Columbus and Cabot were believed by Europeans to have made contact with islands lying east of a vast Asian continent (Figs. 2.4 and 2.6). Not until the 16th-century voyages of Juan Ponce de León and Hernando de Soto, sponsored by Spain, and those by Giovanni da Verrazano and Jacques Cartier, under the French royal banner, did the continuity of North America from Florida to Labrador begin to become an accepted fact and true exploration of North America begin (Fig. 2.7).

Juan Ponce de León

In 1513, Juan Ponce de León, already rich from successful gold mining ventures in Puerto Rico,

received a royal license "to discover and settle the island of Bimini," which was rumored to lie to the north. His voyage passed along the Atlantic side of the Bahamas to the coast of northern Florida (Fig. 2.5). The party clashed with local Indians probably in the vicinity of St. Augustine. Another battle with Indians ensued when a landing was made on the west coast of Florida, probably near San Carlos Bay.

Although nothing of exceptional value was found and the Indians were notably inhospitable, Juan Ponce followed his 1513 discovery of Florida with an attempt at settlement in 1521. Possibly encouraged by the reports of the fabulous wealth being found in Mexico, he equipped a party of 200 colonists with livestock, seed, and equipment for a settlement on the coast of southwest Florida. Here, he probably reasoned, all ships leaving or entering the Gulf of Mexico would find it convenient to trade and take on stores and water. Unfortunately, Ponce had not improved his ability to negotiate with the Indians in the years since his first skirmishes. The Spaniards were driven out shortly after landing by vigorous Indian attacks, and Juan Ponce was mortally wounded.

Ponce's unsuccessful excursion to the Florida mainland was followed by the equally ill-fated adventures of Lucas Vasquez de Ayllon on the coast of South Carolina and those of Panfilo Navarez and Cabeza de Vaca on the Gulf Coast. Spain, by the end of 1528, had experienced a series of failed adventures that provided dearly gained but sketchy geographical knowledge of the southern coastal outline of North America from Texas to South Carolina. The failure to find gold or other great wealth coupled with the presence of seemingly warlike Indians discouraged further Spanish interest in Florida for several decades.

The most significant outcome of Juan Ponce de León's Florida adventures grew from his reports of the powerful Gulf Stream that flows northward along the peninsula's Atlantic coast. Ponce reported that in those waters, "although they had a great wind, they could not proceed forward, but backward and it seemed that they were proceeding well, but in the end it was known that it was in such wise the current which was more powerful than the wind." It was not long before Spanish navigators were regularly returning from Carribean and Central American waters on the Gulf Stream to the

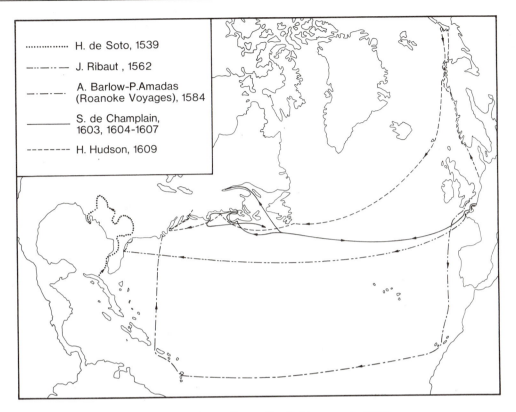

Figure 2.7   Later Transatlantic Voyages to 1609

latitude of the Carolina Outer Banks, and thence eastward to Iberia on the prevailing westerlies (Fig. 2.2). When Spain finally did establish St. Augustine as an enduring outpost on the eastern seaboard of North America in 1565, the motivation to do so was to protect this maritime jugular vein of her New World empire.

Giovanni da Verrazano

The coastal region to the north of Florida was first described by Giovanni da Verrazano. He and others firmly believed that somewhere between the latitude of Florida and the codfish-rich coasts, first sighted by John Cabot, might be found a sea passage to Cathay and the Spice Islands that the recently returned survivors of Magellan's circumnavigation of the world were reporting. This was the basis for the 1523 voyage Verrazano persuaded Francis I of France to support. He made his crossing, using the tried and true technique of latitude sailing, at approximately 32° north latitude. Fearing contact with Spaniards, whom he felt might be in the

Florida area, Verrazano turned his attention to the unknown latitudes to the north.

The chief outcome of Verrazano's reconnaissance of the eastern seaboard was the widespread realization that North America existed as a great independent landmass important in its own right. Thanks to Verrazano's detailed descriptions of the land and its aboriginal inhabitants, North America began to be perceived as a verdant and potentially rich land. Typical of these descriptions is the following, which recounts his entry with the ship's boat into lower New York Bay:

We entered the river into the land for about half a league, where we saw that it formed a very beautiful lake about three leagues [10 miles] in circuit, on which about thirty of their [the Indians] barks were going from one side to the other, carrying an infinite number of people coming from different parts to see us. Suddenly, as befalls in navigating, there rose a strong contrary wind from the sea which forced us to return to the ship and, greatly to our regret, to leave that land, so hospitable and attractive, and we think, not without things of value, all the hills showing minerals [Sauer, *Sixteenth Century North America*, 55].

Verrazano might have provided a description of the Indian-modified landscape around present-day New York had not an onshore wind caused him to retreat to his ship, lying offshore just outside the inlet now spanned by the Verrazano Narrows Bridge between Staten Island and Brooklyn.

Another product of Verrazano's voyage had a major influence on the cartography of North America throughout much of the 16th century. It grew from observations made while he was cautiously sounding his ship, the *Dauphine*, through the hazardous shallows that extend seaward from North Carolina's range of narrow barrier islands now known as the Outer Banks. Perhaps because of poor visibility, Verrazano did not realize that there were narrow inlets between the islands making up the Banks. In his report to the king he wrote of finding, in place of islands and inlets, "an isthmus one mile wide and about two hundred miles long, in which we could see the eastern sea from the ship. . . . This is, doubtless, the one which goes round the tip of India, China and Cathay." To his eager eye, the broad expanse of Pamlico Sound was the Pacific Ocean. Numerous maps drawn in the century following his report prominently showed the "Sea of Verrazano" separated from the Atlantic Ocean by a narrow isthmus in the general area now occupied by North Carolina and Virginia.

Some authorities believe that Verrazano may have elaborated somewhat on his actual observations in an effort to improve his stature in the king's eyes and ensure support for follow-up expeditions. His hopes were not realized because Francis I embroiled France in a disastrous war in Italy, and Verrazano lost his life on an expedition to Central America. Although Verrazano did not live to see it, the concept of a New France on the western rim of the Atlantic had taken root.

Jacques Cartier

Although ten years passed before the French king once again was ready to back a voyage to North America, French fishermen were active on the rich grounds and banks around Newfoundland. Guarded as they were concerning geographical information, they appear to have drawn attention to the Strait of Belle Isle, the long, narrow arm of sea separating the Labrador coast from the northern part of Newfoundland. In 1534 Jacques Cartier was commissioned "to voyage and go to the New Lands and to pass the Strait of the Bay of Castles." Another contemporaneous document revealed that he was expected to "discover certain islands and lands where it is said he should find great quantities of gold and other rich things." It appears that Cartier's expedition was to discover a route to Asia and find treasure-bearing lands along the way. This was a prophetic vision in view of the fabulous wealth the French fur trade in the St. Lawrence Valley–Great Lakes basin ultimately yielded.

Cartier sailed from St. Malo in northern France in late April and arrived off eastern Newfoundland in an amazingly brief 27 days (Fig. 2.5). He explored the coast of eastern New Brunswick and the Gaspé Peninsula, and named "Chaleur" (heat) the large bay separating the two areas. For a short time he believed that Baie de Chaleur might even be the passage to the Pacific. During a detailed survey of the bay named to commemorate the early summer heat, Cartier encountered a large number of Indians who showed a lively interest in trading with the crew. The following extract describing that event documents the beginning of the fur trade that later became Canada's chief source of wealth:

We likewise made signs to them that we wished them no harm and sent two men ashore to give them some knives and other iron goods and a red cap to give to their chief. Seeing this they sent to the shore a party with some of their furs; and the two groups traded together. The savages showed marvelous great pleasure in possessing and obtaining these iron wares and other commodities, dancing and going through many ceremonies and throwing salt water over their heads with their hands. They bartered everything they had to the extent that all went back naked without a thing on them; and they made signs that they would be back on the morrow with more furs. [Chaleur Bay was explored to its head] whereat we were grieved and disappointed. At the head of the bay, beyond its low shore were very high mountains. And seeing that there was no passage we proceeded to turn back [Sauer, *Sixteenth Century North America*, 80].

At least one more large Indian group, of some 300 Micmac, engaged in an active session of bartering in the days that followed and further demonstrated the commercial potential of the region. Although the entrance to the St. Lawrence was not discovered, Cartier's voyage was judged a success. He returned to St. Malo with furs and local Indians to be tutored in French and serve as guides on his next expedition.

Cartier entered the St. Lawrence River and proceeded to explore it the following year (1535), doubtlessly aided by the geographical intelligence the Indians were able to provide. Near the site of present-day Québec, where the St. Charles River joins the St. Lawrence, he decided in September to establish a base for the winter. His description of the area near the important Indian town of Stadacona painted a most attractive picture:

This is as good land as can be found and is highly productive, with many fine trees of the nature and kinds of France, such as oaks, elms, ash, nut trees, plum trees, yews, cedars, vines, hawthorns with fruits as large as damson plums, and other trees, beneath which there grows as good hemp as that of France, and it grows without sowing or labor [*Ibid.*, 86].

Cartier continued upriver with his smallest vessel and two longboats, through a valley he described in similarly glowing terms. On October 2, 1535, more than a thousand Indians at the site of present-day Montreal met his party "with as good a welcome as ever a father gave to his son." The Indian's town, named Hochelaga, was an impressive settlement surrounded by a strong, well-engineered, defensive palisade. Cartier found, within the enclosed town space,

some fifty house . . . each fifty or more paces long and twelve to fifteen wide, made of timbers and covered, roof and sides, by large pieces of bark and rind of trees, some as wide as a table and artfully tied according to their manner. And inside are a number of rooms and chambers and in the center of the house is a large room or space upon the ground, where they make their fire and live together, the men thereafter retiring with wives and children to their private rooms. Also houses have lofts on high in which they store their corn [*Ibid.*, 88].

At the fortified winter camp downriver, the Canadian winter closed in with a ferocity that amazed the Frenchmen. Their position was almost two full degrees of latitude south of St.

Malo and was presumed to have been similar in climate, if not even milder. All might have gone well if an infectious disease had not been spread to the local Indians. Cartier, fearing that they might contract the scourge decimating their neighbors, forbade the Indians to enter the fort or have any contact with the French. It is ironic that this reaction to the Indian's plight was to prove fatal to the Europeans. Cut off from contact with the Indians and the fresh fish and game they provided, the French party was forced to subsist on ship's biscuit and salt meat they had brought from France. Predictably, an attack of virulent scurvy hit the snowbound and vitamin-deficient French; by mid-February almost all were seriously ill. Twenty-five died and forty more were near death before one of the Indians, who had been to France with Cartier, taught them the native remedy—a decoction made from the needles and bark of local evergreen trees. As the party returned to health, contact with the Indians and their supplies of freshly caught fish and game were resumed.

In May 1536, the survivors returned to St. Malo, after completing the longest and most revealing reconnaissance of the heart of what would become, in the following century, New France. No route to Asia was found, but Cartier and Roberval undertook ill-fated settlement attempts in the 1540s. Once again the unbridled ferocity of the Canadian winter proved too great a hardship, and these precursors of Champlain's permanent settlement in New France were abandoned.

Hernando de Soto

At about the same time that Cartier and Roberval's colonization schemes in the St. Lawrence Valley were facing difficulties, Hernando de Soto was undertaking one of the most incredible exploratory adventures in the annals of history. De Soto, already wealthy and influential after fifteen years of treasure gathering in Central America and Peru, turned his eyes to the mainland of what is now the American South. After receiving the necessary royal permissions and privileges, the successful conquistador had little trouble in recruiting an expedition of more than 700 treasure seekers in Spain. A convoy of ten ships was required to move the party, which resembled an invasion force more than a party of explorers. Some 600 soldiers and more than 100 servants and camp followers, along with 200 horses, 300 pigs, and an impressive baggage train, were finally landed on the southwest coast of Florida on May 25, 1539 (Fig. 2.7).

Unlike the other Spanish adventurers who had preceded him, de Soto had no interest in coastal settlement. Rather, he followed the procedure of the conquistadors in Central and South America, where gold and precious objects had been found in the interior rather than on the coastal margins. De Soto proceeded to lead his unwieldy expedition along a rambling route that ultimately touched portions of the present states of Florida, Georgia, South Carolina, North Carolina, Tennessee, Alabama, Mississippi, Arkansas, Louisiana, and Texas. The typical plan would be to capture a local Indian chief and force his tribe to ransom him for food and bearers to carry the camp equipment and baggage to the next major tribal center, where the process would be repeated. As might be expected, the Indians suffered drastically, particularly as they fell prey to the European diseases that formed such an insidious element in the Columbian Exchange, discussed earlier.

The Appalachian Mountains and the Mississippi River were crossed and Plains Indians encountered by the apparently still indefatigable de Soto. From the Plains dwellers he attempted to learn of the route "to the other sea," as the Pacific was termed. In 1542, four years after his landing in Florida, he appears to have decided to return to civilization. On the trail to the coast, Hernando de Soto, sick with fever, died and was committed to a watery grave in the Mississippi River. About 300 Spaniards managed to survive the ordeal and reach the Mexican town of Panuco in the autumn of 1543, empty-handed and dressed in patches of hides taken from Indians. Perhaps the best summary of de Soto's incredible enterprise was provided by the Spanish historian Lopez de Gomara, who wrote, "He went about for five years hunting mines, thinking it would be like Peru. He made no settlement and thus he died and destroyed those who went with him. Never will conquerers do well unless they settle before they undertake anything else, especially here where the Indians are valiant bowmen and strong [Sauer, *Sixteenth Century North America*, 78]."

In the years that followed de Soto's adventure, Florida remained an uninhabited coast vaguely visible in the west to the hundreds of treasure-laden Spanish galleons that sailed along it in the strong north-flowing Gulf Stream. In pointing out the strategic importance that this phenomenon of Atlantic surface circulation lent to Florida for the Spanish, Carl Sauer wrote:

From whatever point of origin—New Spain, Peru, New Granada—shipping to Spain entered the Straits of Florida from the west, to ride the streaming of the sea out of the Gulf of Mexico, through the Bahama Channel, and on north into the Atlantic. At Cape Canaveral the Gulf Stream has a summer rate of flow of seventy miles a day, fifty miles to the east of the Sea Islands of Georgia and South Carolina. . . . This was the *carrera de las Indias* eastbound [*Sixteenth Century North America*, 190].

Jean Ribaut

The possibility of overseas settlement was not ignored by France, one of Spain's emerging European rivals. French Protestants, known as Huguenots, were a minority increasingly under stress in the predominantly Catholic monarchy of the mid-16th century. The Huguenot protector was also the Admiral of France with authority over merchant as well as naval shipping. The idea of overseas colonial refuges for the nonconforming Huguenots was thus encouraged. If such a colony could be established along the Florida coast it could be expected to serve as a valuable base for attacks on the antagonistic Spaniards, whose official policy excluded all other European powers from North America. In addition, a Florida colony might enjoy a more genial, tropical climate than the one bitterly experienced by Cartier.

In February 1562, two French ships under the command of Jean Ribaut and Goulaine de Laudonnière made a fast passage from Le Havre, in heavily Protestant Normandy, to the St. John's River in northern Florida. The local Indians were awed as the French explorers erected a large stone column bearing the royal arms and announced France's annexation of Florida. Ribaut continued north to explore the coast of Georgia and South Carolina, where he found "many other rivers and arms of the sea divide and make many other great islands by which we may travel from one island to another between land and land. And it seemeth that we may go and sail without danger through all the country and enter into the great seas, which were a wonderful advantage." His early description of the Sea Islands, many sounds, and estuaries along this coast was a good one and presaged the development of the Intra-Coastal Waterway of the modern era.

An outpost named Charlesfort was built on Port Royal Sound and garrisoned with volunteers. The main party then sailed for France to raise additional support for a colony. They arrived to find that the long-feared religious war had broken out, and the planned relief for the volunteers on Port Royal Sound had to be abandoned. Not until the spring of 1564 was the Huguenot leadership able to send out another expedition to Florida under the command of Ribaut's lieutenant, Laudonnière. He found the St. Johns River after a quick passage and received an enthusiastic welcome from the Indians. With their advice and assistance, Laudonnière began construction of Fort Caroline a few miles upstream from the river's mouth. The fort was to serve as the French base for further exploration designed to follow up Indian stories of precious metals and other wealth in the interior.

It is fortunate that Laudonnière's party included a gifted artist who was assigned the task of keeping a visual record of the expedition's discoveries. Jacques le Moyne's many sketches and drawings of Florida's landscape and Indians were published as engravings later in the century and constitute the first widely circulated visual account of North American aboriginal life and landscape. Little is known about his training or background except that he was from Dieppe, an important center of cartographic development in the early 16th century. The Dieppe school is famed for its artistically embellished maps that showed details of the flora and fauna of newly discovered lands in addition to their location and configuration.

The Spanish were aware of the French activities in Florida and resolved to remove them from the region. In the late summer of 1565, Fort Caroline was attacked and taken by a force under the command of Pedro Menéndez de Avilés. About 132 French lives were lost in the attack, and a short while later a reinforcing fleet under the command of Jean Ribaut was wrecked by a hurricane along the coast to the south. Making their way north toward Fort Caroline, they were intercepted and brutally massacred by Menéndez, who spared only a few Catholics from the sword in an orgy of killing near the waterway still known as Matanzas Inlet (the place of slaughter), close to modern St. Augustine.

Menéndez, having eliminated the French threat to the vital Gulf Stream sea route, established a center of Spanish control at St. Augustine. This modern Florida city boasts that its date of founding, 1565, makes it the oldest European settled city in North America. For the next two centuries Florida would form a bastion of the Spanish Empire on the Atlantic seaboard of the new continent.

Walter Raleigh

Just as religion played a role in encouraging French exploratory efforts in Florida, it had a fundamental influence in the English exploration of the Carolinas and Virginia. Once Protestant Queen Elizabeth was securely on the throne in England in 1558, the country's latent anti-Spanish sentiment surged to the surface. The Spanish monopoly over all trade with the New World was a major annoyance to seafaring English Protestants sailing from west-of-England ports. Attacks on Spanish fleets and towns by mariners like John Hawkins and Francis Drake signaled the rise of English sea power and inexorably drew the two nations toward war.

It is not surprising that the line between New World exploration and privateer attacks against the Spanish was often blurred in the latter 1500s. Sir Humphrey Gilbert published a tract in 1577 in which he described "how Her Majesty might annoy the King of Spain by fitting out a fleet of war-ships under pretense of a voyage of discovery, and so fall upon the enemy's shipping and destroy his trade in Newfoundland and the West Indies."

After his death, Gilbert's half-brother Walter Raleigh, a particular favorite of Queen Elizabeth, received a patent "to discover, search, find out, and view such remote heathen and barbarous lands, countries, and territories, not actually possessed of any Christian prince, nor inhabited by Christian people, as to him . . . shall seem good, and the same to have, hold, occupy and enjoy to him, his heirs and assigns forever." The English view was that, if the

Spanish were not already occupying and developing New World areas, those regions would be fair game for England's subjects to exploit.

Although Raleigh's precise ambitions are not entirely clear in the historical record, it is safe to assume that any area he undertook to colonize had the potential to be a good base for attacks on the Spanish. Raleigh's thinking also may have been influenced by a growing desire for alternative sources for products traditionally imported from Spain. Because contemporary climatic theories held that regions occupying similar latitudinal positions were similar climatically and would produce the same range of crops, it was reasoned that such products as olive oil, wine, leather, and sugar could be procured from a colony in the Carolina-Virginia area of the New World. It was further felt that the depressed economic conditions prevalent in England could be expected to produce willing colonists.

Raleigh sent a two-ship reconnaissance party under the command of Philip Amadas, a well-qualified navigator, and Arthur Barlow, a capable soldier (Fig. 2.7). The expedition left England on April 27, 1584, and returned to report to Raleigh in the middle of September. Although the identities of the whole party are not known, there is reason to believe that John White and Thomas Hariot were included. On follow-up voyages connected with Raleigh's colonization attempts, White and Hariot provided a superb pictorial and verbal record of the Carolina-Virginia aboriginal landscape and the Indians living in it. (Hariot had been Raleigh's tutor while he was a student at Oxford.)

Barlowe prepared a report entitled "The First Voyage Made to the Coasts of America With Two Barks . . ." for Raleigh at the conclusion of the voyage. He told of approaching the coast near 36° N, "where we smelled so sweet and so strong a smell as if we had been in the midst of some delicate garden abounding with all kinds of odoriferous flowers, by which we were assured that the land could not be far distant." The report described how the small fleet anchored near an inlet through the Outer Banks, entered Pamlico Sound in boats, and formally took possession of the land in the name of Queen Elizabeth (see Corbett, 14–26).

Arriving at Roanoke Island Barlow found "many goodly woods full of deer, conies [rabbits], hares and fowl, even in the midst of summer in incredible abundance." After two days on the island he made contact with the local Indians. The natives were friendly and hospitable and appeared to welcome the Englishmen to their land. Not much time was lost before "we fell to trading with them, exchanging some things that we had for chamois, buff and deer skins." The profitability of the trade was emphasized by Barlowe, who described how a bright tin plate was exchanged for "twenty skins worth twenty crowns or twenty nobles."

Barlowe's report was clearly designed to serve Raleigh as a promotion tract and was well larded with favorable adjectives. Nevertheless, Carl Sauer correctly categorized it as a "perceptive observation" of the flora, fauna, and Indian culture of the Carolina–Virginia region on the eve of its colonization by the English. Like Cartier, Amadas and Barlowe "brought home also two of the savages, being lusty men, whose names were Wanchese and Manteo." It is no coincidence that North Carolina's capital city is named Raleigh and that the two towns on Roanoke Island are named Manteo and Wanchese. Raleigh, with Barlowe's favorable report in hand and the Roanoke Indians on show around London, lost no time in organizing a follow-up venture. His fortunes were greatly enhanced by the favor he won from England's queen, in honor of whom he named the newly explored lands "Virginia."

Roanoke proved lacking as a haven from which attacks could be mounted on treasure-laden Spanish galleons, but it did appeal to a group associated with John White. White was an artist-cartographer whose maps and drawings form an absolutely invaluable record of the land that attracted England's first colonists in North America. With help from Raleigh, White, as governor in 1587, led a group of 110 settlers to reoccupy Roanoke Island and establish the famous "Lost Colony." Leaving a group including his daughter and her baby Virginia Dare, the first English child born in Virginia, White returned home for reinforcements. Unfortunately the long-anticipated war with Spain became official early in 1588. Because the threat of the Spanish Armada loomed large, little could be done to mount a relief expedition for the Virginia pioneers. It was August 1590 before an English force finally reached Roanoke Island, only to find the abandoned colonists gone and the enigmatic word "Croatoan" carved in a tree.

Thus, as the 16th century drew toward its close, practically the whole of the North America's Atlantic littoral had been contacted and much of it explored by Europeans representing the three great empires that would struggle for the next two centuries to control it. The stage was now set for the active and continuous colonization that was to bring about the "Europeanization" of the continent.

ADDITIONAL READING

Books

Collier, J. *Indians of the Americas: The Long Hope.* New York: New American Library, 1964.

Corbett, D.L. *Explorations, Descriptions and Attempted Settlements of Carolina, 1584–1590.* Raleigh, N.C.: Department of Archives and History, 1953.

Crosby, A.W. *The Columbian Exchange: Biological and Cultural Consequences of 1492.* Westport, Conn.: Greenwood Press, 1972.

Cumming, W.P.; Skelton, R.A.; and Quinn, D.B. *The Discovery of North America.* New York: American Heritage Press, 1971.

De Vorsey, L., and Parker, J. *In the Wake of Columbus: Islands and Controversy.* Detroit: Wayne State University Press, 1985.

Driver, H.E. *Indians of North America.* Chicago: University of Chicago Press, 1961.

Duncan, T.B. *Atlantic Islands Madeira, the Azores and the Cape Verdes in Seventeenth-Century Commerce and Navigation.* Chicago: University of Chicago Press, 1972.

Hoffman, B.G. *Cabot to Cartier: Sources for a Historical Ethnography of Northeastern North America, 1497–1550.* Toronto: University of Toronto Press, 1961.

McManis, D.R. *European Impressions of the New England Coast, 1497–1620.* Chicago: University of Chicago Department of Geography, 1972.

Morison, S.E. *The European Discovery of America: The Northern Voyages A.D. 500–1600.* New York: Oxford University Press, 1971.

———. *The European Discovery of America: The Southern Voyages A.D. 1492–1616.* New York: Oxford University Press, 1974.

Quinn, D. B. *North America from Earliest Discovery to First Settlements: The Norse Voyages to 1612.* New York: Harper & Row, 1977.

———, ed. *New American World: A Documentary History of North America to 1612.* 5 vols. New York: Arno Press, 1979.

Sauer, C.O. *Land and Life: A Selection from the Writings of Carol Ortwin Sauer.* Edited by J. Leighly. Berkeley and Los Angeles: University of California Press, 1963.

———. *Northern Mists.* Berkeley and Los Angeles: University of California Press, 1968.

———. *Sixteenth Century North America.* Berkeley and Los Angeles: University of California Press, 1971.

Skelton, R.A.; Marston, T.E.; and Painter, G.D. *The Vinland Map and the Tartar Relation.* New Haven: Yale University Press, 1965.

Taylor, E.G.R. *The Haven Finding Art: A History of Navigation from Odysseus to Captain Cook.* London: Hollis & Carter, 1958.

Vachon, A. *Dreams of Empire: Canada before 1700.* Ottawa: Public Archives of Canada, 1982.

Washburn, W., ed. *Proceedings of the Vinland Map Conference.* Chicago: University of Chicago Press, 1966.

Wroth, L.C. *The Voyages of Giovanni da Verrazano, 1524–1528.* New Haven and London: Yale University Press, 1970.

Periodicals

Geography, journal of the British Geographical Association (Kirk, 1963).

Imago Mundi, journal of the International Society for the History of Cartography (De Vorsey, 1978; Kelley, 1979).

Journal of Historical Geography (Overton, 1981).

Terrae Incognitae, journal of the Society for the History of Discoveries (Juricek, 1973; Quinn, 1976; Thrower, 1979; Vigneras, 1979).

3

The Spanish Borderlands

RICHARD L. NOSTRAND
University of Oklahoma

The term "Spanish Borderlands" refers to modern-day northern Mexico and the tier of states that stretches from California to Florida. It was popularized by Herbert Eugene Bolton and his entourage of student-historians at Berkeley, although Bolton did not coin the term: an unknown editor at Yale University Press suggested it as the title for Bolton's seminal book published in 1921. The "Borderlands" label has one drawback—it is anachronistic, at least when applied to New Spain's vast northern frontier before political borders existed. Its plural use ("Borderlands"), on the other hand, does underscore the area's environmental and cultural diversity, and it does remind us of the difficulties of defining a clear border between Mexico and North America. Whatever its merits or shortcomings, it is a geographical label that is entrenched in the literature and is presumably here to stay.

To Spaniards who lived in the Americas in colonial times, this immense present-day Borderlands was little more than the remote and dangerous northern periphery of Spain's New World empire. Like southern Chile and Argentina at the opposite end of Spain's colonial territory, few settlers were attracted to it because of its apparent lack of minerals and its paucity of tractable Indians. The relatively small number who did nevertheless venture north left an imprint on the land that was similar to that found throughout Spanish America: much of Spanish activity in the Americas was prescribed in the Laws of the Indies (1573) and their recodifications, and a remarkable degree of uniformity characterized Spanish settlements, even on the remote and sparsely populated frontier of North America.

INSTITUTIONAL FRAMEWORK

Spain established an elaborate institutional framework for its colonization of the New World. In the vanguard of frontier occupance were the *presidio* and mission. *Presidios* were garrisoned fortresses built in the form of rectangles with thick ramparts surmounted by parapets and flanked by projecting bastions. Soldiers were charged with maintaining order among neighboring Indians and with protecting missionaries and colonists. Often located within a few leagues of these institutions of conquest were the missions, institutions of Christianization. Missions in New Mexico were church complexes built in Pueblo architectural style adjacent to Indian settlements, but elsewhere in the Borderlands they were large, free-standing, rectangular compounds to which Indians were attracted for purposes of conversion and assimilation.

All *presidios* and missions were eventually to be converted to civil communities—that is, institutions for farmers and artisans that formed the backbone of Spain's colonial efforts throughout the Americas. As prescribed in the Laws of the Indies, civil communities, initially known according to projected size as *pueblos* (places), *villas* (villages), or *ciudades* (cities), were to be land grants of four square leagues or approximately 27 square miles (Fig. 3.1). A gridiron village was located near the center of these grants with the corners of the grid oriented in cardinal compass directions—explicitly, to divert the "four principal winds," but undoubtedly also so that shade would be cast into the streets. A central plaza was to take up four blocks of the grid. Around the plaza were the Roman Catholic church, which was to be elevated and thus more venerated, a palace if the settlement was the seat of government, a customs house, a granary, other institutions, and house lots (*solares*). The most prestigious citizens owned houses fronting the plaza. Beyond the settlement, community land was apportioned to arable fields called *suertes*, common land (*ejido*), pasture (*dehesa*), woodland, and lands reserved for the Crown (*realenga*).

In addition to *presidios*, missions, and civil communities, land grants of several kinds were

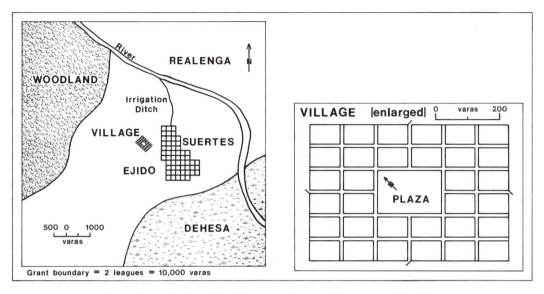

Figure 3.1 An Ideal Civil Community after the Laws of the Indies
(one *vara* = approx. 33 inches; one *league* = 2.6 miles)

awarded in newly occupied areas. In 17th-century New Mexico, *encomiendas*, which were literally "entrustments" of Pueblo Indians rather than grants of land, were issued to large landowners known as *encomenderos*. Because Indians who were so entrusted were often overly exploited for their labor, the institution was eventually discontinued during the 18th century; New Mexico seems to have been the only Borderlands area to have had *encomiendas*. Private land grants issued for stock-raising and farming were also found in New Mexico where, early in the colonial period, they were known as *estancias* or *haciendas*. In California and Texas such grants were called *ranchos*. In the Mexican era (after 1821) a flurry of *rancho* granting occurred in California, while in Texas individuals known as *empresarios* were awarded tracts of land to which they were to introduce a minimum number of colonists within a specified time.

When colonization of the northern frontier did occur, two external points became the springboards for Spanish expansion. After Columbus set foot on what is now believed to have been one of the Caicos islands in the southern Bahamas in 1492, Spaniards spread across the Caribbean, and Havana eventually became the island theater's core area (Fig. 3.2). Havana was the springboard for the colonization of Florida. From Cuba Hérnan Cortés sailed to the vicinity of Veracruz, marched inland, and in 1521 succeeded in toppling Moctezuma and his Aztec Empire. The Aztec capital, Tenochtitlán, became Mexico City, the core area of the mainland and the launching pad for the colonization of New Spain's northern frontier (the present American Southwest).

FLORIDA (1565–1819)

The Straits of Florida was the channel through which the biannual convoys of silver-carrying galleons sailed after the 1520s as they headed north along the Florida coast to catch the prevailing westerlies for Spain. There was need for a port community where these galleons could seek protection from storms and pirates. Yet Spain delayed this decision, and no lasting settlement was established before St. Augustine in 1565. What triggered St. Augustine's founding was the news that the French, who also claimed the area, had established a fort near the mouth of the St. Johns River in 1564 (Fig. 3.3). The next year Pedro Menéndez de Avilés sailed from Spain, paused briefly in Puerto Rico, then went on to Florida where he established St. Augustine on the coast south of the mouth of the St. Johns River. He then

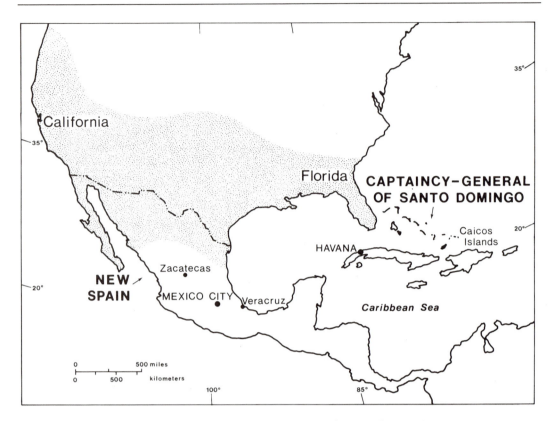

Figure 3.2   The Spanish Borderlands and Colonist Source Areas

cruelly disposed of the unwelcomed French, as discussed in Chapter 2.

The permanent site selected for St. Augustine in 1570 was on the mainland behind a break in the offshore barrier beach islands. A *presidio*, the Castillo de San Marcos, was positioned to guard the narrow entrance to the harbor, and south of the fort stretched the wall-enclosed community of St. Augustine (Fig. 3.3 inset). Although founded before 1573 when the Laws of the Indies were codified, St. Augustine nevertheless embodied those attributes prescribed for civil communities: a plaza, which for coastal communities was to face the water; a Roman Catholic church and the governor's palace fronting the plaza; and beyond the plaza a gridiron street pattern (which in St. Augustine contained the monastery headquarters of the Franciscans, who replaced the Jesuits in 1571). This seat of government and key settlement became the source area for further Spanish expansion. And it was here that Spanish set-

tlers introduced to North America for the first time such items as wheat, barley, olives, oranges, and cattle.

From St. Augustine mission-*presidio* settlements were founded in three directions. First, they were established along the coast from Tampa Bay to South Carolina, a "saltwater" mission field that stretched along the barrier beach islands. Not until the late 1970s was the site of one of these communities, believed to have been Santa Elena, discovered under the golf course of the marine base at Parris Island in South Carolina (Fig. 3.3). The second direction of expansion was behind St. Augustine along the St. Johns River, a relatively unsuccessful "freshwater" mission field. And the third and most successful direction of expansion led across the Florida peninsula to Apalachee Bay, present-day Tallahassee, and on into central Alabama, where settlements were linked by a trail known as the *Camino Real* (Royal Highway). A mapmaker described the highway in

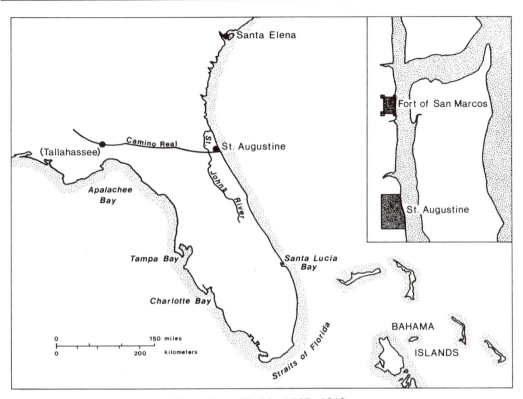

Figure 3.3   Florida, 1565–1819

these terms: "The path is chiefly throe low Pine lands, part of which is wet and boggy after great Rains, is plain and well trod. Crosses many small creeks and branches which have low swamps, that are full of water in wet weather, but fordable." An active trade with local Indians for deerskins and pelts was conducted in this region during the late 17th and early 18th centuries.

Despite this energetic expansion, when Florida became British for a 20-year period in 1763, the only settlement that endured was St. Augustine. Florida had been little more than an impoverished military outpost which, in the absence of riches and the presence of intractable Indians and an unfamiliar environment, had attracted only 3,000–4,000 Spaniards. It had also been a significant drain on the royal treasury. Between 1783, when Spain reacquired Florida,· and 1819, when Florida was transferred to the United States as payment for debts in the Adams-Onís treaty, only St. Augustine was reoccupied. When compared

with the northern frontier of New Spain to the west, therefore, Spain's lasting impact in Florida was indeed modest. As Ralph Brown described it, "Florida . . . was a colony without colonists."

NEW SPAIN'S NORTHERN FRONTIER (1598–1821)

Colonization of New Spain's northern frontier was not the result of one grand march to the north, but of several lesser enterprises separated in time and space. The initial thrust went to New Mexico. In 1536 Alvar Núñez Cabeza de Vaca and three companions reported to Viceroy Antonio de Mendoza in Mexico City that cities filled with treasure existed on a large river far to the north. Four years later Mendoza launched a major expedition under Francisco Vásquez de Coronado to find the now-fabled Seven Cities of Cíbola, which turned out to be the multistory adobe and stone villages of the mineral-poor Pueblo Indians. Coronado's failure to find precious metals ended any major excursions to the north until wealthy Juan de Oñate of Zacatecas, knowledgeable about the peaceful sedentary Pueblo Indians and unconvinced that gold and silver were not to be found, petitioned the Viceroy for permission to colonize New Mexico as a private venture. Permission was granted in 1598.

New Mexico

How many soldier-settlers accompanied Oñate up the Rio Grande Valley in 1598 is not known, yet the majority of the 210 documented colonists, most of whom had been recruited in the Mexico City and Zacatecas areas, had been born in southern and central Spain, especially in Andalucía and Castile. At the confluence of the Chama and the Rio Grande in the northern reaches of the Pueblo Indian realm, Oñate made his capital at the Pueblo village of Caypa, which he renamed San Juan (Fig. 3.4). By Christmas of 1600 he had shifted his capital to nearby San Gabriel. Franciscan missionaries were promptly placed at some of the Indian pueblos. Meanwhile, Oñate explored the area from central Kansas west to the Gulf of California but, like Coronado, found no gold or silver. Accused of misdeeds, including cruel treatment of the Pueblos, Oñate was finally recalled in 1607.

Spanish authorities in Mexico City, persuaded that New Mexico should be retained as a missionary province, sent Pedro de Peralta to replace Oñate as governor. In 1610, Peralta founded Santa Fe. Like St. Augustine, Santa Fe had a plaza fronted by a governor's palace and a Roman Catholic church (but it lacked a gridiron street pattern) and, like St. Augustine, Santa Fe was the region's largest community and its hub of activity. From Santa Fe smaller Indian pueblos were awarded as *encomiendas* to soldier-settlers, a policy initiated by Oñate, and *estancias* or *haciendas* were granted for stock raising and farming. Local Spaniards began to distinguish between two environments located north and south of Cochiti Pueblo, a Rio Arriba (upriver country) that was higher and therefore wetter and more wooded, and a Rio Abajo (downriver country) that was lower and therefore drier but possessing a longer growing season. An increasing number of friars, mean-

while, extended their missionary activities to include the Acoma, Zuñi, and Hopi pueblos in 1629, and eventually to the Paso del Norte District in 1659.

It was to the Paso del Norte District that these Spaniards fled in the Pueblo Revolt of 1680. For seven decades the Pueblo Indians had been forced by the Spaniards to serve as laborers, to grow maize, and to weave cotton textiles called *mantas*. In 1680 these numerically superior Pueblos, in an unprecedented show of unity, joined forces, notably in the Rio Arriba, to attack the 2,500 Spaniards, many of whom lived in Santa Fe. Some Spaniards were taken captive, several hundred were killed, and about 2,000 survivors took refuge in the Paso del Norte District, accompanied by several hundred loyal Pueblos from the Rio Abajo.

Diego de Vargas led the gradual reconquest of the northern reaches of New Mexico beginning in 1693. Santa Fe had to be reoccupied by force and, to secure the capital, a *presidio* was established (the adobe fortress attached to the governor's palace before the revolt had been manned only by volunteers, not soldiers; it therefore was not technically a *presidio*). Additional plaza-centered civil communities were founded at Santa Cruz in 1695 and at Albuquerque in 1706. Moreover, loose agglomerations of small farmsteads known as *ranchos* came to exist along irrigation ditches that paralleled rivers, communities that in the latter 18th century were forced by Plains Indian raids to consolidate within wall-enclosed "plazas." By the close of the Spanish era in 1821, some 30,000 Spaniards effectively occupied the area between Taos and Socorro and between Pecos and Acoma, and they had recently expanded east beyond the upper Rio Grande basin to places like San Miguel (1794?) in the upper Pecos basin (Fig. 3.4).

After the reconquest Franciscans reoccupied many of their missions at the Indian pueblos. The Spanish-born friars, however, were now less intent about forcing Roman Catholicism on their charges. Indeed, they and the other Spaniards with whom the Pueblos came in contact began to grow apart from the Pueblo population. The supply of friars, which seems never to have exceeded 46, was too small to staff all the pueblos and, as the Spanish population increased relative to that of the Pueblos, the friars ministered more and more to the Spaniards. By

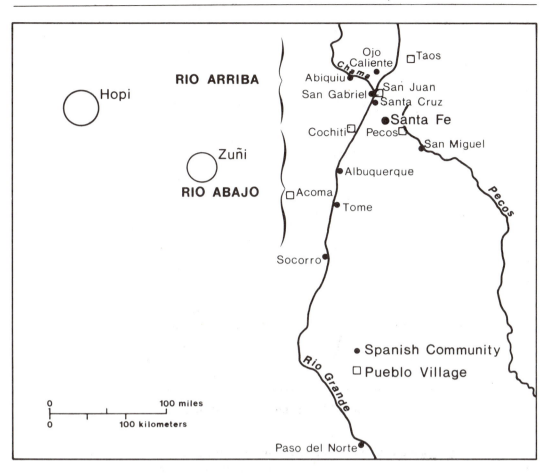

RIO ARRIBA

Hopi

Zuñi

RIO ABAJO

Ojo Caliente

Taos

Abiquiu

San Juan

San Gabriel

Santa Cruz

Santa Fe

Cochiti   Pecos

San Miguel

Albuquerque

Acoma

Tome

Socorro

Pecos

• Spanish Community
□ Pueblo Village

0   100 miles

0   100 kilometers

Rio Grande

Paso del Norte

Figure 3.4 New Mexico, 1598–1821

1821 only five of the nineteen remaining pueblos were staffed with Franciscans.

As Spaniards and Pueblos were going their separate ways, Spaniards and Plains Indians developed a special relationship. During much of the Spanish era Apaches, Comanches, Navajos, and Utes, who completely surrounded the Spanish-Pueblo region, sporadically raided the villages of the Pueblos and Spaniards, carrying off children to be used as slaves. The Spaniards retaliated by capturing Indian children whom they used as domestic servants or sold for much profit in Chihuahua in northern Mexico. Known as *genízaros* to the New Mexican Spaniards, these Plains Indian captives were eventually Hispanicized. Some were allowed to colonize communities of their own, provided that they were at frontier locations. Ojo Caliente (by 1735), Tome (1739), Abiquiu (1744), and San Miguel all began in this way. Others intermar-

ried with Spaniards and were assimilated into the Spanish population. It is not known just how significant this Plains Indian strain was in the *mestizaje* process that created New Mexico's modern-day "Hispanos," yet its existence does help to differentiate Hispanos from Mexican Americans and Mexicans today.

Pimería Alta

Pimería Alta was the northern realm of the Pimas in present-day northern Sonora and southern Arizona (Fig. 3.5). During the 17th century Jesuits had gradually advanced their missionary frontier north along the Pacific-facing slopes of the Sierra Madre Occidental to Pimería Baja. Then, in 1700, the celebrated Jesuit Eusebio Francisco Kino founded Mission San Zavier del Bac in Pimería Alta, and during the next decade he supervised the founding of additional missions and small outlying chapels

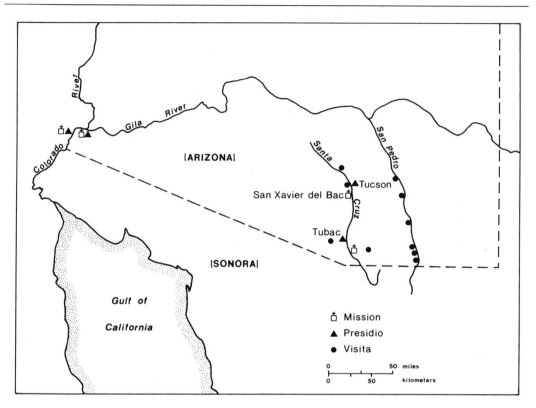

Figure 3.5   Pimeria Alta, 1700–1821

(*visitas*) in the upper Santa Cruz and San Pedro valleys.

After Kino died in 1711, Jesuit activity languished because of the constant raids of Apaches who were the formidable foes of Spaniards and Pima Indians in Pimería Alta. And after missionary efforts were renewed, the Pimas who, like the Pueblos, were no longer willing to accept Spanish subjugation, revolted in 1751. This resulted in the construction of a *presidio* at Tubac in 1752, and then a second *presidio* at Tucson in 1776, by which time Franciscans had replaced the Jesuits, who had been expelled entirely from the New World. Two mission-*presidio* compounds briefly existed near the confluence of the Gila and Colorado rivers about 1780, and a dozen stock-raising grants (*ranchos*) were issued in the vicinity of the Santa Cruz and San Pedro valleys. Yet the history of Spanish activity in Pimería Alta was characterized by cycles of occupation followed by Apache-induced abandonment. In 1821 the area's several hundred inhabitants appear to

have been clustered rather precariously within or near the two *presidios*.

Texas

The third thrust into this northern frontier went to Texas. Once again Frenchmen triggered the Spaniards into action. In the 1680s the French who, like the Spaniards, were jockeying for territory, had briefly established themselves near Lavaca Bay on the Gulf Coast (Fig. 3.6). This prompted the Spaniards in the early 1690s to build several missions and *presidios* in east Texas that also proved to be ephemeral. The French then advanced up the Red River in present-day Louisiana, where they established a fort at Natchitoches in 1714. To stifle this thrust Spaniards responded in 1716 by establishing a mission and later a *presidio* some 15 miles to the west at Los Adaes (Robeline, Louisiana). Between these French and Spanish outposts the small Arroyo Hondo became the international boundary, and Los Adaes was made the capital of Texas. Only in

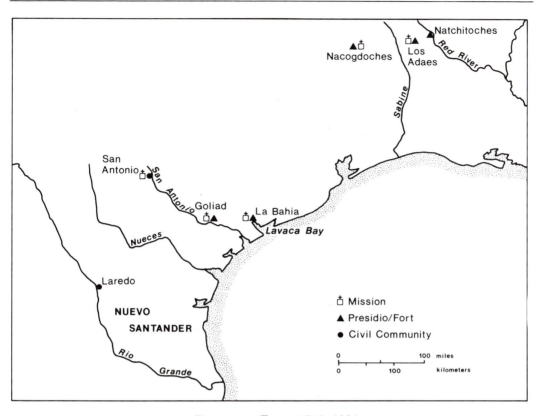

Figure 3.6   Texas, 1716–1821

1819 did the Sabine River become the boundary between Spanish Texas and the state of Louisiana (Fig. 3.6).

Three lasting mission-*presidio* complexes then emerged in present-day Texas: at Nacogdoches in 1716, at the Alamo and elsewhere along the upper San Antonio River in 1718, and at La Bahia near Matagorda Bay in 1722 but relocated to Goliad on the lower San Antonio River in 1749 (Fig. 3.6). After a civil community, later known as San Antonio, was founded near the Alamo in 1731, the Texas capital was relocated from Los Adaes, and San Antonio, like St. Augustine and Santa Fe, became the local seat of Spanish political power and focus of activity. At the close of the Spanish era, some 4,000 Spaniards lived there and at Nacogdoches and Goliad. Meanwhile, on the lower Rio Grande, a civil community was founded at Laredo (1755) and land grants were awarded, but during Spanish times the Nueces River marked the southern boundary of Texas, so that this activ-

ity was in the province of Nuevo Santander. Again we note a persistent theme in the Borderlands—the divergence of cultural and political boundaries. This leaves moot, therefore, the long-term significance of the boundary between Mexico and North America.

Alta California

The final Borderlands *entrada* was directed to Alta California, where southward-moving Russian fur traders posed a threat during the mid-18th century. In 1769 Spaniards converged by land and sea on San Diego where a mission-*presidio* pair was built (Fig. 3.7). Three more such pairs were founded: at Monterey, designated the provincial capital in 1770; at San Francisco (1776); and at Santa Barbara (*presidio* in 1782, mission in 1786). Eventually, a chain of missions 20 strong linked San Diego with San Francisco (in 1823, a 21st link was added to the north at Sonoma) in a pattern that primarily

Figure 3.7   Alta California, 1769–1821

reflected the distribution of Chumash and other smaller Indian groups.

Nestled within this 600-mile coastal concatenation were several dozen *ranchos* and three civil communities: San Jose (1777), Los Angeles (1781), and partly successful Branciforte (now Santa Cruz, 1797). Los Angeles eventually surpassed even Monterey in size, and for a brief time during the Mexican era it also outrivaled Monterey to become the region's capital (Fig. 3.8). Agriculture flourished particularly in the missions where the cultivation of European grains, citrus fruits, olives, and grapes, and the raising of livestock (sheep, horses, and especially cattle) were introduced on a permanent basis. Still, by 1821, California's Spanish population was probably not much larger than the 4,000–5,000 Spaniards who lived in Texas.

Thus, on the eve of Mexico's successful revolt, four outpost clusters stretched from the Pacific to the Gulf of Mexico. Each was similar in its tenuous connections with remote Mexico

and in its isolation from the others. Each was different, however, in its time of initial colonization and in its size of population, factors that would give rise in the American period to several old population subcultures. In the Adams-Onís treaty signed in 1819, a boundary between New Spain and the United States was drawn generously north of the four outpost clusters (Fig. 3.9). This boundary defined what the United States had purchased from France in 1803. It also marked Mexico's northern limits during an era that intruding Anglos ensured would be tumultuous.

THE ANGLO INTRUSION (1821–1848)

Under Mexico this northern frontier was opened officially to non-Mexican traders and colonists. Late in 1821 William Becknell and a companion traveled from (Old) Franklin, Missouri, to Santa Fe with goods to trade. When

Figure 3.8   Los Angeles in 1853 (Courtesy Prints and Photographs Division, Library of Congress)

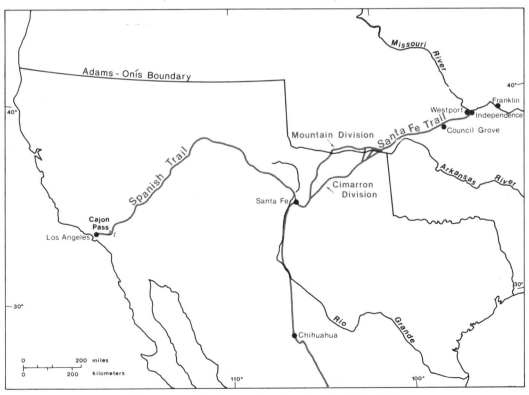

Figure 3.9   Mexico and the Southwest, 1821–1848

they returned to Missouri early in 1822, they sold their merchandise for substantial profit. News of this venture spread quickly and resulted in the Santa Fe trade which, each spring beginning in 1822, saw wagons leave Independence or Westport at the big bend of the Missouri River, form single, more-defensible caravans at Council Grove, take one of two wagon trail "divisions" at the great bend of the Arkansas River, and proceed to Santa Fe (Figs. 3.9, 3.10). In Santa Fe hardware, notions, textiles (including printed cotton calicos), and liquor from the "States" were exchanged for furs and skins, woolen blankets, silver pesos, saddles, and horses and mules from Mexico.

Horses and mules in particular were in great demand but in short supply in Santa Fe. As a consequence, in the winter of 1829–30, about 60 enterprising New Mexicans pioneered a pack trail that led to a California source. Known as the "Spanish Trail" because it followed an old Spanish slave hunting route that led northwest from Santa Fe deep into Ute Indian country, this pack trail was extended southwest across the Great Basin and through Cajon Pass to Los Angeles (Fig. 3.9). Travel occurred between about October and April when temperatures were coolest and grass was most plentiful. In California the New Mexicans traded their

woolen goods for livestock in Los Angeles and at points along the coast. Because there was some thievery, on their departure from California the New Mexicans would be escorted to Cajon Pass where brands and bills of sale were compared. Use of this trail marked the first sustained contact between any of the four Spanish colonial outpost clusters.

The Spanish and Santa Fe trails were used basically for trade, although on the Spanish Trail a small number of New Mexicans did migrate permanently to California, particularly to the upper Santa Ana River near Riverside, and on the Santa Fe Trail some Anglos and French Canadians remained in New Mexico and married local women. The volume and value of trade over the Spanish Trail, which ended in 1846–47, was minor, however, compared with that on the Santa Fe Trail, which continued until 1880. Indeed, New Mexico took on great importance for Mexico as the portal through which coveted American goods were imported. It is not surprising, then, that in a truce called in 1847 midway through the Mexican War, Mexico was willing to cede Alta California and to recognize the Nueces River as the boundary with Texas, but she refused to cede New Mexico.

Alta California, like New Mexico, was in-

Figure 3.10   Las Vegas, New Mexico, in the Late 1860s (Courtesy Denver Public Library, Western History Department)

truded upon during the Mexican era by a relatively small number of traders and interlopers. Trading vessels appear to have been plying the coast of California as early as 1810. Under Mexico such trade was made legal. In July of 1822, the first of many ships from Boston put in at Monterey harbor to register before engaging in trade for cattle hides (to be used for shoes and leather goods) and tallow (to be melted for candles and soap). From Monterey ships proceeded to a number of collection points, including San Francisco Bay (the port for San José), Monterey, San Luis Obispo, Santa Barbara, San Pedro (the port for Los Angeles), and San Diego (Fig. 3.11). On the beach at San Diego hides would be cleaned, stretched, dried, and stored in buildings, and the trading process would be repeated from north to south until there were enough hides to fill the ship's hold. All this is beautifully chronicled by Richard Henry Dana, Jr. (*Two Years before the Mast*, 1840) who, as a common seaman, had made the

voyage from Boston to California between 1834 and 1836.

At the time of Dana's visit, some of Alta California's Franciscans, who had been raising longhorn cattle on extensive mission holdings, had become wealthy in this hide and tallow trade. But this soon ended. In 1834, civil authorities in Alta California began to replace the Franciscans with secular clergy, and they divested the missionary order of its lands, even those occupied by the missions themselves (which were restored to the Roman Catholic church in the 1860s). Known as secularization, this transition merely implemented policy set in motion at the end of Spanish rule, and it was carried out elsewhere in the Borderlands. In California, however, the well-chosen mission lands were regranted as *ranchos*, some 500 of them by the end of the Mexican period. Thus, stockmen, usually Californios but also some Anglos who had been lured to Alta California, replaced the friars as society's wealthy elite.

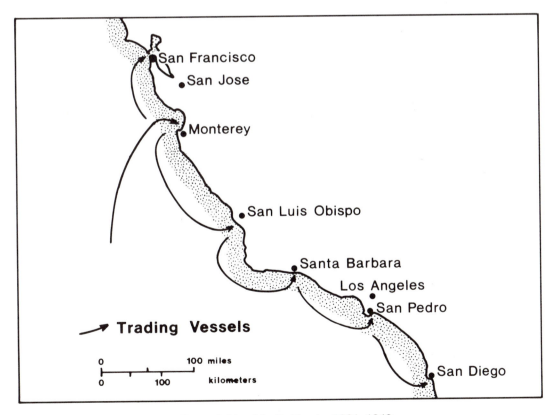

Figure 3.11   Alta California, 1821–1848

Texas in the Mexican era developed quite differently from New Mexico and Alta California. Colonists, not traders, who were encouraged to immigrate through an *empresario* policy, arrived almost immediately in large numbers. At the close of her colonial administration, Spain had initiated a policy whereby persons called *empresarios* would be awarded land provided that they introduce a minimum number of colonists to the land. In 1820 Moses Austin applied for such a grant. When Austin died, his son, Stephen F. Austin, reapplied to the Mexican government and was awarded a huge tract that straddled the lower Brazos and Colorado rivers (Fig. 3.12). In 1823 Austin established his headquarters at San Felipe on the lower Brazos, and Southern cotton planters soon arrived with their black slaves. Additional *empresario* grants were awarded to a variety of peoples: Anglos at Gonzales on the upper Guadalupe, Germans at Industry in the regranted northern reaches of the Austin grant, Irish at San Patricio at the

mouth of the Nueces, even Mexicans at Victoria on the lower Guadalupe. None was as successful, however, as the first grant to Austin.

By the mid-1830s an estimated 30,000 "Anglos" outnumbered the old Tejano group six to one, and problems soon arose between the two groups. Tejanos, who were concentrated in San Antonio and along the lower Rio Grande, were officially opposed to slavery, and they questioned the political loyalty of the newcomers. Anglos, who had settled the coastal plain east of San Antonio, were frustrated with an inept political rule in San Antonio. The upshot was a revolt in which the Anglos (and some Tejanos) declared their independence, eventually defeated the Mexicans in battle, and in 1836 created the Republic of Texas. That Mexico did not recognize the Republic never daunted the rebels who, in 1839, established Austin as their capital on the lower Colorado and who, by continuing to award *empresario* grants, encouraged further immigration. Many of the new

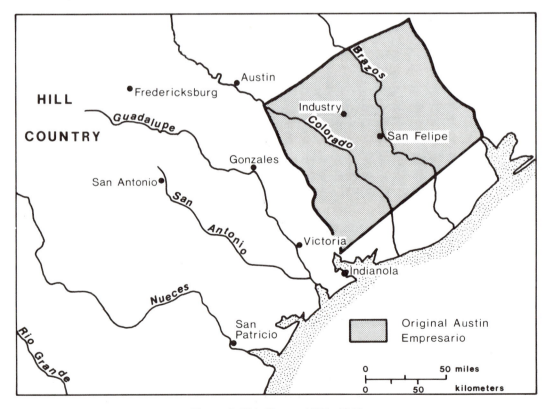

Figure 3.12   Texas, 1821–1848

arrivals were Germans who entered Texas at Indianola and made their way to Fredericksburg and other destinations in the Hill Country (Fig. 3.12). In 1845 Texas was annexed as a state, a move that helped to trigger the Mexican War.

The war between the United States and Mexico was clearly one prompted by an American mentality that, by providential design, the United States was to extend to the Pacific. It was by and large an unpopular war in the United States, but for Mexico it was disastrous. Mexico was forced to recognize the Rio Grande (her Rio del Norte) as her border with recently annexed Texas, and was forced also to cede New Mexico and California north of the Gila River and a line drawn west from it to the Pacific (Fig. 3.13). In 1853 the area south of the Gila was purchased for $10 million by James Gadsden, who was sent by the American government to negoitate such a transaction. This finalized the present-day international bound-ary. The result was that the United States realized her "Manifest Destiny" of extending to the Pacific, and in the process Mexico lost half her national territory.

Living in this former northern half of Mexico were some 100,000 Mexicans, or about 1 percent of Mexico's total population. In the treaty of Guadalupe Hidalgo (1848), these Mexicans were given one year to repatriate or they became American citizens. Several thousand did repatriate by moving to the Mexican side of the Rio Grande, as from Laredo to Nuevo Laredo and from Dona Ana to Mesilla (Fig. 3.13). Those who remained became Mexican Americans, some 75,000 of them in New Mexico and about 12,000 each in Texas and Alta California. Because New Mexico had been only lightly intruded upon by Anglos, Mexican American proportions there were uniformly high. Heavy intrusion to Texas reduced Mexican American proportions everywhere except between the Nueces and the Rio Grande in south Texas

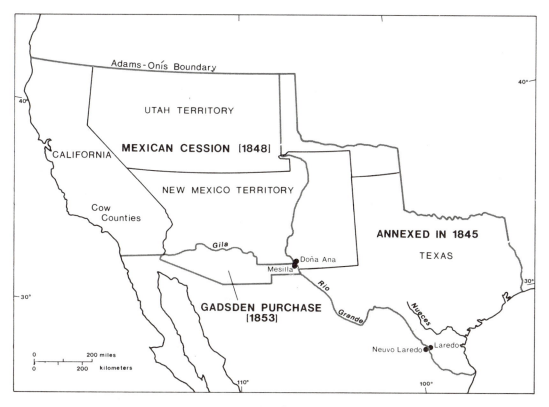

Figure 3.13   The Southwest, 1853

where, to this day, this minority represents 80 to 90 percent of the population. In Alta California, immediately following the war, a heavy influx of gold-seekers decisively reduced Mexican American proportions in the north, while in the "Cow Counties" of Southern California, so called because they remained overwhelmingly pastoral, percentages remained high until a real estate land boom in the 1880s brought in thousands of Anglos.

THE BORDERLANDS LEGACY

Thus, as a result of three events—the annexation of Texas in 1845, the Mexican Cession in 1848, and the Gadsden Purchase in 1853—some 100,000 Mexicans became Mexican Americans, at least nominally. These 100,000 formed three subcultures, an Hispano (as he is called today) in New Mexico, a Tejano in Texas, and a Californio in California. The relatively small Tejano and Californio populations for the most part were soon engulfed by Anglos, although pockets of them persist well into the present century at places like San Antonio and Santa Barbara. Hispanos, by contrast, were not immediately submerged by Anglos, and what happened to them is one of the little-known stories in the annals of the Borderlands.

Drawing on a relatively large population reservoir, Hispanos after 1848 aggressively expanded their frontiers—north to Colorado beginning in the early 1850s, east across New Mexico clear to the panhandles of Texas and Oklahoma by the 1860s, west to Arizona by the 1860s, and south down the Rio Grande almost to the Mesilla Valley. By 1900, about 140,000 Hispanos lived in these five states. Meanwhile, largely because of Anglo discrimination, Hispanos increasingly began to identify with their Spanishness. "Spanish" or "Spanish American" became their preferred self-referents when speaking in English. Roots that went deep into the Spanish colonial era, when now-archaic Iberian speech patterns and folklore examples were introduced, seemed to justify this Spanish consciousness despite protests from Chicano leaders in places like California, who argued that all people of Spanish-Indian or Mexican descent were one people and one culture. In 1980, some 850,000 New Mexican–centered Hispanos identified themselves as "other Hispanics" in the U.S. census.

Mexican Americans, a group that includes the self-consciously Mexican-Chicano element, have outstripped the Hispanos numerically. In the latter 19th century only a few Mexican immigrants went to the Southwest each year, but in the 20th century this trickle grew to flood-like volumes as migrants poured into especially California, Texas, and Arizona, but also into Colorado and New Mexico and, after World War I, even to nonsouthwestern destinations like Chicago. By 1980, more than 8.7 million people, largely residents of the Southwest, listed themselves as "Mexican Americans" in the census, a number that omits a million or more "undocumenteds." Unlike Hispanos, who are an indigenous people, these Mexican Americans are an immigrant people. They constitute a separate subculture. Except for the most-recent migrants, both groups are bilingual and bicultural, and neither has been fully integrated into American society. Both constitute a critically important Borderlands legacy.

That legacy also includes the landscape impress of the forebears of these present-day peoples. A tenet in geography, rather elaborately termed the Doctrine of First Effective Colonization, states that the first group to colonize an area effectively will be of singular importance in shaping the cultural landscape of that area, even though that first group may have been small in numbers and later submerged by others. This doctrine certainly applies to Spaniards: the material things Spaniards built, the way they organized their space, even their toponyms (place names) persist to give character to Florida but especially to the American Southwest.

Many *presidios* and missions were abandoned and gradually crumbled to ruins. Some that endured became the nuclei around which larger settlements grew. Thus, the communities that developed around the Tucson *presidio* and around Mission San Buenaventura became, through inertia, the Anglo-Mexican American cities of Tucson, Arizona, and Ventura, California. Missions that endured also inspired a distinctive "Spanish Colonial" architectural style employed in domestic, civic, and ecclesiastic buildings. Many have been restored and attract thousands of visitors annually (Fig. 3.14).

Civil communities had the "power to attract"—Albuquerque, Los Angeles, and San

Figure 3.14   Mission Santa Ines in the Late 19th Century (Courtesy Denver Public Library, Western History Department)

Antonio verify this. A variety of colonial features persist in them. In the center of each is an open plaza, often a church, and sometimes a palace, as at Santa Fe and San Antonio (Fig. 3.15). Each is laid out on a distinctively oriented grid. That grid, in Los Angeles and elsewhere, was continued during the American period, but only to the original community boundaries where it was then reoriented to follow cardinal compass directions. Thus, even original community boundaries are preserved as part of the street pattern; Hoover Street, which marks the western *pueblo* boundary in Los Angeles, is a case in point.

Rancho boundaries, as later surveyed by Americans, persist today as routes for roads, private landownership boundaries, political (especially county) boundaries, railroad rights-of-way, power-line easements, and drainage ditches. They have even left their mark in street disruptions and distortions.

Features built or laid out, therefore, by a relatively few Spaniards have outlasted the builders to give character to a region now inhabited by millions of Hispanos/Mexican Americans. The Borderlands, particularly its southwestern segment, is one of America's genuinely distinctive cultural regions. It is a prominent example of America's enduring diversity.

ADDITIONAL READING

Books

Bannon, J.F. *The Spanish Borderlands Frontier, 1513–1821*. New York: Holt, Rinehart & Winston, 1970.

———. *Herbert Eugene Bolton: The Historian and the Man, 1870–1953*. Tucson: University of Arizona Press, 1978.

Bolton, H.E. *The Spanish Borderlands: A Chronicle of Old Florida and the Southwest*. New Haven: Yale University Press, 1921.

Figure 3.15   The Plaza-facing Palace of the Governors, Santa Fe, New Mexico, about 1885
(Courtesy Denver Public Library, Western History Department)

Dana, R.H., Jr. *Two Years before the Mast*. New York: World Publishing Company, 1946; originally published 1840.

Garrard, L.H. *Wah-to-Yah and the Taos Trail*. Palo Alto: American West Publishing Company, 1968; originally published 1850.

Jones, O.L., Jr. *Los Paisanos: Spanish Settlers on the Northern Frontier of New Spain*. Norman: University of Oklahoma Press, 1979.

Lecompte, J. *Rebellion in Rio Arriba 1837*. Albuquerque: University of New Mexico Press, 1985.

Meinig, D.W. *Imperial Texas: An Interpretive Essay in Cultural Geography*. Austin: University of Texas Press, 1969.

———. *Southwest: Three Peoples in Geographical Change, 1600–1970*. New York: Oxford University Press, 1971.

Naylor, T.H., and Polzer, C.W., eds. *The Presidio and Militia on the Northern Frontier of New Spain*, Vol. 1, 1570–1700. Tucson: University of Arizona Press, 1986.

Spicer, E.H. *Cycles of Conquest: The Impact of Spain, Mexico, and the United States on the Indians of the Southwest, 1533–1960*. Tucson: University of Arizona Press, 1962.

Stoddard, E.R.; Nostrand, R.L.; and West, J.P., eds. *Borderlands Sourcebook: A Guide to the Literature on Northern Mexico and the American Southwest*. Norman: University of Oklahoma Press, 1983.

Periodical

Annals, Association of American Geographers (Nostrand, 1970, 1975, 1980; Meinig, 1972; Carlson, 1975).

4

France in North America

COLE HARRIS

University of British Columbia

The French penetration of North America began about 1500 and eventually influenced more than half the continent before France lost all her mainland North American territory following the Seven Years' War (1757–63). During this long period France made no spectacular North American conquests, developed a low regard for the potential of newly discovered mid-latitude lands, and sent very few colonists. Overall, North America was a marginal interest, never a preoccupation, and as a result France's long-term impact on the continent was far less than Spain's or England's. Yet France left her broad mark on North America, politically in a country, Canada, which eventually and ironically would grow out of French beginnings, and culturally in the continuing presence of French as a North American language. More than this, the French effort in North America established a northern pattern of European outreach to the New World that would endure long after New France fell. In the first instance, this pattern revolved around staple trades, which, during the French period, were in fish and furs. Although one of these activities was confined to the Atlantic coast while the other drew traders far into the interior, both detached capital and labor from France, placed them in the North American wilderness, and tied them back to France by tight lines of trade. Eventually towns developed at crucial break-of-bulk points and, because France and Britain warred in North America as well as in Europe, these towns became important garrisons, foci not only of trade but also of the military struggle for the continent. Apart from staple trades and towns, and somewhat detached from them, some immigrants turned to farming, usually introducing crops and agricultural techniques from northern France to settings where land was available and markets were poor. Staple trades, towns, and patchy, semisubsistent rural settlements were the ingredients of which the pattern of the French penetration of North America, and of the northern economy, was composed.

THE SIXTEENTH CENTURY

During the latter half of the 15th century, an international fishery, pursued by English, French, Basque, and Portuguese fishermen, operated in the open Atlantic south of Ireland. When John Cabot made known New World fishing grounds, part of this fishery quickly reached out to exploit them, transferring a well-established European economy across the North Atlantic. Breton, Norman, and Portuguese fishermen were in waters around Newfoundland by 1502, perhaps earlier, and French and Spanish Basques were there a few years later. Before the end of the century dozens of ports from southern England to southern Portugal regularly sent fishing ships, each carrying an average of 25 men, to transatlantic fisheries. Of these ports some 60 were French. Usually the voyages were financed in the ports of embarkation, although some merchants in the principal ports or in interior towns owned shares in many ships based in different harbors. Labor was recruited locally. Until recently the only figure we have had for the number of ships involved each year in the French transatlantic fishery was the estimate in 1577 of an English captain, Anthony Parkhurst, that there were 150 French ships in inshore waters around Newfoundland, and perhaps 3,000–4,000 men. This figure is probably low. Recent work with the notarial records in Bordeaux, La Rochelle, and Rouen has established the number of vessels outfitted in these ports for Newfoundland in particular years: 47 from Bordeaux in 1585, 49 from La Rochelle in 1559, 94 from Rouen in 1555. In most years of the 16th century many more ships and men were sent annually from Europe to Newfoundland than to the Caribbean and Central America.

The attraction was one of the world's greatest fishing grounds in shallow waters along the Atlantic coast of North America from southern Labrador to northern New England. There the Labrador Current and Gulf Stream mix, bringing the nutrients that nourish plankton and, ultimately, the bottom-feeding cod. Cod could be caught in great numbers in relatively shallow water close to shore and on offshore banks at depths of 50–100 fathoms. Inshore waters were fished first, and the techniques that would dominate the inshore fishery for at least 200 years soon were well established. The ships that crossed the Atlantic were beached or anchored in New World harbors, where covered wharves were built (or repaired from the previous season) and boats assembled from parts prefabricated in the home port in Europe. Fishing took place from these boats operated close to shore by crews of three who fished with hempen lines and baited hooks. At the end of the day the fish were unloaded at the wharf, where they were headed, split, salted, piled for a few days, washed, and finally dried on beach cobbles, on branches cut and spread out for the purpose (*rances*), or on low drying platforms (*vignaux* or, in English, flakes). Drying required about ten good days, in each of which the cod had to be spread out, turned, turned again if rain threatened, and repiled at dusk. It was labor-intensive work. Shallop-master, header, splitter, and salter required specialized skills, and the shore master had to balance the size of the catch, weather, shore crew, and departure date to produce as much well-cured dried cod as possible for quality-sensitive markets. But much of the labor was unskilled; peasants from overpopulated countrysides, even boys of eight or ten years entered the fishery, providing cheap labor ashore, and extended some of the regional accents and techniques of a still intensely local France across the Atlantic each season. At the end of the fishing season, shore installations were secured as much as possible against weather, natives, and other fishermen, and the dried cod loaded aboard ship. Ship and crew returned to France.

The offshore fishery on the banks developed in the second half of the 16th century and was conducted by ships equipped to fish without landing in the New World. On the banks, perhaps 200 miles from Newfoundland, men stood in barrels on the deck and fished with long baited and weighted lines. The cod they laboriously hauled aboard were headed, split, and stored in the hold between layers of salt. This wet or green cod, much more perishable than the dry-cured variety, was marketed in northern France, principally along the Seine and Loire rivers.

The banks fishery was French and did not require a New World base; the inshore fishery, by contrast, was international and dependent on New World harbors. Until about 1575 the French inshore fishery focused on southeastern Newfoundland, the strait between Newfoundland and Labrador, and eastern Cape Breton Island. In all these locations it competed with Portuguese and Spanish Basque fishermen. On the Labrador shore, Basque whalers came in large ships (up to 600 tons) with large crews (up to 120 men) and built shore installations for rendering blubber that were even more labor-intensive than the work camps of the cod fishery. Only after 1570, as the Danes reasserted control of the Icelandic fishery, did English fishermen cross the Atlantic in numbers; soon English raiding and piracy displaced other fishermen from southeastern Newfoundland. As this happened the French fishery became more dispersed, considerably penetrating the Gulf of St. Lawrence.

The banks fishery made no regular use of the New World coast, and the inshore fishery, which did, relied on European labor. Yet the inshore fishery drew Europeans and natives into contact, and trade in furs began early in the 16th century. There is no evidence that the Beothuk Indians of Newfoundland engaged in this trade; rather, furs probably came from the Micmac Indians in what is now Nova Scotia and northeastern New Brunswick, the Montagnais along the north shore of the Gulf of St. Lawrence, and Iroquoian people along the St. Lawrence River, who probably canoed well into the Gulf to obtain European goods. At first Indians traded with fishermen, but as early as the 1550s small fur-trading companies detached themselves from the fishery and penetrated the Gulf of St. Lawrence. From 1580 French fur traders ventured each summer to Tadoussac at the mouth of the Saguenay River. Like the fishermen they returned home each fall.

During the first century of French activity along the northeastern edge of North America, there was one major attempt to colonize, inspired by Spanish discoveries far to the south. In 1534, Francis I, king of France, authorized Jacques Cartier, a captain from St. Malo, to explore west from the strait between Labrador and Newfoundland, hoping he would "discover certain islands and lands where it is said a great quantity of gold, and other precious things, are to be found." The French court dreamed of another Aztec or Inca empire for the plucking. Instead Cartier found a shore (the north shore of the Gulf of St. Lawrence) "composed of stone and horrible rugged rocks"; he thought the south shore of the Gulf of St. Lawrence was incomparably better, "the finest land one can see, and full of beautiful trees and meadows." He touched on Anticosti Island but missed the entrance to the St. Lawrence River (Fig. 4.1). The next year he was back with more ships and men and, directed by two Indians he had captured the previous year, sailed up the St. Lawrence River as far as the agricultural villages of St. Lawrence Iroquoians near Québec. Cartier and a few of his men went on to Hochelaga, a palisaded village on Montreal island composed, Cartier said, of some fifty houses each some 50 paces long and 12 to 15 paces wide. He returned to spend the winter near Québec, where twenty-five of his crew died of scurvy before Cartier learned of a cure from the Indians: a decoction rich in vitamin C made from the ground needles and bark of cedar branches. As he left Cartier captured several Indians and got away to France.

Like the Indians who enticed Coronado and de Soto into the American West and South with

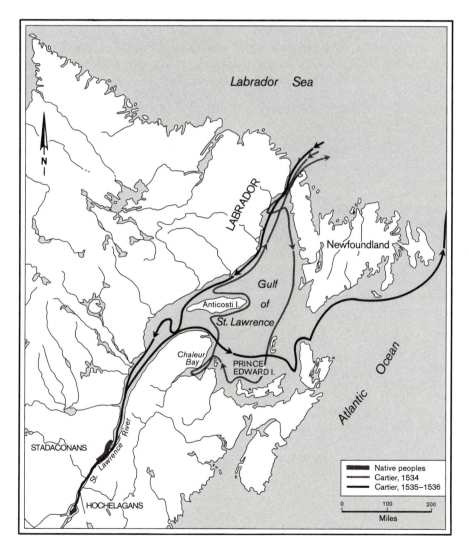

Figure 4.1   Explorations of Jacques Cartier, 1534–1536

tales of gold, Cartier's captives told the French what they wanted to hear. In the kingdom of Saguenay, not far beyond Canada, there were gold and silver, and people (at times with wings and without anuses) who wore woolens like people in France. Although such stories did not get the Indians home—all Cartier's captives, save one girl, were dead by 1539—Cartier set out again in 1541, this time with five ships, several hundred men and women, and livestock. He was to found a colony. The details of Cartier's second winter in North America, spent just above Québec, are less clear than the first, but there was scurvy and there were repeated Indian attacks (Cartier's Indian policy was reaping its reward). In 1542 he packed up and left. His superior in the colonization venture (Jean-François de la Rocque, sieur de Roberval), came out with more colonists; but with a motley collection of aristocrats and criminals, French-Indian relations already soured, and winter ahead, Roberval's prospect was hopeless. His colony lasted less than a year.

In their own terms the Cartier-Roberval voyages were failures. The kingdom of Saguenay had not been found; the gold and diamonds Cartier brought back to France were iron pyrites and mica. Plantation crops could not be grown. There was no obvious route to Asia. The winter was daunting. For more than 60 years the negative results of these voyages discouraged the French from another attempt to colonize northeastern North America, but Cartier and Roberval had expanded enormously the geographical knowledge of the gulf and valley of the St. Lawrence—which henceforth appeared in considerable detail on European maps of North America—and they had established a powerful French claim to a major North American entrant. Basically, they demonstrated the irrelevance in northern middle latitudes of a Spanish model of New World colonization, and left the French where they had been in North America, that is, with an established cod fishery and an incipient fur trade.

FRANCE IN NORTH AMERICA IN 1600

In 1600 the numerous French settlements along the northeast coast of the continent (Fig. 4.2) were all seasonal work camps for a migratory, male labor force drawn from the Atlantic coast of France. There were no women. No society surrounded the fishery—the few Beothuk Indians of Newfoundland did not frequent the fishing camps, at least not when the French were there. Life ashore was an extension of life aboard ship. The ships brought workers to a strange shore, perched them there for a time to accomplish a job, then withdrew them—vehicles of a transatlantic spatial economy that connected European capital, labor, and technique to New World resources. Because there was no alternative New World employment to bid up the value of their labor, fishermen bound for the New World received little more than other French fishermen. Because France was still an intensely regional country, and shipowners recruited men from local hinterlands, there was much variety of local French ways within the common overall pattern of the fishery. Because no one intended to stay and because the leavings from one season could not be counted on to survive to the next, shore installations were quickly, minimally constructed. Behind the more frequented harbors the forest was cut a mile or two inland, while ramshackle wharves, drying platforms, and cabins lined the waterfront.

Perhaps a quarter of the French ships went to the banks and returned directly to France, usually to ports at the mouth of the Seine or the Loire rivers. A large part of the wet (green) cod they carried was destined for the Paris market. The English, who by 1600 were well established in southeastern Newfoundland, deflected the French inshore fishery to the north and southwest. Most ships from western Normandy and northern Brittany (the Gulf of St. Malo) headed for the northern peninsula of Newfoundland and the south coast of Labrador. French Basque shore installations were scattered along the south coast of Newfoundland, on northeastern Cape Breton Island, and on the Gaspé peninsula in the western Gulf of St. Lawrence. By 1600 Spanish Basque and Portuguese competition was weakening as men and ships were commandeered for Spanish military ventures (including the Spanish armada of 1588), and as inflation (initiated by New World bullion) increased costs for Iberian fishermen. Much of the southern European market for dried cod was filled, in 1600, by French and English merchants.

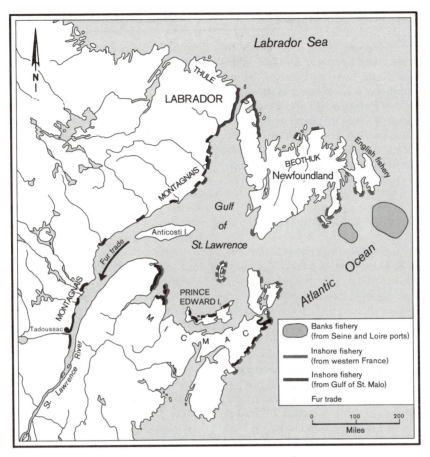

Figure 4.2   France in North America, 1600

At the same time the fur trade was well established in the western Gulf of St. Lawrence. It relied on native labor, drew native and European traders into direct annual contact, and quickly channeled European goods into native economies in payment for furs. The points of annual contact between the westward outreach of European trade goods and the reciprocal flow of native furs were familiar to European and Indian traders. In 1600 a Huguenot, Chauvin de Tonnetuit, armed with a charter from the king, tried to establish a permanent trading post and year-round settlement at Tadoussac. The attempt failed, but a similar effort would be successful slightly farther west a few years later. Whereas the fishery spread a thin, discontinuous rim of French influence along the rocky shores of northeastern North America, the fur trade drew French people and influence inland, up the St. Lawrence.

A century of European contact probably spread European diseases among the Indians of what is now Atlantic Canada. Early in the 17th century a Jesuit missionary reported that the Micmac Indians of Nova Scotia and New Brunswick

are astonished and often complain that since the French mingle with and carry on trade with them, they are dying fast, and the population is thinning out. They assert that before this association and intercourse all their countries were very populous, and they tell how one by one the different coasts according as they have begun to traffic with us have been more reduced by disease.

Along the St. Lawrence River the agricultural Iroquoians whom Cartier encountered in the 1530s were gone in 1600. Perhaps European diseases killed them, but it is more generally assumed that the St. Lawrence Iroquoians were defeated and dispersed about 1580 either by Huron Indians from southern Ontario or by Iroquois from upper New York State. The St. Lawrence Iroquoians may have blocked the westward flow of European goods, thereby upsetting the balance of native power and precipitating the attacks that proved fatal. As the French fur trade spread up the St. Lawrence after 1600, an unoccupied valley—an extraordinary change since Cartier's day—lay before it.

THE SEVENTEENTH CENTURY

Chauvin de Tonnetuit's colony at Tadoussac had failed, but in 1604 another Huguenot trader, Pierre de Gua, sieur de Monts, also obtained a monopoly charter for fur trading, and embarked with colonists. He went to the Bay of Fundy, establishing a first settlement on the St. Croix River, the present border between Maine and New Brunswick, and moved the next year to a more favorable location across the Bay of Fundy at Port Royal. By 1607 when de Monts's monopoly was terminated and he and most of his colonists returned to France, the feasibility of French settlement in the New World had been demonstrated. The next year de Monts's lieutenant, Samuel de Champlain, armed with a one-year trading monopoly, intent upon exploration, and aware that the Bay of Fundy was a cul-de-sac, went to the St. Lawrence River where he selected a strong defensive site at Québec, the head of navigation for large sailing ships, and built a post almost 1,000 miles from the open North Atlantic. The French were now on the St. Lawrence to stay; eventually Champlain's post would become the principal town in New France.

Although Champlain had established a tiny outpost in a depopulated valley, Indians were not far away (Fig. 4.3). Almost immediately Champlain was involved with them. To the immediate north and west were Algonquian-speakers who lived primarily by fishing and hunting: the Montagnais in the Saguenay valley, the Algonquin in the Ottawa valley, and the Nipissing northeast of Georgian Bay. Around the eastern Great Lakes were Iroquoian-speakers, agricultural people who raised corn, beans, squashes, and tobacco, and

who lived in large villages similar to Hochelaga. Of the Iroquoians there were several groups: Huron south of Georgian Bay, Petun just west of the Huron, Neutral around the western end of Lake Ontario, Erie at the southeastern corner of Lake Erie, and Iroquois south of Lake Ontario in what is now upstate New York. The Algonquian-speakers lived in small, well-dispersed bands, but the agricultural Iroquoians were numerous and concentrated, with as many as 3,000 people in a single village. When Champlain arrived at Québec there may have been 20,000 Huron, as many Neutral, and almost as many Iroquois in upstate New York. The St. Lawrence valley was a no-man's-land between the Iroquois to the south and southwest and the Montagnais, Algonquins, and Huron, in alliance, to the north and northwest.

Interested as he was in exploration and trade, Champlain had no choice but to plunge into this Indian world and to take sides in Indian conflicts. In 1609 he sent a young man (Etienne Brulé) to live with the Huron; when Champlain saw him near Montreal the next year he was wearing Indian clothing and speaking Huron. In 1609 and again in 1615 Champlain and his new Indian allies launched campaigns into Iroquois territory, the second an ignominious failure to capture a well-fortified village south of Lake Ontario. Champlain was wounded and carried in a wicker basket much of the way back to Huronia where, more than 500 miles west of Québec, he spent the winter of 1615–16. The French were becoming familiar with Indian ways, had learned to use and repair birchbark canoes, and were acquiring a geographical knowledge of much of the Great Lakes basin. Champlain's last and most remarkable map, drawn in 1632, shows Lake Ontario, Lake Huron, and parts of Lake Superior with considerable accuracy, the largest addition to the European cartography of North America since Cartier. More telling in the long run, Champlain had committed the French to the Algonquins and the Huron—to trade with them, to warfare with their enemies and, for the purpose of trade and movement, to learning their languages and adopting many of their ways.

Yet in the first half of the 17th century, the French fur trade was confined to the St. Lawrence valley. Indians brought furs there, first to

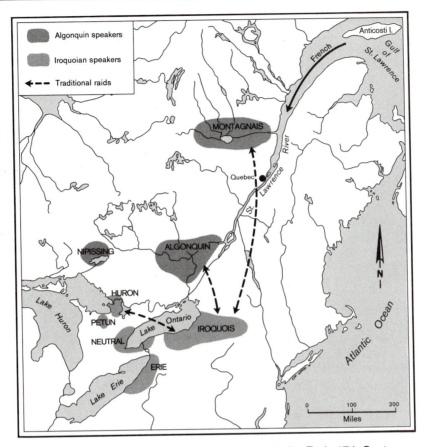

Figure 4.3   Indians Around the St. Lawrence in the Early 17th Century

Québec and later to Trois-Rivières or to Montreal. Initially the Algonquin controlled the trade, preventing French traders from ascending the Ottawa River and exacting tolls from the Huron and Nipissing who traveled to the St. Lawrence. Later, when Iroquois raids had weakened the Algonquin, the Huron and Nipissing came toll-free to Montreal. Jealous of their position as middle men in the trade, they would not let French traders into the interior; Recollet and Jesuit missionaries were admitted to Huronia on condition that they did not trade. During these years Québec, Trois-Rivières, and Montreal were outposts of French trade on the edge of an Indian world, and only the last stage of the fur trade was in French hands.

Although French traders were excluded from the interior, the Indians of the Great Lakes basin faced immense new pressures. The Huron, Algonquins, and Montagnais were allied with the French along the St. Lawrence, the Iroquois were allied with the Dutch at the mouth of the Hudson River, and the two alliances competed with increasing violence. The demand for European goods and the diffusion of firearms (which the Dutch traded freely with their Indian allies and the French withheld from theirs) intensified traditional animosities while disrupting balances of power. In 1634 European diseases, probably carried by Jesuit missionaries, reached the Great Lakes basin and killed approximately half its peoples. By 1639 there were only 12,000 Huron and Petun. Children and old people had been particularly vulnerable; most of the old men, the respected leaders of Indian society, were dead. At the same time villages with missionaries were divided between Christian and pagan factions. Economically, demographically, culturally, and militarily the pre-contact Indian world of the Great Lakes basin was under intense assault, the region in ferment. Nor was the French hold on the St. Lawrence secure. In 1628 an English merchant-adventurer intercepted a shipload of settlers and supplies bound for Québec and captured the post the next year. The French did not recover Québec until 1633.

Eventually, the French-Huron trading system collapsed like a house of cards. Iroquois looting raids against populations weakened by disease and dissension turned to all-out warfare. At first the Iroquois blocked the Ottawa River, allowing only four Huron trading parties to reach Montreal between 1639 and 1648. Then they turned to the population centers. In a series of well-organized campaigns, Iroquois warriors destroyed the Huron villages between 1647 and 1649, the Petun in 1649 in 1650, the Nipissing between 1649 and 1651, and the Neutral in 1651 and 1652. Refugees from these groups and others, fearing the same fate, fled west and north, many of them to settle west of Lake Michigan. Except for the Iroquois south of Lake Ontario and the Shawnee at the forks of the Ohio (dispersed by the Iroquois in 1669 and 1670), the entire eastern Great Lakes basin south to the Ohio valley was depopulated. The scholarly Jesuits, some of whom had lived in Huronia for years, burned their missions, thanked God that so many of the dead had been baptised, and were not again in the territory northwest of Lake Ontario until 1660.

After this horrendous depopulation of the Great Lakes basin, French traders began to venture beyond Montreal to reach Indian groups west of Lake Michigan. Such trade was illegal—the Crown hoped to encourage Indians to return to Montreal and keep French traders out of the interior—but almost impossible to control. After 1654 some Indian traders did make their way back to Montreal each year, but French-Indian trade increasingly took place farther west. By the 1660s there were some 200 French traders and canoemen (coureurs de bois they were called) in the west each year. When the Crown finally legalized the western trade in 1681, the number of coureurs de bois increased and native trading journeys to Montreal stopped.

The French fur trade moved inland along the rivers. It depended on the birchbark canoe, Indian guides, and traders who spoke Indian languages and observed Indian ceremonials. A handful of French traders penetrated a huge, still-Indian territory, reaching out briefly to gather furs at what were soon prearranged trading places and to send them as quickly as possible to Montreal. Soon the lines of trade were hundreds of miles long, and the seasonal round trip from Montreal became impossible. Posts had to be established in the interior and men left to overwinter in them. Fort de la baie de Puants was established on Green Bay in 1670. By 1685 there were French posts on the Mississippi River (reached in 1673 and explored by La Salle to its mouth in 1682) and others north of Lake Superior (Fig. 4.4), all on land that the Indians considered theirs and that they allowed the French to use in return for annual presents. In this fashion several hundred coureurs de bois operated a network of posts extending halfway across the continent, and dominated the trade of the Great Lakes basin. Situated between lakes Huron and Michigan, Michilimakinac became a major entrepôt, receiving furs from the interior and supplies and trade goods from Montreal. There were Jesuit missions at five of the western posts, but after the earlier disasters most of the Jesuits served converted Indians and white traders and did not proselytize vigorously.

The fur trade established the French on the Bay of Fundy (the heart of the territory called Acadia) and along the lower St. Lawrence (the entrance to the territory called Canada). In both locations the mixed, crop-livestock farming of northwestern Europe was feasible. Merchants bent on the fur trade were little interested in agriculture, which involved the great expense of colonization; but the Crown judged that settlers would strengthen the French position in North America and, eventually, provide a market for French manufactures. Hence the stipulation in trading charters that merchant companies bring settlers. Halfheartedly, a few companies did. In this way agricultural settlement began, a somewhat inadvertent by-product of the fur trade.

It is not clear whether de Monts left settlers in Acadia in 1607, but merchants who held trading monopolies in the region after him certainly did. By 1654 there were perhaps 30 families near Port Royal. The Acadian population would grow from this tiny base, to which over the years a few men but virtually no women would be added from outside. In Canada the Crown created a large trading com-

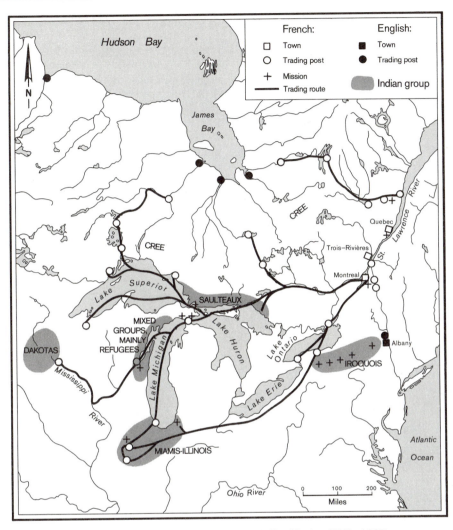

Figure 4.4   The Expanding French Fur Trade, 1679–1685

pany, the Company of New France, in 1627, gave it land title and a monopoly of trade, and required it to establish 4,000 colonists in the next fifteen years. This the company could not do (its first contingent was captured by the English in 1628), but over the years it sent some settlers and granted many seigneuries along the St. Lawrence River in the hope that seigneurs would become colonizers. In 1663 when the Crown revoked the charter of the Company of New France and took over the administration of Canada, there were perhaps 2,500 people of French descent along the lower St. Lawrence. Over the next decade the Crown sent about 1,000 women, many of them from poor-

houses in Paris, and offered inducements to demobilized soldiers and indentured servants to stay in the colony. When royal interest in Canada waned after 1672, only two or three women and not many more men would emigrate from France each year, until the 1750s when some prisoners (salt smugglers) were sent out and soldiers were again induced to stay. In sum, this was a paltry migration of permanent settlers to Canada: over a century and a half only some 9,000 people, almost all young on arrival, most of them male, only about 250 couples married in France. The fur trade, of course, depended on Indian labor and required only a small resident white population, while agriculture as it developed along the lower St. Lawrence offered little to attract investment or labor. The ordinary emigrant who took himself to Canada faced the challenge of pioneering in a forested, northern setting where, in the 17th century, Indians threatened and there was not much market for agricultural products. In these circumstances very few French people chose to emigrate, and the Company of New France, seigneurs, and the Crown were all indifferent colonizers.

Agriculture in Acadia depended on tidal marshland around the Bay of Fundy (Fig. 4.5). The Acadians dyked these marshes, using sods reinforced by branches and logs to build broad dykes some six feet high. At intervals along the dykes there were sluice gates (*aboiteaux*) with clapper valves that closed to the tide. Land so dyked would freshen in a few years and make excellent pasture or ploughland. Soil fertility could be maintained by occasional flooding. The marshes along the Dauphin River at Port Royal were the first to be dyked. By 1670 about 70 farm families lived there; by the 1680s the limited marshland at Port Royal was occupied and settlement spread to the larger marshes at the head of the Bay of Fundy. Behind their dykes the Acadians planted wheat and legumes (beans and peas), their principal field crops, and raised cattle, sheep, and swine. On

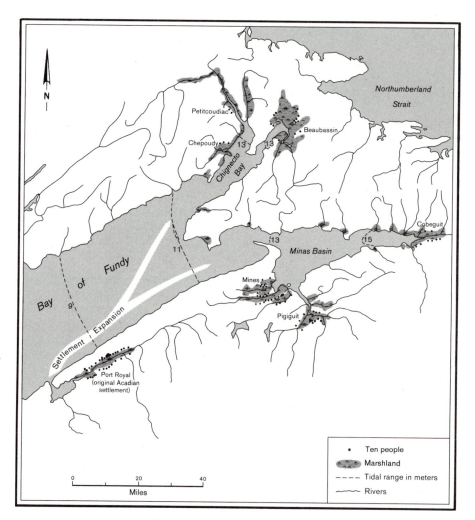

Figure 4.5   Acadian Marshlands

higher ground at the edge of the marshes they built small wooden houses, tended kitchen gardens and a few apple trees, and perhaps cleared a little upland. Supplemented by various gatherings from forest and sea, such farms provided most of the needs of the families who worked them, and a little surplus wheat and beef that entered a coasting trade to Boston. In 1686 there were two small stores in Port Royal, both operated by New Englanders.

After its small, founding migration the Acadian population grew almost entirely from natural increase and was soon demographically balanced. Compared with peasant France, the rate of population growth was high, a result of a lower average marriage age for women and of lower infant and child mortality rates, a reflection, presumably, of improved nutrition. By 1686 there were about 800 Acadians, almost all of them progeny of the founding families. The nuclear family was the primary unit of settlement, but adjacent farm families frequently had the same surname, and ties of consanguinity linked all the settlements around the Bay of Fundy. Acadian material culture, about which we know too little, must have reflected a selection of peasant ways from western France, supplemented by a few borrowings from the Micmac Indians and adapted to the particular environment of the marshlands. Compared with French peasants, the Acadians were relatively detached from economic power. The seigneurial system (the French counterpart of the manorial system in England) was introduced in a few early land grants, but there is no evidence that Acadian farmers ever paid seigneurial rents for land. There were no royal taxes, although when the French held Port Royal a governor and a few troops were usually there and a militia was raised locally. Commercial opportunity was limited because Acadia was a small catchment area for furs, there was no commercial fishing in the Bay of Fundy, and marshland farms produced crops and livestock that were available widely around the North Atlantic. In these circumstances Acadian society was not very stratified; people had enough to eat but there was no wealth. In 1686 the governor's small thatched house in Port Royal was only a little larger than the tiny Acadian houses nearby. Essentially, the marshlands provided a limited opportunity for the French

peasantry but not for many other elements of French society. They became home to a people whose way of life, French in most details, soon had no precise French counterpart.

In rural Canada farming slowly developed after France regained the colony in 1633. The first farms were near Québec on the north shore, and by the 1650s there were others near Trois-Rivières and Montreal—at this period and for some years thereafter only on the north shore because of the Iroquois threat. By 1692, date of an early Canadian census, some 10,000 people lived on farms along the lower St. Lawrence, most within 20 miles of Québec, another patch at Trois-Rivières, and a third on Montreal Island and along adjacent shores (Fig. 4.6). The unit of settlement was the family farm, developed on a lot of 75 to 90 acres held from a seigneur. Some of the earliest deeds of concession of these lots have survived, notarized documents defining the land and the terms by which it was held. From the beginning farm lots were long and narrow (Fig. 4.7), in any given area their long axes parallel to each other and roughly perpendicular to the river. This survey, which came to Canada from Normandy, had been common in areas of new colonization in medieval Europe and would have a long life in Canada. In the 1660s the Jesuits, and then the intendant Jean Talon, experimented with a radial survey intended to group settlement around village squares, but the long lot suited a riparian colony. It was easily surveyed, provided direct access to the river, the colony's highway, and enabled people to live on their own farms yet fairly close to neighbors.

From the beginning rural settlement was dispersed rather than nucleated. Farm families lived on their own land in houses 600 to 1,200 feet apart along the river and made their own agricultural decisions. The open-field village, still common in many areas from which emigrants had come to Canada, was not introduced. Peasants in France had been moving away from the collective constraints of open-field agriculture when they acquired the means to do so, and in Canada, where a riverfront lot was available for the asking somewhere along the lower St. Lawrence at any time during the 17th century, colonial farmers (*habitants*) did so from the beginning. To be sure, the forest was a

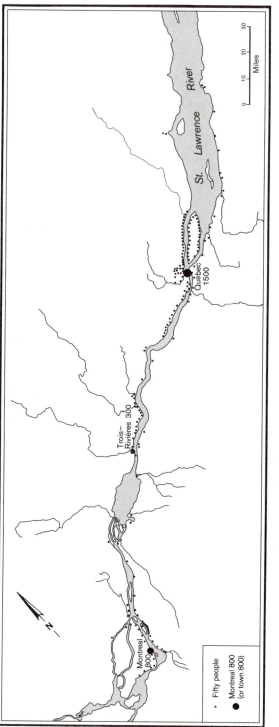

Figure 4.6 Distribution of Population in the St. Lawrence Valley, 1692

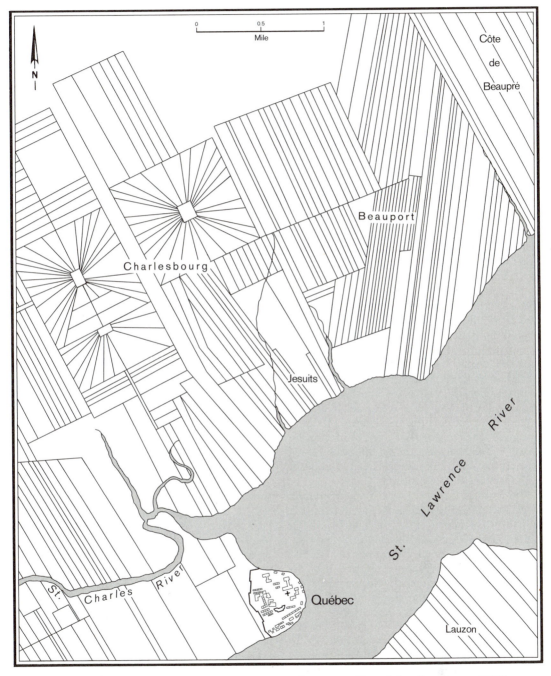

Figure 4.7 The Cadastral System along the St. Lawrence River (after Catalogne, 1709)

daunting barrier that made a farm virtually inaccessible to a destitute immigrant. Most men lived in Canada for some years as a soldier, indentured servant, or wage laborer before trying to farm. Many who eventually tried to clear the forest gave up or soon died. Still, the relative availability of land for farming raised the price of labor well above its French value. Slowly the forest yielded.

The Canadian farm, like the Acadian, was a mixed operation of, generally, the northwest European type. Fields were sown in a two-course rotation of wheat and fallow, occasionally in a three-course rotation with legumes and other grains (usually oats and barley) as well as fallow. The land was rarely manured, seed was poor, and after the initial high returns on newly cleared lands, yields were low—as they were on pioneer farms throughout early North America. With about 15 acres cleared the farm produced some 50 bushels of wheat, hardly enough after feeding a family, putting seed aside, and paying milling charges, land rents, and a tithe (1/26th of the grain harvest) to provide anything for the market. With 30 acres cleared the farm produced about 100 bushels of wheat and probably carried two or three cows, as many swine, a few sheep, and perhaps a pair of oxen. There was a kitchen garden with common French vegetables, herbs, tobacco, and usually a few fruit trees. Such a farm provided for most of the subsistence of a family, paid the seigneurial rent and milling charges and had a modest surplus—some bushels of wheat, perhaps a pig or a calf, perhaps some butter—for sale.

The market, however, was weak. The long, steep decline in the price of wheat and of other agricultural products along the lower St. Lawrence in the 17th century was interrupted only when harvests were bad and few farmers had much to sell. There were no agricultural exports: France or the French West Indies were too far away, and local markets in Québec and Montreal were small. Canadian agriculture developed within this severe constraint. Farms raising many of the crops and livestock of northwestern France could be created. Families could live on them, establishing some market connection, perhaps eventually live a little better than the poor French peasantry, but hardly prosper. The countryside of the lower St. Lawrence admitted people to a limited economic

opportunity that encouraged demographic rather than commercial expansion. In the early years girls married soon after puberty. Later, when the population was more balanced, they married, on average, at 19 or 20, still younger than their counterparts in France or in the English colonies. Families were large and life expectancy relatively long; the population would double in less than 30 years, and most of the increase would be absorbed by farms hewn from the forest.

In these circumstances the Canadian countryside, like the Acadian, was relatively undifferentiated economically or occupationally. Save millers and blacksmiths here and there, almost all heads of households were farmers. Farms of similar age were likely to be similarly developed. Before the end of the 17th century, in the areas of oldest settlement a few peasants worked as much as 50 cleared acres, a substantial farm in Canada, but nothing like the holdings of the wealthiest peasants in many French villages. To a considerable extent the countryside developed within its own momentum, detached from the external economic influences that bore so heavily on the peasantry in France. The farm family and local rural community produced a high percentage of the goods and services that they required. The line of farm houses, the *côte* as it was called, became a loose rural neighborhood frequently reinforced by ties of blood. The parish became a social unit of some importance, although without the responsibility, so onerous in France, to apportion royal taxes. To be sure, at either end of the colony there was employment in a staple trade, toward Montreal in the fur trade and downriver from Québec in the fishery. To enter these worlds was to become a seasonal laborer working for specified terms. A few seigneurs tried to develop large farms on their seigneurial domains; there would be a little wage labor or some form of share cropping. A few merchants were in the countryside in the fall to buy grain and sell cloth, salt, and some ceramic and metal ware. Many peasants were in debt to them. Seigneurs subgranted farmlots in return for annual rents and privileges, such as the monopoly of grist milling. In the early years they often neglected these charges and prerogatives because their sparsely settled seigneuries were unprofitable, but their legal rights were clear, and as the population rose more were exercised. A few bushels of wheat a year could be a heavy charge for a subsistent farmer to pay. The religious orders that controlled some of the best land near Québec, Trois-Rivières, and Montreal were careful record-keepers, and before 1700 the large Sulplician seigneury of Montreal Island was turning a profit; peasants prevaricated as they could in the payment of charges. Edicts and ordinances from the governor and intendant, representatives of royal power, were read and posted in front of parish churches and, in a colony frequently at war with the English and the Iroquois, men drilled in local militias. In sum, the apparatus of power was at hand in rural Canada, but the exercise was often muted by the availability of land and the weakness of the market.

Québec and Montreal, the towns of early Canada, were both much more dependent on their external connections than on the surrounding countryside. At the head of deep-sea navigation on the St. Lawrence, Québec was the colony's port. It received various imports from France (mostly manufactured goods and food stuffs) and sent furs. Montreal, the point of transshipment from small ships and riverboats to canoes, was founded as a mission in 1642 and quickly became the focus of the interior fur trade. Until 1681 some Indians came to trade almost every year, while the expeditions of *coureurs de bois* that began in the 1650s and continued for the rest of the century were outfitted in and eventually returned to Montreal. The Canadian merchants who soon operated in these towns bought French goods, hired labor, operated interior posts, and sent furs to La Rochelle; their warehouses lined the riverfront; and their commerce provided much of the vitality of these first French towns in North America. Québec and Montreal were also administrative and military centers. There were forts and troops in both; in 1688 Montreal was walled for protection against the Iroquois. As the colonial capital, Québec was the residence of governor and intendant and of a considerable bureaucracy. The religious orders erected their finest buildings and maintained most of their staffs in the towns.

In the late 1660s the intendant Jean Talon established a shipyard and brewery in Québec, a tannery nearby, and iron works near Trois-Rivières, and encouraged the preparation of masts and naval stores along the river below Québec. But it was difficult to break the Canadian economy from its export dependence on furs and local dependence on farming. Most of Talon's initiatives collapsed when royal subsidies were removed, victims of the high cost and, often, inexperience of Canadian labor, the smallness of the local market, and the distance to external markets. Saw and grist mills serving local needs emerged in the countryside, and some small ships and boats were built at Québec.

The French migratory fishery all the while maintained a relatively static presence along the Atlantic coast. Techniques for catching and curing cod had changed little since the previous century, but the organization of the fishery did become more concentrated and, here and there, people began to overwinter. In France the fishery came to depend on a few ports: principally Havre-du-Grâce (mouth of the Seine) and Sable d'Olonne (south of the Loire) in the green fishery; and St. Malo, Granville, La Rochelle, and the Basque port of St.-Jean-de-Luz in the dry. Firms that specialized in the transatlantic fishery operated out of these ports, sending out ships that were considerably larger (on average perhaps 90 tons) than those of the 16th century. Their destination in the northwestern Atlantic was limited in the north by Thule Eskimos, who drove French fishermen off most of the Labrador coast and raided across the Strait to Newfoundland, and in the south by fishermen from New England, who increasingly controlled the Atlantic coast of Nova Scotia. The English migratory fishery remained entrenched in southeastern Newfoundland. The French held the rest of Newfoundland and the Gulf of St. Lawrence. Along these French shores the fishery focused increasingly on proven, reliable harbors: Percée and Gaspé in the western gulf, Plaisance in southern Newfoundland, and a number of harbors along the bleak, ice-bound coast of northeastern Newfoundland, a region judged to be uninhabitable.

Elsewhere fishing ships began to leave behind caretakers to look after shore installations over the winter. Eventually, a few merchants began to stay as well. Such men (called *habitants-pêcheurs* by the French and planters by the English) controlled at least one fishing property and a few boats, hired migrant labor, and purchased supplies from and sold dry fish to the ships that came each year from France. They were small links, close to the resource, in an elaborate, transatlantic commerce. In both the French and English fisheries the advantages and disadvantages of the resident system were fiercely argued throughout the 17th century, but the system endured and gradually strengthened. As it did, women and children appeared in the fishing harbors; populations became a little more stable. Yet there were not many such residents. Plaisance in southern Newfoundland, the largest French settlement along the Atlantic coast of North America in the 17th century, had about 20 families in 1689, all of them dependent on the fishery and on ships and labor that came each year from France. The settlement was a fishing camp with a few families and a small garrison added (most of whom also participated in the fishery), a residential toe-hold in a still largely migratory French fishery that sent some 400 ships and 10,000 men across the Atlantic each year.

FRANCE IN NORTH AMERICA ABOUT 1700

In 1700 fewer than 20,000 people of French background were scattered across North America from Newfoundland to the Mississippi. The overall pattern of their distribution had been set by the cod fishery and fur trade, and at the beginning of the 18th century many people still lived in, and many more worked seasonally in, settlements that were essentially the work camps of these staple trades. Directed toward rocky, inhospitable shores, the fishery had almost no New World multipliers, whereas the fur trade drew Europeans inland, generating towns and agricultural settlements. By 1700 Québec and Montreal were well established, and most French-speaking residents in North America lived on farms that had little to do with staple trades (Fig. 4.8).

The fur trade continued to be riverine, expansive, and interracial; the cod fishery remained maritime, static, and European. The fishery, as it always had, relied on European labor, discouraged European-Indian contact, and drew fishermen to familiar shores year after year. The fur trade, dependent on an easily depleted continental resource and on native labor, drew French traders far into the continental interior, and Indians and Europeans together. By 1696 there were some twenty French posts west of Montreal, eight of them in the Mississippi watershed; all were tied in one direction to networks of Indian trade and in the other by canoe routes to Montreal and by ship across the Atlantic to La Rochelle, the French port of entry for almost all Canadian fur. Yet both the cod fishery and the fur trade were staple trades dependent on overseas markets. Both created wilderness settlements dominated by the specialized techniques, work routines, and transportation connections of a staple trade, and inhabited by migratory, male work forces. Put another way, both separated place of work from place of residence, detaching French capital and labor from their larger social contexts and placing them where neither tradition nor community but rather the terms of work in a staple trade would shape social relationships. In settlements near the resource a few trade-related tasks were accomplished by largely migratory work forces with as little expenditure as possible. In the fishery wharves, dry platforms, washing cages, oil vats, and cabins were put up along a shore; in the fur trade a few squared-log buildings could be constructed in days behind equally hastily erected palisades.

Although both the cod fishery and the fur trade depended on towns, the urban base of the cod fishery remained almost entirely transatlantic. Plaisance was a tiny settlement; most ships, crews, and profits of the fishery returned to France, strengthening French firms and building imposing merchant houses in some French ports. As the fur trade pushed inland, however, it required New World towns. In Acadia where the fur trade was small and scattered, Port Royal was barely a village in 1700. But in Canada in that year there were some 2,000 people in Québec and perhaps 1,200 in Montreal. Although visitors from France described them as "miserables bourgs," they were by far the most comprehensive settings of French life in North America. Their waterfronts—the lower towns—were given to commerce: warehouses, stores, cabarets, and the artisanal activities of a port. Farther from the waterfronts—the upper towns—land use was more open and institutional: forts and barracks; residences of officials; hospitals, churches, seminaries and other buildings of

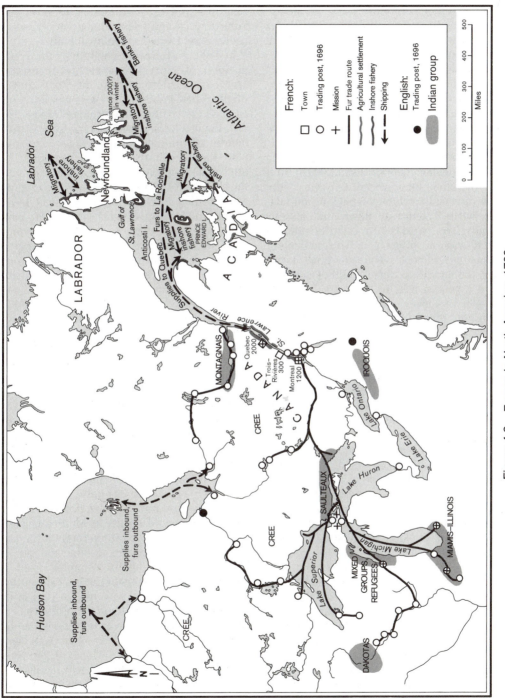

Figure 4.8　France in North America, 1700

religious orders. These towns were occupationally diverse and socially stratified, reproducing within the limits of such small places much of the fine meaning of French social hierarchy. They relied on the surrounding countryside for much of their food, and on France or the North American interior for almost everything else. The availability of land in the countryside had driven up urban wages and probably had increased the mobility of labor, conditions that favored the importation of labor-intensive manufactures and discouraged skilled, local craftsmanship.

In 1700 about 1,200 people lived around the marshes of the Bay of Fundy and 13,000 in rural seigneuries along the lower St. Lawrence—the bulk of the resident, French-speaking population of North America. In these rural settings the family farm, weakly connected to external markets, was the primary unit of settlement and economy. People lived in small farmhouses, perhaps 18 × 28 feet, built of round or squared logs and usually thatched. The simplest walls were made of vertical posts dug into the ground. More-durable houses had stone sills and either timber frame walls (variously infilled, but usually with squared logs laid horizontally) or solid walls of horizontal logs (usually cross-notched or dovetailed at the corners). Such building techniques had been common in medieval France when the forest was at hand, had largely lapsed when it was not, and reappeared where wood was again abundant. Houses built with them clustered around the Fundy marshes and lined the St. Lawrence River, one house much like its neighbor, one farm much like the next. Most crops, livestock, tools, and agricultural practices came from France. Beyond the farm were the myriad relationships (some of blood) of the local community; usually a grist mill and a parish church; and perhaps a seigneurial manor, only a little more pretentious than the peasant house. Farther away there was a town—a place that was known and sometimes visited, that sent out merchants who supplied goods beyond the capacity of local fabrication, and took farm surpluses. In some areas there was still danger of Indian attack, and for some young men there was contract labor in the fishery or the fur trade. But in large part the peasant horizon was local, and compared with France it was less beset by economic demands. As the staple

trades tended to detach specialized labor and capital from France, so these mixed agricultural economies tended to detach a peasantry. As Montreal and Québec tended to reestablish French social and occupational variety, so the countryside tended to diminish both.

In 1700, as from the beginning, the French position in North America was contested. Thirty years before, in 1670, the Stuart court in England had granted the Hudson's Bay Company all the territory that drained into Hudson Bay. English forts, established on the Bay at the mouths of the major rivers, began competing with the French for the interior trade. The English had replaced the Dutch at the mouth of the Hudson River and, allied with the Iroquois, were trading into the southern Great Lakes. There was a large English fishery in Newfoundland, and English colonies, many times more populous than New France, along the eastern seaboard. In sum the English presence in North America was far more substantial than the French.

Nevertheless, at the end of the 17th century in North America, military momentum was with the French. French forces captured the English forts on Hudson and James bays in the 1680s, although the English recaptured one of them, Fort Albany, in 1693 and held it. French troops destroyed several Iroquois villages south of Lake Ontario in 1693 and 1697, forcing the Iroquois to treat for peace, although the Hudson-Mohawk route to the Great Lakes remained in Iroquois-English control. In 1690 a marine attack by New Englanders on Québec failed miserably. In 1697 the French Crown, faced with a glut of beaver pelts, was confident enough to close most interior posts, assuming the Indians would return to Montreal. Far to the south it established three forts on the Gulf of Mexico—at Biloxi, at Mobile, and on the Mississippi River about 45 miles from its mouth—hoping to contain the English south of the Appalachians and to control access to the interior. In fact the continental interior was vast and porous, and there was not nearly enough manpower to seal it off, least of all from illegal traders operating out of Montreal. In Newfoundland the predicament was similar. In 1696–97 a combined force of French troops and Canadians under Pierre le Moyne d'Iberville sacked almost every English settlement in Newfoundland but, as there was not manpower to hold these settlements, the English fishery returned when the attackers withdrew. In these years the one French loss in North America came a little later in Acadia. The small fort at Port Royal withstood two assaults in 1707, but fell in 1710 to a force of some 3,500 New Englanders. By the terms of the Treaty of Utrecht (1713) that ended the long French-English war known as the War of the Austrian Succession, France confirmed English title to peninsular Acadia, ceded Newfoundland (while retaining fishing rights in the north), and returned the forts on Hudson Bay. France had bargained for European advantage with North American territory and had disastrously weakened her North American position.

CHANGES IN THE EARLY EIGHTEENTH CENTURY

The Treaty of Utrecht forced adjustments east and west in the French position in North America. The French migratory fishery to northern Newfoundland, protected by landing privileges, continued much as before, whereas the French fishery in southern Newfoundland, migratory and residential, moved across Cabot Strait to Cape Breton Island, which was still in French hands, and quickly reestablished itself there. On Cape Breton Island, the residential component of the fishery grew; some merchants adopted the New Englanders' practice of sending small schooners to the offshore banks. The best harbor on the island was at Louisbourg where, in 1717, the French Crown decided to build a major fortification to protect the entrance to the Gulf of St. Lawrence. A geometrical town plan was superimposed on a straggling fishing village, and massive low walls, designed to withstand artillery bombardment, were slowly built. When completed in the 1730s, Louisbourg was the largest fortification in North America, an early 18th-century fortress town built in the precise military geometry of the Vauban style on a low, frequently foggy peninsula protecting an excellent harbor that had become one of the busiest in North America (Fig. 4.9).

After the Treaty of Utrecht the French also moved quickly to restore their earlier position in the west. The ban on interior trade was lifted. Michilimakinac was reopened in 1712–

13, and trade was soon restored to the Illinois-Michigan posts. Agricultural settlement began in the Illinois country: at Vincennes on the lower Wabash and at Kaskaskia on the Mississippi above the Ohio. Colonists came from Canada, which supplied and administered these settlements until the Illinois country was made part of the colony of Louisiana in 1717. By the early 1720s there were several posts along the lower Great Lakes from Fort Frontenac at the eastern end of Lake Ontario to Detroit, their purpose to exclude English traders, while French posts north of Lake Superior cut into Hudson's Bay Company trade. Detroit and Michilimakinac became major entrepôts, receiving supplies from Montreal and furs from the west. In the 1730s traders from Montreal reached the northern Plains, establishing posts on the Red and Assiniboine rivers. By the 1740s they were on the Saskatchewan River, some 2,500 miles by canoe from Montreal. Freight canoes had become larger, carrying six men rather than three as earlier in the century. As the lines of the French carrying trade lengthened, more French labor was required in the west; by the early 1740s there are records of about 500 men leaving Montreal each year, most of them voyageurs hired to paddle canoes loaded with supplies and trade goods to specified destinations and to return with packs of fur.

To the south France moved to strengthen her hold on the lower Mississippi River and, thereby, on the whole Mississippi valley. In 1717, after almost two decades during which French settlement along the lower Mississippi had been little more than a garrison, the Crown granted a merchant company title to, and a trading monopoly in, Louisiana for twenty-five years. The company was to establish 6,000 settlers and 3,000 slaves. The next year it founded New Orleans, and began granting large properties that the company assumed would be worked primarily by indentured servants brought from Europe. Immigrants were recruited in France, the Low Countries, and Germany, and several thousand French convicts were sentenced to deportation to Louisiana. Few convicts left France, however, fewer reached Louisiana, and only a handful survived there. Some Canadians arrived overland from Montreal, but white labor was scarce and expensive. In these circumstances the company

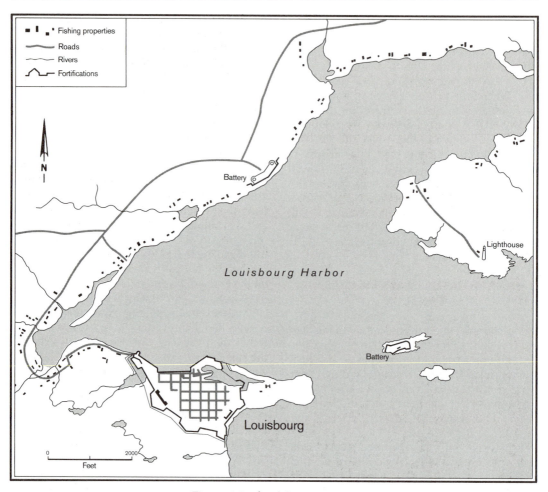

Figure 4.9   Louisbourg, 1742

turned increasingly to black slaves, the characteristic plantation labor force on the French sugar islands (Guadaloupe, Martinique, and St. Domingue, the western third of Hispaniola). By 1731 when the company's monopoly was terminated and the Crown assumed control of Louisiana, there were more blacks than whites in a non-native population along the lower Mississippi of about 4,000. Plantations worked by slaves were the principal units of production.

And yet, an export staple was not established. Sugar was a marginal crop, not competitive with island production. Mid-latitude grains grew poorly in a subtropical climate. Citrus fruits, figs, and pineapples, which did well, had no export market. Cotton could not yet be ginned. Rice, indigo, and tobacco were more promising and became the principal plantation products together, on some of the larger plantations, with lumber and naval stores. Furs and hides (deer and buffalo) from the interior were also exported but, essentially, the struggling Louisianan economy depended on agricultural land, much of which was occupied by Indians. Initially amicable French-Indian relations soured as Indian lands were appropriated. Skirmishes and small wars broke out in which the Indians had the short-term advantage of surprise and the French the long-term advantage of fire power. Between 1729 and 1731 the Natchez, approximately 3,000 Indians living along the Mississippi some 190 miles above New Orleans, were dispersed, many of them to St. Domingue as slaves.

While these developments were taking place

along the lower Mississippi, the very different settlements along the lower St. Lawrence and in Acadia expanded within well-established patterns. There was virtually no 18th-century immigration to Acadia and, until the last decade of the French regime, little enough to Canada. Birthrates remained high; in each area the average annual population increase was more than 2 percent, most of it absorbed in the countryside where farmland was available. By 1740 there were about 40,000 French-speaking people in the St. Lawrence valley, and some 8,000 around the Bay of Fundy. Settlement had spread along the St. Lawrence River, reducing the gaps between Québec and Montreal, following minor tributaries, and extending well below Québec on the south shore (Fig. 4.10). All the habitable marshes around the Bay of Fundy were occupied by 1740, and Acadian settlement had begun on Prince Edward Island. Agricultural practices did not change, but for a time there was a little more commercial opportunity because Louisbourg created a relatively accessible market. A little Acadian wheat and some cattle found their way there in most years, usually in tiny, Acadian-built ships. Merchants from Québec also began to supply Louisbourg and to expand their cabbotage in

the gulf (to supply fishing stations). From 1727 to 1742 an average of ten Canadian ships a year carried flour, meat, butter, and lumber to Louisbourg, and a few went on to the sugar islands. Then, in 1742, these trades were disrupted by the first of a succession of poor harvests along the lower St. Lawrence. Wheat prices rose, but there was no surplus for export, a condition that continued to the end of the French regime, putting a heavy lid on the agricultural economy, breaking a promising commercial connection between Canada and Louisbourg and a more tenuous one with the West Indies, slowing urban growth, and weakening the St. Lawrence colony.

The urban population in Canada and Acadia grew much less rapidly than the rural. Port Royal (renamed Annapolis Royal in 1713) remained what it had been when the New Englanders captured it—a fort and garrison with a village nearby, except that after 1710 the garrison and many of the villagers were English-speaking. With the impetus of expanding trade Québec grew quickly from 1727 to the early 1740s, but even in 1744, the date of an enumeration of the parish of Notre-Dame de Québec, only some 4,700 people were in the town. Montreal was little more than half as

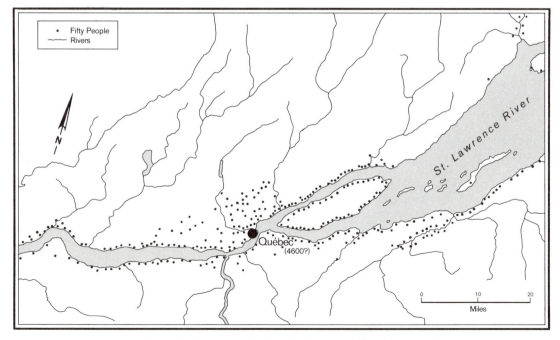

Figure 4.10   Population Distribution near Québec, 1739

large. The fur trade required the towns but generated little urban growth because most of the goods traders exchanged for furs came from France. By 1744 agricultural exports had stopped; furs, a valuable export, required only two or three ships a year. Imports involved more ships, but the small colonial market for French manufactures and foodstuffs and for West Indian molasses and rum was soon satisfied. The size of civil and clerical administrations, and even of garrisons, changed slowly. Québec and Montreal were small, stable towns in the first half of the 18th century, their economies established and circumscribed, their populations growing slowly.

FRANCE IN NORTH AMERICA
ABOUT 1750

In the middle of the 18th century France claimed a vast crescent of North America from the Gulf of St. Lawrence to the mouth of the Mississippi (Fig. 4.11). Such a claim was intended to deflect European rivals; within much of New France the French deferred to Indians, who regarded the land as theirs and still controlled it. Yet the French dominated the two main continental entries and far outdistanced English traders in the interior, building posts and trading through thousands of miles of Indian territory. French settlement was hardly in proportion: some 60,000 people of French descent along the lower St. Lawrence River, perhaps 2,000 along the lower Mississippi more than 3,000 miles away, more than 1,000 in the Illinois country, a few hundred around the lower Great Lakes, more than 10,000 Acadians around the Bay of Fundy (most living in British territory), and just over 5,000 people on Cape Breton Island, including those at Louisbourg. After 150 years of French activity there were fewer than 80,000 French-speaking settlers in North America. The French migratory fishery, still large and inflexible, continued to northern Newfoundland and into the gulf. Overall, the French-speaking settlements were a collection of patches strung somewhat diagonally across a continent, some linked to each other by trade, but the collection as a whole dispersed, underconnected, and vulnerable.

In the early 1750s the French fur trade reached its zenith (Fig. 4.12). Perhaps 700 men from Montreal Island and seigneuries nearby traveled west each year, many of them to overwinter at interior posts. English traders were checked along the Great Lakes, and Montreal traders competed around the large perimeter of Hudson's Bay Company trade. The whole Great Lakes basin and upper Mississippi valley were, briefly, in French control; in 1754–55 80 percent of the North American fur trade was French, almost all of it passing through Montreal and Québec and thence, in a few ships a year, to La Rochelle. In the same year almost a million quintals (one quintal = 112 pounds or about 50 kilograms) of dried and green cod from the French fisheries in the northwestern Atlantic returned to France in several hundred ships; a relatively tiny quantity of cod went to the sugar islands. A variety of agricultural products, naval stores, and lumber was shipped from New Orleans to the sugar islands or to France. These trades were not interconnected; they all bypassed the mixed farms along the lower St. Lawrence and in Acadia, on which most French-speaking people in North America lived. It is true, however, that Kaskaskia, Vincennes, and other French settlements in the Illinois country sent salt beef, pork, and flour to Louisiana. The farms at Detroit and near Montreal provided foodstuffs and manpower for the fur trade, and some farms near Québec supplied the gulf fisheries. But the ships that brought imports from France to Québec usually sailed in ballast to Louisbourg, hoping for a cargo there. In the early 1750s the building materials and most foodstuffs imported at Louisbourg came from New England. Canadian agricultural exports had dried up. Even Acadia, close by, was a fitful supplier: a few cattle, a little grain, some knitting, a few wooden tools—a tiny fraction of Louisbourg's annual imports. Increasingly in the early 1750s Louisbourg was a mart for New Englanders, where French manufactures, West Indian rum and molasses, Cape Breton fish, and New England foodstuffs and building supplies were traded and bills of exchange earned on French firms. Prosperous merchants in Louisbourg traded into the North Atlantic rather than toward Canada, Acadia, or Louisiana. Despite many official projects to the contrary, it had not proved possible to create an integrated commerical system out of the differ-

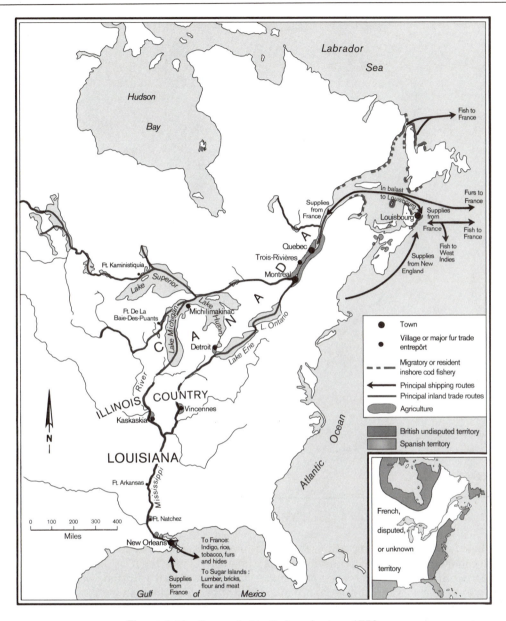

Figure 4.11   France in North America, ca. 1750

ent, widely separated spatial economies of New France.

Therefore, there was no one urban hierarchy. New Orleans controlled the Mississippi trade north to the Illinois country, Québec and Montreal controlled the St. Lawrence trade, and Louisbourg participated in North Atlantic trade. All were well connected to France and, excepting Québec and Montreal, little connected to each other. Yet all were colonial

French towns with important commercial, military, and administrative functions. Commerce dominated their waterfronts, and institutional buildings their upper towns. Merchants, colonial officials, and officers dominated their social structures. Urban society was sharply hierarchical, status-conscious, and deferential although, as in other towns of the day, people of very different standing lived side by side. In many ways the towns of New France resem-

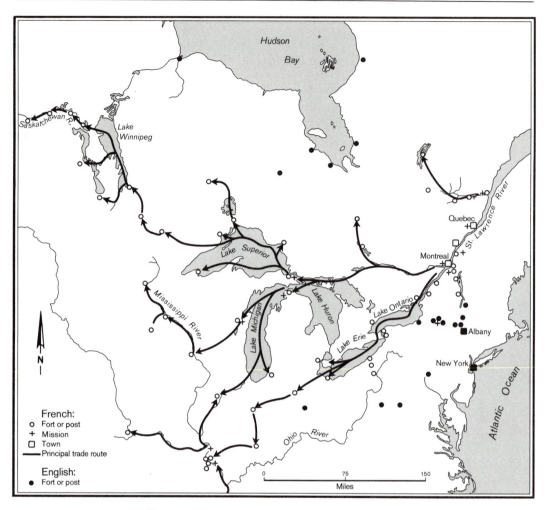

Figure 4.12 The French Fur Trade, early 1750s

bled their French equivalents. Montcalm, the French commander at Québec, considered that Québec, which had just over 5,000 people in 1750, was as fine as any town in France after the first ten. Of course they were new, they were not centuries of architectural accretion, and they were composed of people of many regional backgrounds. In New Orleans there were many black and some Indian slaves in a population of perhaps 1,200. In all the towns the cost of labor was high. There were no guilds, apprenticeship was much less defined than in France, and small labor-intensive manufactured goods were usually imported. In Québec rough footwear was made locally, whereas most fine shoes came from France, although there were skilled craftsmen—wig-

makers, cabinet-makers, sculptors, and silversmiths—in the town as well as the rougher trades associated with the port and with construction. The oldest and largest of the towns of New France, Québec was the most like a French provincial capital.

Of these towns Louisbourg has been the most closely studied. Its economy was dominated by trade (including the fishery) and by the garrisons, and its society by colonial officials, officers, and merchants. There was a great deal of occupational mobility, but the occupational choice was limited because almost all manufactured goods were imported. Officers participated in the fishery, *habitants-pêcheurs* became innkeepers or importers. Shoes, cloth, most clothing, kitchenware, and fine furniture came from France. Inexpensive furniture came from New England. Culturally, Louisbourg was a melting-pot, drawing people from many parts of France, from elsewhere in Europe, and from Acadia, Canada, and even New England. Its women were more likely to be North American born than its men; husband and wife characteristically came from different regional backgrounds. In six houses along one waterfront block lived heads of households or their wives born in France, Portugal, Louisbourg, Acadia, and Canada; and, at the social extremes, the *commissaire-ordonateur* (the principal civil official in Louisbourg) and a fisherman's widow.

Because a good deal of Louisbourg has been rebuilt after much research, its 18th-century appearance is accurately known. The architecture of all the principal buildings reflected current French taste, just as the layout of fortifications reflected current French military engineering. The appearance of lesser buildings, most of them of timber-frame construction variously infilled, was less bound to current style and more dependent on techniques of construction. Gardens, always small in Louisbourg, were laid out geometrically, as was the town itself which, like New Orleans, was a rectangular grid of streets, walled. In Québec and Montreal officials discouraged wooden buildings because of the fire hazard. By 1750 most houses were of stone, their shingle or plank roofs punctuated by spare dormers and massive chimneys. Usually they were built continuously on narrow lots. Size was gained by height; the largest houses of successful merchants had four stories above the basement. In New Orleans, where local stone was not available, most buildings were of timber-frame construction with brick infill. Otherwise the architectural styles and the techniques of construction of the northern towns also prevailed in New Orleans.

In 1750, as earlier, rural Acadia and Canada remained somewhat detached from this urban world. Some 13,000 Acadians had dyked all the available marshes, and many of them, fearful of English intentions and short of land, were moving to Prince Edward Island, still in French hands. Acadian agriculture remained what it had been in 1700: mixed, largely subsistent, family centered, and primarily dependent on the marshlands. Acadian society may have be-

come a little more stratified, although there is very little evidence one way or the other and no suggestion of wealth in any settlement around the Bay of Fundy. A few Acadians had become farmer-merchants, masters of tiny ships that they sailed to Boston or Louisbourg. Essentially the Acadians remained a peasantry who, by the mid-18th century, were several generations removed from France. Descended from a tiny founding population, they had coped with a common and very distinctive environment and, although there were imported goods in their houses and English troops at Annapolis Royal, had mixed relatively little with the larger world of the North Atlantic.

By the early 1750s some 50,000 rural people of French descent lived along the lower St. Lawrence, almost all of them members of farm families. As the population grew the countryside became somewhat more differentiated. There were now several agricultural villages housing a priest (*curé*) and perhaps the seigneurial family, a few artisans and perhaps a merchant agent or two besides farm families. More seigneurs were able to profit from their land rent and domainal farms; manor houses became more common and a little larger. A few merchants in Montreal and Québec prospered from their dealings in the countryside, while a few farmers in long-settled areas near the towns worked as much as 75 acres of cleared land and relied on hired labor. As they lived near the quarries that served Québec and Montreal, their houses were usually of stone. Yet the continuing availability of land somewhere in the colony, if not near the parental farm, and the weakness of the export economy slowed the pace of social and economic differentiation. The countryside could still yield a rough living for most, and was only slowly yielding much more for a few.

In the Illinois country opportunities were quite different. The largest concentration of French settlement was in five villages, inhabited by some 1,000 whites and 500 black and Indian slaves, along the Mississippi River between the Missouri and the Kaskaskia. Father Vivier, the Jesuit who served these settlements, estimated that two-thirds of their agricultural production was exported. Wheat, beef, pork, and some livestock on the hoof were sent to New Orleans, destined for the sugar islands. Corn, which was not exported, yielded abundantly and was the food of cattle, slaves, and natives. The largest landholder in the village of Kaskaskia worked some 500 acres of arable land and owned sixty slaves (including some women and children) and many hundred cattle, swine, and horses. Most settlers had very little arable land and presumably lived primarily from hunting and the hide trade, but almost 70 percent of white families were slave-owners. In the Illinois country, French settlement from Canada had reached a bounteous land suitable for arable and pastoral farming and within range of a market. A small, ethnically mixed population was growing rapidly, its economy vigorous, its society sharply stratified. Vivier considered the Illinois country the pivot of the French effort to hold the vast continental crescent between the Gulf of St. Lawrence and the Gulf of Mexico. In many ways he was right, but a few villagers far in the interior were a fragile pivot for continental ambition. The region needed more settlers and more years than it was ever allowed.

Almost 500 miles along the river south of Kaskaskia, a garrison fort at the mouth of the Arkansas River was the most northerly outpost of French settlement on the lower Mississippi and a way point for convoys to and from the Illinois country. A few settlers had farmed there until driven off by the Chickasaw in 1748. At Natchez, some 190 miles farther south, there was another garrison, again penned in by the Chickasaw, and good but underused tobacco land. At Pointe-Coupée, halfway between Natchez and New Orleans, agriculture was more secure, tobacco being the principal crop. There was a German settlement 20 miles above New Orleans; below the town both banks of the river were occupied almost halfway to the sea. Throughout these plantations blacks considerably outnumbered whites (a census of 1763 enumerated 4,539 blacks and 2,966 whites along the lower Mississippi). Slaves were used to produce subsistent crops such as potatoes, corn, and vegetables, to work in rice, indigo, and tobacco fields, and as laborers in saw mills, brickyards, and in the preparation of naval stores. Some forty ships were reported to have called at New Orleans in 1750, most coming from Martinique and St. Domingue for lumber and bricks. The colony also exported a variety of goods to France—principally indigo, tobacco, rice, furs, and hides—but

in 1750, as previously, Louisiana was a considerable financial liability to the French Crown. The settlements along the lower Mississippi were set around by hostile natives and still had not established an export staple. After the initial burst of immigration in the first years of the merchant company, the population had grown very slowly.

A plantation worked by slaves was an efficient means of harnessing year-round work for labor-intensive, market-oriented productions in tropical or subtropical environments. It was unsuited to the weakly commercial, seasonal agricultural economies of northeastern North America, while the cod fishery and the fur trade, both labor-intensive, had also solved the problem of labor very differently. Some 8,000–10,000 fishermen still crossed the Atlantic each year from France. In fishing harbors in northern or western Newfoundland, on the Gaspé Peninsula, or on Cape Breton Island, these men and boys were accommodated minimally, worked incessantly, and subjected to iron discipline. The lots of fisherman or shore worker in the fishery or of slave on a plantation were not very different except that for one there was eventually a return voyage, some pay, and some choice of subsequent work—but not very much choice for poor people. The fur trade continued to rely on Indian hunters and trappers spread across much of the continent, and on a relatively small number of whites to maintain trading posts. By 1750 Fort Detroit, the largest entrepôt in the fur trade, was a walled village with a winter population of 400; far to the northwest along the Saskatchewan River in western Canada, new forts comprised a few buildings behind hastily built palisades—minimal winter accommodation for a few whites living among little-known and untrusted Indians.

CONCLUSION

The French position in North America, vast, scattered, and underpopulated, was lost during the Seven Year's War. In 1755, before the war officially began, British officials in Acadia, distrusting the French-speaking population they loosely governed and encouraged by Boston merchants who stood to earn lucrative contracts, decided to deport the Acadians. Many Acadians fled to Canada or to the Gulf of St. Lawrence, but many others were caught and sent to the English colonies to the south. When

Louisbourg fell in 1758 after a massive siege, the French could no longer protect the gulf. Acadian refugees there were rounded up and sent to England or France. In 1759 another large British force laid siege to Québec and after a summer's bombardment took the town. Surrounded, the French army in Montreal capitulated the next year. New France was lost. The British effort to take it had cost some £80 million, the French defense about a twentieth as much. At the end, as throughout, France's involvement in North America had been half-hearted. Furs from Canada were only 5 to 10 percent of the value of French colonial imports, 1 to 2 percent of the value of all imports. Louisiana had been an expense rather than a revenue. The fisheries seemed more important than either Canada or Louisiana. France bargained for them and, in the Treaty of Paris ending the Seven Year's War, retained fishing privileges in northern and western Newfoundland and two small islands, St. Pierre and Miquelon, south of Newfoundland. Canada and all of Acadia were ceded to Britain; Louisiana was ceded to Spain. From a French perspective the loss of New France was not devastating and might even encourage the English seaboard colonies, freed from French threat, to revolt.

In North America the fall of New France changed the control but not the pattern of the spatial economy. The Acadian lands were reoccupied by New Englanders who would soon practice much the same semisubsistent agriculture as their predecessors. Louisbourg was abandoned and demolished, but the fisheries continued, with the French migratory fishery now confined to northern Newfoundland and to St. Pierre and Miquelon. In the St. Lawrence valley Montreal and Québec retained their older functions under new management. Their populations declined after the conquest, then grew very slowly. The countryside remained French-speaking, and rural life stayed much as it was. The connection with the west quickly resumed, employing the techniques and reoccupying and expanding the space of the Montreal fur trade at the end of the French regime. Increasingly the merchants were English-speaking. Plantation agriculture continued in the lower Mississippi valley, now in Spanish hands, to which, over the years, many Acadian refugees made their way. The different econo-mies of the former French possessions in North America were no more integrated than they had been under the French.

Early in the Revolutionary War American troops attacked Canada, assuming that the French-speaking inhabitants of the St. Lawrence lowlands, recently conquered by the British, would rally to the American cause. A few did, the invaders captured Montreal and laid mid-winter siege to Québec. But British troops held the town, local support for the Americans evaporated and, in the spring when British reinforcements arrived, the invaders fled. The old French colony along the St. Lawrence had held against its former enemies and at the end of the war was the core of the British position in North America. In the peace settlement of 1783 an international border was drawn from the St. Lawrence River through lakes Ontario, Erie, Huron, and Superior, placing Grand Portage, the principal entrepôt on the north shore of Lake Superior, on the American side. A canoe route beyond Lake Superior to the northern Plains was barely retained, while the more southerly reach of the St. Lawrence fur trade into the Ohio valley and the Mississippi valley was lost. The small, vigorous, quite distinctive, but too belated settlements in the Illinois country would soon merge in the tide of American westward expansion. In the east, Newfoundland remained British, as did the territory the French called Acadia, renamed Nova Scotia. In effect, Britain retained the original French economies in North America: the cod fishery and the fur trade based on the St. Lawrence, the towns which the fur trade had created, and the semisubsistent agricultural economies that had emerged in its train— patches of settlement bounded by uncultivable land and separated by distance along the northern edge of North American agriculture. Over the years the fur trade and cod fishery would continue, as detached as ever from each other. Other staple trades would reach into northern North American space, and towns would emerge to serve them. Agriculture would continue in patches, and none of the patches would be very well connected to each other. Economic, social, and political life would evolve within this fractured economic space, along the northern inhabitable edge of a continent, as it had done throughout the French regime.

ADDITIONAL READING

Books

Clark, A.H. *Acadia: The Geography of Early Nova Scotia to 1760*. Madison: University of Wisconsin Press, 1968.

Dechêne, L. *Habitants et marchands de Montréal au XVIIᵉ siècle*. Montreal: Plon, 1974.

Eccles, W.J. *The Canadian Frontier, 1534–1760*. New York: Holt, Rinehart & Winston, 1969.

Giraud, M. *Histoire de la Louisiane française*. 4 vols. Paris: Presses Universitaires de France, 1953 and subsequently.

Harris, R.C. *The Seigneurial System in Early Canada: A Geographical Study*. Madison: University of Wisconsin Press, 1966; 2nd ed. Montreal: McGill-Queen's University Press, 1984.

Harris, R.C., and Warkentin, J. *Canada before Confederation: A Study in Historical Geography*. New York: Oxford University Press, 1974.

Heidenreich, C. *Huronia*. Toronto: McClelland & Stewart, 1971.

———. *Explorations and Mapping of Samuel de Champlain, 1603–1632*. (Cartographica, 17, 1976).

La Morandière, C. de. *Histoire de la pêche française de la morue dans l'Amérique septentrionale*. Paris: Maisonneuve et Larose, 1962.

Sauer, C.O. *Sixteenth Century North America: The Land and the People as Seen by the Europeans*. Berkeley and Los Angeles: University of California Press, 1971.

The Historical Atlas of Canada, Vol. 1, *Canada before 1800*. Toronto and Montreal: University of Toronto Press / Les presses de l'université de Montréal, 1987, forthcoming.

Trigger, B. *The Children of Aataentsic: A History of the Huron People to 1660*. Montreal: McGill-Queen's University Press, 1976.

Trudel, M. *The Beginnings of New France 1524–1663*. Toronto: McClelland & Stewart, 1973.

5

The Colonial Origins of Anglo-America

ROBERT D. MITCHELL
University of Maryland, College Park

This enterprise may staye the spanishe Kinge from flowinge over all the face of that waste firme of America, if we seate and plante there in time.

Richard Hakluyt, *A Discourse Concerning Western Planting*, 1584

If you Plant, where Savages are, doe not onely entertaine them with Trifles and Gingles; But use them justly, and gratiously, with sufficient Guard nevertheless: And doe not winne their favour by helping them to invade their Enemies, but for their Defence it is not amisse. And send oft of them over to the Country that Plants, that they may see a better Condition than their owne, and commend it when they returne.

Francis Bacon, *Of Plantations*, 1625

The "planting" of a new society, devoutly wished by the geographer and writer Richard Hakluyt and the philosopher-statesman Francis Bacon, has been enshrined by Americans in a complex vision of an heroic past, a unique "mythology of creation." This vision, replete with references to rugged, individualistic pioneers winning the continent for civilization and culminating in the fight for freedom and independence, remains vivid in the popular if not the scholarly imagination. The revisionist scholarship of the past 20 years, on the other hand, has plunged us into debate about the origins of the new societies created in North America.

England entered the world of European colonization of the Americas rather late. Its principal achievement by 1700, more than 250,000 settlers distributed sparsely and discontinuously from southern Maine to South Carolina with few settlements more than 50 miles from the coast, appears modest in the light of the demographic growth and territorial expansion of the 18th and 19th centuries. But viewed in comparison with Spanish colonization, with its marginal interests in North America, or French colonization, with its marginal locations in the north, English settlement proved quite successful. More important, this pioneer population was principally responsible for creating both the foundation for and the delineation of a new American culture and society that later genera-

tions gradually transformed into the more familiar world of the late 20th century.

The study of Anglo-American origins is one of the more controversial issues in American historiography. Some observers have argued that the creation of the new society was based primarily on elements of English life that were transferred selectively across the Atlantic and, metaphorically speaking, transplanted in the new land, took root, and flourished. Continuity of life between the Old World and the New was, therefore, paramount. This view contrasted with the earlier interpretation of Frederick Jackson Turner, who emphasized the formative influences on a new society of a moving American settlement frontier increasingly distant from Europe. Others have argued forcefully that the characteristics of the new land itself were critical in defining the principal features of 17th-century life. Pioneer settlers had to adapt to a variety of environmental circumstances, seemingly familiar and unfamiliar. In so doing, they modified both their environments and their European heritages.

Debate has also ensued over the precise geographical configuration of these new colonial settlements. Are they best described in terms of a rapid convergence and simplification of English traits into three regions of cultural integration, the so-called hearths of southern New England, the lower Delaware Valley and southeastern Pennsylvania, and the tidewater Chesapeake? Or were early colonial settlements more diversified and more complex? If diversity is a more appropriate theme, what were the characteristics of its regionalism and for how long did this diversity endure? And to what extent are the differences found in these early settlements to be explained basically in terms of distinctions made between communitarian, subsistence societies and those of more liberal, individualistic, and commercial orientation?

These issues and questions allow us, therefore, to identify three major themes in our quest for Anglo-American origins. The first theme is the configuration and transfer of the values, institutions, and practices of English life to the Atlantic coast of North America during the 17th century. Second, we need to examine the spatial reorganization and landscape expression of these elements in new North American environments. Third, it is also important for us to identify the spatial and temporal changes that occurred in the colonies during the century and that provided the framework for continuity, expansion, and convergence during the 18th century.

ENGLAND ON THE EVE OF COLONIZATION

English administration of territories overseas was not a novel experience. As the largest, most populous, and most southerly area of the British Isles, England had administered territories in France until the middle of the 15th century. Later generations of Tudor monarchs devoted considerable attention to reorganizing the British Isles into an English-dominated national territorial system. Wales and Cornwall had been integrated into an English state structure by the middle of the 16th century. Scotland remained relatively untouched until the Union of the Crowns under James I in 1603. English monarchs devoted most attention to Ireland during the later 16th and early 17th centuries; and it was in Ireland that several early colonial founders—Humphrey Gilbert in Newfoundland, Walter Raleigh at Roanoke Island, and several members of the Virginia Company of London—received part of their training in colonization and in the military subjugation of non-English populations. When the English

turned their attention to transatlantic enterprises by the 1560s, therefore, they did so within the context of prior administrative, legal, and military experience.

The 4 million people who comprised the English nation in 1600 were organized into some forty shires or county communities, more than 700 boroughs, and about 9,000 rural parishes. English life was overwhelmingly rural, agrarian, and provincial. Only London, with 250,000 inhabitants, had more than 20,000 people. Even by the end of the century 85 percent of England's 6 million people still resided in the countryside (Fig. 5.1). English life was thus characterized by considerable regional diversity, a diversity that tended to foster much insularity and provincialism. This provincial world, nevertheless, was focused on a widely shared set of values, symbols, and institutions. Belief in social order and stability, hierarchy and inequality, aristocracy and patriarchy, and individual responsibility within a recently transformed Protestant society was associated with symbols of nature and the pastoral, of communal and agrarian living, of emerging national identification, and strong upper-class preoccupation with the past. The institutions that molded these characteristics into patterns of everyday living were those associated with family and kin, rural neighborhood and community, the manor and local government, church and parish, land and property, and civil and common law.

The conventional view of English regionalism holds that a basic division existed between a lowland zone of open-field arable farming associated with nucleated villages and hamlets in the south and east and an upland zone to the west and north of enclosed fields, hamlets, and dispersed farms, with more pastoral activities. It is now clear that rural England was more complex than this. We can identify several principal farming types, field systems, settlement patterns, and vernacular (folk) housing forms, all of which overlapped to create a myriad of regional subtypes.

In southern and eastern England, from which three-quarters of 17th-century colonists came, there were four principal regional societies and economies with several subtypes. In southeastern England, a wood pasture economy prevailed based on barley, wheat, and rye, peas and beans, sheep, cattle, and localized pig

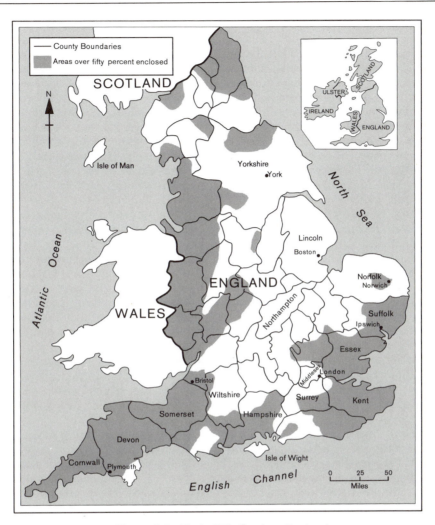

Figure 5.1   Early 17th-Century England

production. This system was associated with irregular and sometimes open-field systems, hamlets and dispersed farms in which timber-framed rectilinear houses predominated. In the Home Counties around London large manors and individual farms were engaged in wheat, oats, vegetables, cattle, and pig production in the valleys with a shift to sheep farming on the surrounding chalk hills. Midland England supported a more varied, mixed farming economy based on open and commonfield farming, with large villages under a strong manorial system in the east; this pattern gave way farther west to a more complex arrangement of villages and open fields interrupted by areas of enclosure and more dispersed settlement. To the east,

barley, wheat, rye, oats, peas and beans were commonly cultivated in association with cattle, pigs, and poultry; to the west, greater emphasis on rye and oats, cattle and sheep was evident. Timber-framed rectilinear houses and hall and parlor houses were common throughout the region. In the southwest, a more open pasture economy prevailed based on barley and oats, cattle and sheep rearing. This system was associated with small enclosed fields, dispersed farmsteads, and long farmhouses with connected service buildings, and merged into open-field systems, hamlets, and hall and parlor houses to the east.

Provincial England was also a relatively spatially restricted society. Country folk showed little interest in national affairs or even in re-gional issues. Strong association with place of birth, with family loyalty, participation in com-munity and church affairs, and limited contacts with the rest of the country fostered an often intense local attachment. Most people seldom strayed beyond the local parish and the local market town. Geographical mobility was dis-couraged officially among the lower classes of husbandmen, tenants, laborers, and paupers. Travel on roads and waterways was slow and limited, especially during periods of inclement weather. Within local communities the land-owning classes, especially the aristocracy and the gentry who filled most provincial political and administrative offices, provided a continu-ity with the past. Their interest in family-in-herited estates, political offices, trading connec-tions, and in geneology and heraldry perpetuated the continuity of the local provin-cial scene.

Yet significant changes occurred in English society during the 17th century that affected both the pattern of emigration to the Americas and the relations between the "mother coun-try" and her colonies. Foremost among these was the drive toward national-political integra-tion alluded to earlier. This was exemplified by the concomitant establishment of the Ulster Plantation in northern Ireland (a colony of sub-jugation) and the Jamestown Plantation in Vir-ginia (a trading venture) during the first decade of the century. It was expressed further in the bitter civil war of the 1640s, the subsequent Puritan republic of the 1650s, the restoration of a Catholic monarch in 1660, and the so-called Bloodless Revolution of 1689 that finally as-sured Anglican Protestantism as the faith in perpetuity of the British Crown.

A second measure of change was the increas-ing concentration of economic and political power in London and the challenges to the traditional order in the city and adjacent Home Counties. London became a magnet for the disaffected, the unemployed, and the ambi-tious provincials who were responding to long-run social and economic changes in the coun-tryside. Agricultural reorganization in the form of increased farm enclosure (Fig. 5.1), greater emphasis on commercial agricultural speciali-zation, and a weakening of manorial institu-tions began to affect extensive areas of south-ern and eastern England by mid-century. The

fragility of a 35–40 year life span generally made the yeoman, husbandman, and lesser tenant and laboring classes, who comprised the bulk of rural populations, willing to accept authority, patriarchy, and inequality as part of the natural order of things. But vulnerability to famines, plagues, wars, and the economic deci-sions of larger landholders could lead also to social unrest, institutional modification, and to religious revivalism. The spread of Puritanism (originally devised as a derogatory term) in the late 16th and early 17th centuries was one such response to perceived change.

Third, the emergence of new commercial and mercantile classes, partly supported by agrar-ian reform and by profits in New World ven-tures, began to produce a gradual redistribu-tion of wealth, power, and status away from the traditional landowning classes to more ur-ban-oriented merchants and artisans and to those farmers who sought to take advantage of the increasing pace of agricultural and trading enterprise. Many transatlantic migrants were derived from such populations, people ulti-mately unwilling to accept the limitations im-posed on property ownership, wealth accumu-lation, social mobility, or religious practice at home.

The migrants to North America, neverthe-less, brought with them a set of cultural as-sumptions about the world that was deeply embedded in the familiar provincial society of rural England. They expected to reproduce much of this world in their new surroundings in North America, within the limitations of their slim geographical knowledge. What dis-tinguished their behavior above all was their sense of cultural mission that equated right with Christian faith, might with military power, social order with private property and individual worth, and civilization with the sub-dued pastoral and small-town landscapes of lowland England.

THE NEW WORLD ENVIRONMENT

The 60,000–odd English settlers who migrated to the American colonies before 1660 encoun-tered a world both new and seemingly familiar. Glowing, propagandistic reports of early ex-plorers and pioneer settlers gradually gave way to more measured, often critical views of the environments encountered. An almost universally expressed opinion was that the immense, forested wildernesses found almost everywhere inland from the Atlantic coast were a challenge to civilized English settlers. The intellectual historian Perry Miller's evaluation of the Puritan's "errand into the wilderness" identified the particularly acute sense of mission transmitted to New England. Wild landscapes reflected wild people unable or unwilling to subdue nature for purposes of civilized settlement.

The environments encountered by the pioneer settlers, however, varied significantly in space and in time. Seventeenth-century climatic patterns appear to have been slightly cooler and drier than 20th-century patterns throughout the Atlantic region. Conditions were relatively temperate during the first two decades of colonization, with coastal climates perhaps a few degrees cooler and precipitation in general a few inches less than at present. In 17th-century terms, however, relatively harsh conditions prevailed during the 1630s and 1640s; a more temperate situation was the rule from the early 1650s until the extremely harsh winters of the 1680s and 1690s. A general amelioration of climate set in again until the deterioration of the 1730s and 1740s. These fluctuations, while locally variable, probably produced slightly shorter frost-free seasons than at present. This would mean about a 160–165 day season in eastern Massachusetts (some 50 days less than in southern England), 200–205 days in the Virginia tidewater, and 275–280 days in the South Carolina low country. What this meant in real terms for settlers north of the Carolinas, however, was that climatic patterns were more extreme than in the mother country: summers were hotter (by 10°–20° F.), drier, and more humid, and winters longer, colder (by 10°–20° F.), and snowier. While early settlers in Massachusetts could bemoan their settlement experience in a cold, barren, mountainous, rocky "desert," a visitor to South Carolina could write later that the climate in general was very pleasant and delightful. If the summer months were bothersome to some people, fresh air, shade, summerhouses, and cool bathings provided relief.

What these experiences meant in ecological terms was that there were no major barriers, except the variously dense to open, mixed deciduous forests, to the direct transfer of English crops and farming practices to the colonies, although local adjustments had to be made. In New England, the rather stony, leached, and only moderately productive soils and frequently dry early summers tended to favor the growth of maize rather than wheat; the harsh winters created a need for more elaborate feed and shelter practices for livestock. In the Virginia tidewater, the hot, humid summers, brackish and saline water, and extensive marshlands made settlement more difficult, and the widespread occurrence of malaria initially caused higher death rates than farther north.

It was, however, the presence of the native Indian populations that provided the most significant encounters for the early settlers (Fig. 5.2). It is clear from recent research that the Indian societies that came into contact with the colonists were mere remnants of the populations who had occupied the Atlantic coastal zones during the early 16th century. Earlier calculations of a paltry 500,000–600,000 Indians east of the Mississippi have now been expanded at least fourfold to between 2 million and 2.5 million. Such numbers were not encountered during the 17th century because Indian-European contacts through disease transmission (smallpox, measles, influenza, bubonic plague), warfare, and Indian retreat had reduced native populations east of the Appalachians to probably less than 200,000 by the early 17th century.

It has been customary to suggest a broad homogeneity and unity of outlook among native populations through such designations as the "Eastern Woodland Indians." But the unity can be recognized only at a macro-level ("Indian" and "European") and the homogeneity scarcely at all. Beyond a general outlook or shared worldview, the diversity of Indian life was even greater than that of English life. The Indians shared, nevertheless, not only a set of forested environments, but a philosophy of life that differed in significant respects from the assumptions entertained by the colonists. Fundamental to the Indian world was the indivisibility of the natural and human spheres of existence. The distinction between "man" and "nature" held so profoundly by the Europeans was incomprehensible to the natives. This had important implications for Indian perceptions

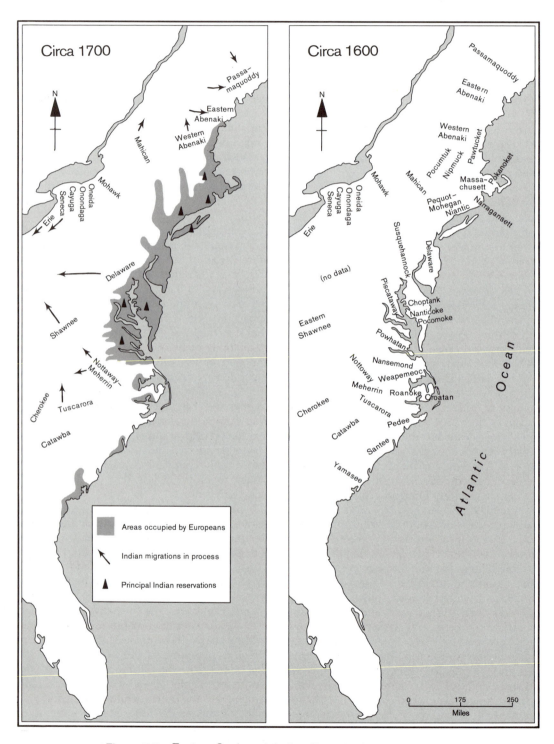

Figure 5.2   Eastern Seaboard: Indian Groupings, 1600 and 1700

of and access to resources. Private ownership of land as an alienating right in perpetuity was unknown. Rights of access to land and water were more varied. Whether in the creation of long-term family hunting territories, privately used garden plots, or communal gathering and hunting practices, the general principle was usufructory. Rights of access were equated with rights of regular use; where persistent use had been terminated, rights of access were once again theoretically "open." Thus the Dutch, who began occupying Manhattan in 1626, had "bought" the island for a mere 60 guilders from local Indians who were in the process of migrating farther north. The natives, no doubt, were pleasantly surprised by the generous "gift" from the strange visitors for territory to which they no longer had claim.

These basic differences in outlook were critical to contact, because the settlers who came under the aegis of English commercial companies eventually came to stay. The struggle for land that ensued has dominated Indian-American relations ever since. The settlers did not come to share the land but to alienate it from the natives by purchase (from an English perspective), by manipulation, and by outright conquest. Even such a seemingly enlightened proprietor as William Penn could legitimize his acquisition of territory only through written treaty, contract, and purchase, means of land negotiation unfamiliar to the Indians. What justified the taking of Indian territories in English eyes was the belief above all that the natives had not made sufficient or efficient use of the land. The English could do better.

There was some general relationship, although hardly a neat correlation, between Indian economic, linguistic, housing, social, and political patterns in eastern America. In general, the hunting and gathering bands of Algonquian language stock that occupied much of northern and central New England were the smallest groups in numbers, the most nomadic (using portable tipis), and the least socially complex societies encountered by the early Europeans. From southern New England and central New York southward, however, an enormous variety of organizational patterns existed based upon a widely shared horticultural base of corn (at least four varieties), beans, squashes, and several dozen other cultivated and wild plants used in the absence of domesti-

cated animals except for small dogs and the feral turkey. Forest clearance was achieved through cutting and burning underbrush and girdling larger trees so that they rotted gradually. The ground was prepared with a rough hoe, and planting of corn, bean, and squash seeds was done with a digging stick in mounds almost a foot high and four to six feet apart. New land was cleared on a regular basis as yields declined, in a system we describe today as a slash-and-burn, field rotation cycle. Early colonists frequently described as "Indian old fields" areas cleared in this manner for cultivation or areas burned over for hunting purposes. The domesticated plant diet was supplemented by the gathering of wild roots, berries, nuts, and fruits, by both salt- and freshwater fishing, and by the hunting of game (particularly deer).

It was this hunting component that most confused early English observers. The Indians' pre-plow cultivation practices were comprehensible to the settlers, and indeed surplus Indian crops helped the pioneers at Jamestown and Plymouth to survive the early years of agricultural experimentation and to make corn (maize) rather than European small grains a suitable foodstuff and feedstuff during the 17th century. Hunting, however, was a different matter. It was acceptable to the English as a sport indulged in mainly by the landed classes in England, but as a permanent occupation it offended the English sense of civilized humanity. Hunting of this kind was the mark of "savage" rather than civil behavior.

Europeans found a similar absence of a civilizing influence in Indian social organization. Despite a gradual appreciation of the complexities of group arrangements from supra-band organizations lacking clear leadership patterns to complex hierarchies and multiple chiefdoms, such as the Powhatan "Confederacy" in tidewater Virginia or the "Nations" of the Iroquois in central New York, and the generally larger populations and more stable settlements associated with such complexity, Europeans consistently refused to accept such characteristics as the mark of civilized people. What especially condemned the natives from a European perspective was their "heathenism," their ignorance of the Christian god and of Christian salvation. English desire to acculturate and ultimately assimilate the Indian into colonial soci-

ety and culture was predicated on the elimination of the savage and the heathen elements of
Indian life, a proselytizing task that was
adopted most intensely by the Puritan churchmen of Massachusetts. The transformation of
the American wilderness into an English garden meant not only the introduction of English
resource practices, but also a cultural transformation of the natives into a darker-skinned
semblance of civilized English men and
women. The subsequent history of Indian-
American relations has demonstrated the painful futility of such aspirations. The creation of
colonial society was to be accomplished without serious Indian participation. Intercultural
contacts continued through trading connections, military alliances, or the survival of
"mixed blood" populations on reservations,
but always within the larger context of a dy-
namically moving, Indian-contested, interior
settlement frontier that was to leave the area
west of European settlements as a temporary
"reserve" for declining Indian populations (Fig.
5.2).

SETTLEMENT, POPULATION, AND TERRITORY

The early failures of private colonization
schemes during the 1570s and 1580s, such as
Gilbert's in Newfoundland and Raleigh's in
North Carolina, partly convinced English administrators that the state should provide political, if not financial, aid in encouraging commercial trading companies to create permanent
bases in North America. The establishment of
such commercial outposts was an elaboration
of informal and often haphazard contacts made
previously by fishermen, lumbermen, speculative merchants, and illegal traders (Fig. 5.3).
More formal steps were taken in April 1606
with the founding of the twin companies, The
Virginia Companies of London and Plymouth.
Each company, reflecting the vague geographical knowledge of the time, was granted a wide
swath of coastal territory within which to
found profitable resource contacts (Fig. 5.4).
The St. George settlement in southern Maine
was abandoned after the winter of 1607, but the
Jamestown settlement, despite a shaky beginning, survived to provide the nucleus of the
Virginia colony.

The Jamestown settlement emerged in mag-
nificent isolation until 1614, when the Dutch,
who were emerging as the preeminent trading
nation in Europe, and who were already har-
assing Spanish convoys in the Caribbean, demonstrated an interest in the fur trade of the
Hudson valley. They founded a trading post,
Fort Nassau, just south of the future site of
Albany, ten years before plans were made for a
permanent settlement on Manhattan. Almost
concomitant with these activities was the establishment of the Plymouth colony north of Cape
Cod by Puritan Separatists in 1620, which survived as a distinct colony until 1691. This was
followed by the massive immigration (some
16,000 settlers) of more moderate Puritans to
Massachusetts Bay and adjacent areas between
1629 and 1640. Farther south, Lord Baltimore
founded his Maryland colony at St. Marys in
1634, and four years later a few score of Swedes
and Finns established the short-lived colony of
New Sweden (1638–55) on the lower Delaware
River. From these tentative and discrete foundations, Anglo-America began to take shape.
By mid-century, about 46,000 settlers had distributed themselves along the Atlantic coast
and up the major river valleys from the rocky
shores of southern Maine to the marshy lowlands of Norfolk, Virginia (Fig. 5.5). Increasing
settlement densities and geographical expansion were most evident in the Virginia tidewater and eastern shore, around Massachusetts
Bay, and up the Hudson and lower Connecticut valleys.

Population grew to over 250,000 during the
second half of the century. The latitudinal distribution did not change significantly, except
for the first isolated settlements in the Carolinas around Pamlico Sound and Cape Fear in
North Carolina and in the vicinity of Charles
Town in South Carolina (Fig. 5.5). But considerable settlement consolidation had occurred in
eastern Virginia and the Chesapeake Bay in
general, along the lower Delaware River, and
along the northern coast from northern New
Jersey to New Hampshire. Inland penetration
had reached the general vicinity of the fall zone
in Virginia, and up the central Connecticut
valley, but further expansion and consolidation
failed to occur in the Hudson valley. The settlement of northern and western New England,
as well as most of New York and Pennsylvania
and almost all of the Carolinas, therefore, was
delayed until the 18th century.

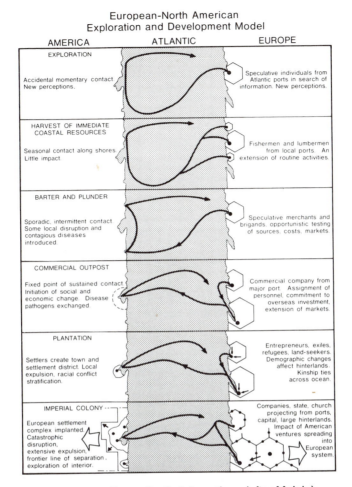

European-North American
Exploration and Development Model

Figure 5.3   Transatlantic Interactions (after Meinig)

Population growth patterns also reflected this general distribution (Table 5.1). Rates of immigration varied considerably during the 17th century. Most colonies experienced very rapid rates of growth as a result of initial immigration, a pattern that generally slowed down in the latter part of the century. Immigration rates tended to be highest during the 1630s and 1640s (especially in Virginia and Massachusetts), during the 1660s (especially in the Chesapeake), and during the 1680s and 1690s (especially in Pennsylvania and because of the Chesapeake slave trade). The results of these differential patterns by 1700 were two colonies with 55,000 to 60,000 settlers (Virginia and Massachusetts) and two others with 25,000 to 30,000 settlers (Maryland and Connecticut). New York's growth had proven to be erratic rather than steady until the 1690s, while Pennsylvania was in the process of attracting the most massive immigration levels of the entire colonial period.

Population growth and settlement expansion hardly occurred in a territorial vacuum. English colonial schemes contrasted starkly with the homogeneity and standardization that were more characteristic of official Spanish and French colonial policies. What is most remarkable about the English experience was not only the volume and rate of population growth, but its institutional variety. Instead of one centralized and consolidated imperial system, there were 13 separate colonies (with Plymouth absorbed by Massachusetts in 1692 and Georgia founded in 1732). They were administered from London, to be sure, but each had its own

Figure 5.4   17th-Century America: Principal Territorial Disputes

distinctive political structure and operations. English colonies had been founded under a variety of schemes. Some, like Virginia and Massachusetts, began as company ventures only to become royal colonies under direct Crown administration; others, such as Maryland and Pennsylvania, originated as proprietory colonies in which the proprietors operated initially with little external interference; while still others, notably Connecticut and Rhode Island, were chartered corporate colonies that had broken away from Massachusetts. This variegated arrangement reflected a practical rather than an ideological orientation in English colonialism. No other contemporary imperial system could have produced a Puritan Massachusetts, a Quaker Pennsylvania, or a Catholic Maryland.

Territorial variation and rivalry were not only the spice of colonial life, they were also the source of heatedly disputed boundary problems (Fig. 5.4). Many boundary issues remained unsettled until after the American Revolution, while some lingered on into the 20th century. Such problems originated because of the diverse ways in which colonial grants were drawn up and because of the vagueness with which neat lines drawn on maps were translated on the ground. The most glaring omission was any sense of geographical understanding of the interior beyond the coastal zone. Many colonial grants and subsequent colony bounda-

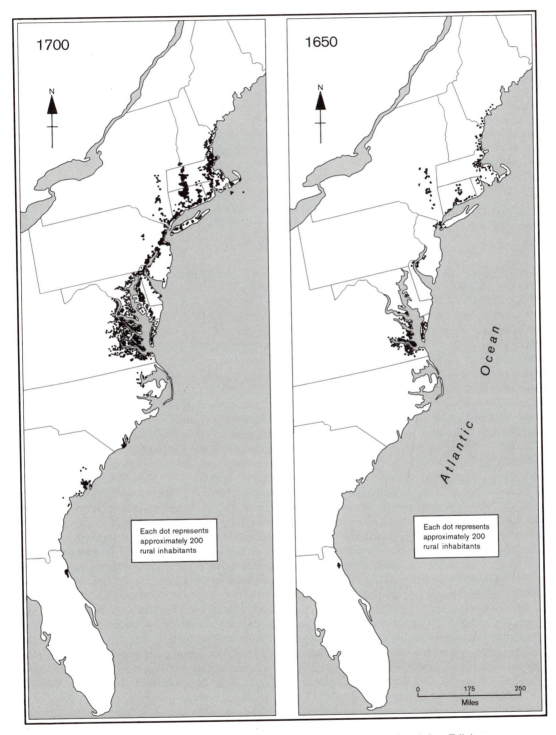

Figure 5.5   17th-Century America: Population Distribution (after Friis)

Table 5.1   American Colonies: Estimated 17th-Century Populations

Colony	1630	1640	1650	1660	1670	1680	1690	1700
New Hampshire	500	1,055	1,305	1,555	1,805	2,047	4,164	4,958
Plymouth	390	1,020	1,566	1,980	5,333	6,400	7,424	—
Massachusettsa	906	9,832	15,037	20,082	30,000	39,752	49,504	55,941
Rhode Island	—	300	785	1,539	2,155	3,017	4,224	5,894
Connecticut	—	1,472	4,139	7,980	12,603	17,246	21,645	25,970
New York	350	1,930	4,116	4,936	5,754	9,830	13,090	19,107
New Jersey	—	—	—	—	1,000	3,400	8,000	14,010
Pennsylvania	—	—	—	—	—	680	11,450	17,950
Delaware	—	—	185	540	700	1,005	1,482	2,470
Maryland	—	583	4,504	8,426	13,226	17,904	24,024	29,604
Virginia	2,500	10,442	18,731	27,020	35,309	45,596	53,046	58,560
North Carolina	—	—	—	1,000	3,850	5,430	7,600	10,720
South Carolina	—	—	—	—	200	1,200	3,900	5,704
Total	4,646	26,634	50,368	75,058	111,935	153,507	209,553	250,888

aMassachusetts includes Maine, and also Plymouth after 1691, although official totals do not reflect this.

ries were simply latitudinal lines with overlapping claims and indeterminate western boundaries. Thus, eastern-bounded colonies such as Massachusetts and Connecticut, as well as those from New York southward, extended their territorial claims as far as the Mississippi River. Disputes between adjacent colonies were frequent, such as those engaging Connecticut and New York between the 1660s and 1728; Pennsylvania and Maryland between the 1680s and 1732 (and finally surveyed by Mason and Dixon between 1763 and 1768); and Virginia and North Carolina between the 1660s and 1715. The resolution of the status of interior lands beyond the Appalachians was to be one of the major problems facing the new nation in 1783.

Territorial organization below the colony level was based upon English conceptions of local government and private property. Population in the company colony of Virginia was organized initially on an irregular pattern of small units known as English hundreds, with monthly courts meeting at particular plantations. By 1634, an English county form of government was introduced that provided the initial foundation for local territorial organization in the colonies south of Pennsylvania (Fig. 5.6) and ultimately for all of the United States. Counties generally ranged in size from 200 to 450 square miles before devolving into new

counties late in the century. County courthouses were located so that local residents could make the round trip in no more than a day's ride. Although counties were often subdivided into or synonymous with church parishes, the parish system proved to be a less viable unit than in England, and counties remained the principal receptacles of civil government.

North of the Chesapeake, however, county systems were slower to emerge and were preceded, especially in New England, by townships (Fig. 5.6). The New England town or minor civil division reflected the more socially cohesive, group settlement that characterized the region. Towns generally ranged in size from 50 to 100 square miles, much smaller and more intimate units of territorial organization than counties in the Chesapeake. The principal internal focus was the centrally located meeting house that functioned initially not only as the place for town meetings, but also as the local church and social hall. This arrangement probably encouraged a greater sense of community and individual participation in decision-making in New England than in the more loosely organized county system.

The acquisition of land was a prime goal of most 17th-century immigrants. Land grants were assigned on an individual basis generally on a fee simple (ownership) principle or on

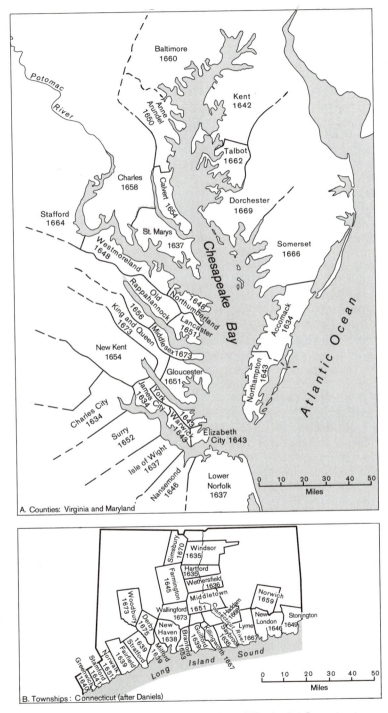

Figure 5.6   17th-Century America: Local Territorial Organization

leasehold. The dispersed individual family farm and household formed the basic unit of social and spatial structure throughout the colonies. The result has been the most dramatic imprint of European culture on the American landscape: the creation of individual property (cadastral) boundaries outlined by fields, fences, walls, and town lots and delineating one private territory from another. Despite their common heritage, colonial land grant patterns varied considerably between colonies (Fig. 5.7). In New England towns, for example, individual landholdings tended to be laid out in a more careful fashion than elsewhere, often accompanied by areas of common land for livestock. In the Chesapeake, a more irregular metes and bounds survey system was employed, grants tended to be distributed more haphazardly along stream valleys, and overlapping boundaries led frequently to prolonged court litigation. Grants were often assigned names, such as Ashley's Hope or Franklin's Folly, that highlighted the aspirations and the experiences of early landowners. A third cadastral form occurred in Dutch New York where land was assigned under a modified manorial (patroon) system. Large grants in the Hudson valley, sometimes exceeding 100,000 acres, were allotted by the Dutch West India Company to prominent colonial investors whose responsibility it was to redistribute some of the land in small parcels to long-term tenants. These three land assignment systems reflect, in a sense, the principal regional variations of 17th-century life that had emerged by the 1680s, the Chesapeake, New England, and the Anglo-Dutch world of New York–New Jersey.

THE CHESAPEAKE WORLD

The creation of a new society in tidewater Virginia ran counter to the creation of "a normal English colony," because it proved to be a riskier venture than anticipated. The establishment of a trading station at Jamestown Island proved tenuous because of site limitations and the uncomfortable dependence on local Indians for sustenance. The direct transfer of English resource practices, moreover, was hampered by high death rates from malaria and poor nutrition, by the initial failure of English grains, and by the low nutritive value of native

grasses for livestock. One of the first acts of adaptation was the adoption of Indian staple foods and cultivation practices. Corn, beans, and squashes were grown by means of hoe-hill cultivation methods without the use of the plow. (Plows remained rare objects in Chesapeake farming until the end of the century.) A second adaptation was the "seasoning process" whereby new immigrants arrived in spring or early fall to avoid the summer heat, humidity, and disease. A third adaptation was the discovery in 1614, through trial and error, of the commercial viability of tobacco (*Nicotiana tabacum*). This crop was to provide a profitable basis for the young settlement despite the belief of the colony's treasurer, Sir Edwin Sandys, that one could not build a colony on smoke.

The commitment to tobacco cultivation for export, however, required considerable amounts of land for its success. This had two important implications. First, land could be acquired only from the native population. This produced a struggle for land with the Powhatan that by 1650 had resulted in two native uprisings, the removal of Indian populations from the tidewater, and the creation of small spatial enclaves, or "reservations," for the few surviving natives. Second, tobacco cultivation in the absence of systematic crop rotation resulted in significant reductions in yields and soil fertility after three or four years. This encouraged the development of a field rotation system whereby additional acreages were cleared for cultivation, leaving former tobacco lands in prolonged fallow for up to 20 years. Land also became a device used by officials in Virginia and Maryland to attract immigrants through a headright system that granted anyone who brought in immigrants 50 acres per potential settler. This tactic, however, highlighted the critical need for labor.

Tobacco production was a high labor-intensive activity by English standards. Its 15–month cycle required heavy labor inputs for brush clearance, field preparation, transplanting, weeding, suckering, harvesting, drying, and packing in barrels (hogsheads) for delivery to ships for export to London. The Virginia Company's solution was to import large numbers of young, male indentured servants from England. Thus, early Virginia society was characterized by distinct differences in social status between tobacco planters and their hired ser-

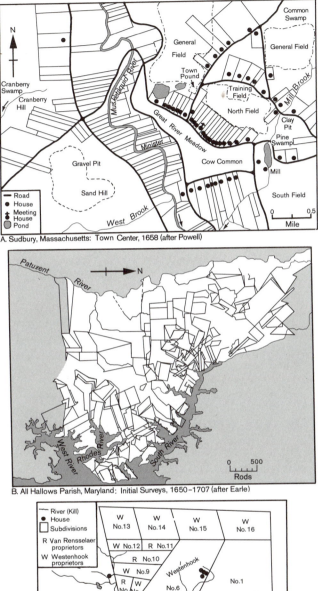

A. Sudbury, Massachusetts: Town Center, 1658 (after Powell)

B. All Hallows Parish, Maryland: Initial Surveys, 1650–1707 (after Earle)

C. Part of Rensselaer Manor, New York: Land Allotments, 1685– (after Kim)

Figure 5.7   17th-Century America: Patterns of Land Subdivision

vants, a hierarchical structure that was to be magnified after mid-century by the immigration of sons of the English gentry sent to manage the family estates in the Chesapeake and to form the elite of colonial society. A second striking characteristic was the fact that few entire families came directly from England. This created initially a sexually unbalanced population and left many colonists with the responsibility of creating family structures without recourse to parental approval or extended family support.

The settlement consequences of a tobacco world were equally significant. Individual plantations were dispersed irregularly along the shores of the Chesapeake and up the major rivers, often spaced a mile or two apart. Early plantation structures were not designed to last. English cottages of simple rectilinear or hall and parlor design were built of wood, with the spaces between the planks wattled and daubed with clay, and a wood-framed clay or stone chimney attached at one end (Fig. 5.8). A tobacco barn, a simple log or plank structure for drying and curing the leaves during the winter, was the first outbuilding to be constructed. Only toward the end of the century were more elaborate frame housing structures built with board and batten exteriors to ensure insulation.

The establishment of Maryland in 1634,

Figure 5.8   A Maryland Tobacco Plantation (Historic St. Mary's City)

much to the consternation of Virginians, added a new element of diversity into the Chesapeake. Lord Baltimore had no intention of creating a tobacco colony on the Virginia model. Rather, his ideal was a semifeudal society based on manorial land tenure, a traditional landed gentry and aristocracy, a strong family nexus, nucleated village settlement, religious toleration, and a diversified economy of fur trading, mixed farming, and craft manufactures. Such a model of stability and hierarchy did not materialize because the need to keep the colony solvent meant a commitment to rapid economic development, a commitment already worked out in Virginia. Thus, within a decade Maryland's pioneer generation was involved in a tobacco production system and an overseas trading link forged previously by its southern neighbor. The two colonies shared a tobacco-dominated world that was exporting between 4 million and 5 million pounds of tobacco annually to England by the 1650s.

Regional distinctions remained, however. At the colony level, Maryland's proprietory structure created an unusually divisive political tendency, the proprietory prerogative, whereby political decisions made by both elected and appointed officials could be ignored by the proprietor. This political tension was exacerbated by religious division. Many of the early landowners were Catholic, including several Jesuits, eager to create a Catholic haven in the colonies; most of the early indentured servants were English Protestants. This circumstance intensified the distinction between landowners and servants. Within both colonies there were also subregional differences. Virginia's three tidewater peninsulas, with their emphasis on water transportation, offered a rather different settlement experience from southern Maryland, where rivers offered fewer barriers to movement, and both areas differed from the more isolated Eastern Shore across the bay (Fig. 5.6).

The final touches to this Chesapeake world were made during the second half of the century. Between 1660 and 1700, the population of Virginia and Maryland increased from 35,000 to 88,000 people. Although immigration remained an important source of population, natural increase had become the principal contributor to growth. The first truly Creole generation had been created in the Chesapeake by this time, a

generation with no direct association with England. This undoubtedly further contributed to an "Americanization" of the region's inhabitants. Young women tended to marry at about 21 or 22 years of age and young men at about 24 or 25, at least two or three years earlier than their peers in England. Families were relatively small, with two or three surviving children per family, compared with five or six in New England, because women seem to have stopped having children earlier. Infant deaths remained common, and death rates were higher than in New England. Most people who survived could expect to live at least into their early forties in the Chesapeake (and some into their seventies), during which time at least one-third of all adults were widowed and remarried, few grandparents existed, and orphans abounded.

The composition of the region's population also changed during the latter part of the century. The principal change was the shift from English indentured servant labor to African slave labor, beginning in Virginia during the late 1670s and in Maryland by the early 1680s. This shift, made initially for economic reasons, had profound effects on Chesapeake society because it raised important moral issues and it placed an already hierarchical class structure on a caste foundation. Slaves were permanently unfree, and their offspring were born automatically into slavery. Racial distinctions became an ingrained part of social differentiation; to be "negro" was to be unfree and ultimately to be inferior. Employed on plantations as field hands and domestic servants, Africans were to be excluded, like Indians, from the "normal workings" of an English colony.

Fewer than 1,000 Africans existed in the Chesapeake in 1660. Indentured servants continued to be imported from England at the rate of 1,000 per year. But during the 1660s, economic conditions in England improved, and the supply of servants dropped significantly by the early 1670s. At the same time, the increasing volume of slaves available from western Africa, principally for Portuguese Brazil and the Caribbean islands, had reduced the cost of a male slave. Between 1670 and 1700, more than 12,000 slaves were imported into the Chesapeake. The change was dramatic. Until the late 1670s in Maryland, for example, servants outnumbered slaves by more than four to one; by 1700, slaves outnumbered servants by almost four to one. Almost 15,000 slaves existed in the Chesapeake by this time, concentrated in the lower and middle peninsulas in Virginia and in southern Maryland, comprising 15 percent of the Chesapeake's population. Slave-holding, however, remained an exception in the tobacco world. Fewer than 20 percent of all planters could afford slaves, and 90 percent of slave-owning planters owned only one or two. The social basis of Chesapeake life, nevertheless, had been recreated on a vastly different basis from that of England, a fact that was to have dramatic repercussions for future American society.

Economically, the Chesapeake became increasingly immersed in a commercial, tobacco world. Tobacco exports increased from about 9 million pounds in 1670 to 35 million pounds by 1700. These exports represented more than 80 percent of the total value of all mainland colonial goods sent to England by the end of the 17th century. Trade continued to be conducted on a straight consignment system whereby sloops and small ships would collect tobacco hogsheads from wooden landings along the rivers and deliver them to larger, ocean-going vessels anchored in the bay. The entire system was based on good fortune, trust, and credit. Planters lost all control over their product after it had left their landings, trusting that it would arrive safely in England, be sold for a good price by their merchant connections in London, the profits less commission be credited to their London accounts, and the goods that they requested arrive intact on the return voyage. No money changed hands, the credits from tobacco sales being balanced (and usually outweighed) by the debits of the planters' purchases in England. To add to the planters' concerns, tobacco prices fluctuated considerably during the century. They were high initially, but stabilized at lower levels by the 1630s and declined further during the 1660s and 1670s, before plunging into prolonged depression for the rest of the century while fluctuating wildly from year to year.

Most planters rarely sent more than four or five hogsheads (variously weighing from 600 to 900 pounds each) to London in a season. This would have been the product of from 3 to 5 acres of land within plantations that ranged in size from 200 to 400 acres. A typical planter by the end of the century had between 15 and 20

acres cleared for crops, with more acreage (6 to 8) in corn than in tobacco or in English grains (4 to 5), as well as a kitchen garden of vegetables and herbs, a small apple or peach orchard, a few cattle, pigs, and perhaps sheep, a horse or two, and a collection of fowl. Labor would be supplied from some combination of servants and slaves such that each adult male could harvest 1 to 1.5 acres of tobacco.

The relative self-sufficiency of the plantation unit in terms of basic foodstuffs, feedstuffs, fuel, and clothing was enhanced by the pool of plantation craftsmen (especially carpenters, coopers, and blacksmiths) generally available within a five- to six-mile radius. This level of local support had important implications for the Chesapeake's settlement structure, particularly a distinct absence of towns.

The provision of local services and the conduct of the tobacco trade were highly decentralized throughout the 17th century. The dispersed arrangement of tobacco plantations, their relative high level of self-sufficiency, the simple organization of the consignment system, the absence of further tobacco processing within the region, and the relatively limited demand for manufactured goods precluded the creation of an urban network. A service hierarchy did exist, but the highest-order place was London, 3,000 miles away. No settlement within the Chesapeake had attained more than 500 people. The new capitals of Virginia and Maryland, Williamsburg and Annapolis, respectively, were less than ten years old in 1700, and neither contained even a hundred houses. Local services were supplied by country storekeepers and merchant-planters. Activities at county courts, ferry sites, and churches were periodic and intermittent and seldom sustained sufficient nodality to encourage further settlement concentration.

By the end of the century there was distinct evidence of regional homogeneity within the Chesapeake. The commitment to a tobacco-plantation-slave system with its consequent class structure was widespread. Life was overwhelmingly rural, agrarian, dispersed, and decentralized. This was true whether one lived in peninsular Virginia, southern Maryland, or on the Eastern Shore. In the latter region the first faint signs of dissatisfaction with the uncertain boom-and-bust life of tobacco production became evident. A few planters began to diversify their farm production by increasing their acreage of corn and wheat and improving their livestock production, a process of diversification that was to become more pronounced during the 18th century.

THE NEW ENGLAND WORLD

Despite a common English heritage, the settlers of early New England initially created a different settlement experience from their Chesapeake counterparts. The Plymouth and Massachusetts Bay colonies brought a different kind of settler to America, who was to create a contrasting form of colonial society. The early Puritan colonists, of diverse persuasions, came with a distinct sense of purpose, even of destiny. Governor John Winthrop wrote in 1630: "For wee must consider that wee shall be as a citty upon a hill. The eies of all people are uppon us." Their desire to worship in their Protestant faith freely and without official interference created a distinctive pattern of population migration. People came more often in family groups, even occasionally as entire congregations, from specific locations in England. They encountered environments in southern New England that bore broad similarity to conditions they had left in western Europe. And they encouraged other Puritans to follow them in a kind of linked-chain migration that reinforced the regional characteristics of their home territories. The initial result was a more faithful attempt to reproduce the diversity of English provincial life than anywhere else in the New World.

The Separatist settlement at Plymouth remained isolated from the rest of New England until 1692, when the Confederation of New England was created under Massachusetts dominion. The 120 original Plymouth pioneers occupied an Indian-held territory that had been devastated by disease in 1616, an event the new settlers viewed as "providential," a conscious act of God that paved the way for their divinely inspired occupance. Despite a life of urban exile in London or in the Netherlands, the settlers recreated much of the life they had remembered in provincial England. Indian corn, beans, and squashes were integrated with the more familiar English small grains, peas, cattle, pigs, and fowl, and the use of the plow, into a closer reflection of English rural life than in Virginia. Settlements were organized into loosely arranged villages and then gradually into dispersed farmsteads. Houses, of rectilinear or hall and parlor design, were one to one and a half story clapboard structures with central or end chimneys and thatched roofs. A small barn, cowshed, pigpen, garden, and apple and pear orchard generally completed the components of the "homelot." Farms, ranging from 30 to 100 acres in size, were relatively small by Chesapeake standards, but this excluded the common acreages used to pasture livestock. Spring wheat, corn, peas, beans, and squashes were sown in May; English grasses were sown later to provide hay for wintering the animals; the wheat and vegetables were harvested in early August, while the corn was allowed to stand until September. Life in Plymouth Colony remained quiet and provincial until its 10,000 inhabitants were incorporated into Massachusetts in 1692.

The Massachusetts Bay Colony to the north proved to be a more dynamic settlement. Between 1629 and the early 1640s almost 16,000 immigrants came to Massachusetts and established Boston, named after its Lincolnshire counterpart (Fig. 5.1), as a town focus and commercial port. Settlers came from a variety of English regions. Some had come from the communal, open-field, village worlds of parts of East Anglia and eastern Yorkshire. Others came from more individual, enclosed-farm areas of Wiltshire and the "West Country." And still others had left such bustling East Anglian towns as Ipswich and Norwich. In their spread outward from Massachusetts Bay, they created townships within which they attempted to reproduce their familiar worlds of provincial England. Within the semi-planned towns, land was assigned on an agreed-upon basis. In some towns this meant an initial attempt to create agricultural villages with elongated farmsteads of 20 to 30 acres radiating out from the village; in others, land assignment was made in individual lots of 100 to 200 acres on which each family established its own family farm; while in still others, settlers founded small service centers in which merchants and craftsmen could conduct their activities most conveniently.

The end result of all this pioneering was a complex regional mosaic of colonial life, a series of "little Englands," subject to differential patterns of change during the rest of the century. Some towns remained relatively stable, with small families, low rates of population growth and turnover, and primarily subsistent and limited-surplus agriculture. Such was the case in central Massachusetts and eastern Connecticut. Other townships, often immediately adjacent, appear to have experienced a contrasting situation of large families, rapid population growth, sharply declining man-land ratios, high rates of migration, and rapid transition to commercial agriculture. Such was the case around Massachusetts Bay, in the Narragansett Bay area of Rhode Island, and in the lower and middle Connecticut valley.

There were, on the other hand, forces of centralization that mitigated these provincial variations. Foremost among them was the centralizing tendency displayed by the Massachusetts General Court in Boston, in providing the legal and political basis for an acceptable Puritan commonwealth, and by influential churchmen, such as John Cotton and Increase Mather, who provided the intellectual and spiritual basis for an acceptable Puritan life. Resistance to such conforming trends was a persistent feature of the early New England world. This caused a veritable diaspora from the Massachusetts Bay Colony itself of disaffected and disinherited settlers, most notably Roger Williams, who helped to found new settlements at Providence, Rhode Island (1636), at New Haven (1638), at Newport (1639), and in the lower Connecticut valley (late 1630s).

If religious beliefs and practices both united and divided early New Englanders, concern over the "Indian menace" created an English singularity of purpose. Two complementary attitudes developed toward the Indian. First, the Puritans believed themselves to be superior to the natives as users of land; this conviction was strengthened by the belief that it was God's will that they should subdue and conquer both the American wilderness and its inhabitants. The result was a series of skirmishes in Massachusetts during the 1630s that led to Indian defeat and the first legal instigation of the reservation concept in North America. Further Indian uprisings occurred during the 1640s (the Pequot Wars), as they did also in the Chesapeake, leading to further reduction in Indian numbers and space, especially along the Rhode Island–Connecticut coast and in the lower Connecticut

valley. By 1660, the few thousand remaining Indians in southern New England were largely confined to reservations (Fig. 5.2). Only then did the second attitude, paternalism leading to proselytization, come to the fore. At least 14 "praying towns" comprising several hundred missionized Indians had been founded in Massachusetts, and several others existed in Plymouth Colony. Surviving natives in these settlements were encouraged to convert to Christianity and to adopt an English farming way of life. Other less assimilable Indians rallied around a new leader, Metacom ("King Philip" to the English), in 1675 in a last-ditch effort to retain their lands and their way of life. The failure of the uprising left all of southern New England in the hands of the colonists.

The early pattern of localism and regional diversity that characterized English settlement was modified during the 1670s, after two generations of settlement. By 1680, the 68,500 settlers of Plymouth, Massachusetts, Rhode Island, Connecticut, and New Hampshire (founded as a royal colony in 1679) were distributed from the coast of southern Maine south to New York and inland up the Connecticut valley to the New Hampshire border. Certain distinctive regional patterns had emerged by this time. The township, with its agricultural population, centrally located church and meeting house, and its small urban centers, remained dominant and spread wherever New England settlers migrated—to Long Island, the central Hudson valley, and to East Jersey. Almost everywhere the rural settlement pattern was one of individual, dispersed farmsteads (Fig. 5.9); outside of Plymouth only about 20 farm villages had been founded successfully, and few of these survived intact into the 18th century.

Distinct patterns of regional economy had also emerged by 1680. It is possible to identify at least three zones of economic activity. The broadest zone comprised the agricultural townships of eastern and central Massachusetts, northern Rhode Island, and central and northern Connecticut. Subsistence farming prevailed in these areas based on corn, wheat, barley, rye, flax, vegetables, fruits, cattle, pigs, and sometimes sheep. Farms ranged from 50 to 150 acres and were declining in size as they were subdivided for the next farming generation. Surplus products were few and were sold

IN 1667

The Bird Homestead
in Dorchester
(Bird-Sawyer)

1 Parlor, 2 Kitchen,
3,5,6, Bedrooms,
4 Woodshed,
7,8, Storage.

1ST FLOOR

2ND FLOOR

C.W.S.

Rooms of the
Bachelor's Cabin:

1 Living Room
2 Kitchen
3 Bed Room
4 Woodshed
Ladders   up & down

IN 1637

Thomas Birds Place
in Dorchester
(now the Bird-Sawyer Homestead)

C.W.S.

Figure 5.9   Farm Evolution in Massachusetts (Historic American Buildings Survey)

locally; labor was supplied by family members and an occasional hired hand. Communities tended to be close-knit and relatively egalitarian, to experience low levels of population turnover, and to have low levels of wealth differentiation. Much of the research on New England towns during the 1960s and early 1970s focused on such communities, thus creating an impression of all New England life during the 17th century as being stable, egalitarian, even harmonious. Such an interpretation has, in turn, been challenged by more recent research that suggests this image to have been less applicable to other New England areas.

This revisionist depiction is certainly more applicable to settlement evolution along Massachusetts Bay, where such foundings as Salem (1626) and Boston (1630) were predicated on port sites, fishing activities, craft concentrations, and mercantile trade. Boston came to dominate this relatively densely occupied region of small fishing villages, inland market centers, and compact commercial farms. The town became the regional entrepôt for most of southern New England, primarily because of its function as the center of Massachusetts government, the focus of craft and artisan activities, and its preeminence as the principal port for overseas trade that was enhanced by its connections with prominent London merchants (Fig. 5.10). The settlement, founded on a narrow peninsula, expanded inland on several areas of reclaimed land that almost doubled its area by 1700. Boston grew from 3,000 inhabitants in 1650, or some 20 percent of the colony's population, to almost 7,000 people in 1700, which made it the largest town in North America. With about 20,000 residents of the bay area living in urban centers by the end of the century, there was a growing demand for foodstuffs and processing raw materials. Farming in the region, therefore, became more commercialized, producing grains, meat, pork, and vegetables for Boston and its neighbors. Boston merchants, in turn, exported grain, cattle, naval stores, and dried codfish to western Europe and the Caribbean. They had extended their enterprise by the end of the century into shipbuilding and carrying goods for areas that possessed few vessels of their own. The evolution of trade around the Narragansett Bay followed a somewhat similar pattern. Newport, with a

Figure 5.10   Boston's First Townhouse, 1657–1711 (Courtesy Harvard University Press)

population about one-third that of Boston by 1700, dominated other urban centers, such as Providence, principally because it functioned as the outlet for corn, cattle, and sheep products from the large farms (200 to 300 acres) around the bay, and as a principal importer of molasses, sugar, and rum that were initially shipped to Boston to purchase imported English manufactured goods.

A third regional zonation emerged along the Connecticut coast and up the Connecticut valley as far as western Massachusetts. This region was characterized by small coastal towns, such as New Haven and New London, that were involved in local and coastal trade, and by rapidly growing centers in the Connecticut valley, such as Hartford and Springfield. The fertile soils of the valley helped to make the area the "breadbasket" of late 17th-century New England. Wheat, corn, barley, meat, and pork were the principal commercial products sent through local market centers to Boston or to the Caribbean. Farms were generally larger (200 to 300 acres) than in the subsistence farming areas outside the valley. Social stratification through land aggrandisement was more pronounced, tenancy was more common, and population turnover was more rapid than in adjacent subsistence areas. Merchant entrepreneurs, unlike the merchant-planters in the Chesapeake, were not content to make profits and accumulate debts, but reinvested their earnings in land acquisition, lumbering, craft industries, and shipping. These investments, in turn, created further growth in the New England economy that was to distinguish the entire region's achievements from those of the tobacco-committed Chesapeake.

THE ANGLO-DUTCH WORLD

The area that was to fall eventually between the Chesapeake and the New England settlements was quick to receive its own distinct European imprint. Five years after Henry Hudson, on behalf of the Dutch government, explored north of Manhattan in 1609 and brought back beaver pelts and skins, the Dutch established their fur-trading post at Fort Nassau. Thus began Dutch colonialism in the New World, which was to involve not only the New Netherlands but also ventures in Brazil, the Guyanas, and the Caribbean.

The New Netherlands, which stretched eventually from the lower Delaware River to Long Island and north to Albany, was an unusual and even paradoxical settlement. Founded as a centrally controlled company colony of the Dutch West India Company (1621), interested in the fur trade and in disrupting Spanish activities in the Caribbean, it was forced to establish a settlement policy that turned out to be more feudalistic in tone than anything created in the mother country. New Amsterdam, begun at the southern tip of Manhattan in 1624–25, created a focus for the colony. Within five years company settlers had built a fort and battery, about 30 tree-bark houses and, symbolically, a stone countinghouse. All goods traded with the Indians or with the outside world had to pass through this new settlement. The company, advancing beyond Virginia Company practice, established three statuses. Highest in status were the wealthy, urban, merchant investors who formed the directorship of the company in the Netherlands; next were company employees, such as soldiers, clerks, and hired farmers, who received a subsistence and a salary in the New Netherlands; and third were autonomous individuals who received company benefits for deciding to emigrate to the New World at their own expense.

Yet the colony was plagued by a chronic labor problem that was exacerbated by the company's restrictive land policy. Control of the fur trade at Albany was to be a company monopoly. But even a successful trading colony required support services. The company's solution was to grant large tracts of land to prominent Dutch investors, described as *patroons* (patrons), who would be responsible for encouraging immigrants to settle on their lands. Land tenure was to be established on a feudalistic basis rather than on the freehold basis that was to become widespread in the English colonies. The result was that settlers would receive enough land to create working farms, called *bouweries*, but would remain as tenants, rather than owner-occupiers, subject to annual quitrent. Only four large patroonship grants were made during the Dutch colonial period, each with at least an eight-mile river frontage. But only the largest of these, the patroonship of Rensselaerswyck, which encompassed more than 800,000 acres on both sides of the Hudson River including Albany, successfully attracted settlers (Fig. 5.7). This patroonship had more than 200 tenants by 1650, but tenancy proved unattractive, population turnover was high, and few farming families were created.

The company's intent, therefore, to create a socially stratified society dominated by merchants and officials in New Amsterdam and Albany and by manorial landowners in the Hudson valley, did not materialize. While the fur trade and coastal trade with the English colonies grew, agricultural settlement and development lagged. Despite a successful subsistence agriculture and even a trading surplus in wheat and rye, the chronic shortage of settlers encouraged the company to maintain a liberal immigration policy to attract colonists from any conceivable source. This policy had three long-term results. First, it encouraged an extremely culturally diverse population. As the leader of the Dutch Reformed church described it in 1655, "we have here Papists, Mennonites and Lutherans among the Dutch; also many Puritans or Independents, and many Atheists and various other servants of Baal under this Government, who conceal themselves under the name of Christians; it would create a still greater confusion, if the obstinate and immovable Jews came to settle here," which they did a few years later. More than a dozen languages were to be heard in the streets of New Amsterdam, from English and Dutch colonists as well as from French Huguenots, Walloons, settlers speaking various German dialects, and colonists from Spain and Portugal, and Scandinavia, and African slaves speaking various languages and dialects. Second, many of the new immigrants who wished to take up land avoided the Hudson valley and dispersed into Long Island and New Jersey where company policies were less stringently enforced. New England Puritans, who moved into eastern and central Long Island during the 1640s and 1650s, formed an integral part of the New Netherlands and many swore allegiance to the Dutch colony. Other Puritans and Dutch settlers moved to New Jersey, opposite Manhattan, and along the lower Delaware River, where they encountered Swedish and Finnish settlers who had established fur-trading posts and small farms focused on Fort Christina (Wilmington, Delaware). New Sweden, however, was not to last, and its 500 settlers were incorporated into the New Netherlands in 1655, adding to the colony's already heterogeneous population. Third, the company's strong centralized control and the absence of local government institutions did not strike a responsive chord in many immigrants. The combination of cultural pluralism and weak public institutions was to produce increasing political factionalism and growing tension between the company and its settlers.

By the early 1650s, during the governorship of Peter Stuyvesant, the colony's population had barely reached 2,000 inhabitants. Despite reforms instigated by Stuyvesant that decentralized government and trade and granted land on a more liberal basis, the New Netherlands remained a weak and vulnerable colony. The fur trade was proving to be a disappointing investment, an Indian invasion of Manhattan and adjacent New Jersey had disrupted settlement, and the English had enacted the first of their navigation acts that were designed in part to reduce Dutch trade with English colonies.

Much of the growth of the New Netherlands occurred during the last decade of its existence, between 1654 and 1664. When the English captured New Amsterdam in 1664 they acquired a loosely defined colony of 8,000 settlers, about 5,000 of whom were of Dutch origin and another 600 of African origin. Population was unevenly distributed. More than a fifth of the population was located on Manhattan, 1400 in New Amsterdam, and the rest in dispersed farms and the village of Haerlem. Half the remaining colonists occupied adjacent river valleys (kills) and flats of east Jersey and Staten Island to the west, Jonas Bronck's (Bronx) place to the northeast, and Long Island from the village of Breuckelen to the Puritan settlements of Southampton. The Hudson valley was thinly populated with few concentrations of settlement between Manhattan and Beverwyck (Albany) except for the 100 settlers around Esopus (Kingston).

The Dutch legacy was more than a few place names and a great assortment of settlers. It included an operational fur trade, relatively good relations with the Iroquois, an extensive landholding system, and the entrepôt of New Amsterdam. The bustling, fortified town, stretching as far north as Wall Street, with its narrow curving streets (except for Broad Way), some 200 three- and four-story, step-gabled, red and black tiled row houses backed by kitchen gardens, more than 35 taverns, imposing statehouse, East River wharf, main canal, and windmill, presented the most unusual urban appearance in 17th-century North America.

Few immediate changes occurred in the area as a result of the change in territorial control. Dutch cultural and property rights were upheld, and most settlers chose to remain. The land granted to the Duke of York, however, was unwieldy. No serious attempt was made to pursue his claims in Maine and Connecticut, but the New Netherlands was divided by the granting of New Jersey to Lords Berkeley and Carteret. This broke the territorial unity of the Hudson valley and reemphasized the regional contrasts between East and West Jersey. By 1700, East Jersey's 8,000 settlers had had their Dutch heritage diluted by an influx of New England Puritans and Scots Presbyterians. West Jersey's 6,000 settlers represented a stronghold of English Quakerism, closely associated with Pennsylvania.

New York was to continue as an unusual colonial experience. It was to be a colony that had not originated with English settlers; its hastily assembled charter was to leave the Duke of York with virtually absolute powers, to the detriment of representative government at the provincial level; and its persistent pluralism worked against unity and promoted local and regional rivalries. The result was a highly factional, dual colonial society in which Anglo-American influences were slow to replace the Dutch heritage.

The extensive land-grant system continued under the Duke of York. The patroonship tradition was extended with the creation of 16 large manorial grants in the Hudson valley and on Long Island, ranging from a few thousand acres to almost 200,000 acres in size. No immigration requirements were stipulated, a leasehold system prevailed, and many manors became speculative enterprises. Yet survey boundaries were often vague and tenants difficult to attract. The result was a relatively slow growth in population until the 1690s (Table 5.1).

The colony contained more than 19,000 inhabitants in 1700. They continued to be concentrated mainly on Manhattan (4,500 settlers) and on Long Island (7,000 settlers). Fewer than 5,000 settlers occupied the Hudson valley; most of them lived in isolated Dutch rural communities or in the settlements of Kingston, Albany, or Schenectady. Included in the provincial total were about 1,300 Africans, comprising 7 percent of the population; some were free, but the majority worked as laborers or domestic servants in Manhattan or as field hands on Hudson valley estates. Economic development and an increase in agricultural acreage occurred with the growth of population during the 1680s and 1690s. The fur trade continued to be an important, but declining, element in the colony's diversifying economy; it remained in the hands of Dutch traders in Albany. English officials, however, continued to seek Iroquois support for the struggle against the French. This strategy, in effect, allowed the Iroquois to play the English and French off against each other until the 1750s. Agricultural expansion on Long Island and intermittently in the Hudson valley took place along familiar colonial lines—general farming based on corn, European grains, and flax, with some specialization in wheat, beef, pork, apples and, in some areas, small-scale lumbering. These characteristics were reflected in the occupational structure and export trade of the port of New York. Flour-milling, brewing, and shipbuilding were prominent activities; bread and flour, furs, beef, pork, and lumber were major exports in the coastal and overseas trades. New York suffered, however, from the control exerted by Boston merchants in both of these trading arenas.

Anglicization of the colony was a process pursued only gradually by English officials. Although an English system of counties was introduced in 1683, Dutch cultural and social patterns remained intact. Indeed, the number of Dutch Reformed congregations expanded from 11 in 1664 to 29 in 1700. What emerged was an increasing factionalism between the older Dutch elite and the emerging Anglo-Dutch establishment. This tension came to a head in 1689 when a group of Dutch burghers rebelled unsuccessfully against the newer, more individualistic tone set by an English administration. The result was a wholesale introduction of English institutions, from English common law and a new judicial system to the establishment of the Anglican church in Manhattan and surrounding counties. Older Dutch settlers could only view these changes with a sense of wry frustration. They were initiated by the new occupiers of the English throne, William and Mary, associated with the Dutch House of Orange.

TRANSPOSITION

The 1680s proved to be a watershed in the shaping of colonial America. Not only was coastal Indian resistance eliminated by this time and the sustained commitment to slave labor initiated in the Chesapeake, but two other events epitomized the ambiguous heritage of the 17th century. The first was the founding of Pennsylvania in 1681 by William Penn, a prominent member of the Society of Friends ("Quakers"); the second was the successful experimentation with rice cultivation in the vicinity of Charles Town, South Carolina, toward the end of the decade.

Pennsylvania, based on the utopian vision of Penn, was to emerge as the population phenomenon of the late 17th century. The colony increased from a handful of settlers in 1681 to almost 18,000 by 1700. Penn's policy of avowed religious freedom, easy land acquisition, and active overseas recruitment encouraged the first sustained immigration of continental Europeans to an English colony. German-speaking settlers, of both church (Lutheran, Reformed) and sectarian (Moravian, Mennonite) persuasions, mingled with English and Welsh Quakers in the rich farmlands of southeastern Pennsylvania. They created a diversified economy and society based on 100–200 acre farms producing corn, small grains, and livestock products with the use of family and hired labor, together with a variety of small crafts, and the founding of the planned town of Philadelphia between the Delaware and Schuylkill rivers. Pennsylvania thus came to symbolize the heterogeneous, yeoman-farming, free labor world of the colonies north of the Chesapeake.

The creation of Charles Town, on the other hand, symbolized in exaggerated form the commitment to a more provincial, plantation-slave-staple world characteristic of the colonies south of Pennsylvania. The Carolinas, granted by Charles II to eight noblemen in 1664, had languished in uncertainty and neglect. The Spanish in Florida destroyed most settlement attempts made during the 1660s; a few isolated communities had survived in the Albemarle Sound section of North Carolina where farmers had been trickling in from Virginia since the 1650s. English immigrants made a successful settlement at Charles Town, between the Ashley and Cooper rivers, in 1670. The 1,000 settlers in the area by 1680 were exporting provisions to the English sugar islands and deerskins to England. The influx of planters from the heavily exploited island of Barbados during the 1680s quickened the search for a regional resource staple. The successful cultivation and husking of rice was achieved in the coastal uplands bordering the tidewater swamps by 1690, and exports to Portugal and the Caribbean had reached 400,000 pounds by 1700.

The commitment to rice production transformed a struggling farm population into a plantation society. Rice placed heavier demands on labor than did tobacco. The Fundamental Constitutions of Carolina, designed to create a colony neither "a numerous democracy" nor "an unrestrained aristocracy," became skewed in favor of the latter as the need for African slaves became paramount. The impact of slave labor was evident by 1700. Although North Carolina (10,700) had almost twice as many settlers as South Carolina (5,700), only 4 percent of its population was slave, compared with almost 43 percent farther south. Slavery in early South Carolina showed another twist; more than 700 slaves were of Indian origin, the result of wars and trade with inland Indian groups.

CONCLUSION

"Thus in the beginning," wrote the philosopher John Locke, "all the World was America. The English colonist [has] thereby removed her from the state of Nature, wherein she was common, and hath begun Property." The imposition of a European world on a native world, largely through the operations of English institutions, had created a new Atlantic America literally from scratch. What had been created was not simply a geographical extension of England. The process of migration and diffusion was itself a complex and selective one. Those who came and stayed founded a colonial system that was English in outline but

American in content. Continuity existed between colonial and English societies, but often through more simplified and more hybridized agencies than were to be found in the mother country.

English visitors at the end of the century would have found much that was familiar. The virtual ubiquity of the English language would have permitted them to converse freely. They would have appreciated the dedication to the familiar values of liberty, property, and profit functioning through equally familiar if less elaborate legal, political, religious, and business institutions. The creation of boundaries, on the landscape and in the imagination, that had not existed previously would have met also with general approval: provinces, counties, and towns; property boundaries; fields with familiar crops and livestock; a skeletal road system; and the beginnings of urban life.

But in the transposition of the New World environment from a wilderness inhabited by savage heathens to the "middle landscape" of English pastoral civility, the experience had also transformed the colonists. The English visitors, if they had remained long enough and traveled far enough, would have found much to intrigue and even to disturb them. The sparsity of population, the often considerable distances between settlements, and the remaining vast stretches of forest might have proven unnerving. The summers would have been uncomfortably hot and humid, and the winters almost frighteningly cold and bitter north of the Carolinas. New crops, such as corn, squashes, and tobacco, would have generated interest, but the generally casual and extensive nature of cultivation likely would have drawn expressions of disapproval. Countering such impressions would have been admiration for the relatively high material living standards, the ease with which land could be acquired, the ubiquity of dispersed farm units with recognizable architectural styles, and the generally egalitarian societies to be found, at least north of the Chesapeake.

Yet the creation of 17th-century Anglo-America was based not only on the successful exploitation of wild environments, but also on the manipulation of non-European peoples. What might have given the visitors pause was the presence of two much-modified European institutions, the reservation and the plantation. The shaping of early America had been accomplished at the expense of the native population. Although English fascination with Indian exoticism would remain, the Indian world was upheld as an experience to which civilized Europeans could not revert. Violence, removal, and confinement were to be the consequences of Anglo-American advance. Although similar specialized staple-producing, agricultural units could be found in southern Europe, the institution of slavery that accompanied such units in America had no English precedent. The perpetual enslavement of imported Africans, while rationally acceptable in economic terms, created moral, cultural, and racial fissions in colonial society that not only differentiated colony from metropolis, but also colony from colony and social class from social class as Anglo-America began the 18th century.

ADDITIONAL READING

Books

Allen, D.G., and Hall, D.D., eds. *Seventeenth-Century New England*. Charlottesville: University Press of Virginia, 1985.

Axtell, J. *The European and the Indian: Essays in the Ethnohistory of Colonial North America*. New York: Oxford University Press, 1981.

———. *The Invasion Within: The Contest of Cultures in Colonial North America*. New York: Oxford University Press, 1985.

Cronon, W. *Changes in the Land: Indians, Colonists, and the Ecology of New England*. New York: Hill & Wang, 1983.

Daniels, B. *The Connecticut Town*. Middletown: Wesleyan University Press, 1979.

Darby, H.C., ed. *A New Historical Geography of England*. Cambridge: Cambridge University Press, 1973.

Dodgshon, R.A., and Butlin, R.A., eds. *An Historical Geography of England and Wales*. New York: Oxford University Press, 1978.

Earle, C.V. *The Evolution of a Tidewater Settlement System: All Hallow's Parish, Maryland, 1650–1783*. Chicago: University of Chicago Department of Geography, 1975.

Everitt, A. *Changes in the Provinces: The Seventeenth Century*. Leicester: Leicester University Press, 1972.

Greene, J.P., and Cole, J.R., eds. *Colonial British America: Essays in the New History of the Early Modern Era*. Baltimore and London: Johns Hopkins University Press, 1984.

Innes, S. *Labor in a New Land: Economy and Society in Seventeenth-Century Springfield*. Princeton: Princeton University Press, 1983.

Jennings, F. *The Invasion of America: Indians, Colonialism, and the Cant of Conquest*. Chapel Hill: University of North Carolina Press, 1975.

Kim, S.B. *Landlord and Tenant in Colonial New York: Manorial Society, 1664–1775*. Chapel Hill: University of North Carolina Press, 1978.

McCusker, J.J., and Menard, R.R. *The Economy of British America, 1607–1789*. Chapel Hill: University of North Carolina Press, 1985.

McManis, D. *Colonial New England: A Historical Geography*. New York: Oxford University Press, 1975.

Nash, G.B. *Red, White, and Black: The Peoples of Early America*. 2nd ed. Englewood Cliffs: Prentice-Hall, 1982.

Powell, S.C. *Puritan Village: The Formation of a New England Town*. Middletown: Wesleyan University Press, 1963.

Rutman, D.B. *Husbandmen of Plymouth: Farms and Villages in the Old Colony, 1620–1692*. Boston: Beacon Press, 1967.

Sauer, C.O. *Sixteenth Century North America: The Land and the People as Seen by the Europeans*. Berkeley and Los Angeles: University of California Press, 1971.

Tate, T.W., and Ammerman, D.L., eds. *The Chesapeake in the Seventeenth Century: Essays in Anglo-American Society and Politics*. New York: W.W. Norton, 1979.

Periodicals

Annals, Association of American Geographers (Harris, 1977; Mitchell, 1983).

Geographical Review, journal of the American Geographical Society (Earle, 1977).

Journal of Historical Geography (Lemon, 1980; O'Mara, 1982; Wood, 1982).

Proceedings, International Geographical Congress (Meinig, 1976, section 9).

William and Mary Quarterly, journal of the Institute of Early American History and Culture (Henretta, 1978; Kupperman, 1984).

6

Colonial America in the Eighteenth Century

JAMES T. LEMON

University of Toronto

The founding of Pennsylvania in 1681 and of Georgia in 1732 confirmed what had become clear earlier in North America: that Europeans, mostly British, were here to stay. Between 1700 and 1775 the population of the eastern seaboard colonies grew nearly ten times, as did the area occupied. This expansion was reflected in the growth of the economy and the spread of population. Economic specialization and diversification were both evident, and living standards continued to remain high. Spaces between the discrete settlements of the 17th century were filled in along the coast, especially south of the Chesapeake. The result was an increased sharing of colonial experiences leading toward greater homogenization and broader regional expressions. Colonists initiated the massive overtaking of much of the continent that was to be a feature of the next century. As the 18th century progressed, neither the natives nor their allies in New France could hold back this interior movement. Yet, even as the French were defeated at Québec in 1759 and the British became undisputed masters of North America, British rules and regulations came unstuck in the 13 colonies. By 1775, most settlers had come to see themselves as Americans despite the fact that the colonies appeared to be converging demographically and socially with the mother country. The first successful colonial revolt in the New World was to produce a robust new nation poised to create its own stamp on North America and the world. The new northern colonies in Canada, partly peopled by American loyalists, would gradually achieve their own self-governance over the next 200 years.

POPULATION: GROWTH, EXPANSION, AND COMPOSITION

Growth

By 1775 the population of the 13 colonies had reached almost 2.5 million, compared with only 250,000 in 1700, a tenfold increase (Table 6.1). Between 1700 and 1775 the rate of growth averaged about 3 percent: even higher before 1750 and falling gradually thereafter. This rate was very rapid for the time; the population jumped from one-twentieth to about one-third of Britain's. The gap would continue to narrow after 1776 so that, by 1820, the population of the United States had surpassed that of Britain. In contrast to many poor Third World countries today with similar rates of growth, the colonies possessed the space, resources, and organization to maintain the highest standard of living in the world. Few experienced starvation or even malnutrition. The gloomy, late 18th-century prediction of the English Reverend Doctor Thomas Malthus—that high population growth would eventually outstrip resources and lead to starvation—was irrelevant in white and even in black America, where people continued to spread themselves over more and more land, land that the native Indians gradually were forced to give up.

In the mid-18th century, Benjamin Franklin, a newspaper editor and social philospher living in rapidly growing Philadelphia, described population change quite accurately. In his *Observations Concerning the Increase of Mankind*, he saw that earlier and more frequent marriages and larger families were drawing America's total population closer to Britain's. He predicted correctly that economic power also would eventually shift across the Atlantic. Let us consider first the process of demographic growth.

Birthrates continued to be high, although probably no higher than in parts of western Europe. Between 1720 and 1760 in New England births averaged around seven children, about the same as in England, but still higher than in the Chesapeake. Earlier marriages, however, partly accounted for the more rapid growth of population in America. Although few married as teenagers in England or in America, women married on the average at 21

Table 6.1   Estimated Populations of the American Colonies, 1700–1780

Colony	1700	1720	1740	1760	1780
(Maine)a	—	—	—	20,000	49,133
(Vermont)a	—	—	—	—	47,620
New Hampshire	4,958	9,375	23,256	39,093	87,802
Massachusetts	55,941	91,008	151,613	202,600	268,627
Rhode Island	5,894	11,680	25,255	45,471	52,946
Connecticut	25,970	58,830	89,580	142,470	206,701
New York	19,107	36,919	63,665	117,138	210,541
New Jersey	14,010	29,818	51,373	93,813	139,627
Pennsylvania	17,950	30,962	85,637	183,703	327,305
Delaware	2,470	5,385	19,870	33,250	45,385
Maryland	29,604	66,133	116,093	162,267	245,474
Virginia	58,560	87,757	180,440	339,726	538,004
North Carolina	10,720	21,270	51,760	110,442	270,133
South Carolina	5,704	17,048	45,000	94,074	180,000
Georgia	—	—	2,021	9,578	56,071
(Kentucky)a	—	—	—	—	45,000
(Tennessee)a	—	—	—	—	10,000
Total	250,888	466,185	905,563	1,593,625	2,780,369

aNot organized as provinces or states by 1780. Maine part of Massachusetts; Vermont part of New York (disputed); Kentucky originally an extension of Virginia, and Tennessee of North Carolina.

and men at 24 in the colonies. While the age of marriage fell in England during the 18th century, in the latter half of the century women took their vows on the average three years later, and men two than a century before. Later marriages in England functioned as a birth-control measure. So, in America continued earlier marriages led to earlier births, thus adding more quickly to the population. Yet women who bore children earlier tended to stop earlier. This would help to explain why American families would appear not to have been much larger than those in England, even though white growth remained much more rapid. The black reproduction rate slowly became similar to whites, as the sex ratio came into balance late in the century (Table 6.2).

While high birthrates were the basis for rapid 18th-century growth, low death rates and immigration were contributing factors. In some regions of continental Europe, growth was kept in check by extremely high death rates, particularly among infants, as high as 40 per thousand yearly. In America, estimates have been calculated at from 15 to 25, probably only slightly below the English rate. By 1700 the birthrate had fallen and generally stabilized, with some

exceptions. Communicable diseases brought on by unsanitary water and sewage conditions increased the rates in more densely settled cities, if not nearly as seriously as in much larger London. The hazards of fishing and whaling and losses from war, especially in mid-century, took a toll of men, particularly in New England. Childbirth complications led to the death of one in every six or seven mothers. In England approximately two-thirds of those born lived to the age of 15, and perhaps three-quarters did so in America. And chances were high of survival beyond then to the biblical three score years and ten. Death rates among blacks were not substantially different, and far lower than in the morbid working environments of the Caribbean sugar islands.

The low rates of death were the result of a healthy population; colonial Americans were a people of plenty. More than enough food, a diverse and excellent diet, adequate clothing, an abundance of wood for winter fuel, low levels of communicable diseases with only occasional epidemics in rural areas and, not least, modest working hours for much of the year—all kept premature death largely from the door. Although unacceptable by mid-20th century

Table 6.2   Comparison of White and Black Population by Region, 1700 and 1775 (in percentages)

	1700			1775		
	White	Black	Percentage of total population	White	Black	Percentage of total population
Lower South	81	19	6	59	41	17
Upper South	77	23	35	63	37	31
Middle	92	8	21	94	6	24
New England	98	2	37	97	3	26
West	—	—	—	83	17	1
Total population	89%	11%	100%	79%	21%	100%
(Population in millions)	0.22	0.03	0.25	1.94	0.52	2.46

Lower South: Georgia, South Carolina, North Carolina.
Upper South: Virginia, Maryland, Delaware.
Mid-Atlantic: Pennsylvania, New Jersey, New York.
New England: Connecticut, Rhode Island, Massachusetts, New Hampshire, (Vermont).
West: Kentucky, Tennessee.
Note: 1775 interpolated from 1770 and 1780 figures. Percentages do not add to 100 because of rounding.

standards, one and a half infants (statistically) of seven born failed to survive, so that the completed family perhaps reached 5.5 children, compared with about 5 in England. Actual households were larger, on the average, because many families kept servants. Although colonial demographic growth remained impressive, economic growth occurred largely by the expansion of this population repeating the setting up of new farms. Only slowly did America catch up to Britain's level of overall development; there were few signs of this before the 19th century. It could be argued, however, that Britain's more successful expansion overseas by 1750 in comparison with France or Spain was partly a consequence of a healthy population. America continued and eventually improved upon British conditions.

Immigration into the mainland colonies was heavier after 1700 than before; about 370,000 Europeans and 250,000 Africans emigrated between 1700 and 1775. The influence of immigration on 18th-century population growth was obviously marked. Yet over time the *relative* importance of arrivals fell considerably. One estimate suggests that white immigration between 1700 and 1775 added 25 percent to the population. By the 1770s, after a decade of slower movement, whites born outside the colonies possibly added up to no more than 10

percent. The number of blacks in 1700 was little more than 30,000, but the impact of their immigration persisted longer because of the increasing importance of slavery. Although new immigrants brought new and fresh ideas and great energy, the chief implication of the rising proportion of American-born whites meant that fewer had experienced British or European life. While the Atlantic could be crossed more speedily and more safely in larger ships than was the case in the 17th century, the ocean ironically became more of a gulf, perhaps weakening and distorting images of the homeland. This may have made independence easier. An unknown but probably small number of settlers eventually returned to the Old World, an option that blacks, of course, did not enjoy.

Distribution and Expansion

Regionally, all colonies grew in numbers, but considerable population shifts occurred (Tables 6.1, and 6.2; Fig. 6.1). The oldest settled areas, the upper South (Chesapeake) and New England, together dropped from nearly three-quarters of the colonial total to less than three-fifths. Virginia, however, maintained the lead as the most populous province. Massachusetts, partly because of a lower birthrate, lost second place to Pennsylvania, the major success story of the century. New England produced the

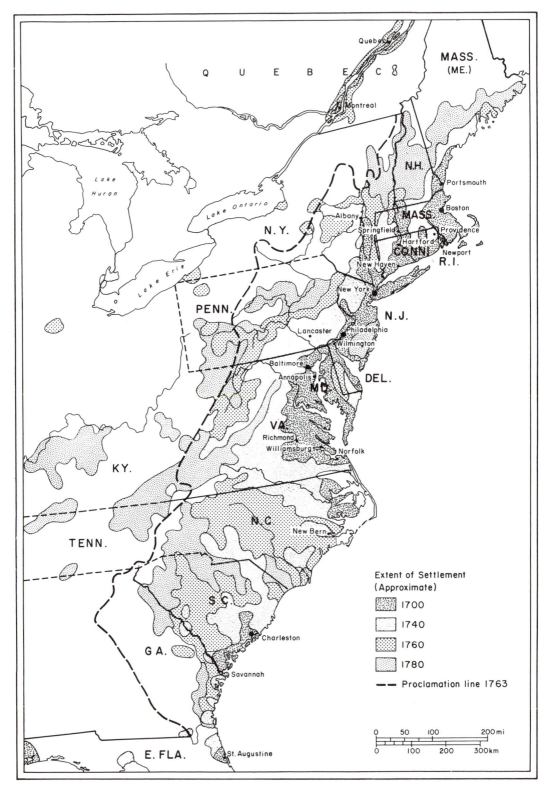

Figure 6.1   Population Distribution, 1700–1780

slowest growth, rising only 7 times between 1700 and 1775. By contrast, the lower South jumped by a factor of 27, as the Carolinas and Georgia expanded rapidly. The Middle Colonies grew 11 times, and the upper South by a factor of 9. The Mason-Dixon line drawn between Pennsylvania and Maryland divided the population almost equally to the south and north by 1775. Almost 90 percent of the rapidly increasing black population was located south of the line.

By 1700 settlements were virtually contiguous from Norfolk, Virginia, to Portland, Maine; south of Norfolk only small discrete settlements were established, the largest around Charleston (Charles Town). Penetration inland everywhere was still limited—no more than 30 miles above tidewater, except up the Connecticut and Hudson valleys.

By 1740 almost all of southern New England was occupied except the rougher, interior hill lands. Settlers were moving west from the Hudson along the Mohawk valley. Much of New Jersey was filled except for the southern pine barrens. The strongest thrust was in southeastern Pennsylvania, up to 150 miles to the west, and in Maryland and Virginia where settlers were spilling beyond the tidewater on to the Piedmont and even beyond the Blue Ridge. Immigrants landing at Philadelphia provided much of this impetus toward the backcountry. In the lower South population was confined largely to northeastern North Carolina and up the valleys from the coast.

Almost all land east of the Appalachian Mountains was populated by the time of the Revolution, as well as many fertile valleys within the Appalachians in northern New England, and the western reaches of Pennsylvania, Maryland, and Virginia. Beyond the mountains the Nashville Basin of central Tennessee and the Bluegrass country of Kentucky beckoned. By then the Carolinas were virtually occupied, while Georgians still largely hugged the coast and the South Carolina border. The 2.5 million people in the 13 colonies who were on the verge of unification had produced a rate of geographical expansion that equaled the rate of population growth.

Population was overwhelmingly rural because nearly all families engaged in production from the soil. Densities of rural population varied with the timing of settlement, with access to seaports and the coast, and with the quality of the land. After a thickening of the original settlement of an area, the population leveled off at densities that were relatively low when compared with much of lowland England. At least this was true in Pensylavania; much of Chester County to the west of Philadelphia achieved densities of 30 to 40 persons per square mile by 1760. Another stage of thickening began about 1790, partly as a result of new forms of manufacturing organization and the intensification of agricultural land use. But a more strictly social reason can be advanced: landholding was a widely respected virtue. Hence people spread out over a much greater area than necessary from a strictly economic point of view, even given the relatively low level of technology of the period. Not everyone bought land, but the majority did. In the Chesapeake and southern New England, the thickening may have continued closer to the economic, or better, Malthusian limits than in Pennsylvania, but there was no material reason for anyone to starve in affluent America.

In 1775 only about 5 percent of the population lived in urban places, where agricultural activity was limited to garden plots, if at all. In fact, the proportion of urban dwellers may well have fallen during the period, even while most of the seaports and new inland towns continued to grow. The urban places seem to have been able to handle the regional needs of the more rapidly increasing rural population. The highest urban-to-rural ratios actually occurred during the 17th century in most colonies; once established, seaport towns could service the ever-increasing rural populations reasonably well. Other processes contributed to the slower growth of urban population. Boston, the largest city before 1740, stagnated after then, and the scarcity of urban places remained characteristic of the Chesapeake tobacco-producing areas. Not until well after the War of Independence did urban populations begin to surpass rural growth. But even in 1850, after the decade of most-rapid urban growth ever in the United States, the urban population stood at only 15 percent.

Composition

By national origin, race, and religion, the people of the 18th century became more heterogeneous than before, including what had been very English New England and Virginia. By 1775 the number of colonists with English ancestry may have fallen to two-thirds of the white population and to nearly half of the total population. Although estimates of various groups are virtually impossible to make (even working backward from the problematic 1790 census and with other data), it is clear that other parts of the British Isles, especially northern Ireland (Ulster) but also lowland Scotland and south Wales, sent people to the colonies. The so-called Ulster Scotch-Irish settled thickly in Pennsylvania, the backcountry of the southern colonies, and in New Hampshire. They may have accounted for 250,000 people, or one-tenth of the total population. The Welsh were most conspicuous in eastern Pennsylvania, the Scots in the Carolinas and in East Jersey. Beginning in the 1680s, German-speaking settlers arrived from the Rhine Valley and Switzerland in increasing numbers until 1755, when flows stopped during the French and Indian War, and did not reach the same levels again until the middle of the 19th century. In 1775, 250,000 colonists, approximately one in ten, were of German ancestry, with Pennsylvania easily the most preferred province. Like the Scotch-Irish, many German-speaking settlers went to the backcountry of Maryland, Virginia, and the Carolinas. The Dutch who had come in the 1620s expanded their numbers but still added up to less than 5 percent (about 100,000), especially in New York and New Jersey. Except for some Germans, most settlers, and even more so their descendants, spoke English. Presciently, Ezra Stiles of Connecticut predicted that English would likely "become the venacular tongue of more people than any one tongue on Earth except the Chinese."

Historical interpretation in the late 19th century and well into the 20th attempted to draw sharp distinctions in attitudes and practices between ethnic groups, particularly between German-speaking groups and the Ulster Scotch-Irish in Pensylvania. More recent scholarship does not support this view. Distinctions have been drawn also within national groups and even among blacks on the basis of Old World regional origins. But all the secondary and tertiary differences pale before the enormous gulf between black and white in colonial America. By 1775 blacks constituted one of every five persons, up from one in ten or so in 1700, reflecting the continued forced immigration from West Africa (Table 6.2). Regionally, blacks increased in all southern colonies, reaching at least one-third of the population there (excluding Delaware) and almost 55 percent in South Carolina. In the North, only in the city of New York did blacks represent as much as 10 percent. These numbers signaled a social question of major political importance: at least 90 percent of blacks were slaves, and most of the few freed blacks in the North remained on the bottom rank of the social hierarchy.

While the treatment of, and attitudes toward, blacks remained a serious problem, even after they fell proportionately in the overall population after 1800, the issue of the Indian was of a totally different order. Although the destruction of Indian populations through disease transmission had largely ceased, surviving Indians continued to be pushed westward. During the 18th century several groups, such as the Iroquois Confederacy, and the Cherokees and Creeks in the Southeast, remained formidable adversaries, especially in the 1750s and 1760s. But the British government's proclamation of 1763, which marked off the watershed of rivers flowing directly into the Atlantic as the settlement limits to the colonies, did not prevent resentful settlers from entering land at least reserved temporarily for Indian populations (Fig. 6.1). Indeed, some settlers were already there before 1763, symbolizing the inability of authorities to stop independent searches for new agricultural lands.

Although most early Americans were of Protestant religious persuasion, religious affiliations were as diverse as population compositions. Bishops did appear eventually in the Church of England overseas, but traditional ecclesiastical arrangements were weakened considerably. In fact, the Church of England found itself increasingly in a minority position except in the tidewater South, as did an even smaller number of Roman Catholics. Eighteenth-century America continued and expanded the trend toward diversity that began in the Protestant Reformation in 16th-century western Europe. Eighteenth-century groups replicated European regional denominations: the reformed Calvinistic tradition was represented by Presbyterians largely from northern Ireland and Scotland, and by the Reformed churches of the Netherlands and the west German states; the Lutheran church tradition from adjacent states in Germany was strongly represented; and the anabaptist dimension of the Reformation was continued through Baptists from England and Wales, together with Mennonites, Amish, Dunkers, and others from Germany and Switzerland. Almost every strand of theological possibility within the Christian framework was found in England and thus also in America, most obviously in Pennsylvania and adjacent provinces. Friends, pejoratively known as "Quakers" because of their vibrant rhetoric, were prominent from 1680 onward, following a half-century after the so-called Puritans of New England. By 1700 the latter had evolved from their hard-line Calvinism that stressed otherworldy salvation into Congregationalism, and others would develop Unitarianism later. Methodism was yet another English development that would become powerful in America, but it was only gathering steam between 1750 and 1775. It is ironic that as a working-class group in England, Methodist churches elected bishops, although in a more democratic fashion than in the established Church of England (renamed Episcopal after the American Revolution). This European melange was the basis for 19th-century religious developments that increasingly became generated internally. Although American religious pluralism has been renowned, 17th-century England, especially, was the basis for this diversity. Blacks, while retaining some West African religious practices, gradually took on Christian forms, especially those of the Baptists.

The implications of these national and religious patterns varied. Certain national distinctions persisted, and occasionally antagonisms came to the fore. Because the majority were of English ancestry, they did not see themselves as an "ethnic" group, and few writers since then have considered them so. How people behaved in organizing their households and community life, and their economy, differed only in secondary ways from one ethnic group to another. English legal, customary, and governing institutions remained the basis for action, and set the ground rules and the limits to colonial ambitions.

Among non-British settlers social associations derived from religious beliefs were stronger than those emanating from national backgrounds. In contrast to Europe and even England by 1700, religious groups had to learn to live with one another as "denominations," more or less as equals. The Quakers, for example, had to accept others after their early dominance in West Jersey and Pennsylvania. Lutheran and Reformed groups, not originally friendly in Germany, often shared buildings for worship in the colonies. This is not to say that some denominations did not carry more status than others, a persistent fact in American life. High-income persons in cities were frequently Anglican. In the rural South the aristocracy was Anglican, while poor whites were Baptist and also increasingly Methodist. As a consequence, the congregation was extremely important in defining community life. There were, in addition, connections of pluralistic religion to society through what might be called aesthetic and moral individualism. The frequent public revivals, most conspicuous in the so-called Great Awakening of the 1740s, were emotional outlets for substantial numbers of people. And no one could escape the "Protestant ethic" with its emphasis on individual success through action. Religion in America bolstered personal initiative through theological pronouncements strongly stressing individual salvation and exhibited by worldy improvement, balanced to a lesser degree by more general communitarian concerns.

SETTLEMENT PATTERNS AND TERRITORIAL ORGANIZATION

As people spread themselves over the 18th-century landscape, they continued to organize themselves spatially. The terms *rural* and *urban* provide one set of spatial parameters; another set concerns local, county, regional, and national levels of organization and, in our case, the British Empire and the Atlantic world.

The distinction between rural and urban settlement, while time-honored in the literature and the censuses, cannot be rigidly applied to colonial America. If the hustle and bustle of trading, of the courts, and of the ale and coffee houses were concentrated in densely built-up cities, clusters of a few houses, a tavern, and perhaps a church at many crossroads were hardly distinguishable from the countryside. In fact, reversing the picture, many functions associated with urban life were also found in the country. This was most obvious on large southern plantations. Recently, greater attention has been paid by scholars to non-farming activities by farmers themselves and not only by those stating particular occupations. Manufacturing—that is, processing goods extracted from the soil and indirectly from animals or from stone—was frequent outside of towns.

Dispersed Rural Settlement and Property

Land in both city and country continued to be viewed as a resource and as property. With property, there were dealers, speculators, and lawyers to handle transactions that included government operations, such as courts for resolving disputes, registry offices for recording deeds, and then legislative and regulatory bodies, and so on, to taxes for the support of public service systems. As Ben Franklin said, "nothing is more certain than death and taxes." Much of colonial political life revolved around the level of taxation, most conspicuously when Britain taxed its colonies without providing them with representation in the British Parliament.

Although all institutions were important, the family and then the local community continued to be the most basic. Located on the land held by a family were the farmstead—house, barn,

other outbuildings such as a piggery, smokehouse, bake oven, and springhouse. The land was divided into woodlots and fields of hay, pasture, and grain, connected by lands to the cluster of buildings, with adjacent garden and orchard. A lane led to the public road usually only a short distance from the farmstead. Other similar farms were nearby but usually were beyond earshot (Fig. 6.2). A church or religious meeting house and a store or tavern were not far away, and together they completed the rural scene.

Irregularity in the shapes of lots largely marked settlement in every 18th-century colony, as shown in today's aerial photographs and road patterns. One exception was in Pennsylvania, where the settlers in the first two decades after 1681 were located within presurveyed rectangular lots and townships (Fig. 6.3). But after the first ranks of lots and townships were occupied, Penn and his officers failed to follow through. Settlement subsequently occurred where the first people into an area, after obtaining a warrant from the Land Office (though often not), had their chosen land surveyed. Although many people settled near friends and relatives, they sought land with adequate drainage and a good water supply. The ad hoc process led, as in the 17th century,

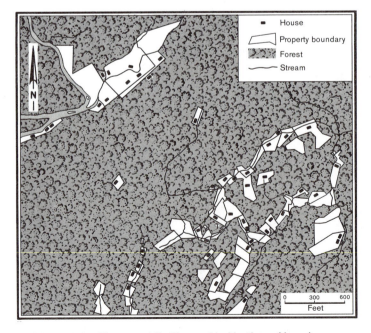

Figure 6.2   Dispersed Settlement in Northern New Jersey,
Middle of the 18th Century (after Wacker)

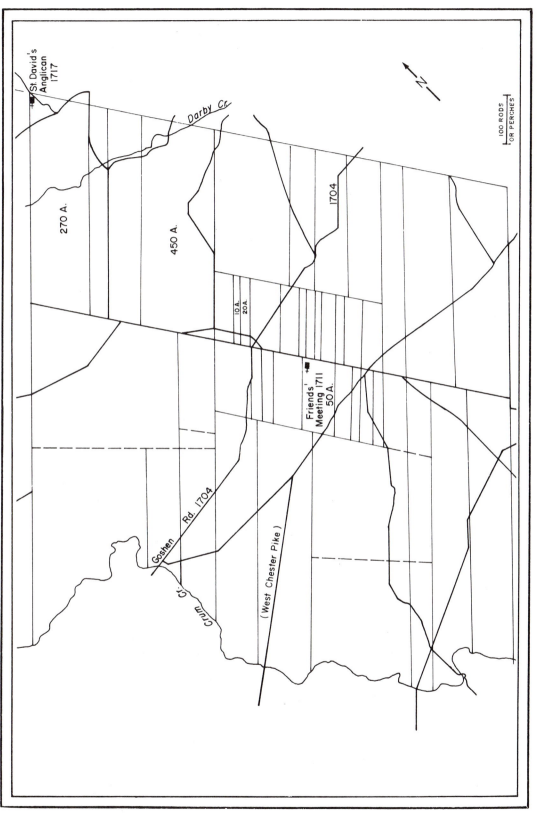

Figure 6.3 Newtown, Pennsylvania (after Lemon)

to an irregular pattern with much overlapping. Resurveying and court cases resulted. In 18th-century New England, however, regularity continued to be more common on good land. Not until after the American Revolution was the priority of survey reestablished on a grand scale in the American Rectangular Survey system. Whether regular or not, the layout of adjacent farms presents a familiar image of dispersed settlement to North Americans continuing the trend of the "enclosure movement" in England, where 75 percent of agricultural land had been enclosed by hedges by 1760.

In the 1680s William Penn encouraged his Quaker coreligionists to live in close proximity. But only one or two agricultural villages were laid out in Pennsylvania. One might have expected Mennonites and Amish, who arrived later, to have expressed their cooperative spirit on the land. But they took up large holdings (200–300 acres) and dispersed. A small number of Moravians in Pennsylvania and North Carolina did live communally for a time, and even more tightly shared possessions, but most occupied dispersed settlements by the end of the century. The organizers of the last colony established, Georgia, brought all kinds of marginal people from the streets of London to set up Savannah as an utopian community with communal ownership and operation. Again there was failure; indeed Savannah and Georgia soon replicated Charleston and South Carolina with slaves and plantations. Thus, a dispersed pattern of settlement was overwhelmingly the norm, varying from small to medium-sized holdings of ordinary farmers in all colonies, to large plantations in the South with slave quarters, to large patroons or manors in New York with tenants, or to small holdings (mostly craftsmen and laborers) who lived close together not by design, but simply because their lands were tiny.

The dispersed spatial pattern and the irregularity reflected the social aims of the settlers. While they did not reject community organization (and no society can), they sought considerable independence from tight community structures, particularly through ownership of land. Although freehold or fee simple allowed virtually unlimited power over a piece of property to be used or rented by the owner, the right was not quite absolute; in the 18th century in some proprietary colonies, settlers and

their descendants had to pay quitrents, or ground rents, to the proprietors and pay taxes. Absolute control was also limited by public needs. Symbolically, until 1776, the British sovereign owned all land (even in proprietary colonies) and granted the rights of use and exchange. After 1776 the people as a whole did, hence the use of the term "commonwealth" for states such as Massachusetts and Virginia.

Independent tenure signified three interrelated values: status, exchange, and use. Holding land established respect from others and so enhanced a sense of well-being. Although many tenant farmers in Britain enjoyed considerable status and security of tenure, vast numbers of tenants and owners on small plots found life difficult. In America the existence of so much land meant that many could own land, which created a leveling effect on society. There were, as we have observed, some holders of large properties in the southern colonies and in New York, as well as among land speculators in all colonies. For most property-holders, the ability to provide land for their offspring, either through gifts before death or through wills, was considered important in maintaining family status.

Tenancy continued to be significant and even increased in the 18th-century colonies. In affluent southeastern Pennsylvania, a quarter to a third of families did not own land in 1760. Their status among neighbors varied. Some were substantial families who, as in England, remained in that condition; others were smallholders with skills to sell; and still others, inmates and married families living in households of others, had low status. But most tenants in Pennsylvania held a higher position than poor renters, for example, on Maryland's proprietary lands. In the tidewater South poor tenants (and owners) maintained their status only in comparison with slaves, who possessed no standing at all.

All property, including land, carried exchange value. When a holding passed from father to one or two or even three sons, the other children were paid by those with money, acquired land elsewhere, or were given some other valuable consideration. A money value was attached to all kinds of work and commodities. While advocating community solidarity, William Penn sold land, first to wealthy speculators called "First Purchasers," and then to land companies that were responsible for settling people from Britain. Leases for rented land specified the value in money, the term of years, and certain obligations on the renter and sometimes on the owner. Like Britain and much of the Western world by 1700, the upper rank of society reeked of calculation. The value of slaves was reckoned carefully. In their wills middle-status men frequently were careful to specify the goods and/or money their widows should receive, apparently not always trusting their children to provide for their mothers. But no part of early America was outside the pressures of land, commodity, and labor markets. Lands with easier access to external trade—those nearer ports and with better quality soils—were certainly the most valuable.

Use value refers to the immediate or end consumption of a good: food, clothing, shelter, or some service. Land was cultivated, grazed by livestock, and forests cut; how much home production and how much exchange of material goods and of services will be considered below. The land produced a superabundance of goods most of the time in most places, so that people had plenty of time and energy over the year for other activities. Control over resources provided the security to do so.

Early Americans, even more than their counterparts in western Europe, were individualistic, stressing the autonomy of the nuclear family. The 18th-century household might be extended at times to include grandparents as well as servants and apprentices, and to depend on labor for harvesting and other work . But the independent organization of activity on a piece of land was central. Farms were businesses even while directly providing goods for use. The independent farm and other operations were also a way of life, the "natural" way to organize society.

Local Government

Yet it would be a mistake to overstate the independence of families from the social milieu, both local and regional. They and their properties were located formally within minor civil divisions and counties in each province. They were responsible to those who governed and were expected to participate in local affairs, in some areas even if they did not hold property. All heads of households were named on the tax rolls. Less formally they belonged to congregations, trading areas, and kin and other social networks.

Minor civil divisions continued to be labeled with English terms—towns, townships, hundreds, or parishes. The particular label depended on the timing of settlement and on the ideological concerns of the founders. The proper names of places often was the collective decision of the first settlers, and were sometimes named after the home place in Europe, a biblical site, a saint, or the local Indian name. The higher-level local region was called the county almost universally after 1700 (parishes in South Carolina were the equivalent of counties) and they were frequently named after English counties or persons.

The size and shape of local and county units varied considerably, and so did the terminology defining officials. When counties finally appeared in the North, they were larger than in the South. Individually they embraced as many as forty towns and townships and populations of 15,000 to 25,000 by 1775. The splitting of large counties occurred only after 1780, but even then northern units remained larger. By contrast, in the Chesapeake the typical tidewater counties included about 5,000 white and 2,000 black settlers, within an area only a quarter to a third the size of those farther north. Inland on the Piedmont, counties were larger and, despite later divisions, attained sizes comparable with those in the North. Shapes varied greatly, generally following topography more than arbitrary lines.

By 1700 local and county powers were generally well defined by provincial legislature and councils. But like all the earlier colonies, Pennsylvania and Georgia went through a period of what might be called experimentation in sorting out powers at different levels. The customary view of the division of powers between the local and county levels holds that in New England the towns predominated; in the South, the county; and, as one might expect, in the Middle Colonies they were more balanced. But such sharp distinctions are no longer valid. Local administration was found everywhere. In Pennsylvania, it has been suggested recently, a larger and indeed expanding role emerged during the century for township officials such as constables, overseers of the poor, road supervisors, fence viewers, and poundkeepers. But their power was circumscribed by very limited taxing power. That local positions were rotated among men suggests not only local egalitarian democracy, as in New England, but also that they were seen primarily as obligations and less as routes to higher status, as in the case of more sought-after county and provincial offices. Also paralleling New England, Pennsylvania township meetings elected most officials, but also nominated candidates for constables, who were then appointed by county justices.

In the North some county officials were elected and others appointed by provincial authorities. Justices who presided over the courts were powerful figures. The keeping of public order—of trying persons for criminal acts, resolving disputes over lot boundaries that could be dealt with locally, recording of inheritances, debts, verbal attacks, and the like—continued to be a central concern. Maintaining records such as deeds and wills was another critical role. In all colonies, representatives in the legislature assumed considerable influence in running their counties.

In the South the much smaller counties close to tidewater took on more of the local power than in the North. In Maryland the parishes only created in 1692 were apparently not very important, because they were abolished in 1776; but, as elsewhere, people served on juries. In Virginia, despite the counties being even smaller, parishes retained some functions, mainly to raise money for the Anglican clergy. One of the more interesting secular obligations of the vestry or parish government was "land processing." Because inaccurate surveys had led to so many law suits, the assembly ordered vestries to view property lines and renew markers every four years.

Churches and Other Local Networks

Churches probably provided partial social cement at the local level. But as in England, denominational preferences divided people, and theological disputes within congregations could separate neighbors. By 1700 many local communities had more than one church, even in New England where the Congregational churches, and in Virginia and Maryland where the Anglican (Episcopal) church, had been officially established by the provincial authorities.

The importance of other local institutions is hard to measure. Local trading and work patterns were not only economic in the sense of people competing with one another, but social in bringing people together. These cut across town and county boundaries. Barn raisings and husking bees, celebrated in the 19th-century literature as signs of voluntary cooperation, probably did not bring every neighbor out. Kinship ties were perhaps the strongest local glue, often reaching over boundaries like trade ties. If extended families were not common, celebrations certainly were. Funerals were as important as weddings, and more so than baptisms, in bringing families together and were often shared with neighbors. Neighboring everywhere was important for casual, usually uncontroversial, conversation as well as for crises. Although encouraged in some provinces, schools were probably infrequent in the 18th century and normally only for the elite; children learned mainly at home, or as apprentices. Black children too learned manual skills, but also a special set of abilities—to be deferential to owners yet maintain the integrity and solidarity of their families and the community of slave barracks on plantations. Black rebels against the social system could pay dearly with their lives.

Whatever the variations, the working of local government and other ventures in each colony was basically the same. In fact, 18th-century America operated very much like Britain, and some authors have argued for a stronger anglicization of institutions over the century. Ripples of differences were ironed out in the meting out of justice and in the managing of society and the public environment. It is paradoxical that taking neighbors to court may have been one of the ways society held together. Certainly it strengthened the legitimacy of legal institutions. At the same time, the wide variety of positions and distribution of powers between the local level and the county enhanced democratic participation, possibly more so in the North than in the South.

Higher Authorities

Places within counties were located within colonies and within a larger imperial system. The New England provinces had come under royal governors just before 1700, and New Jersey, Maryland, and the Carolinas would soon follow. If the governors and their executives were responsible to the Crown and Parliament, the legislatures were run by the colonial leaders.

Tensions between the two were frequent, culminating finally in the events of 1776. Colonial representation in the House of Commons in London might well have headed off separation. But the existence of colonies peopled predominantly by migrants from the homeland of Britain was unprecedented. As Britain, like America, haltingly moved toward wider representative government, it was not clear to enough people of authority in Britain how to reach a more democratic way of governing colonies. In Canada it took from 1791 to 1931 (even 1982) to work out an acceptable system of self-government under the Crown.

Urban Development and Regional Organization

Although most settlers and their descendents lived in rural communities, urbanization continued in the 1700s as many new places were established to service the increasing population. A hierarchy of places in all colonies or regions appeared much more obvious than in the 17th century, enough so that a central-place model can be applied. Theoretically, a central-place system has one large center, two at the second level, and more and more at the third, fourth, and even fifth levels. The larger the place, the larger its hinterland. The regions of smaller places nest, as it were, within the larger ones. The range and intensity of services and goods define where a place fits. Population and function reflect one another, as does the level of wealth. The real world does not neatly fit the theory, but it does provide a useful starting point and a model for comparison.

Before 1700 the promoters of colonies founded capitals for maintaining public order, facilitating commerce and trade, and focusing provincial social life. By 1700 Boston, New York, Philadelphia, Newport (Rhode Island), and Charleston were well established at the top of their colonial regional hierarchies, all under London as the dominant center. Still, only Boston exceeded 5,000 people. On the Chesapeake Bay no large center had appeared, and indeed few urban places, in the conventional sense. By 1775 Philadelphia and New York (both with about 25,000 people, as large as provincial cities in Britain), followed by Boston (16,000), Charleston (12,000), Newport (11,000) and the two new cities of Norfolk (6,250) and Baltimore (6,000) had become the leading places as the pattern filled in.

Philadelphia and its region provide the case closest to central-place theory (Fig. 6.4); describing it first will permit a clearer understanding of other areas. In 1681 Philadelphia was established as the capital at the same time as the province was founded. Government operations, such as the provincial courts, the land office, and regulatory bodies, provided people with jobs directly and, in turn, multiplied other occupations to supply them with goods and services. Merchants dealing with fur traders, inland shopkeepers, and farmers settled in the town, a small-scale replica of London in its early years. Many occupations organized by merchants and associated with shipping added to its strength. Ships were built, manned, and supplied with food to sail the Atlantic, bringing imports from England and elsewhere and taking exports to the West Indies, southern Europe, and Britain. As Boston had thrived earlier in the carrying trade, so did Philadelphia to a degree, although the produce of the region, notably wheat, flour, beef and pork, was more prominent.

In addition to governmental and economic functions were the central structures of the churches. The yearly meetings of Friends brought in prominent Quakers, many of whom were leaders in local economic affairs, who came to transact business. Quarterly meetings corresponding with the county courts also met there, and other church bodies held regional meetings. From the beginning Philadelphia was the richest place in the colony; many merchants and top government officials earned high incomes through trade, administrative salaries, and speculation in land. Hence the glitter of good living was more conspicuous than in the countryside. As the century progressed Philadelphia prospered further; in 1775 it shared with New York the title of "metropolis" in the British Empire after London. If its administrative region was restricted to the province, its economic and social hinterland extended far beyond, into half of New Jersey, Delaware, and the eastern shore of Maryland, and into the Appalachian valleys of Maryland and Virginia. After 1750 it had to share some of the latter areas with the rapidly growing port of Baltimore.

The second-level places were the county capitals or seats. For decades, Philadelphia overshadowed Chester and Bristol (Bucks County),

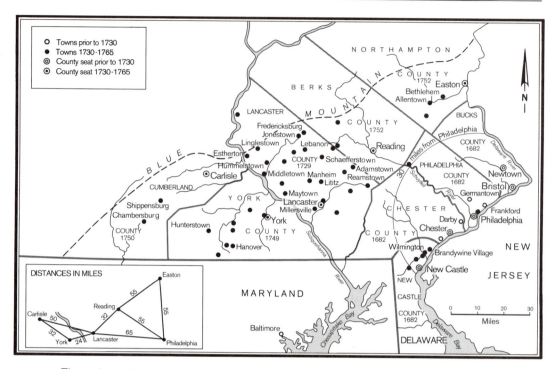

Figure 6.4   Urbanization in Southeastern Pennsylvania, 1652–1765 (after Lemon)

Burlington, Salem, and Gloucester in New Jersey, and New Castle in Delaware, so much that they failed to grow significantly. Their status could not overcome the far stronger economic pull of Philadelphia nor the relatively greater importance in earlier years of the central government. But eventually, as the increasingly populous backcountry prospered, the obvious need for further and stronger counties and county towns arose.

Lancaster in 1729 and four more towns in the 1740s and early 1750s were laid out by the Penn family or their friends, successfully earning revenues from subdivided urban lots. In fact, by 1775 Lancaster resembled an English market town and was recognized as the largest inland town in America, a miniature Philadelphia with about 3,000 people. Its courthouse set in the central square was a busy place. The local government paved the streets, built bridges, ran the marketplace, even eventually piped water. The creation of these colonial counties and county seats for governing, trade, and social interaction was a successful case of collective planning. They were far enough from Philadelphia, centrally accessible in their counties, and large enough to encourage strong

growth. Intensification came later from further county subdivision.

Some post–1776 county seats were created by private entrepreneurs in anticipation of county status. Harrisburg, named after its founder, soon became not only a county seat but also capital of the state, more central to the population than Philadelphia. But some that became seats had been laid out earlier by speculators. Indeed, between 1740 and 1775 they established more than 50 places, two-thirds of them in the late 1750s and early 1760s. Town-making then and later came in waves as investors sought to cash in on subdividing, although only a few were very successful. Thus third and fourth levels of towns appeared; the former were accessible economically, while many in the fourth rank gained little activity or status for their developers. Some managed to become villages of a hundred people by 1775, but others never got off the drawing boards. Crossroad hamlets provided a final level in the urban hierarchy. Their taverns provided lodging, food, and drink to waggoners and other travelers; on main roads, taverns were as frequent as every two miles. Like larger towns, local taverns or stores housed post offices after

1776 to serve surrounding populations. Thus in Pennsylvania we can think of a hierarchy of five levels; even if it fails to fit the theory precisely, it comes closest in early America, though in other colonies the same processes were at work.

We must also note the intrusion of "religious" manufacturing and mining towns into this service-oriented pattern. Moravian Bethlehem combined both aspects; Germantown was set up soon after Philadelphia with a strong contingent of weavers, and several mills followed. Other towns developed at milling sites. By 1775, at Brandywine village adjacent to Wilmington (a third type of town noted above), clusters of mills had appeared to take advantage of the fall of water. Mines and iron works induced "urban villages," too. Soon afterward, textile manufacturing factories appeared at waterfall sites, also in New Jersey and New England, further complicating late 18th-century urban patterns.

In other regions the urban systems fit the model less clearly. In New England the original founding of a string of seaports and fishing villages created a point pattern along the coast. Rhode Island was small but Newport had to share economic and political power with Providence. Connecticut was originally two colonies with two capitals, so that New Haven and Hartford continued to be more or less equal. In Massachusetts, while Boston was the dominant center, in the Connecticut valley Springfield continued to be central, although it was less focused on the fur trade than it earlier had been. Settlement from the east and the west only coalesced west of Worcester in the mid-1700s. Other inland urban places were settled slowly, partly because shorter distances rendered access to coastal towns easier than in Pennsylvania. Besides, the whole area west of the Connecticut River fell more and more under New York's economic dominance that undercut Hartford, New Haven, and even Boston by 1775. Political and economic dimensions of activity did not fit as closely as in Pennsylvania.

New York also dominated New York province, as one might expect, although Albany up the Hudson paralleled Springfield in its relative autonomy, more than any county town in Pennsylvania. Along the Hudson and on Long Island, counties and their towns were established. New York also controlled East Jersey, while Philadelphia controlled the west, more or less along the line between the original two colonies. New Jersey, even when it was unified, could not generate a first-rate center; politics and economy again were divided geographically.

The upper South experienced the most complex pattern of urban growth. Before 1700 urbanization had been slight for several reasons. First, the tobacco trade was organized from London to a far greater degree than was the grain and livestock production in the North, which was controlled more directly by Boston, New York, and Philadelphia merchants who had more economic leverage relative to London. Second, the numerous small counties inhibited strong secondary towns. Many courthouses controlled by large planters were virtually free standing without urbanization. Third, large planters dominated economic life and, in a sense, their plantations operated as urban places. The larger Chesapeake planters possessed relatively more power than farmers in the North. Fourth, many plantation owners shipped from their own wharves on the deeply indented coasts without the need to be serviced by central places. Despite a good deal of talk about the need for market shire towns, English-style, none had appeared.

Where the tobacco trade continued to dominate in the 18th-century the situation held to a large degree. The creation of Williamsburg as Virginia's capital in 1699 confirmed this. Unlike northern capitals, the flow of activity was far more discontinuous. Only four times a year, when the legislature and courts met, did large planters and their entourages and merchants converge on the place. Annapolis, Maryland's capital after 1694, attracted only a modest number of merchants. Economic transactions were thus secondary to administration and the social whirl. Tidewater planters increased their power in the 18th century, further dampening urbanization in the best tobacco-growing areas. Tobacco inspection warehouses were set up in the 1730s in Virginia and the 1740s in Maryland to ensure good quality, but did not induce a great deal of urbanization. Factors or agents of Scottish merchants from Glasgow set up stores in the Virginia Piedmont and strengthened the "forward linkage," the control overseas.

But Virginia and Maryland did experience profound settlement changes, especially after

1740. The Piedmont and Great Valley regions, as they were settled, took on more of a northern quality. Mixed grain and livestock farming came to dominate land use, as it did in Pennsylvania. Baltimore took off at mid-century to compete with Philadelphia in controlling this backcountry. By this time it had become unnecessary to combine the capital with major economic activities. Small Annapolis remained the capital, a disjunction that came to be even more obvious after 1775. The rising overseas demand for wheat led merchants to turn Baltimore into an important milling center using local falls, as in Wilmington, which drew not only on Maryland and Virginia, but also on Pennsylvania west of the Susquehanna River. Richmond too emerged as an important if smaller city after 1730. After the Revolution it became the capital and a milling site, causing Williamsburg to atrophy. Some entrepreneurs took advantage of the heads of navigation and falls, as well as backcountry crossroads, to found new settlements that added further levels to the settlement hierarchy. Finally, Norfolk rose to prominence early in the century, trading corn and livestock for West Indian rum and sugar. By the time it was burned by the British in 1776 it was already slowing down, because its merchants did not enter the rising wheat trade.

In the lower South the picture was also complex. In North Carolina, which had separated from South Carolina in 1691, urbanization was slight in 1775 even when compared with Virginia. This was the result in part of the lack of a large local center, the late and relatively slow settlement from the coast at various points by different groups, the spilling over of Virginia settlers into the northeast, the influx from the north into the Piedmont and backcountry by settlers from the Middle Colonies and others who had immigrated via Philadelphia, and the invasion of tobacco planters into the northeast and then gradually toward the southwest. In the southeast, Wilmington and other towns shipped naval stores—pitch and tar from pine trees. In the Piedmont more towns like Salem emerged as wheat became important. Again, as in eastern Virginia, small counties meant fewer large shire market towns.

Charleston was the largest place in the South, an exception before Norfolk and Baltimore arose. In 1700 it may have reached 2,000, only to slow again until the 1730s. Then it reached about 12,000 in 1775, about half the size of Philadelphia and New York and not far behind Boston. Beside its status as capital, its merchants dealt with the Indian trade, engaged in re-exports to the West Indies and, especially after 1730, financed the rice and indigo trades. In the 1760s they tapped the expanding wheat production of the backcountry for export as the wheat belt emerged southward through Maryland, Virginia, and North Carolina to South Carolina. A distinctive social feature was Charleston's summer resorts for rich planters. While northern merchants built suburban villas and Virginia's planters visited Williamsburg quarterly, Carolina's planters sought summer sea breezes to escape from oppressive heat and malaria on their tidewater plantations. Other coastal ports appeared: Georgetown and Beaufort, and Savannah in Georgia, replicating Charleston's style. In the backcountry small places such as Camden emerged slowly.

Even though urban populations were exceedingly modest by modern standards, urban places obviously played an important role in organizing points for administration, trade and commerce, and social life. Where these fit together, most clearly in Pennsylvania, the system was most regular—at least at the second level of county seats. Baltimore's rise signified a separation of economic and political activities; a big city could prosper without being the capital. Perhaps it was a harbinger of the future; after 1776 Philadelphia lost the capital to Harrisburg and New York to Albany, without economic harm. Indeed, London was the undoubted center of the empire in all respects until 1776. It would continue as America's major financial center, and even as an important social and cultural focus, for decades to come.

MATERIAL LIFE: AGRICULTURE, INDUSTRY, TRADE AND COMMERCE, AND INCREASING INTERREGIONAL TIES

The rise of Baltimore signaled a separation of the economy from public administration. But in a real sense, a strong degree of autonomy from direct regulation had been practiced much earlier in Britain. Money values were attached to property, goods, and services, even when barter rather than money was used for exchange. Merchants, shopkeepers, millers and many farmers kept account books, for reckoning with others. Contracts were signed when necessary, although many were informal. If there were fewer attempts to control prices as the century wore on than in early 17th-century urban places, legislated and customary standards for weights and measures could hardly be avoided, nor could taxes, even if they were minimal. The discipline of prices set in London markets were the basis for those in Philadelphia, New York, Boston, and far into the countryside. And those with economic power could dictate economic events to a degree. One could say that in all colonies there was a free enterprise economy, but there were limits. Adam Smith's famous treatise *The Wealth of Nations*, published in 1776 and often cited in support of the "hidden hand" of the market, was far more sensitive to social needs than we generally realize.

Farming

In contrast to today, the production, processing, and distribution of food, fiber and wood, and brick and stone were far more decentralized and small-scale. Whereas virtually every consumer today depends on the huge corporations for groceries and other goods, in the 18th century most goods were produced at home or locally on farms and in shops. This did not mean complete self-sufficiency, as has often been stated in past writings. Smallholders could produce a good deal in their gardens, but had to trade their labor for wheat or flour and for hay. Even more well-off persons practiced trades as well as farming. They sold farm produce to millers and others for export as well as for local trade. Regionally, New England imported wheat from colonies to the south. From time to time crop failures occurred, creating short-term dependency, although the soil generally provided a high standard of living. Those who were marginal in the society were more likely to be socially, rather than materially, deprived. They acquired debts they could not repay and could not provide property for their children. This was especially conspicious in the tidewater South, where small planters became increasingly dependent on large planters or on Scottish factors of overseas merchants for credit and imports of English goods. Obviously, too, slaves provided their labor for production, but had little say in distribution.

Farms produced a wide range of crops and livestock. The number of improved acres was the prime determinant of how much of the production was consumed at home and how much was sold. Few new techniques in caring for land and livestock were devised during the 18th century, and they probably did not account for much increase in productivity. Among grains, wheat and Indian corn were the most important for food and trade, the latter relatively more so in the South and New England, the former in the Middle Colonies (Fig. 6.5). Parts of New England continually suffered from stem rust, a disease of wheat. Wheat expanded into the southern backcountry and even into the Chesapeake after 1730. In southeastern Pennsylvania, central New Jersey, and along the Hudson, wheat production was emphasized on the best land. Most wheat was milled into flour for bread, and much entered trade regionally and increasingly overseas as markets opened up in the Caribbean during the 1740s.

Corn was used both for human consumption, primarily as corn meal, and increasingly for fattening livestock. Rye was grown primarily for whiskey and barley for beer and, to a considerable extent in New England, for bread. Oats were raised for horses and, according to the famous English commentator, Samuel Johnson, for Scotsmen's porridge, although persons of other ethnic groups ate it also. Buckwheat was a minor crop; apparently the poor made it into pancakes. In South Carolina and adjacent Georgia along the coast, rice became increasingly important after 1730, especially for export.

Garden crops and orchards provided a large but unknown share of vegetable and fruit. The addition of potatoes early in the century to the turnips, peas, cabbage, and herbs earlier brought from Europe was an important step. Pumpkins, squash, and beans from the Indians were still widely grown. Fruit was preserved, fed to animals in the late summer and fall, and pressed into cider and distilled into brandy. In New England at least, cider became more important than beer. Hay, with improved English grasses, clover, and alfalfa, was a major crop for feeding animals in the winter, obviously more so in the North. For much of the year animals ranged on pasture or in woods; many were raised on rangeland beyond the limits of settlement.

In all regions pork in its various forms was preferred over beef, and mutton and lamb were of lesser importance. Cows provided milk,

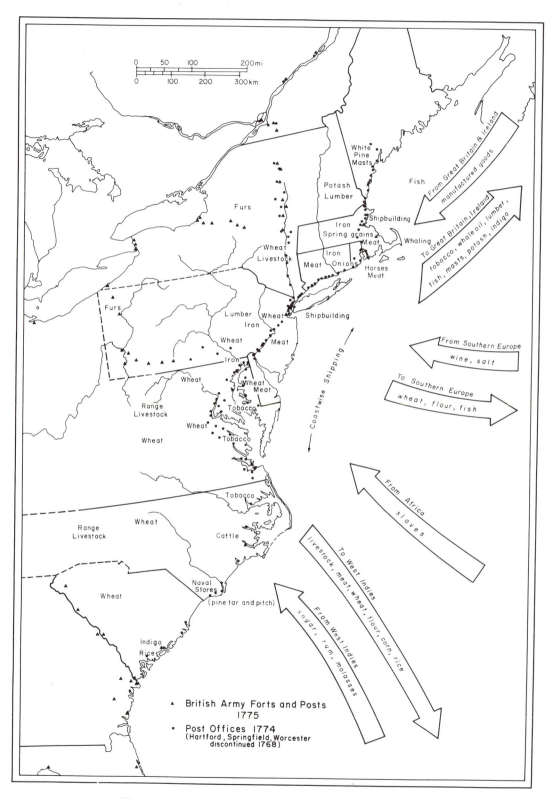

Figure 6.5 Colonial Trade and Economic Activity, 1775

some of which was converted into cheese and butter. Improved cattle breeds adapted to different environments appeared by the early 1770s, chiefly from English stock. New England may have raised more livestock than elsewhere: coastal Massachusetts emphasized sheep and fattened cattle were raised in the backcountry, while horses were especially important in Rhode Island. Horses or oxen ploughed, harrowed, and pulled carts. As commercial production of wheat expanded, especially in Pennsylvania and adjacent regions, four-horse teams pulled large wagons loaded with wheat to merchant mills increasingly concentrated near the coast. Riding, buggy, and racing horses bred for speed, not strength, were widespread; the finer the horse, the higher the status of the owner. Chickens, often referred to as "dunghill fowl" because they scratched around in manure heaps, have probably been underestimated by scholars as a source of protein (eggs and flesh). Geese and ducks provided food and feathers for bedclothing. The now-extinct passenger pigeon and deer also added to the supply of animal products. Bee-produced honey was used to sweeten bland foods, and in New England and New York maple syrup was popular. Sugar was also imported increasingly from the West Indies to supply the needs of urban dwellers and, gradually, those in the countryside as well.

Linen from flax grown on small plots, together with wool fleeces from sheep, provided fabric for clothing, bedding, curtains, and other uses. Wool was probably more important in New England than elsewhere. Dye crops were grown to add color: in South Carolina indigo, introduced from the Old World and yielding a rich blue color, became an important export to England and other colonies. Spinning was undertaken by women at home, but weaving was primarily a male occupation, and not only among the poor. In contrast to early 20th-century assertions of the "golden age of homespun," British woolen and Irish linen cloth were widely sold in America. On some farms, hemp, grown particularly in Virginia's Piedmont and Great Valley, was made into rope and bags. Farms, plantations, and even smallholdings thus produced what seems an almost endless array of goods for use and sale.

Tobacco, as in the 17th century, remained the key commercial crop of the Chesapeake tidewa-ter. Over the century it contracted from some areas and its production expanded somewhat into North Carolina and on to the southern Virginia Piedmont. Large planters increased their production at the expense of smaller ones; the inspection acts of the 1730s and 1740s favored the larger producers. Since they were more likely to produce good-quality tobacco rather than "trash," inspectors accepted relatively more of what the large planters grew. Small planters grew only an acre or two, while the largest planters produced up to 60 acres on two or more plantations. In the latter half of the century, as tobacco specialization became less competitive, large planters tended to diversfy into more crops, especially wheat and corn.

In terms of agricultural practices, an average farm of 125 acres in Lancaster and Chester counties in Pennsylvania, between 1760 and 1775, devoted about 25 acres to grain, including 8 in wheat and 8 in corn. Possibly another 20 acres grew hay, and a few acres were devoted to flax and hemp, and garden and fruit crops. On the average farm were 6 or 7 cattle, 3 or 4 horses, 6 to 10 pigs, and 6 to 12 sheep. In New England most farms were smaller; in the plantation South farms continued to be considerably larger. The extent of woodland on farms decreased over the century in older settled acres, but large acreages remained for fuel and lumber (and speculation). Near cities cordwood was consumed in large amounts and exhausted easily accessible supplies, and iron-making used up forests through the burning of charcoal.

Yields of crops and livestock were lower than today. Most 18th-century commentators pointed to an average of 10 bushels of wheat per acre, the other grains being somewhat higher. Cattle on the hoof may have averaged 700 pounds, pigs 175, and horses 1,000 pounds. Critics of agriculture after 1750 complained of the low yields and the small size of cattle. But when one considers the low population levels by European standards, production was more than adequate for home use, local trade, and export. Manure fertilized gardens and orchards, but not usually grain fields. By the 1760s lime came into wider use as a rejuvenator of fields and so also did rotations with clover for hay. New evidence of higher yields in older-settled eastern Massachusetts in the early 1770s suggests more fertilizing or at least more care than we usually associate with colonial farming. The usual way to renew worn-out fields was through resting, or long fallows of up to 20 years. Tobacco and corn were particularly severe in this regard. This did not mean that farms were abandoned, for which there is no evidence. Even later abandonments were not the result of exhaustion beyond the possibility of renewal; rather it was the consequence of the land not being good enough to support the level of commercial production needed to pay for farm properties.

Not all farms or households were able to produce their dietary needs. In 1771, 24 percent of households in Massachusetts held inadequate land, and 38 percent could not reach minimum requirements for self-sufficiency, at least as measured by grain. This is based on a somewhat more conservative estimate of need calculated for individual families and households than in other studies. Since undernourishment was not widespread, two-fifths or more of households bought grain and probably meat and hay from neighbors or from the open market. The inadequate diets of Boston's poor, for example, was a matter of food distribution, not of the inability of the country to produce. In mid-century no "agricultural crisis" hit New England, the region least able to feed itself. Indeed, better management of storage led to better and more-varied diets throughout the year than in the previous century. As a result, local trading was widespread, far more so than scholars previously have thought.

Households without adequate production had to pay their neighbors and storekeepers for local and imported goods. At least in the northern colonies and in parts of the South with few slaves, men worked as farm laborers for the more substantial farmers and as craftsmen selling their goods. The more affluent farmers needed the labor of these people and also often housed servants. Many of these were indentured immigrants who paid for their travel across the Atlantic by selling themselves for several years, generally from four to seven. Others were poor married "inmates," born in America. Although it is probably true that many families with mature unmarried children could for some years provide most of the work, it has become clearer through recent studies that interdependency was far more common than scholars once believed. The lower the

income, the more likely people were to be dependent.

Although farms needed work every day, seasonal patterns were distinct. Between May and July the first crop of hay was mown with a scythe. Harvesting of grain was most intensive in June (and July in New England) when winter grain ripened—wheat and rye sown the previous September. Spring grains—oats and barley—came later. A second hay crop often was harvested after winter grain, at least south of New Hampshire. Cutting grain with sickles was extremely time-consuming and had to be done quickly before the kernels fell out of the heads. Many people had to be mobilized. Poor residents of Lancaster, Pennsylvania, for example, were drawn to the fields at harvest time. Sickles were in fact used because the worker grasped a sheaf of several stocks close to the ground for cutting to prevent spillage. Scythes fixed with cradles (and allowing a reaper to stand up rather than bend over) may have come into widespread use by 1760 for cutting some grains. Either way, sheaves had to be stacked for further drying, then hauled into the barn. This was followed by threshing (by wooden flails) which, if prices were high after harvesting, had to be done quickly.

Slaughtering livestock often needed outside help, particularly in the late fall. Clearing land of trees demanded arduous labor, and some men specialized in doing this. Some farmers engaged in other crafts in slacker times, and some persons specialized in the weaving of cloth, bricklaying, carpentry, clockmaking, haircutting, and so on. Even if permanent farm laborers were less common than in England at the time, the picture now emerging is less unlike the mother country than previously had been considered. The fact that the wages for labor remained higher in the colonies than Britain underlines the continuous need for workers not only in the cities and mines and iron works, but also in the countryside.

The South continued to differ from the North in its labor requirements. The longer growing season and the specialized types of crop—tobacco, rice, and indigo—demanded more and continuous labor, as did upland cotton after 1775. Thus the need for slaves had arisen where these crops predominated. The expansion of wheat, however, led to a deemphasis on slave labor in much of the backcountry South.

Many farmers with smaller holdings acted more like northern farmers in using wage labor; indeed, the export wheat boom of the late 1760s and early 1770s helped to force up wages. Indentured servants became more prominent once again, as they had been in the 17th century. Large plantations introduced wheat but also continued to produce tobacco. Needing less labor, larger planters sold surplus slaves, a pattern that would become especially obvious after 1790 when cotton began its march to the west in the South Atlantic and Gulf Coast plains. It is clear that planters, large and small, adjusted their labor needs and costs to changing economic conditions.

Although farming occupied most rural people's time, a gender division of labor was apparent. Men were largely responsible for the preparation of fields, care of most livestock, cutting wood, and selling produce. Women did help in reaping grain; they were also mostly responsible for the garden and the flower beds; and they also managed the homes. Even though widows were the only women to possess legal standing as persons, undoubtedly many, if not most, wives were influential in many, even major decisions. Law and practice did not, as always, correspond.

Industry

By 1775 the making of iron had become an important colonial industry, accounting for about 15 percent (30,000 tons) of world output. Iron was produced in all colonies, because "bog" iron and hardwoods for charcoal were widely available. In Pennsylvania, Maryland, and New Jersey more than 100 furnaces and forges turned out pig iron and its second stage, bar iron. Many made finished products such as stoves, pots, and kettles, despite Parliament's attempt to limit the production of final products to Britain and prevent colonial manufactured goods from competing with those of the mother country. Blacksmiths, who fashioned horseshoes and bands for barrels put together by coopers, and wheelwrights were to be found everywhere, while coopers were concentrated at major milling sites.

Iron production was the largest-scale operation in the economy. A good deal of capital was needed to buy mineral and timber rights, to construct a furnace and forge and other equipment, to house workers and their families, and

to buy food and the like. Hope Furnace in Rhode Island often employed up to 75 men by the 1770s; about half were laborers engaged in cutting and hauling wood. Some highly skilled workers received high wages; founders and charcoalers especially were in great demand. If the latter turned out poor charcoal, the iron ore could not be heated to the right temperature for good quality pig iron. Compared with the scale of steel production beginning in the 1840s, the level of colonial iron production was small, and many operations were intermittent. Yet these works were the basis for the larger iron and steel mills of the 19th century.

Small-scale and intermittent operations were true also for most other industries. Milling of flour from wheat and weaving of cloth concentrated some people at particular sites; the conversion of weaving from human to waterpower was beginning during the late colonial period. Even though Manchester and Leeds in England led the way in cotton and woolen goods, America was not far behind. Shipbuilding stood out as the major industry on the river edges in cities and towns from Pennsylvania to Maine. By 1775 the long-protracted "industrial revolution" that was to provide the basis for 19th-century industrialization was underway in the northern colonies.

Trade

The pace of trade quickened over the 18th century, although far more slowly than in 19th century. Local trading was widespread and became intensified. Little is known of its extent because most scholars, until recently, have underestimated the degree of interdependency among farmers. Around 1770, 90 percent of the corn and more than 80 percent of the wheat produced in Virginia was consumed there, but how much entered internal trade is unclear. Some goods were sold at formal markets and at fairs, but increasingly most produce was handled by farmers or through dealers such as shopkeepers and merchants. In most towns pedlars hawking produce competed increasingly successfully with marketplace stallholders. Cattle were driven from rangelands in the backcountry for fattening near markets on the coast. Some of the pig iron produced at furnaces was sold to those who traded specialized goods. The range of goods in local and intraprovincial trade was extremely varied and must have been substantial.

External trade, of which more is known because scholars have investigated the issues more closely, expanded enormously. To England alone, the value of exports tripled between 1720 and 1770, then briefly in 1775 reached four times that level (Table 6.3). Even

Table 6.3   Value of Exports to and Imports from England, 1700–1776 (in pounds sterling)

	Exports	Imports
1700	395,021	344,341
1720	468,188	319,702
1740	718,416	813,382
1760	761,099	2,611,764
1775	1,920,950[a]	4,202,472[b]
1776	103,964	55,415

[a]Prewar peak.
[b]Prewar peak year of 1771.

so, it amounted to only 9 to 12 percent of colonial gross output around 1770. Throughout the 18th century the value of commodity exports continued to be outweighed by imports, but the financial burden was balanced by earnings on shipping, insurance, and other business, as well as by British military spending in the colonies. The Navigation Acts restricted some colonial trade into channels set by Parliament, but they were not a major impediment to growth. Indeed, under the umbrella of the British Atlantic trading network, the colonies prospered. After independence the trade continued to expand, after an initial period of readjustment at the end of the 18th century.

Exports from the South exceeded those from the North by almost two to one. In the period between 1768 and 1772 (the years with complete customs accounts), the South on the average sent out commodities valued at three-fifths of the roughly £ 2,500,000 sterling (pound sterling, £, was worth about $5 then). The North exported £ 900,000, nearly equally divided between the Middle Colonies and New England. By far the largest amount was Chesapeake tobacco, almost a third of all commodities shipped. Rice, indigo, wheat, bread and flour, Indian corn, boards, and barrel staves were also important southern exports. Bread and flour were the major exports of the Middle Colonies, although meat, iron, and potash also

contributed. The New England list was more diverse, with fish, livestock, whale oil, potash, and lumber standing out; the towering white pines of Maine became the masts of ships in the Royal Navy.

Great Britain, the West Indies, and southern Europe were the chief destinations of these exports (Fig. 6.5). As the major "enumerated" commodity under the Navigation Acts, tobacco was shipped to Britain. Shipments ranged from 35 to 50 million pounds (by weight) annually during the 1720s and 1730s; from 50 to 65 million pounds during the 1740s; from 60 to 80 million pounds during the 1750s; from 70 to 80 million pounds during the 1760s; and between 97 and 105 million pounds during the early 1770s before the outbreak of the Revolution. Most of it was re-exported to France (despite the wars), Germany, and other European countries by London merchants and, especially after 1750, by Scottish merchants from Glasgow. Between 1750 and 1775 the Scottish merchants increased their share of the tobacco trade from one-third to one-half. Their centralized control over this crop, both the forward and backward linkages, suppressed urbanization and a merchant class in the Chesapeake region, as we saw earlier. Indigo (900,000 pounds by 1757) too went to England for use as a dye in the textile and clothing industries. Most of the grain, flour, and bread were taken to the West Indies and southern European countries, the latter developing as major customers only after 1750. About two-thirds (50 million pounds) of Carolina and Georgia rice production also had southern European destinations by the 1770s. In all, between 1768 and 1772, about 58 percent of colonial exports went to Britain and Ireland, 27 percent to the West Indies, 14 percent to southern Europe, and less than 1 percent to Africa. Excluding tobacco, Britain's level fell behind that of the West Indies. Obviously, the luxury weed remained of paramount importance.

Imports continued to grow, in fact at a faster rate than exports. The West Indies sent sugar, molasses, and rum (derived from sugar) to the colonies, although rum was distilled from molasses in the colonies, especially in Rhode Island and Massachusetts. Southern Europe provided wine and salt. Of the goods valued at £ 3,600,000 brought into the colonies in 1760, however, only 20 percent was of West Indian origin and 2 percent of southern European origin. About four-fifths came from Britain, especially England (Table 6.3). The colonists spent money on consumer goods: woolen and linen cloth, finished clothing, hardware and metal goods, tea (from India), glassware, spices (from the East Indies), drugs, fine furniture, and many other ordinary and luxury products. It has been noted that slaves were clothed in British goods, and even that "homespun was not for the exigencies of the masses." The colonists' needs seemed insatiable and so were more and more locked into an expanding British industrial system; in turn, Britain depended more on the colonial market. Although British laws inhibited colonial maufacturing of iron and textiles to some extent, the cheapness of British goods was the major factor leading to increased imports over the period. These figures do not account for the trade in human beings that was needed if major economic expansion were to occur and profits to be made. Around 1770 payments yearly for people added £ 200,000 for slaves and £ 80,000 for indentured servants to the commodity deficit of £ 1,120,000. This human traffic was handled mainly by British merchant ships.

The colonies as a whole were able to balance the great annual debt around 1770 of £ 1,600,000 in three major ways. Shipping services and related earnings on insurance and commissions for managing trade on the Atlantic contributed £ 820,000. This amount, largely earned by the New England and Middle Colonies in the carrying trade, is a clear sign that merchants on this side of the Atlantic were increasingly significant contributors to the organization of commerce in the British Empire. The second category in balancing the books was the direct contribution of about £ 400,000 by Britain to military and naval defense expenditures, by 1770 an ambivalent blessing to America (Fig. 6.5). Most of the salaries of British civil servants, many placed to collect custom dues, were apparently paid from taxes in the colonies, especially after 1750. The remaining £ 40,000 debt was paid by metal money (specie), little of which was in circulation, or by recycling debt. Most of the "money" crossing the Atlantic was in the form of "bills of exchange," more or less like checks in recent times.

Much has been made in the past of the debts owed to British creditors by large plantation owners in the South, especially, and by merchants in the northern cities. It is now believed that colonial indebtedness was modest and most individuals did not chafe under the load. Most businessmen understood the functioning of credit; economic development through capital investment depended on this flow. The tiny amount of taxation was a bigger problem—political far more than economic—since it was levied without representation. The presence of British army and navy units, even though they brought money to balance the trade deficit, seemed less necessary after the final defeat of France in 1763. By 1791 Americans owed British merchants twice as much as in 1776; credit indeed made the world go around.

Finally, interregional trade became increasingly significant, although calculations are not as complete as for external trade. Besides trading goods raised by one another, the colonies also redistributed imports and collected goods for export. It has been estimated that at least £ 1,300,000 yearly entered the coastal trade around 1770, about a quarter of the external trade. Because the data are based only on the main ports, that amount is probably lower than the actual colonial total, because many small ports were also engaged in coastwide activity. New Englanders were the major actors in this interregional drama. Gradually through the 18th century, their region became more dependent on the wheat of the Middle Colonies and, less so, on the Chesapeake. The affluent inhabitants of New England were able to exercise their preference for wheaten white bread over the rye and cornbread, eaten by the "ruder" sorts of people. Although interregional trade was mainly a marine activity, the overland movement of mail intensified (Fig. 6.5). Weekly service linked most places; service between large cities occurred daily. These connections brought leaders of all colonies into closer contact and so led the way to unity in 1776.

Economic Growth and Incomes

The expansion of the colonial economy thus was especially significant between 1700 and 1775. Most of the growth arose from the extension of settlement, that is, by adding more people, far less from new technologies and city building as was to occur in the 19th century. By 1775 the colonial gross product had reached £ 35,000,000 sterling, according to one estimate ($2,300,000,000 in 1980 prices). This amounted to about 40 percent of Britain's gross product, compared with a tiny 4 percent in 1700. Per capita annual income of £ 13 ($845 in 1980 terms) was the highest in the world and probably had been after the first trying years of the 17th-century settlements.

Real incomes on the average probably rose modestly over the period. With the possible exception of New England, the rate of income growth accelerated after 1730, particularly in the late 1740s and 1750s. Overall the rate may have reached 0.5 percent a year between 1750 and 1775, certainly not as rapid as in some decades of the past two centuries. Economic development—that is, the intensification of activity and not just the extension of more people doing the same things—may have been the result of improved business practices and the strength of the "invisibles" noted above. Little can be attributed to labor- and land-saving improvements in agriculture. Milling for export came to be concentrated at coastal points, such as Baltimore, Wilmington, and Richmond, because it was cheaper to carry wheat for export there than to convert it to flour inland. This was a clear sign of tighter organization. But new technological devices were only beginning to appear in manufacturing and in agriculture. The economic quickening of the 1780s in England and soon after in the mid-1790s in the United States can be attributed largely to factories and machines and more rational farming methods such as the "scientific" rotation of crops.

LATE COLONIAL SOCIETY: DEPENDENCE AND INDEPENDENCE

The United States has been characterized as a "business society," meaning that the aims of businessmen dominate profit making through free enterprise and possess the right to keep and use the money as they see fit. Certainly, such a view is stronger in the United States than elsewhere in the world. The 18th century exhibited a clear tendency in that direction. A British traveler in 1744 noted Albany merchants whose "whole thoughts . . . turned upon profit and gain which necessarily makes them live retired and frugall." This is a confirmation of what has been referred to as the "Protestant ethic" (although one could apply the term to

many Catholics as well). Religion in America has indeed bolstered individual action. Also, the elimination of English titles, such as lord, knight and squire, in the new nation appears to have been a step away from ranked aristocratic society. But "gentleman," "esquires," and "officials" topped the asset holders. Besides, the business ethnic was strong in Britain, where many of the nobility and their sons engaged in commerce. The large planters of the Chesapeake and Charleston lived as if they were titled, and many merchants in northern cities built country estates just as successful merchants did in England. More ordinary white people in America drawn from Europe had, however, on balance greater opportunity and therefore were addicted with the expansionist view. Subsequent developments in the 19th century confirmed this trend.

Wealth, if less so than at the present time, was concentrated in fewer hands than is often thought. The elite class, making up no more than 20 percent of the population, held (by one calculation) 68 percent of total assets by 1775. They increased their share over time, but this tendency was already apparent at the time of initial settlement. The poor increased over time, although their condition was more likely to fluctuate over time. In the Middle Colonies the distribution was probably less skewed than in the New England or in the southern colonies. The importance of large planters and their slaves actually resulted in the rural population in late colonial America holding as much of the average wealth as those in cities. In New England wealth was more focused in urban places, although most rural New Englanders were not poor in basic needs. In Boston, and also at times in New York and Philadelphia, the poorest strata did suffer want, but mainly because those with the power were little interested in ensuring a minimum decent standard of living for everyone. The building of poorhouses after 1750 and minimal provision for indigents in hospitals did not solve the problem.

Class divisions were thus apparent in the distribution of wealth. Most people, rural and urban, were middle class or "middling sorts," as they often said then. They were affluent enough to add to their worldly goods; in well-off rural Chester County, Pennsylvania, in virtually every township a clockmaker crafted elegant grandfather clocks, a sign of status for buyers. Occupational distinctions even in cities did not separate an industrial class to nearly the same degree as in the 19th century. There were strikes and what was referred to then as "mob" action, such as British officials experienced at the Boston Tea Party. Marginal farmers rebelled periodically in some colonies, as in the Regulator Movement in North Carolina during the late 1760s, because they lacked money to pay bills. They agitated in fact for government-printed currency (something taken for granted today) and for easier credit terms on land. Even though ownership was far more widespread than in Britain and tenancy less frequent, a minority did not easily share the largesse. Because land was relatively cheap and accessible, however, new family farms continued to spring up on the frontier.

In the South the presence of blacks—by 1775 half the population—resulted in a peculiar set of class relations. The potential threat of a slave uprising pushed rich Anglican planters and poorer Baptist and Methodist whites into a tacit alliance; one needed the protection of the other. Ironically, white poverty may have been more widespread among southern whites because of this. Blacks diverted attention from the rich/poor division by being a "class," yet clearly lower than the bottom group of whites. In Britain the working people were not as deferential to the rich as in the southern colonies. When blacks rebelled or committed crimes, the penalties were often severe, but no more brutal than the torture and executions meted out to free blacks and slaves in New York City who did not stay in their place. Slavery and, since the 1860s, the "otherness" of blacks created the greatest dividing line in the southern half of North America, making it strikingly different from the rest of the Western world. The deepening of this chasm began during the 18th century. If slavery was disliked by many, its persistence did not, however, prevent the North and South joining together in 1776.

Equally important, therefore, were unification and westward expansion. The colonies indeed coalesced. The discrete and separate English colonies of the 17th century grew together and so had to live together. By 1776 they were poised for nationhood, despite the fact that independence was not intended initially by many. The occupation of native lands to the west strengthened the cause of nationality and, within a century and a half, the United States had become the world's most powerful country. The westward movement also prolonged the colonial reality that Americans were a people of plenty, the most affluent society ever known. But plenty meant waste. Only in the late 20th century have Americans generally become aware that the United States' and the planet's resources cannot sustain the excesses set in motion by the assumptions of colonial settlers and spread by the ideology of the new nation after 1783.

ADDITIONAL READING

Books

Cappon, L.J.; Petchenik, B.B.; and Long, J.H., eds. *Atlas of Early American History: The Revolutionary Era, 1760–1790.* Princeton: Princeton University Press, 1976.

Clemens, P.G.E. *The Atlantic Economy and Colonial Maryland's Eastern Shore: From Tobacco to Grain.* Ithaca: Cornell University Press, 1980.

Daniels, B.C., ed. *Town and Country: Essays on the Structure of Local Government in the American Colonies.* Middletown: Wesleyan University Press, 1978.

Earle, C.V. *The Evolution of a Tidewater Settlement System: All Hallow's Parish, Maryland, 1650–1783.* Chicago: University of Chicago Department of Geography, 1975.

Greene, J.P., and Pole, J.R., eds. *Colonial British America: Essays in the New History of the Early Modern Era.* Baltimore and London: Johns Hopkins University Press, 1984.

Henretta, J.A. *The Evolution of American Society, 1700–1815: An Interdisciplinary Analysis.* Lexington: D.C. Heath, 1973.

Jones, A.H. *Wealth of a Nation to Be: The American Colonies on the Eve of the Revolution.* New York: Columbia University Press, 1980.

Lemon, J.T. *The Best Poor Man's Country: A Geographical Study of Early Southeastern Pennsylvania.* Baltimore: Johns Hopkins University Press, 1972; New York: Norton, 1976.

McCusker, J.J., and Menard, R.R. *The Economy of British America, 1607–1789.* Chapel Hill: University of North Carolina Press, 1985.

McManis, D. *Colonial New England: A Historical Geography.* New York: Oxford University Press, 1975.

Merrens, H.R. *Colonial North Carolina in the Eighteenth Century: A Study in Historical Geography.* Chapel Hill: University of North Carolina Press, 1964.

———, ed. *The Colonial South Carolina Scene: Contemporary Views, 1697–1774.* Columbia: University of South Carolina Press, 1977.

Mitchell, R.D. *Commercialism and Frontier: Perspectives on the Early Shenandoah Valley.* Charlottesville: University Press of Virginia, 1977.

Nash, G.B. *The Urban Crucible: Social Change, Political Consciousness, and the Origins of the American Revolution.* Cambridge: Harvard University Press, 1979.

O'Mara, J. *An Historical Geography of Urban System Development: Tidewater Virginia in the 18th Century.* Downsview: York University Department of Geography, 1983.

Pawson, E. *The Early Industrial Revolution: Britain in the Eighteenth Century.* New York: Barnes & Noble, 1979.

Perkins, E.J. *The Economy of Colonial America.* New York: Columbia University Press, 1980.

Russell, H.S. *A Long Deep Furrow: Three Centuries of Farming in New England.* Hanover: University Press of New England, 1976.

Wacker, P.O. *Land and People: A Cultural Geography of Preindustrial New Jersey: Origins and Settlement Patterns.* New Brunswick: Rutgers University Press, 1975.

Walton, G.M., and Shepherd, J.F. *The Economic Rise of Early America.* New York: Cambridge University Press, 1979.

Wolf, S.G. *Urban Village: Population, Community, and Family Structure in Germantown, Pennsylvania, 1683–1800.* Princeton: Princeton University Press, 1976.

Zuckerman, M., ed. *Friends and Neighbors: Group Life in America's First Plural Society.* Philadelphia: Temple University Press, 1982.

Periodicals

Agricultural History, journal of the Agricultural History Society (Lemon, 1967).

Annals, Association of American Geographers (Mitchell, 1972; Harris, 1977).

Geographical Review, American Geographical Society (Lemon, 1966).

Journal of Economic History, journal of the Economic History Association (Kulikoff, 1979; Galenson, 1984; Jones, 1984).

Journal of Historical Geography (Harris and Guelke, 1980; Lemon, 1980; Wood, 1982 and 1984).

Perspectives in American History (Earle and Hoffman, 1976).

William and Mary Quarterly, journal of the Institute of Early American History and Culture (Henretta, 1978; Kulikoff, 1978; Pruitt, 1984).

PART III

EXPANSION

1780s–1860s

What good man would prefer a country covered with forests and ranged by a few thousand savages to our extensive Republic, studded with cities, towns, and prosperous farms, embellished with all the improvements which art can devise or industry execute, occupied by more than 12,000,000 happy people, and filled with all the blessings of liberty, civilization, and religion.

President Andrew Jackson, 1830

The possession of land is the aim of all action, generally speaking, and the cure for all social evils, among men in the United States. If a man is disappointed in politics or love—he goes and buys land. If he disgraces himself he betakes himself to a lot in the West. If the demand for any article of manufacture slackens, the operatives drop into the unsettled lands. If a citizen's neighbours rise above him in the towns, he takes himself where he can be monarch of all he surveys.

Harriett Martineau, Society in America, 1837

And is this French Canadian nationality one which, for the good merely of the people, we ought to strive to perpetuate, even if it were possible? I know of no national distinctions marking and continuing a more hopeless inferiority. The language, the laws, the character of the North American continent are English . . . It is to elevate them from that inferiority that I desire to give to the Canadians our English character.

Lord Durham, Report, 1849

7

A Robust New Nation, 1783–1820

SAM B. HILLIARD

Louisiana State University

The 1783 Treaty of Paris was a remarkable document. Despite the bitter opposition of both France and Spain, Britain agreed to a proposal that granted to the United States an area that extended from the Atlantic to the Mississippi and from the Great Lakes to within spitting distance of the Gulf of Mexico, virtually all the territory sought by an ambitious Continental Congress. It was a huge area, extending far beyond the zone effectively occupied by the former British colonies, a fitting reward for the group of visionaries who dreamed big dreams. One could argue, though, that the nation's grand outlines were determined some two decades before by an earlier Treaty of Paris (1763), the one that marked the end of the Seven Years' War. At that time, almost all Americans lived east of the Appalachians, but hundreds, perhaps thousands, of adventurers had already crossed the divide along its entire length on missions that ranged from simple wanderlust to grand ideas of commercial empires. Stimulated by the opportunities to trade with the Indians and a desire to keep both Spanish and French interests at bay, Indian traders, scouts, land speculators, military men, and explorers followed streams through the mountains and into the headwaters of the Ohio, Cumberland, and Tennessee rivers. Farther south, Carolina traders moved easily across the Gulf Plains, even trading with the Choctaws and Chickasaws along the Mississippi. With the outbreak of fighting in the West, even more were to make the trek and return with stories of its promise. Thus, by the close of the conflict in 1763, the geography of the Appalachians was well known to residents of the Atlantic colonies.

The Treaty of 1763 erased all European opposition to Britain east of the Mississippi. France was expunged completely from the mainland, and (except for New Orleans) Spain was limited to the area west of the Mississippi River. Britain reigned from the Arctic to the Gulf, but her triumph was short-lived. Even before the document was penned, events were underway

that would make moot all the careful designs of the Crown. The events were not political machinations of an enemy, but the quiet and deliberate moves of American Englishmen who sought new land and the freedom to look after it themselves.

The young nation's press for the Mississippi as its western boundary was grounded on more than mere territorial proclamation. Not only was precedent set by the boundaries of the 1763 treaty; the two intervening decades had seen Americans pouring into the West, establishing residence claims that were difficult to ignore at the bargaining table. Complicating the issue of frontier settlement was the Proclamation Line of 1763, a futile attempt by the Crown to regulate westward movement. It limited non-Indian settlement to the area east of a line running from Maine along the Appalachian Divide through central Georgia to the St. Marys River in Florida. The area west of that line was envisioned as an Indian Reserve and the Proclamation Line established to protect it. But the line was quickly breached by both treaty and the clandestine movement of squatters. By 1770 scattered settlements sprang up along the Ohio River and its tributaries and in favored locations farther south. Settlers pushed west through Pennsylvania to the Ohio and downriver to establish posts along the Great Valley into the western North Carolina valleys (now eastern Tennessee) and over the plateau into the Nashville Basin. Thus, by the time of the Revolution, America could claim, by right of occupancy, a huge area west of the Proclamation Line. All told, as many as 100,000 people may have been living west of the imaginary line established in 1763. It is small wonder that the Continental Congress insisted from the outset of negotiations on the Mississippi River as its westward boundary. The boundary as of 1783 was, in effect, political recognition of de facto claims that had existed since the earlier Treaty of Paris.

The boundary agreed upon in 1783 led from the mouth of the St. Croix River to its source and then due north to the southern boundary of Québec. It then followed the 1763 Québec line southward and westward to the St. Lawrence River, up the St. Lawrence to Lake Ontario and thence westward in a manner that bisected Lakes Ontario, Erie, Huron, and Superior, and on to the Lake of the Woods and the Mississippi River. The western and southern boundary followed the mid-line of the Mississippi south to the 31st parallel (approximately 60 miles downriver from Natchez), east along that parallel to the Chattahoochee River, down the Chattahoochee to its confluence with the Flint, and then in a straight line to the head of St. Marys River, which it followed to the sea (Figure 7.1). Later boundary disputes involved a strip 100 miles deep in what later became lower Alabama and Mississippi claimed by Spain (the Yazoo Strip), and the boundary between the United States and New Brunswick. Confusion over the extreme northwestern corner in what is now Minnesota resulted from a lack of knowledge about the Mississippi River's source. The boundary was changed in 1818, but the northward bulge in the boundary at Lake of the Woods remains today to remind us of the earlier misunderstanding. The new nation could claim a territory of nearly one million square miles, twice the area of the 13 original states, and three to four times the area effectively occupied by the 3 million souls that made up the United States in 1784.

THE GEOGRAPHY OF FEDERALISM

The birth of any organism is fraught with danger, and the new nation was no exception. The First Continental Congress met in Philadelphia in 1774, inaugurating a series of debates and actions that resulted in the creation of a new and unique nation. In less than two decades, the 13 small and separate colonies, with no precedent to guide them and little in common except a British heritage, declared themselves independent, secured recognition from foreign powers (including an alliance with France), defeated Great Britain, and negotiated a peace treaty with generous territorial provisions.

The major issue confronting those leading the new nation was a simple one: what kind of government should there be? Having lived their lives as free Englishmen, the founding fathers were resolute in their defense of liberty, but the immense size of the continent and its fragmentation into individual colonies raised the issue of two levels of government, state and national. Most considered themselves citizens of a particular state, yet were faced with the necessity of uniting for purposes common to all. Even so, no one wished to see the Crown replaced by an equally obnoxious and overpowerful central government. The result was a confederation in which each state retained almost complete sovereignty. So fiercely did the states guard their independence that the union almost failed to function. Congress had no power to regulate interstate activities, and revenues and armies had to be raised by requests to the states. It was government by supplication.

Recognizing the unworkability of the government under the Articles of Confederation, the legislatures of Virginia and Maryland issued an invitation to a conference at Annapolis in 1786 to discuss governmental revision. Only five states were represented at Annapolis, but out of that conference grew a proposal for delegates from the several states to meet in Philadelphia for the purpose of discussing revision of the Articles of Confederation. Thus the constitutional convention was born.

Despite the delegates' strong loyalties to their home states, the chaotic conditions in the years following the Revolution had convinced a majority of the delegates that a stronger national government was necessary, but bitter debate would ensue before the remarkable compromises necessary for "a more perfect union" were reached. The initial proposal called for revision of the Articles, but as discussion lengthened it became obvious that an entirely new document was needed. The result was a constitution that provided the basis of the government of the new nation.

The new constitutional government might best be described as a representative democracy defined by the cardinal principles of popular sovereignty and limited government. Specific limitations were placed on both the state and national governments in a number of places, especially in the Bill of Rights, indicating deep distrust of government at all levels. The Constitution provides for a tripartite government consisting of executive, legislative, and judicial branches, reflecting the principle

Figure 7.1   The New Nation as Outlined by the Treaty of Paris (1783)

of separation of powers. The American Congress is bicameral; that is, it consists of two bodies, a Senate and a House of Representatives, both of which must approve legislation before it goes to the executive for approval. This dual organization resulted directly from the arguments over representation. In the initial proposal by Edmund Randolph, the Virginia Plan, representation was to be according to population, but those delegates representing states with small populations objected, preferring instead the New Jersey Plan, which called for equal representation from each state. The resulting compromise called for two legislative bodies, one (the House) consisting of representation according to population, and the other (the Senate) having two senators from each state. The terms of office differed also, being six years for the Senate, while the entire House must stand for reelection every two years. Of particular interest to scholars interested in studying the past is the practice of holding decennial censuses. Having established the policy of representation according to population, the government was faced with the task of determining how many people lived in each political unit. Thus we have an official population count every ten years.

One of the paramount questions of the period and one that still lingers is the question of states' rights versus national sovereignty. The national government's powers are delegated, while the states have reserved and inherent powers. In its designated field the national government is supreme, protected by the judiciary; but in studying the Constitution one is struck by the obvious efforts to circumscribe federal powers rather than to issue a *carte blanche*.

Of equal concern to the founding fathers was the fear of an all-powerful federal government meddling in the affairs of individuals. European experience had engendered concern over the power of a central government and its potential for tyranny. Thus an early attempt to erect safeguards against such intrusions was begun even before ratification. A body of ten articles guaranteeing individual rights was adopted as the first ten constitutional amendments. Because they deal specifically with individual liberties they are known as the Bill of Rights and, because of their adoption so closely following the adoption of the Constitution itself, are generally considered virtually a part of the document. On the whole, the Bill of Rights guarantees such specific rights as freedom of speech, of religion, of the press; protection from unreasonable detention, search, and seizure, and security of personal possessions and domiciles; and such procedural rights as trial by jury. The wording of Amendment Ten reveals clearly the inherent fear of governmental power: "The powers not delegated to the United States by the constitution, nor prohibited by it to the States, are reserved to the States respectively, or to the people."

Once the Constitution had been laden with a protective coating of amendments, the debate shifted to the question of a national capital. What kind of place should it be, and where should it be located? To many delegates, who had convened in no less than eight different places, the idea of a permanent seat was appealing. Despite widespread suspicion of a powerful national government, it was obvious to all that proximity to the new capital would be advantageous. A number of offers were made by existing cities, but opinion seemed to favor the selection of a site unsullied by previous occupancy. The usual lobbying forces were present, representing financial and sectional interests, but the choice of a site on the Potomac River represented an acceptable compromise. Supported strongly by Washington, Jefferson, and Madison, the area was agreed upon only after an agreement was made in which southern forces would support legislation that would ensure federal assumption of state war debts.

The result was a 10-mile square laid out astride the Potomac in Maryland and Virginia. The site of the capital city itself was chosen by Major Pierre Charles l'Enfant, a young French engineer who had served in the Revolution. Although Washington reluctantly dismissed the fiery Frenchman, his plan of diagonal avenues superimposed upon a rectangular grid remains a hallmark of the federal city.

POLITICAL FUTURE OF THE WEST

The political status of the newly acquired land was an open question. All of it was claimed by one or more of the original 13 colonies. Altogether, seven states had western claims extending from Lake Superior south to the 31st parallel (Fig. 7.2). Virginia claimed the largest area—all the new western lands from the mountains to the Mississippi River that lay north of 36–1/2 degrees north latitude. It was overlapped by several other claims. Connecticut claimed an intermittent strip that extended to the Mississipi River, a part lying in western Pennsylvania. Massachusetts argued for a part of western New York and a strip that extended to the Mississippi across what later became Michigan and Wisconsin; and New York had a nebulous claim based on Indian negotiations that included most of the Old Northwest and south to the Tennessee River. North Carolina's claim extended westward to the Mississippi,

Figure 7.2   State Claims to the Public Domain

the area that later became the state of Tennessee. Georgia's claim also extended to the Mississippi, conflicting in the north with a narrow strip also claimed by South Carolina, one that proved imaginary because of misconceptions about the headwaters of the Savannah River, and in the south with Spain (the Yazoo Strip). The conflict with Spain resulted from an agreement between Spain and Britain that the boundary would run along latitude 32° 28' rather than the 31st parallel.

The acquisition of this huge body of land stimulated lively debate over its future. The claims of the seven states, based on colonial charters or agreements, were countered by appeals to the common good and the obvious fact that all 13 had shed blood in its defense. The matter was brought to a head when Maryland, goaded by the adamant position of Virginia over the issue, refused to sign the Articles of Confederation. The stalemate was broken when New York ceded its western claims. Other states followed, but it took some 20 years for all claims to be relinquished. Even then most states managed to gain something from their claims, usually the right to grant lands to veterans or to sell them outright. The result of these territorial cessions was the creation of a huge body of land owned not by individual colonies or states, but by the new nation itself. Thus, for the first time, the United States was a landowner, and the new territory became known as the Public Domain. Not all the western lands were included, but approximately 220 million acres eventually became part of this Public Domain, the creation of which was a milestone in North American development. It greatly enlarged the area of the new nation and also changed its character, for the organization, administration, division, and distribution of that domain remained a central political issue for most of the next 100 years.

The conflict over western lands involved more than sovereignty. It meant the right to dispose of the land for use by individuals (soil rights) according to the dictates of the states, which meant money for their empty treasuries. From New England to Georgia the states rushed to dispose of their lands before political events could rob them of the chance. Massachusetts relinquished its claim to sovereignty in western New York in return for the right to sell 6 million acres west of the "Preemption Line," a north-south line running through western New York from Lake Ontario to Pennsylvania. Massachusetts disposed of the land in the accepted fashion of the time—it sold to land developers who subdivided and resold to individuals. After passing through the hands of several speculators who failed to meet their obligations, the tracts were eventually settled, as were others sold by both Massachusetts and New York. Connecticut also kept part of its Ohio claim, the Western Reserve, which it promptly sold to both speculators and prospective settlers. Of all the attempts to make quick profit on western claims, Georgia's example was perhaps the most flagrant. In 1789 and again in 1795 it sold some 25 million acres located in what later became Alabama and Mississippi to several land companies. The sales were later repudiated by the state, but the courts finally resolved the matter in favor of the speculators. Even as the debate on relinquishing claims to western land raged, North Carolina and Virginia were busy getting rid of their lands located across the mountains. By the time Kentucky and Tennessee had become states in 1792 and 1796, respectively, most of their lands had already passed into private hands. Virginia also reserved the right to settle veterans' claims by granting land in a huge tract north of the Ohio between the Scioto and Little Miami rivers known as the Virginia Military Reserve.

Once the Public Domain became a reality, the new nation was faced with the very practical matter of what to do with it. Conflicting state and federal claims and their attendant land sales had not discouraged westward migration, and these new settlers were quick to demand certain rights and services, among them the right to organize into self-governing units. Once organized they could petition to enter as new states or simply break away to form a western nation. In addition, there was the question of land speculation. Since before the French and Indian War easterners had coveted western lands, and a number of persons had massive development schemes in mind, which they presented to both state and federal governments. It was a period of great turmoil and a critical one for the new nation. Clearly, something had to be done. In 1784 a Congressional Committee consisting of Thomas Jefferson, Jeremiah Chase, and David Howell presented a plan to Congress that provided the means for dividing the western lands into states and administering the new units until their acceptance into the union as states. This "Plan for the Temporary Government of the Western Country" (the Ordinance of 1784) set parallels and meridians as boundaries for the 10 states to be established northwest of the Ohio River (more were planned for the southwest), provided for self-government in each state, and specified the means of achieving statehood. Intrinsic in the document were certain guarantees of freedom and the principle of creating new states that were not subservient to the 13 original states. The Ordinance of 1784 was adopted but with a number of Jefferson's innovations deleted, such as the classically inspired state names like Sylvania, Polypotamia, and Polisipia. The Jeffersonian proposal (of 1784) was superceded by the Ordinance of 1787, frequently referred to as the Northwest Ordinance, which remained in effect during the settlement era. The Northwest Ordinance provided for a "territorial period" during which government was effected through a governor, secretary, and three judges, all congressionally appointed. As population increased an assembly was to be elected, and when the population reached 60,000 the territory could frame a constitution and apply for admission to the Union on equal terms with the original states.

DIVIDING UP THE LAND

The Northwest Ordinance of 1787 dealt with the matter of government in the territories, but the survey and distribution of land had claimed the attention of the Continental Congress somewhat earlier. Land surveying and distribution had been underway for nearly two centuries in the colonies, resulting in a complex of practices that differed from place to place. Colonists had long employed a western European system of survey known as "metes and bounds" that might be described as part geometry, part topography, and part consensus. The use of natural features as boundaries and identifying monuments had long been in use, but with the development of instruments for measuring angles and laying out straight lines a bit of geometry was added. It became standard practice in colonial America to lay out tracts of land using the compass and chain. In many

cases, natural features, most commonly streams but occasionally roads and ridge crests, served as partial boundaries, but the remaining sides consisted of straight lines connecting specified points marked on the land by trees, stakes, pins, or stones called "monuments." Careful recording of all pertinent information permitted reconstruction on paper either in verbal or cartographic form, or both. Such records constituted legal descriptions and were fundamental to the orderly transfer of land throughout the country. The system differed little from that employed in Britain at the time, but the context in which surveying took place greatly complicated the process. Not only did the surveyor have to chop his way through uncleared forests, he had to establish points on lands essentially devoid of prior markers.

The concept of private land ownership in fee simple eventually became universal, and all colonial governments were forced to establish land policies. Some established relatively rigid rules regarding land disposal, specifying the manner of allocation and survey. The best known model was New England, where towns often were laid out into tracts to be granted or sold to individuals. In general, such parcels were surveyed prior to their transfer, a system often lauded for its orderliness. Other colonies had simply granted land through the issuance of warrants that entitled the bearer to a certain number of acres, the location of which was unspecified. Although the latter system was widespread, it eventually became identified with the southern colonies and was in effect throughout the settlement period. A major advantage of the southern system was its flexibility. The prospective settler simply obtained a land warrant and then selected the tract he wanted. Those who arrived first had the best choices, but new lands became available for settlement at such a rapid rate that many simply bypassed the poor sites in favor of tracts farther in the wilderness. The system encouraged rapid settlement, especially when coupled with the headright or some other system of granting virtually free land. Contrasting sharply with the rather open system in the South was the New England town settlement. Beginning early in the "theocratic era" of the early 17th century, New Englanders established the practice of surveying entire towns or townships into parcels, a practice that supposedly discouraged settlement outside established towns. Furthermore, the policy of survey *prior* to settlement was firmly established. In fact the two systems differed more in the manner in which land was divided, granted, or sold than in the method of survey. Chain and compass (or circumferentor) were used in surveying individual tracts in Georgia or in township surveying in New Hampshire.

In the hectic years following independence, those states having unclaimed land continued to grant or sell land in the traditional fashion; some permitted unrestricted access to settlers who simply squatted where they wished and later filed claim for their land under headright law. With the creation of the new nation and its Public Domain, the debate over land policy intensified. Some wished to continue the southern policies, while others sought to impose more rigid standards. As early as 1784 Jefferson's committee on public land drafted an ordinance that provided the germ for what later became the system of land survey now commonly identified with the American landscape. The geometric regularity of its six-mile square townships divided into 36 square sections is so well known by American historians and geographers that little detail is needed here. Perhaps less known is the evolution of concept and the myriad variations that were used during the early years. The initial proposal called for the creation of *hundreds*, each measuring ten *geographical* (not statute) miles square. The geographical mile was defined as 6086.4 feet, and each hundred was to be divided into 100 square-mile lots containing 850.4 acres each, rather than the 640 acres accepted on today's standard (Fig. 7.3). There is evidence that Jefferson had even more radical reform in mind. He considered dividing the geographical mile into 10 furlongs and the furlong into 10 chains, each consisting of 10 paces, a system quite similar to the British furlong, chain, and fathom. Surveying would have been done using a chain one-tenth of a furlong in length, thus each geographical mile would have been 100 chains to the side and each square mile would have contained 1,000 (reformed) acres. The hundred would have contained 100 square miles or 100,000 acres. All lines were to be run either north-south or east-west, resulting in a network of cardinally arranged square parcels. The word *hundred* was

based on current usage in Virginia, Maryland, and Delaware at the time, having been introduced from England where it had been used as a common subdivision of the shire or county during the 16th and 17th centuries. The proposal of 1784 differed from earlier usage in that it assigned the quantitative number *hundred* to the ancient term. In final form the land ordinance abandoned the geographical mile, the term *hundred*, and the reformed chain. Instead, the 66-foot Gunter chain and the 5,280-foot statute mile (80 chains) were used. The term *hundred* was replaced by the New England term *township*, and the word *section* took the place of *lot*.

Although ample antecedents may be cited, the American Rectangular Land Survey System represented a radical departure from previous land disposal systems in that it was uniformly rectilinear in appearance, stipulated survey prior to sale, and resulted in units of a standard size. It was first employed in eastern Ohio, where the famous "seven ranges" were laid out immediately west of the Ohio River and, though modified in detail, remained the standard throughout the Public Domain.

It would be misleading to give the impression that the new federal survey system was an immediate and unqualified success or that it was a paragon of accuracy. It did, in fact, have a profound impact on the American landscape, but it took more than half a century to establish the tradition of consistency and accuracy that carried it across the continent. The early years were marked by indecision and accommodation to the point where one might properly ask if it was any improvement over the land disposal systems of the colonial period. It was a period of discovery when trial and error set the guidelines, and the results were surprisingly various. A brief look at two examples, Ohio and Louisiana, will serve to illustrate the clumsy beginnings. Because all surveyors at the time used the same instruments and methods, the federal system was far from the "radical" innovation it is usually regarded. As a counterpoint to the federal system, we will also see how Georgia chose to survey and distribute her own "public domain."

Ohio was admitted to the Union in 1803, but for years surveyors had tramped its forests to run boundaries, chop trees, and measure land for new settlers. Tennessee, Kentucky, and Ver-

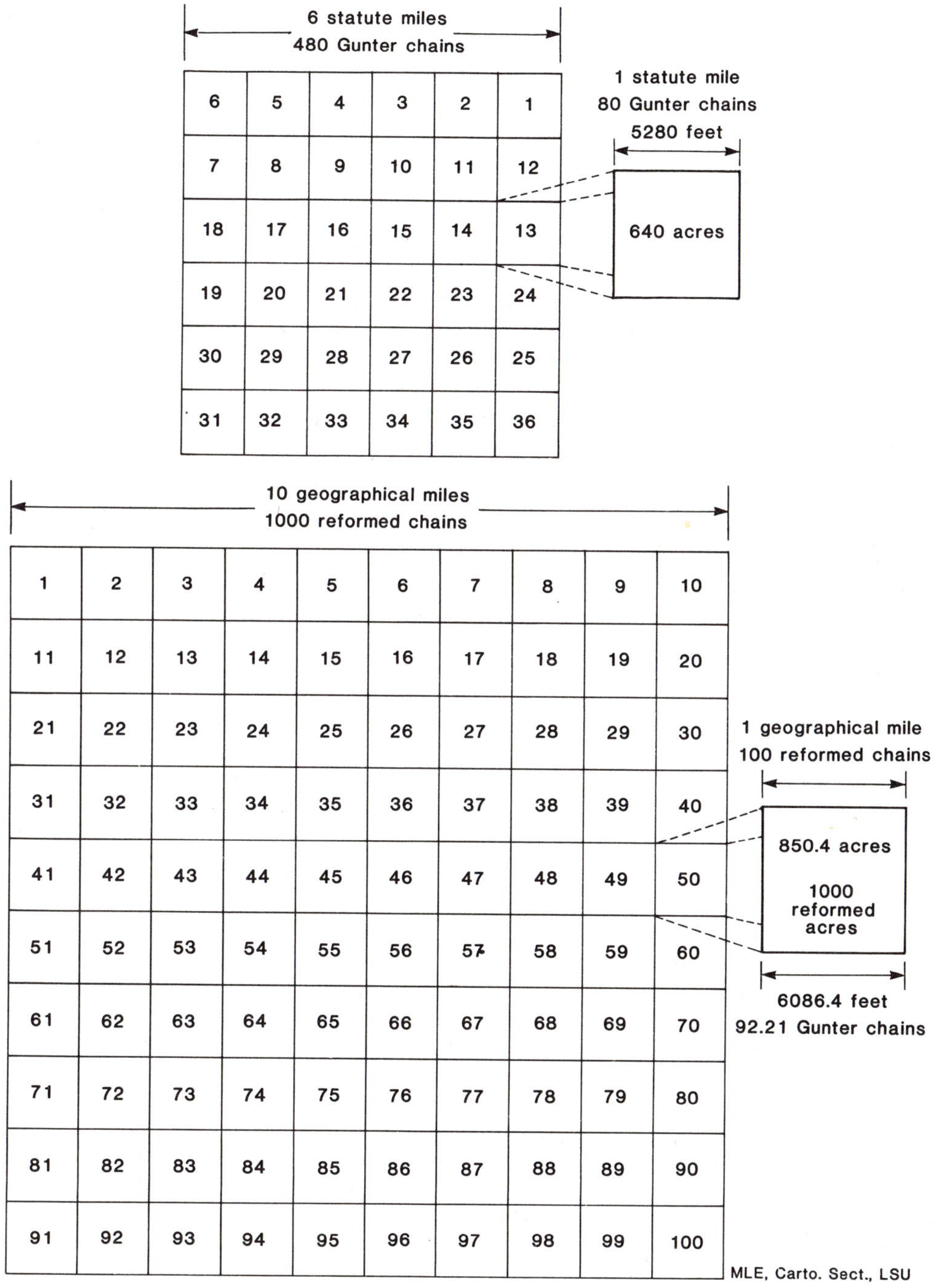

Figure 7.3 Scale Comparison of the Original Jeffersonian Plan for "Hundreds" with Present-day Township

mont preceded it into the Union, but Ohio was the first state created from the Public Domain, and served as a laboratory in which the government surveyors would put into practice the often nebulous rules a demanding Congress had imposed. Surveying began in 1785 and was accomplished in piecemeal fashion over several decades. Because of the existence of state claims (Virginia and Connecticut), sales to private land companies, and the fact that Indian claims were ceded in variable sized chunks, surveying was done in blocks of land ranging in size from a few square miles up to several hundred square miles.

Altogether, the state was surveyed in nearly 20 districts (Fig. 7.4A), all more or less rectangular except the Virginia Military Reserve where irregular tracts were common, but even here rectilinear tracts were the rule (Fig. 7.4D). The first federal lands to be surveyed were the original Seven Ranges bordering the upper Ohio River. Beginning at a wooden post at the highwater mark on the north bank of the Ohio River where it crossed Pennsylvania's western boundary, a group of surveyors headed by the geographer Thomas Hutchins ran a line westward, marking the actual beginning of federal surveying. This Geographers Line formed the northern boundary of the first tracts surveyed. Seven ranges were laid out during the years 1785–87, and the townships were numbered from the river northward, resulting in a somewhat confusing pattern of numbers (Fig. 7.4C). The 36 sections within each township were numbered beginning in the southeast corner. The pattern established in the Seven Ranges was followed later when the Ohio Company Purchase lands were surveyed, the exception being township subdivision, which was modified to provide a number of 262–acre lots, according to company rules (Fig. 7.4B).

Further deviation from the standard occurred in the U.S. Military Reserve (Fig. 7.4A, number 13) where townships were divided into 25 rather than into 36 sections. All military warrants were issued in multiples of 100-acre units; thus a 16,000-acre unit subdivided much more easily than the standard 23,040-acre township. Additional five-mile-square townships were surveyed in both the Connecticut Western Reserve and the Firelands, the latter being further subdivided into quarter-townships of 4,000 acres each, while townships in

the former were surveyed into rectangular or square lots of various sizes. The remaining Ohio lands were surveyed as they became available through Indian treaties. Each survey had its own peculiarities, especially in the numbering of townships and the subdivision of sections, but standardization slowly evolved and accuracy improved. During this period the practice of numbering townships and ranges from base lines and meridians was established, and sections were numbered beginning in the northeast corner.

The purchase of Louisiana in 1803 added greatly to the Public Domain, but it also brought a new challenge to federal surveyors. Not only were they entrusted with the task of establishing the rectangular system, they were instructed to survey and plot all tracts claimed under colonial regimes: French, Spanish, and English. The most renowned of these was the French long lot, a feature of the *arpent* system (from the French unit of measure), one that granted linear tracts alongside large streams. Louisiana topography was amenable to the practice, for in much of the state the only well-drained land lay adjacent to the streams. In much of Louisiana long lots were granted in tiers 40 or 80 arpents deep, leaving adjacent swampland unclaimed and unsurveyed (Fig. 7.5C).

Despite the fact that much of the land in southern Louisiana had been granted previously, the federal system had considerable impact. First, it provided a comprehensive survey of existing grants. Second, it established a system of township and range lines within which all landholdings were identified, and it surveyed the unclaimed part of the state into the traditional square-mile sections. A third, though little known, feature was that it also borrowed from the French system by surveying in long lots where conditions were favorable (Fig. 7.5A). The resulting system consisted of a grid of six-mile-square townships and ranges superimposed over all previous grants, some containing the usual 36 sections and others containing irregular tracts of British, French, or Spanish origin or a combination of two or more types (Fig. 7.5B).

Georgia was not a part of the Public Domain, but her unique solution to the task of land disposal invites attention. The state, having granted the eastern fourth of the state under

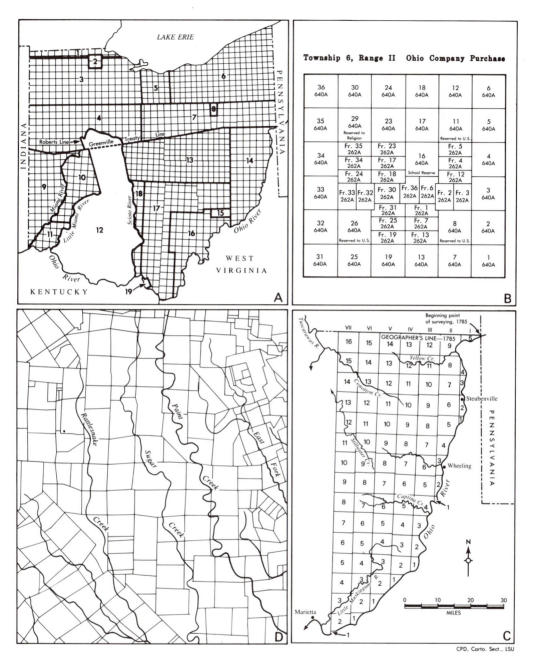

Figure 7.4   Survey Districts of Ohio

A 1. Michigan Meridian Surveys, 2. Twelve Mile Reserve, 3. North and East of First Principal Meridian, 4. South and East of First Principal Meridian, 5. Firelands, 6. Connecticut Western Reserve, 7. Ohio River Base, 8. Muskingum River Base, 9. Miami River Base, 10. Between the Miamis, 11. Symmes Purchase, 12. Virginia Military Reserve, 13. U.S. Military Reserve, 14. Original Seven Ranges, 15. Donation Tract, 16. Ohio Company Purchases, 17. East of Scioto, 18. Scioto River Base, 19. French Grants.

B Township from Ohio Company Purchase.

C   Detail of Original Seven Ranges.

D   Sample of approximately 400 square miles taken from the Virginia Military District.

headright law (either colonial or state) and having endured a number of land scandals, devised a scheme to survey the western three quarters of its area and distribute it equitably among the citizenry. In a total of six lotteries, beginning in 1805 and lasting until 1832, the

state surveyed and granted (with only nominal charges) the western three-fourths of the state. It was a radical system of land disposal, and an equally radical survey system was devised to accomplish its purpose (Fig. 7.6). The newly ceded Indian lands were first organized into

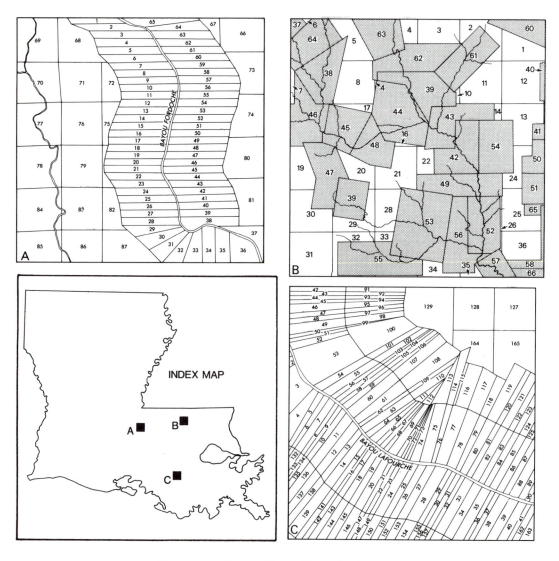

Figure 7.5   Sample Townships in Louisiana

A Combination of American long lot and standard mile-square sections.
B Township in the Florida Parishes showing prior grants (shading) amid land unclaimed
at the time of survey.
C French arpent grants along Bayou Lafourche in two tiers of lots each 40 arpents deep.

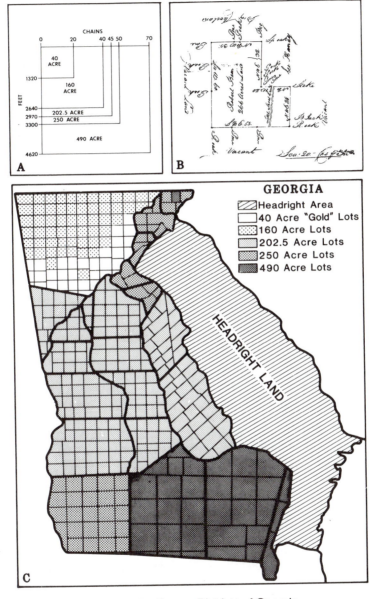

Figure 7.6   Survey Districts of Georgia
A   Lottery lots varied in size.
B   Sample grant in headright area.
C   Lot size varied from 40 to 490 acres.

counties, then surveyed into land districts that, in turn, were subdivided into square lots of varying sizes. Individual lots were numbered and identified by land district and county. Each land lot was plotted on a separate piece of paper and deposited in a drum to be drawn at public lottery and matched with a name drawn from another drum containing the names of eligible registrants. Of special interest is the choice of land lot size, which ranged from 40 to 490 acres. The seemingly odd lot sizes resulted from the creation of square plots whose dimensions are specified in chains. Most Georgia land districts (and lots) are arranged cardinally, the exceptions being in Baldwin and Wilkinson counties where they are laid out from a base line running N45E. No attempt was made to conform to meridians or parallels, thus adding further variety to the evolving republican landscape.

LAND SALES

An essential feature of the federal land system was survey prior to sale; during the early years the former proved easier than the latter. Complicating the issue was the lack of agreement on just how land sales were to be conducted. The financiers' view, most ably presented by Hamilton, saw in western land the means for raising revenues to settle debts, but just how the money would be raised remained unresolved for years. The easiest way was to sell land in large chunks to those with the means to purchase entire townships and let the buyer resell in smaller parcels to prospective settlers. The practice had been in effect during the very early years, for example, in the Ohio Company lands and in that contained in Symmes Purchase also in Ohio. But disappointing results led many to argue that the government should sell directly to individuals, eliminiating the speculators. Land sales in the Seven Ranges also proved disappointing, partly because of continuing Indian presence in the area but also because no one wanted or could afford to buy land in huge tracts. Given the technology of farming of the period, most farms were smaller than 200 acres, thus even a single section (640 acres) was out of the question, let alone the 23,000 acres an entire township contained. Furthermore, the more egalitarian view, as espoused by Jeffer-

son, envisioned a West filled with yeomen farmers of modest means who would provide the republic with the fund of human resources it needed. Vast areas still lay unclaimed, moreover, within several of the original states. Vermont, Maine, and New York competed directly with the West for settlers, and in the South fully three quarters of Georgia lay open, although Indian claims persisted for some years. A few tracts in what later became Kentucky and Tennessee also still beckoned.

Debate over land policy continued throughout the late 18th and into the 19th century. In fact, it became even more heated as new areas were opened up. The purchase of Louisiana in 1803 nearly doubled the nation's land, adding greatly to the reservoir of vacant land. Debate eventually polarized into two factions, those favoring a liberal land policy with low prices, sales in small parcels, and credit, and those who wished for high-priced land that would bring in more money and discourage wholesale migration. Land policy vacillated between the two extremes for a time, but by 1820 liberal land policies prevailed. Potential settlers could buy as little as 80 acres at a minimum of $1.25 per acre, although full payment was required in cash. Prices went lower, and credit became available eventuating in virtually free land with the passage of the Homestead Act in 1862, but decades would pass before that milestone was reached. Land sales increased dramatically in the early 19th century, from less than 100,000 acres in 1800 to nearly 3 million acres in 1819. Total land sales amounted to nearly 20 million acres from the opening of land offices through June of 1820.

INDIAN LAND CESSIONS

Along with its new real estate, the Public Domain, Congress also acquired the sole power to deal with the American Indian. The Indian policy that evolved reflected the accepted custom among European powers of distinguishing between political sovereignty and soil rights, the former representing claims of jurisdiction, while the latter was taken to mean "use of the land," such as tillage. Europeans claiming political sovereignty by right of discovery created colonies with little regard for the wishes or rights of the aborigines. By 1733 the mother country had established (or licensed) colonies all along the eastern seaboard, thus extending British law over a vast domain. But she also recognized the Indian's soil rights, which could not be taken away arbitrarily. Thus, free title to land could be gained only after the Indian title had been extinguished by formal treaty. British policy was adopted with few changes by the United States. The inherent contradiction in declaring sovereignty over a people while still recognizing them as groups of nations with whom treaties were signed would appear obvious, but such was the case. Beginning in 1784 the new nation entered into treaty after treaty with many Indian tribes, the process not ending until nearly a century later (1871) with an act that "no Indian nation or tribe . . . shall be acknowledged or recognized as an independent nation, tribe or power with whom the United States may contract by treaty."

Literally hundreds of treaties were contracted, but for our purposes those that ceded land for white settlement in the Old Northwest and Southwest are at issue here. The process was a long and complex one, involving diplomacy, intrigue, coercion, and outright fraud. It was complicated and compromised by lack of tribal organization and conflicting tribal claims on the part of Indians, as well as by a disastrous inconsistency on the part of the federal government. On the one hand insisting on formal treaty ceremonies with the various tribes while permitting, or at the very least ignoring, white encroachment onto Indian lands, the government gave little indication that it would go very far in honoring its agreements. Exacerbating the difficulties was the instability associated with an expanding frontier and the vagaries of a new and experimental democracy. The result, though seemingly chaotic, was that white settlement progressed steadily at the expense of Indian, until virtually all the land east of the Mississippi had passed into white ownership and the original inhabitants were exterminated, assimilated, or removed to reservations located west of the Mississippi (Fig. 7.7).

The first cessions were made where white pressure for land was most intense: western New York, western Pennsylvania, Ohio, Kentucky, Tennessee, the Carolinas, and Georgia. During the 18th century, treaties with the Six Nations of New York (the Iroquois), with twelve tribes in Ohio and Indiana, and with the Cherokee and Creek tribes in Tennessee and Georgia ceded land adjacent to established areas, thus opening up new areas for settlement. The two most notable agreeements affecting the area north of the Ohio were the Treaty of Fort Stanwix (New York) in 1768 and the Treaty of Greenville (Ohio) in 1795, the former relinquishing Indian claims in western New York and northwestern Pennsylvania, and the latter releasing nearly two-thirds of what later became Ohio, including a part of Indiana. Additional tracts in southern Indiana and Illinois were ceded in 1795. In a 1785 treaty with the Cherokee at Hopewell, tracts in Tennessee and the Carolinas were opened for white settlement, all cessions being adjacent to land already occupied by whites. In Georgia, a huge strip stretching in an arc from the Blue Ridge Mountains of South Carolina to within 30 miles of the coast near Savannah was ceded by the Creeks five years later.

During the first decade of the 19th century, cessions were added that quadrupled the area already ceded (Fig. 7.7). Two tracts in northern Ohio and a third extending into eastern Michigan were ceded by treaty with the Wyandot, Ottawa, Chippewa, Munsee, Delaware, Shawnee, and Potawatomi tribes. Additional tracts in southern Indiana and Illinois were ceded, almost all adjacent to previous cessions as the pressure of increasing white population served both to inflame Indian tempers and to goad government officials into action. Conflicting Indian claims in Wisconsin, Illinois, and Missouri took years to settle, but huge areas were ceded during the years between 1803 and 1808. Farther south, Indian resistance was more organized, although white pressure for action remained intense. The Cherokees ceded large tracts bordering the Nashville Basin and the Tennessee River and a small tract in northern Georgia, while the Creeks gave up the area east of the Ocmulgee River in Georgia. In the Old Southwest, the Choctaws ceded the land from Mobile to the Mississippi in three tracts, the westernmost forming the Natchez District, an early mecca for cotton planters. The following decade (1810–19) saw the elimination of Indian claims to virtually all of Ohio and most of Indiana and Illinois, but large areas of the Old Southwest remained in the hands of the Cherokees, Creeks, Choctaws, and Chickasaws, the last not being relinquished until 1835.

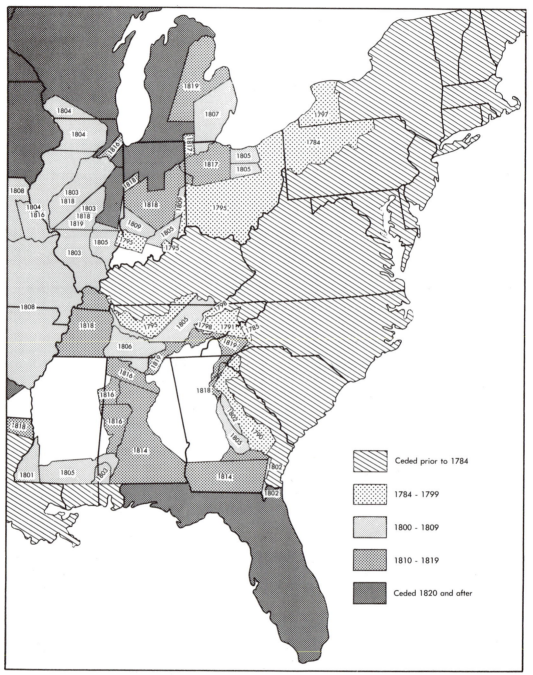

MLE, Carto. Sect., LSU

Figure 7.7   Indian Land Cessions, 1784–1819

The fate of Indians occupying these lands was varied, as were the attitudes toward the so-called "Indian problem." Outright warfare was much less common than is popularly supposed. Most eastern tribes had been in contact with whites for a century or more, and many were actively engaged in agriculture and commerce. Those in the Southwest grew cotton and kept cattle and hogs; some even owned black slaves. Many simply became assimilated in the burgeoning population, while others were moved to reservations. Proposals to relocate the Native Americans to areas set aside only for their use were voiced from time to time. A number of treaties called for the establishment of reservations that were never surveyed; others were abolished before any action to relocate Indians was taken. The reservation movement eventuated in the "permanent Indian Reserve" that originally included virtually all of what later became Kansas and Oklahoma, to which the remnants of a number of tribes would eventually be moved after 1835. The story of Indian removal is a sorry one, indeed. Forced onto smaller and smaller plots of land, they became the object of derision and pity. It was argued at the time that removal to some place distant from white settlements would permit them to recapture their former ways of life and live in peace, but few would make the trip and fewer still would live tranquil lives. But that is part of another story.

A GROWING AND EXPANDING POPULATION

At the close of the Revolution the bulk of America's population lay east of the Appalachians in a broad swath from the Merrimack River in New Hampshire to the Savannah River in Georgia. Population was densest and most concentrated in southern New England and the mid-Atlantic area; south of the Potomac, the settled area widened to include all the Coastal Plains and the Piedmont and extended into Georgia. Massachusetts, Rhode Island, Connecticut, New Jersey, and Delaware may be said to have been settled effectively, but most of New Hampshire, Maine (still a part of Massachusetts), New York, Pennsylvania, Virginia, North Carolina, and Georgia still had sparsely occupied areas. Even Maryland and South Carolina had some western lands yet available for settlement. By the time of the first federal census in 1790, the new nation could boast a population of nearly 4 million, of which slightly over 100,000 lived west of the mountains. In the 30 years following the first census, states were added to the union and population more than doubled, to 9.6 million. More important, a radical shift westward had occurred, with more than 2 million inhabitants, nearly a quarter of the nation's total, being counted west of the Appalachians (Table 7.1).

By 1790 more than 100,000 settlers already occupied Kentucky and Tennessee west of the Appalachians. Major western population clusters were to be found in western Pennsylvania, the Bluegrass Basin of central Kentucky, and along the Cumberland River in central Tennessee. The frontier had expanded northward in New England to include southern Maine and most of central New Hampshire and Vermont. The Watauga–Holston settlements in east Tennessee had grown enough to declare themselves the short-lived independent state of Franklin, challenging the authority of North Carolina and hoping for admission as a new state by a sympathetic Congress.

However impressive the movement across the mountains following the French and Indian War had been, it was but a trickle compared with the flood that followed in the 1790s. The conclusion of Jay's Treaty in 1794 removing British claims from the Old Northwest, the Treaty of San Lorenzo in 1795 that ceded Spanish claim to the Yazoo Strip, and the Treaty of Greenville with the Ohio Indians in the same year cleared the way for massive migrations into the interior of the continent. Interrupted only briefly again during the War of 1812, the tide of people swept over the land until initial occupancy had been completed.

The westward movement was not simply a giant wave of population that surged over the mountains from the East. It changed pace as political, economic, and frontier conditions dictated, sometimes grinding to a halt for a time only to surge again when opportunity beckoned. It was selective in both the routes chosen and the land taken up. The migration was keenly sensitive to topography, perceived land values, land availability, and Indian presence. It was intimately associated with so many variable conditions that the story cannot be told

Table 7.1   Populations of the States, 1790–1820

State	1790	1800	1810	1820
Maine	96,540	151,719	228,705	298,335
New Hampshire	141,885	183,858	214,460	244,161
Vermont	85,425	154,465	217,895	235,981
Massachusetts	387,787	422,845	472,040	523,287
Rhode Island	68,825	69,122	76,931	83,059
Connecticut	237,946	251,002	261,942	275,248
New York	340,120	589,051	959,049	1,372,812
New Jersey	184,139	211,149	245,562	277,575
Pennsylvania	434,373	602,365	810,091	1,049,458
Delaware	59,096	64,273	72,674	72,749
Maryland	319,728	341,548	380,546	407,350
Virginia	691,737	807,554	877,683	938,261
West Virginia[a]	55,873	78,592	105,469	136,808
North Carolina	393,751	478,103	555,500	638,829
South Carolina	249,073	345,591	415,115	502,741
Georgia	82,548	162,686	252,433	340,989
Alabama	—	1,250	9,046	127,901
Mississippi	—	7,600	31,306	75,448
Louisiana	—	—	76,556	153,407
Tennessee	35,691	105,602	261,727	422,823
Kentucky	73,677	220,955	406,511	564,317
Ohio	—	45,365	230,760	581,434
Indiana	—	5,641	24,520	147,178
Illinois	—	—	12,282	55,211
Total	3,938,214	5,300,336	7,198,803	9,525,362

[a]West Virginia did not become a state until 1863; data shown are for that part of Virginia that later became West Virginia.

here in detail. The burgeoning population needed land; but before land was sold it had to be surveyed, and before survey it had to be cleared of Indian title. In many cases the temporal sequence was not followed so neatly; some settlers simply squatted wherever they wished, expecting to secure title later. Many pioneers were well ahead of government officials, creating unrest among the Indians and thereby hastening the process of Indian removal.

This great human tide was choosy simply because it had a good idea of what it wanted and where to find it. The previous late-colonial generation had probed the frontier's edge along its entire length, learning about topography, vegetation, soils, and drainage. Unlike the hordes of immigrants who moved directly from European cities to the treeless prairies some 70 years later, typical settlers of the period between 1790 and 1820 were either American-born or had spent considerable time along the east coast before setting out. They knew the value of oak and maple forests as soil indicators; they also knew where water and salt could be found. They sought out mill and ford sites quite early, and kept close to navigable lakes and streams, expecting to "float" their products to market. Furthermore, they established towns, churches, schools, roads, stores, even factories as soon as was humanly possible, for they cherished no ideals about an idyllic refuge in the wilderness. They moved west to build new homes, but such homes were to be part of civilized communities in which commerce and industry would be nurtured alongside the arts. This tide was made up from a variety of parent ethnic and national groups, such as the so-called Scotch-Irish, English, Irish, French, German, and the Dutch, but their backgrounds were far less distinct than those of the previous generation because they had become Americans. To be sure, one encountered alien tongues and dialects in the wilderness, but the transformaton was underway, and a new nation was being built.

Given such expertise and goals, we should not be surprised at the changing distribution of population (Fig. 7.8). Settlers poured out of New England and New York along the Mohawk Valley, detouring into favored sites until Lake Erie was reached. The stream then moved along the lakeshore on to the western reserve of Ohio where 3 million acres of vacant land lay waiting. Farther south the route led westward from Ft. Pitt (Pittsburgh). Two routes were open: one led overland directly westward into the Seven Ranges; the other simply used the Ohio River as a highway. By 1800 much of the land bordering the river had been settled, but land could be found only a short distance inland. The Ohio Company Lands (Fig. 7.4) lay waiting, as did those of other surveyed tracts. Both the Virginia and the U.S. Military Reserve had land aplenty. Military warrants were sold openly, and thus both areas were settled by veterans and non-veterans. By 1800 real estate activity was feverish over eastern Ohio, and within two decades much of the land was sold, although intensified settlement and cultivation came more slowly.

South of the Ohio, speculative activity was much less notable. Few large tracts were opened for sale, so settlement was on a smaller scale. Furthermore, the topography of Kentucky and western Virginia discouraged large-sized contiguous farms, restricting settlement to favorable spots, usually the flat valley bottoms adjacent to streams. Uplands were settled only when valley land was taken; even then slope and soil type were important, and most settlers wisely avoided very steep slopes and sandy soils. By 1820, white settlement blanketed almost all of Kentucky and Ohio and large parts of Indiana and Illinois. Tennessee was effectively occupied, except for the lands lying between the Tennessee and Mississippi rivers, which was held by the Chickasaws until 1818.

Migration into the Gulf States was just as dramatic if less continuous as that in the Old Northwest. Emanating from four major sources, population swept through the area. The oldest of these nodes were lower Louisiana (established in 1699) and eastern Georgia (es-

tablished in 1733). By the time of the Creek treaty of 1790, settlers were pouring into Georgia from Virginia and the Carolinas. Subsequent land cessions encouraged movement farther west, but after Jackson's defeat of the Indians in 1814, many "leap-frogged" into Alabama. Louisianians were less aggressive than Georgians, but a gradual movement upriver from New Orleans had taken the best drained levee lands, creating a surplus population ready to take up tracts in the Natchez District when it was opened in the first two decades of the 19th century.

The two remaining sources of settlers were at the opposite poles of Alabama. The east Tennessee settlements had expanded downriver into Alabama, while the somewhat older settlement at Mobile moved north. Thus Alabama was opened by a pincer movement from both north and south (Fig. 7.8). By 1820 population in Alabama, Mississippi, and Louisiana had grown to almost 360,000 settlers, enough for all three areas to be admitted as states (Fig. 7.9). The rapid growth was similar to that of the Old Northwest during the same period, although the total number of settlers north of the Ohio River by 1820 totaled more than 780,000 settlers, indicating distinctly different rates of frontier expansion in the new nation's northern and southern thrusts prior to the 1830s.

THE FRONTIER ECONOMY

The westward flood of population following the Revolution resulted from a variety of factors and conditions that were common to most North American frontiers. Differential social and political conditions, land prices, and taxes served to entice or drive people westward. Such motivations were common to all parts of the continent, and thus the westward movement may be seen as a giant wave with smaller ripples occurring where special conditions prevailed. But the movement was much more than a mass migration of people to new lands; it was a transfer of the attitudes, institutions, and occupations that had developed along the eastern seaboard during nearly two centuries of occupation. It also carried along a variety of plants, animals, and material objects with which settlers would transform the western

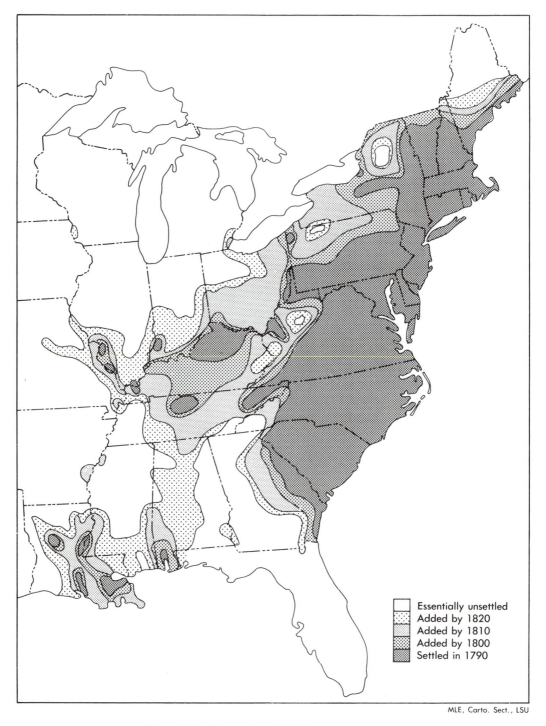

Figure 7.8   Expansion of Settlement, 1790–1820

Figure 7.9   The Creation of New States, 1791–1848 (excluding California)

landscape. For the most part, the new settlers represented little more than an expansion of the culture and societies that had developed in the East. This was particularly true in the Old Northwest, where pioneers were engaged in the same kind of agriculture their fathers had developed in the New England and Mid-Atlantic states. Conditions in the Gulf South were somewhat different because, of the region's three cash crops, rice, cotton, and sugarcane, the latter two were relatively new.

Overwhelmingly European in origin but tempered by the American experience, the American Culture (if that be the correct phrase) had itself matured to a state in which broader regional differences were discernible, and nowhere were they greater than in the patterns of rural economy. Even by 1790 the South had developed a strong dependence on certain crops, notably tobacco, rice, indigo, and cotton, while farther north a more diversified agriculture based on grains and livestock was the rule. Even this distinction is oversimplified, because most agriculturalists achieved a high level of subsistence by keeping a number of livestock and growing a variety of food crops. It is tempting to refer to the southern specialty crops as "cash" crops, but such a characterization obscures the fact that many crops and animals served as "cash" items throughout the new nation. Thus wheat was as much of a cash crop in parts of New York and Ohio as tobacco was a cash crop in Virginia and Kentucky. As might be expected, such regional diversity was reflected later in the developing areas of the West, for migration was decidedly zonal. The upper Midwest was settled largely by New Englanders and upstate New Yorkers; the Gulf Plains by Georgians, Virginians, and Carolinians; and the central Midwest became the domain of migrants from the Mid-Atlantic states. The Ohio Valley, including all of Kentucky, much of Tennessee, and southern Ohio and Indiana, received a variety of settlers, principally from Virginia but many also from Maryland, Pennsylvania, and North Carolina. Obviously, such broad generalizations are not without exceptions, but they serve to delineate the regional patterns of rural economy and culture established west of the Appalachian divide.

The very earliest agriculture focused on survival. Food for family and stock had highest priority, but subsistence farming soon developed a commercial element. Corn, wheat, and livestock were sold to incoming settlers, and within a few years both eastern and foreign markets were eyed. Transportation problems in such an isolated area seemed insurmountable at first, but enterprising westerners found ways of marketing goods that were unthinkable a generation earlier. High-value goods could be hauled out by wagon, but the relatively bulky goods, such as corn, cotton, meat, and wheat, were floated downriver to New Orleans. Livestock, particularly cattle but also horses, mules, and hogs, were driven overland, a practice that continued for half a century or more. Eventually, the Great Lakes–Erie Canal waterway greatly eased the difficulties for the Old Northwest, but throughout the antebellum period the relative isolation of western farmers remained a nagging problem.

In the South many conditions were similar, but the production system and crop emphasis were different. Virginia and North Carolina had long enjoyed prosperity associated with the world market for tobacco, but farther south the emphasis had been on indigo, rice, and was now turning to cotton. Cotton, grown in small quantities along the South Carolina–Georgia coast, came to be a preferred raw material for light textiles. This sea-island variety commanded premium prices but was limited to favored coastal locations. A hardier variety, upland or green-seeded cotton, was more widely grown but production was hampered by the difficulty of separating lint from seed, a problem solved by the development of the mechanical cotton gin in the early 1790s. Stimulated by this innovation and by the seemingly limitless world market for the new fiber (especially in industrial Britain), cotton producers swept across the Gulf South. Southern producers were in a somewhat better position than those in the Old Northwest because of the orientation of major rivers. Both Mobile and New Orleans served huge hinterlands, so that cotton moved easily into the ocean trade, where the major disadvantage was the long voyage necessary to reach both eastern American and European ports. It is a remarkable testimony to the transportation technology of the time that cotton growers in northern Alabama and the Nashville Basin sent their goods on a journey of more than 1,500 miles to New Orleans, where it then had to travel some 5,000 miles more to reach Liverpool. It is small wonder that eastern entrepreneurs dreamed of a direct route from the eastern cities into the interior.

Although it would be misleading to talk of agricultural specialty regions before 1820, we can identify incipient nodes of production in the West. Cotton was the raison d'être of the western South with three areas showing early productions: the Tennessee Valley of Alabama and adjacent Nashville Basin, central Alabama, and the lower Mississipi valley in Louisiana and southwestern Mississippi. Development of the process of sugar granulation in Louisiana in the 1790s encouraged its production along major waterways adjacent to New Orleans. Both sugar and cotton production expanded rapidly, supplementing the existing culture of indigo and livestock in Louisiana, although sugarcane remained largely limited to the area south of the 31st parallel because of its need for a long growing season of more than 220 days. Farther north in Tennessee and Kentucky, agricultural practices mirrored those of Virginia and North Carolina, a diversified production of livestock and grains, supplemented by the culture of tobacco and hemp in favored locations. Both the Nashville and Bluegrass basins offered the best conditions, and both became centers of population and economic activity. Both wheat and corn were widely grown, the latter providing feed for livestock and the raw material for whiskey.

The Old Northwest developed along several lines. The southern part concentrated on the production of corn and hogs, and pork-packing became a major industry. Dairying became a notable feature of the Western Reserve in northeastern Ohio. Corn and wheat were widely grown, the former being a staple for both man and beast, while the latter found its way to markets in Canada and New Orleans. Livestock were kept by virtuallly all farmers, reflecting the practices of those prevalent a generation earlier in New England and the Mid-Atlantic states. Mule breeding emerged in Ohio in response to the demand for draft stock, and sheep were quite numerous in the eastern hill country. By the end of the second decade of the 19th century the major outlines of the western economy had already developed. No one could talk seriously about a Cotton Belt or a Corn Belt at that time, but the ingredients necessary for their development were in place. In the following decades farm production increased dramatically as new outlets and markets developed, uniting the three great resource regions—Northeast, Middle West, and South—into a national system.

ADDITIONAL READING

Books

Bartlett, R.A. *The New Country: A Social History of the American Frontier, 1776–1890*. New York: Oxford University Press, 1974.

Bidwell, P.W., and Falconer, J.I. *History of Agriculture in the Northern United States, 1620–1860*. Washington D.C.: Carnegie Institution, 1925; New York: Peter Smith, 1941.

Cappon, L.J.; Petchenik, B.B.; and Long, J.H., eds. *Atlas of Early American History: The Revolutionary Era, 1760–1790*. Princeton: Princeton University Press, 1976.

Gray, L.C. *History of Agriculture in the Southern United States to 1860*. 2 vols. Washington D.C.: Carnegie Institution, 1932; New York: Peter Smith, 1958.

Hibbard, B.H. *A History of the Public Land Policies*. New York: Macmillan, 1924; Madison: University of Wisconsin Press, 1965.

Kelsey, D.P., ed. *Farming in the New Nation: Interpreting American Agriculture 1790–1840*. Washington D.C.: Agricultural History Society, 1972.

Pattison, W.D. *Beginnings of the American Rectangular Land Survey System, 1784–1800*. Chicago: University of Chicago Department of Geography, 1957.

Rohrbough, M.J. *The Trans-Appalachian Frontier: People, Societies, and Institutions, 1775–1850*. New York: Oxford University Press, 1978.

Royce, C.C. *Indian Land Cessions in the United States*. Washington: Government Printing Office, 1900.

Schwartz, S.I., and Ehrenberg, R.H. *The Mapping of America*. New York: H.M. Abrams, 1980.

White, C.A. *A History of the Rectangular Survey System*. Washington: Government Printing Office, [1983].

Yazawa, M. *From Colonies to Commonwealth: Familial Ideology and the Beginnings of the American People*. Baltimore: Johns Hopkins University Press, 1985.

8

Regional Economic Development West of the Appalachians, 1815–1860

CARVILLE EARLE
Miami University of Ohio

Few countries have grown so fast on so many fronts in so short a time as the United States between the American Revolution and the Civil War. In just eight decades, Americans expanded their territory threefold, their population fifteenfold, their economy twentyfold, and their urban population thirtyfold. They also prospered. Americans in 1860 had twice as much income per capita as they did in 1780; their economy in 1860 ranked third in riches after Britain and France. The American achievements are all the more remarkable when compared with the rest of the world outside of Europe. In that world accustomed at best to steady-state economies or at worst to a decay of living standards, the United States counterpoised the example of growth, prosperity, and progress.

The exceptional success of the American economy in the first half of the 19th century has attracted a wide range of commentary and interpretation. Attention has centered on two issues: economic growth, or the increase in income per capita, and economic development, or the nature of investments in transportation, communications, urbanization, and manufacturing that transform agricultural economies to higher levels of productivity. In the case of the United States, the geographical dimensions and the diversity of the nation almost of necessity resulted in varying regional patterns of growth and development. During the period under study, a predominantly commercial, agrarian nation divided into a mosaic of at least three distinctive economic regions. The northeastern states experienced an increase in manufacturing and urban population. The South, including the older states of the Old Southwest, persisted on an agrarian track with special emphasis on cotton and slavery. In the West, including the Ohio basin and the Great Lakes vicinity, developments tended toward diversified grains and livestock, usually produced by family farms or free labor and marketed through an elaborate urban transport system.

This chapter focuses on the role of trans-Appalachian agriculture in American economic growth and development. The principal proposition put forth is that expansion into this vast region, extending from the Great Lakes to the Gulf of Mexico and from the Appalachians to the 100th meridian, increased both aggregate and per capita output of the national economy. Productivity changes arose from a variety of sources, the most significant of which was the evolution of three specialized agricultural regions, the Cotton, Corn, and Wheat belts. These regional staples, with their distinctive production and marketing functions, shaped equally distinctive trajectories in the development of systems of labor, rural and urban settlement, and commodity marketing.

AMERICAN ECONOMIC GROWTH AND DEVELOPMENT

The spectacular achievements of the American economy between 1815 and 1860 have occasioned a rich literature of interpretation and theory. At least three separate but overlapping perspectives may be identified. The first, and the best known, theory regards the investment in social overhead capital and the emergence of a leading sector of growth (railroads) as essential preconditions for economic "take-off" and sustained growth. The second thesis, which is related to the first though differing in its attentiveness to space, is Douglass North's regional export base model. North's model envisions regional specialization and trade interdependence as the causes of national economic growth. The third thesis shares North's emphasis on regions and agricultural exports while maintaining that growth was the consequence of intraregional changes in agricultural productivity and the development ramifications of staple crops. Our review examines these theories and pertinent criticism.

The United States in 1800, according to Walt Rostow, was a low-growth economy poised for rapid economic growth. The transition required a substantial investment in social overhead capital. America channeled these investments into transportation infrastructure: first into roads, river navigation, and canals, and later into the extension of the railroad. These inventions, innovations, and improvisations all operated to lower transport costs and to facilitate commerce and exchange within the nation. The noted historian George Rogers Taylor earlier made the same point in labeling these years as ones of "transportation revolution." Although Rostow's critics have discounted the role of railroads in American economic development, they must concede the more significant point of the role of transportation improvements in the expansion of the American market.

A preoccupation with aggregate economic performance, however, overlooks regional variations and interdependencies in the American space economy. American economic growth may be regarded as a spatial process involving regional economic specialization and interregional trade. The United States after 1815 divided into three regions—the industrial Northeast, the cotton South, and the diversified grain and livestock Middle West—all linked by interregional trade flows. The motor of economic growth, according to North, was the cotton South. Cotton export earnings, in his view, created a large southern market for midwestern provisions and northeastern manufactured goods. Southern demand thus triggered economic growth and development in other parts of the nation.

This tidy spatial model of economic growth touched off a volley of empirical criticism. The theorized trade flows, however plausible according to neoclassical economic theory, simply did not exist. With respect to the West–South trade, several studies demonstrated only a modest flow of provisions to southern markets. Complementary studies of plantations revealed that most of them produced sufficient corn and pork for their own needs. As for the North–South trade in manufactures, recent work has indicated an equally limited ex-

change. The one interregional trade link of economic significance seems to have been the commodity flows between Northeast and Middle West.

The breakdown of North's model poses some vexing questions. Why did Americans defy economic theory that suggests the profitability of regional specialization and trade? Why did southern cotton planters raise corn and pork at a time when cotton specialization ensured greater profits? That strategic decision eliminated regional complimentarity and precluded large-scale trading for provisions with the Middle West. Similarly, if southern planters spent modestly on midwestern provisions and on northeastern manufactures, then on what indeed did they spend their money?

The answers to these questions have been slow in coming, yet we may report on one recent interpretation emphasizing growth as an intraregional process. Diane Lindstrom, in her study of the Philadelphia region, views growth as taking place within relatively autonomous regions. The engine for economic development, in her view, consists of the growth of population and internal markets. As aggregate consumer demand increases within the region, entrepreneurs in the urban center expand their scale of operations, and invest in manufactures that displace the importation of foreign goods. Growth becomes a function of the size of the market, division of labor, and sectoral shift to manufacturing. This neoclassical interpretation of economic growth, however, is constrained in its generality. All of the United States was not Philadelphia, and one is left to ponder why New York City developed in quite different ways; or why rural commercialism prevailed in the cotton South; or why the West tended to reenact after 1840 the Philadelphia experience.

One of the difficulties with these theories of regional economic growth is their neglect of agricultural practice. In a nation in which the majority of the population practiced farming or planting and in which agriculture as late as 1860 contributed perhaps 60 percent of commodity output, its economic role is of necessity critical. More specifically, Robert Gallman has demonstrated substantial productivity gains in American agriculture beginning in the 1820s—a decade in which the Erie Canal commenced operation and settlement poured into the trans-Appalachian country. On the eve of the Civil

War, this territory produced three-quarters of the American cotton crop, three-fifths of its corn, and nearly half its wheat. Although the literature on agricultural productivity gains is diffuse, sufficient evidence suggests their association with the emergence of the cotton-, corn-, and wheat-producing regions west of the Appalachians. In the case of wheat, the introduction of the reaper in the 1850s increased acreage and output per worker. Similarly, the use of riding cultivators sped the process of corn tillage and permitted planting more acres per worker. In cotton and corn cultivation, the shift westward into relatively drier regions of the Mississippi valley reduced the extent of grass invasion of the cotton fields, thereby permitting an expansion in the acres tilled per worker. In each of these regions, changes in environment and technique increased agricultural output per worker by 25 percent or more.

In addition to its contribution to American economic growth, midwestern agriculture significantly shaped the patterns of regional economic development. Elaborating on the staple theory of development, articulated especially by Robert Baldwin, Ronald Hoffman and Carville Earle have identified distinctive production and marketing functions for regional agricultural stages. The former affect rural labor, settlement patterns, and regional urban wage rates; the latter, transport development and urbanization. The key staple production function is the seasonality of labor demand. Broadcast (seeds scattered by hand) cereal grains require few days of labor, while at the opposite extreme planted crops require many days (particularly in the task of tillage). Wheat farmers consequently hired day laborers for the short harvest in early summer, while cotton planters wanted slaves for the long periods of planting, tillage, and picking. Rural settlement reflected these divergent demands for labor. Northern farmers resided on family farms and drew on rural laborers, and cotton planters resided on slave-labor plantations.

Staple seasonality also determined the level of regional urban wage rates. In farming regions, rural laborers experienced long periods of unemployment and small annual earnings; hence a relatively low urban wage offer induced them to migrate to city jobs. Conversely, in the cotton South where rural whites labored much of the year as small planters or overseers, rural earnings were higher, as was the urban wage required to lure them to the city. Contemporary estimates from the 1850s suggest that unskilled urban wages in the Cotton Belt doubled those of the upper Middle West. Accordingly, midwestern urban entrepreneurs could hire two workers for every one hired by their southern counterparts. The seasonality of broadcast cereal farming created a wage structure and a pool of cheap labor that facilitated urban growth and the expansion of manufactures.

Regional urban wage rates, derived under different staple regimes, help to account for the remarkable contrast in city size in the Middle West and South, but the location and growth of cities also reflect differences in the marketing functions of staples. Perishable, high-weight, and high-bulk commodities such as wheat, corn, and livestock imposed considerably higher marketing margins than cotton or tobacco. Illinois corn shipped to New York City in the 1850s carried a 50 percent margin for middlemen in the urban transport system. By contrast, cotton customarily had margins of 7 to 10 percent. Although middlemen earnings were small, rarely accounting for more than a fifth of the economic base of northern or southern cities, they constituted the foundation for the spatial structure of regional development. Transport routes and urban centers, aligned with respect to staple flows from farm to market, established the spatial sectors and nodes wherein urban and manufacturing growth might agglomerate.

These three theoretical perspectives on the "take-off" of the American economy—transportation, regional economies, and agriculture—provide the structural framework for interpreting the trans-Appalachian region from 1815 to 1860. The geographical processes that unfolded there played a strategic role in the exceptional success of the early American economy.

THE POLITICAL-ECONOMIC CONTEXT FOR AMERICAN "TAKE-OFF"

In 1815, the Atlantic world was at peace and would remain so, more or less, for several generations. In the afterglow of Napoleon's defeat, European statesmen boasted of effecting a balance of international power and a durable peace. Americans, meanwhile, were relieved that the war-weary British were satisfied to conclude the War of 1812 in a draw. With peace in sight, European and American traders and manufacturers forecast halcyon days. They anticipated a resumption of international trade (made secure by the British Navy), an expansion of domestic investment, and general prosperity.

Americans adapted swiftly to the new political-economic environment. Despite their relative prosperity as neutral traders during the Napoleonic Wars, Americans welcomed peace and the new era of free trade trumpeted by European political economists. Indeed, the philosophy of a liberal, laissez-faire economy was one of the central premises of the American federal Constitution written a quarter of a century earlier. With peace at hand, many Americans joined the classical European economists in the belief that the impersonal market would operate at maximum efficiency and engender limitless economic growth and development. Americans laid the basis for a transportation revolution in this instant of renewed economic confidence.

THE TRANSPORTATION REVOLUTION AND TRANS-APPALACHIAN AGRICULTURAL EXPANSION

The United States began its "take-off" into economic growth in this buoyant atmosphere of peace and anticipated prosperity. Transport improvements led the way. Two years after the Napoleonic Wars, the state of New York authorized funds for the construction of the Erie Canal, which would link midwestern grain farmers with New York City and European markets. At the same time, Mississippi River entrepreneurs proclaimed their shallow-draft steamboat a success when the *Washington* made the trip from New Orleans to Lousiville in 25 days. Both events signaled confidence in the international economy and in the potential of the trans-Appalachian region. But an effective union between them required a solution to the high costs of inland transportation. It was imperative that American freight rates decline from the prohibitive levels of wagon transport.

Freight charges by wagon stood in excess of 15 cents per ton-mile on even the best roads. Farmers rarely shipped agricultural goods more than 100 miles. For farmers living in the vicinity of Pittsburgh, the costs of transporting crops overland often exceeded the price at Philadelphia markets.

Navigable rivers and flatboats offered a far cheaper mode of transport for midwestern farmers. Downriver flatboat rates were less than 2 cents a ton-mile as early as 1800 and, at these rates, farmers in Pittsburgh sometimes shipped goods over 1,700 miles via the Ohio and Mississippi rivers to New Orleans and several thousand miles by ship to Philadelphia (which by land was 300 miles distant). The drawback of the flatboat was that it could not operate economically upstream. To solve this problem river people began experimenting with the steamboat. They pronounced their experiments a success in 1817, and upstream freight rates fell sharply in the next decade (Fig. 8.1).

But neither the steamboat nor the flatboat served the entire region. Canal proponents offered wider accessibility to regions distant from navigable waterways. Two types of canal systems served the trans-Appalachian country. The Erie Canal, opened in 1825, carried interregional trade between the Great Lakes periphery and eastern markets; numerous other Ohio canals constructed during the late 1820s and early 1830s served as intraregional feeder routes into the Great Lakes and on to the Erie system. Ohio ranked second in canal mileage after New York in 1830, and had surpassed the Empire State a decade later. As construction proceeded, canal freight rates fell quickly, reaching less than a cent per ton-mile by the early 1840s—nearly two decades after that rate had become commonplace on the western rivers (Fig. 8.1).

The trans-Appalachian country had gained two outlets for its products by the early 1840s. The northern third of the region shipped cheaply via intraregional canals to the lakes and then to the Erie Canal, and the southern two-thirds shipped via flatboat and steamboat down the Mississipppi trunkline to New Orleans. A third outlet, however, was in the offing. The Baltimore and Ohio Railroad introduced the first steam locomotive railroad to the country in 1828. Although the potential of rail-

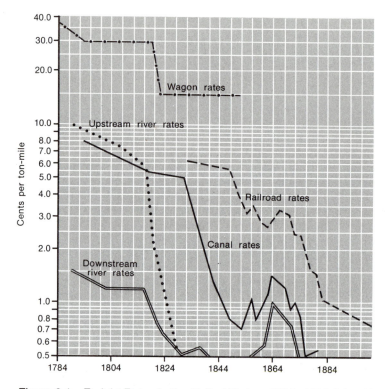

Figure 8.1   Freight Rates in the United States, 1784–1900 (after North)

roads was widely recognized, their diffusion proceeded slowly, perhaps because of the heavy investments required. Investments in rail and in canals stood at roughly the same level until the mid-1840s—in 1840 nearly $15 million was invested in canals and $14 million in railroads. The bulk of rail investment before 1840 occurred in the northeastern states but, as freight rates fell and the British opened their grain market to foreign producers, investment shifted westward. The Middle West accounted for a third of U.S. rail investment in 1851 and, two years later, more than a half. At that date, midwestern railroad investment totaled nearly $50 million, while the national investment in canal construction stood at about $4 million, annually.

By the mid-1850s all this investment in railroads had established an elaborate intraregional rail net in the Middle West as well as a few direct trunkline routes to eastern markets. The intraregional rail net served as an adjunct to interregional routes such as the Lake Erie system, the southern river route, and the direct rail lines to New York City, Philadelphia, and Baltimore. The principal entrepôt cities of the Middle West are easily identifiable by counting the number of rail routes radiating from them. On the northern perimeter, Cleveland, Toledo, Detroit, Chicago, and Milwaukee were rail hubs for the flow of agricultural goods to the lakes or along interregional routes. On the southern and western perimeter, the railroad centers of Cincinnati and St. Louis gathered the shipments of interior produce for dispatch to New Orleans (in the case of Cincinnati after 1857 goods were shipped up the Ohio to Pittsburgh or Wheeling and then east by rail). To these entrepôts must be added the interior rail hubs of Indianapolis and Dayton, which served a special function in the emergent Corn Belt (Fig. 8.2).

The trans-Appalachian country north of the Ohio River was well served by river, canal, lake, and rail carriers. The region by 1860 contained a third of the nation's rail mileage, and the vast majority of farmers had accessibility to distant markets. Few of them lived more than 20 road miles from relatively cheap transportation routes.

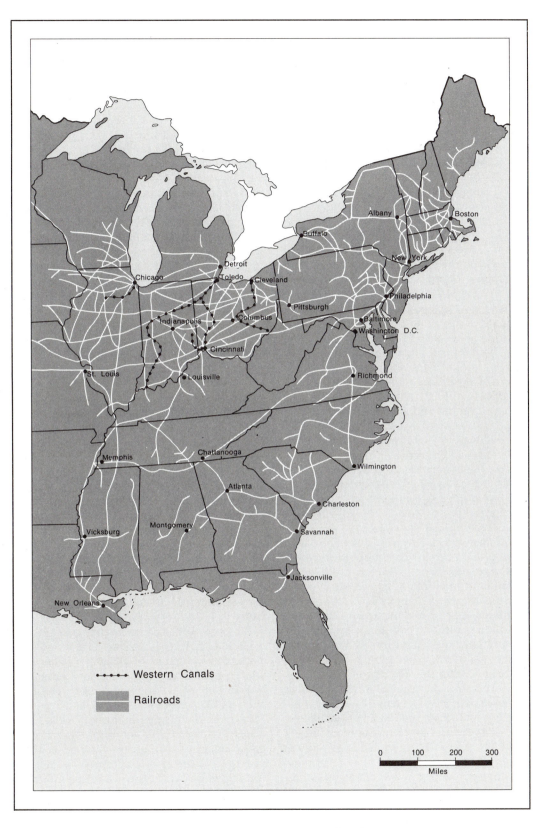

Figure 8.2   Railroads and Western Canals, 1860

South of the Ohio River, market accessibility was not as widespread as in the Middle West. The combination of river navigation and rail connectors, however, effectively served the Old Southwest. Rail mileage in the region between 1850 and 1860 increased from 400 to 4,000 miles. Although a few of these railroads, such as the Mobile and Ohio, the New Orleans, Great Northern, and Jackson; and the Mississippi Central, competed directly with river routes, the vast majority of lines connected interior planters to river ports. The principal cities lay along the trunkline rivers (New Orleans and Memphis on the Mississippi River, Louisville on the Ohio River, and Mobile and Montgomery on the Alabama River) or on tributary rivers (Nashville on the Cumberland, Chattanooga on the Tennessee). Despite the plenitude of rivers and a modest rail network, inaccessibility was a problem in large sections of the trans-Appalachian south. Before 1860 a journey of 20 miles and more separated planters and farmers from rail or river transport in eastern Kentucky, east-central Tennessee, north-central and southeastern Alabama, southern Mississippi, southwestern Louisiana, and northwestern Arkansas (Fig. 8.3). The far greater accessibility offered by midwestern rails reduced these isolated areas by 1860 to tiny islands located usually on the margins of the Corn Belt and the Wheat Belt.

Accessibility to low-cost transportation spurred commercial agriculture in the trans-Appalachian west. Even relatively isolated stretches of the South successfully participated in the market by producing corn and hogs for plantations in the Cotton Belt. Regional population growth reflected the impacts of the transportation revolution and the expansion of commercial agriculture. The trans-Appalachian area accounted for just one-seventh of national population in 1810 but more than two-fifths of it in 1860. During the first phase of the transport revolution, population growth centered on the Mississippi valley states. Nearly half the region's people lived in Kentucky and Tennessee in 1820. Two decades later the spatial effects of the Erie Canal–lakes feeder canal system shifted growth northward. Ohio's population soon equaled the population of Kentucky and Tennessee; by 1860, following the spread of the intraregional rail net over the Middle West, the region contained the three most populous

states in the trans-Appalachian country and more than 60 percent of its total population. Even more impressive was the expansion of improved agricultural acreage in the trans-Appalachian area. Whereas midwestern population between 1810 and 1860 grew thirteenfold (from 1 million to 13 million), the quantity of improved acreage increased eighteenfold (from 4.4 million to 80.6 million acres; Fig. 8.4). Improved acreage per capita doubled during the course of this period, with the most sizable gain occurring between 1810 and 1820—the timing of which tends to confirm the significance of the initial stage of the transport revolution. The revolution's second (canals) and third (railroads) stages spread the benefits of low-cost transport and the improvements in agricultural land.

As the transport revolution cascaded over the Appalachians, American agriculture experienced a dramatic spatial reorganization. This new agricultural heartland contained by 1860 just two-fifths of the American population, yet produced three-fourths of the nation's cotton, three-fifths of its corn, half of its wheat, and a large share of whiskey, hemp, tobacco, sugar, livestock, and livestock products. Of all these western products, cotton was king. New Orleans received by river almost two-fifths of all American cotton as early as 1825; a decade later, that city and Mobile accounted for half of all cotton receipts; and by 1860 they, together with the youthful Texas ports, received three-fourths of the South's entire crop. No other American commodity export compared with cotton. The fiber contributed 39 percent of the value of American exports from 1816 to 1820, 63 percent from 1836 to 1840, and thereafter about half.

The trans-Appalachian country also aggrandized the production of cereal grains and livestock, although more slowly than was the case with cotton. Midwestern farmers produced just 15 percent of national wheat output in 1820, but 31 percent in 1840 and 46 percent by 1860. Even more significant, the Middle West dispatched ever larger shares of regional output to domestic and foreign markets. In 1820, perhaps no more than 12 percent of its crop left the region (almost exclusively downriver to New Orleans). Two decades later, about 27 percent departed (300,000 barrels of flour to New Orleans and 5 million bushels of wheat

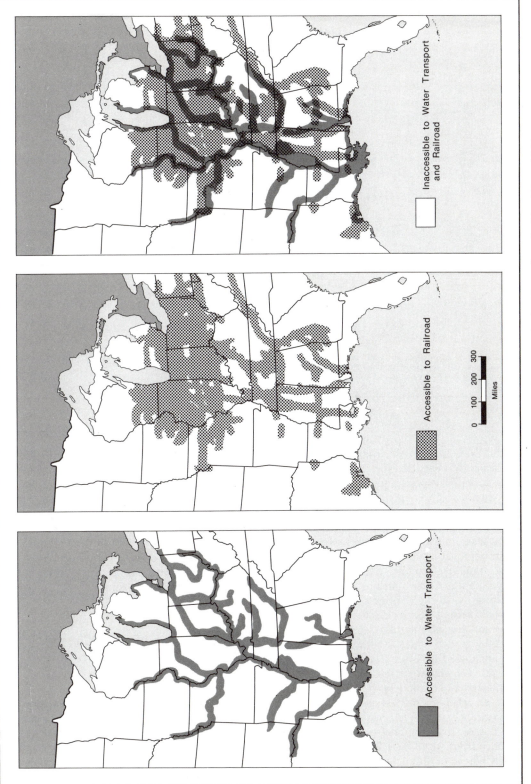

Figure 8.3   Accessibility to Railroads and Water Transport in the Trans-Appalachian West, 1860

Accessible to Water Transport

Accessible to Railroad

0   100   200   300
Miles

Inaccessible to Water Transport
and Railroad

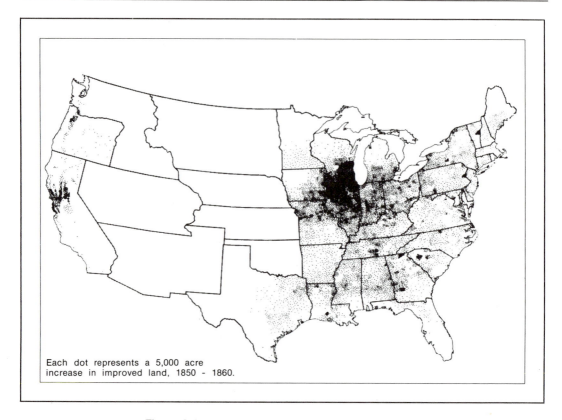

Figure 8.4   Increases in Improved Land, 1850–1860

via the Erie Canal). After the British repealed their Corn (Wheat) Laws in 1846, regional exports rose in response to higher prices. By 1860, regional shipments amounted to 56 million bushels or 70 percent of total midwestern wheat production. Like cotton planters to their south, western wheat farmers were closely tied to extraregional markets by 1860.

The trans-Appalachian west also engrossed the production of corn and its derivative commodities: livestock, pork and beef, and whiskey. Less than a quarter-century after the Napoleonic Wars, the middle section of the area (the Ohio valley states together with Tennessee, Iowa, and Missouri) produced nearly 60 percent of national corn output. Unlike the commercial orientation of cotton and wheat, however, relatively modest amounts of corn (or corn equivalents in livestock, meat, and whiskey) entered into regional exports. Of a total region output in 1839 of 188 million bushels (when wheat output totaled 26 million bushels), less than 3 percent of the corn crop left the

region. Trans-Appalachian farmers in 1857 exported almost 9 percent of their total corn production of 492 million bushels. Corn exports from the seven-state middle section had risen from 3 percent to almost 9 percent; meanwhile the Middle West dispatched 70 percent of its wheat, and the cotton South shipped out more than 90 percent of its cotton. Corn and livestock remained in the Middle West for purposes of household consumption or for intraregional markets.

PATTERNS OF AGRICULTURAL COMMERCE IN THE TRANS-APPALACHIAN COUNTRY

The extension of commercial agriculture progressed rapidly after 1815. Cotton planters relied on distant markets as early as 1820; the same may be said for midwestern wheat farmers by the 1850s. Corn and livestock farmers, however, had just begun the transformation when the Civil War erupted. Their thorough-going commitment to the market awaited postwar improvements in refrigerated transport and institutional changes in the regulation of the meatpacking industry. Nonetheless, an elaborate, multimodal transportation system provided most farmers and planters with access to interregional and international markets.

Three gateways connected the Middle West with external markets. These were, in chronological order, the southern river routes, the northern Erie Canal system (later complemented by rail), and the eastern rail lines of the Pennsylvania and the Baltimore and Ohio railroads. Of the three routes, the southern dominated western trade until the mid-1830s, when the effects of the Erie Canal–lakes–Ohio feeder canal system began making inroads. By 1850, the northern route had captured half the shipments from the west, while the southern river route retained just 45 percent. The rapid expansion of commerce via the Erie Canal reflected its capture of the grain trade in the upper Middle West (the periphery of the Great Lakes). The southern route, which had taken virtually all midwestern trade to 1830, took just 62 percent in 1835, 44 percent in 1844, and 29 percent by 1853. The Erie route, meanwhile, had captured nearly 40 percent of the trade by 1840 and more than 60 percent by 1853. Even the lower Middle West along the Ohio River diverted its trade from the southern water route. Cincinnati, which in 1853 shipped more than 90 percent of its goods south, reversed direction and shipped its products upriver to the termini of eastern railroads by 1860.

The centerpiece of the southern route was the Mississippi River and its navigable tributaries. In the earliest years of settlement, flatboats offered cheap, downriver freight rates. Lacking alternative low-cost transportation, western settlement congregated along navigable waterways. Riverine settlement was reinforced by the successful adaptation of shallow-draft steamboats to southern waters in the 1810s. The steamboats lowered upstream freight rates, permitting the dispatch of imported goods from New Orleans as far north as the Ohio valley. By the mid-1820s, nearly half of New Orleans's trade originated in the Ohio valley, the other half coming from the Mississippi valley south of St. Louis. Well over half of the interior receipts at New Orleans consisted

of diverse provisions—corn, flour, pork, beef, and whiskey—mostly from the Ohio valley. Bulk grain shipments were rare because wheat spoiled in the heat and humidity and, in any event, New Orleans had modest storage facilities. Similarly, New Orleans merchants favored the shipment of cornmeal and barreled corn (in the ear) over sacked corn (shelled) until the mid-1830s.

During its period of western hegemony, New Orleans and upriver towns flourished. As the principal entrepôt for a drainage basin in excess of 1 million square miles, New Orleans's river receipts rose from less than 100,000 tons of goods in the 1810s to 1.2 million tons by 1840. The Crescent City rose from a small town of 17,000 persons in the 1810s to fifth rank among all American cities; its population of 102,000 in 1840 almost precisely matched Baltimore's. The busy port annually received 2,000 to 3,000 flatboats and steamboats during the 1830s and transshipped the bulk of these goods on to ocean-going vessels. Upriver from New Orleans, hundreds of landings, wood stations, towns, and cities connected the river with interior producers. Of the various settlements along the trunkline the three largest in 1840 lay in the Ohio valley: Cincinnati with 46,000 people and 1,600 miles from New Orleans; Pittsburgh, 31,000 people and 2,063 miles distant; and Louisville, 21,000 persons, was 1,442 miles distant. The fourth-ranking city was St. Louis on the Mississippi, 1,242 miles from New Orleans with a population of 16,500 (Fig. 8.5).

The growth of New Orleans's tributary cities (Cincinnati was the sixth largest city in the nation in 1840) was closely tied to their trade in diversified, bulky, and perishable provisions. These cities assembled interior produce and improved its value by reducing bulk and perishability. Corn, for example, was shelled and sacked, barreled, milled into meal, or made into whiskey. Mills ground wheat into flour. Livestock was slaughtered and barreled in brine or cured into bacon and hams. Its packing industry earned Cincinnati the title of "Hogopolis" by 1840. The pace of life was brisk in these cities which received wheat in the summer, hogs in the fall and winter, and corn in the spring.

Closer to New Orleans, river ports were smaller and quieter than the cities upriver. A town of several thousand was a rarity, and

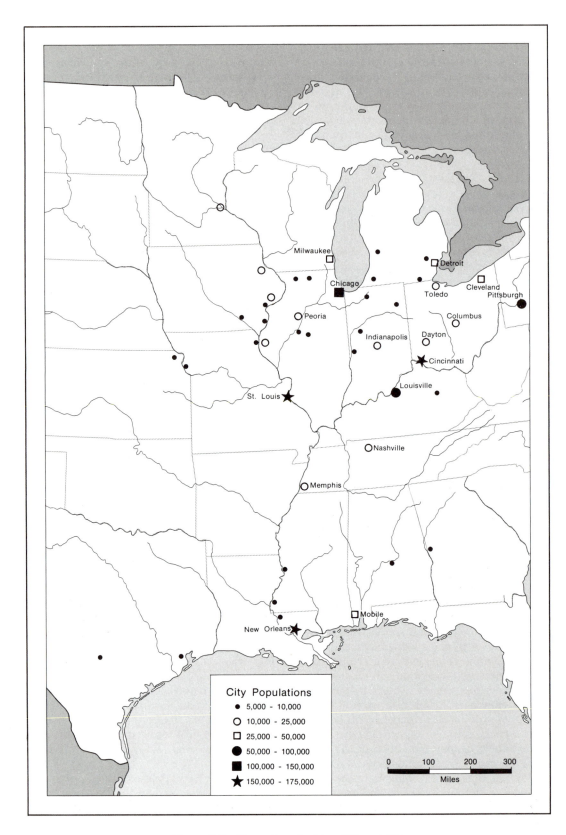

City Populations

- 5,000 - 10,000
- 10,000 - 25,000
- 25,000 - 50,000
- 50,000 - 100,000
- 100,000 - 150,000
- 150,000 - 175,000

Milwaukee
Chicago
Detroit
Cleveland
Pittsburgh
Toledo
Peoria
Columbus
Indianapolis
Dayton
Cincinnati
St. Louis
Louisville
Nashville
Memphis
Mobile
New Orleans

0   100   200   300
Miles

Figure 8.5   Trans-Appalachian Cities, 1860

trade was generally dull except during August to November, the cotton shipping season. Located at intervals of roughly 75 to 100 miles along the river, a good day's journey by steamboat, these towns functioned as collection points and markets for local cotton planters. Slaves and small white planters carted the baled cotton to town. Requiring neither processing nor elaborate storage facilities, the cotton just sat awaiting the steamboats. The transshipment of cotton to New Orleans-bound steamboats was the principal function of these towns.

Although New Orleans monopolized the interior trade, it shared the cotton trade with the neighboring port of Mobile, Alabama. Located at the mouth of the Alabama River, the port of Mobile serviced the successful cotton planters of central Alabama and northeastern Mississippi. Cultivating rich prairie and bottom lands along the Alabama, Tombigbee, and Black Warrior rivers, these planters produced good yields of cotton, which they sent by steamboat to Mobile. By the late 1830s, cotton receipts in Mobile amounted to almost half those in New Orleans; the young port housed more than 20,000 persons by 1840 and was about the size of Louisville.

New Orleans's hegemony over the western trade endured until the late 1830s when the northern gateway—the multimodal system of western canals, lake boats, and Erie Canal boats—offered stiff competition. The new rival carved out a trade zone stretching south into central Ohio and northwest along the edges of Lakes Erie and Huron. As the northern route expanded, the principal ports assumed a rank-size distribution: in 1840, Buffalo (population 18,000) was about twice the size of the second-ranking city, Detroit; triple the size of third-ranked Cleveland; and quadruple the size of fourth-ranked Chicago. During the next decade, however, the western ports grew faster and Chicago, with nearly 30,000 people, moved into second place, with Milwaukee competing with Detroit for third rank.

Although the northern gateway stimulated urban growth, the lake ports were smaller than the river ports on the southern route. The former handled the flow of bulk grains, particularly wheat and corn, while the processing industries associated with Ohio River ports were relatively scarce. Consequently, the largest lake port, Buffalo with 42,000 people in 1850, was slightly smaller than Louisville, about half the size of Pittsburgh, and a third the size of Cincinnati.

The pace of urban growth on the northern route accelerated with the spread of railroads in the Middle West after 1846. Lake ports added the function of staple processing to their economic base. Before the railroads, crops were shipped via the lake system. The lake trade, however, was suspended each November by wind and ice and was not resumed until spring. The interregional rail routes, via the northern and the eastern gateways, permitted year-round shipments of higher-value goods. Bulk-reduction processing made headway in several lake ports; Chicago, for example, shipped increasing quantities of flour and dressed hogs (in winter to provide natural refrigeration). Live hogs and cattle, destined for the tables of urban Easterners, also moved through the enormous Chicago stockyards. By 1860, 15 rail lines funneled staples into Chicago (the city's storage capacity for grain in that year exceeded the total tonnage of the South's entire cotton crop). Chicago's population swelled in 1860 to 112,000. Buffalo at 81,000 had lost ground, because much trade now went direct via rail. Meanwhile Detroit, Cleveland, and Milwaukee all rested at populations of 40,000 to 45,000 (Fig. 8.5).

Chicago's exceptional growth—travelers regarded it as an American wonder—was based on its dual trade via rail and the Erie system. Equally important was its proximity to the emergent agricultural regions—the Wheat Belt of northern Illinois and southern Wisconsin and the Corn Belt, with associated hogs and cattle, of central Indiana and Illinois. These staple regions were gravitating to the north and west—a direction favoring the growth of Chicago over all other lake ports.

On the eve of the Civil War, the commerce of the trans-Appalachian west had been thoroughly restructured. Although the largest cities occupied the old southern route—New Orleans, St. Louis, and Cincinnati ranged between 160,000 and 175,000 people—the trade of the Old Northwest flowed principally to the eastern and northern gateways. The lake ports, especially Chicago, gained ground over river ports to the south. New Orleans, once the master of the Mississippi valley, suffered from hinterland capture. In 1860, the Crescent City retained the lucrative cotton trade of the lower Mississippi and some provisions trade from the Tennessee and Cumberland rivers, but the city's share of trans-Appalachian trade had diminished to about 25 percent, scarcely any of which came from north of the Ohio River.

REGIONAL ECONOMIC SPECIALIZATION IN THE TRANS-APPALACHIAN WEST

The radical realignment of western commerce and the shifting loci of urban growth were part and parcel of a broader restructuring of agricultural regions west of the Appalachians. As the territory assumed the role of the nation's agricultural heartland, it also divided into regional chambers of specialized production. Three principal regions emerged during the two decades before the Civil War: the Wheat Belt of the upper Middle West; the Corn-Hog Belt of the lower Middle West and the upper South; and the Cotton Belt in the lower South (Fig. 8.6). Supplementing these were the more-localized regions of lumbering in the coniferous forests of Wisconsin and Michigan; scattered areas of burley tobacco and hemp production in the upper South; and the sugar country of subtropical Louisiana.

A major theme of regional agriculture is its westward gravitation. Usually this spatial drift is explained as a natural and inevitable tendency of the frontier, but in actuality it involved a host of interrelated climatic, agronomic, and technological factors. In the case of cotton, three-fourths of the nation's cotton was raised west of the Appalachians by 1860, and indeed 55 percent came from the three states of Alabama, Mississippi, and Louisiana. Within these states, intensive cotton production centered on three areas: (a) the rich alluvial bottomlands of the Mississippi valley from Baton Rouge to Natchez and its tributaries in the state of Mississippi; (b) the black prairies of central Alabama and northwest up the Tombigbee River; and (c) the region surrounding Memphis on the Mississippi.

More than any other western crop except sugar, cotton's geography was critically affected by climatic conditions. For optimal production, cotton requires a long growing season

of 200 or more frost-free days. Today, that isoline runs from the Georgia–South Carolina border northwest to the tip of southeastern Missouri and then west to Oklahoma; but in the mid-19th century, when cooler temperatures prevailed, the line lay farther to the south. The antebellum Cotton Belt evolved in a region that was one to two degrees cooler than at present and was drier as well. The area of drier conditions formed a triangle with its apex in the Mississippi valley and its base extending from Alabama to Texas—a triangle that enclosed the core of the Cotton Belt in the 1850s.

Cotton's gravitation into this triangle was a rational response to more-optimal agronomic conditions. In this cooler and drier zone cotton planters alleviated two of their most severe problems, weed growth and fungus diseases. Drier conditions retarded the invasion of crabgrass into the fields during the first two months of cotton's growth. Whereas Old South planters in a rainier environment commonly complained that they tilled weeds four times or more in spring, western planters usually escaped with just three cultivations. And because tillage was the principal bottleneck in cotton planting, a reduction in cultivation frequency permitted an expansion of cotton acreage per worker (by 3 to 4 acres) and of output per capita. In addition, cotton disease was less of a problem for western planters, while to the east, the Agricultural Society of South Carolina searched in vain for a solution to cotton plant rust.

Although wheat stood at the opposite latitudinal extreme from cotton, it too experienced a rapid westward shift before the Civil War. Until the early 1840s Ohio led the nation in wheat production, but by 1860 the Wheat Belt had shifted several hundred miles northwest to northern Illinois and southern Wisconsin. This migration would not have been possible without the easy access provided by rail and lake carriers, yet many areas adjacent to the Great Lakes enjoyed similar locational advantages. More critical, perhaps, was the drier and cooler climate in the new Wheat Belt. Plant diseases such as wheat rust and the "wheat blast" that plagued farmers in Indiana and Ohio in the 1850s were less serious in the northwest. The area west of Lake Michigan had two other advantages for wheat production. First, according to the agricultural historian Allan Bogue,

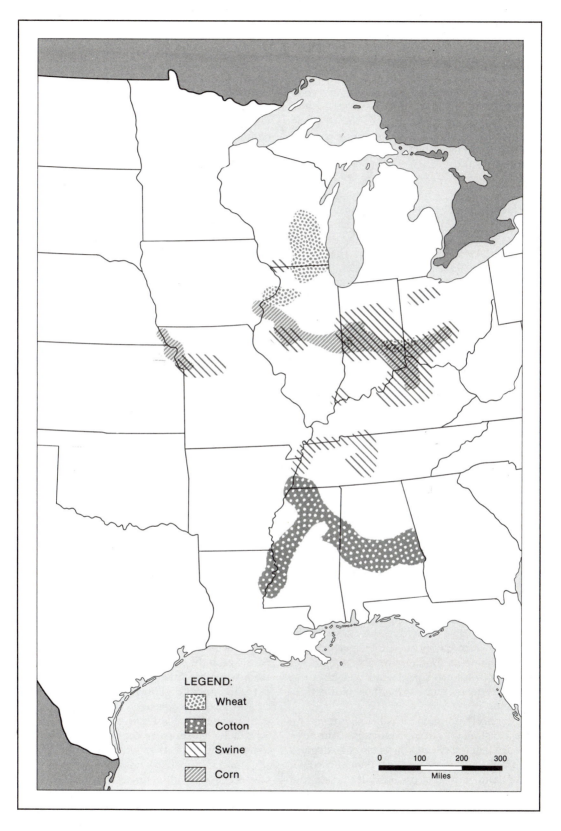

LEGEND:

▓ Wheat

▒ Cotton

╱ Swine

▨ Corn

0   100   200   300
Miles

Figure 8.6   Generalized Core Regions of Staple Production in the Trans-Appalachian West, 1860

was its location on the prairie margin. The region's uneven surface of ridges and trees moderated winter soil temperatures by comparison with the open prairie to the south. Hence the risk of winter killing from heaving and thawing diminished in the prairie margin. Second, the relatively drier springs permitted a shift from fall-sown winter wheat to spring-sown wheat. In the drier fields the farmers could plant their wheat in early spring and provide sufficient time for maturation. Although other areas of the country persisted in raising wheat, none of them in the 1850s rivaled the spatial concentration of the Wheat Belt, and few rivaled it in yields.

Corn, the third great crop of the trans-Appalachian region, flourished in a wide variety of environments from the gulf to the Great Lakes, but its core region lay in the latitudinal band of 39 to 41 degrees and in a longitudinal range from Columbus, Ohio, to Davenport, Iowa. In this region, and particularly on its eastern margins, Corn Belt farmers also specialized in hogs (Fig. 8.6).

In the creation of this belt-shaped region, climatic conditions played a key role. South of the Corn Belt, farmers occupied a more-humid environment that presented considerable problems for row-crop tillage. Weeds such as Johnson grass, Bermuda grass, and yellow nutsedge were chronic pests, invading cornfields and requiring more tillage and labor than in the Corn Belt. Moreover, southern grasses often demanded tedious hand-hoed tillage, whereas Corn Belt farmers escaped with lighter cultivations. The considerable popularity of riding cultivators in the Corn Belt was unmatched in the South, where these new machines were relatively ineffectual on vigorous weeds. Because tillage rates tended to be faster in the Corn Belt, farmers increased their acreage in corn (in some cases doubling the per-worker acreage of southern corn farmers), which also reinforced the economic advantage of this sinuous zone.

To the north of the Corn Belt cooler temperatures constrained corn production. Although the Corn Belt today extends as far as 44 degrees north latitude, conditions were generally cooler in the mid-19th century Middle West, and corn's optimal thermal limits (a heat supply of 50° F. or more for a period of 4 to 5 months) stood at 42° to 43° N, or roughly the southern Wisconsin border (Fig. 8.7).

Favorable climate alone would not have made the Corn Belt into a preeminent agricultural zone. Equally important was the intensive railroad construction that lashed the region together during the 1850s. Few areas of the nation rivaled the rail mileage constructed in southeastern Ohio, central Indiana, and central Illinois (Fig. 8.8). Indiana, for example, constructed more than 1,000 miles of rail lines between 1849 and 1853—half of the state's total mileage as of 1860; and in the same period, southwestern Ohio acquired most of its antebellum trackage. In these places, the interior cities of Indianapolis and Dayton emerged as rail hubs, with seven and five rail lines entering them, respectively.

This feverish pace of railroad building was prompted, in part, by intraregional specialization and trade. The new lines facilitated the shipment of cash grain from Illinois and Iowa to the eastern margins of the Corn Belt, with its emphasis on hogs as well as corn. Although the new rail lines suffered from overbuilding, competition, and declining profits, corn farmers and hog raisers reaped the benefit of lower freight rates. Cheap transport fostered subregional differentiation in the Corn Belt. The western Corn Belt specialized in feed grain that was shipped to the livestock markets of Chicago, St. Louis, and other Mississippi River ports, or to the eastern corn-hog complex. The eastern Corn Belt specialized in hogs that were directed eventually to Ohio River ports and to pork markets in the South, or to eastern cities such as Baltimore, Washington, and Philadelphia.

The westward migration of antebellum agriculture involved far more than an extension of commercial farming and planting. The specialized belts of cotton, wheat, and corn significantly accelerated the pace of American economic growth. During the period from 1839 to 1859, when the American population rose by 60 percent, agricultural output doubled. The principal source of increasing output per capita lay with the new set of environmental-agronomic conditions existing in the trans-Appalachian west. Cooler and drier weather in the Mississippi and Ohio valleys conferred an ecological advantage on producers of row crops. Drier conditions during the growing season retarded weed growth among the rows of southern cotton and midwestern corn, thereby reducing labor input at tillage and increasing acreage per

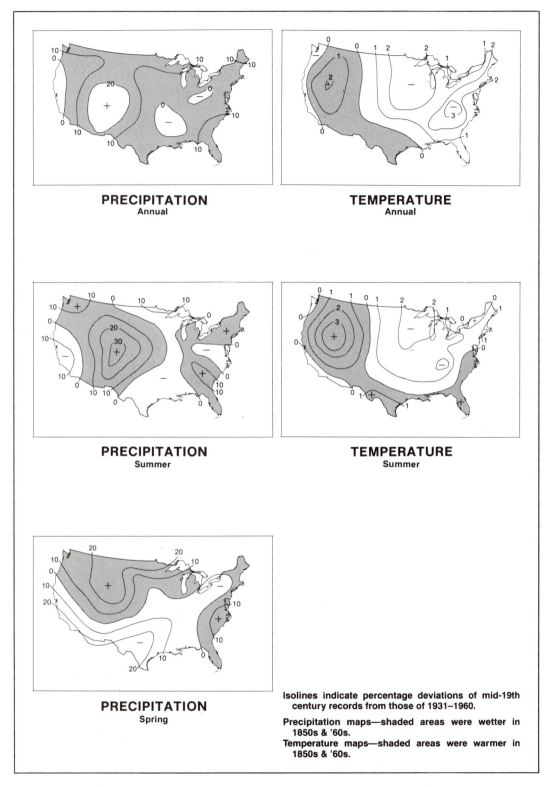

PRECIPITATION
Annual

TEMPERATURE
Annual

PRECIPITATION
Summer

TEMPERATURE
Summer

PRECIPITATION
Spring

Isolines indicate percentage deviations of mid-19th
century records from those of 1931–1960.

Precipitation maps—shaded areas were wetter in
1850s & '60s.
Temperature maps—shaded areas were warmer in
1850s & '60s.

Figure 8.7   Precipitation and Temperatures in the Middle of the 19th Century,
Compared with 1931–1960

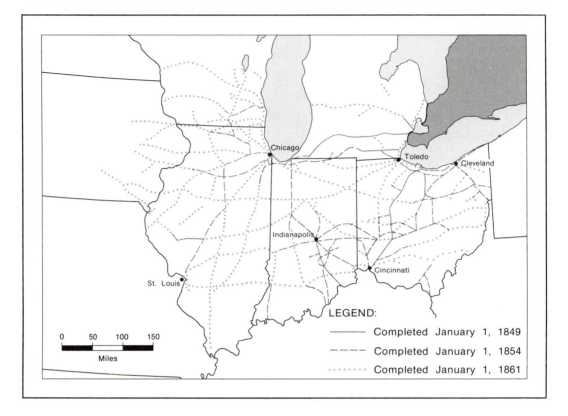

Figure 8.8   Midwestern Railroad Construction, 1849–1861

worker. The more-western planters and farmers cultivated their fields in May and June just three times, on average, as compared with the four or more cultivations customary eastward. During the roughly 60 days available for tillage and at the usual tillage rate of an acre a day, western row-crop capacity stood somewhere between 19 and 20 acres per worker, while in the more humid conditions to the east, row-crop capacity was 15 acres or less. Drier conditions, by easing the tillage constraint, permitted a 25 percent increase in row-crop acreage per worker. Productivity gains were even greater in the Corn Belt of the 1850s, when the introduction of riding cultivators lifted the acreage capacity above 20 acres. These new cultivators, which tilled at double the hand rates, proved particularly successful in the Illinois prairies where light plowings sufficed. In more-humid regions, east and south of the Corn Belt, weeds grew more vigorously and required tedious methods of hand-hoeing; cultivators were not adopted widely.

Wheat production also experienced productivity gains in its westward migration. Some of the more-serious problems in wheat production—rust, winter kill, and the brevity of the harvest period—were alleviated in the Wheat Belt of northern Illinois and southern Wisconsin. Per acre yields of wheat rose from less than 20 bushels to around 30 bushels because wheat rust and blight did less damage in the drier environment and because losses from winter kill were less in this rolling, prairie margin than in the open prairie to the south. Indeed, the problem of winter kill was avoided altogether by the diffusion of spring-sown wheat varieties, which was contingent on relatively dry springs and hence early access for plowing and sowing this broadcast grain. Finally, the gently rolling topography allowed mechanical reapers to operate with little difficulty on the region's gentle slopes. The introduction of the machine sped up the harvest rate. The precise gain is controversial, but a 20 to 50 percent improvement over hand rates of an acre a day appears most plausible. Put differently, given the stringent ten-day bottleneck of wheat harvest, a worker using a reaper harvested 12 to 15 acres as opposed to perhaps 10 with a scythe or cradle. The productivity advantage of the Wheat Belt over eastern producers can be summed up as follows: a yield-per-acre increase of 10 bushels and an acreage-per-worker increase of two to five acres; these translate into a gain of 20 to 50 bushels per worker over eastern outputs of 200 bushels per worker. The Wheat Belt, thus, conferred a productivity gain of between 10 to 25 percent.

The American economy reaped substantial productivity gains from the western extension of agriculture and the emergence of specialized staple regions possessed of favorable environmental endowments. Perhaps the most significant improvements in productivity occurred in row crop acreage per worker. Cotton and corn experienced a 25 percent gain in acreage per worker. Broadcast grains, most notably wheat, enjoyed more modest acreage gains of 10 to 25 percent. A second source of productivity gains was in higher yields per acre. Wheat Belt yields in the 1850s were half again those of most farmers to the east. Cotton and Corn Belt gains in yields were somewhat smaller. More fertile soils, undoubtedly, accounted for some of these increases in yields, but less well appreciated are the more-subtle environmental advantages of drier growing seasons, fewer weeds, and less plant disease. This ecological endowment, and its agronomic advantages, provided a sound logic for the western migration of agricultural production and specialization in the context of the expanding markets of the first half of the 19th century.

STAPLE REGIONS
AND SETTLEMENT SYSTEMS

Although productivity gains accrued in all these new agricultural regions, each region sculpted distinctive patterns of rural and urban settlement appropriate to its staple crop. At one extreme was the Cotton Belt with its assemblage of plantations, many though not all with slaves, and small towns; at the other extreme was the Wheat Belt typified by family farms, a sizable free labor force, and a hierarchy of towns and cities. More ambiguous in settle-

ment pattern was the Corn Belt landscape, which drew upon slave labor in its outliers south of the Ohio River and upon free labor north of it.

These variations in regional settlement represented in part a cultural transplantation of eastern settlement patterns but, more significantly, they constituted an adaptation to the unique labor requirements of each staple crop. In wheat cultivation, the demand for labor was highly seasonal, with the most critical time occurring in the frantic summer harvest period of ten days to two weeks. Wheat was thus a "few-day" crop, and farmers hired seasonal wage labor for the harvest; even at the high daily wages prevailing in the Middle West in the 1850s, a hired hand cost about $20 while a year-round slave costed out at nearly $60. In cotton planting, by contrast, planters preferred slaves when they could afford them. Cotton was a "multiple-day" crop with labor demands stretching from spring planting and tillage to late summer and autumn picking. Raising this demanding row crop required 120 days of labor stretched out over eight months; hence cotton planters rarely, if ever, hired wage workers, for their costs would have been double those of a slave.

Corn is the most interesting American staple because it is an "intermediate-day" crop, which often compelled in corn farmers an ambivalence about the most efficient supply of labor. As a row crop, corn required considerable attention from spring planting through early summer tillage; but afterward, the crop presented several options because harvesting did not have the urgency associated with wheat or cotton. Sometimes corn was left in the field well into winter and was harvested casually by family members; other times it was mowed down by livestock; and in still others it was cut, shocked, barned, and shelled. Because of this variety of harvest options, corn farmers generally worried about the labor bottleneck of tillage time in what they called the "crop season"— the four months from April through July. By the 1850s, corn farmers discovered that it cost them nearly the same to hire a wage worker for the "season" as it did to use slave labor. Consequently, corn growers south of the Ohio River, where slavery was legally permissible, often used slaves, while midwesterners used free hired hands. Many midwesterners, however, recognized the economic superiority of slave labor and, during the 1850s, explicitly advocated its introduction north of the Ohio River.

Rural settlements, in turn, accommodated the unique regional labor requirements. In the Wheat Belt, family farms drew on three sources for farm labor: sons, local agricultural laborers and townsmen, and itinerant workers arriving by train from Chicago, Milwaukee, and other points. The most reliable harvest labor, of course, was the sons of farmers. A wheat farmer with a teen-aged son calculated that together they could harvest 20 acres; hence, knowing labor was assured, he planted 20 acres of wheat in the fall or early spring. Consequently, the reliability of family labor was an inducement to high fertility. Illinois women in 1860, for example, averaged over four children during their child-bearing years, and at least one of these was old enough to do harvest work. A more-fluid source of labor was the reservoir of local farm laborers. They typically made up a fifth to a third of the adult male labor force in the Wheat Belt. Even less reliable were the itinerant workers who came from more-distant places. The convergence of these labor flows at the time of wheat harvest made for a bustle of activity, but the pool of workers was soon spread thin. Farmers rarely hired more than a few harvest workers and, as a result, farm size was constrained. The average wheat farm contained in 1860 about 50 to 70 acres in improved land, and double or triple that amount in total acreage. Less than half of the improved land was in wheat (somewhat more if farmers used mechanical reapers). The remaining acreage was planted with corn, oats, rye, barley, and grass. Every farm had livestock too, but their numbers were modest when compared with Corn Belt farms.

Juxtaposed with the Wheat Belt's rural landscape of moderately sized family farms and its fluid labor force was an urban system of sizable dimensions. Chicago and Milwaukee, the principal entrepôts for the Wheat Belt, broke into the middle and upper rank of American cities by 1860. Hinterland towns, such as Peoria and Rockford, also flourished. Urban growth and wheat farming were intertwined at several levels. The most obvious tie between country and city was the commodity marketing and forwarding function of urban centers. Their contribution to economic base, however, according

to recent calculations by Earle and Hoffman, was considerably less than that required to explain the size of Wheat Belt towns and cities. A more-subtle and more-decisive factor explaining the large populations of these cities lay in the tie between wheat farming and labor supply. The rural labor supply in the Wheat Belt experienced underemployment as a result of wheat's acutely seasonal regime. The brief wheat harvest made it extremely difficult for rural workers to accumulate capital and climb the agricultural ladder toward farm ownership. For most laborers, the Wheat Belt represented a waystation for migration either west to cheaper lands or east to the region's burgeoning towns and cities. The plight of the wheat laborer was a bonanza for the region's urban entrepreneurs, who tapped these workers as a low-cost source of labor. In Chicago in the 1850s, for example, the transfer wage—the annual wage required to lure a rural laborer from the countryside to unskilled labor in the city—stood at about $180 to $200 per year. These were the lowest unskilled urban wages in the nation and about half those of the cotton South. Urban labor in the Wheat Belt was cheap precisely because rural work and earnings were so extremely seasonal and brief. Wheat Belt cities and towns were the beneficiaries of cheap labor. Their entrepreneurs hired more workers per unit of labor cost than their counterparts in the rest of the nation. The Chicago urban system, despite a regional economic base identical to that of Mobile's, employed nearly twice as many workers in its urban labor force.

The rural and urban landscape shared many, but not all, features with the Corn Belt to the south. Corn farmers also resided on family farms of modest size and drew upon rural wage labor, although south of the Ohio River slaves were used. Cities and towns were integral features of the region. Corn Belt farmers were served by the Middle West's second- and third-largest cities—Cincinnati serving the eastern half, St. Louis the western half. Chicago too made inroads in central Illinois and central Indiana.

The similarities in the Corn and Wheat Belt landscapes, however, obscure fundamental differences in rural seasonality and labor supply. Corn, as noted earlier, is a row crop and its peak labor demands occur during the "crop season" from April through June. This short period of time determined how much corn could be planted. A good worker, tilling at a rate of an acre a day and doing each field thrice, cultivated a maximum of 20 acres of corn in 60 days. Some farmers increased per-worker acreage by introducing faster riding cultivators, but their diffusion in the Corn Belt before 1860 was modest. The typical Corn Belt worker, therefore, probably cultivated about 20 acres. Farm size in the Corn Belt, because of the tillage constraint, was small. Farm expansion depended on the availability of rural laborers, who made up anywhere from an eighth to a third of the rural labor force—clearly, an insufficient number to satisfy every farmer. The labor constraint on corn acreage thus helped to fix the typical Corn Belt farm in central Illinois in 1859 at 163 acres, 105 of which were improved. Corn Belt farms were somewhat larger than those in the Wheat Belt partly, perhaps, because corn farmers also used their hired hands to harvest some wheat and other small grains and to do the haying.

The Corn Belt further differed from the Wheat Belt in its emphasis on livestock, and particularly swine production. By 1860, the eastern half of the Corn Belt had integrated corn and swine production effectively; hogs were turned loose in the corn fields on occasion, or the standing crop was cut, taken to the barn, and fed on demand. In the western half of the Corn Belt where swine were fewer, corn was cut, shocked, shelled, and shipped as feed grain to external markets.

The corn-hog complex typical of southwestern Ohio and east-central Indiana also appeared south of the Ohio River, but producers in the Kentucky bluegrass and Nashville basin regions suffered market setbacks during the 1850s. Tennessee and Kentucky led the nation in swine production at the beginning of that decade and, on a per capita basis, middle Tennessee tripled the national average. By 1860, however, these states experienced a 20 percent decline in swine numbers and surrendered national leadership to Indiana and Illinois. Although improved swine weights offset some of the decline in southern swine, its principal cause was the collapse of the Cotton Belt market for corn and pork. Cotton Belt planters in Alabama, Mississippi, and Louisiana diversified their operations, adding corn, cowpeas, and swine, and concurrently satisfied most of the food needs on their plantations. The result was that corn production in these cotton states rose by 18 percent during the 1850s, as compared with a 5 percent gain in the upper South; and swine numbers in the cotton states declined by less than 5 percent, compared with a 20 percent drop in the upper South. Changes in the agricultural organization of cotton plantations increasingy deprived the upper South of its principal market for corn and pork.

The settlement fabric of the Cotton Belt was woven out of three strands: the multiple-day labor demands of the staple, the rationality of slave labor, and the expansion possibilities of slavery (Fig. 8.9). Cotton's labor demands stretched from late winter seeding through spring planting and tillage to fall picking. Because of the lengthy labor period, cotton planters expanded operations through the acquisition of slaves rather than hired labor. This expansion path, however, was obstructed by a rapid rise in slave prices during the prosperous 1850s. The price of prime male slaves rose from $1,500 to $2,000—a level far exeeding the resources of family plantations that grossed perhaps $300 a year from cotton planting. Many small planters as a result eschewed slaves and relied on their wives and children. Slaveless plantations in the cotton South increased from 39 percent of the total in 1850 to 48 percent in 1860. Even in the legendary Mississipi alluvial region, noted for its grand plantations, non-slave plantations rose from 20 percent to 36 percent during the decade. Similarly, the Cotton Belt in central Alabama recorded an increase in non-slave plantations from 21 to 29 percent. Concurrently, slaves were concentrated numerically among the larger planters (those having 15 or more slaves) and spatially in the high-yield Cotton Belt areas of the Mississipi valley and the black prairie lands of central Alabama and northeastern Mississippi (Fig. 8.9).

Plantation scale in these favored areas increased in direct proportion to slave labor. Scale economies were at best modest because cotton output was closely regulated by a worker's tillage capacity. No matter how many slaves were added to the plantation, each slave's tillage capacity was limited to 15 to 20 acres of row crops. Large planters tried to circumvent the tillage bottleneck by compelling slaves to cultivate from sunup to sunset, rain,

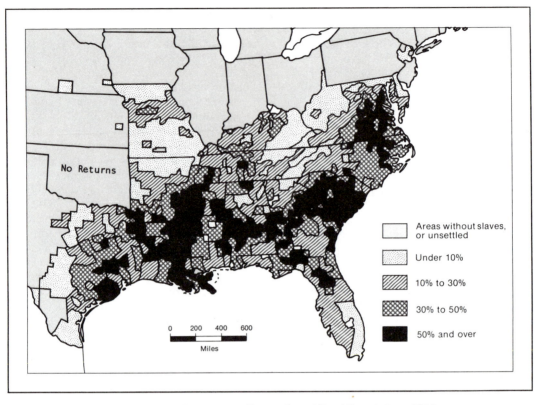

Figure 8.9   Slaves as a Proportion of Total Population, 1860

shine, and holidays, and in gang systems, but these strategies produced only marginal gains. From an economic standpoint, therefore, a large plantation was an expanded version of the many small plantations cultivated by family labor. That is not to say that the social organization of large plantations did not differ; indeed, scholars of the slave experience have pointed out the ironic virtues of large slave plantations in offering slaves a richer black cultural life, in preserving black folk culture, and in providing some economic mobility within the slave system.

Plantations large and small also shared in the process of economic diversification beginning in the 1840s and accelerating in the 1850s. Southern cotton planters, in switching some of their cotton land into corn and hog production, behaved in a seemingly irrational fashion. Perhaps, as some scholars have suggested, their combination of cotton and corn acreage in a two-to-one ratio (customarily planting 12 acres of cotton and 6 of corn) may have been a hedge against the uncertainty of cotton prices. At least planters fed themselves and their families when prices fell. But in the late 1840s, and especially in the 1850s, cotton prices were not falling. Quite the contrary: prices rose in response to international prosperity and the heavy British investment in textile mills. Diversification for the purpose of self-sufficiency seems unlikely during a period of rising cotton prices. A more-plausible explanation of diversification centers on planter efforts in maintaining soil fertility under an exhaustive crop such as cotton. Soil exhaustion had long been a serious problem for planters, and they had few options to combat the problem. One option, applying commercial fertilizers, was exorbitantly expensive; a second option, wearing out the land and migrating west to fresh lands, was customary until the early 1840s. Then a third option arose with the discovery by soil science of the nitrogen-fixing properties of leguminous plants. With this knowledge, planters devised an ingenious crop rotation scheme. It combined corn and the leguminous plant cowpeas with cotton to restore soil fertility far more cheaply than by the previously available options. This rotation system began with exhausted cotton land. Planters restored soil fertility by planting corn in the spring and, in July after tillage, intercropping cowpeas in the corn rows. By fall, cowpeas climbed the corn stalks, and their roots restored nitrogen to the worn-out soil. Planters then turned their hogs into the fields to mow down the corn and the cowpeas. The following spring, the restored land was available for two more years of cotton cropping. When fertility declined again, the land was turned back into corn and cowpeas. By planting a ratio of two acres of cotton to one acre of corn per worker (up to the tillage constraint of 18 acres in row crops), the planter was assured of steady cotton yields as well as adequate supplies of corn and pork—much to the dismay of producers in the upper South.

The southern cotton plantation had evolved by 1860 into a diversified agricultural production unit relying upon either family or slave labor. The plantations produced cotton for the market, corn and cowpeas for swine, and corn and pork for human consumption. This remarkably self-sufficient domestic economy, however, was curiously incidental to the southern goal of preventing soil exhaustion. Although the transformation in crop choice and diversification was widespread in the cotton South, it seems to have progressed farthest among the largest slave plantations such as those in the Natchez District on the Mississippi. But despite obvious differences in slave numbers (50 or more were usual), wealth, and material opulence, these large plantations produced cotton, corn, hogs, and cowpeas in almost precisely the same manner as did their smaller neighbors. Small cotton planters also were relatively prosperous during the 1850s, but the rapid rise in slave prices prevented them from pursuing the expansion path of slave acquisition taken by wealthy planters.

AGRICULTURAL REGIONS AND THE COMING OF THE CIVIL WAR

The economic superiority of slaves or free labor west of the Appalachians was clear-cut in the cotton South and the Wheat Belt but ambiguous in the Corn Belt. Slaves were far more efficient in the production of cotton, and the adoption of slave labor provided opportunities for an increasing scale of operation. Consequently, plantations with more than 1,000 acres and 100 slaves were juxtaposed with small farms reliant on family labor. Free labor, conversely, was more efficient in the production of wheat, but the hiring of daily or monthly wage workers seriously crimped expansion possibilities. The seasonal labor pool mobilized at harvest was always insufficient for the needs of all wheat farmers. Although some farmers expanded wheat acreage by adding mechanical reapers, mechanization of the farm was still in its infancy. Extremely large wheat farms were uncommon, and such a scale of operation awaited the postbellum period when massive seasonal labor pools were transported by passenger trains into the Great Plains wheat regions. Large agricultural holdings, in sum, were possible in the cotton South, although coexisting with family plantations, while in the Wheat Belt of the Middle West, farm size was constrained by labor scarcity. The landscape consisted of family farms of 100 to 200 acres supported by a substantial landless rural force.

For corn farmers, with their intermediate demands for seasonal labor, the choice of labor systems was problematic both morally and economically. They tended to be ambivalent about the preference for slaves or wage labor. As Alexis de Toqueville noted in the 1830s and Frederick Law Olmsted observed in the 1850s, some corn farmers preferred slaves, while others hired labor for the "crop season." This choice was merely an economic one south of the Ohio River where slavery existed legally. But north of the river, slavery was prohibited by the various state constitutions, and the advocacy of slaves in corn farming inflamed political and moral passions. During the 1840s, numerous midwestern Corn Belt farmers declared the economic superiority of slave labor and openly advocated its legalization in state constitutional conventions. On a purely economic basis, the pro-slavery farmer made sense. The costs in 1850 of hiring a free worker for four months were virtually identical with the annuallized costs of a prime male slave. In the next ten years, as free wages rose more rapidly than slave prices, slavery gained the advantage—the annual costs stood at $72 for free labor and $60 for slave labor.

Although the nation was preoccupied with the extension of slavery into the western territories of Kansas and Nebraska, a far more critical struggle over slavery threatened to fracture the Middle West. Corn Belt farmers, many of them from northeastern states, proposed the extension of slavery into Illinois, Indiana, and Ohio; in reaction, wheat farmers in the upper Middle West—for whom slavery was uneconomic as well as immoral—lent vigorous support to antislavery parties. The 1848 presidential election returns in Illinois reveal the unstable fault line between antislavery wheat farmers and ambivalent or pro-slave corn farmers (Fig. 8.10). In this election, the candidate for the antislavery Free Soil Party, Martin Van Buren, drew the vast majority of his support from northern wheat-farming areas. This geographical division deepened during the 1850s. Following the controversial Kansas-Nebraska Act in 1854, which repealed the Missouri Compromise of 1820 that prohibited slavery north of 36 degrees and 30 minutes north latitude, the Wheat Belt solidly supported the newly risen, antislavery Republican Party. In the campaigns of 1858 and 1860, the Wheat Belt formed a bulwark of support in Abraham Lincoln's unsuccessful bid for the Senate and his victorious bid for the presidency.

The pivotal role of the Middle West in the impending Civil War has been eclipsed by a preoccupation with slavery in the western territories. The leading presidential candidates in 1860, Lincoln and Stephen Douglas, were from Illinois, and Lincoln's narrow margin of victory was won largely in his home state and in Indiana. Although Lincoln won the election by a comfortable margin in the electoral college, these results are deceptive. If 18,000 voters in Illinois and Indiana and 500 in California had switched votes to the leading opposition party, Lincoln would have been denied a majority in the electoral college and the election would have been thrown into the House of Representatives (where, undoubtedly, he would have lost). The Middle West, and more particularly its wheat farmers, preserved Lincoln's narrow victory—a victory that virtually guaranteed southern secession.

Southerners understood correctly Lincoln's position of preserving the union and eradicating slavery, but they did not appreciate fully the basis of his fear. The greatest danger in slavery was not its existence in the South, nor even its extension into the western territories; the real danger lay in its expansion, via corn farmers, into the Middle West. Lincoln had witnessed the constitutional and electoral offensive of Corn Belt farmers on behalf of slavery. He witnessed the antislavery reaction that barely defeated slave advocates in the state constitutional conventions and lost to them in the 1858 Senate race. Lincoln's presidential victory, however, did nothing to change the economic advantage of slaves over free labor in the Corn Belt. Lincoln understood that efforts to legalize slavery in the Middle West would persist until relative labor costs shifted in favor of free labor (which was unlikely) or until the institution of slavery was eliminated as a labor choice. As long as slavery existed in the nation, corn farmers would be tempted to use it. Lincoln would have appreciated the observations of a perceptive southerner who noted that "where a real interest, and a question of abstract morality conflict in a Yankee's mind, abstract morality will suffer a grievous overthrow."

CONCLUSION

The story of trans-Appalachian settlement between 1815 and 1860 is bittersweet. On the one hand, the occupation of the region resulted in marvelous economic achievements. Agricultural productivity gains were substantial as the Middle West responded to external markets and transport improvements by regional specialization. It is fair to say that the trans-Appalachian region had assumed the role of the nation's agricultural heartland by 1860. The region's endowments were considerable. Aside from excellent and extensive navigable rivers and gentle topography, the Middle West enjoyed a relatively cooler and, in a corridor along the Mississippi valley, drier climate than at present. These subtle climatic differences helped to make farming and planting easier and more productive.

A mosaic of specialized staple regions consequently emerged, and each region developed distinctive patterns of rural and urban settlement. In the Cotton Belt, plantations ranged from small family operations to large-scale

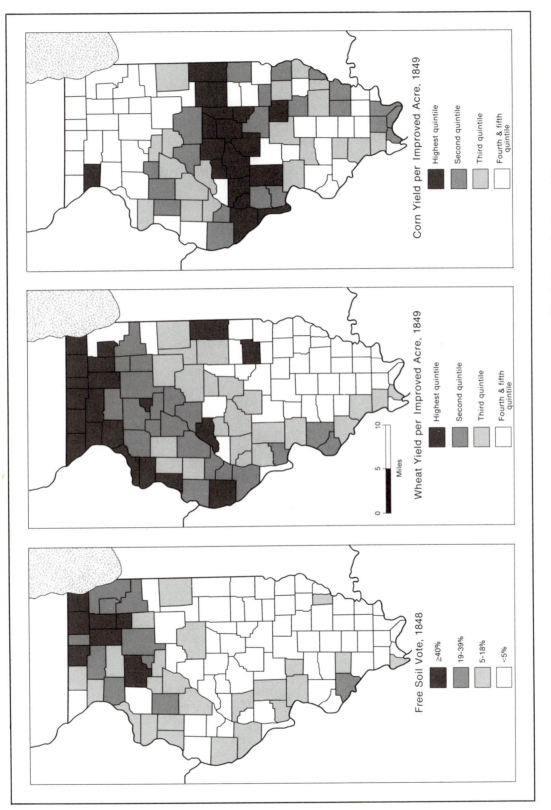

Figure 8.10 Antislavery Politics and Agricultural Production in Illinois During the Late 1840s

slave production units. The economic efficiency of slaves in cotton production provided an expansion path that was unavailable for Wheat and Corn Belt farmers, who relied on a less-predictable, seasonal pool of wage workers. Although a landscape of family farms, 100 to 200 acres in size, prevailed in both the Wheat and Corn Belts, the causes of these settlement patterns were unique to these staple crops and the seasonality of their labor demands. In the Wheat Belt, farm size was constrained by the harvest labor bottleneck of ten days to two weeks, while in the Corn Belt, farm size was fixed by tillage capacity during the two months of May and June. Not until after the Civil War would mechanization of corn tillage and wheat harvest reduce the stringency of these constraints on the family farm.

The bitter side of trans-Appalachian development, on the other hand, pertains to the viability of slavery not only in the plantation South, but by the 1850s in the lower Middle West as well. Slavery's efficiency and profitability in the Corn Belt jeopardized the delicate geopolitical balance constructed out of assorted compromises in the first half of the century. In this case, however, the vanguards of slavery were midwestern corn farmers rather than the southern slavocracy. As of 1860, the economic geography of labor and staples, particularly corn, had pushed the nation to its greatest impasse.

ADDITIONAL READING

Books

Bidwell, P.W. and Falconer, J.I. *History of Agriculture in the Northern United States, 1620–1860.* Washington D.C.: Carnegie Institution, 1925; New York: Peter Smith, 1941.

Bogue, A.G. *From Prairie to Cornbelt: Farming in the Illinois and Iowa Prairies in the Nineteenth Century.* Chicago: University of Chicago Press, 1963.

Curti, M. *The Making of an American Community.* Stanford: Stanford University Press, 1959.

David, P.A. *Technical Choice Innovation and Economic Growth.* Cambridge: Cambridge University Press, 1975.

Davis, C.S. *The Cotton Kingdom in Alabama.* Philadelphia: Porcupine Press, 1974.

Fishlow, A. *American Railroads and the Transformation of the Ante-bellum Economy* Cambridge: Harvard University Press, 1965.

Fogel, R.W., and Engerman, S.L. *Time on the Cross: The Economics of American Negro Slavery.* 2 vols. Boston: Little, Brown, 1974.

Gates, P.W. *The Farmer's Age: Agriculture, 1815–1860.* New York: Holt, Rinehart & Winston, 1960.

Genovese, E. *The Political Economy of Slavery.* New York: Pantheon, 1965.

Gray, L.C. *History of Agriculture in the Southern U.S. to 1860,* 2 vols. Washington D.C.: Carnegie Institution, 1932; New York: Peter Smith, 1958.

Haites, E.F.; Mak, J.; and Walton, G. *Western River Transportation: The Era of Early Internal Growth, 1810–1860.* Baltimore: Johns Hopkins University Press, 1975.

Hilliard, S. B. *Hog Meat and Hoecake: Food Supply in the Old South, 1840–1860.* Carbondale: Southern Illinois University Press, 1972.

Jakle, J. *Images of the Ohio Valley.* New York: Oxford University Press, 1977.

Kelsey, D.P. *Farming in the New Nation: Interpreting American Agriculture 1790–1840.* Washington D.C.: Agricultural History Society, 1972.

Klingaman, D.C., and Vedder, R.K., eds. *Essays in Nineteenth Century Economic History.* Athens: Ohio University Press, 1975.

McManis, D. *The Initial Evaluation and Utilization of the Illinois Prairies, 1815–1840.* Chicago: University of Chicago Department of Geography, 1964.

North, D.C. *The Economic Growth of the United States, 1790–1860.* New York: W.W. Norton, 1966.

Parker, W.N., ed. *The Structure of the Cotton Economy of the Antebellum South.* Washington D.C.: Agricultural History Society, 1970.

Paullin, C.O. *Atlas of the Historical Geography of the United States.* Washington D.C.: Carnegie Institution of Washington and The American Geographical Society, 1932.

Phillips, U.B. *Life and Labor in the Old South.* New York: Grosset & Dunlap, 1929.

Potter, D. *The Impending Crisis, 1848–1861.* New York: Harper & Row, 1976.

Pred, A. *Urban Growth and City Systems in the United States, 1840–1860.* Cambridge: Harvard University Press, 1980.

Rostow, W. *The Stages of Economic Growth.* Cambridge: Cambridge University Press, 1960.

Scheiber, H.N. *Ohio Canal Era.* Athens: Ohio University Press, 1969.

Shob, D.E. *Hired Hands and Plowboys: Farm Labor in the Midwest, 1815–1860.* Urbana: University of Illinois Press, 1975.

Taylor, G.R. *The Transportation Revolution, 1815–1860.* New York: Holt, Rinehart & Winston, 1951.

Ward, D. *Cities and Immigrants: A Geography of Change in Nineteenth Century America.* New York: Oxford University Press, 1971.

Whitaker, J.W., ed. *Farming in the Midwest, 1840–1860.* Washington D.C.: Agricultural History Society, 1974.

Wright, G. *The Political Economy of the Cotton South.* New York: W.W. Norton, 1978.

Periodicals

Agricultural History, journal of the Agricultural History Society. (Gallman, 1972).

American Historical Review, journal of the American Historical Association. (Earle and Hoffman, 1980).

Geographical Review, journal of the American Geographical Society. (Muller, 1976).

Manchester School of Economic and Social Studies. (Baldwin, 1956).

Monthly Weather Review. (Whal, 1968; Whal and Lawson, 1970).

9

The Northeast and Regional Integration, 1800–1860

PAUL A. GROVES

University of Maryland,
College Park

At the dawn of the 19th century the United States had fewer than 5.5 million inhabitants, of whom about 900,000 were slaves. Life expectancy at birth remained low (40 years), the country was largely rural (94 percent of the population was non-urban), transportation and communications were poor, and the population was concentrated along the eastern seaboard from Georgia to New Hampshire. North of the Potomac River lived almost three-fifths of the U.S. population; most of the remaining two-fifths were located to the south, with a small fraction west of the Appalachians.

The distinction between the Northeast and the South was reinforced throughout the first half of the 19th century by the increasing levels of urbanization and industrialization in the North, and by the increasing dependence of the South on a rurally based, staple crop economy. In 1800 the four largest cities in the United States, New York, Philadelphia, Baltimore, and Boston, were all in the Northeast. Thirty-three settlements were defined as urban in 1800; 28 of these were in the Northeast. The Northeast was not highly urbanized in 1800, for only one in ten of its residents lived in urban places; in the South the proportion was about one in fifty. The slave population was strongly concentrated in the South, with only Maryland of the northeastern states having a large slave population.

This pattern was transformed as the new nation emerged in the decades prior to 1860 (Fig. 9.1). Westward expansion pushed the settlement frontier beyond the Mississippi River (Table 9.1), while new forms of transportation

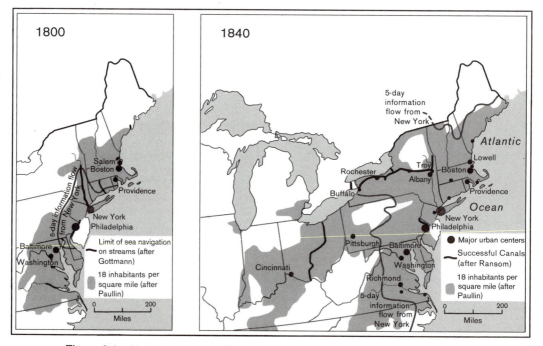

Figure 9.1   Northeast: Urban Centers and Population Density, 1800 and 1840

Table 9.1   U.S. Population by Region, 1800–1860 (population in thousands)

	1800	1820	1840	1860
Northeast	3,040	4,862	7,343	11,468
	(57)	(51)	(43)	(36)
South	2,208	3,917	6,369	10,260
	(42)	(41)	(37)	(33)
West	49	839	3,408	9,785
	(1)	(8)	(20)	(31)
Total United States	5,297	9,618	17,120	31,513

Note: Figures in parentheses indicate proportion of total U.S. population.

In this and all other tables the Northeast is defined as New England (Maine, New Hampshire, Vermont, Massachusetts, Rhode Island, and Connecticut) plus the Mid-Atlantic states (New York, New Jersey, Pennsylvania, Delaware, Maryland, and the District of Columbia).

(steamboat, canal, barge, and railroad) bound the existing ecumene more tightly together. Foreign trade and the capital accumulated by merchants in the seaport cities provided an economic base for the rapid growth of the major mercantile centers. The transformation of the national economy through the dual processes of industrialization and commercialization of agriculture placed new demands on both urban and rural America. The cities were receiving grounds not only for migrants from rural areas, but increasingly for immigrants from western Europe. During the period from 1820 to 1860, between 5 and 6 million immigrants, the majority of Irish and German origin, landed in the United States. Their numbers swelled the city populations of New England and the Mid-Atlantic states; few settled in the southern states.

At the beginning of the 19th century, therefore, the Northeast was the most economically developed region in an infant national economy. It was an area ready to take advantage of the shifting fortunes of international trade, and of early transportation development in the form of turnpike roads, canals, and railroads. It was the first area in North America to experience the impact of industrialization. Industrial growth transformed the landscape of eastern Massachusetts, southern New Hampshire, and Rhode Island and created additional impetus to

growth of the other mercantile cities. The region was a core area with a periphery that would extend generally westward as transportation and trade pulled it into a closer economic relationship with the core. For the Northeast (as core) this meant bridging the Allegheny section of the Appalachians. Once this was done, an emergent Middle West would be linked more fully with the Northeast and would itself experience the impact of urbanization and industrialization. The Northeast, in this view, can be seen as a staging ground for extending economic development to, for example, Ohio, Illinois, Indiana, and Michigan.

As the American economy grew, each of the major northeastern seaports—New York, Baltimore, Boston, and Philadelphia—developed a network of economic relationships with its hinterlands and, more important initially, with the Atlantic trade. Standing at the contact of these two realms, one inward-looking and the other outward-looking, the seaports assumed the role of "hinges" linking the development of these two foundations of the national economy. The period from 1790 to 1807 was one of massive maritime expansion, and the mercantile cities of the Northeast were the prime beneficiaries. New York, during this period, took a commanding lead among American seaports that it has retained ever since.

During the period from 1800 to 1860, the Northeast lost its role as the major populated region of the United States. The region accounted for 57 percent of total population in 1800, but this had declined to 36 percent by 1860. By the latter date, the population of the United States was about equally divided between the Northeast, the South, and the West (Table 9.1). Yet, the Northeast accounted for almost two-thirds of manufacturing employment and 17 of the 30 cities in the nation with populations of 25,000 or more (Table 9.2). Nor, of course, was its population static; an increase of 8.5 million included a disproportionate number of the foreign-born population.

The Northeast was an innovative area throughout this period. Here the dual, and inextricably linked, processes of urbanization and industrialization were initially played out. Transportation improvements produced more efficient links to other regions yet, by 1860, the emerging national economy occupied only the area east of the Mississippi River. The problems

Table 9.2   U.S. Cities of 25,000 Population or More by Region, 1800–1860

	1800	1820	1840	1860
Northeast	4	4	6	17
South	—	2	2	5
West	—	—	1	8
Total United States	4a	6b	9	30

aIncludes Boston (24,937).
bIncludes Charleston (24,780).
Note: The suburbs of New York (Brooklyn), Philadelphia (Spring Garden, Northern Liberties, Kensington, Southwark), Boston (Charleston, Roxbury, Dorchester, and Cambridge) and Pittsburgh (Allegheny) are included in the population totals for those cities in this and all subsequent tables.

of urban-industrial growth—shortage of housing, poor urban amenities, child labor, immigrant populations—were all found initially in the Northeast. The area grew from a sparsely populated region with major urban development limited to the major ports, to a core area that acted as innovator and director of a growing nation. Such developments created a number of tensions. First was the tension between the larger dominant cities and their hinterlands, particularly if the latter were congruent with the political unit of the state. New York, for example, early in the century experienced the distinction and perceived prejudice toward New York City at the expense of "upstate." The dominance of Baltimore within Maryland provides an additional example. Second, within each of the regions, growing tensions emerged between rural areas and rapidly growing urban centers. The rural areas were afflicted with changing market conditions related to western competition and with the growing demands of the northeastern cities for labor as well as for food and raw materials. Agriculture was in flux over much of the early 19th century, and reorganization and readjustment took their toll. Third, within the major urban areas a cleavage developed between the older native populations and the newer foreign-born populations over competition for work and housing. Finally, increased political tension between the North and the South had particular impact on border states like Maryland.

TRADE AND TRANSPORTATION

The period from 1790 to 1810 marked a high point in America's dependence on foreign trade as a vehicle for development. The leading sectors in the period of substantial economic development from 1793 to 1807 were the shipping and export industries, the latter including exports of American products as well as the reexport of foreign goods. War between Britain and France (the Napoleonic Wars) lasted, with one major interruption, from 1792 to 1815. This tied up the shipping trade of France, Britain, and major European countries and gave the neutral United States a massive advantage in world trade. The United States transported sugar, coffee, cocoa, pepper, and spices from the West Indies to Europe and carried manufactured goods from Europe to the rest of the world. In addition, domestic exports grew as cotton production spread through the South and as demand increased from the cotton textile plants of Britain.

The passage of the Embargo Act in 1807, followed in 1809 by the Nonintercourse Act, slowed U.S. trade expansion, and the outbreak of war between the United States and Britain in 1812 brought an end to the era. A measure of the growth of trade in this period is provided by a comparison between 1790 data and the peak year for trade in 1807. In 1790, exports totaled $20.2 million, reexports $0.3 million, and imports for domestic use $23.5 million; the figures for 1807 were $108.3 million for exports, $59.6 million for reexports, and $85.1 million for imports. Foreign trade was generally more important to the economy than domestic trade until the second decade of the century. The vagaries of war and its aftermath, however, caused large variations in this foreign trade; for example, exports in 1808 as a result of the 1807 Embargo Act were only 20 percent of the total for 1807.

The decade from 1810 to 1820 has been called the great turnabout in American economic development. During and after the 1810–1820 decade, foreign trade declined in relative importance vis-à-vis domestic trade as the hinge seaports looked increasingly to the national rather than to the international economy. The earlier period of foreign-trade prosperity had permitted capital accumulation and laid a foundation for future economic expansion. The capital market was made more efficient through the extension of banking and insurance. An influential merchant and banking clan evolved, the growth of urban centers extended the domestic market, and turnpike roads were built to permit foodstuffs to be moved to the expanding seaports. Most of these gains from trade accrued to the Northeast and particularly to the ports of New York, Boston, Philadelphia, and Baltimore. Between 1790 and 1820, New York's population grew fourfold, Boston's threefold, Philadelphia's more than twofold, and Baltimore's nearly fivefold. In addition, New York established a dominance that it would never relinquish.

Domestic trade that predated the War of 1812 was dominated by very short intraregional movements. Henry Adams commented in 1800, "In becoming politically independent of England, the old thirteen provinces developed little more commercial intercourse with each other . . . than they had maintained in colonial days. . . . Each group of States lived a life apart." Such internal trade that occurred at the beginning of the 19th century was confined to the immediate hinterlands of the seaports. Boston engaged in commerce with eastern Massachusetts and northern New England, Philadelphia with the Delaware valley and southeastern Pennsylvania, Baltimore with the Chesapeake Bay and western Maryland, and New York with the Hudson valley, Connecticut, and northern New Jersey. Accessibility by natural waterway, whether river or bay, was the major determinant of hinterland size.

After the War of 1812, the settled areas west of the Alleghenies remained commercially isolated, but the Northeast and South began an increasing level of trade. The Northeast, particularly via New York, redistributed European and domestic finished goods, while the South's increasing commitment to cotton and other staples such as tobacco, sugar, and rice produced a reciprocal trade. Trade was based on available, inexpensive transportation that highlighted waterway (sea, river, canal) movement over land (turnpike, road) transportation. Until the advent of interregional railroad transportation in the 1850s, the lines of trade were set by the availability of water transportation. The limited role of overland transportation in long-distance trade was a function of its cost. An 1816 Senate committee report indicated that the

cost of importing a ton of goods from Europe was about $9.00, or roughly the cost of moving the same ton of goods 30 miles overland. Such high costs did not totally prevent overland movement. In the early 1820s, prior to the opening of the Erie Canal, the Pittsburgh Pike from Philadelphia carried about 30,000 tons of goods annually, and the National Road from Baltimore about 10,000 tons. In addition, roads were the initial, albeit short, link for producers (whether farmers or manufacturers) to move their merchandise to the steamboat, canal barge, or sailing vessel.

From 1800 to 1860, New York, Baltimore, Philadelphia, and Boston were the four largest cities in the Northeast as well as in the United States. Coastal trade was an important economic component in the growth of each city, but each attempted to enlarge its hinterland area in other ways. Early turnpikes, particularly in New England, had provided a minimal road system, but building costs were high and travel slow and expensive. A few major turnpikes—the Lancaster Turnpike and the Cumberland Road—were financially successful, and by 1815 eastern Pennsylvania, New York, New Jersey, and southern New England were served by fairly good roads between the chief commercial cities. Although the building of turnpikes between 1800 and 1830 and a later boom in plank road construction (1844–57) are highlighted in any discussion of transportation development, the humble country road was equally important for its function of providing the initial link to the major carriers of merchandise. It was the road that linked the farmer and his surplus crop to the canal and the railroad.

Yet it was the building of the Erie Canal (1817–1825), financed by the state of New York, that demonstrated the advantages of hinterland expansion. New York via the Erie Canal and its feeders tapped into the Great Lakes and the upper midwestern market in a strikingly short period of time. The Erie Canal was the major element in a series of canals connecting it to other important water transportation routes. The Champlain, the Oswego (linking the Erie to Lake Ontario), and the Ohio (to Olean on the upper Allegheny River) were all financially successful canals. More important, they extended the role and regional dominance of New York City. Other major cities attempted to follow suit. Construction of the Chesapeake and Ohio began in 1828 and extended canal transportation some 184 miles from Washington, D.C., to Cumberland, Maryland. Philadelphia, attempting to address the potential loss of trade to New York, completed the Main Line Canal, which included a portage railroad, to Pittsburgh in 1834.

Other canals, including the Delaware Division, linked the anthracite fields of eastern Pennsylvania to the Delaware River. These in turn were connected by canals across New Jersey or New York State, and became important as carriers of anthracite to New York City and to New England markets. By 1840, the nation had 3,326 miles of canals but few were long-term successes. The Erie Canal and its feeders were the notable exception. After 1846, the railroad, the steamship, and the telegraph became the standard vehicles of transportation and communication. Between 1851 and 1854, the Erie, the Baltimore and Ohio, the Pennsylvania, and the New York Central railroads provided all-weather overland transportation from the Northeast to the west. By the outbreak of the Civil War railroads extended across the eastern third of the country. In 1840, railroads were found in all of the northeastern states, but their function was essentially as feeder lines to the existing canal system. By 1840, 3,328 miles of railroad line had been built, almost two-thirds of which was in the Northeast; by 1850, total national mileage stood at 8,879, with the proportion in the Northeast almost identical. An intensification of the system in the Northeast occurred and many independent lines were combined, but still most traffic remained within its own system. For example, even as late as 1860, more than 80 percent of the traffic on the Pennsylvania and the Baltimore and Ohio railroads did not move beyond those systems.

By 1860, railroad mileage nationally had reached 30,636. As the railroad spread west, so too did the telegraph. Now communication was not bound to overland transportation time. This benefited the bankers, investors, and entrepreneurs of the Northeast in supplying information necessary for economic decisions. The advent of the ocean-going steamship after 1848 confirmed the role of New York and other Atlantic ports as the American termini of the trans-Atlantic runs.

Each pair of major northeastern cities was linked by large volumes of trade. The only weak link was between Philadelphia and Baltimore, cities that were segmented by an extremely roundabout sea route to the south of Cape Charles at the mouth of Chesapeake Bay. The coastal commodity flows between these cities between 1820 and 1860 were of three types: agricultural or raw material production from the port of origin, manufactures produced in the port of origin or its hinterland dependents, and redistributive shipments. Boston receipts included flour, corn, oats and other grains from Baltimore, Philadelphia, and New York, both for its own use and for the mill towns of its hinterland. Also to Boston came hides and leather from Baltimore, Philadelphia, and New York for the boot and shoe industries of the area around Lynn; anthracite coal, steam engines, and manufactured goods from Philadelphia; and foreign imports from New York. Philadelphia receipts included shoes and textiles from Boston both for local consumption and for redistribution, and English dry goods and other foreign imports from New York. New York coastal receipts included shoes and textiles from Boston, many of which were forwarded to the west and south by local merchants; industrial commodities from Philadelphia, many of which were reshipped to southern ports; coal from Philadelphia; and flour, coffee, and tobacco from Baltimore. Baltimore's acquisitions included leather products from Boston, foreign imports from New York, and manufactured goods from Philadelphia.

This massive coastal water traffic was not, however, the totality of interurban trade. Each of the four major cities had an important set of connections to those smaller urban places in its own hinterland. Boston had trade with the coastal ports of Maine and with the closer ports of Salem and Portsmouth; Baltimore had the Chesapeake Bay commerce and the downstream Susquehanna River trade. Philadelphia traded with places along the Delaware River as well as with areas to the west of the city, especially after completion of the Main Line Canal to Pittsburgh in 1834. New York had a flourishing trade with Providence, Bridgeport, New Haven, New London, and Norwich and, most significant, an important riverine trade with Albany and such smaller Hudson valley towns as Poughkeepsie, Newburgh, and Kingston. Before the opening of the Erie Canal in 1825, there were large flows of flour and grain from Albany to New York and of imports and manufactured goods in the opposite direction. After the opening of the Erie Canal this traffic increased dramatically, sufficient to propel Albany to the sixth-largest urban center in the Northeast by 1840. By 1860, Buffalo, Albany, Troy, Rochester, and Syracuse (a line of cities paralleling the Erie Canal) were all among the largest 15 places in the Northeast (Table 9.3).

While interaction *within* the developing northeastern system was high, important connections to the South (particularly New Orleans and Mobile), as a function of the cotton trade, and to Europe should be noted. New York's cotton triangle was the most important component of this trade. At the three corners of the cotton trade were the cotton port (New Orleans, Mobile, Charleston), the European port (Liverpool or Le Havre), and New York. While a normal direct run of cotton from, say, New Orleans to Liverpool would seem logical, New York acquired a strong grip on the cotton

trade by channeling cotton from the South through New York to Europe. After the War of 1812, New York maintained its leadership in cotton trade from the South to the Northeast and to Europe, although by the late 1830s and early 1840s Boston was capturing an increasing share. The shippers in New York consolidated the city's position after 1822 by establishing regularly scheduled packet lines to the major cotton ports of Europe (Liverpool, Le Havre, and London). The return run from Europe to New York carried imported merchandise as well as immigrants. Shipped to the southern ports, for their own consumption or for redistribution up the Mississippi–Ohio River system, were such European imports as lace, wine, books, cutlery, woolens, and fine cotton goods, in addition to New England–produced furniture, coarse textiles, and sheeting, New York–produced clothing and soap, boots and shoes from Massachusetts, and harnesses and saddlery from Newark, New Jersey.

The Northeast, through its trade, commerce, and manufacturing growth in the first half of the 19th century, emerged by 1860 as the most-diversified and -developed region in North America. As regional definition occurred such that the Northeast, South, and Middle West came to be thought of as displaying discriminating features, the Northeast emerged as the dominant area for organizing the emergent national economy. The nature of the linkage between these three regions has been subject to varying interpretation, however. Fishlow concluded that "interregional exchange was a prominent feature of American antebellum development but not as a result of interdependence among all regions." In particular, what developed in trade between the Northeast, the South, and the Middle West was not trilateral, but bilateral trade. Trade between the South and the Middle West was always of limited importance to both regions in the antebellum period. The South was not a major market for midwestern produce nor in dire need of imported foodstuffs. In its rate of growth it stands in sharp contrast to exchange between Middle West and Northeast. While consumption of midwestern produce by North and South was at approximate parity in 1839, the former was absorbing three times as much by 1860. Flow patterns diverge most distinctly in the 1850s as the extension of east-west transport routes

Table 9.3   Northeast U.S.: Population of Major Urban Places, 1800–1860 (by 1860 population rank; population in thousands)

	1800	1820	1840	1860
New York	61	131	360	1,093
Philadelphia	62	109	220	566
Boston	25	54	119	298
Baltimore	27	63	102	212
Buffalo	—	—	18	81
Pittsburgh	—	7	31	77
District of Columbia	14	33	44	75
Newark	—	—	17	72
Albany	5	13	34	62
Providence	8	12	23	51
Rochester	—	—	20	48
New Haven	4	7	13	39
Troy	—	5	19	39
Jersey City	—	—	3	37
Lowell	—	—	21	37
Syracuse	—	—	—	28
Hartford	4	5	10	27
Portland, Maine	4	9	15	26

Note: Populations of less than 2,500 are not included.

drew the commerce that had once been trans-shipped via New Orleans. From the beginning, high-valued merchandise was able to bear the cost of transportation and entered the Middle West from the Northeast; by 1839 the Middle West already depended more heavily upon the Northeast than the South for its imports. By 1860, the advantage had grown enormously; almost ten times as much of western purchases came from the Northeast than up the Missis-sippi River. This occurred in the context of a rapid increase in the domestic market. The North, unlike the South, always fared better in exports to other regions than abroad. The Northeast found itself during the early 19th century in a dynamic role, with urbanization and industrialization proceeding on a broader scale than elsewhere, but also with the need to respond to competition from the Middle West, particularly in agricultural produce. For exam-ple, whereas New England was a deficit area (consumption exceeded production) in both wheat and corn during the period between 1839 and 1859, the states from New York to Maryland, while always being deficit states in corn, moved from a surplus in wheat produc-tion in 1839 to a deficit in 1859. This was a direct effect of western competition. Thus, tra-ditional crops like wheat became less important while agriculture reorganized to take advan-tage of the expanding urban markets.

READJUSTMENT AND REORGANIZATION

As the Northeast established itself as the "eco-nomic core" of the new nation, a series of readjustments in its economy occurred as the American ecumene increased in size. Nowhere was this clearer than in agriculture. Unfortu-nately, the careful measurement of agricultural change awaits the first U.S. Census of Agricul-ture in 1840. That, and the succeeding census reports, identify two dimensions of change in northeastern agriculture. First, production in corn, oats, barley, and hay increased from 1840 to 1860, while production of wheat, rye, and potatoes showed an absolute decline (Table 9.4). All crops (with the exception of oats) showed a relative decrease, however, so that the proportion of U.S. crop production ac-counted for by the Northeast declined. Second, the Mid-Atlantic states were more productive

Table 9.4 Northeast U.S.: Production of Selected Crops, 1840–1860 (thousands of bushels, except where noted)

	1840	1850	1860
Wheat	31,960	36,175	30,514
	(37.7)	(36.0)	(17.6)
Corn	46,939	70,590	84,564
	(12.4)	(11.9)	(10.1)
Oats	56,418	62,425	83,032
	(45.8)	(42.3)	(48.1)
Rye	13,987	12,020	13,680
	(75.0)	(84.7)	(64.8)
Barley	3,548	4,172	5,962
	(85.2)	(80.7)	(37.7)
Hay (thousands of tons)	7,989	9,662	10,420
	(78.0)	(69.8)	(54.6)
Potatoes	78,160	45,237	65,324
	(72.0)	(68.8)	(57.3)

Note: Figures in parentheses equal proportion of total U.S. production.

than New England (Table 9.5). By 1860, New England was producing a larger proportion of U.S. hay and potatoes in comparison with its population size, but a lower proportion of most other crops. The Mid-Atlantic states were more productive; rye, barley, oats, hay, and potatoes were all disproportionately high.

Until the second decade of the 19th century, agriculture in the Northeast had incorporated few of the changes identified with the agri-cultural revolution in England. While pockets of commercial farming existed, many farms were self-sufficient units, growing food for home use and trading small surpluses at the local store for salt, sugar, or iron products. Cultivation was expensive and exploitive, sys-tematic crop rotation and fertilizers generally absent, and livestock neglected. Oxen were the main draft animals, and cattle were relatively poor producers of either meat or milk. Where commercial agriculture existed it was tied, loca-tionally, to adequate transportation. Thus, early in the century the Hudson and lower Mohawk valleys were specializing in wheat production and the Connecticut valley in corn.

The advent of *large-scale* commercial agricul-ture depended strongly on the growth of re-gional, non-farm demand. The population of the Northeast more than doubled in the first four decades of the century and, by 1840, there

Table 9.5   Northeast U.S.: Concentration of Selected Crops and Animals, 1840–1860

	1840		1850		1860	
	N.E.	M.S.	N.E.	M.S.	N.E.	M.S.
Wheat	0.2	1.2	0.1	1.2	0.1	0.7
Corn	0.2	0.4	0.2	0.4	0.1	0.3
Rye	0.8	2.2	1.0	2.6	0.7	2.2
Barley	1.5	2.2	0.7	2.6	0.8	1.1
Oats	0.5	1.3	0.5	1.3	0.6	1.6
Hay	2.3	1.6	2.1	1.6	2.1	1.3
Potatoes	2.5	1.3	2.6	1.4	1.9	1.5
Dairy cows	—	—	0.8	0.9	0.8	0.9
Hogs	0.2	0.5	0.1	0.3	0.1	0.3
Sheep	1.5	1.3	0.9	0.9	0.8	0.8

N.E. = New England. M.S. = Mid-Atlantic states. Numbers equal crop production or animal numbers by region as % of U.S. total, divided by population by region as % of U.S. total. Thus in 1850, New England's proportion of total U.S. rye production was equal to its proportion of the U.S. population.

were six major cities as well as a host of minor urban places. The early growth of a limited number of large mercantile cities gave way to a broad-scale growth of towns and cities under the impetus of manufacturing. At the stage that large concentrations of non-farm populations existed, one of the prerequisites for an increase in the role of commercial agriculture had been met. The second prerequisite was the necessity for effective transportation to move farm goods to the urban markets. Nothing was more important to the farmer than access to market. Local access roads, turnpikes, canals, and railroads all contributed to the transformation of a subsistence-plus agriculture to a predominantly commercial one. As the Northeast urbanized and developed a transportation infrastructure, farmers could specialize in what they could produce best and move their products to market at ever-decreasing cost.

A clear example of adjustment in light of these factors is provided by New York State. The completion of the Erie Canal had an important impact on the central and western parts of the state as well as upon the Hudson valley. The former region became a major wheat producer with high yields and good-quality grain centered on the Genesee valley. Hudson valley producers were not commercially competitive with this new wheat area and turned to dairying instead. Cheese and butter became major products, and a beginning was made in or-

chard production. The largest market for these products was, of course, New York City. This process of readjustment was later repeated with the rapid development of wheat production in Ohio, Indiana, and Illinois. As Genesee valley development had caused Hudson valley readjustment, so the development of new western wheatlands made the Genesee less competitive. Before 1840, New York flour was moving *west* out of Buffalo. In 1840, Buffalo received 1 million bushels of wheat from the west and, by 1855, more than 8 million bushels. By 1860, New York no longer held its place as one of the five largest wheat-producing states in the nation.

Initially, agriculture in the Northeast was adjusting itself to changing intraregional conditions (massive population growth, increasing levels of urbanization, and the development of manufacturing), but it soon had to reckon with an extraregional force, competition from the western states. As Kirkland has indicated, "The changing conditions in the East scattered the seeds of regeneration as well as decay." Industrialization drew young men and women to the factories, but the resultant urban communities provided large and consistent markets for foodstuffs. Some agricultural products were too bulky to pay long-distance freight charges; others were perishable and needed to be grown close to the market. The Northeast responded in two ways. First, the techniques of farming were improved sufficiently to provide partial competition with the Middle West. Second, and more important, a shift to crops and live-stock responded directly to the new economic conditions of the Northeast. It was in this latter area that agricultural invention and innovation appeared as never before.

While agricultural societies, such as the Philadelphia Society for Agriculture, founded in 1785, flourished throughout the region, they were elitist and impractical. A more-effective organization for the diffusion of new ideas was started in 1810 in Pittsfield, Massachusetts; this was the agricultural fair. The Berkshire Agricultural Society was established to perpetuate this custom and, by 1858, a list of such boards and societies in the United States numbered over 900. Such societies through their fairs demonstrated machinery and exhibited live-stock; some operated experimental farms and imported improved cattle. In 1862 the federal government showed its direct interest in the agricultural sector by establishing the U.S. Department of Agriculture. Its duties were to "acquire and to diffuse . . . useful information on subjects related to agriculture." Through the diffusion of information by these channels farmers became more scientific; they had, in effect, accepted their own agricultural revolution.

The growing cities and towns of the Northeast created a strong demand for dairy products, eggs, vegetables, beef, pork, mutton, dray horses, carriage horses, and the hay and grain to feed such animals. Around each major city a market gardening and a dairy industry developed. The production of fluid milk was of particular importance and continued to expand as other facets of the dairy industry, notably cheese and butter production, moved westward. Feeding cattle for beef was concentrated in the Connecticut valley, which supplied the Brighton Market near Boston, and in southeastern Pennsylvania to the west of Philadelphia. Many of these cattle were locally raised, but cattle were still being driven from Ohio to Philadelphia and Baltimore markets as late as 1850. Specialization in butter and cheese making developed north of New York City and in upstate New York after the completion of the Erie Canal. Around other cities the sale of fluid milk had largely supplemented cheese and butter production by 1840.

Eastern wool production enjoyed its greatest prosperity in the 1830s. The domestic manufacture of woolen goods was firmly established and, by 1840, the farmers of the Northeast accounted for 60 percent of the country's sheep. Wool production was limited to the hilly regions of the Northeast on marginal land largely unfit for crops. Merino sheep, with their fine wool, had been imported from Spain to Vermont as early as 1810. Their wool commanded premium prices and, by the 1830s, Merino sheep were widely distributed over the Northeast with an attendant improvement in flocks.

As the northeastern farmer became progressively more commercial, his cash income was used to procure clothes, tools, and furniture produced in the towns and cities of the area. The family farm as an economic unit became less important as sons and daughters migrated to the cities and mill towns. A second transforming influence—western competition—caused the eastern farmer to adjust still more.

The opening of the Erie Canal and the extension of the railroad system beyond the Alleghenies in the 1840s brought steadily increasing quantities of western products to eastern markets. From the Middle West came wool, wheat, and pork in large quantities and at prices low enough to discourage local northeastern production. Sheep raising in New England declined nearly 50 percent between 1840 and 1850, with a further 35 percent decrease in the following decade. Eastern wheat growers, suffering from soil deterioration and crop blights, could not compete with midwestern wheat. In 1840, the three major wheat-producing states (in rank order) were Ohio, Pennsylvania, and New York; by 1860 they had been supplanted by Illinois, Indiana, and Wisconsin. The driving of cattle from Ohio to the eastern markets had practically ceased by 1860; cattle were now sent east by railroad. Hog production in the Northeast also declined; the number of hogs in New England, for example, dropped from 749,000 in 1840 to only 326,000 in 1860. Hogs could be brought in by railroad, as with cattle, to be slaughtered at the market.

If northeastern farmers lost their ability to compete with western wheat, wool, and pork, they took advantage of their proximity to the large urban centers of the region. More attention was given to vegetable farming and supplying fluid milk. Cheese and butter making also increased. By 1860 the Northeast accounted for more than 70 percent of the nation's cheese production and more than 50 percent of its butter. More hay and forage were grown in 1860 than in earlier years; potato production (particularly in Maine) increased dramatically; and orchards were planted to supply the cities' needs. The fruit and vegetable industry was dependent upon a middle-class urban market, improved transportation, and nursery production of young trees. All of these were in place by 1860.

Agriculture in the Northeast thus was changed by urban demand and western competition. Local farmers were forced to specialize in milk, butter, cheese, vegetables, fruit, and hay which, because of their bulk or perishability, escaped western competition and found markets in the expanding urban centers close by.

INTEGRATION AND DIFFERENTIATION

The period from 1815 to 1860 saw the Northeast improve its function as the economic core of the newly emergent nation. The early mercantile cities competed for regional and national domination as new forms of transportation (canals, railroads, steamships) provided the potential for more efficient linkages in external trade as well as in internal expansion. Thus, the Northeast as a region became more spatially integrated. In addition, it was more fully industrialized and urbanized than either the Middle West or the South. Its early mercantile cities, built upon trade and wholesaling, shifted investment progressively to manufacturing after 1820. In eastern Massachusetts such capital industrialized a basically rural landscape through the development of the cotton textile and shoe industries; in Philadelphia urban manufacturing came earlier and in greater volume than in its neighbors of New York City and Baltimore; to the south the new federal capital of Washington, D.C., also emerged.

The mercantile cities of Boston, New York, Philadelphia, and Baltimore were to dominate the Northeast and the nation for much of the 19th century. James Vance's basic thesis holds that "the earliest support for enlarged cities, beyond the encouragement offered by the population in the close vicinity comes from whole-saling—only a single entrepôt in each major region will rise to large city size on the basis of wholesale trading." Thus, the early mercantile cities acted as points of collection and distribution in an enlarging and westward-expanding urban system. The census date at which cities reach a population of 50,000 supports this concept. New York (1800), Philadelphia (1800), Baltimore (1820), and Boston (1820) all reached that level before any other American cities (Table 9.6). In 1840, New Orleans reached that

Table 9.6	Population Growth of Selected Mercantile Cities, 1800–1840		
	1800	1820	1840
New York	60,515	130,881	360,323
Philadelphia	61,559	108,809	220,423
Boston	24,937	54,024	118,857
Baltimore	26,514	62,738	102,313

goal, and by 1850 the trans-Appalachian cities of Cincinnati, Pittsburgh, and St. Louis as well as Albany were new additions. Thus, the location of the early major mercantile centers and the northeastern region are synonymous. A littoral settlement pattern existed in 1800, with a regional economy severely curtailed by limited transportation facilities. As the trading complex developed, the interior entrepôt serving as a "primary collecting point for resources shipped back to the original entrepôt" is formed. In the case of New York City (the major mercantile center), Albany, Rochester, and Buffalo can be identified as interior entrepôts by 1840. The wholesale-trading mechanism was the basis for the development of the largest places in the Northeast's urban hierarchy. A second set of mid-sized places developed as industrial towns. By 1830, a number of these had emerged in New England—particularly Lynn, Springfield, Lowell, Providence, and Warwick.

The Mercantile City

The mercantile city focused on the waterfront (Fig. 9.2). There the functions of the city were performed: the loading and unloading of vessels, the warehousing of goods and materials awaiting distribution into the city or farther inland and containing items to be shipped via coastal vessel to other mercantile ports or over-

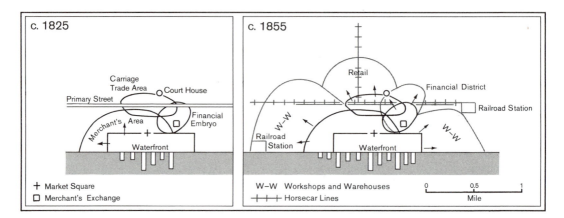

Figure 9.2   The Mercantile City and the Emergence of Downtown (after Muller)

seas, and the financial districts and merchant exchange where the many and various financial transactions (insurance, credit exchange, and the like) occurred. Beyond lay the courthouse, the final arbiter of mercantile conflict. All these functions were organized with reference to the "point of attachment" (the docks) to the outside world (Fig. 9.2). Beyond lay the residences of the wealthy. Charles Dickens described Baltimore in 1842 as "a bustling busy town with a great deal of traffic of various kinds and in particular of water commerce. That portion of the town that it most favors is none of the cleanest it is true; but the upper part is of a very different character and has many agreeable streets and public monuments." Thus the middle and upper classes separated themselves from the commercial waterfront area.

The mercantile city was also compact. Baltimore in 1830 packed its 81,000 residents into an area measuring 2¼ miles by 1½ miles, and no part of the built-up area was more than 1½ miles from the developed waterfront. Residential densities were high. The fact that most people moved on foot and most goods by horse and cart produced a highly condensed city structure. Many people worked at their place of residence. Except for commerce-serving (shipbuilding, ship repairing, for example) and entrepôt industries (processing of tobacco, sugar, and other raw materials) the dominant form of manufacturing organization was the artisan shop. This contained production, sales, and residence in the same location, and the vast majority of tailors, bakers, cobblers, tobacconists, and blacksmiths were organized in this

manner. There were few large manufacturers. In the early 1830s there were probably no more than ten factories with 100 or more employees in all of the major mercantile cities of the Northeast combined. In New York, the largest plant employed 200 workers; in Baltimore, the Stockton and Stokes' coach-making operation employed 80; but in Boston there was no establishment employing more than a hundred. While mercantile cities are characterized by small-scale, dominantly artisan manufacturing, steam power was beginning to be used in foundries, machine shops, and cotton textile plants. Baltimore in 1833 had 32 steam-powered plants, using small horsepower engines. By 1838, only 45 plants in Baltimore and 59 in Philadelphia were utilizing this newer form of power.

Mercantile cities have been characterized as compact, dominated by pedestrian and horse and cart movement, with noxious industries (tanning, slaughtering) pushed to the periphery. The central area was interspersed with artisan manufacturing, but the waterfront provided a basis for functional segregation (Fig. 9.2). Not until 1827 in New York and the 1850s in most other mercantile cities was the horse-drawn omnibus introduced. This provided for the privileged few—25,000 riders per day in New York in 1837—an escape from the high mercantile city densities.

Industrialization

As the sequential transportation improvements of canal, steamship, and railroad more fully integrated the area east of the Mississippi, the

Northeast experienced the parallel growth of industrialization and urbanization (Table 9.7). The mercantile cities acted as source areas for capital for merchant capitalists who were seeking new areas for investment. Thus, two major streams of change occurred: the larger urban places became attractive locations for manufacturing, and new industrial towns developed, particularly in New England, and became urban places as a function of their industrial origins.

Early industry in the Northeast was predominantly household manufacture (the "family factory") in which farm homes were the units of production. The process was of self-provision, "a fertile ground in which invention might germinate," and thus from the basically rural areas of southern and eastern New England came a flood of inventions. But waterpower was the energy for the American Industrial Revolution, which had its roots in the cities of the Northeast and the countryside of New England. The first cotton spinning mill was set up by Samuel Slater at Providence in 1790. The first true industrial city in America, as opposed to the existing large mercantile centers, was Lowell, established by "The Proprietors of the Locks and Canals of the Pawtucket Falls of the Merrimac River in Massachusetts."

The growth of the national market (to nearly 10 million people by 1820) and demands by New England shippers for goods to trade increased the pressure on domestic entrepreneurs to produce more staple products (cheap and durable textiles, metal products, wooden ware, and the like). The capital to engage in such production had been earned by New England merchants. The industry to which the new American system of manufacture was applied was, as in Britain, that of cotton textiles. Earlier developments in the cotton textile industry in such places as Pawtucket, Slatersville, and Manchester had been relatively small, producing yarn and thread for use in handweaving, and had utilized whole families as their labor forces.

In 1814, Francis Cabot Lowell and Patrick Jackson organized the Boston Manufacturing Company, utilizing capital earned in the shipping trades. Their first mill built in that same year at Waltham was an integrated mill. Utilizing baled cotton purchased from southern merchants, the factory produced a plain, coarse, inexpensive white sheeting. The enormous success of the Waltham mill encouraged the Boston capitalists to repeat the undertaking. The next great venture was Lowell, followed by Chicopee and Holyoke in Massachusetts, Nashua and Manchester in New Hampshire, and Biddeford and Lewiston in Maine. By 1855 in Lowell, for example, 52 integrated mills employed 13,187 people of whom nearly 9,000 were women. Five years earlier, the Merrimack Manufacturing Company was employing 2,145 operatives and there were five other mills with employment exceeding 1,000. In Lowell, boardinghouses were constructed initially to house the female workers attracted from the surrounding areas by employment opportunities. By the 1850s, however, many immigrant

Table 9.7   Northeast U.S.: Manufacturing Data, 1860

	Establishments		Employment		Average employment per establishment	Value added ($000's)	
New England	20,871	(14.8)	391,836	(29.9)	13.9	223,076	(26.1)
Middle States	53,286	(37.9)	551,243	(42.0)	10.3	358,211	(41.9)
Northeast	74,158	(52.7)	943,079	(71.9)	12.7	581,287	(68.0)
Rest of U.S.	66,475	(47.3)	368,167	(28.1)	5.5	272,970	(32.0)
Total U.S.	140,633	(100.0)	1,311,246	(100.0)	9.3	854,257	(100.0)

Note: Numbers in parentheses equal proportion of U.S. total.

women were employed in the mills, particularly in the lower-paid cording and spinning departments. The Irish in Lowell were "a dominant factor of Lowell life" by 1860, and this was repeated in other mill towns like Providence and New Haven. Large mills in a rural setting with their attendant boardinghouses, interlaced with industrial canals to harness the waterpower, characterized this archetypical industrial town. The mill towns that developed in northern New England as a consequence of the Waltham enterprise had their antithesis in the Providence region. While the Boston-financed cotton textile plants of eastern Massachusetts were large integrated plants, highly dependent on female labor, the Providence-financed Rhode Island–Connecticut cotton factories were smaller, with a greater reliance on male labor. This phase of industrial-urban growth produced a new set of cities with industrial, rather than mercantile, origins (Fig. 9.3). While the wholesaling functions for the Waltham system cities remained in Boston or Portland (Maine), the towns attracted retail trade. Provi-

dence grew upon demands generated by the small industrial towns of Rhode Island and Connecticut, as well as upon its function as the port from which southern cotton was redistributed to local mills. Thus, by 1860, both Lowell and Providence were among the largest 25 cities in the United States.

An important effect of any rapidly growing dominant industry, cotton textiles being no exception, is the linkages created by that industry—forward linkages in the form of consumer goods (men's clothing, cotton goods) and backward linkages expressed in an important demand for textile machinery. Usually, many textile mills produced their own machinery but, as the industry grew larger in scale, specialized textile machinery producers emerged who often, in turn, broadened their production line to include machine tools, stationary engines, and locomotives. In Lowell, for example, by 1845 the Lowell Machine Shop, which had begun as a textile machinery manufacturer, was producing machinery, locomotives, and stationary engines with an employment force of 900 men.

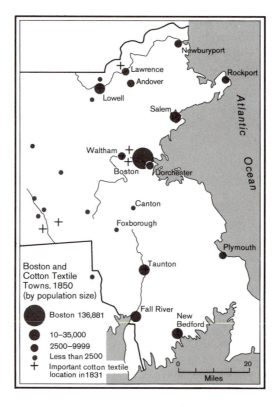

Figure 9.3   Cotton Textile Towns in Eastern Massachusetts: 1831 and 1850

The backward linkage into textile machinery had further important linkages into the iron casting, metal working, and machine tool industries. This process of demand created through both forward and backward linkages was of increasing importance as the United States emerged as an industrial nation by the 1860s.

The cotton textile industry was matched in its concentration in New England by the woolen industry and the production of boots and shoes. Each of these industries was strongly geared to a national rather than local market and operated at scales substantially above the average for the United States. Massachusetts was the dominant location for both industries. In the 1850s, the value of the output from the New England woolen mills increased dramatically, and by 1860 the region accounted for two-thirds (by value) of U.S. production. Between 1830 and 1860, the boot and shoe industry of New England adopted the factory system, and by the latter date the sewing machine was transforming the industry in a parallel manner to that experienced in the clothing industry. For boots and shoes, as with the cotton and woolen industries, Boston was the dominant wholesaler. The boot and shoe industry in 1860 was the largest manufacturing industry (by employment) in the nation and was highly concentrated in eastern Massachusetts, particularly in Lynn and Worcester. The product was wholesaled through Boston, with probably 50 percent of output remaining in the Northeast. In similar fashion, close to 75 percent of coastal shipment of cotton goods from Boston remained in the Northeast.

The introduction of steam power brought yet another element to the New England manufacturing complex. The Waltham system, expanding in the mid-1840s, reproduced the Lowell industrial model by utilizing both waterpower and female boardinghouse-lodged labor at Lawrence. At the same time, the Wamsutta Company in New Bedford created a cotton mill based on steam power and male labor drawn from the existing port town. Lawrence and New Bedford demonstrate two distinct forms of industrial development utilizing different power sources and labor segments, albeit at a large factory-scale level. Fall River, originally dependent on limited waterpower but experiencing increasing pressure to expand, had, by

1860, converted to steam power and was on the threshold of preeminence as a cotton textile town.

Yet outside of New England, the major cities dominated manufacturing employment. While Boston accounted for only 11 percent of Massachusetts's manufacturing employment, New York City, Philadelphia, and Baltimore employed 45 percent or more of their respective states' industrial workers (Table 9.8). Thus, three distinct locational patterns emerged: the New England form of small to medium-sized town dominated by manufacturing (Lowell, New Bedford, Lynn, Lawrence, Manchester); the large city (New York, Philadelphia, Baltimore, Boston) building on its mercantile heritage; and the processing centers (Albany, Rochester, Troy) concentrated along the Erie Canal transportation corridor (Fig. 9.4).

Large city manufacturing was dominated in the Northeast by New York City and Philadelphia. Like all large cities they benefited from high levels of local demand, but they slowly sought to expand their markets in certain products from local to regional to national levels. The major manufacturing cities were characterized by a broad range of manufacturing output with a handful of dominant industries. Thus, in Philadelphia in 1850 textiles and the clothing trades hired about one-third of all industrial workers. Yet the building trades, boot and shoe manufacture, heavy industry, and metalling all absorbed between 5 and 10 percent of the labor force, and five more industries, including hat making, food production, and printing, employed between 2 and 4 percent. New York showed a similar pattern; textile mills, garment factories, ironworks, breweries, distilleries, flour mills, meatpacking plants, and the largest shipyard in the nation producing ocean clippers, sailing vessels, and steamships were all part of the city's manufacturing structure. In all the major port cities, agricultural processing was also important; sugar refining, flour milling, brewing, and slaughtering were part of the urban landscape.

Three other factors encouraged the development of such cities. First, as the dominant port cities they were the recipients of vast numbers of immigrants. Between 1840 and 1860, more than 4.25 million immigrants arrived in the United States of whom more than 3 million were of German or Irish origin. The availability

Table 9.8   Northeast U.S.: Manufacturing Data for Selected States, 1860

	% of U.S. population	% of U.S. manuf. employment	Female % of state manuf. employment
Massachusetts	3.9	16.6	32.7
Boston (11.2)			
Lowell (6.1)			
New Bedford (5.2)			
New York	12.3	17.6	23.1
New York (44.8)			
Pennsylvania	9.2	16.9	17.8
Philadelphia (44.6)			
Pittsburgh (5.0)			
Maryland	2.2	2.2	23.6
Baltimore (59.4)			
New Jersey	2.1	4.3	23.0
Newark (33.7)			
Rhode Island	0.6	2.5	36.0
Providence (34.3)			

Note: Figures in parentheses after the important manufacturing centers show proportion of state manufacturing employment.

of labor, a problem in New England industrialization, was not a concern for the large city manufacturer. The immigrant populations swelled city labor forces while adding to the burgeoning consumer market. By 1860, foreign-born populations (a measure that grossly underestimates their cultural impact) exceeded one-quarter of the populations in all but one (Washington D.C.) of the ten largest cities of the Northeast (Table 9.9). Black populations were insignificant except in the so-called "border cities" of Baltimore and Washington, D.C.

Second, these cities, as a function of their mercantile dominance, were points of capital accumulation where entrepreneurs saw opportunity through investment in manufacturing. They also possessed the physical structures—port facilities, warehousing, and transportation connections into their enlarging hinterland areas—and the banking and insurance institutions necessary for integrated output.

Third, the availability of steam power allowed for a higher concentration of particular manufacturing types than would otherwise have been the case. Waterpower sites limit industrial concentration; steam power has no such built-in constraint. Yet steam power was not utilized in all industries and in all sizes of industrial establishments. In Baltimore, in 1860, only 80 of 1,147 manufacturing establishments used steam power. In Philadelphia, in 1850, only 10 percent of all employers utilized steam engines or water wheels, and these innovations were confined largely to textiles and heavy industry. The application of steam power was highly selective and related more to product than to size of enterprise, and steam power was expensive in comparison with other energy sources. This relationship is clear in Baltimore in 1860. Fewer than 5 percent of all industrial plants in the city employed more than 50 workers, yet these establishments accounted for more than one-half of all employment. Such large-sized establishments accounted for fewer than 30 percent of steam-powered plants. The concentration in the use of steam power was more directly associated with particular industries—iron foundries, metal-working, machine production, food processing, and planing and woodworking. Steam power was also more expensive at this time than waterpower at virtually all locations in the Northeast; thus its utilization required evidence of strong necessity.

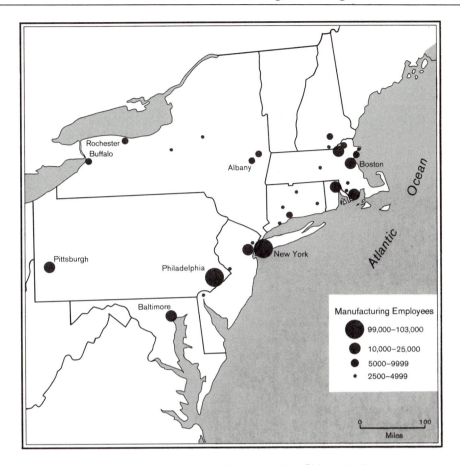

Figure 9.4   Northeast: Manufacturing Cities, 1860

The Erie Canal corridor had at its eastern terminal an industrial district focused on Albany and Troy. This was an important center for lumber, brewing, and flour milling, as well as one of the nation's major iron producers. In addition, Troy had important cotton mills. Rochester and Buffalo were at the western end of the Erie Canal corridor and were important points of connection to the increasingly important midwestern wheat states. Their manufacturing was dominated by flour milling. Rochester, for example, had only two cotton mills to go with its 23 flour mills.

By 1860, cities were industrializing and factory towns were fast becoming urban. This process was dominated by the Northeast, where 72 percent of manufacturing employment and 68 percent of "value added" by manufacture were concentrated. Size of establishment in the Northeast was twice the national average. By 1860, although the four largest cities in the nation were in the Northeast, their positions were being challenged by the newer centers of Cincinnati, St. Louis, and Chicago. Yet in manufacturing, the Northeast was totally dominant; of 23 places where manufacturing employment exceeded 5,000, only six were outside the Northeast (Table 9.10). New York and Philadelphia dominated with 15 percent of the nation's manufacturing employment. From an urban perspective, a number of regional centers (New York, Philadelphia, Baltimore, and Boston), edging toward metropolitan status, had emerged. These centers dominated large hinterland areas, were industrial, wholesaling, and financial centers, and were important beyond their statistical status as the "points of organization" within the emerging national economy. Between 1840 and 1860 the Northeast was the area of urban and manufacturing

Table 9.9   Northeast U.S.: Foreign-Born and Black Proportions of Population in the Ten Largest Cities, 1860

	% of foreign-born in total population	Most numerous foreign-born group	Next most numerous foreign-born group	% of blacks in total population
New York	48	Irish	German	2
Philadelphia	29	Irish	German	4
Boston	36	Irish	British-American	1
Baltimore	25	German	Irish	13
Buffalo	46	German	Irish	1
Pittsburgh	37	Irish	German	2
District of Columbia	18	Irish	German	18
Newark	37	Irish	German	2
Albany	34	Irish	German	1
Providence	25	Irish	English	3

innovation, a model (albeit imperfect) that would be restructured and modified as the nation grew and which itself would be subject to readjustment in the process.

The Nation's Capital

While economic power became vested in the large cities of the Northeast during the antebellum period, the nation's political center was a new, planned city straddling the Potomac River. Section Eight of Article 1 of the Constitution gave Congress power to set up "a district not exceeding ten miles square" to be "the seat of the government of the United States." Thus the nation's capital was to be a maximum of 100 square miles in size. The Residence Act of 1790 gave the president the power to choose a location on the Potomac River. The site chosen by President Washington included the existing settlements of Georgetown and Alexandria. Once the site had been selected, Washington acted with despatch to hire Pierre Charles L'Enfant to plan the city. The plan, drawing heavily for inspiration on European design, was essentially a grid overlaid with a radial pattern. The President's House (today's White House) and the Capitol would be joined by a grand avenue (the Mall). The federal government transferred from Philadelphia to Washington in 1800.

Thus, a new city was born with an initial population of some 14,000 people; this included a Georgetown total of 3,000 and an Alexandria count of 5,000. The District of Columbia grew dramatically during the first half of the 19th century. As the nation grew, the federal capital assumed greater responsibilities and attracted population, both white and black. Black Americans, in particular, sought to locate in the capital and, by 1860, 18 percent of its residents were black. This was a far higher percentage than was found in any city to its north. It was characterized, therefore, as a political and administrative town that had incorporated into its boundaries the bustling ports of Georgetown and Alexandria. Its manufacturing base was limited, and its commercial strength was tied strongly after 1828 to the beginning of construction of the Chesapeake and Ohio Canal to Cumberland, Maryland. The canal was of limited success, particularly after the construction of the Baltimore and Ohio Railroad (from 1830 on). The commercial success predicted for the Chesapeake and Ohio Canal was particularly demoralizing to Alexandria. In 1846, the federal district lost one-third of its total area with the retrocession back to Virginia of the area south and west of the Potomac. By 1860, however, Washington, D.C., had 75,000 residents, a population not attained through mercantile strength or an industrial base but largely through its attractions as the nation's capital.

THE NORTHEAST IN 1860

Between 1800 and 1860 the proportion of the U.S. population located in the Northeast fell from 57 percent to 37 percent. In 1860, the Northeast had only 1.3 million residents more than the South and only 1.7 million more than the Middle West. Yet the Northeast, in the words of David Ward, "supported a sizeable industrial production and was the center of the expanding American economy." While the United States experienced the dual linked processes of industrialization and urbanization, it was the Northeast that was in the forefront of these developments. In 1860, with 37 percent of the total U.S. population, the Northeast contained 72 percent of total American manufacturing employment. With only 12 percent of

Table 9.10   Northeast U.S.: Manufacturing Cities with 5,000 or More Manufacturing Employees, 1860

	Population	Manufacturing employment	Manuf. employ. as % of pop.	Female % of manuf. employ.
New York	1,092,791	102,969	9.4	25.2
Philadelphia	565,529	99,003	17.5	30.9
Boston	297,673	24,445	8.2	22.8
Newark	71,941	18,851	26.2	27.4
Baltimore	212,416	17,054	8.0	27.4
Lowell, Mass.	36,827	13,236	35.9	65.3
New Bedford	22,300	11,297	50.6	5.9
Pittsburgh	77,233	11,151	11.9	19.1
Providence	50,666	11,142	22.0	26.8
Lynn, Mass.	19,083	9,588	50.2	39.0
Troy, N.Y.	39,235	8,826	22.5	54.6
New Haven	39,267	7,474	19.0	42.0
Lawrence, Mass.	17,639	7,150	40.5	55.4
Manchester, N.H.	20,107	7,000	34.8	64.9
Rochester	48,204	6,706	13.9	21.4
Albany	62,367	5,821	9.3	22.9
Buffalo	81,129	5,578	6.9	6.2

Note: Outside the Northeast, only Cincinnati (29,501 manufacturing employees), St. Louis (9,352), Richmond (7,474), Louisville (6,679), Chicago (5,360), and New Orleans (5,062) had 5000+ manufacturing employees in 1860.

the U.S. population in cities of 25,000 or more, the Northeast had 21 percent of its population in cities of that size (Table 9.11). As late as 1860, only New Orleans, St. Louis, Cincinnati, and Chicago had populations that were of remotely comparable size to the major U.S. cities of New York, Philadelphia, Boston, and Baltimore.

As a region, the Northeast experienced urbanization and industrialization before any other. As Thomas Cochran has observed, "while the United States of 1850 . . . was still agricultural as measured either by employment or production, its Northeast had gone through the first and critical phases of industrialization." Large markets permitted higher levels of specialization. Thus the first firms producing for a national, rather than a regional or local, market were in the Northeast, manufacturing textiles, clothing, boots and shoes, and stoves. The Northeast, therefore, not only acquired urban and industrial characteristics before any other region, but it was the economic core from which manufactured goods, in particular, were sent to less urbanized areas and to which farm products flowed. It was, in short, the central area of economic organization for the entire American economy. The industries of the towns and cities of the Northeast became the basis for the emerging manufacturing belt. David Meyer has argued that "by 1860 . . . the key regional industrial systems of the manufacturing belt were established." This belt stretched from St. Louis to Baltimore and Chicago to Detroit, but it was the eastern portion, that part lying in the northeast region, that was dominant.

As a region that was more economically developed by 1860 than any other, the Northeast experienced a number of "firsts." Urbanization and industrialization were paramount, but the telegraph, the ocean-going steamship, the "penny" press, and the department store were all of northeastern origin. It was here also that cities first confronted problems associated with size and diverse, high-density populations.

Yet because of its high level of development it was increasingly bypassed by immigrants to the United States. In 1850, almost 60 percent of the total number of foreign-born inhabitants lived in the Northeast. Progressively, the proportions declined in the Northeast as the Middle West and Northern Plains and the growth of inland cities attracted more immigrants. This was part of a more general phenomenon that

Table 9.11   Northeast U.S.: Population, Urbanization, and Industrialization, 1860

	Total manufacturing employment		Female % of manufacturing employment	% of total U.S. population	% population in cities of 25,000+
New England	391,836	(29.9)	32.9	10.0	15.2
Mid-Atlantic states	546,243	(41.7)	20.8	26.5	28.3
Northeast	938,079	(71.6)	25.9	36.5	20.9
U.S. total	1,311,246	(100.0)	20.6	100.0	11.9

Note: Percent of U.S. total in parentheses.

persists to the present, the high mobility of the American population. This mobility was expressed by 1860 not just in the traditional rural-to-urban migration, but also in increased levels of inter- and intraurban movement.

The "new" Northeast was a prototype for many of the processes—economic, political, social, and cultural—that were played out on larger gameboards as the American ecumene enlarged. Perhaps the most important was the development and linking of mass production and mass consumption. As real family incomes improved in the Northeast, city retail structures were increasingly democratized. In 1862, A.T. Stewart opened his modern department store in New York City. This symbolized the realization that the consuming public was able to purchase more than basic necessities. Such consumer palaces were, as Daniel Boorstin indicates, "symbols of faith in the future of growing communities." They identified the central

business district of the American city into the 20th century.

While the Northeast by 1860 was the most economically diversified and advanced region within the nation, not all parts of the region shared equally in these impressive gains. Areas of northern New England, the Appalachians, and the Alleghenies were relative "backwaters." If urbanization and industrialization produced positive economic results, they also produced many negative social effects. The northeastern towns and cities in 1860 were often overcrowded, with poor housing, inadequate urban services, and limited transportation. Yet they were productive, innovative, and bustling. The marked social and economic differences (as well as incipient racial cleavages) that increasingly characterized the American city as the 19th century unfolded were evident, therefore, in the Northeast by the onset of the Civil War.

ADDITIONAL READING

Books

Adams, H. *The United States in 1800*. Cornell: Cornell University Press, 1964.

Bidwell, P.W., and Falconer, J.I. *History of Agriculture in the Northern United States 1620–1860*. Washington: Carnegie Institution, 1925; New York: Peter Smith, 1941.

Boorstin, D.J. *The Americans: The Democratic Experience*. New York: Random House, Inc., 1973.

Cochran, T.C. *Frontiers of Change: Early Industrialism in America*. New York: Oxford University Press, 1981.

Cochrane, W.W. *The Development of American Agriculture. A Historical Analysis*. Minneapolis: University of Minnesota Press, 1979.

Danhof, C.H. *Change in Agriculture: The Northern United States, 1820–1870*. Cambridge: Harvard University Press, 1969.

Dickens, C. *American Notes and Reprinted Pieces*. London: Chapman & Hall, 1843.

Dublin, T. *Women at Work: The Transformation of Work and Community in Lowell, Massachusetts 1826–1860*. New York: Columbia University Press, 1979.

Gates, P.W. *The Farmer's Age: Agriculture, 1815–1860*. New York: Holt, Rinehart & Winston, 1960.

Gilchrist, D.T. *The Growth of Seaport Cities, 1790–1825*. Charlottesville: University Press of Virginia, 1967.

Gottmann, J. *Megalopolis. The Urbanized Northeastern Seaboard of the United States.* New York: The Twentieth Century Fund, 1961.

Hershberg, T., ed. *Philadelphia: Work Space, Family, and Group Experience in the 19th Century.* New York: Oxford University Press, 1981.

Kirkland, E.C. *Industry Comes of Age: Business, Labor and Public Policy, 1860–1897.* New York: Holt, Rinehart & Winston, 1961.

Pred, A. *Urban Growth and the Circulation of Information: The United States System of Cities, 1790–1840.* Cambridge: Harvard University Press, 1973.

————. *Urban Growth and City-Systems in the United States, 1840–1860.* Cambridge: Harvard University Press, 1980.

Taylor, G.R. *The Transportation Revolution, 1815–1860.* New York: Holt, Rinehart & Winston, 1951.

Trollope, A. *North America.* London: Chapman & Hall, 1862.

Vance, J.E., Jr. *The Merchant's World: The Geography of Wholesaling.* Englewood Cliffs: Prentice-Hall, 1970.

————. *This Scene of Man: The Role and Structure of the City in the Geography of Western Civilization.* New York: Harper & Row, 1977.

Ward, D. *Cities and Immigrants: A Geography of Change in Nineteenth Century America.* New York: Oxford University Press, 1971.

Ware, C.F. *The Early New England Cotton Manufacture.* Boston: Houghton Mifflin, 1931.

Warner, S.B. *The Urban Wilderness: A History of the American City.* New York: Harper & Row, 1972.

Periodicals

American Economic Review (Fishlow, 1964).

Annals, Association of American Geographers (Pred, 1966).

Geographical Review, journal of the American Geographical Society (Muller and Groves, 1979).

Geographical Magazine, (Muller, 1980).

Journal of Economic History, journal of the Economic History Association (Taylor, 1967; Crowther, 1976; McIlwraith, 1976).

Journal of Historical Geography (Muller, 1977; Meyer, 1983; Wood, 1984).

Journal of Urban History (Glasco, 1975; Doucet, 1982).

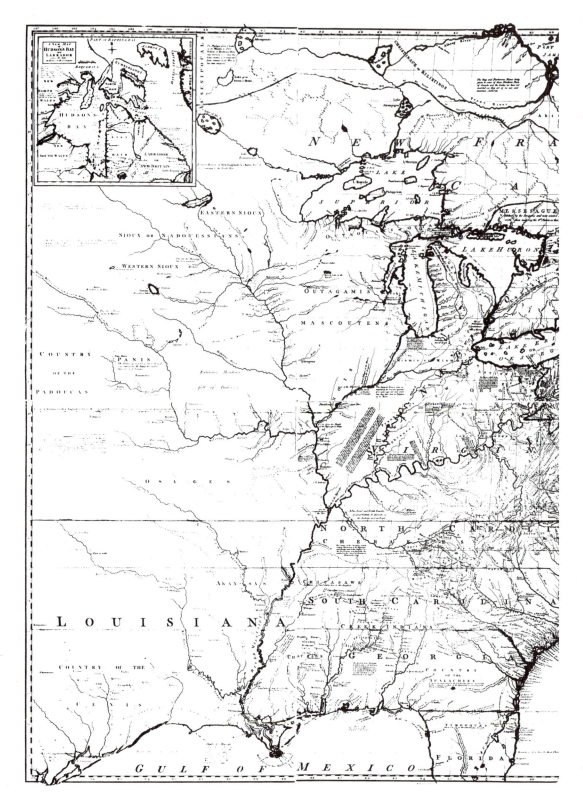

Figure 10.1   The Mitchell Map of North America, 1755

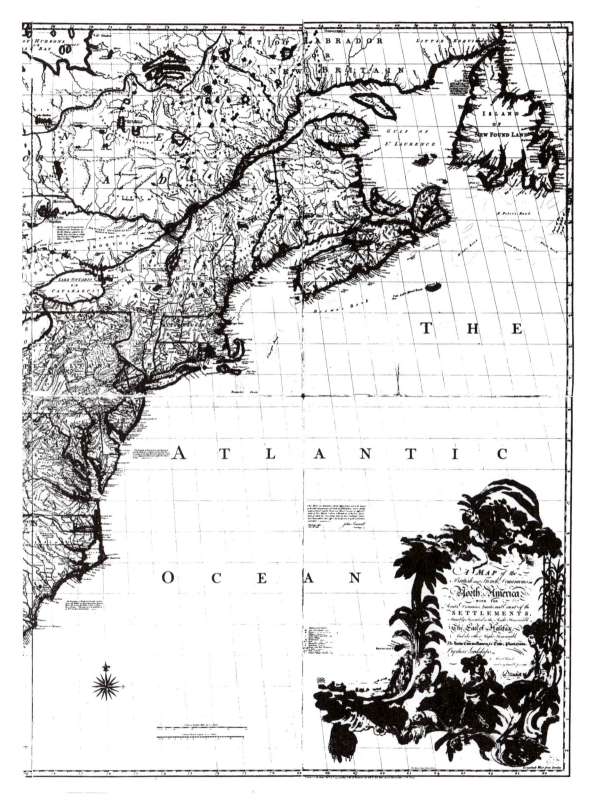

British North America, 1763–1867

THOMAS F. McILWRAITH
University of Toronto

In 1755, John Mitchell published "a map of the British and French Dominions in North America" (Fig. 10.1). Tinted copies show a patchwork of territorial units bearing scant resemblance to the provinces and states today, yet this map was used until the early 20th century to fix boundaries as English-speaking peoples took over the continent largely explored by Frenchmen. The official end to "the French dominions" was still eight years away, but Mitchell used modern English names throughout, just to be ready. When the end came, two British islands—St. Pierre and Miquelon, off Newfoundland—were ceded to France, and continue to this day as token remnants of the once-great French claims in North America. Elsewhere, from Florida to Hudson Bay, from Newfoundland to the Mississippi valley, along the Atlantic seaboard, across the Appalachians, and around the Great Lakes, the land in 1763 was British.

Britain was supreme at sea, and 18th-century North America was ocean-oriented. In the next 100 years that grip was to diminish, however, not because of any weakening at sea but because a landward focus developed. America was less and less an obstruction to British global aspirations and increasingly a homeland in its own right. Mitchell's map was barely into its second edition before the American Revolution outdated it once more; the Monroe Doctrine (1823) and reciprocal free trade between the United States and British provinces to the north (1854) are only two of the political signs of the trend. Old coastal towns, individually linked to an overseas metropolis, had to share attention with Ohio or Ontario, where self-standing systems of transportation and urban places were evolving. Land took on value and domestic economies grew up; social structure went far beyond simple kin and family organization. Settlement frontiers generally advanced, but some sputtered and stalled and occasionally even retreated in a most un-Turnerian manner. Despite its unimaginable

vastness, in parts of the continent usable space was becoming a precious resource by the 1860s.

This chapter is concerned with those parts of North America never included within the United States. Figures 10.2 and 10.3 show population change and trends in selected economic indicators for this broad northerly territory—British North America—and are the basic elements upon which to build an account of a century of achievement.

British North America contained fewer than 300,000 people in the 1760s, about two-thirds of them native and one-third European. Fewer than 10,000 natives remained in the Atlantic region, bypassed survivors of much larger populations 150 years earlier. Nearly 80,000 lived in the Great Lakes woodlands and the extensive regions from Hudson Bay westward to the Rockies, and were active participants alongside Europeans in the fur trade. The remainder—100,000 on the Pacific slopes, in the Mackenzie valley, and throughout the Arctic—had yet to see white faces.

Of the Europeans, some 70,000 were French-speaking Roman Catholics, mostly family farmers, subsisting in the St. Lawrence valley. Traditional farming techniques, limited involvement in the western fur trade, and a decaying feudal social structure (seigneurialism) in the shadow of the walled towns of Québec and Montreal placed this group on the outer margins of world affairs in the middle of the 18th century. Another 20,000 or so were nearer the center of the action, in the Atlantic cod fishery. Half of these, who maintained the old style of traveling outward to the fishing banks from Europe each season, perhaps never saw land, much less occupied it; the remainder fished out of countless villages sprinkled around the mainland shores and the eastern parts of Newfoundland. Several thousand first-generation New Englanders were to be found along the shores of the Bay of Fundy, often taking up farmlands recently vacated by French Acadians, who had been forcibly expelled from

Figure 10.2 Population, 1760s–1875

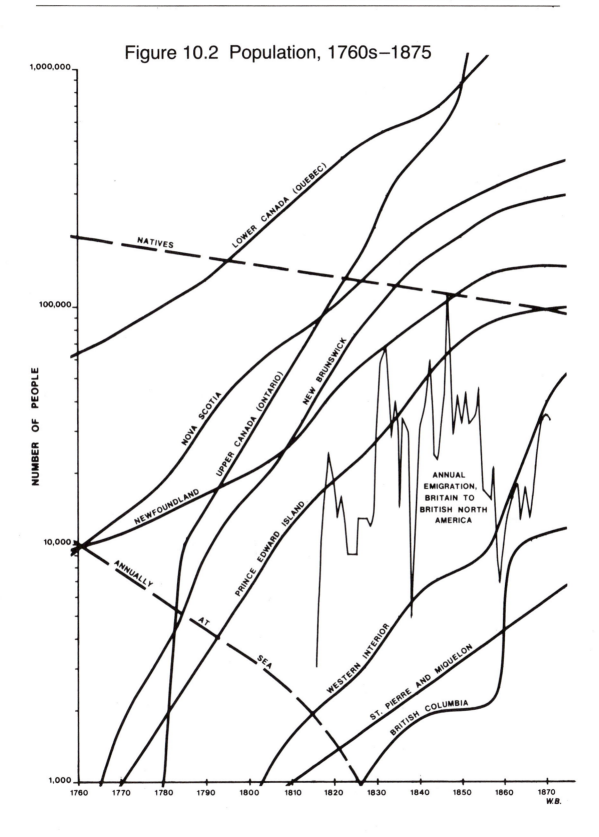

Figure 10.3 Trends in Selected Indicators

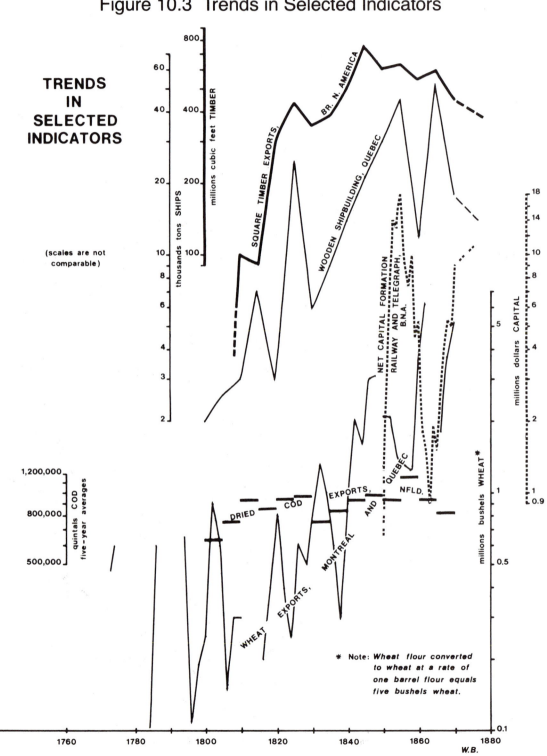

the region by the British between 1755 and 1757. A commercial, aggressive spirit characterized these people. Halifax, a military town of 8,000 persons founded in 1749, was the sole outpost of British urbanity beyond the 13 colonies.

The gaps in Mitchell's map were gradually filled in by the reports of further discoveries, and a quickening succession of scientific evaluators added a new depth of continental understanding. The observations of, among many, Titus Smith, Jr. (a botanist), William Logan (a geologist), Louis Agassiz (a geomorphologist), Paul Kane (a native artist and ethnologist), and military topographer-artists such as J.F.W. Desbarres, Thomas Davies, and James Cockburn, established beyond question that a huge landmass with manageable—but rarely outstanding—vegetational and climatic characteristics lay open for use. And it proved an attraction. By the 1860s, British North America had more than 3 million inhabitants, ten times that of a century earlier. Numbers doubled every 20 years, compared with once every 35 years today, and settlement in Ontario during the 19th century proceeded at a still faster rate (Fig. 10.2).

In 1867, the provinces of Ontario, Québec, New Brunswick, and Nova Scotia formed a federation, Canada, with its own legislature. Newfoundland, Prince Edward Island, Manitoba, and British Columbia looked on with interest, and all but Newfoundland joined within six years. Had Huck Finn's balloon drifted northeastward on that mass of humid Gulf of Mexico air that regularly makes a friendly invasion of eastern Canada, he would have gazed down on a patchwork of regions virtually indistinguishable from his own. British traditions persisted in Canada, enlivened by a reviving French element, and a feeling was developing that the differences, whatever they might be, had to be defended. Identifying, celebrating, and maintaining "Canadianness" is a lasting legacy of the century when British North America turned inland from the sea.

THE CHANGING NATIVE WORLD

Between the 1760s and 1860s, many native groups were overtaken by alien cultures, both European and displaced native, with predicta-

ble loss of patrimony. By and large, the surrender was quiet and virtually without violence. Alterations in military alliances, commerce, land claims, mission work, and attitudes toward benevolence all accelerated the erosion of native independence. By 1867, assimilation, deportation, isolation, neglect, and extinction had occurred, all pointing to the subtle yet unassailable conclusion that native people were becoming misfits in their own homelands.

The Eastern Woodlands Groups

In the Atlantic region, native and European were well acquainted by the 1760s (Fig. 10.4). In an ages-old seasonal pulse, 10,000 hunters and gatherers took game in the interior regions of Newfoundland, the northern Appalachians, and north shore of the Gulf of St. Lawrence during the winter, and migrated to the coasts for a summer's fishing. This rhythm matched that of the migratory European fishermen, large numbers of whom appeared offshore each spring and then retreated overseas in the late fall, and meetings had been inevitable. There was a potential complementarity here, but the natives could teach Europeans little about the Grand Banks cod fishery, nor render attractive service.

As the shorelines of modern-day New Brunswick filled with white settlements after 1783 and timber camps began appearing in the interior about 1800, the 3,000 to 4,000 surviving Micmac and Malecite there quietly gave up their old migratory ways. A few tried, unsuccessfully, the western Newfoundland fur trade in the 1830s, but showed resettlement to be impractical. These staunchly Roman Catholic peoples, who had been close allies of the expelled French, were among the first victims of British neglect of natives in British North America. It would happen again. A more definitive outcome was in store for the Beothuk of Newfoundland, who were cornered on their island and hunted to extinction in the 1820s. The least affected in this period were the Naskapi of the north shore of the Gulf of St. Lawrence. With the poorest harbors and land hopeless for forestry or farming, these stretches of coast remained largely undisturbed well into the 20th century.

Woodland peoples living north of the Great Lakes pursued similar seasonal migrations to the interior in the winter and the larger lakes in

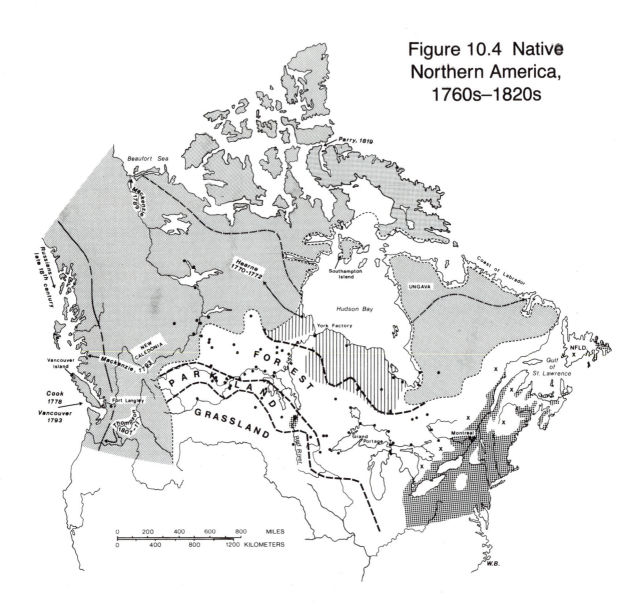

Figure 10.4 Native Northern America, 1760s–1820s

Native societies virtually unaware of European peoples in 1810s

Native population becoming substantially influenced by European activities between 1760s and 1810s

Continuing interaction between Natives and Europeans from before 1760s and on beyond 1820

Areas of European settlement by 1820s; Natives extinct or largely disregarded

X   Native refuge or vacant land; little or no interest to Europeans after 1800

•   Trading posts, 1780s

–––––   Southern limit of Inuit

– – –   Eastern limit of Pacific Coast societies

the summer. But here it was the remote wintering grounds, rich in fur, that interested the Europeans, and a partnership developed between Algonquins in the winter woods and Europeans at the shores. But it was not a symbiosis; as European self-confidence and knowledge of the land grew, they took over the middleman function and bypassed the natives. By the 1820s Algonquins in a wide arc south of Hudson Bay were ravished by disease brought on by starvation and cultural destitution. Both the Roman Catholic and Anglican churches were active in this region by mid-century, administering a mixture of social welfare and religious teaching to less than half the native numbers of a century earlier.

Throughout the Great Lakes, the end of French rule left a power vacuum, complicated by the economic stress of Britain's suspension of annual gift-giving. Some natives still aligned themselves with Britain in the American Revolution, however, and after peace was declared in 1783, were displaced to newly surveyed townships north of Lake Erie and Lake Ontario. After fighting for Britain one last time in the War of 1812, Indian warriors were obsolete. The British attempt to make the agricultural Mohawk into family farmers may have made sense, but to try it on Algonquins was a naive affront. But it established a significant precedent for placing Indians on reservations as nonnative settlement advanced. As the varying quality of land became clear to white settlers and the number of natives diminished by the forces of disease and privation, reserves shrank, and some Indians were relocated to remote areas of poor-quality land, such as Manitoulin Island in Lake Huron. Once again, old partnerships dissolved and the natives were shunted aside.

The Western Interior, Pacific, and Arctic

The Black Hawk wars of the 1830s may be regarded as the desperate strikes of frightened Woodland peoples with their backs to the wall—in this case unfamiliar grasslands. Ojibwa and Cree, Woodland tribes living northwest of Lake Superior, spread into the transitional parklands and onto the plains before 1800, induced by the energetic rivalry between fur traders from Montreal and Hudson Bay (Fig. 10.4). Once involved in a grassland way of life, these groups, plus the Assiniboine

of the parkland belt, could not readjust to the forest. The horse and buffalo hunts forever changed their lives. Even some Iroquois went west after 1794 but, in the longer sweep of events, this was merely a postponement of the end of native self-determination.

Since its incorporation in 1670, the Hudson's Bay Company fur trade had gradually spread to the plains, but trapping and transporting was done by natives. After 1770, however, the Montreal rivalry drew bay dwellers to the interior (Fig. 10.4). The natives' role as middlemen had so diminished by 1790 that many turned to hunting bison, a food source for the trade and increasingly valued for buffalo robes. When food production was taken over by a few thousand Scottish settlers in the 1820s, and when the supply of robes petered out with the extermination of the great bison herds by 1865, native independence came to an end. Enlightened conservation measures initiated by the Hudson's Bay Company after 1821 could not reverse the ecological damage of the rivalry, and outbreaks of diseases, such as measles in the 1830s, added to the misery. Gradually, a long, peaceful coexistence had quietly fallen apart. From the transition sprang the Métis, mixed-blood peoples (mostly French-Indian) who numbered more than 8,000 in 1857 (Fig. 10.5). Their rebellious reaction to alleged British disdain for civil rights brought troops, a police force, and settlers into the Manitoba region after 1870, assuring the final demise of grassland societies.

The Indians of the Pacific coast had yet to encounter Europeans in the 1760s. When scattered British, Spanish, and Russian explorers' ships first appeared in the inlets of Vancouver Island and the mainland, and Alexander Mackenzie, in the employ of Montreal traders, arrived overland in 1793, each was at the extreme end of a different tether and posed little threat. The tribes of the northwest coast have been recognized as among the most-advanced culturally of any in the Americas, and in the benign climate they had evolved a rich economy and society based upon riverine, estuarine, and marine habitats. An estimated 100,000 natives easily held their own.

The rich Pacific slopes and intermountain regions yielded their treasure to Europeans with little involvement by natives. For a brief period between the 1780s and 1810s, Nootka

Figure 10.5 "Métis Encampment," oil on canvas by Paul Kane
(Courtesy Royal Ontario Museum, Toronto)

and Haida Indians joined the new seaotter fur trade with China. Tlingit of Alaska provided some foodstuffs for the Russians, but smallpox in the 1830s ended the relationship. While the natives were indeed accomplished salmon fishermen, no external market yet existed for their catch, nor were they engaged in the whale hunts that developed after 1820. The Hudson's Bay Company, which acquired Pacific coast rights after 1821, commenced selling farm lots on Vancouver Island in the 1840s to augment its own farm production at Fort Langley, but natives were not involved. The British Columbia region was a place for grab-and-run exploitation, without regard for indigenous peoples. When gold drew 20,000 fortune-seekers to New Caledonia in 1858, the native population was halved to 30,000 within fifteen years.

Finally, the far north remained the undisturbed home to several thousand tundra Indians and Inuit throughout the 100 years. A Moravian mission established in Labrador in 1771 was exceptional. The Hearne, Mackenzie, Parry and Franklin expeditions and Hudson's Bay Company forays as far as the Yukon and eastern Alaska were purely exploratory. The tundra lay beyond the domain of the fur trade, and even lands east of Hudson Bay did not start producing furs until the mid-19th century. The appearance of American whalers around Southampton Island and in the Beaufort Sea after 1860 was a sign of the future, but until that time missionaries, not traders, were the principal influence.

Native Canadians were regarded by Europeans as useful guides and hunters, but little more. When the hunt was over—the furs depleted or the foe vanquished—they were not further adopted into the new European world. It is a remarkable fact that beaver pelts found a ready market at the very moment in history when explorers started reaching inland in America, for neither wheat, nor woodpulp, nor iron ore, had they been sought, would have produced the same working arrangement. Hunting was a native habit, and we may speculate that the fur trade, for all its recorded destructiveness to traditional societies, nevertheless softened the impact of the meeting of the two cultures. The relatively peaceful relationship that had existed between the two groups may be seen as a legacy of the fur trade.

TIDAL BRITISH NORTH AMERICA

Territorial and Political Geography

The Treaty of Paris, closing the Seven Years War in 1763, divided authority northward from Massachusetts (which then included Maine) into four parts (Fig. 10.6). The British province of Nova Scotia was the old Acadian area, and Québec the entrance to the fur trade; both had vague or arbitrary inland limits. Newfoundland (a non-colonial British claim) and St. Pierre and Miquelon (French territory) provided each mother-nation with landing places for the Atlantic fishery.

The American Revolution made it necessary to fix the northeastern boundary of the United States, resolved near the coast in 1817 and further inland in 1842. No other international decisions were called for in the region, but substantial refinements occurred prior to 1825. Nova Scotia was balkanized into four pieces, encouraging a mosaic of parochial settlement that has thwarted all attempts at Maritime union, starting as early as the 1830s. The shores of Newfoundland were traded back and forth with Québec and were opened to French and Americans for landing and curing fish, but supposedly not for settlement. Newfoundland was simply a rock in the sea, and any potential political unity was suppressed by the international significance of the fishery.

Britain's claims on the Pacific, dating from Cook's discovery in 1778, were challenged at various times by Spaniards, Russians, and Americans. Had the final settlement been made eastward from the coast and before 1815, precedent suggests that the Columbia River would have formed part of the boundary. By the time the stakes became high enough to force a solution in the 1840s, however, Britain was clearly satisfied with simple geometric solutions. Extending the 49th parallel through to the Pacific followed precedent and suggests that Britain was only moderately committed to the Pacific area. Yet it is a mark of the continuing focal nature of the sea itself that the coastal colonies of Vancouver Island and New Westminster came together as the single province of British Columbia in 1866.

The Seaward Focus

The settlement of Newfoundland, Labrador, and the northern half of the Gulf of St. Law-rence is the unpremeditated result of changed perceptions of the resources swimming in the surrounding seas (Fig. 10.7). Places such as the Gaspé and Newfoundland had little agricultural potential and were not occupied as goals in themselves. Yet between 1780 and 1830, 100,000 people (three-quarters Irish) established new homes in the coves and tickles from Bonavista around the southeast coast of Newfoundland and westward to Fortune Bay. More than 3,000 French (Acadians and St. Pierrais) and British occupied the forbidden west shore, and 10,000, mostly from Jersey, settled the Gaspé region; 900 more fished out from the Magdalens. As early as the 1740s, members of seasonal fishing parties from Britain had developed the habit of passing the winter in Newfoundland as watchmen for the drying tables and other modest assets that marked the beginnings of the dried fish industry. This was conducted from shore in small boats and was more lucrative than the ship-based salted fish industry it was destined to supplant by the early 19th century. The new economics of cod thus set the stage for permanent family settlement after 1780 (Fig. 10.8). The installation of a year-round governor in 1807—his predecessors had been on hand only during the summer—and the establishment of private property ownership rights in the next decade showed that a real colony was in the making.

The decline of the annual migration was helped by the dangers of being at sea during the Napoleonic Wars (1793–1815), and it brought about the demise of the great English West Country merchant monopolies and the interruption of their provisioning. Cheaper foodstuffs came from New England, transforming Newfoundland into an outpost of the United States by 1840. A new marketing strategy, the truck system, evolved in the Gaspé to manage the Gulf of St. Lawrence fish stocks against overharvest by larger and larger numbers of solo operators. Resident managers kept fishermen perpetually indebted to them by supplying fishing gear in exchange for guarantees to buy the season's catch. And the catch could be substantial, for year-round residence permitted the development of other fisheries. The number of seals taken on the coast of Labrador and in the Gulf of St. Lawrence increased sevenfold between 1805 and 1830. A winter cod fishery, with light salting, devel-

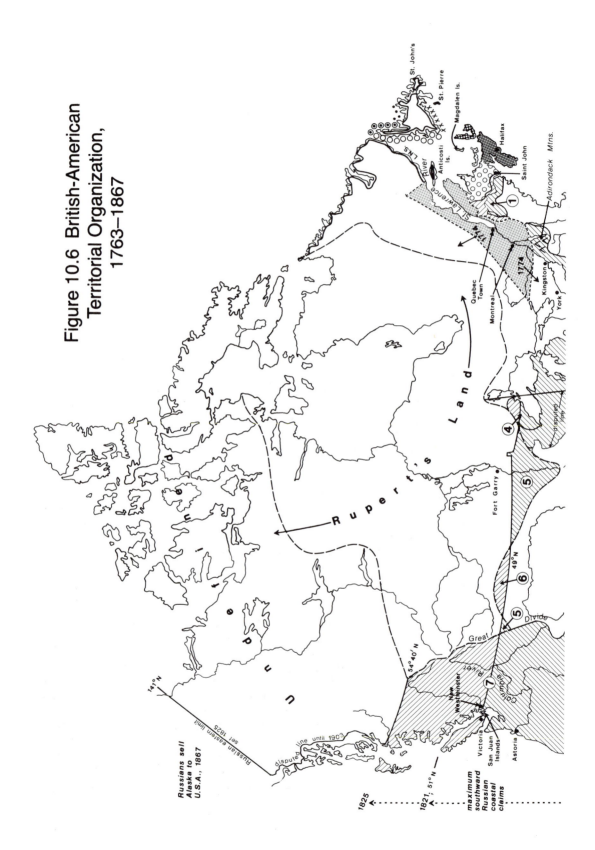

Figure 10.6 British-American Territorial Organization, 1763–1867

MILES

KILOMETERS

1812; 38° N

42° N

0 200 400 600 800

0 400 800 1200

W.B.

80° N

Mississippi River

Ohio River

Cairo

Territorial Claims and Disputes Resolved 1783 - 1867

To British North America

To United States

1. Maine boundary, fixed 1842
2. Trans-Appalachian area, unchallenged by British 1774
3. Quebec Act claim, conceded by British 1783 and confirmed by treaty 1815
4. Quetico region, dispute 1826 - 1842
5. Rupert's Land, to U.S.A. 1818
6. Louisiana Purchase land, to Britain 1818
7. Oregon-Columbia region, dispute 1818 - 1846; San Juan Islands boundary, fixed 1871

Nova Scotia 1763

subdivided into

St. John's Island, 1769 (renamed Prince Edward Island, 1798)

New Brunswick, 1784

Cape Breton Island, 1784 - 1820 (formerly Ile Royale)

Newfoundland 1763

including Coast of Labrador to 1774, and after 1809

Lower north shore (L.N.S.) to 1774, and 1809 - 1825

Anticosti Island and Magdalen Islands to 1774

Quebec 1763

expanded to Ohio and Mississippi rivers, and Rupert's Land, 1774

including Coast of Labrador, 1774 - 1809

Lower North Shore, 1774 - 1809 and after 1825

Anticosti Island and Magdalen Islands after 1774

France 1763: St. Pierre and Miquelon Islands

fish-curing rights on Newfoundland Island, 1774 - 1783 ●●●●●● 1774 - 1904 ◉◉◉◉ 1783 - 1904 ○○○○

xxxxxx United States 1818

fish-curing rights on Newfoundland Island

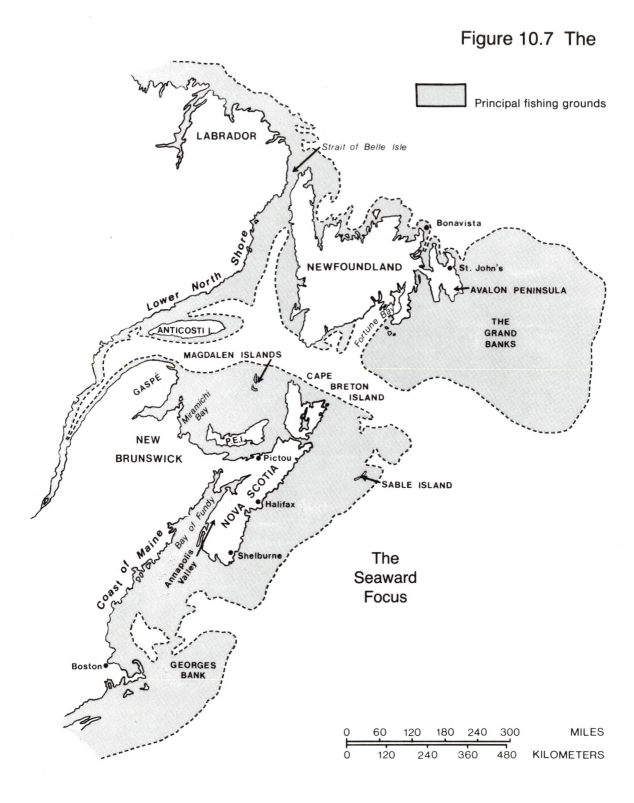

Figure 10.7 The

Principal fishing grounds

The Seaward Focus

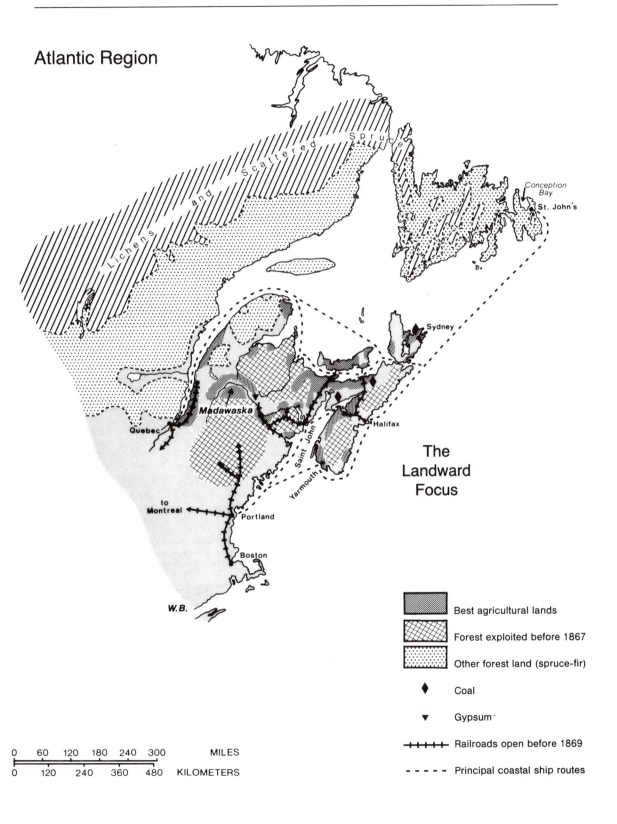

Atlantic Region

Lichens and Scattered Spruce

Conception
Bay

St. John's

Sydney

Madawaska

Quebec

Halifax

Saint John

Yarmouth

The
Landward
Focus

to
Montreal

Portland

Boston

W.B.

Best agricultural lands

Forest exploited before 1867

Other forest land (spruce-fir)

♦ Coal

▼ Gypsum

+++++ Railroads open before 1869

- - - - - Principal coastal ship routes

0	60	120	180	240	300	MILES
0	120	240	360	480		KILOMETERS

Figure 10.8 A Newfoundland Outport: Brigus South, Newfoundland, 1963
(Courtesy C. Grant Head)

oped along the south shore of Newfoundland, and salmon, lobster, mackerel, and herring all were attractions for a swelling U.S. market after 1820.

But it was cod on which this world turned and, when the English fish trade declined about 1840, Newfoundland found itself with an underemployed, immobile, and scattered population, which included numbers of nonfishing landholders. Farmers and fishermen became subsistent and reverted to the jack-of-all-trades conditions of isolation, while life elsewhere in America was tending toward specialization. Newfoundland was slipping behind, and the simpler way of life persisted until the outport centralized resettlement scheme of the 1960s.

The coastline of the rest of Atlantic Canada in the years between 1760 and 1810 was alive with new and revitalized settlement, much of it by refugee groups. Nearly 3,000 German and French Protestants were fleeing from religious oppression; 35,000 United Empire Loyalists were displaced by the American Revolution; the free blacks of Halifax had escaped slavery.

By 1800 as many of 8,000 of the Acadians deported in 1755 had returned, joining the descendants of the 2,000 who never left. Some people came voluntarily, including thousands of Highland Scots: Roman Catholic, conservative, and committed to family. New Englanders had been spreading northward along the Maine coast for years, and for 7,000 of them the Bay of Fundy was the next stopping place.

Newcomers fished for oysters and scallops, carried coal, timber or gypsum, built and worked ships, or filled hundreds of positions in naval services centered in Halifax during the Napoleonic Wars. Others turned to farming in the limited pockets of suitable land, especially in the Annapolis River valley, the head of the Bay of Fundy, the Miramichi, or on Prince Edward Island, "the garden of the gulf." But production was uncertain. People who had been starving in Cape Breton in 1833–34 were exporting produce to Newfoundland in the late 1840s. The old Acadian marshlands were worn out. Three thousand United Empire Loyalists, who had migrated to the rocky shore at

Shelburne, Nova Scotia, in 1784, found a site that had no sustaining agricultural possibilities. With no prospect of rivaling Halifax, and few people interested in fishing, all but 300 had moved on by 1790, mostly to promising farmlands in the Lake Ontario region. Shelburne symbolizes the Maritimes' inability to be agriculturally self-sufficient, let alone a food exporter.

Inland Atlantic Canada

The inland regions of Atlantic Canada were for the most part heavily forested and of great value in a wooden age. Thus when the mast and ship timber of Maine became unattainable in 1776, Britain turned to the interior of New Brunswick as the next best alternative (Fig. 10.7). From 1806 until 1849, preferential tariffs further encouraged the exploitation of the hardwood and pine forests, and ruthless, undisciplined cutting allegedly occurred. Land management and environmental concern were absent, and even the destruction caused by the great Miramichi fire of 1825 was easily forgotten. A complex system of inward provisioning and outward log drives developed in the Saint John, Restigouche, and Miramichi river basins, and an imperfect symbiosis evolved between woodsmen and bush farmers. Timber created massive demands for eastward cargo space before the 1850s and many a vessel sailed once only, eastward, to be dismantled overseas for reusable timbers and lumber. The crews returned on immigrant vessels in ballast.

Timber preferences came to an end in 1849, but exports held up for a further twenty years, thanks to reciprocity (duty-free trade in primary products) with the United States between 1854 and 1866, and to a shipbuilding industry that had decided to stay with wood, despite the rise of steam and iron. Decline of the New Brunswick forest industry was gradual, and until nearly 1900 Maritime yards were building small wooden vessels for the coastwise trade and fishing, becoming ever more anachronistic and less competitive as time wore on.

The interior of New Brunswick was not well suited for farming, and in general the removal of the forest was not a prelude to agriculture. The principal exception was the valley of the Saint John River, Loyalist country where a mixed dairy and grain economy well served the city at the mouth. Far upstream, almost at the Québec border and spilling over into Maine,

lay the "republic" of Madawaska, a rare enclave of good farmland that was establishing itself as a major potato region, rivaled only in that crop by Prince Edward Island. Otherwise, eastern Nova Scotia, central New Brunswick, Gaspé, Cape Breton, and Newfoundland provided no more than the most meager subsistence.

In 1828, the General Mining Association was organized in Halifax to develop the coal reserves at Sydney, Pictou, and the Chignecto isthmus. Rising coal exports, plus gypsum, grindstones, lime and bricks, offset declines elsewhere, but Pennsylvania anthracite and bituminous coal held the edge in eastern U.S. markets, especially after 1866. From being a favored colonial region of Britain, the Maritimes were becoming colonial outposts of the United States, but without special status.

Tidal Towns and Transport

By the 1840s the transformation of the Newfoundland fishery to a New World operation was complete, and the final step was the emergence of the Newfoundland entrepôt. The choice of St. John's as the seat of government clinched its position as the successor to Waterford, Bristol, and Plymouth in the British Isles. No colonial town so dominated its hinterland as did St. John's; its population of 29,000 in 1870 was about one-fifth that of the entire island.

Halifax, founded in 1749, existed for defensive reasons, continuing the role of the previous French forts at Louisbourg (1713–58) and Plaisance, Newfoundland (1690–1713). Merchant Loyalists and pre-Loyalists who settled there saw this town of 3,000 as inheritor of the trading mantle borne by Boston prior to the revolution, and Halifax was indeed a vital landing in the British Empire throughout the Napoleonic Wars. After 1815, however, the dockyard was transferred to Bermuda, leaving only a diminished peacetime naval role and unfulfilled hopes of Halifax ever becoming a manufacturing town.

Halifax adapted gracefully to its reduced importance and grew from 10,000 to 25,000 people in the half-century before Confederation. Any political enmity that might have supported equal merchant centers in both Halifax and Boston dissipated rapidly after the Napoleonic Wars, however, and the free-trade era that followed generated rivalries that were fundamentally economic. Halifax became the focus for coastwise traffic from Yarmouth to Cape Breton, and for reshipping. American grain, British manufactures, West Indian sugar products, and local minerals and dried fish were exchanged there, and reciprocity and the American Civil War kept the warehouses busy. But Halifax was poorly situated to become British North America's New York; that role fell to Montreal. The rerouting of Cunard ocean liners away from Halifax to terminals in Québec and New York in the 1840s symbolized the plight of Halifax and, as the polemicist T.C. Haliburton suggested, Nova Scotia's fading sense of self-confidence.

From its founding as a Loyalist center in 1784, Saint John, New Brunswick, grew rapidly to a city of 10,000 by the 1830s, effectively drawing upon the timber and foodstuffs in its upriver hinterland to support a major urban shipbuilding center (Fig. 10.9). From the 1830s to nearly 1860 Saint John was the Maritimes' leading city, outranking Halifax in manufacturing strength. Forty percent of the nonfishing tonnage built in Atlantic Canada at mid-century was from Saint John; only 13 percent came from Halifax. A suspension bridge spanned the harbor mouth in 1853, a visible step not matched in Halifax until the next century. The promise of railroad links to Montreal or Boston further fueled the euphoria but, in the end, a conservative business community hanging on to a technologically obsolete, labor-intensive industry sealed Saint John's fate.

Frequent food shortages and a staples economy made the Maritimes dependent upon external areas, and consequently vulnerable to political pressures. Manifest Destiny—the U.S. doctrine that viewed British North America as diminishingly British and ripe to fall into the republican camp—was threatening, and concerned figures in Saint John and Halifax sought each other's support against it. Boston's proximity to the Maritimes, plus New York's improved access to the St. Lawrence and Lake Ontario after 1820, threw the St. Lawrence and Maritimes into defensive postures and prompted discussions of overland transport between these two regions. A celebrated military trek across the Appalachians in the winter of 1813 had demonstrated the isolation of the Atlantic and inland areas, and showed that security within British North America was no simple matter, however invincible Britain's position at sea may have been.

A proposal for an all-British railroad between New Brunswick and the Montreal area in the 1840s won the support of the Loyalist population in the Saint John valley, many of whom had kinfolk in the Lake Ontario region (Fig. 10.7). But the costs of crossing miles of empty country around the hump of Maine were beyond the Maritimes' means. British entrepreneurs in the St. Lawrence–Great Lakes region, setting economic goals higher than political ones, had built a railroad on the shortest route to the sea, terminating in 1853 at Portland, Maine. A ferry between Portland and Saint

Figure 10.9 Saint John Waterfront, circa 1840 (Courtesy New Brunswick Museum)

John or Halifax closed the gap. It was not a solution to satisfy nationalists, however, nor was passage assured in winter; yet it stood until the Canadian route was completed in 1876.

The Maritimes were not swallowed up by the United States, despite fears. Rather, overland links to central Canada drew the Maritimes into Canada, a circumstance which Maritimers soon viewed as only a slightly lesser evil. For central Canada by the middle of the 19th century was emerging as the focus of colonial power, and railroads expected to draw inland trade and commerce to the Atlantic coast and away from the United States actually worked in reverse, gradually pushing the Maritimes out to the periphery. The Atlantic trunkline railroads came to be centered in the Great Lakes area, reaching eastward. They foreshadowed by a generation equivalent experiences with Canada's Pacific railroads, bridging still vaster emptiness to the west.

While external railroads were changing the Maritimes' position in America, it is paradoxical that improvements to internal communications were making the region more integrated and thus more accessible to outside influences. Railroads took shortcuts between Halifax and the Bay of Fundy (1857) and between Saint John and the Gulf of St. Lawrence at the Prince Edward Island ferry terminal in 1869 (Fig. 10.7). Other lines reached Pictou and Fredericton, the New Brunswick capital. But the sea was a continuing influence, and a mixed system of land and water facilities persisted in the Maritimes long after railroads had achieved sole supremacy farther inland.

The Atlantic region is a study in the persistence of cultural tradition through isolation. Land was valued as a base for fishing, but also cursed for its niggardliness. The concept of land ownership for its own sake—the engine that drove so much of the inland settlement—remained weak, and Newfoundland was particularly old-worldish in this respect. Isolation reinforced homogeneity of settlements, preserved today as a patchwork of dialects, fraternalism, and vernacular buildings. So while much of North America was a construction camp in the 19th century, Atlantic Canada had already peaked. By 1867, it was a post-pioneer region with a lingering commitment to staple commodities, ill-suited to the processes of industrialization and urbanization moving to center stage elsewhere in the continent. Being only modestly endowed with resources was turning out to be a liability, and Atlantic Canada was one of the first regions of decline in North America.

The Pacific

Fort Victoria, founded on Vancouver Island in 1843, was to British interests on the Pacific what Halifax had been on the Atlantic a century earlier: a fixed presence against burgeoning American activity. The colony of Vancouver Island was formed in 1849, three years after the Oregon Treaty had fixed the mainland boundary along the 49th parallel and left Victoria uncomfortably close to the United States (Fig. 10.6). Protected by British seapower, and made naval headquarters on the Pacific in 1862 (replacing Valparaiso, Chile), Victoria quickly shed its Americanness and developed the image of cultivated Englishness that has been its trademark ever since. Six thousand settlers lived there in 1863.

The Fraser River gold rush in 1858 gave the region a second focus. Twenty thousand people scrambled 600 miles inland by boat and pack trail, only to leave within a few years after the workings quickly ran out. More enduring were wool, tallow, and hides, marketed since the 1840s, plus canned salmon (replacing the salted variety), and coal. The trees were too big to be felled efficiently and sawn up, and until new logging technology was in place in the 1880s, only those trees that could be felled into coastal waters were readily merchantable. San Francisco was a major market. Altogether, except for the gold, the resource picture was remarkably like the Maritimes. But unlike the East, British Columbia had a future. In 1871 it became a province in Canada, committing itself to being the western anchor of the Dominion, provided that an overland railroad was built.

QUEBEC AND ONTARIO

Territorial and Political Geography

Britain's procedures for incorporating New France into an English-speaking continent after 1763 kept on changing, as successive colonial administrators tackled a world far different from the homeland. First, in 1763, strict boundaries enveloped the St. Lawrence settlement and free landownership was proposed (Fig. 10.6). The few hundred British who replaced French administrators were expected to be supervising assimilation, which was presumed to be proper and even inevitable. In reality, however, seigneurial life changed imperceptibly, while such chaos prevailed on the Indian reserve lands throughout the Great Lakes, threatening several hundred traders, that new rules were deemed necessary. Under the Québec Act (1774), Québec was extended to the Ohio and Mississippi rivers, and French institutions—religion, language, law—were guaranteed throughout. But then, beginning in 1784, the north shores of Lake Ontario and Lake Erie began filling with Loyalists who resented French customs, especially seigneurial duties. They were modern North Americans, bent on owning, not renting, land; and in 1791 the Constitution Act accommodated them by setting up a new, landlocked colony—Upper Canada—with British institutions.

Québec shrank to a remnant, now called Lower Canada and with much the same limits as in 1763. Thus isolated, it grew and intensified in Frenchness, buoyed by a regular rate of population increase between 3 and 4 percent, despite the absence of immigration from France. In 1837 a mild revolt by farmers in both Canadas against entrenched authority renewed calls for assimilation, and many French believed that two outbreaks of cholera in that decade were extermination plots. Thus, union of Upper and Lower Canada in 1841 (named the Province of Canada) appeared to be a dangerous political step to the French people. In fact, by this time their presence was unassailable, and when seigneurialism officially ceased in 1854, the occasion was really a minor postscript to the transformation of French Canada into a solid North American phenomenon. If physical coherence may be listed as a factor in "la survivance" and in the roots of Québec nationalism, then the boundary decision of 1791 surely stands as one of the most seminal events in British history.

One more time the region split, becoming the provinces of Québec and Ontario in the new Dominion of Canada in 1867. The two founding societies were thus firmly established in what was to become the nation's heartland, and

have ever since engaged in refining the art of peaceful coexistence.

The Québec Act of 1774 had another important implication. By setting the boundary through the middle of Lakes Ontario and Erie to 80°W (near the present western boundary of New York State), Britain effectively conceded upstate New York to the rebellious colonials (Fig. 10.6). With the French retrenching, and settlement moving westward through the Mohawk River valley, American pioneers took possession of the best inland route south of the St. Lawrence almost by default. Through this territory would pass the Erie Canal in 1825, serving the rich Genesee wheat region. Under different circumstances, the Great Lakes naval engagements of the War of 1812 might never have occurred and New York City been less dominant. But the middle-of-the-lakes boundary line of 1774 set the precedent, and in 1783 Britain agreed to its extension, essentially as it is today, to the western end of Lake Superior. The utility of a drainage basin within a single jurisdiction was denied two generations before railroads made unified watersheds less critical to interaction.

Further territorial decisions affirmed the inevitability of what William Gilpin, an American pamphleteer, called "the hereditary line of progress." By and large, British negotiators lacked the resolve of their American counterparts, and Canadians have viewed these decisions at least partly as sellouts. These included the 49th parallel, which sliced across the plains in 1817, and its extension from the Rocky Mountain crest to the Pacific in 1846; the Maine–Québec–New Brunswick boundary (1842); the Quetico area (1842); and the San Juan Islands (1871) (Fig. 10.6). Canada was firm in at least one instance, however, rejecting an American attempt in the 1840s to buy a strip of land around the north end of the Adirondack Mountains in New York State for a proposed canal between the St. Lawrence River and Lake Champlain.

Settlement and Economy

"The Canadas" (Upper and Lower) are not commonly studied as a single unit, yet in economic terms they were one, regardless of cultural contrasts. The English speculated in crown land near Toronto and in seigneuries near Montreal for a common reason. The entire area was exposed to the continental thrust, the pioneer agricultural spirit, the rise of a commercial economy, and to budding industrialization. Lower Canada had to overcome an obsolete social system, while Upper Canada suffered no preexisting traditions on the ground. Localized environmental, cultural, and economic reasons produced varied responses to what was, nevertheless, a universal quest for rich and meaningful lives.

A few dozen Scots in Montreal picked up the French trading spirit and, with experienced French voyageurs working for them and with security gained by the Québec Act, mounted an intense, debilitating rivalry with the Hudson's Bay Company fur traders. Until 1802, when war caused prices to slump, furs accounted for two-thirds of the value of Québec exports, and grain, spirits, and wholesaling also prospered, especially in the 1790s. Montrealers made the first improvements to navigation on the St. Lawrence River, built a road between Lake Ontario and Georgian Bay in 1795, and consolidated the Thunder Bay (Grand Portage) trading post and the canoe-and-road portage route onward to the Red River. Montreal traders reached as far inland as pre-industrial technology would allow; when overextension killed their enterprise in the 1820s, sixty years would pass before the railroad once again placed them firmly in the prairie economy.

Between 1784 and 1791, 10,000 United Empire Loyalists from the United States established rural communities along the shores of Lakes Erie and Ontario, at the western end of the St. Lawrence River, and on land directly north of New England known as the Eastern Townships (Fig. 10.10). They made up only 2 percent of the estimated 500,000 Anglo-Americans opposed to the Revolution, which suggests that one had to be intensely motivated (or harassed) to give up roots for the cause of empire. Many came later, adding to the 100,000 English-speaking residents who were established on the British side of the Great Lakes by 1810. The Americanness of Upper Canada by 1815—fully 75 percent—was a decisive factor in the longer history of the province, but seems not to have contributed to the outcome of the War of 1812. Loyalism, despite its enduring image as a noble gesture to one's sovereign, might reasonably be seen as a polite, thin veil over well-established economic motives and geographic reality.

Settlers showed up in Canada, because that was where the next most accessible and rewarding-looking land was at the end of the 18th century. Naturally, the attraction was the free land grants for which both Loyalists and opportunists were eligible, either in recognition of wartime service or simply by being there. But those who supported the Revolution also received their rewards in land in the United States, and it would appear that few land-seekers in 1800 were unable to acquire at minimal expense a choice piece somewhere in America. It was a buyer's market, in a porous borderland, and each country was trying to consolidate its sovereignty by establishing a resident population.

Upper Canada was a community planned by Lieutenant-Governor John Graves Simcoe before he even set foot in the colony in 1791. His ideal was a British class system complete with town lots, gentry estates, and reserves for the Church of England and the Crown. Military regiments would be the focus of town life, and a rectangular grid of roads would bind town and countryside together with geometric elegance. This plan was as ill suited as the seigneurial system had been, however, and only the gridwork of farmlots and roads (somewhat adapted to physiography) materialized. On the land, too few bona fide settlers opened farms, while all around were speculative holdings, as large as 50,000 acres in some cases. It was a great land-grab, and by 1819, the year absenteeism was outlawed, three-quarters of Upper Canada land south of the Canadian (Precambrian) Shield was in private hands, yet barely 10 percent was cleared for farming (Fig. 10.11).

Upper Canada emerged in the half-century after 1820, becoming relatively less "Yankee" but no less English-speaking as overseas migration resumed following decades of war. An ethnic and denominational brocade developed as settlers filled the gaps of the Loyalist era in a fashion quite unlike the frontier zone of the United States. Group settlement, such as McNab and Talbot, was rare (Fig. 10.10), and utopian communities scarcer still. Some 150,000 new persons came into the St. Lawrence valley between 1825 and 1832. Principally Scots, Ulster Scotch-Irish, and English, they included artisans, families escaping the gloom of industrial towns, and prosperous farmers astute enough to quit farming while ahead.

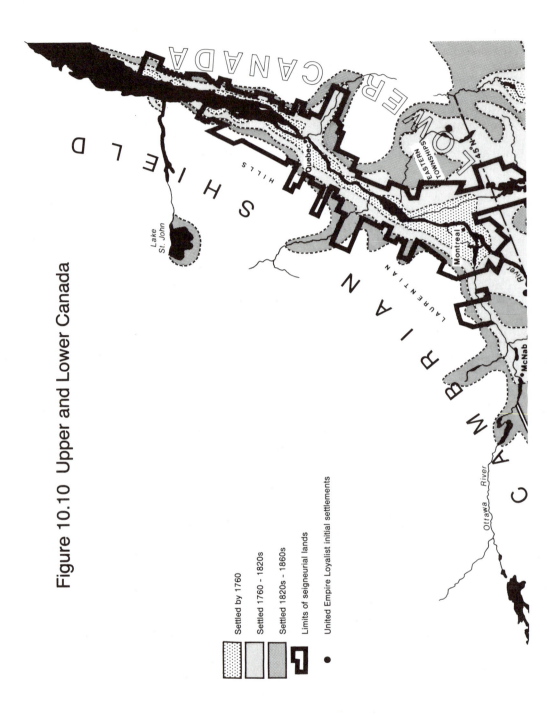

Figure 10.10 Upper and Lower Canada

Settled by 1760

Settled 1760 – 1820s

Settled 1820s – 1860s

Limits of seigneurial lands

• United Empire Loyalist initial settlements

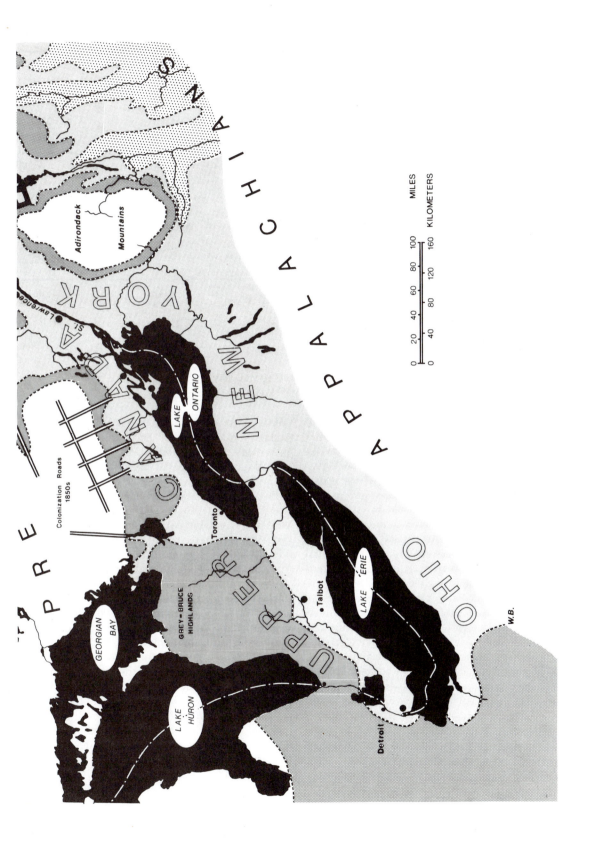

PRECAMBRIAN

APPALACHIAN

NEW YORK

Adirondack Mountains

St. Lawrence

Colonization Roads 1850s

LAKE ONTARIO

Toronto

GEORGIAN BAY

GREY–BRUCE HIGHLANDS

UPPER

LAKE HURON

LAKE ERIE

Talbot

Detroit

OHIO

W.B.

MILES

KILOMETERS

0 20 40 60 80 100
0 40 80 120 160

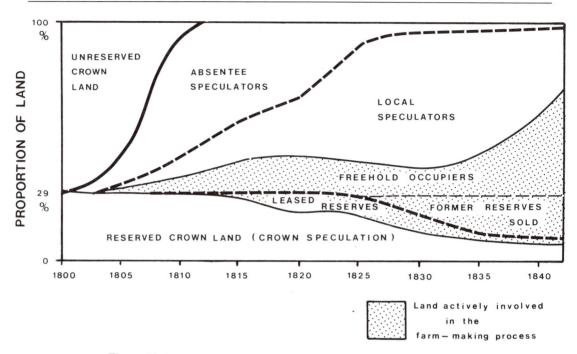

Figure 10.11   Upper Canada Land Disposal, Hypothetical Example

Discharged military pensioners added an element of gentility in a few townships, frequently introducing a type of mixed farming quite out of step with the export-based style of the pre-industrial, non-urban America. Several thousand immigrants put off taking up land (at least temporarily) to fill construction jobs building the Welland or Rideau canals, the two show-piece public works of the period. These heavily capitalized stone structures brought substantial quantities of specie into an economy chronically strapped for cash.

But the majority of pioneering immigrants paid the small registration fee that allowed them a number of years to start farming and gain title. For most it was their first experience with landownership and the principal goal in emigrating. Success lay in the unpaid, volunteer labor of men, women, and children toiling together. The public purse was entirely too small even to support roadbuilding, and it was rare indeed for professional builders to be commissioned (or act speculatively) to make a farm or a mill for a client. It was typical woodland pioneering, at the rate of one or two acres cleared per year, until a manageable farm unit of about 35 acres of field was achieved. Even

allowing for woods, two farms could easily be made on one survey lot. Each successful settler was thus a speculator, holding an attractive parcel for children or for sale in the next round of infilling.

British immigration reached new heights by the 1840s (Fig. 10.2), and many newcomers suffered terribly during their journeys on poorly equipped timber ships that offered cheap fares. Upper Canada's population doubled in ten years and had surpassed Lower Canada's by 1851. The annual amount of new farm acreage in upper Canada soared from 10,000 in 1825 to more than 200,000 within twenty years, and the total farmland exceeded that of Lower Canada by about 1855. Many of the 80,000 refugees of the Irish famine after 1847 went into farming on the last substantial tract, the Grey-Bruce highlands, which rapidly filled with Scots at this time. Others took jobs in the forests, in railroad construction, and as general labor in the larger urban centers. Still others heard of greater opportunities in the American Middle West, and moved on. There even was talk of Manitoba, where private land-ownership became legal after 1840, and a steamboat on the Red River and wagon road to

Edmonton in 1859 improved access. But such talk was premature when places like Illinois were such attractive alternatives.

There were many signs that the era of easy land in Canada was drawing to a close, among them rising farm prices, construction of fences to define individual properties, and government support for underdrainage of wetlands. The province sought to continue the settlement process by once again offering free lands along colonization roads running into the Canadian Shield (Fig. 10.10), but word spread during the 1850s that little decent land existed in those parts and that Canada was past its prime. Among those moving on west after mid-century were many children of immigrants for whom the original family farm could not be further subdivided below 50 acres. This was not 18th-century New France with its long lots indefinitely riven into unmanageable slivers, but a far more rootless society in which families, not lands, were split up.

As Upper Canada and the Eastern Townships filled, the landscape mellowed (Fig. 10.12), but an undercurrent of instability persisted, part of the process of cultural mixing. Church buildings, often three or four in a single village, signaled the diversity. The Church of England, Roman Catholics, five or six versions of Methodism, three Presbyterian denominations, plus Baptists and various sects, all endeavored to reestablish spiritual consciousness in raw communities. The Methodists—the roots of today's United Church of Canada—

became predominant, their circuit riders acting as wandering central places for a scattered flock, while the Church of England stayed put in misguided anticipation of parishioners coming to it. The circuits faded as an urban society emerged, leaving a populist church strongly in place.

All this time the rural French society had been turned inward, pioneering upon vacant land within the familiar seigneuries. Even the Catholic church seemed to have forsaken the rural French, the number of priests having fallen between 1760 and 1830 while the population grew seven times. It was a resolute, self-sufficient body of habitants that finally overflowed the seigneurial confines in the 1830s and moved on to the farmlands of the Eastern Townships and adjacent Upper Canada or the barrens of the Gaspé, into the timber camps stretching from the Ottawa River valley to Lake St. John, or to new labor opportunities in Montreal and southern New England (Fig. 10.10). Wherever they went they became interspersed with English-speaking people and, in the timber areas along the Laurentian fringes to the north, intermarriage of French and Irish Catholics was commonplace after mid-century. By the 1860s fears that French survival was still threatened made emigrants to the United States look unpatriotic, and a degree of divine inspiration was bestowed upon settlement schemes in northern Québec sponsored by the revitalized Roman Catholic church.

Canada was the agricultural heartland of

Figure 10.12   The Rural Ontario Landscape (Thomas F. McIlwraith)

British North America (Table 10.1), and wheat was the principal product (Figs. 10.3 and 10.13). Wheat and flour made up one-third to one-half of all Upper Canada tonnage shipped down the St. Lawrence in the second quarter of the 19th century, and a well-established farm might produce 300 bushels per season, making flour for sixty people. The best land lay west from the Grand River toward the American border, where the growing season was 40 days longer than at Québec City. Severe winters determined that spring-planted wheat be grown east of Kingston, despite its lower market price.

Canadian wheat production received an artificial stimulus between 1815 and 1846 under the rules of the British Corn (wheat) Laws, which gave it a preferred position in British markets. The milling industry along Lake Ontario also was encouraged by the special status given to the flour of American wheat imported into Britain if ground in British North America. After 1832, however, substantial quantities of wheat and flour, originally destined for overseas markets, were diverted inland from Montreal to support Lower Canada as it converted from export grain into livestock and mixed commercial farming for the enlarging home market. Other foodstuffs from Upper Canada, headed eastward through the Erie Canal, never got past the burgeoning eastern American cities, and in 1835 and 1836 British wheat surpluses actually flowed west to cover deficiencies in the United States. Upper Canada occupied a fall-back position for the Atlantic world, a place to turn to when all other sources failed, and a land of barns bursting with surplus in those years when supply exceeded needs.

Ontario's prominence in wheat declined after 1860. The debilitating alternation of wheat and fallow was gradually replaced by a crop rotation that included wheat perhaps only one year in seven. Better educated farmers appreciated that restorative crops—clover, peas, or grasses—planted in the intervening years offered an opportunity for raising livestock, and the mixed-farming economy that emerged was well suited to serve the needs of more and more city dwellers. The rebuilding of seasonal roads for year-round use, the rise in school attendance, the passing of the rudimentary log house, and development of a rural tenantry of farm laborers all were signs that the new Province of Ontario had passed the pioneer stage.

Beyond the suitable agricultural lands lay the Canadian Shield and Appalachian uplands, cloaked with forests and underlain with minerals. By 1820, the hardwoods and pineries of the Ottawa valley and countless smaller streams were providing millions of board feet of square timber cheaply rafted to the Québec depot for overseas shipment (Fig. 10.3). When preferential duties ended in 1849, the Canadas turned

Table 10.1   Farmland and Population, 1851

	Land cleared for farming		Population		
	(000's) acres	%a	(000's)	%b	
Upper Canada	3,000	35	900	33	3.6 acres per capita in 3/4 of all cleared farmland
Lower Canada	3,500	40	900	33	
New Brunswick	800	9	300	11	2.4 acres per capita in 1/4 of all cleared farmland
Nova Scotia	1,000	11	400	14	
Prince Edward Island	400	4	80	3	
Newfoundland	little	1	150	6	
Total	8,700 +	100	2,730	100	

aPercent of total land cleared for farming.
bPercent of total population.

to the huge inland American market for construction lumber, and that trade built up substantially under reciprocity.

Mines were rare before Confederation. Several bog iron sites and two iron ore pits were developed, and a major silver strike was made on Lake Superior in 1868. Stone was widely used in construction, and distinctive brick farmhouses were showing up everywhere in Ontario by 1870, evidence of widespread clays. Glacial sands and gravel were uncovered in the course of railroad construction after 1850, and became the source of the all-weather road that was universal soon after Confederation. Finally, petroleum was first pumped near Sarnia in 1859, the same year it was discovered in northwestern Pennsylvania.

Transport and Urban Places

For wheat and flour traders the Great Lakes was an imperfect transport system, and their inability to deliver that first big crop in 1802 demonstrated the problem. To the nation whose entrepreneurs made the best improvements lay the spoils of a vast, rich American Middle West fronting on Lakes Erie and Michigan. The contest was between Montreal, gatekeeper for the trade of Upper Canada (and collector of customs) and New York City. The Erie Canal was a bold initiative and technological triumph that gave the Americans access to Lake Erie for barge-load traffic in 1825, and set the British to catching up (Fig. 10.13). By 1832 the Welland and Rideau canals had matched it, but already the Oswego branch of the Erie assured Americans that Lake Ontario traffic could still find its way to the Hudson. By the time steamboat canals had been completed on the St. Lawrence in 1847, tonnage through Albany was five times that passing Montreal, and the enlarged, rebuilt Welland Canal was being used at less than one-seventh of its capacity.

Outscored on the water, the British continued the challenge with the first of several bursts of railroad construction in the 1850s. The Grand Trunk Railway of Canada was designed to provide year-round transportation for the intensively settled stretch of Canada between the Michigan border and Québec City, and also to draw American traffic away from the Erie Canal to the St. Lawrence (Fig. 10.14). Its completion in 1860 was politically significant, but it

was a debt-ridden and underutilized liability, somewhat out of step with the swelling North-South trade. Other pre-confederation railroads at first functioned simply as shortcut portages for established water routes. During the 1850s, four lines opened between Lake Ontario and Lake Huron, and half a dozen more were chartered. Each reinforced continental interaction, as did railroads between the Montreal area and New England. Gradually gaps were filled in—bridges across the Niagara River in 1854 and 1873, ferries at Sarnia and Windsor in the 1860s—and the portage function was virtually eliminated once track gauges became uniform in the 1870s. Long before that, American railways had reached Chicago from the east and provided nontransfer, single-mode transport for grain, which entirely bypassed the Lakes, the Grand Trunk line, and Canada.

Railroad prospectuses in Canada tended to focus upon through traffic rather than local business: a line between Lake Ontario and Lake Erie that would replace the Welland Canal, a line to bring cordwood from the Canadian Shield to heat Toronto houses, another with ice from Lake Simcoe, or several to carry lumber from the Ottawa valley or Laurentian highlands to American markets. Only gradually were wayside station houses and siding tracks added to the bare bones of a typically underfunded endeavor. But as mixed farming developed, the milk train came to be part of the railroad's repertoire, enhancing its role as a regional carrier and creating the dominance of the terminal town.

The development of urban places was quite different in seigneurial and English-speaking parts of Lower and Upper Canada. The non-commercial economy of French Canada produced endless linear street-villages—"rangs"—that retarded the emergence of nucleated settlements. Millsites and churches were the most important nodes away from the river landings and, with the exception of Montreal and Québec, virtually no communities numbered more than 5,000 inhabitants (Table 10.2 and Fig. 10.14). Lower Canada's population in towns of 1,000 or more fell from 25 percent in 1760 to 10 percent in 1825, and still had not recovered forty years later. In 1825, one French person in twenty was in a town, compared with one English person in three.

Upper Canada and the Eastern Townships

Figure 10.13 The Wheat Economy

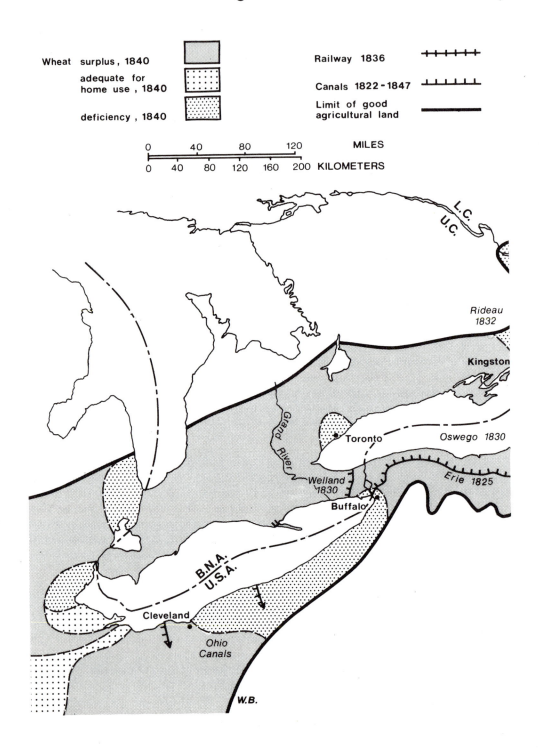

Wheat surplus, 1840

adequate for
home use, 1840

deficiency, 1840

Railway 1836

Canals 1822-1847

Limit of good
agricultural land

MILES
0   40   80   120

KILOMETERS
0   40   80   120   160   200

L.C.
U.C.

Rideau
1832

Kingston

Toronto

Oswego 1830

Grand River

Welland
1830

Erie 1825

Buffalo

B.N.A.
U.S.A.

Cleveland

Ohio
Canals

W.B.

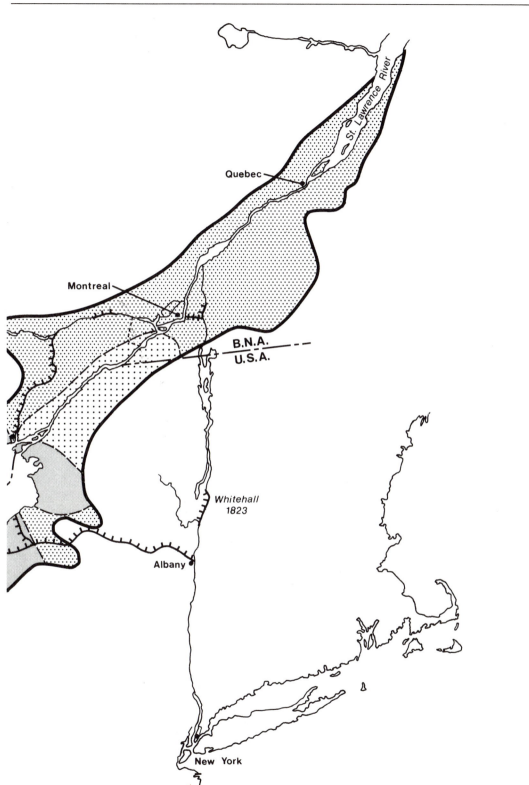

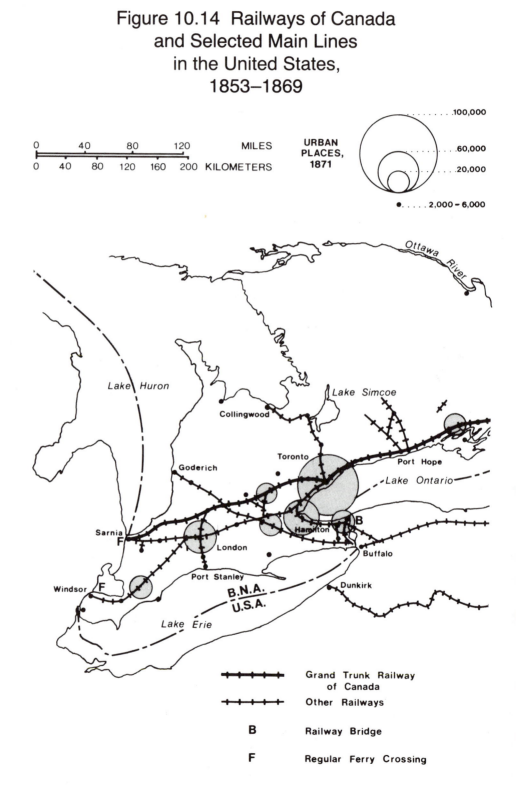

Figure 10.14 Railways of Canada
and Selected Main Lines
in the United States,
1853–1869

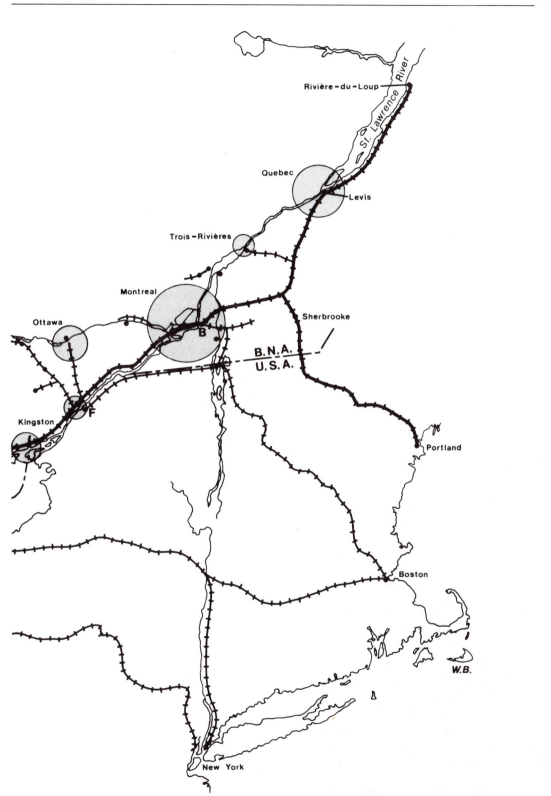

Rivière-du-Loup

St. Lawrence River

Quebec

Levis

Trois-Rivières

Montreal

Ottawa

B

Sherbrooke

B.N.A.
U.S.A.

Kingston

F

Portland

Boston

New York

W.B.

Table 10.2 Urban Characteristics, 1851 and 1871

Towns (population size)	Lower Canada		Upper Canada	
	1851	1871	1851	1871
25,000 plus	76a	73	22	25
5,000–25,000	0	9	29	29
1,000–4,999	24	18	49	46
Number of people in towns of more than 1,000	131,000	229,000	139,000	327,000
Percent of total population in towns of more than 1,000	14.7	19.2	14.6	20.2

aNumbers are percentages of total urban population.

were, in contrast, born to trade, and a hierarchy of nucleated settlements was evident during the farm-making era (Table 10.2). Snow-packed winter roads, lakefront granaries, and lakeboats had served the grain trade adequately, and also had introduced mills, warehouses, merchant forwarders, and bankers, scattered widely and poised to serve industrialization as it developed in the 1860s. Vigorous campaigns began in the 1840s to finance plank roads, and then railroads, to bind it all together. These may have diverted money from industrial investment in the era of take-off in the eastern United States, but a growth in manufacturing firms in Upper Canada from 60 in 1841 to 260 in 1867 is notable. Textiles and machinery in the Grand River valley, woolens west of Ottawa, farm machinery in Lake Ontario shore towns, and a wide variety of machine shops in Hamilton and Toronto were signs of a manufacturing sector that would blossom from this small-town base after 1867.

Toronto, a major new city of the 19th century, grew from 2,000 in 1825 to 67,000 in 1867, the third-ranking city in British North America. With the warming of relations between Britain and the United States during the second quarter of the century, the military threat to British North America diminished, replaced by the new challenge of economic dominance, first commercial and later industrial. Toronto belonged to this new order, emerging as the main city along Lake Ontario by consolidating the importing function, with its substantial markups. In the 1830s a dozen towns strove for preeminence, all of them recipients of inland grain

for export and many in due course holders of railroad charters. But all fell back, with the wholesale center of Hamilton the last to go (in the 1870s) as more and more main roads and railroads converged on Toronto. Upon Confederation in 1867, Toronto assumed a major administrative role as capital of the Province of Ontario. It had a fine harbor, a lakefront transport corridor built on reclaimed land, and was about to embark upon a substantial program of municipal services that would assure undeterred growth and the spatial specialization of functions familiar to industrializing cities in the last third of the century. Its course was set.

Montreal became the metropolis of the St. Lawrence valley and eclipsed both Québec, the anchor for the attenuated New France settlement throughout two centuries, and Kingston, a one-time French fort at the upper end of the St. Lawrence. Montreal's population passed Québec's in the 1770s, and by 1815 a line of steam tugs on the river helped to redirect transshipment activity from Québec to Montreal. The latter town's wall was demolished in the 1820s and, despite loss of the fur trade, the economy accelerated after the harbor was rebuilt in 1832. Commerce dominated manufacturing through most of the century, and a fine townscape emerged (Fig. 10.15), crowned by Mount Royal Park, laid out by Frederick Olmstead, the designer of New York's Central Park. Rejection of the marginal 18th-century Atlantic world and adoption of a continental role propelled Montreal to the forefront of Canadian cities, where it stayed for fully 100 years.

Québec represented the traditional reasons

Figure 10.15   A Montreal Terrace in the 1860s (Courtesy McCord Museum, McGill University, Montreal)

for isolated urban places in British North America: a staple export depot and a military and administrative center. But overseas timber exports faded after 1860, and the last British garrison was withdrawn in 1871. The railway project with which Québec entrepreneurs intended to win back control of the Great Lakes became instead a feeder line to Montreal, firmly restating Québec's place in Montreal's sphere of influence. Québec became the capital of the Province of Québec in 1867, but was as poorly situated as Saint John or Halifax to participate in the emerging continentality of British North America. As for Kingston, it had experienced a brief glorious moment as provincial capital between 1841 and 1844, and some fine buildings were constructed. But stripped of that function and no longer a naval base because of the 1817 treaty with the United States that forbade warships on the Great Lakes, Kingston entered a long gentle decline.

In both Canadas relatively independent urban hierarchies began to form toward midcentury, evidence of the rise of mixed agriculture

and manufacturing. Both Montreal and Toronto established regional markets that supplemented their traditional roles in international trade, and such an enduring rivalry developed that Canada today has no clearly primate city. The relative immiscibility of the French- and English-speaking societies is part of the explanation, but so too is economic geography. Aggressive entrepreneurs in each of two distinctive inland agricultural regions carved out niches for themselves with considerable success, and neither could "buy out" the other. It is interesting that in 1822, an attempt by English-speaking Montreal merchants to annex themselves to Upper Canada failed. Had the plan gone through and the entrepreneurs moved to Toronto from Montreal (as they did in the 1970s), quite possibly Toronto would be alone at the top today.

The administrative separation between 1791 and 1841 had been critical, and by the 1820s Upper Canada was well on its way to becoming the heartland of British North America. This was a place of expansive thinking: the Simcoe

Plan, large farm lots, big canals, and expensively designed railroads. All anticipated growth that would catch up sooner or later. While the writer Thomas Haliburton ridiculed Nova Scotia's dithering, the spirit of progress flourished a thousand miles inland. And unlike old Québec, residents of Upper Canada spoke the common North American language, were growing wheat demanded in the United States, and dwelt astride the westward routes. It was in the thick of the continental action, and while that meant power it also presaged the danger of becoming a colony of the United States, a threat that would become more acute as industrialization developed.

INSIDE AND OUTSIDE

It was common for British military officers stationed in Canada to pass the time painting or sketching, or writing novels, poetry, and plays. Captain John Richardson was one of this dabbling fraternity, and his 1834 play *Wacousta* dramatized a garrison mentality that was rooted far back in the country's history. To Richardson, early Canada was characterized by an inside—within fortress walls a sanctuary for the Europeans—and an outside, filled with savages. (This is arguably an inversion of the circumstances, for the natives were actually the insiders and the European interlopers the outsiders.) Richardson's image has been perpetuated in the literature and, by 1867, the roles had indeed become reversed in much of British North America. Throughout the Great Lakes, St. Lawrence, and Atlantic regions, reservations were the shrunken remains of the inside that natives had once considered home, now occupied by a society poised on the brink of industrialization and urbanization.

British North America of the 1860s was a vast landmass, scantily populated and far from displaying a consensus. The one recognizable heartland was Québec, but it had little of the procreative powers of continent-wide settlement displayed by New England or the Pennsylvania-Chesapeake area. The Atlantic area and Ontario were reception regions: the former being discrete pigeon-holes where small homogeneous communities might take up North American ways at faster or (more commonly)

slower pace; the latter being a crossroads of English, Scots, Irish, Maritimers, New Englanders, Pennsylvanians, and New Yorkers, all mixed together in one of America's principal eclectic landscapes. It was more an area of emulation than of innovation. In many ways, Ontario in 1867 was to the future Canada what Pennsylvania had been to the United States a century earlier. But whereas the Quaker State had distanced itself socially and economically from Britain, its most influential progenitor, Ontario (and Canada generally) was unable to put the same mileage between itself and the United States. There was no type of clean start, wrenching though it might be, that spells independence, and therein lies the root of Canada's continuing self-doubt.

The cultural landscape of the 1860s must have shown the effect. New York temple–style houses stood on the north shore of Lake Erie; Cape Cod houses in southwest Nova Scotia. The Pennsylvania barn was about to appear in western Ontario, while handsome middle-class terraces of New York-Boston-Edinburgh-brownstones ascended Montreal's mountain (Fig. 10.15). Even the seigneurial lands were sprouting American classical or British gothic styles in place of generations-old Norman structures, and Virginia rail fences ran everywhere. Particularly in Ontario, the cultural landscape was still raw, and new structures, rather than altered ones, were normal. Distinctively Canadian landscapes were indeed rare.

British North America was immature, certainly beside Britain, but even in relation to the United States. It was a place for pragmatists, not philosophers or even dreamers. There were no transcendentalist thinkers, no Hudson River School artists, no Tench Coxe to eulogize industrialization. Only in Québec an author—F.X. Garneau—and a subject—"la survivance" (French survival) stirred men's hearts. The skyline was still mainly trees, or dories at sea; steeples and chimneys were scarce in this horizontal landscape. A domestic frontier was truncated; whereas the United States had a Middle West in which to develop agricultural populism, Canada had only the impenetrable Canadian Shield with its tradition of hit-and-run staples exploitation. That all-important "middle ground" between city and wilderness, of which Leo Marx has written, was yet to be found. Instead of extolling a truly warm inside,

Canadian literature has dwelt on the dark, gothic, wilderness, and survival themes that led Captain Richardson to see the vast land as outside his comprehension.

British North America did display one distinctive, abiding link to the old country: the use of the name Victoria. From coast to coast the monarch's name was applied to urban places, bridges, railways, steamboats, municipal halls, townships, a Methodist mission, a coal mine, and countless streets, as well as later to an entire era. Victoria Day, the Queen's birthday, is still a statutory holiday. It is ironic that many of these Victorias owed their well-being principally to the United States. Victoria, British Columbia, lay just beyond the reach of San Francisco, while residents and horses from Victoria County, New Brunswick, found seasonal employment in southern Maine. Victoria Foundry, Hamilton, and the Victoria Railway, northeast of Toronto, had American investors or American customers.

Here, then, was British North America in the 1860s, ever so subtly different from the United States, but sufficiently different that the border, for all its porosity, was a discernible influence. And British North America itself was divisible, too. The Atlantic region was more and more outside the oceanic world, yet never became truly inside North America with Confederation; British Columbia was much the same. Many from the east coast found their metropolitan focus in Boston, where a club for Maritime expatriates was formed in 1853. Québec, once on the fringes of the Atlantic world, created its own enclave on the fringes of the North American world, and it would have a slow struggle back into the mainstream. Ontario started beyond the fringe, but found its inland location was consistent with the emergent continental orientation. Canals and railroads had made Ontario accessible, just as deep keels and fore-and-aft rigging had opened the oceans three or four centuries earlier. Ontario's problem has been to reconcile overseas and North American ambitions, and the province has found itself both inside and outside at the same time. The western interior plains were indeed central to a vanishing way of life for Indians and mixed bloods but, along with the Arctic and Cordillera, were external to the current focus of human activity in North America. The Confederation year, 1867, has been recognized as a political benchmark. Huck Finn would have wanted a new map, but for life in British North America it was neither an end nor a beginning.

ADDITIONAL READING

Books

Atwood, M. *Survival: A Thematic Guide to Canadian Literature.* Toronto: Anansi Press, 1972.

Dictionary of Canadian Biography. Toronto: University of Toronto Press, 1966–1986, particularly vols. 4–10.

Fingard, J. *Jack in Port: Sailortowns of Eastern Canada.* Toronto: University of Toronto Press, 1982.

Fischer, L.R., and Panting, G.E., eds. *Change and Adaptation in Maritime History: The North Atlantic Fleets in the Nineteenth Century.* St. John's: Memorial University of Newfoundland, 1985.

Fisher, R. *Contact and Conflict: Indian-European Relations in British Columbia, 1774–1890.* Vancouver: University of British Columbia Press, 1977.

Gagan, D. *Hopeful Travelers: Families, Land, and Social Change in Mid-Victorian Peel County, Canada West.* Toronto: University of Toronto Press, 1981.

Gentilcore, R.L. and Head, C.G. *Ontario's History in Maps.* Toronto: University of Toronto Press, 1984.

Harris, R.C. *Two Societies: Life in Mid-Nineteenth Century Quebec.* Toronto: McClelland & Stewart, 1976.

Harris, R.C., and Warkentin, J. *Canada Before Confederation.* New York: Oxford University Press, 1974.

Historical Atlas of Canada, Vol. 1; *Canada before 1800.* Toronto and Montreal: University of Toronto Press/Les presses de l'université de Montreal, 1987, forthcoming.

Houston, C.J., and Smyth, W.J. *The Sash Canada Wore: A Historical Geography of the Orange Order in Canada.* Toronto: University of Toronto Press, 1980.

Judd, C.M., and Ray, A.J., eds. *Old Trails and New Directions: Papers of the 3rd North American Fur Trade Conference.* Toronto: University of Toronto Press, 1980.

Keefer, T.C. *Philosophy of Railroads.* Toronto: Andrew H. Armow, 1850. (See "Introduction" by H.V. Nelles to 1973 edition published by University of Toronto Press.)

Klinck, C.F., ed. *Literary History of Canada.* Toronto: University of Toronto Press, 1965.

Krech, S., ed. *The Subarctic Fur Trade: Native Social and Economic Adaptations.* Vancouver: University of British Columbia Press, 1984.

Louder, D.R., and Waddell, E., eds. *Du continent perdu à l'archipel retrouvé. le Québec et l'Amerique française.* Quebec: Les presses de l'Université Laval, 1983.

Mannion, J.J., ed. *The Peopling of Newfoundland: Essays in Historical Geography.* St. John's: Memorial University of Newfoundland, 1977.

McCann, L.D., ed. *Heartland and Hinterland: A Geography of Canada.* Scarborough: Prentice-Hall of Canada, 1982.

Ouellet, F. *Economic and Social History of Quebec, 1760–1850.* Ottawa: Carleton University Press, 1980.

Stelter, G.A., and Artibise, A.F.J., eds. *Shaping the Urban Landscape: Aspects of the Canadian Building Process.* Ottawa: Carleton University Press, 1982.

Upton, L.S.F. *Micmacs and Colonists: Indian-White Relations in the Maritimes, 1713–1867.* Vancouver: University of British Columbia Press, 1979.

Weaver, J.C. *Hamilton, An Illustrated History.* Toronto: James Lorimer, 1982.

Webster, D.B. *Georgian Canada: Conflict and Culture.* Toronto: Royal Ontario Museum, 1983.

Wood, J.D., ed. *Perspectives on Landscape and Settlement in Nineteenth Century Ontario.* Toronto: McClelland & Stewart, 1975.

Wynn, G. *Timber Colony: A Historical Geography of Early Nineteenth Century New Brunswick.* Toronto: University of Toronto Press, 1981.

Periodicals

Acadiensis: Journal of the History of the Atlantic Region (special issue, 1981; Ryan 1983).

American Review of Canadian Studies, journal of the Association for Canadian Studies in the United States (special issue, 1984).

Cahiers de Géographie de Québec (Courville, 1980; special issue, 1984).

Canadian Historical Association, *Historical Papers* (Smith, 1971; Gaffield, 1982).

Canadian Historical Review (Sutherland, 1978).

Canadian Papers in Rural History (McInnis, 1982; Akenson, 1982).

Histoire Sociale/Social History (McCalla, 1983).

Journal of Economic History, journal of the Economic History Association (McIlwraith, 1976).

Journal of Historical Geography (Ray, 1975).

PART IV

CONSOLIDATION

1860s–1920s

The depravity of the business classes of our country is not less than has been supposed, but infinitely greater. The official services of America, national, state, and municipal, in all their branches and departments . . . are saturated in corruption, bribery, falsehood, mal-administration . . . The great cities reek with respectable as much as non-respectable robbery and scoundrelism . . . I say that our New World democracy . . . is, so far, an almost complete failure.

Walt Whitman, *Democratic Vistas*, 1871

I understand that you are going to stay some time in California. Do you mind my giving you a little advice? . . . Do you understand anything about revolvers? . . . Then you are safe . . . You invite your own death if you lay your hand on a weapon you don't understand. No man flourishes a revolver in a bad place. It is produced for one specified purpose and produced before you can wink.

Rudyard Kipling, *From Sea to Sea*, 1889

The truth is, that the majority of non-Anglo-Saxon immigrants since the Revolution, like the majority of Anglo-Saxon immigrants before the Revolution, have been, not the superior men of their native lands, but the botched and unfit: Irishmen starving to death in Ireland, Germans unable to weather . . . the post Napoleonic reorganisation, Italians weed-grown on exhausted soil, Scandinavians run to all bone and no brain, Jews too incompetent to swindle . . . Here and there, among the immigrants, of course, there may be a bravo, or even a superman . . . but the average newcomer is, and always has been, simply a poor fish.

H.L. Mencken, *Prejudices*, 1923

11

Settling the Great Plains, 1850–1930: Prospects and Problems

DAVID J. WISHART

University of Nebraska

> The finest soil you ever dreamed of—a veritable land of Canaan.
>
> Rolvaag, *Giants in the Earth.*
>
> A nameless, blue-green solitude, flat, endless, still, with nothing to hide behind.
>
> Ibid.

Throughout O.E. Rolvaag's epic novel of Norwegian settlement in southeastern South Dakota in the 1870s, a central conflict divides the pioneers' reactions to the Great Plains. The soil is so rich that the head of the pioneer family becomes almost drunk with excitement as he plans the empire he will build in this "Promised Land." His wife, however, confined to their crude sod house surrounded by vast plains, sees only the isolation and grinding poverty of frontier life. This conflict between the fertile promise of the soil and the practical difficulties of living in a remote and climatologically marginal land is a primary defining characteristic of the settlement of the Great Plains.

The Great Plains is an extensive, sometimes flat, but generally rolling area stretching from the Coastal Plain of Texas to the coniferous forests of Canada, and from the Rocky Mountains to a largely indistinct merger with the Middle West and the South to the east. The international boundary between the United States and Canada bisects the northern Plains along the 49th parallel, marking no major division on the land, but offering a political basis for dividing the region for purposes of study into the American Great Plains and the Canadian Prairie Provinces. This chapter focuses on the American Great Plains.

The Great Plains was settled late and rapidly, but with considerable difficulty, by Euro-Americans. Pioneer settlement began with the Kansas-Nebraska Act of 1854, progressed westward in waves of advance and retreat, and ended with the Dust Bowl and Depression of the 1930s. Although abandoned lands were quickly put back into cultivation as soon as the rains returned and prices recovered after 1940, the era of pioneer settlement was over. A region of net in-migration became a region of net out-migration.

The two main environmental problems that have faced settlers in the Great Plains are climatic variability and sheer distance. The climatic hazards are many—extreme summer and winter temperatures, blizzards, hail, and high winds—but the key factor is periodic drought. Periods of 35 days or more without rain can be expected each year, and extended droughts of years' duration have occurred on about a 20–year cycle since the area was opened to Euro-American settlement. Not all parts of the Great Plains are equally susceptible to drought. In general the frequency of 30–day droughts increases westward across the Plains. The major extended droughts of the 1890s and 1930s desiccated the entire region. The dry years of the early 1950s, however, affected mainly the southern Plains, while North Dakota and Montana received near-normal precipitation. Rainfall also varies locally so that, quite literally, one farmer's good fortune may be another farmer's failure.

Despite agricultural adjustments, persistent efforts by optimists to increase the rainfall, and government aid, which provides some cushion against drought, the pulse of life on the Great Plains still reverberates to the rhythm of the fluctuating climate. As recently as 1981, almost all Nebraska was declared a disaster area because of drought, hail, and insect damage.

The problem of distance, on the other hand, has been progressively overcome through transportation improvements. The significant innovations were the railroad and the automobile. The railroads extended into the Great Plains after 1860, breaking settlers free from the Missouri River, which had previously been their main link to the markets and supplies of the eastern United States. The railroad became, in Isaiah Bowman's words, "the forerunner of development, the pre-pioneer, the baseline of agriculture." In the areas between the rail lines, distance remained a serious problem until the 1920s, when automobiles came into common use, revolutionizing mobility and giving a new flexibility to settlement decisions. Even in the last quarter of the 20th century, however, isolation remains a reality of life on the Plains, particularly in the sparsely populated interstices between the main lines of transportation and settlement.

The settlers who advanced to the western borders of Iowa and Missouri in the early 1850s were not daunted by the environmental problems of the Plains. Enthusiasm for the organization of Nebraska Territory was at a fever pitch. Even before the Kansas-Nebraska Act had officially opened the central and northern Plains to Euro-American settlers, a provisional government for Nebraska had been formed in Missouri, and frontiersmen had crossed the Missouri River and were squatting on Indian lands. Far from being dismissed as a desert, a reputation given to the area by the early 19th-century explorers Zebulon Pike and Stephen Long, the Great Plains were now praised in the Missouri newspapers as a "beautiful country . . . soon to belong to the white man, and be made to blossom like a rose."

EASTERN NEBRASKA BEFORE 1870

To sponsoring politicians like Stephen A. Douglas of Illinois, the main purpose of the Kansas-Nebraska Act (1854) was to open up a corridor for a transcontinental railroad that would unite the country from coast to coast. To the local settlers, Nebraska and Kansas territories offered new opportunities for cheap land, speculation, and the various activities associated with supplying other settlers. First, however, the area had to be bought from the Indians, and this involved a major shift in federal Indian policy.

Since 1803, when President Jefferson purchased Louisiana from France, the Great Plains had been seen as a depository for Indians who were blocking the progress of westward expansion in the eastern United States. In the 1820s and 1830s the relocation of the Cherokee, Choctaw, Chickasaw, Creek, and Seminole from the southeastern United States to Indian Territory (later Oklahoma) and of the Shawnee, Delaware, Wyandot, Ottawas, and many other groups into what is now Kansas put this removal policy into practice. By the late 1840s, however, with tens of thousands of emigrants crossing the central Great Plains to Oregon and California each year, the "Permanent Indian Frontier" was no longer feasible, and it was replaced by the reservation policy. Indians would be restricted to small areas that were remnants of their former domains or in Indian Territory.

By 1858, much of what would become the states of Kansas and Nebraska in the following decade had been ceded by the Indians (Fig. 11.1). The Indians (or some of each people, at least) gave their consent to these sales, but as the Secretary of the Interior Caleb Smith admitted in 1862, "it is well known that they have yielded to a necessity which they could not resist." Forced to sell by pressure from the federal government and by their own desperate circumstances, the Indians relinquished their lands for a pittance. The Pawnee, for example, were given 22 cents an acre for almost 10 million acres in central Nebraska, and were left with a 288,000-acre reservation on the Loup River.

Payments to the Indians generally were made in kind—agricultural equipment, seeds, livestock, clothes, and food—and the services of blacksmiths, laborers, and farmers. The objective was to break the Indians of their communal and nomadic ways and to convert them into individual farmers so that they would become self-sufficient and ready for assimilation into the larger American society when the frontier again enveloped them. This spatial restriction and cultural assault only added to the turmoil of the eastern Plains Indians, whose populations had been decimated by epidemics of cholera and smallpox over the preceding century. Moreover, the reservation policy was never given a chance to work because the reduced Indian lands were encircled by settlers in the following two decades, and many Plains

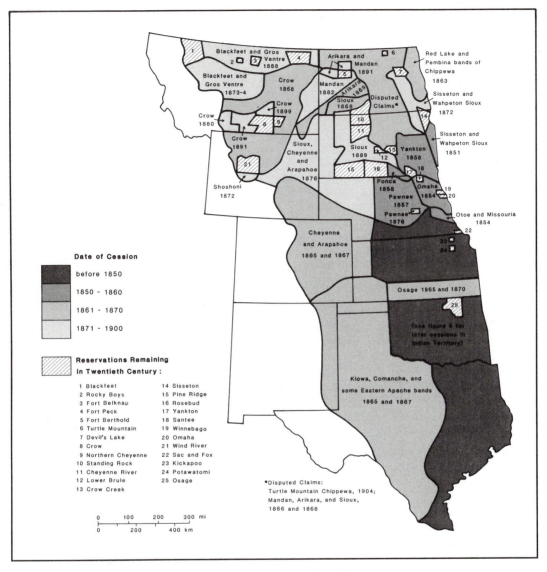

Figure 11.1   Indian Cessions on the Great Plains, 1830–1900

Indians were pressured into migrating to Indian Territory.

With most of the Indians cleared from the eastern portions of Kansas and Nebraska territories, the way was open for resettlement by European immigrants and by Americans. By 1860, the counties adjacent to the Missouri River in Nebraska, plus a wider belt of counties in Kansas, had population densities of more than two persons per square mile (Fig. 11.2). Most settlers stayed near the Missouri valley, where abundant timber and water and access to imported supplies made pioneering relatively easy. The main westward extensions of population were along the Platte and Kansas river valleys, but virtually every stream and creek flowing into the Missouri had its own, small fingers of settlement. Open prairies were avoided because it was too difficult and costly to break the sod.

By 1860 there were 28,826 settlers in Nebraska, already well in excess of the local Indian population. The majority came from previous frontier areas in Ohio, Illinois, Iowa, and

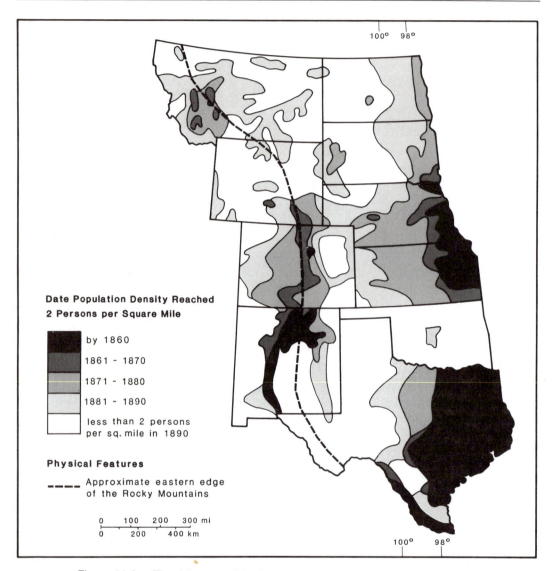

Figure 11.2   The Advance of the Frontier on the Great Plains, 1860–1890

Missouri. Almost one-quarter were foreign-born, with British, Irish, and Germans the dominant groups. Settlers came by steamboat from St. Louis, disembarking at the various towns along the river, or they crossed by ferry from Iowa and Missouri, paying a one dollar fare for their loaded wagon and team of horses. As is typical of frontier areas, the settlers were mostly young adults and children, and the men outnumbered the women.

Before 1862 most of the land was purchased under the Preemption Act of 1841, which al-

lowed settlers to buy 160 acres at $1.25 an acre. Ex-soldiers could obtain 160 acres free through government-issued land warrants. After 1862 the Homestead Act introduced the era of virtually free land: any adult citizen, or person who intended to take out citizenship, could file for 160 acres of public land, pay a nominal registration fee and, after residing on the land for five years and showing proof of cultivation, receive title from the government. Homesteaders could also receive immediate title after six months by paying $1.25 an acre. Land values in

Iowa already averaged $2.50 an acre in 1860, so the attraction of the new frontier areas, with cheap or free land, was strong.

Yet Nebraska was not really a farming frontier in these early years of settlement. In 1860, no county had more than 7 percent of its land area in improved pasture or crops. Agricultural technology was limited, and although land was cheap the costs of cultivation and fencing were high. Corn was the main frontier crop, followed by oats and potatoes. Most of the harvest was locally consumed, although after 1858 a small surplus was marketed in St. Louis and in Colorado.

Almost three-quarters of the population in territorial Nebraska lived in nucleated settlements, from small hamlets of fewer than 20 people to embryonic towns like Omaha and Nebraska City. By 1856, Omaha had 200 buildings and 1,200 inhabitants and was a bustling commercial center with warehouses, hotels, stores, a bank, and blacksmith shops. Like Sioux City to the north and Kansas City to the south, Omaha grew as an outfitting center linking the frontier areas to a national trade network. The main activities of Omaha's population were construction, wholesaling, and speculation. City lots already cost $1,000 to $2,000 in 1860 and were increasing in value at a rate of 50 percent a year. More immediate profits were to be made in the rapidly developing cities than on the land.

In common with most frontier areas, geographic and occupational mobility was high. Many settlers moved on to Colorado, Utah, and California after only a short stay in Nebraska. The small town of Omadi in northeastern Nebraska, for example, was virtually depopulated by an exodus to the Colorado mines in 1859. Across the Missouri River from Omadi, in Sioux City, 66 percent of the 142 working men who were there in 1860 were gone a decade later. Mobility was particularly high among young, low-income laborers, many of whom stayed in Sioux City only long enough to earn a downpayment on land. People with large investments in the community tended to stay, forming a "socioeconomic elite" who dominated Sioux City at least until the 1890s.

Nebraska's population had increased to 122,993 by 1870, and Kansas had almost three times that number. The Civil War and a nationwide financial crisis beginning in 1857 had slowed settlement, but even with these constraints, densities of more than 50 persons per square mile were common along the Missouri River in both states. Railroads had enhanced the positions of Sioux City, Omaha, and Kansas City as gateways to the Plains, and the economic structures of these towns were far more complex than they had been in 1860. Railroads penetrated west of the Missouri, and the Kansas Pacific and Union Pacific spanned the Plains. The railroads permitted the expansion of commercial farming, and by 1870, 52 percent of Nebraska's population were classified as farmers.

Settlers advanced westward along the Platte and Kansas valleys to about the 98th meridian (Fig. 11.2). This is the line that historian Walter Prescott Webb designated an "institutional fault" between the humid East and the semiarid Great Plains. Webb believed that settlers halted at this boundary, stalled until adjustments could be made in institutions and ways of life. It is true that significant adaptations were made in the process of settling the High Plains to the west of the 98th meridian but, contrary to Webb's thesis, there was no hesitation at this line, at least not in the central Great Plains, where the advance of the frontier was spearheaded.

EASTERN DAKOTA TERRITORY IN THE EIGHTEEN-SEVENTIES AND EIGHTIES

Before the Railroads

Dakota Territory, like the eastern portions of Kansas and Nebraska, was a pre-railroad frontier in its early years. In 1870 settlers were concentrated in the southeastern corner of the territory, in the river valleys of the Missouri and its north bank tributaries, the James, Vermillion, and Big Sioux (Fig. 11.3). This area had been prepared for resettlement by the Yankton cession of 1858. The Yankton were given a reservation of 430,000 acres on the north side of the Missouri, just west of the town that adopted their name. The reservation was well suited for agriculture and, by the mid-1870s, many of the Yankton were cultivating individual plots, raising sheep, and wearing "citizens' dress." Still, living conditions were poor and death rates high. Vaccination prevented major losses from smallpox and cholera, but pulmo-

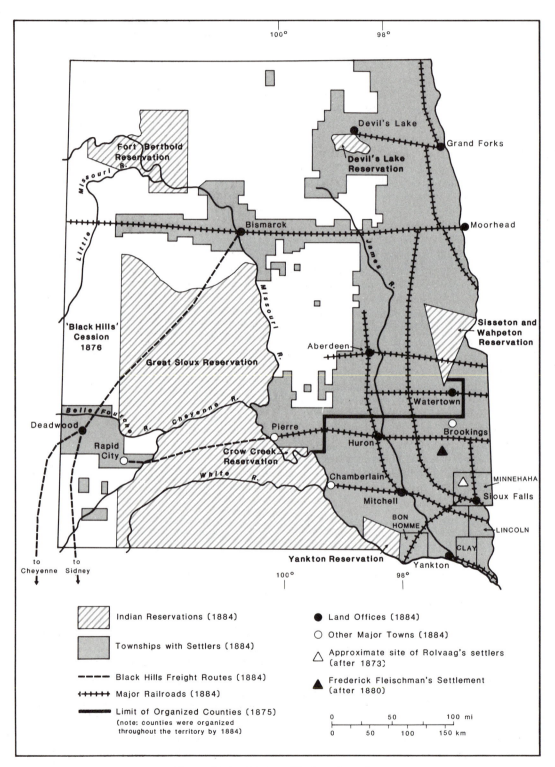

Figure 11.3   Dakota Territory in 1884

nary and respiratory diseases continued to take a heavy toll. The Yankton agent attributed the high death rate to "extreme poverty," poor housing, and the harsh climate, but the rapid change in diet from traditional foods to government provisions (white flour, sugar, and lard, primarily) must also have weakened resistance.

There was no rush of settlers to Dakota Territory until 1868. The disruption and inflation of the Civil War years slowed migration to the frontier in general, and cheap land was still available in the more accessible and temperate regions of eastern Nebraska and Kansas. Locally, drought and grasshopper infestations in 1864 and 1865, and violent clashes with the Santee Sioux in Minnesota and bands of the Dakota Sioux to the west of the Missouri River after 1863, gave the new territory a bad reputation. By 1868, with economic recovery, a growing military presence on the northern Great Plains that eventually subdued the Indians, and the arrival of the Illinois Central Railroad at Sioux City, the stage was set for the first Dakota boom.

Sioux City was the main entry point into Dakota Territory until 1873. After reaching the railhead at Sioux City, settlers boarded steamboats for Yankton or Vermillion, then headed up the James and Vermillion river valleys to the nearest available cheap land. The completion of the Dakota Southern Railroad from Sioux City to Yankton in 1873 facilitated this process, and the Dakota Southern carried thousands of Americans (mostly from Minnesota and Iowa), Norwegians, Swedes, Czechs, German Russians, and Hutterites to their new homes. In 1871 an Immigration Bureau was established, and representatives were dispatched to the New York docks and the Chicago rail terminal to lure immigrants with glowing reports of Dakota Territory. Germans from the steppes of Russia were particularly sought because they were already skilled grassland farmers.

Most immigrants, however, found their way to the frontier by following well-defined migration routes that connected previous neighborhoods and social networks in Europe, often through intermediate settlements in the Middle West, to new emerging communities in Dakota Territory. It was not so much a process of planned group migration (although this did occur, as in the case of the Hutterites) as a reassembling over a period of years of families and acquaintances who were linked through letters and native-language newspapers.

In Dakota Territory, migrants settled "in neighborhoods of their own." Swedes, for example, were concentrated in Clay County, to the east of the Vermillion River; Czechs, German-Russians, and Hutterites settled in Bon Homme County, to the west of the James; and Norwegians pushed up the Big Sioux River into Lincoln and Minnehaha counties (Fig. 11.3). Even within national groups, immigrants tended to cluster in communities that reflected their regional origins in the old country.

The first Dakota settlement boom ended in 1873 when the nation entered a five-year period of economic depression. Settlers also had their first protracted exposure to the environmental hazards of the Plains. Extremely cold winters and irregular rainfall brought hardship to many settlers, but the grasshopper plagues of 1873, 1874, and 1876 finally left the region destitute. Crop failures and high interest rates combined to produce large numbers of farm foreclosures.

This period of settlement is vividly captured in Rolvaag's *Giants in the Earth*, a work of fiction, but one with a true sense of time and place. Rolvaag's settlers had been fishermen in central Norway who migrated by steamship to Quebec. They set out for the frontier, pausing in southeastern Minnesota, where there were well-established Norwegian communities. After filing a homestead claim at the Sioux Falls land office in the spring of 1873, Per Hansa and his family and friends pushed out into the prairies. Fifty miles northwest of Sioux Falls the settlers stopped at Spring Creek, a site that had been selected by one of the men in the previous fall (Fig. 11.3). They stayed close together, settling adjacent quarter sections, knowing that they would need the group support.

Per Hansa came to the frontier with only $30, which meant improvisation and deprivation. The improvised home was a sod house, which was regarded as a temporary structure until such time as timber, an expensive item in the early years of settlement, could be imported for frame buildings. Timber for fuel and for the willow thatch on the sod buildings was hauled 35 miles from the valley of the Big Sioux. Potatoes were the initial sod crop, but the Norwegian settlers were convinced that this was "soil for wheat, the king of all grains." The wheat crop flourished until the grasshoppers descended, leaving the fields stripped to the soil.

The settlers stayed only because poverty had deprived them of the ability to leave. They persisted through the hard times, and by 1881 Per Hansa was owner of 480 acres. In addition to the initial homestead, he probably had purchased 160 acres through the Preemption Act, and another quarter-section through the Timber Culture Act (1873), which had been passed in an effort to increase the number of trees on the Great Plains.

The community survived through combined effort. One of their number served as a school teacher, another as a Justice of the Peace, and soon a frontier minister brought organized religion to Spring Creek. Other Norwegians settled nearby. But the plains environment continued to threaten the settlers. Per Hansa finally died in a blizzard while attempting to reach a doctor in the James River valley.

Many migrants to Dakota Territory, particularly the Americans, came to the frontier alone. Frederick A. Fleischman, for example, homesteaded in Kingsbury County in 1880 (Fig. 11.3). He started with $425 with which he built a small frame house and invested in a wagon, a team of horses, and some farm machinery. Fleischman paid to have 20 acres of prairie broken, and in the fall of the first year he harvested 181 bushels of wheat. Encouraged by this initial success, he returned to Wisconsin, married, and brought his wife back to the Dakota homestead in time for spring planting. Eventually, the Fleischmans raised ten children, a valuable asset on a family farm.

In 1882 a good harvest produced an income of $1,242, enough to cover expenses and provide a comfortable living by the standards of the time and place. But the price of wheat went on a downward spiral after 1882 and did not recover until after the drought and depression of the 1890s. While many others failed, the Fleischman family endured because of luck, intelligence, and austerity. They were lucky in starting farming during two years of good rainfall and high wheat prices, which allowed them to gain a foothold. When wheat prices fell, they diversified, so that even during the hard times there was some income from the sale of eggs, milk, lard, and meat. But the family survived mostly because they tightened their belts: in 1894 when the income from the farm was only

$95, they became virtually self-sufficient and spent only $30 on groceries and provisions. Conditions improved after 1895, and the Fleischmans enjoyed a period of relative prosperity in the first two decades of the 20th century.

The Impact of the Railroad

By the later 1870s, Dakota Territory was a railroad frontier and experiencing a surge of population growth. In the year following June 30, 1879, more than 2 million acres of government land were disposed of under the Homestead, Preemption, and Timber Culture acts. This was more than one-quarter of all the land alienated in the nation that year. From 1880 to 1883, 200,000 settlers moved into east-central Dakota Territory. This was a zone of overlap between the Corn Belt of southeastern Dakota, which had been largely settled before 1873 via the Missouri River, and the emerging spring Wheat Belt, which was settled after 1878 in an east-west movement of people following the railroad tracks (Fig. 11.3).

The arrival of the railroads at the eastern border of Dakota Territory, and their extension westward after 1878, eclipsed Sioux City's role as gateway city to the northern Great Plains. A series of formerly insignificant towns, such as Sioux Falls and Grand Forks, became the main portals for settlers heading west and the primary exit points for agricultural products destined for eastern markets. The railroads also truncated the Missouri River route. Steamboat traffic declined after a peak in 1867, and Chicago and Minneapolis supplanted St. Louis as the main wholesaling centers for the northern Plains.

The railroad changed the pace and nature of pioneering. Settlers were recruited by railroad companies that wanted their government land grants filled with people and their boxcars filled with grain. The railroad companies joined the Immigration Bureau in sending agents to Europe and New York, and throughout the United States they set up booths at county fairs to demonstrate the rich agricultural rewards of settling on the northern Plains. Most immigrants now boarded trains for the frontier, unless the trip was of a short distance or the price of a ticket too high. They came by the thousands in the spring, often to be met at the station by railroad representatives who would direct them to their quarter-sections. This re-cruitment process displayed a strong ethnic bias. Non-English-speaking immigrants from northern Europe and Russian-German Menno-nites were sought because it was believed that they would "work harder, complain less, and produce more than anyone else."

Settlers were tied to the railroad by their reliance on wheat, which accounted for 60 per-cent of all the improved land in the new state of North Dakota in 1889. Wheat farmers were obliged to live within 20 miles of the railroad because haulage over a longer distance would consume all their profits. The Census Bureau estimated that it "costs the ordinary farmer more to carry each bushel of wheat a mile than it now does the railroad to carry a ton."

The North Dakota settlers included native-born Americans from the Middle West, first-generation Canadians from Ontario, German-Russians in their tightly organized com-munities, Germans directly from Europe and German-Americans from Wisconsin, and tens of thousands of immigrants from the overpop-ulated rural districts of Norway and Sweden. On the frontier the non-English-speaking set-tlers tended to marry within their groups, pre-serving the ethnic mosaic that was established with the initial settlement. These groups, how-ever, mingled in the course of making a living. Occupational and geographic mobility was a way of life; 40 percent of North Dakota home-steaders worked off their farms for periods during the early years.

After 1880 the frontier was much more closely tied to national economic networks than it had been in previous years. The nationwide system of railroads, a national bank system, and vertically integrated corporations that con-trolled the supply and distribution of products, all brought the frontier into closer contact with the more settled parts of the country. Mail order houses and canned goods introduced diversity to the consumer on the frontier. The diet of the Fleischman family, for example, was expanded after 1895 to include imported fruits and vegetables and a wide variety of canned goods.

This was an era of increasing economic spe-cialization, and the range of goods and services that the new Plains towns offered reflected this trend. In addition to the general store, there were now butcher shops, hardware stores,

grain elevators, and lumberyards. Whereas the small establishments were generally locally owned, most frequently by native-born Ameri-cans, the elevators and lumberyards were con-trolled by large companies based outside the region. By 1889, Minnesota was producing one-third of the nation's lumber, much of it des-tined for the treeless northern Plains, and cor-porate giants such as Pillsbury of Minneapolis dominated the grain trade.

The morphology, spacing, and prospects of the towns were largely dictated by the railroad. The central courthouse square plan, common in the eastern United States, was replaced on the northern Plains by the "T-town," where the square grid was oriented to the railroad tracks, with their accompanying elevators, lumber-yards, and standardized depots. The railroad companies spaced the towns along the tracks to serve as grain collection points for the sur-rounding farms. This relatively dense settle-ment fabric was an anachronism within a few decades of its creation. Established in a horse and buggy era when the spread of a town's hinterland was limited by slow and costly movement, the towns were too many when the automobile expanded the range of circulation in the 20th century. Those distant from the lifeline of the railroad, in particular, could not compete, and many stagnated and died. The growing mechanization of agriculture, result-ing in increased farm sizes and declining rural population, also removed customers from the services that the economy of the small towns depended upon. The towns that survived, either because of favored location or enterpris-ing citizens, benefited from the extra business that had previously been conducted at smaller, more local centers.

While the eastern Great Plains was filling up with settlers, the drier and more remote coun-try to the west of the 100th meridian was occu-pied by Indians, miners, and cattlemen. After the Civil War, hundreds of thousands of cattle were driven north from Texas each year to the boom towns at the railheads in Kansas and Nebraska, where they were bought and shipped to eastern markets. The cattle were moved in even greater numbers to the western ranges in Colorado, Montana, and Dakota Ter-ritory, where gold and silver discoveries had created bustling exclaves of settlement in 1859, 1862–64, and 1874, respectively. The final destinations for the drives were the reservations of Indian Territory and the northern Plains. Meat and stock were furnished to the Indians as one form of payment for their lands and as an alternative to the bison, which by the 1870s was facing extinction. Nothing symbolizes the deteriorating circumstances of the Plains Indians as accurately as this shift from bison hunting, which had allowed mobility, independence, and effective resistance, to the "feeding" policy on the reservations, which emphasized dependency and defeat.

THE WESTERN GREAT PLAINS, 1865–1900

Restricting the Indians

By 1865, while the Indians of the eastern Great Plains were making difficult adjustments to reservation life, the nomadic hunters of the western Plains remained relatively unchallenged in the possession of their lands. In fact, the 1851 Treaty of Fort Laramie had defined and confirmed the territories of the Dakota Sioux, Cheyenne, Arapahoe, Crow, Assiniboine, Gros Ventre, Mandan, and Arikara in an attempt to reduce intertribal conflict over contested hunting grounds. The Fort Laramie Treaty also recognized the right of the United States to establish roads and military posts in these territories. This clause became a contentious issue after 1862, when gold was discovered in Montana and miners converged on the northern Rockies. Army posts were built along the Missouri River and along the Bozeman Trail through Wyoming to protect the two main routes to the gold fields. Relations between the United States and the western Indians deteriorated to a state of intermittent warfare that continued until the last resistance was stamped out on the snowswept plains of Wounded Knee, South Dakota, on December 29, 1890.

The federal government's response to the escalating conflict on the western Plains after the Civil War was the Peace Policy, a combination of brutal military suppression and well-intended paternalism. The emphasis of the Peace Policy varied from time to time, depending on who was commissioner of Indian affairs, and from place to place, according to degrees of Indian resistance. At the heart of the Peace Policy was the idea of the reservation. The

Indians would be collected into two large districts, one in Indian Territory, the other to the west of the Missouri River in Dakota Territory. This would not only remove the Indians from the central Plains where the advance of settlers was most rapid, but would also restrict the movements of the bison hunters, tying them down to specific places where government agents could teach them "self-sustaining habits."

In 1867 and 1868, at the Councils of Medicine Lodge Creek (Kansas) and Fort Laramie (Wyoming), vast areas of the western Plains were sold to the United States. At Medicine Lodge Creek, the Kiowa, Comanche, Southern Cheyenne, and Arapahoe, and some bands of the Apache ceded their lands on the High Plains of Texas, New Mexico, Colorado, and Kansas and were placed on reservations in Indian Territory. At Fort Laramie, the Crow, Northern Cheyenne, and Arapahoe, and the seven bands of the Dakota Sioux agreed to major cessions of their hunting grounds in return for subsistence rations and guaranteed reservations. The Crow, for example, received a cash-equivalent of 3.6 cents an acre for 30 million acres of land in Wyoming and Montana and a 6 million-acre reservation to the south of the present town of Billings (Fig. 11.1).

In subsequent years, the reservations created by the Treaty of Fort Laramie were reduced through additional cessions of lands often in direct violation of earlier treaties. The 1876 surrender of the Black Hills by the Dakota Sioux and the Northern Cheyenne and Arapahoe, for example, was made under duress and without the necessary signatures of three-quarters of the tribal population. The Black Hills cession is still unfinished business in the 1980s, a matter of dispute between the federal government and the Ogalalla Sioux and between the Ogalalla Sioux and the Northern Cheyenne.

The Peace Policy distinguished between those Indians who capitulated and settled on the reservations and those who resisted and continued to roam. As Commissioner of Indian Affairs Francis Walker explained in 1872, the policy was that "The Indian should be made as comfortable on, and as uncomfortable off, their reservations as it was in the power of the Government to make them." On the reservations, missionaries were appointed as agents in the hope that they would reduce administrative corruption and put the Indians on the Christian path. Massive amounts of rations were delivered to the agencies to sustain and pacify the Indians. The rations were given to the heads of individual families so that the power of the chiefs and the communal basis of Indian societies would be weakened. Frequently rations were withheld by agents as a punishment or means of coercion.

The "feeding policy" did not work well. Rations were dispensed irregularly from agencies located predominantly along the Missouri River. This was convenient for the government, which could transport the bulky annuities by steamboat, but difficult for the Indians, many of whom still camped in bands in remote parts of the reservations. Not until 1890 were substations established to dispense rations more locally. Even then, many of the non-food rations that the government handed out were sold to traders for a few cents. The shelves of the secondhand store in Gordon, Nebraska, just to the south of the Pine Ridge Reservation, were well stocked with government clothes in the 1890s, sold by the Indians at a going rate of 25 cents for a pair of shoes and 75 cents for a suit of clothes.

Off the reservation the Indians found it increasingly difficult to resist the growing force of the American military. By the 1870s there were 25,000 troops on the northern Great Plains. The number of military posts was increased from 3 in 1860 to 38 in 1878. Most of the forts were located at the agencies along the Missouri River, and served the dual function of regulating the Indians and keeping the river route open. Forts were also built on the western Plains to protect railroad and telegraph construction crews, as well as on the routes to the goldfields. The extension of the railroads into the Plains, improving communication lines for the army, and the virtual elimination of the bison herds, depriving the Indians of their economic base, foreshadowed the end of Indian resistance. After the massacre at Wounded Knee the military presence on the northern Plains was greatly reduced.

Despite statements to the contrary in various treaties, the reservations were seen by many in the Indian Office as temporary expedients on

Figure 11.4   Guthrie, Oklahoma, May 2, 1889 (Courtesy Oklahoma Historical Society)

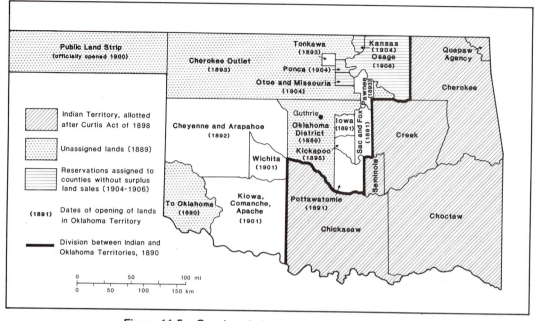

Figure 11.5   Cessions in Indian Territory, 1889–1906

the way to assimilation. This was made clear in 1887 when the Dawes Act imposed allotments on the Indians, an action that had been under consideration for decades. Each Indian would be given an individual plot, generally 160 acres, and encouraged to farm. The remainder of the reservations, after allotments had been made, would be sold as "surplus lands" to settlers. The result was another massive erosion of the Indian land base. The 1.7 million-acre Fort Peck Reservation in eastern Montana, for example, was created in 1888 as a redefined homeland for 1,178 Yankton and 713 Assiniboine (Fig. 11.1). During the following twenty years the Indians lived on rations, produce from small gardens, and income from grazing leases. Allotments were introduced on the reservation in 1908. By 1912, 700,000 acres had been allotted, mainly along the southern border of the reservation, and the remainder of the reservation was opened to settlers. The proceeds from the sales were put into irrigation projects and cattle purchases, but even in 1925 less than 5,000 acres were in crops, and many Indians were still dependent on rations.

Allotments were also the means of extinguishing Indian title to much of Indian Territory. The first area to be opened for settlement was the unassigned Oklahoma District, which was filled by a stampede of homesteaders on

April 22, 1889. Towns sprang up on the prairie overnight, tent and clapboard cities of men (very few women at first) where a semblance of order was maintained by the military (Fig. 11.4). Settlers came from all parts of the United States, attracted by country that offered better prospects than the drought-prone lands that remained as frontier in Kansas and Nebraska.

In 1890, Indian Territory west of the lands of the Five Civilized Tribes was redefined as Oklahoma Territory. With the exception of the Kansas, Osage, Ponca, and Otoe and Missouria reservations, which were converted into counties and allotments without surplus land sales, the reservations in Oklahoma Territory were allotted and the surplus lands sold to settlers in the decade following 1891 (Fig. 11.5). The eastern part of Indian Territory, home to the Five Civilized Tribes since the removals of the 1820s and 1830s, was largely allotted during the first decade of the 20th century. The Cherokee, Creek, Choctaw, Chickasaw, and Seminole gave up their special status as self-governing nations following the Curtis Act of 1898 and took citizenship along with their allotments. In 1907 Indian Territory and Oklahoma Territory were combined into the new state of Oklahoma.

The transition to farming on individually owned plots was made far more successfully on the eastern than on the western Great Plains. Many of the Omaha in eastern Nebraska, for example, and the Pawnee in eastern Oklahoma were farming on allotments and living in frame houses by 1900. But on the drier western plains, which had never been farming country for the Indians, attempts to cultivate the land generally failed. On the Pine Ridge Reservation in the 1890s, corn, turnips, and other vegetables did germinate, but were "scorched away" in the heat of the August sun. Consequently, very few of the Ogallala of Pine Ridge were settled on allotments by 1900. Unless irrigation was provided, as on the Crow Reservation in Montana, grazing proved a more successful adaption to changed circumstances for the Indians of the western Plains, but rations continued to be a main means of subsistence well into the 20th century (Fig. 11.6).

The Black Hills Mining Frontier

In 1874, long-standing rumors of gold in the Black Hills were confirmed as fact. By the end of 1876 (before the Blacks Hills had been officially ceded from the Indians), there were 5,000 people in Deadwood and another 15,000 in mining camps within a ten-mile radius. In 1879 a correspondent for the *New York Tribune* visited Deadwood. He found a lively town. The main street was lined with frame buildings, adorned with sham fronts to give a "metropolitan appearance" (Fig. 11.7). The residential areas consisted of small "but tastefully built cottages," with a Chinese quarter at the bottom of Main Street. Deadwood had gambling halls, an "abundance of saloons," a variety theater, schools, churches, and three banks, each with more than $500,000 in deposits. Wage rates were high, but so was the cost of living, because of the need to import food and other supplies. Profits were to be made as readily in supplying the area as in mining. One enterprising man brought $3,000 worth of goods up from Cheyenne in 1877 and sold them within a day for $10,000. Deadwood was also full of lawyers because mining gave rise to "almost endless" litigation.

Deadwood, like Denver and Helena but unlike most Plains towns, was founded without the aid of the railroad. The first tracks did not reach the Black Hills until 1886, when a branch line was laid north from the Chicago and

Figure 11.6   Ration Day Issue at the Commissary, between 1889 and 1891
(Courtesy Nebraska State Historical Society)

Figure 11.7   Main Street, Deadwood, Dakota Territory, ca. 1880 (Courtesy Nebraska State Historical Society)

Northwestern at Chadron, Nebraska, and not until 1905 was Rapid City connected east by rail to Pierre. The lure of gold and silver was strong enough to pull settlers hundreds of miles ahead of the railroad. Moreover, unlike wheat, gold could bear the high costs of overland transportation. So for more than a decade Deadwood and the other mining areas in the Black Hills were connected to the outside world by difficult, and often dangerous, stagecoach routes. Before 1880, the most important connections were to Sydney, Nebraska, and Cheyenne, Wyoming. After 1880, when the Chicago and Northwestern reached Pierre and the Northern Pacific pushed west through Bismarck, the Black Hills were increasingly supplied overland from the east (Fig 11.3).

As in Colorado and Montana, the presence of a large mining population in the Black Hills was a strong incentive for local food production. By 1879 the valleys of the Black Hills were supplying wheat, oats, and potatoes to the mining camps. The development of stock raising on the plains around the Black Hills was even more significant. The first drives from Texas into southwestern Dakota Territory (other than to the reservation) took place in 1877, as soon as the land was acquired from the

Indians. For a brief period the cattlemen dominated the western Great Plains from the Rio Grande to the Canadian prairies.

The Open-Range Cattle Kingdom

The "day of the cattleman" actually lasted about two decades, from 1866 until the late 1880s. It was one of the few occasions when the region was integrated lengthwise, instead of being fragmented by lateral connections to the east and west (Fig. 11.8). The predominant east-west orientation was reestablished in the 1880s when much of the open range was settled and fenced by homesteaders.

The transfer of almost 6 million steers from Texas to the railheads and ranges of the central and northern Great Plains from 1866 to 1885 made patent economic and ecological sense. During the Civil War, when the conventional outlets to eastern markets were blocked, a reservoir of more then 3 million cattle built up in the Coastal Bend and Cross Timbers regions of Texas and spilled over on to the southern High Plains. The economic logic of the cattle drives, as the entrepreneur Joseph G. McCoy realized in 1866, was that a three-year-old steer worth less than $10 in Texas would bring at least $35 at the Chicago stockyards and as much as $70 at

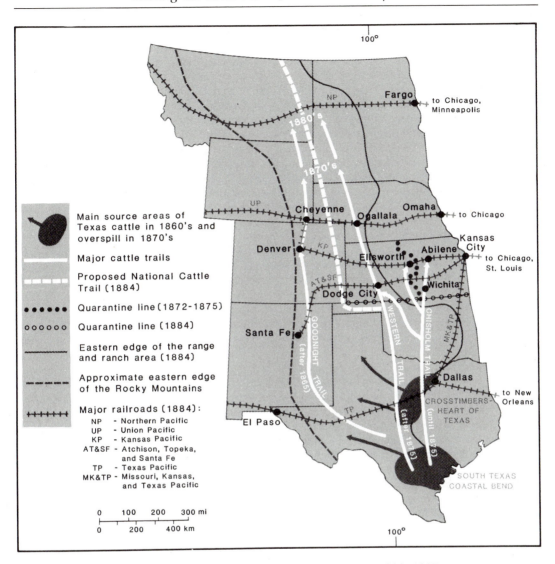

Figure 11.8   The Open Range Cattle Kingdom, 1866–1887

the New York market. McCoy was instrumental in creating the first Kansas cattle town at Abilene in 1867, where cattlemen could meet buyers and where the Kansas Pacific Railroad provided the link to eastern markets.

The ecological reason for the trail drives involved the complementary nature of the southern and northern ranges. The southern plains of Texas, with their mild winters, were excellent breeding grounds where a herd could be increased by 80 to 90 percent each year. But the cattle did not add flesh well on the mesquite grass of Texas. On the northern Great Plains, on the other hand, severe winters kept the

annual calf "crop" at less than 45 percent, but cattle fattened well on the nutritious short-and mixed-grass prairie. A two-year-old Texas steer could add 200 pounds in two years on the Montana range at a cost of no more than $1.25 a year. The four-year-old steer would be worth $25 to $45 at the railhead. The trail drives, therefore, consisted of one to two-year-old steers that were moved to the northern ranges for fattening and mature steers that were driven to the cattle towns and shipped directly to the packing houses in Kansas City and Chicago.

As the period progressed, the cattle trails and

transshipment points were dislodged westward as the railroads penetrated the Plains, drawing the farming frontier in their wake. Quarantine laws, enacted to prevent the spread of Texas (splenic) fever from the longhorns to the local cattle, also caused the trails to veer to the west. Abilene flourished from 1867 to 1872, then surrendered the trade to Ellsworth and Wichita. By 1877 the Chisholm Trail to Wichita was blocked by fences and quarantine legislation, and Dodge City took over as the major cattle town. Dodge City, and Ogallala, Nebraska, were the main transshipment points in the 1880s during the last years of the open range cattle era on the central Great Plains (Fig. 11.8).

The cattle towns were both more and less than their reputations: less, because they were never as violent as legend has made them; more, because they were important commercial centers, with banks, saloons, hotels, grocery houses, clothing stores, bootmakers, lawyers, and prostitutes, all connected in one way or another to the cattle trade. They were temporary boom towns that cashed in on the cattle trade, then made the necessary adjustment to the more mundane world of serving the surrounding ranching and farming population.

By 1885 there were an estimated 7.5 million cattle on the western Plains from Indian Territory to the Canadian border. Settlement patterns on the open range were oriented to the streams because cattle needed to graze within six miles of water. The herdsmen secured the rights to the land along the rivers, often by manipulation of the land laws. In the Nebraska Sand Hills, for example, stock owners employed their herders at "liberal wages" to take out Timber Culture claims in the lush hay meadows that lie between the dunes. These lands were used "rent free, tax free, and interest free" for many years with no pretense at fulfilling the conditions of the law. By 1885, many herdsmen on the northern Plains were fencing the range in order to gain firmer control over the water supplies and in anticipation of the wave of homesteaders that was about to engulf them.

Many of the early cattlemen who grazed their herds on the open range were typical frontier entrepreneurs who had moved to the West at an early age and accumulated capital in such activities as trading or land speculation. They were owner-operators who made the most of what the historian Louis Pelzer called the "golden age of ranching," when their control of the open range was unchallenged, prices were high, and the only overhead was the cost of stock cattle. After 1880 these individual owners and small partnerships were bought out by major corporations and foreign investors. In Cheyenne County, in the Panhandle of Nebraska, the 13 operators who controlled the range in 1880 had sold their interests to two corporations—the Ogallala Land and Cattle Company and the Bay State Live Stock Company—by 1885. This same process of consolidation of holdings on the open range occurred throughout the western Great Plains in the early 1880s. Standard Oil controlled large acreages on the range in the Cimarron Strip in Indian Territory (using Oil as a brand), and European aristocrats invested heavily in the industry in Colorado, Wyoming, and Montana.

This second wave of investment was only just beginning when the bottom dropped out of the industry. The Texas cattlemen suffered greatly after 1884, when Kansas extended its quarantine laws against splenic fever across the entire state, blocking the northern drives (Fig. 11.8). On the northern Plains, overstocking of the range led to a deterioration in the quality of the cattle. The poor quality, combined with the accumulation of years of high production that resulted in oversupply at the markets, caused the price of beef to fall from $5.60 per 1000 lbs. at Chicago in 1884 to $4.75 in 1885. Collusion between the major meat companies, Armour and Swift of Chicago and Kansas City, also kept the market prices low. The final blow was dealt by the severe winters of 1886–87 and 1888–89, which reduced the herds by 40 to 60 percent throughout the northern Plains. The owners tried to recoup their losses by dumping their remaining stock on the market, and the price of beef at the Chicago stockyards plummeted to $3.75 per 1000 lbs. by 1889.

Even if the cattlemen had survived these economic and climatic reversals, their period of control of the western ranges was over. The whole weight of the federal government, as expressed in the land laws, favored the homesteader over the cattleman. In ideology, at least, it was considered unAmerican for few owners to dominate the range where thousands of homesteaders could be settled. The

Texas cattle interests made a last attempt to salvage their industry by introducing a bill in Congress in February 1885 to establish a National Cattle Trail, a six-mile-wide "free highway" stretching from western Indian Territory to Canada that would be reserved from private ownership (Fig. 11.8). But the grid of barbed wire fences was rapidly being laid across Kansas and Nebraska, choking off the trails and restricting the open range to smaller and smaller areas and to remote refuges, such as the Montana plains.

Homesteading on the Western Great Plains, 1878–1900

In 1890 the U.S. Census Bureau declared that the unsettled area was "so broken into by isolate bodies of settlement" that it was no longer possible to identify a distinctive frontier line. A surge of settlement in 1878 and 1879, then again from 1883 to 1887, carried the farming frontier across the mythical barriers of the 98th and 100th meridians into the short-grass plains of Kansas, Nebraska, and Colorado. By 1890, this westward moving frontier had merged with the irrigated oases that were scattered along the Colorado Piedmont. To the north, the new state of South Dakota was settled to the Missouri River (with an outlier of 32,559 people in the Black Hills), and the railroads were rapidly pushing the spring wheat frontier across North Dakota. To the south, the resettlement of Oklahoma and Indian territories was imminent, and Oklahoma District already appeared on the population map (Fig. 11.2).

In Texas the southern frontier had been blocked at the eastern edge of the Great Plains from 1860 to 1875 by the Kiowa and Comanche, which may explain why Walter Prescott Webb, a Texan, believed that the entire Great Plains frontier stalled at the 98th meridian for several decades. Even when the Indian threat was removed, farmers were slow to migrate west of the Cross Timbers because of remoteness from markets and the prevailing belief (fostered by the cattle ranchers) that West Texas would never be farming country. The extension of the railroads beyond the Cross Timbers and through the Panhandle after 1880 changed both the image and economic potential of West Texas, prompting, and to a great extent promoting, the boom of 1887–90. The cotton frontier advanced 100 miles along its entire length

and, in the Panhandle, wheat fringed the railroad tracks that cut through the heart of sparsely populated cattle country.

On the central Great Plains, settlers were seduced into the marginal farming lands beyond the 100th meridian by years of good rainfall (particularly 1883–87) and an intense propaganda campaign launched by federal and state agencies, townsite promoters, and the railroads. To a large degree this was a speculator's frontier, with genuine farmers following on the second wave of settlement. Speculation varied in scale from local entrepreneurs who filed claims for the purpose of relinquishing them when the area became more settled and land values climbed, to absentee landlords like William Scully, who amassed 225,000 acres of farmland in Illinois, Missouri, Kansas, and Nebraska. Nowhere was the discrepancy between the ideal of the yeoman farmer and the reality of the speculator's frontier more blatant than in Nance County, in central Nebraska, which was created out of the abandoned Pawnee reservation in 1879. Virtually all the land was sold by 1883, with 14 individuals or partnerships each acquiring more than 2,500 acres. Most of the land was resold to settlers within a few years of purchase, indicating the intent of speculation. This was particularly ironic, because the Pawnee had been preached to for decades that the way to become an American was to work diligently on a 160-acre plot.

The promoters of Plains settlement had at their disposal a "perfect recruiting device" in the theory that rainfall was "following the plow." The illusion was inculcated into the receptive minds of the settlers that rainfall would increase as they broke the prairie sod and planted trees. Scientific backing for the idea came from Samuel Aughey and Charles D. Wilber in Nebraska and Franklin B. Hough of the Department of Agriculture, who theorized that loosening the soil and planting trees would make more water available for evaporation, leading to saturation of the atmosphere and increased rainfall. Constructing facile arguments from dubious experiments, Aughey, Wilber, and Hough predicted that the Great American Desert would soon be transformed into a "rain belt" through the farmers' own efforts. School textbooks, state atlases, railroad promotional pamphlets, local horticultural societies, and the Federal Division of Forestry all conveyed this hopeful, but fallacious, message. Many scientists disclaimed the theory, but the settlers were left alone to realize its folly in the desperate years of the 1890s.

There was nothing illusory, however, about the value of the railroads in easing the burdens of settling the western Great Plains. Branch lines sprouted from the main tracks after 1878, making it easier for settlers to get into the country and bringing supplies and markets closer to formerly isolated communities. By 1885, virtually all of Nebraska east of the 98th meridian was within 12 miles of a railroad, and even in the western part of the state the Burlington, Union Pacific, and Sioux City and Pacific railroads brought the frontier into close contact with the more settled parts of the country.

The editors of the widely read journals *Rural Nebraska* and *The Nebraska Farmer* advised the settler to bring $200 to $300 to the frontier to cover the costs of housing, fencing, and sod-breaking. But many settlers moved with little except hope for the future. They could not afford railroad land or other accessible land that had already been improved. So they moved out ahead of the main wave of settlers and stuck it out in isolated areas, waiting years, often in vain, for the tracks to be laid into their counties.

One such settlement occurred in Osborne County in north-central Kansas. The first farmers reached the area in the 1870s, driving the ranchers into the hills, then out of the district altogether. Most came with very little,

one settler reportedly bringing "nine children and eleven cents." This was a self-contained community; there was no other choice, because the nearest railroad station was 60 miles away. A settler with a few cows was considered a rich man. Food was plain and entirely locally raised; sorghum molasses was the settlers' sugar, rye their coffee, and cornmeal their staple. The main crop was corn, planted in small fields with the aid of an ax, worked with a hoe, and cut with a knife. Wild plants, such as dandelion leaves, sheep sorrel, and plums, added some variety to the diet and kept scurvy at bay. The settlers lived in sod houses, often shoveled out of banksides, sometimes with flowers planted on the roofs (Fig. 11.9). At their best, the sod houses were efficient insulated dwellings, staying warm in winter and cool in summer; at the their worst, they were dark and dank, infested by mosquitoes and bedbugs, and attractive shelter for rattlesnakes. Life was tedious and lonely, especially for the women who worked in the fields, made the clothes, kept the house, and walked great distances to sell butter, lard, and eggs at the nearest town. Despite these hardships, the old-timers who told these stories to the Kansas historian John Ise remembered their pioneer days with fondness, recalling a simpler life when friendships were binding and the connection with the land brought a satisfaction that has since been lost.

Lying at the heart of Webb's thesis is the argument that settlers could not advance on to the western Great Plains until major adjust-

Figure 11.9   "Our Home": Dugout near McCook, Nebraska, 1890s (Courtesy Nebraska State Historical Society)

ments were made in their "ways of life and living." There is no doubt that various inventions—Glidden's barbed wire, for example, and the self-governing windmill, both of which came into general use in the 1880s—facilitated settlement. But adaptions to the semiarid grasslands took place slowly and in face of opposition from settlers who did not want, or did not have the means, to change their methods of farming. It was easier to believe that the environment was adapting to them by becoming more humid.

Corn remained the dominant crop throughout western Kansas, western Nebraska, and even eastern Colorado in the 1880s. In years of good rainfall, corn thrived on the newly turned sod and was useful both as a feed and as a food crop. But corn could not endure the drought that returned in 1887 and lasted, with only brief respites, until 1896.

The drought dessicated the western Great Plains from the Texas Panhandle to the Canadian prairies. In eastern Colorado, rainfall fell from its average of 16 inches a year to 8 inches in 1895. Grasshoppers and low market prices compounded the farmers' distress. Large parts of the western Plains were depopulated. The abandoned farmhouses and the stream of broken settlers, their futures foreclosing with their farms, stood as stark evidence of what Harlan Barrows called "the first great crushing defeat" of the American farmer.

The population map for 1900 shows this dramatic retraction of the frontier in the central Plains, despite the renewed immigration that occurred after 1896. Many of the failed settlers headed for the newly opened lands in Oklahoma Territory, which filled up so quickly that by 1900 there was no evidence on the population map to suggest that the area had been held out of settlement for fifty years: the bands of population density ran across Oklahoma from Kansas to Texas without refraction (Fig. 11.10).

The drought forced adjustments on the farmers of the western Plains. The illusion of increasing rainfall was finally laid to rest, and irrigation and dry farming were increasingly advocated as solutions to the problem of moisture deficiency. New drought-resistant crops, such as Turkey Red wheat, gradually replaced corn, and in eastern Colorado many farmers turned to livestock raising. A more accurate view of the area was forged from the failures of

the 1880s and 1890s, but as with every drought on the Great Plains, many of the lessons were quickly forgotten when the rains and prices revived.

TWENTIETH-CENTURY FRONTIERS

A comparison of the 1900 and 1930 population density maps for the Great Plains states clearly reveals that much of the area was settled on 20th century frontiers (Fig. 11.10). In fact, more land was disposed of under the Homestead Act (and its enlarged versions of 1909 and 1916, giving 320 and 640 acres respectively) from 1898 to 1917 than in the previous three decades. From 1900 to 1910, millions of acres were plowed up in central North Dakota, western Kansas, and Nebraska, and parts of western Texas and Oklahoma. From 1910 to 1919 the main thrust of settlement was through western North Dakota into eastern and central Montana. When the devastating drought and rapid decline in wheat prices halted the settlement boom on the northern Plains after 1919, the focus shifted to the southern Plains. This was the last great farming frontier in the United States. It was also the prelude to the Dust Bowl.

By the 1920s at least five major agricultural regions could be distinguished on the Great Plains. In the south, the Cotton Belt extended west across the red soil prairies of central Oklahoma and out on to the fertile sandy loams of the Texas High Plains as far west as Lubbock. To the north, stretching from the Texas Panhandle to western Nebraska, lay the winter Wheat Belt. Separating the winter Wheat Belt from the spring Wheat Belt of the Dakotas and Montana was the western extension of the Corn Belt, an area of mixed crop and livestock production characteristic of northern Kansas and southern and eastern Nebraska. On the western fringes of the Great Plains, in south-central Montana, Wyoming, western South Dakota, and with an eastern outlier in the Nebraska Sand Hills, cattle and sheep raising were the primary activities, unless irrigation allowed local crop production.

Each of these agricultural belts was oriented to, and largely controlled by, cities located mainly to the east of the Great Plains. The railroad provided the essential connections, and only the most isolated parts of the Plains

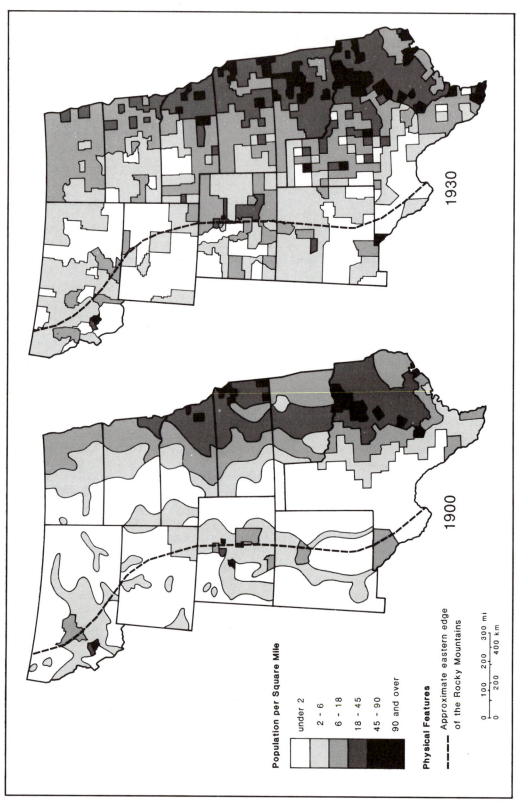

Population per Square Mile

under 2

2 - 6

6 - 18

18 - 45

45 - 90

90 and over

Physical Features

Approximate eastern edge
of the Rocky Mountains

| 0 | 100 | 200 | 300 mi |
| 0 | 200 | 400 km |

1900

1930

Figure 11.10 Population Density on the Great Plains, 1900 and 1930

remained more than 25 miles from the tracks. Fort Worth, for example, was the "gateway and focus of West Texas," channeling cotton and livestock products to the east. The Texas Panhandle, however, was connected by the Atchison, Topeka, and Santa Fe to Kansas City, the capital of the winter Wheat Belt. Omaha, and ultimately Chicago, were the main hubs of the Corn Belt, while Denver's Plains hinterland extended from eastern Colorado and western Kansas to Wyoming. On the northern Plains, Minneapolis millers and bankers, in alliance with railroad companies, controlled the storage, pricing, transportation, and marketing of spring wheat.

The diversity of farming types tends to obscure common characteristics of early 20th-century Plains settlement. These were mechanized frontiers where settlers came, and left, by railroad and automobile. They were frontiers where the small farmer had a poor chance of success: the marginal nature of the environment necessitated large acreages, which were difficult to work without the new gasoline-powered tractors and combines and prohibitively expensive to fence. Few people had the resources for such heavy capital investments, unless they went into debt and faced the consequences of foreclosure when grain prices went on a downward spiral, as in the 1920s. Increasingly, this was a speculator's frontier where a few people with money and ambition could acquire vast holdings by manipulating the land laws or buying out failed small farmers for a few dollars an acre. Many of the failed farmers, or settlers too poor to buy good farming land in the first place, became tenants. By 1930, more than 60 percent of the farmers in Texas and Oklahoma were tenants, and in general the Great Plains was second only to the South as a region of tenancy. Finally, agriculture on the Plains (particularly in the wheat belts) became monocultural, where a single crop dominated the landscape, producing ecosystems that were highly simplified and, therefore, highly unstable.

Pioneering in Montana, 1900–1930

Even as late as 1910 only 4 percent of Montana was improved for agriculture. Most of the improved land was in the Rocky Mountain valleys, where oats and wheat had been grown since the 1860s to feed the mining population.

By 1905 some irrigated agriculture was practiced on the Montana plains, in the valleys of the lower Yellowstone and Milk rivers, but eastern and central Montana was primarily open-range country thinly populated by cattlemen, sheepherders, and Indians.

The cattlemen came into Montana in the 1880s, some driving their stock across the mountains from the Pacific Northwest. The cattle thrived on the blue grama and needle-and-thread grasses and, by 1894, the year the Montana open-range business peaked, the eastern two-thirds of the state was organized into 17 large round-up districts. The Indians, including the Blackfoot, Gros Ventre, and Assiniboine, posed little threat to the newcomers. They had ceded their homelands in the last three decades of the 19th century and were confined to reservations located mainly in the dry grassland country to the north of the Missouri and Milk rivers (Fig. 11.1).

The Montana homestead boom began in 1909, following the passage of the Enlarged Homestead Act. The railroads were already in place to bring the settlers in. In the peak year of 1910, 21,982 Homestead applications were filed at the Montana land offices, almost as many as in all the years combined from 1869 to 1905. Homestead entries continued to be made at an average rate of 14,911 a year until 1919. Most of the settlers came from North Dakota, Minnesota, and other midwestern states, with western Canada and Washington also important source areas.

Montana received above-average rainfall from 1906 to 1915, and farmers enjoyed bumper crops. Then drought struck in 1916, intensified in 1918 and 1919, and lasted through the early 1920s. Homestead filings decreased sharply. With the reestablishment of grain production in Western Europe and Russia after the war, wheat prices halved from 1918 to 1921. Farmers who had considered it their "patriotic duty" (as well as the route to success) to borrow more money, buy more land, and grow more wheat during the war years found themselves faced with declining land values and debts that they could not pay. By 1925 one out of every two Montana farmers had lost his land through foreclosure. Even the drought and Depression of the 1930s took a lighter toll on Montana than the collapse of the 1920s.

The drought aggravated the already terrible

living conditions on the Montana Indian reservations. When Hugh L. Scott, a member of the Board of Indian Commissioners, inspected the Blackfoot and Fort Belknap reservations in 1920 he found the range dessicated and the tribal cattle starving. Many of the Indians were also starving. Conditions were particularly severe among the traditional full bloods, who lived separately from the other Indians. Most were old, many were blind, and all were dependent on government relief. The Indians were inadequately clothed, poorly sheltered, and the sanitary conditions at the agency boarding schools were described as "dangerous." Scott observed that many of the homesteaders in the vicinity of the reservations were also destitute but, unlike the settlers, the Indians had nowhere else to go.

In 1930 Isaiah Bowman, president of the American Geographical Society, visited Garfield County, located on the dry, short-grass plains of eastern Montana. He found a sparsely populated frontier, predominantly ranching country, without a single mile of railroad or telegraph line. Garfield County's infant mortality rate was one of the highest in the United States, and the landscape of sod houses and tarpaper shacks stood as witness to the recency and impermanency of settlement. Bowman saw signs of "amelioration" in living conditions: the increased ownership of automobiles, the appearance of frame dwellings, and the prospect, always a year or two ahead, that the railroads would extend into the county, putting the rancher and dryland farmer on an equal competitive footing with producers in more accessible areas. But the railroads never came to Garfield County, and the trend of declining population that was already underway in 1930 has continued to the present.

The End of Pioneering: The Southern Great Plains in the 1920s and 1930s

The last extensive area of the Great Plains to be plowed up and settled was the short-grass country of western Texas and Oklahoma, eastern Colorado and New Mexico, and southwestern Kansas (Fig. 11.10). The boom began in 1900, as soon as rainfall and confidence recovered from the setbacks of the 1890s, accelerated under the stimulus of wartime grain demands, continued despite dry years in 1910 and 1915

and falling wheat prices in the 1920s, and ended in 1931 with the return of the Great American Desert to the Plains.

From 1920 to 1930, the High Plains counties of Texas, Oklahoma, and Kansas added 197,045 people, an increase of 260 percent. This was perfect land for mechanization—extensive, flat, and without the impediments of stumps and stones. Soon the farmers were investing in gasoline-powered tractors, disc plows that pulverized the surface soil, and combines that could harvest 500 acres in two weeks. By 1930, more than three-quarters of the farmers in the winter Wheat Belt owned combines.

The refined transportation and production technology gave rise to a new type of entrepreneur, the absentee or suitcase farmer. Farming from a distance was already underway by World War I (and in fact had been common at a local level since the beginnings of settlement), but the big expansion occurred in the spring and winter Wheat Belts in the 1920s. Suitcase farmers typically owned widely dispersed lands that they visited for only a few weeks each year to harvest one crop and plant the next. They concentrated on wheat as the best chance for short-run profits. By 1933, in nine counties in western Kansas, more than one-quarter of the farmers lived more than one county away from their lands; most were from the established wheat country of central Kansas. Some of the absentee owners were farmers back home; others included bankers, lawyers, doctors, real estate agents, even preachers. In one sense, the suitcase farmers were making an intelligent adjustment to farming on the semi-arid margins by spreading their risks from place to place and from occupation to occupation. In another sense, they epitomized the attitude that land was no more than a context for making money. The landscape of suitcase farming, with its absence of dwellings, or at the most a tent or portable bunkhouse, was a surface expression of the fact that farming was becoming divorced from attachment to place.

As farmers moved out into the southern Plains, agricultural experts urged them to diversify and to practice dry farming techniques. But farmers were reluctant to diversify because, despite the risks, wheat had a better chance of producing a salable product than any other crop and was well suited to mechanized production. Moreover, there is an inertia to farming, an investment in experience and specialized equipment, and few farmers had the savings to see them through the transition to a more diversified base. Farmers did adopt drought-resistant varieties of wheat. They also learned from their own or from their neighbors' successes and failures to plant early so that the crops were well established before the intense heat of the summer, and to cultivate frequently to establish a moisture-preserving mulch. But other recommended techniques, such as well irrigation and summer fallowing, were largely avoided by farmers intent on maximizing short-run profits or, quite simply, surviving.

Dry farming was not enough to secure settlement on the southern Great Plains when drought and depression struck in the early 1930s. By 1937, 20 counties in the southern High Plains, centered on the panhandles of Texas and Oklahoma, were severely damaged by wind erosion, and the forage value of the range had been depleted by more than 75 percent. In Cimarron County, Oklahoma, in the very heart of the Dust Bowl, virtually no wheat was harvested from several hundred thousand acres. Mortgages on land and debts on equipment could not be met. By 1934, the total rural debt in the county was $4.75 million, or $5,500 per farm. Over the decade the farm population fell by 40 percent. The agricultural collapse brought down entire communities as banks closed, implement dealers lost their market, and real estate dealers lost their clients. The pioneer settlement of the Great Plains came to an end in the worst ecological disaster in American history.

POSTSCRIPT

In 1936 a committee of experts presented its recommendations to President Roosevelt concerning the future of the Great Plains. The committee blamed the Dust Bowl on the settlers' lack of understanding of the differences between the humid environments of the eastern United States and the subhumid lands of the Great Plains. The problem lay not only in unadapted methods of farming, but more fundamentally in "attitudes of mind" that had been ingrained through generations of pioneering in the country east of the Plains. These included the beliefs that nature must be con-

quered, that resources are limitless, and that landownership carries privileges but not obligations. These assumptions had powered frontier expansion, but on the Plains they came up against environmental limits and resulted in ecological catastrophe.

Among its recommendations, the committee urged that most of the land in dry farming, particularly the wheat and cotton regions, should be put into pasture for livestock. This recommendation echoed the earlier advice of John Wesley Powell and Willard Johnson, both of whom had recognized that the Great Plains was not merely an extension of the Middle West, but a unique region of inconstant climate and variable agricultural potential. It is significant that all three critical appraisals came in, or at the end of, a serious drought when adversity brought a temporary realism and willingness to look at the region as a whole. It is also significant that their recommendations were largely forgotten as soon as the hard times passed.

By 1950, fully 90 percent of the land plowed up in the 1920s was back in crops. In addition, several million acres that had never been plowed were put into wheat in the central and northern Great Plains by 1950. Despite stabilizing influences, such as government subsidies, built-in crop insurance, and improved varieties of crops and methods of farming (including expansion of irrigation and widespread use of summer fallow), crop failure is still common on the Plains, particularly in the reoccurring drought years, as in the early 1950s and mid-1970s.

The ambivalent nature of the Great Plains— fertile yet fragile—has never been as evident as in the early 1980s. Sophisticated technology, large-scale corporate production, and the intensive application of fertilizers and pesticides have produced bumper crops. Harvests have recently been so large, while international markets have been reduced, that overproduction is now the major problem, despite government programs that have left more than 30 percent of the wheat land idle. Falling prices and rising costs again have brought record numbers of Plains farmers to the brink of foreclosure.

The gains in production have been accompanied by serious ecological and social costs. Terraces, shelter belts, and other conservation practices that were established in the 1930s have been eliminated to accommodate larger machines and pivot irrigation systems. Over much of eastern Nebraska, 25 tons of top soil per acre are being lost each year, and erosion rates reach 100 tons per acre annually on the margins of the Sand Hills where cultivation is being extended into a grazing region. Whereas irrigation has secured farming in some areas, the "mining" of the Ogallala acquifer has left only a ten-year supply of water in West Texas. On the northern Great Plains coal, oil, and uranium interests now vie with the farmer and rancher for land and water. It is evident that, in addition to the uncontrollable climate, new environmental constraints produced by human activities now pose further problems for the future settlement of the Great Plains.

Meanwhile, as agriculture has become more capital-intensive, the trend of rural depopulation has continued. The number of farms in Nebraska declined from 134,000 in 1935 to 70,000 in 1973 and has continued to decrease by an average of 1,000 a year since that time. The rural landscape is emptying. Abandoned farmhouses, their porches sagging and empty windows gaping, stand as evidence of a time when the Great Plains was the last great agriculture frontier for homesteaders. No doubt future booms will restore prosperity, if not population, to the Plains. But if the past offers any lesson, it is equally certain that drought and depression will never be far behind.

ADDITIONAL READING

Books

Barker, E.C., ed. *Readings in Texas History*. Dallas: The Southwest Press, 1929.

Barrows, H.G. *Lectures on the Historical Geography of the United States as Given in 1933*. Chicago: University of Chicago Department of Geography, 1962.

Blouet, B.W., and Lawson, M.P., eds. *Images of the Plains: The Role of Human Nature in Settlement*. Lincoln: University of Nebraska Press, 1975.

Blouet, B.W., and Luebke, F.C., eds. *The Great Plains: Environment and Culture*. Lincoln: University of Nebraska, 1979.

Bowman, I. *The Pioneer Fringe*. New York: American Geographical Society, 1931.

Dykstra, R.D. *The Cattle Towns*. Lincoln: University of Nebraska Press, 1968.

Emmons, D.M. *Garden in the Grassland*. Lincoln: University of Nebraska Press, 1971.

Fite, G.C. *The Farmers' Frontier, 1865–1900*. New York: Holt, Rinehart, Winston, 1966.

Great Plains Committee, *The Future of the Great Plains*. 75th Congress, 1st Session, House of Representatives, Doc. No. 144, February 10, 1937.

Haines, N.E., ed. *Economics, Sociology, and the Modern World*. Cambridge: Harvard University Press, 1935. See chapter by Ise.

Hewes, L. *The Suitcase Farming Frontier*. Lincoln: University of Nebraska Press, 1973.

Holt, O.H. *Dakota*. Chicago: Rand McNally, 1885.

Hudson, J.C. *Plains Country Towns*. Minneapolis: University of Minnesota Press, 1985.

Jordan, T.G. *Trails to Texas*. Lincoln and London: University of Nebraska Press, 1981.

Kappler, C.J. *Indian Affairs: Laws and Treaties*. Vol.

2. Washington, D.C.: Government Printing Office, 1904.

Kraenzel, C.F. *The Great Plains in Transition*. Norman: University of Oklahoma Press, 1955.

Malin, J.C. *The Nebraska Question*. Ann Arbor: Edwards Brothers, 1953.

Meinig, D.W. *Imperial Texas: An Interpretive Essay in Cultural Geography*. Austin: University of Texas Press, 1969.

Nimmo, J., Jr. *Report on the Internal Commerce of the United States*. Washington, D.C.: Government Printing Office, 1885.

Paullin, C.O. *Atlas of the Historical Geography of the United States*. New York: American Geographical Society, 1932.

Pelzer, L. *The Cattlemen's Frontier*. Glendale: A.H. Clark Co., 1936.

Powell, J.W. *Report on the Lands of the Arid Region of the United States*. Washington D.C.: Government Printing Office, 1879.

Rolvaag, O.E. *Giants in the Earth*. New York: Harper & Row, 1927.

Royce, C.C. *Indian Land Sessions in the United States*. Washington D.C.: Government Printing Office, 1900.

Webb, W.P. *The Great Plains*. Boston: Ginn & Co., 1931.

Worster, D. *Dust Bowl: The Southern Plains in the 1930s*. New York: Oxford University Press, 1979.

Periodicals

Annals, Association of American Geographers (McIntosh, 1975; Hudson, 1976).

Great Plains Quarterly, journal of the Center for Great Plains Studies (Silag, 1982).

12

The Far West, 1840–1920

DAVID HORNBECK
California State University,
Northridge

The area west of the Rocky Mountains played an important part in the development of the United States. In spite of this distinctive role, the typical historical view of this region places it within the framework of the last westward moving frontier, a scheme that all but ignores the fact that the American frontier skipped over the Great Plains and Rocky Mountains into a western region already settled by other European cultures. The Far West was a series of regional frontiers in which solutions to environmental problems required new methods that, in turn, created distinct and often unique differences among places. As a detached frontier, the Far West was a frontier moving eastward, bringing with it a robustness and a vibrancy forged from diversity. This vitality made it different in almost all aspects from the more traditional westward-moving frontiers of the 18th and 19th centuries.

The Far West, initially, was an imperial frontier, where the United States competed with other nations for territory; here the United States completed its shape and realized the ideals of manifest destiny (Fig. 12.1). But it was gold that made the Far West a real part of the United States. A tide of miners in search of instant wealth simultaneously created agricultural, transportation, mining, and urban frontiers, each populated with an amalgam of peoples—Asian laborers, European settlers, Mexican stockmen, commercial speculators, squatters, and health-seekers. It was this mix of people and events that gave the Far West a unique personality in the 19th century, a distinct regional frontier with only ephemeral links with the eastern United States.

ABORIGINAL OCCUPANCE

"Diverse" is probably the most apt description of the first inhabitants of the Far West. Approximately 250 tribes, or ethnic units, were spread over the area in varying patterns and distributions (Fig. 12.2). The area was extraordinarily complex linguistically, with about 22 major language families split over 116 mutually unintelligible languages. The most fragmented area was California, with 14 language families and about 80 mutually unintelligible tongues.

Although differences among native inhabitants were great, there were regions in which subsistence patterns were similar enough to group tribes regionally on the basis of greater subsistence similarities within the resulting regions than between them. These economic features can be grouped into five broad regions: the Northwest Coast, the Plateau, California, the Great Basin, and the Southwest. This regional division rests on specific ecological adjustments, because the overriding feature of all Indian tribes in the Far West was their mixed diets of wild plants, seeds, land mammals, and fish. Gathering, hunting, and fishing were in some combination the main bases of Indian economies, with gathering usually dominant.

Fishing was the paramount activity for the Northwest coastal tribes. In the Plateau region, fishing was likewise extensive, because salmon was the dietary mainstay, with wild roots and berries providing the balance of the Indian subsistence base. In California, marine resources were dominant among the coastal and riverine environments while, outside these narrow ecological bands, acorns and pinenuts were consumed. Great Basin inhabitants tended to gather many types of plants, although seed bearing plants prevailed. In the Southwest, domesticated crops were an important part of the diet, with wild plants of lesser importance. Throughout the Far West, Indian tribes acquired food resources from their neighbors (who usually lived in different ecological zones) through ceremonial feasts, trade, raids, or common consent to joint access to an area. Hunting was both common and an important activity, but it tended to be secondary to gathering and fishing activities.

The least diverse aspect of the far western

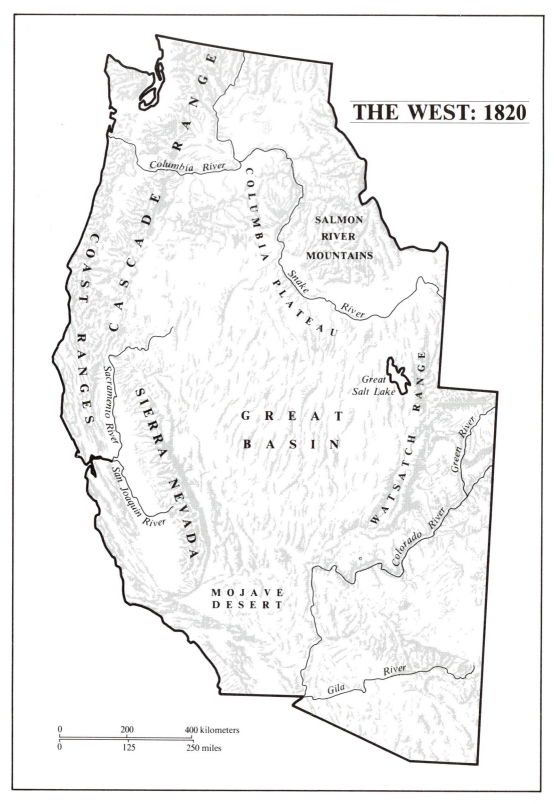

THE WEST: 1820

COAST RANGES

CASCADE RANGE

Columbia River

COLUMBIA PLATEAU

SALMON
RIVER
MOUNTAINS

Snake River

Sacramento River

SIERRA NEVADA

San Joaquin River

Great
Salt Lake

G R E A T
B A S I N

W A S A T C H   R A N G E

Green River

Colorado River

M O J A V E
D E S E R T

Gila River

0   200   400 kilometers
0   125   250 miles

Figure 12.1   Physical Features of the West

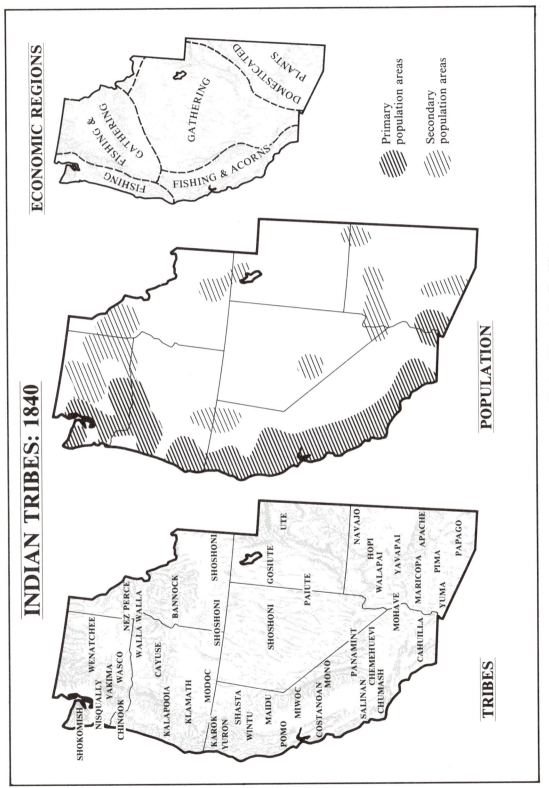

Figure 12.2   Distribution of Indian Tribes in the Far West

Indians was their tribal distribution and density. Without widespread agriculture, Indians relied heavily on the gathering and hunting of local resources. Thus there was a strong relationship between environmental quality and aboriginal density. In general, the marine and riverine environments with their wealth of food sources supported higher population densities than the interior regions and the areas away from rivers. Permanency and compactness followed a similar pattern, ranging from seminomadic family camps of ten people in the Great Basin to permanent villages of a thousand or more along the rich Santa Barbara coast. California, by far the most densely populated region, was the home of some 300,000 Indians. With about 5 percent of the land area of the United States, California contained at least 12 percent of its total native population.

While the Europeans were everconscious of the Indian after contact, native dependence on the local environment for subsistence was not generally appreciated. Early perceptions of the Far West as endowed with abundant natural resources led to exploitation by Spain, Britain, Russia, and the United States, with little regard for the subsistence patterns and needs of the Indians. Early cropping and trading gave way to colonization and farms, each resulting in a substantial disruption in the gathering and hunting environments of the Indians and causing in turn a decline in their numbers. For example, the California Indians were reduced from a population of 300,000 in 1770 to less than 30,000 by 1870. European diseases cannot be overlooked as an important factor in the decline of the Indians, but the alteration of their environment was equally significant.

EXPLORATION

The first European penetration into what is now the American Southwest was by Spanish explorers in the 16th century, searching for the fabled Seven Cities of Cibola. The region initially held out the promise of rich rewards, and Spain sought to replicate the success Cortez had enjoyed in central Mexico. Treasure and riches, however, were not to be found. It took two centuries for Spain to receive any reward and, when it came, it was in the guise of spiritual rather than material wealth. The chris-

tianization of the Indians along the California coast, in central Arizona, and in the upper Rio Grande valley was the only reward Spain received for 200 years of effort. The British also entered the Far West, but not until the latter part of the 18th century. They focused their energies on the Pacific Northwest and sought riches from the exploitation of beaver, sea otter, and trade with local Indians. The United States quickly followed Britain into the Pacific Northwest, competing for similar rewards. These early excursions by Spain, Britain, and the United States not only revealed the broad extent of the area and its diverse environments, but also brought about conflicting territorial claims.

Although American seamen had traded along the northern Pacific Coast in the latter part of the 18th century and an American ship had navigated a short distance up the Columbia River in 1792, the United States' involvement in the Far West did not begin in earnest until the Louisiana Purchase in 1803. This acquisition inaugurated the first transcontinental expedition to explore the newly acquired region. The expedition, led by Lewis and Clark between 1804 and 1806, not only surveyed the geography of the upper Missouri River, Rocky Mountain, and lower Columbia River regions, but it also brought public attention to the Far West by illustrating its varied and abundant resources (Fig. 12.3).

The Lewis and Clark expedition was followed by a far-reaching plan of John Jacob Astor, whose Pacific Fur Company attempted to occupy the Columbia River Basin in 1811. The plan was to send an overland party via the Missouri, Snake, and Columbia rivers to rendezvous at the mouth of the Columbia with a ship sent around Cape Horn. From there, the parties would trade for furs in the Pacific Northwest in order to ship them to China. The War of 1812, the tremendous distances involved, and local difficulties with Indians spoiled Astor's bid to establish a fur trading center, but the venture was not a total failure. The expedition established Fort Astoria, at the mouth of the Columbia River, signifying yet another U.S. claim to the Far West. The expedition also blazed a new trail across the Rocky Mountains to the Pacific Ocean which, with its famous South Pass, would become eventually the Oregon Trail.

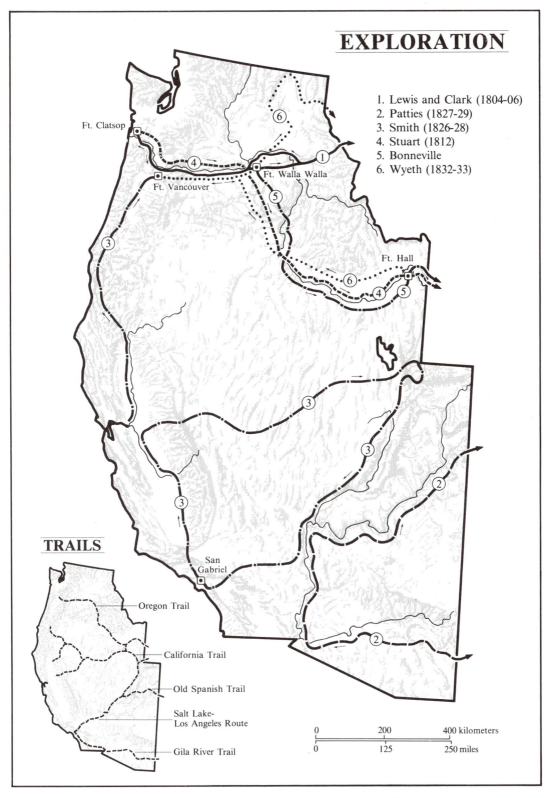

EXPLORATION

1. Lewis and Clark (1804-06)
2. Patties (1827-29)
3. Smith (1826-28)
4. Stuart (1812)
5. Bonneville
6. Wyeth (1832-33)

Ft. Clatsop

④

Ft. Walla Walla

Ft. Vancouver

⑤

①

③

⑥

Ft. Hall

⑥ ④ ⑤

③

③

②

③

San Gabriel

② ②

TRAILS

Oregon Trail

California Trail

Old Spanish Trail

Salt Lake-
Los Angeles Route

Gila River Trail

| 0 | 200 | 400 kilometers |
| 0 | 125 | 250 miles |

Figure 12.3   Early Exploration Routes in the Far West

The Far West was not contiguous with the pioneer fringe of the United States and, as Astor's venture well illustrated, distance was a formidable problem. Although the Lewis and Clark and the Astor expeditions both represented important steps toward defining the extent of the Far West, it was not until the 1820s that the region was seriously explored. Between 1820 and 1840, the breadth and extent of the Far West were investigated by one of the most colorful and unique "frontier types" in American history, the mountain man. Working for one of the many fur trading companies or for themselves, the mountain men explored the Far West in search of beaver and adventure, defying Mexican law and causing considerable alarm among British trappers in the Oregon Country.

The decade of the 1820s was an exciting one for western exploration. Between 1825 and 1830, Peter Skene Ogden pushed south from the Willamette valley in Oregon to California, discovered the Humboldt River, explored the northern shore of the Great Salt Lake, and journeyed from the Humboldt Sink to the Colorado River, becoming the first white man to cross the Great Basin north to south. One of America's greatest explorers, Jedediah Smith was the first to travel from the present-day Southwest into California, returning to California, veering north to Oregon and then eastward to the Rocky Mountains, becoming the first white individual to explore the Far West from east to west and from north to south. In 1824, Sylvester and James Ohio Pattie were the first to explore the Gila River and, along with Ewing Young, walked the rim of the Grand Canyon in 1826. In 1828, the Patties made their way from Santa Fe to Southern California, the first to travel the soon-to-be-popular southern route. In 1829, a Mexican mule trader named Antonio Armijo linked California with New Mexico by blazing the Spanish Trail.

During the 1830s, American trappers and traders made their way across the Rockies into the Far West in greater numbers, exploring its resources and extolling its beauty. Joseph Walker, Jim Bridger, Kit Carson, and many others so successfully defined the Far West that, by the 1840s, would-be farmers, miners, and merchants were making their way west along easily identified trails. The mountain men had accomplished a great deal: they sent thousands of furs down the Missouri River into the American economy, brought about confrontation between the Americans and the British in the Oregon Country and the Spanish in California, discovered mountain passes, and identified fertile valleys for future farmers. Yet, for all that was known, the Far West remained to be mapped. By the 1840s the region had changed, beaver had declined substantially, and mountain men so familiar with every corner of the country became the guides for a new kind of explorer—those who would begin to map the Far West. The government needed more information about the vast expanse of territory at its western boundary, accurate locations of topographic features and, especially, detailed maps of possible routes westward. Charles Wilkes, John C. Fremont, and William H. Emory were among those early government explorers who began to provide this needed detail on maps. Fremont wrote glowing accounts about the Far West as a "Pastured Paradise." Emory, on the other hand, anticipating permanent settlement, reported that "No enterprise could survive without cooperation of water." The California gold rush of 1848 stimulated a whole new need for maps, those that located and identified mineral resources. These, in turn, brought new government-sponsored surveys into the Far West. As the area came under permanent settlement in the 1850s, government surveys were turned toward mapping the real potential of the Far West, its agricultural land.

UNITED STATES ACQUISITION OF THE FAR WEST

Although the mountain men explored and exploited large areas of the Far West, they did not establish permanent territorial rights for the United States. The region was open country, destined to become the last meeting ground between imperial rivals in North America. In the first quarter of the 19th century, Spain, Britain, Russia, and the United States each laid claims to parts of the area. Spain was the first to organize permanent settlements in present-day Arizona, New Mexico, and coastal California. Spanish claim to a much larger area was reduced in 1819 by the Adams-Onis treaty, in which Spain surrendered to the United States all of its claims north of 42°N. The agreement further provided for a western boundary to the Louisiana Territory. The treaty between the United States and Spain left Russia, Britain, and the United States all jockeying for the Oregon Country. At first, Russia attempted to seize a share of the Oregon Country by asserting territorial rights as far south as 51°N latitude, but the Monroe Doctrine and the size and presence of the British Navy forced Russia to reconsider. In 1824 and 1825, Russia signed treaties limiting its claim as far south as 54° 40′N latitude. With Spanish and Russian claims thus limited, only the United States and Britain were left to vie for the Oregon Country, the last unclaimed part of the Far West. Rather than press for immediate and permanent division, both parties signed a treaty of joint occupancy.

Britain's claims to Oregon were based on the coastal explorations of James Cook in 1778 and George Vancouver in 1792, and the overland explorations of Alexander MacKenzie. The strongest claim in Britain's favor was that the Hudson's Bay Company owned permanent posts in the area. The United States, on the other hand, laid claim to Oregon on five counts: the discovery of the mouth of the Columbia River by the American sea captain James Greg in 1792; the Louisiana Purchase; the expedition of Lewis and Clark; the location of Fort Astoria built by the Pacific Fur Company; and, finally, that Spain had transferred to the United States her claim to the area running north of 42°N latitude to 54° 40′N latitude, and from the Pacific Coast to the crest of the Rocky Mountains. Neither Britain nor the United States wanted to quarrel over so distant a land. Thus in 1827, they renewed their joint occupancy of the Oregon Country indefinitely, with the proviso that either nation could end the agreement with one year's notification. In the 1820s Oregon could have gone to either nation, the territory being awarded to the nation that was able to attract the greatest number of permanent settlers. Britain was clearly winning the race during the 1820s and 1830s.

Religion helped to settle the Oregon Country for the United States. Beginning in 1834, a number of churches began to establish missions in the area to convert the Indians to christianity. Glowing letters describing agricultural possibilities began to circulate through-out the United States, causing widespread interest in the Oregon Country. The rising interest in Oregon's agricultural potential came when the United States was feeling the impact of an economic downturn in 1837 and, to many, Oregon appeared to be the place to begin anew. Oregon became the prime focus for westward migrants and, by the early 1840s, more than a hundred farms and 500 settlers dotted the lower reaches of the Willamette valley. The number of new settlers continued to increase and, by 1846, approximately 8,000 American settlers permanently occupied the area. Facing increasing American settlement, Britain capitulated the Oregon Country to the United States and agreed to the present-day boundaries.

Settlement was also the key element of American acquisition of the remaining portion of the Far West. After Oregon, California became the next target for American expansion. California in the 1840s was hardly in a position to resist the westward push of American settlers. Isolated from Mexico, rural, and largely unexploited, California's small population was unable to stem the aggressive tide of American immigrants claiming the land as their rightful and manifest destiny.

Manifest Destiny can be viewed in many different lights. At once it was justification and reason, cause and effect. It was an aggressive philosophy calling for military expansion into the Far West, while it was projected as an idealistic, nonviolent program for settlement. The many faces of Manifest Destiny were complicated and took various expressions, but at its simplest it provided a nationalistic philosophy and a justification for geographical expansion. The prospect of gaining new territory was justified in several ways. A push westward would assure the possibility of the rich trade with the Orient; it would prevent French and British designs on the West; it would gain control of San Francisco Bay; and it would help to educate the "backward" Mexicans. The target for Manifest Destiny was California, for here was the terminus, the culmination of the westward march of American settlement.

Throughout the 1830s and 1840s, a number of Americans and other foreigners came to California because of the profitable hide and tallow trade by sea between California and Boston. Others came to take up the land. At first, the number of new settlers was small—approximately 400 foreigners had settled in California by 1840. By 1841, however, overland immigration from the United States began to increase the number of Americans in California. For the most part, these newcomers settled in the interior, because the coastal areas between San Diego and San Francisco continued to be occupied by Mexicans. With increasing numbers of Americans on Mexican soil, the annexation of Texas by the United States against the wishes of Mexico in 1845, and growing jingoistic attitudes throughout the United States, war broke out between Mexico and the United States in 1846. The war ended in 1848 with the United States receiving the area south of Oregon. Thus, between 1846 and 1848, the United States added the entire Far West to its land area. Except for the Gadsden Purchase in southern Arizona and New Mexico in 1853, the contiguous territory of the United States was set by 1848. Acquisition of the Far West was the apogee of Manifest Destiny (Fig. 12.4).

SETTLEMENT OF THE FAR WEST

By 1848, the sweep across the continent was complete; British domination and Mexican occupation had been overcome. The Far West offered new and exciting vistas that would delight Americans and engage their imaginations. The problem, however, was to people the new land. In the Far West, only three areas had permanent settlement at the time of acquisition by the United States: the Willamette valley, the Great Salt Lake Basin, and coastal California. In general, migrants carry their cultural and social habits with them to new places: newly settled areas usually reflect much of the character of the migrants' former homes. As might be expected, the Far West defies this generalization; it was not to become a cultural mirror of Eastern frontiers. Rather, because of great distances, rugged and semiarid environments, and various culture groups, it created new patterns that tended to set it apart from even the Great Plains. For those migrating westward,

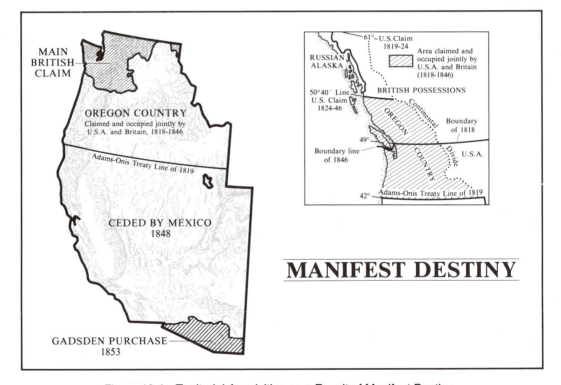

Figure 12.4   Territorial Acquisition as a Result of Manifest Destiny

the choices were clearly different: farming in the Willamette valley, Mormonism in the Great Salt Lake Basin, or mining in the goldfields of California (Fig 12.5).

Of these three settled areas, the Willamette valley was most like the Eastern frontier, with many of the newcomers being transplants from Missouri, Indiana, Illinois, and Kentucky. A variety of factors promoted Oregon settlement: the economic depression caused by the Panic of 1837, patriotic feelings associated with "winning" Oregon for the United States, alluring tales of fertile soil for excellent farming opportunities, possible trade with the Orient, and also the very momentum of westward movement itself. The actual settlement of the valley began in 1841; within a year, more than 100 hopeful settlers had arrived in the region. A provisional government was formed in 1843, and its success was the result in part of the influx of 1,000 new settlers that year alone. With the organization of the Oregon Territory in 1848, the population continued to increase steadily to more than 13,000 inhabitants by

1850, 90 percent of whom lived in the Willamette valley. In the 1850s, new areas in Oregon became the focus of settlement, with migrants moving north into the Cowlitz valley and south into the Rogue River and Umpqua valleys.

In contrast to the Oregon Territory, the early settlement of the Great Salt Lake region was undertaken for very different reasons. The first Americans to settle the area were members of the Church of Jesus Christ of Latter Day Saints, known also as Mormons. The Mormons did not go west by choice. Rather, their migration was forced because of religious persecution, political action, and to some extent their economic prosperity. They had been driven earlier from Kirkland, Ohio, to Independence, Missouri, and from there to Nauvoo, Illinois. The trek from Nauvoo to the Great Salt Lake was under the leadership of Brigham Young. The first 1,500 Mormons arrived in the Salt Lake Basin in 1847. Although Young intentionally settled in a harsh environment, irrigation and planned settlement soon led to prosperity. By 1850, there were almost 12,000 Mormons in the

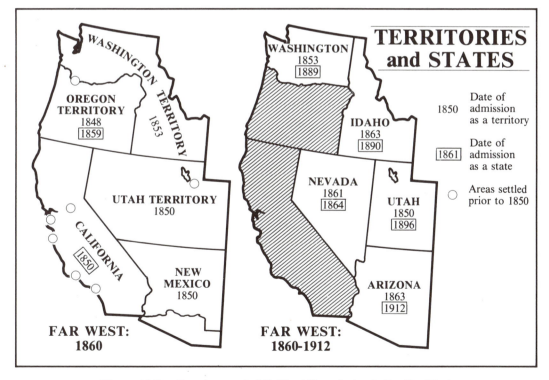

Figure 12.5   Development of Political Boundaries in the Far West

Salt Lake Basin. Throughout the 1850s, the number of Mormon settlements increased by 100 and were spread from Idaho south to the Colorado River.

While initial settlement of Oregon and the Great Salt Lake area can be characterized as pioneering efforts by transplanted settlers from the Ohio valley and the Middle West, the settlement of California was entirely different. California was not initially settled by Americans, but had been occupied by Spain since 1769; hence, when the Americans finally arrived they found a preexisting society. California's early population was based on the establishment of three frontier institutions for settling the land: presidio, pueblo, and mission. Spain, however, did not people its new land vigorously, and California's non-Indian population had reached only 3,000 by 1821, when independent Mexico began to govern California. Under Mexico, California's non-Indian population grew to approximately 12,000 by 1845, most of whom were concentrated at various locations along the coast. Los Angeles was the largest town, but new arrivals began to populate the Sacramento valley on the eve of the war between Mexico and the United States. By the end of the war, California's population was about 16,000, but the discovery of gold in 1848 caused such a tremendous influx of people that, by 1850, the U.S. census enumerated more than 93,000 people in the state.

It was from the fringes of the Far West—the Great Salt Lake region, the Willamette valley, and coastal California—that the region finally began to take shape (Fig. 12.6). In the 1850s, new territories and states emerged, giving definition to the area as the population increased and new areas were settled. The California gold rush provided the initial impetus to move west, but other areas also attracted settlers and benefited from the tide of westward movement. High prices for farm goods and forest products in the goldfields led many a newcomer to turn north to the fertile lands and the forests of southern Oregon. The discovery of gold on the Rogue River in 1851 caused a rush that brought even more people to southern Oregon, many of whom found farming ultimately more profitable than mining. The region north of the Columbia River was separated from Oregon in 1853 and named Washington Territory. The new territory also benefited from California's rapid surge in population, particularly the areas around Puget Sound. Here were excellent harbors, vast forests, abundant water power for mills, and the prospect of a ready and seemingly insatiable market for timber and lumber in San Francisco.

On the eastern side of the Cascades and west of the Rockies is an area of more than 200,000 square miles drained by the Columbia River and its tributaries. Bypassed by early pioneers who thought the country too dry for exploitation, the area around Walla Walla began to gain a few settlers by the late 1850s. As miners flooded the region after the discovery of gold along the branches of the Snake River, these early farmers found a ready market in the new mining areas. As word spread, more and more settlers began to take up land throughout what would become known as the "Inland Empire" of eastern Washington, the Palouse region.

The settlement of the vast areas of the Great Basin required many new settlers; far more people than those attracted from wagon trains moving west. The Mormons sent missionaries throughout the United States (and various other countries of the world) to preach Mormonism and urge converts to resettle in Zion. The response was immediate. Salt Lake City became a staging area for thousands of converts beginning new lives in the Great Basin. Settlement of the hot and dry Great Basin followed a well-defined set of procedures, much like those used by Spain to settle its northern frontier in North America. First, exploring parties found locations where settlements could be established viably. A "call" for settlers was then issued and, as the new settlers arrived, communal efforts established agriculture first, homes second, and a town last. Central to Mormon settlement was the village surrounded by large fields to which villagers commuted daily. The villages were similar, each with wide streets, irrigation ditches, and large blocks divided into homes and gardens. By 1860, the Mormon church, using this procedure, had spread settlement south of Salt Lake City into Arizona, north into Idaho, and west into the Great Basin and California.

The population of the Far West increased fivefold between 1860 and 1890, yet the three early settlement areas continued to dominate the overall settlement pattern (Table 12.1). In California, the coastal section continued to at-

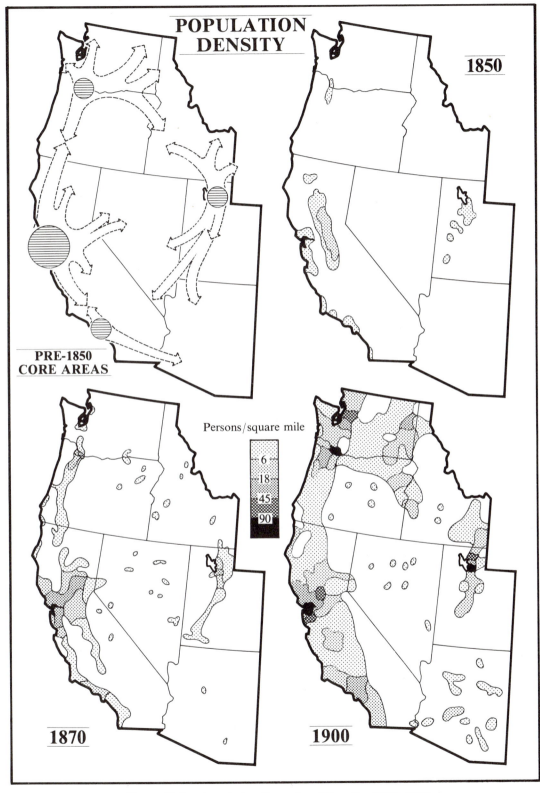

POPULATION DENSITY

1850

PRE-1850 CORE AREAS

Persons/square mile

6
18
45
90

1870

1900

Figure 12.6   Population Spread and Density, 1850–1900

Table 12.1   Populations of the Far Western States, 1850–1920 (in thousands)

	1850	1860	1870	1880	1890	1900	1910	1920
Arizona	—	—	10	40	88	123	204	334
California	93	380	560	865	1,213	1,485	2,378	3,427
Idaho	—	—	15	33	89	162	326	432
New Mexico	62	94	92	120	160	195	327	360
Nevada	—	7	42	62	47	42	81	77
Oregon	13	53	91	175	318	414	673	783
Utah	11	40	87	144	211	277	373	449
Washington	—	12	24	75	357	518	1,142	1,357
Total	179	585	921	1,513	2,484	3,216	5,465	7,220
% of U.S.	0.7	1.8	2.4	3.0	3.9	4.1	5.8	6.7
Total U.S.	23,067	31,184	38,116	50,189	63,070	77,257	93,402	107,436

tract the most immigrants, although increasing numbers of newcomers were being drawn to the rich and fertile Central Valley. After 1880, southern California began to attract large numbers of immigrants and, by 1890, California had two major population centers, in San Francisco and Los Angeles. Throughout the latter part of the 19th century, the Willamette valley remained a popular destination for immigrants, as did the Great Salt Lake region. The Puget Sound area, like Los Angeles, began to attract large numbers of new settlers and became the only intensely settled area to develop after the United States acquired the area. In general, settlement of the Far West by 1890 was an embellishment or expanded version of the 1850 pattern. Settlement still was clustered around the periphery, but there were newly populated areas in the interior along the Columbia and Snake rivers and in the Great Basin. The Great Basin was dotted with settlements mainly in response to mining activities or the presence of the railroad. A real attempt began after 1870 to settle the interior permanently, particularly after the railroad provided easy connections with the East.

The population of the Far West tripled between 1890 and 1920 to almost 7 million. Each state increased in population, but California continued to outpace its western rivals. Washington overtook Oregon as the second-largest state, primarily on the basis of the large number of newcomers taking up agricultural land in eastern Washington. The major change in the settlement pattern during this thirty-year pe-

riod was the rapidly increasing population of southern California and the retreat from the Great Basin back to the periphery. By 1920, the earliest settled areas remained important population centers, and the basic settlement patterns of today had been established. Between 1850 and 1920, Americans successfully and progressively had occupied the periphery of the Far West, leaving most of the hot and dry Great Basin to future pioneers.

URBAN DEVELOPMENT

The Far West experienced a tumultuous period of growth and expansion in the 1850s. The discovery of gold brought a tide of miners who sought instant wealth in the goldfields. For many, their stays in California and the other mining regions were to be only temporary visits, long enough for them to become wealthy and then return home and enjoy the rewards of their adventures. A few did become rich, although most did not become as rich as they had anticipated. Some returned home, but many remained in the Far West to settle a frontier that had leaped 2,000 miles in a single bound. For those who stayed and the others who followed, the Far West frontier posed the problem of how to exploit and develop a region so isolated and so different from what they had known or expected. The economy of the region, nevertheless, grew at a remarkable rate.

For the Far West, but especially for California, the economy changed suddenly from a pastoral, subsistence-oriented economy to one of commerce, services, and industry, long before a rural farm population had developed to support it. Mining brought about the change and for many years was able to sustain the economy (Fig. 12.7). Eastern capital and local initiative boosted development even when it was apparent that the California goldfields were producing diminishing returns for the labor and capital invested in them. Other areas also held out the promise of new riches: southern Oregon in 1852, the eastern Sierras in the late 1850s, western Washington and Idaho in the 1860s, and scattered regions throughout the Great Basin until 1890. Mining had been transformed by 1865 into a highly capital-intensive industry controlled by large companies that now employed miners as wage laborers. This was a sharp contrast with early mining, which had been basically a man-by-man treasure hunt on a grand scale. Yet this early mining led to the exploration and opening up of the Far West, generating the capital that catapulted the area into a highly urbanized economy.

The vast amounts of wealth pouring out of the mines made the region remarkably urban in nature long before a rural network of production units had developed sufficiently to support an urban economy. In the East, cities had been "jumping-off" points to the frontier, but in the West cities themselves were an integral part of the frontier. The urban frontier was an uncoordinated and "detached" set of mining camps, speculative towns, market centers, military posts, religious settlements, railroad towns, and port cities, each competing for instant recognition and for control of a hinterland. Literally thousands of settlements were founded between 1850 and 1880, most of which failed as quickly as they were created. Towns located in the earliest settled areas had an advantage and often became focal points of early city growth. Coastal California, with an urban network already in place from Hispanic settlement, the Willamette valley, and the Great Salt Lake region, each saw the rise of large regional cities (Table 12.2).

San Francisco, the primary gateway to the mining regions of California, grew rapidly in the 1850s. New mining strikes in Nevada,

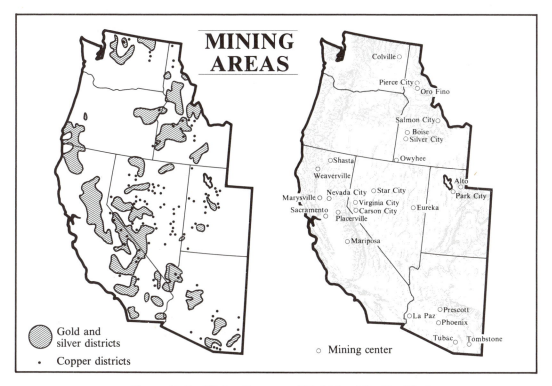

Figure 12.7   Mining Towns and Districts of the Far West

Table 12.2   Major Cities in the Far West, 1860–1920 (population in thousands)

	1860	1870	1880	1890	1900	1910	1920
San Francisco	57	150	234	299	343	417	507
Sacramento	14	16	21	26	29	45	66
San Jose	—	9	13	18	22	29	40
Oakland	2	11	88	49	67	150	216
Los Angeles	4	6	11	50	103	319	577
Long Beach	—	—	—	1	2	18	56
San Diego	1	2	3	16	18	40	74
Portland	3	8	18	46	70	207	258
Salt Lake City	8	13	21	45	54	93	118
Seattle	—	1	4	43	81	237	315
Spokane	—	—	—	20	37	104	104
Phoenix	—	—	—	3	6	11	29
Tucson	—	3	8	5	8	13	20
Albuquerque	—	—	—	4	6	11	15

along with an expanding local agricultural base, assured San Francisco of a strong economy. By 1860, with a population of 234,000, it dwarfed its nearest rivals and was beginning to establish hegemony over the entire Far West. San Francisco became a great commercial emporium, almost a city-state, commanding lumber and agricultural products from the Pacific Northwest, gold and silver from the interior, and cattle from southern California. With its own sources of capital, primarily from mining, San Francisco dominated the early stages of urban growth in the Far West. The region immediately surrounding the city reflected its dominance: Sacramento, San Jose, and Oakland, with 9,000 to 16,000 inhabitants in 1870, were essentially satellites of San Francisco. By 1880, San Francisco (Fig. 12.8) and its surrounding region was the most urbanized area in the West and contained a population of almost 360,000, greater than all other cities in the Far West combined or any single state outside of California.

The emergence of other large cities in the Pacific Northwest between 1850 and 1880 was in response to local settlement, but their early growth greatly depended on San Francisco's voracious appetite for raw materials and agricultural products (Fig. 12.9). Portland was founded in 1845 as a market center for the Willamette valley and later became a commercial leader for exporting products from the Columbia River Basin to San Francisco. Portland was able to reach eventually into the interior and command the trade for the entire region,

whereas in reality the town was little more than a regional center dominated by San Francisco. Seattle, founded in 1851, remained hardly more than a mill town supplying lumber to San Francisco until the last decade of the 19th century.

The urban center least affected by San Francisco was Salt Lake City. Planned in 1847, Salt Lake City was the focus of the Mormon church. With thousands of converts arriving in the city yearly, Salt Lake City was assured of constant growth. It was able to take advantage of its position astride one of the major overland trails to the West and engage successfully in a variety of commercial and trade ventures. The establishment of towns in Utah was firmly under the control of the church, which carefully located towns in order to maximize locational advantages and resources. By 1880, 400 towns had been founded in the Great Basin, mostly along the western edge of the Rocky Mountains from Idaho to Arizona. As the center of the Mormon church, Salt Lake City thrived and, while not rivaling San Francisco in commerce or mining, it firmly controlled its own hinterland, maintaining its distinction and separateness from San Francisco.

After 1880, many cities were able to take advantage of continued immigration, consolidate early economic gains, and move out from under the hegemony of San Francisco. Although San Francisco, Portland, and Salt Lake City continued to attract urban dwellers, the transcontinental railroads helped other cities establish their respective urban identities. The

Figure 12.8   San Francisco, 1874 (Courtesy California State Library)

last two decades of the 19th century and the early years of the present century can be characterized as a period of emergence for those newly maturing cities that challenged and eventually surpassed the original centers of American settlement. With the aid of the railroads, Los Angeles and Seattle exceeded even their own expectations. Los Angeles grew from 11,000 in 1880 to 576,000 in 1920, surpassing San Francisco as the largest city in the Far West. Seattle increased during the same period from 3,500 to 315,000 to become the largest city in the Pacific Northwest. Long Beach, Tucson, and Phoenix would eventually become large cities, but their major growth would come primarily in the 20th century.

Cities in the Far West lacked the strong industrial base of their eastern counterparts. Instead, they had large service and distribution sectors, well out of proportion to their manufacturing and agricultural bases. Manufacturing was represented in all cities, but the value of products ranked very low in all but San Francisco, the ninth-largest U.S. city in 1880, but rated only twenty-fifth in manufacturing. The need to import agricultural products dur-

ing the early years of urban growth stimulated specialized agricultural development in the immediate areas, but city growth quickly exceeded the capability of farmers to satisfy the local demands. To satisfy these needs, cities reached well beyond their hinterlands, affecting agricultural development throughout the Far West.

ECONOMIC GROWTH

Even though cities provided a ready market, agriculture in the Far West was difficult, beset with the problems and hardships of unfamiliar climates and varying physical conditions. Unlike the humid East, where familiar and traditional agricultural methods and crops could be transferred from one area to the next, the Far West, like the Great Plains, required modifications and adaptations in farming methods and types of crops grown. The three settled areas were the only agricultural nuclei, and each exhibited a distinct set of environmental and locational problems. Farmers in Oregon, where agriculture was most advanced, coped with

Figure 12.9   Astoria Harbor, Oregon, 1881 (Courtesy Oregon Historical Society)

clearing heavily forested land and considerable rainfall. Mormon settlers struggled with plowing ditches for their first efforts at irrigation farming. Much of the agricultural land in California along the accessible coast was being used by the Mexican rancheros for extensive cattle grazing. Miners-turned-farmers had to cope not only with farmland far from the urban markets, but also with bewildering, long summer drought. Yet, the rapid population growth caused by the Gold Rush made farming almost from the start a commercial enterprise in California.

The immediate impact of the gold rush on agriculture in the Far West was to create a demand that far exceeded supply. Farmers in the Willamette valley quickly moved to supply California by creating a mixed agricultural base, and the few farmers in California experimented with a variety of crops, hoping to find those that would be commercially viable in an arid environment. Mormon farmers, meanwhile, were affected by the gold rush only in that they enjoyed the opportunity to provide agricultural products to pioneers heading west. Although demand for agricultural products

was high, the total amount of improved land in the Far West in 1850 was very small, approximately 180,000 acres, two-thirds of which was in Oregon.

In general, the Far West did not appear at first to have a great future in farming, except to supply its own urban markets. In addition to unfamiliar climates, there was no economical way to reach eastern markets, and labor was in short supply. Nevertheless, in the decades following 1850, experimentation in crops and methods demonstrated that agriculture could be profitable (Fig. 12.10). New areas were being opened to settlement, railroads were beginning to solve the problems of isolation and inaccessibility, dry land farming and irrigation offset rainfall deficiencies, and the introduction of new kinds of machinery compensated for labor shortages. By 1880, the Far West had over 14 million improved acres with a considerable proportion devoted to specialized commercial crops. Bonanza wheat farms spread throughout the Central Valley of California, fruit and vegetable farms were found all along the coast, and cattle ranches dominated Southern California. In the Pacific Northwest, mixed grain,

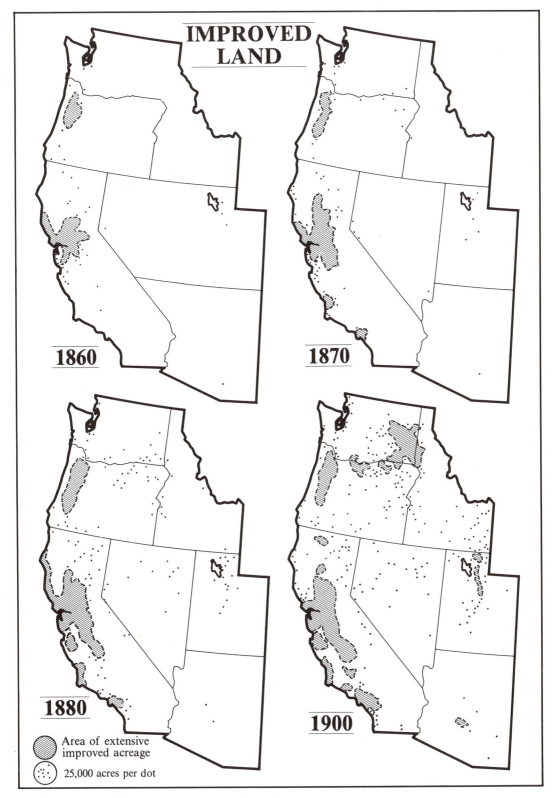

IMPROVED LAND

1860

1870

1880

1900

Area of extensive
improved acreage

25,000 acres per dot

Figure 12.10   Improved Land, 1860–1900

vegetables, and fruit had emerged as the primary crops. The Mormons emphasized a mixed agriculture with less attention to commercial markets.

The agricultural frontier worked itself out between 1900 and 1910. Crop patterns stabilized, environments were more carefully assessed, markets were established, transportation problems were solved, and the amount of irrigated acreage increased significantly. In California, wheat declined in importance as a commercial crop and was replaced by vegetables as the state began to enter the era of commercial marketing of farm products. In the Willamette valley and west of the Cascades, mixed farming continued, while dairy farms and fruit orchards emerged as commercially viable enterprises. The Mormon agricultural experience continued as mixed farming, but there was emphasis on changes, such as experimentation with sugarbeets. Continuing their search for fertile lands, the Mormons expanded into the region of the upper Snake River and established farms and communities there. After 1880, the rolling hills of the Columbia Plateau were transformed into one of the premier wheat-growing regions in the United States, the Palouse. Characterized by huge farms, large amounts of machinery, and a single crop, this boom resembled the earlier patterns of the wheat bonanza in California.

The Columbia Plateau was the last agricultural frontier in the Far West. Farmers who followed thereafter were forced into deserts or dense forests. Farming much of the Far West required costly capital inputs, primarily for irrigation, costs that were too much for the private sector to bear. If new areas were to be found, it would have to be with the federal government as a partner. The government, in turn, moved to assist agriculture by building dams in sections of Idaho and central Washington to stimulate irrigation and fruit production. The Roosevelt Dam on the Salt River provided central Arizona with water—the prime ingredient for its agricultural base. In California, damming of the lower Colorado River in the 1900s turned the Imperial Valley into a veritable winter garden. These and many other government-sponsored projects had illustrated by 1920 that profitable commercial agriculture in the Far West had to depend on the twin inputs of irrigation and government capital.

During the early years of settlement, cities provided farmers with their primary commercial markets. By the end of the 19th century, however, farmers had focused their efforts on supplying eastern and European cities. The ability of far western farmers to market their crops outside of the region came with the railroads and associated improvements in shipping methods. In general, the entire economic spectrum of the Far West followed closely the development of transportation. During the last quarter of the 19th century, the railroads opened up vast stretches of the Far West to profitable settlement, encouraged immigration, stimulated urban growth, and set in motion new economic patterns.

The first railroad to span the Far West was completed in 1869. By 1883, four transcontinental railroads were in operation: the Union Pacific and Central Pacific, the Southern Pacific, the Santa Fe, and the Northern Pacific. A fifth, the Great Northern, was extended from the Great Lakes to Puget Sound in 1893 (Fig. 12.11). Other short lines were added to the system, crisscrossing the Far West and connecting cities or mining areas with nearby urban centers. The addition of railroads to the Far West had an immediate impact on the economy. Before the first rail lines spanned the continent, Portland and especially San Francisco had been able to use their coastal locations to great advantage. As port cities, they could control the flow of goods into and out of the interior. The railroad broke up this regional monopoly by allowing other cities to reach eastern manufacturing and trading firms directly. Eastern firms were able to flood the Far West with cheap manufactured goods and undercut local western manufacturers. Quick to capitalize on the emerging western markets, the railroads encouraged and often sponsored an eastward flow of raw materials, thereby obtaining profits from freight in both directions. The railroads also brought in new capital. Mining had been the major source of capital for the development of agriculture, irrigation projects, lumbering, fishing, and manufacturing, and for the railroads themselves. With the Far West more easily accessible, however, eastern capital became more prevalent in the development and exploitation of western resources. As this capital moved into the Far West on a large scale, the economy began to move toward a "colonial" economy, in

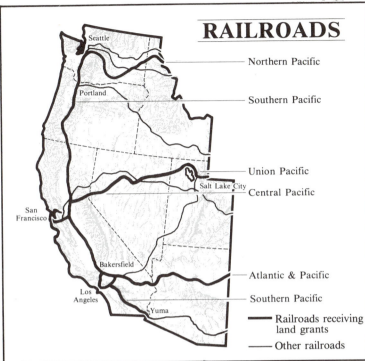

RAILROADS

—— Northern Pacific

—— Southern Pacific

—— Union Pacific

—— Central Pacific

—— Atlantic & Pacific

—— Southern Pacific

—— Railroads receiving land grants

—— Other railroads

Seattle
Portland
San Francisco
Salt Lake City
Bakersfield
Los Angeles
Yuma

Figure 12.11   Major Railroad Routes
in the Far West

which raw materials were exchanged for manufactured products. This situation was not stabilized until the middle of the 20th century.

The economic transformation of the Far West brought about by the railroads was also reflected in settlement and urban growth patterns. Railroads controlled vast amounts of land awarded to them by the government, and enticed new settlers to come west and buy railroad land. In this manner, railroads opened the wheat country east of the Cascades, California's San Joaquin Valley, southern California, and central Arizona. The railroads in these areas meant not only new settlements, but also a shift from livestock grazing to cereals, and eventually to irrigated specialty crops. In some areas, they transformed agriculture into a branch of commerce.

The most spectacular effect of the railroad was on urban growth. The Far West was a dynamic region, with constant movement and change, particularly in the development of new towns. Each new town competed to become a metropolitan center but, without a rail facility, its chances of survival were slim. The railroads

were instrumental both in founding new towns and also in enhancing those already in existence. Seattle, Tacoma, and Spokane grew quickly after the arrival of a railroad. Probably no city owed its growth to the railroad more than Los Angeles, a city so often associated with the automobile. The city of Los Angeles was in the enviable position of having two rail connections with the East, the Southern Pacific and the Santa Fe. The competition between the two lines resulted in fares so low that thousands of settlers were encouraged to come to Los Angeles and to buy land from the largest landowners in the region, the railroads.

The economic advance of the Far West was nothing short of spectacular, even by North American standards. In a matter of thirty years, the region was transformed from an ephemeral economy based on anticipated quick returns in mining to an area where agriculture and commerce became the cornerstones of life. The railroad was especially instrumental in building and contributing to an economy that would increasingly become more involved in extractive industries. Although the railroad brought change, it also ended the Far West's isolation and thereby its pioneering stage.

CONCLUSION

The early development of the Far West is far from being fully understood. Many of the themes touched upon above need further explication and more detailed commentary. Nevertheless, one overriding theme that appears throughout the historical geography of the Far West, from aboriginal occupance to the 20th century is diversity, a diversity reflected in its biophysical environments as well as in its human populations. Indian occupance was marked by tremendous differences from place to place. The differences went unnoticed, for the most part, by early trapper-explorers, who were more concerned with identifying and exploiting environmental differences. The human geography of the Indian and the explorer was quickly pushed aside once Spain, Britain, and the United States began to compete earnestly for the Far West. Each approached the region from different perspectives and directions, and each in turn created regional frontiers that would remain throughout the 19th century and influence and anchor the West's growth and development. Once the United States had quieted all competing imperial claims to the land, it faced the prospect of peopling a land that was not, nor would ever become, a cultural mirror of its westward moving frontier. The discovery of gold, and the subsequent rush to claim it, heightened and extended the diversity of the entire area. Mining, instant urbanization, specialized agriculture, and spiraling growth in-

tensified differences that, in turn, became engrained in its human geography.

As yet, the Far West has failed to attract the amount of scholarly research necessary to summarize adequately the tremendous diversity within the region. Unlike other American frontiers, few in-depth studies have dealt with agriculture, settlement, population, city formation, and economic growth. In the westward-moving frontier schemes of many geographers and historians, the Far West is often overlooked, except for the California gold rush, leaving the region only vaguely understood. The Far West should not be considered as a simple extension of a continually westward-moving frontier from the Atlantic, but rather as an eastward-moving frontier from the Pacific with its own unique history and indigenous historical geography.

ADDITIONAL READING

Books

Allen, J.L. *Passage Through the Garden: Lewis and Clark and the Image of the Northwest.* Urbana: University of Illinois Press, 1975.

Arrington, L.J. *Great Basin Kingdom: An Economic History of the Latter-Day Saints.* Cambridge: Harvard University Press, 1958.

Barth, G. *Instant Cities: Urbanization and the Rise of the San Francisco and Denver.* New York: Oxford University Press, 1975.

Bartlett, R.A. *Great Surveys of the American West.* Norman: University of Oklahoma Press, 1962.

Bowen, W.A. *The Willamette Valley: Migration and Settlement on the Oregon Frontier.* Seattle: University of Washington Press, 1978.

Dicken, S.N., and Dicken, E. *The Making of Oregon: A Study in Historical Geography.* Portland: Oregon Historical Society, 1979.

Fogelson, R.M. *The Fragmented Metropolis: Los Angeles 1850–1930.* Cambridge: Harvard University Press, 1967.

Goetzman, W.H. *Exploration and Empire: The Explorer and Scientist in Winning the American West.* New York: Alfred A. Knopf, 1966.

Hornbeck, D. *California Patterns: A Geographical and Historical Areas.* Palo Alto: Mayfield Publishing Company, 1983.

Jackson, R.H., ed. *The Mormon Role in the Settlement of the West.* Provo: Brigham Young University Press, 1978.

Jolinek, L.S. *Harvest Empire: A History of California Agriculture.* San Francisco: Boyd & Fraser, 1979.

Jorgenson, J.G. *Western Indians: Comparative Environments, Langauges and Culture of 172 Western Indian Tribes.* San Francisco: W.H. Freeman & Co., 1980.

Lotchin, R.W. *San Francisco, 1846–1856: From Hamlet to City.* New York: Oxford University Press, 1974.

Luckingham, B. *The Urban Southwest: A Profile History of El Paso, Albuquerque, Tucson, and Phoenix.* El Paso: Texas Western Press, 1982.

Merk, F. *Manifest Destiny and Mission in American History: A Reinterpretation.* New York: Alfred A. Knopf, 1963.

Meinig, D.W. *The Great Columbia Plain: A Historical Geography, 1805–1910.* Seattle: University of Washington Press, 1968.

Peterson, R.H. *The Bonanza Kings: The Social Origins and Business Behavior of Western Mining Entrepreneurs, 1870–1900.* Lincoln: University of Nebraska Press, 1977.

Pomeroy, E. *The Pacific Slope: A History of California, Oregon, Washington, Utah, and Nevada.* New York: Alfred A. Knopf, 1966.

Reps, J.W. *Cities of the American West: A History of Frontier Urban Planning.* Princeton: Princeton University Press, 1979.

Rodman, P. *Mining Frontiers of the Far West, 1848–1880.* New York: Holt, Rinehart & Winston, 1963.

Rodman, P., and Etulain, R.W. *Frontier and the American West.* Arlington Heights: AHM Publishing Corp., 1977.

Sale, R. *Seattle: Past to Present.* Seattle: University of Washington Press, 1976.

Wheat, C.I. *Mapping the Trans-Mississippi West, 1540–1861.* 5 vols. San Francisco: Institute of Historical Cartography, 1957–63.

Winther, O.O. *The Transportation Frontier, 1865–1890.* New York: Holt, Rinehart & Winston, 1964.

Wishart, D. *The Fur Trade of the American West, 1807–1840: A Geographical Synthesis.* Lincoln: University of Nebraska Press, 1979.

13

Population Growth, Migration, and Urbanization, 1860–1920

DAVID WARD

University of Wisconsin,
Madison

During the period of mass immigration that began in the mid-1840s and ended in the mid-1920s, the population of the United States increased from about 17 million to more than 105 million (Table 13.1). This sixfold increase was unparalleled elsewhere in the Western industrializing world; the populations of the United Kingdom and Germany, for example, grew at about half that rate. Even before the onset of mass immigration, extremely high rates of natural growth had doubled the population of the new nation in less than 25 years, but toward the end of the 19th century natural growth rates declined as the excess of births over deaths diminished. During the 1870s death rates were as high as 22 per thousand and birthrates exceeded 40 per thousand. By the decade of World War 1, death rates had declined to about 15 per thousand, but birthrates had dropped more dramatically to just over 25 per thousand. Net migration rates fluctuated from decade to decade, reaching a maximum of 10 percent between 1880 and 1885 and, after declining to less than 3 percent during the depression of the mid-nineties, increased once again to a level of 7 percent between 1905 and 1910. The proportion of the white population born abroad increased from about 13 percent in 1850 to almost 20 percent in 1890 and then declined to 17 percent by 1920, but the proportion of people of foreign birth and parentage together reached its maximum level of 45 percent in 1920 (Table 13.1). Overall, immigration probably doubled the rate of growth among those of European ancestry, but in the absence of a substantial immigrant contribution the relative proportion of blacks in the total population dropped from more than 15 percent in 1850 to less than 10 percent in 1920.

This unparalleled rate of growth among the white population was accompanied, as in many parts of Europe, by a rapid rate of urbanization. Unlike Europe, the diverse resources of an

Table 13.1   U.S. Population Composition and Growth, 1840–1920 (in percentages)

	Population (in millions)	Urban	Black	Foreign parentage	Foreign born
1840	17.1	10.8	16.8	n.d.	n.d.
1850	23.2	15.3	15.7	n.d.	12.9
1860	31.4	19.8	14.1	n.d.	17.9
1870	39.8	25.7	13.5	19.0	19.6
1880	50.2	28.2	13.1	22.5	17.8
1890	62.9	35.1	11.9	25.0	19.9
1900	76.0	39.7	11.6	27.6	18.1
1910	92.0	45.7	10.7	27.8	18.0
1920	105.7	51.2	9.9	28.0	16.9

n.d. = no data.

undeveloped frontier stimulated high levels of interregional migration to non-urban settings as well. Between 1790 and 1850, the urban proportion of the total population more than tripled to reach 15 percent and increased by a similar margin in the suceeding six decades, so that by 1910 more than 45 percent of the population lived in urban settlements (Table 13.1). Toward the turn of the 19th century, the city-ward movement of people far exceeded migration to a greatly diminished frontier. By 1920, the population of the United States surpassed 100 million, and for the first time a narrow majority was urban. The impact of foreign immigration on both the size and the ethnic composition of the American population had for long aroused anxieties among the native-born and, in 1924, entry restrictions, which had been applied to Orientals as early as the 1880s, were extended to include all foreigners. Thereafter, a precipitous drop in foreign arrivals compounded the longer-term effects of a declining rate of natural growth and brought a period of unprecedented population growth to an end.

THE ORIGINS AND DESTINATIONS OF MIGRANTS

Restrictive legislation was in part provoked by changes in the volume, sources, and destinations of immigrants after about 1880. Approximately 33 million foreigners entered the United States in the century prior to comprehensive immigration restriction, but only one-third of this total had actually arrived by 1880. During the succeeding forty years, an average of about 6 million people arrived in each decade, with more than 8 million newcomers entering the United States in the first decade of the 20th century (Table 13.2). After 1880, the source areas of immigrants expanded from northwestern Europe to include southern and eastern sections of the continent. Prior to that date, about 85 percent of all immigrants came from the British Isles, British America (Canada), the German states, Switzerland, Scandinavia, and the Low Countries, but during the decade of World War I these areas accounted for barely 20 percent of the total arrivals. Immigrants from the Austro-Hungarian and Russian empires as well as from Mediterranean Europe provided more than one-half of the new arrivals in the last decade of the 19th century and overwhelmingly dominated the immigrant stream from Europe in the two subsequent decades (Fig. 13.1). Immigration from Latin America and the Orient also increased markedly after 1880. Although their contribution to the total flow remained less than 10 percent, both groups had a profound impact on the populations of western states.

Debates on the desirability of immigration increasingly focused on the tendency of the more recent arrivals to congregate in the slums of large cities of the Northeast and Middle West. On the basis of both Old World sources and American destinations, a distinction was made between "old immigrants" who had arrived before about 1880 and "new immigrants" who had landed after that date. The distinction, however, did become the source of prejudicial evaluations of the new immigrants and the basis of the ethnic quotas that were established by the immigration restriction legislation of the 1920s. In contrast, the contributions and experiences of the old immigrants were reevaluated in a more positive light. Northwest Europeans were viewed as part of the broader culture from which American values were derived. Their rapid assimilation into American society was further facilitated by their participation in the frontier movement and their more balanced distribution between urban and rural settings. With the striking exception of the Irish, most old immigrant groups did indeed contribute to the settlement of the midwestern frontier in larger proportions than most new immigrants. Parts of the rural Middle West were, however, a mosaic of ethnic communi-

Table 13.2   Decennial Immigration to the United States, 1820–1919

	1820 to 1829	1830 to 1839	1840 to 1849	1850 to 1859	1860 to 1869	1870 to 1879	1880 to 1889	1890 to 1899	1900 to 1909	1910 to 1919
Total in millions	0.1	0.5	1.4	2.7	2.1	2.7	5.2	3.7	8.2	6.3
Percent of total from:										
Ireland	40.2	31.7	46.0	36.9	24.4	15.4	12.8	11.0	4.2	2.6
Germany[a]	4.5	23.2	27.0	34.8	35.2	27.4	27.5	15.7	4.0	2.7
United Kingdom	19.5	13.8	15.3	13.5	14.9	21.1	15.5	8.9	5.7	5.8
Scandinavia	0.2	0.4	0.9	0.9	5.5	7.6	12.7	10.5	5.9	3.8
Canada[b]	1.8	2.2	2.4	2.2	4.9	11.8	9.4	0.1	1.5	11.2
Russia[a]	—	—	—	—	0.2	1.3	3.5	12.2	18.3	17.4
Austria-Hungary[a]	—	—	—	—	0.2	2.2	6.0	14.5	24.4	18.2
Italy	—	—	—	—	0.5	1.7	5.1	16.3	23.5	19.4

[a]Continental European boundaries prior to the 1919 settlement.

[b]British America to 1867; Canada includes Newfoundland; Canadian immigration was not recorded between 1886 and 1893.

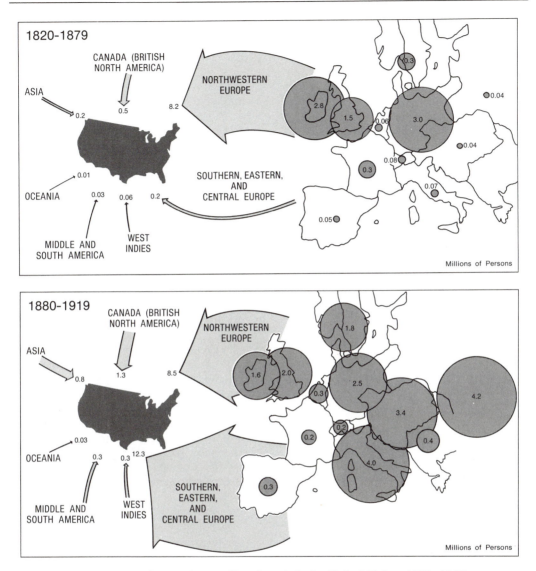

Figure 13.1   Source Areas of Immigrants to the United States, 1820–1919

ties, and for most groups assimilation was not necessarily rapid. Moreover, the declining intensity of frontier settlement recorded regional shifts in economic growth and opportunities to which native as well as foreign-born migrants responded. Indeed, the most striking feature of both old and new immigrants was their avoidance of the South throughout the entire period of mass immigration. A commercial agricultural system largely based upon the intensive use of black labor and a decidedly slow rate of industrialization offered few attractions to foreign immigrants.

Immigrants from southern and eastern Europe were more highly urbanized than the earlier arrivals from northwestern Europe, yet in 1920 the long established Irish remained the second most urbanized group (Table 13.3). Almost 87 percent of the Irish-born lived in cities and this proportion was exceeded only by the Russian immigrants. More than 80 percent of all Poles, Hungarians, and Italians lived in cities, but fewer than 70 percent of several other new immigrant groups were classed as urban. Among the recently arrived Yugoslavs and Czechs, for example, the degree of urbanization was little different from that of the longer established German-born. Moreover, while only two-thirds of the Germans were urban residents, they accounted for 11 percent of the total foreign-born population of American cities, and only the newly arrived Russians and Italians contributed more to the total foreign population (Table 13.3). Certainly, some ethnic

Table 13.3   Urban Residence of Foreign-Born White Population, 1920

	Percent of group urban	Percent of total foreign-born urban population	Total foreign populations (in millions)
Foreign-born white	75.5	100.0	10.36
Russia	88.6	12.0	1.24
Ireland	86.9	8.7	0.90
Italy	84.4	13.1	1.36
Poland	84.4	9.3	0.96
Hungary	80.0	3.1	0.32
United Kingdom	75.0	8.4	0.86
Austria	75.0	4.2	0.43
Canada	74.5	8.1	0.84
Yugoslavia	69.3	1.1	0.12
Germany	67.5	11.0	1.14
Czechoslovakia	66.3	2.3	0.24
Scandinavia	54.6	6.5	0.34

and national groups of the new immigration settled almost exclusively in cities, but as late as 1920, old immigrants still accounted for almost half of the foreign-born urban population. This distinction of the "old" and the "new" clearly neglected the effects of length of residence in the new country on both the distribution and assimilation of immigrants and also obscured major differences in the experiences of individual groups within each category. Changes in the proportion of immigrants with urban destinations was probably no greater than among native Americans who migrated before and after 1880. Some of these native-born urban migrants were, of course, the children of immigrants who had settled on the land earlier in the century. Others were southern-born blacks who established patterns of migration that were to expand dramatically once foreign immigration was restricted.

These cumulative geographic consequences of rapid population growth, high rates of migration, and accelerated urbanization resulted from literally millions of individual decisions that were provoked by an almost endless combination of specific motives. Most migrants were in search of new employment and, at any given time, information on the availability of opportunities in specific destinations was restricted. Moreover, centers of expanding employment were rarely fixed, and information was often incomplete, if not erroneous. Consequently, migration was rarely a single event, and frequent moves were often responses to expanding agricultural and mining frontiers and to the growth of manufacturing industries in the Northeast and Middle West. During the past twenty years high rates of population turnover have been documented in both urban and rural settings throughout the second half of the 19th century. The large volume, high frequency, and sequential pattern of migration usually occurred in the form of a network or "chain" of destinations within which relatives and friends provided short-term security and reliable information.

Frequent migration and population turnover did not obliterate the cumulative locational effects of the selective migration of different ethnic, religious, and racial groups from their ancestral or adopted source regions. Although most immigrants shared their new destinations with other groups, and although in time many of their ancestral traits disappeared, their ethnic identities in the United States were often associated with their initial regional concentrations rather than with their cultural hearths in the Old World. Long before mass immigration, English immigrants to the New England and Chesapeake colonies, when they spread westward, were identified as "Yankee" and "southern" rather than as English-American. Similarly, French colonists to Québec and Acadia retained their original labels long after their subsequent moves to Louisiana and New England, respectively. The Mormons, defined by their religious beliefs, were originally organized in upstate New York but today are most closely identified with their adopted state of Utah. Other groups have retained their immigrant label, but their ethnic identity is now closely associated with their original concentrations within the United States. People of

Norwegian ancestry, for example, are strongly associated with sections of Wisconsin and those of Swedish descent with parts of Minnesota.

These uneven patterns of distribution in part record national and regional differences in the impact of industrial capitalism, which set well-defined limits to the routes and destinations of most migrants. The disruptive effects of industrialization on rural crafts, domestic manufacturing, and farming virtually forced emigration from many parts of Europe. During the 1840s, crop failures savagely compounded this agrarian distress, and these critical conditions in the Old World rather than any complete awareness of opportunities in the New World probably initiated mass emigration. Once established, however, the immigrant flow also responded to upswings and downswings in the American business cycle and to regional shifts in economic growth within the United States.

THE INITIAL IMPACT OF MASS IMMIGRATION: 1860

The regional destinations of those foreigners who had arrived in the first surge of mass immigration were clearly established by 1860. Of more than 4 million foreign-born people, 37 percent were concentrated in the Mid-Atlantic region and an identical proportion in the Middle West, while another 11 percent were to be found in New England (Fig. 13.2). Fewer than 10 percent of the foreign-born had settled in the South, and the majority of these people were concentrated in Baltimore, New Orleans, Louisville, and other ports and river towns which encircled that dominantly rural region. Prior to the start of mass immigration, native-born Americans had moved westward in substantial numbers, and each coastal concentration of colonial Americans had expanded in a somewhat latitudinal fashion. Most migrants from the Southeast (Georgia and South Carolina) moved into the lower Mississippi valley, while those from the Mid-Atlantic region pushed west along the Ohio valley into the middle Mississippi valley. Those from the Upper South (Virginia, Maryland, and North Carolina) migrated to both sections of the Mississippi valley, while the majority of New Englanders moved into the Great Lakes region by way of the Mohawk

Gap, through which the Erie Canal was dug. The westward extension of this northern trajectory of frontier settlement lagged far behind those farther south, for New Englanders had initially found land available in upstate New York and Upper Canada (Ontario). By the time New Englanders began to settle the westerly sections of the Great Lakes region, they were joined by large numbers of immigrants primarily, but not exclusively, from the German states and Scandinavia. The pioneer populations of Wisconsin and Minnesota included extremely high proportions of foreigners. The Irish contribution to this proportion was, however, decidedly modest. Consequently, the regional distributions of the Irish and continental Europeans exhibited some striking contrasts as early as 1860.

These regional tendencies are revealed by a crude index of deviation that indicates the degree to which a given group is under- or overrepresented in relation to regional distribution of the population as a whole (Table 13.4). The index has been computed for regional clusters of states on the basis of similarities in their ethnic compositions (Fig. 13.2). The Irish were heavily overrepresented in the Northeast, and although immigrants from the German states were also well represented in the Mid-Atlantic region, there were relatively few of them in New England. In the Middle West, the Germans were as highly overrepresented as were the Irish in New England. Of all immigrant groups, the English were the most evenly distributed among these regions, and only in Missouri, Iowa, and the Kansas Territory were they slightly underrepresented. The Scots closely paralleled the settlement patterns of the English, but the Welsh were strongly overrepresented only in the Mid-Atlantic region. Of the other smaller groups, those from British America (Canada), including many whose parents were born in the British Isles, were strikingly prominent in New England and some sections of the Middle West, while immigrants from Scandinavia, Holland, and Switzerland were almost exclusively concentrated in Michigan, Wisconsin, and Minnesota.

Although substantial proportions of most immigrant groups had participated in the settlement of the Middle West, the Irish were a striking exception. To be sure, Irish laborers were involved in the construction of canals,

Table 13.4   Regional Representation of Selected Foreign-Born Groups, 1860 (index of deviation)

	Ireland	Germany	England	Scotland	Br. America
New England	1.9	0.2	1.0	1.2	2.8
Mid-Atlantic	2.0	1.4	1.7	1.6	1.0
E. Midwest	0.7	1.6	1.3	1.2	1.4
N. Midwest	1.3	3.6	2.6	1.9	2.7
S. Midwest	0.7	1.6	0.8	0.8	0.8
Total in thousands	1,611	1,301	432	109	250

Note: Index of deviation = percent group / percent total population in each region.
See Figure 13.2 for regional boundaries

railroads, and cities in the West, but very few settled on the land. Famine conditions yielded a high proportion of impoverished and sickly migrants who lacked the skills and resources to move beyond the ports of arrival. Indeed, in the absence of specialized cheap passenger services, Irish immigrants became the westbound ballast of Atlantic sailing ships, compensating in revenue for the difference in bulk between eastbound cargoes of raw materials and return loads of manufactured goods. The New Brunswick lumber trade, in particular, provided cheap passages to the Maritime Provinces, from where many Irish immigrants moved on to New England. Eventually, the greater frequency of ships between Liverpool and New York directed the Irish emigrant traffic to these ports.

The majority of German immigrants also landed in New York, but initially the routes of commodity commerce had influenced their destinations too. Many German-speaking people from Alsace-Lorraine and adjacent sections of the Rhine valley traveled to the United States on cotton freighters returning from Le Havre to New Orleans. They moved on to the Middle West by way of the Mississippi. Immigrants from northwestern Germany utilized the tobacco ships that plied the route from Bremen to Baltimore, from where the majority moved inland by way of the Ohio valley. Others found their way to New York after short voyages across the North Sea to the ports of the east coast of England and then overland to Liverpool. Once the emigrant traffic became a specialized and scheduled service and the pressures for immediate emigration subsided, the vast majority of all foreigners arrived at New York and, with the rapid development of

steamship services after the Civil War, this dominance became even more pronounced. Deteriorating and at times catastrophic conditions in the Old World strongly directed the initial courses of emigration but, increasingly, economic growth in the United States became decisive in the regional allocation of immigrants.

REGIONAL DESTINATIONS: 1860–1890

Following the resumption of mass immigration with the end of the Civil War, the majority of immigrants continued to come from northwestern Europe, and most arrived during two major surges that peaked in the early 1870s and again in the mid-1880s. The completion of a transcontinental railroad system and the rapid advance of trunklines into the western states had facilitated the westward expansion of settlement and development. Railroad construction had also been rewarded by huge government grants of land adjacent to their routes and, consequently, the railroads had a vested interest in the rapid alienation of their holdings. To speed up settlement, they sent agents to Europe to publicize the potential of their holdings and provided special discounted fares from rural Europe to the American West. Several midwestern states created immigration agencies that also facilitated the diffusion of information on conditions and opportunities on the American frontier but, ultimately, it was the personal networks of knowledge compiled from emigrants' correspondence that provided the most persuasive influences on the decision to migrate.

Under these circumstances, the proportion

of immigrants who moved directly inland from the ports of arrival increased markedly. In 1860, approximately equal proportions of immigrants were housed in the Mid-Atlantic region and in the Middle West, but by 1890 about 45 percent of all foreign-born residents lived in the latter region and just under 30 percent in the former (Fig. 13.2). While many immigrants continued to settle in Ohio, Michigan, and Illinois, the largest gains were made in Wisconsin, Minnesota, and the Dakotas. Here, immigrants were often a majority of the new settlers, but farther south in Iowa, Missouri, Kansas, and Nebraska, the substantial native-born migration exceeded that of foreigners. Nevertheless, Scandinavian, Dutch, Swiss, and German immigrants were all well represented in varying degrees throughout the Middle West. With the exception of the Germans in the Mid-Atlantic region and the Swedes in New England, these groups were not prominent in the Northeast (Table 13.5). Although they were often identified as new immigrants, almost 120,000 Bohemians (Czechs) were recorded in the U.S. Census of 1890, and their regional distribution was little different from that of other groups from

continental northwestern Europe. In particular, there were striking concentrations of Czechs in and around Omaha, Nebraska. The Swiss and Scandinavians were also overrepresented in the Pacific Northwest and the northern sections of the Rockies. Throughout this vast expanse of new settlement, newly arrived immigrants often reestablished and even elaborated their ancestral patterns of life in the form of church centered or congregational societies. Although they quickly adapted to the agricultural practices and market orientation of American life, many rural groups have retained a distinct ethnic identity to this day. Among many striking examples of these persisting ethnic groups are the Dutch in and around Kalamazoo, Michigan, and the Swiss of New Glaurus, Wisconsin.

California had also attracted some of the immigrant groups who had settled the Middle West and the Northwest, but here the British, Irish, Italians, and Portuguese were also well represented. The distinctive ethnic tone of California and adjacent sections of the Southwest was, however, set by the prominence of the Chinese and Mexicans. Mining and railroad

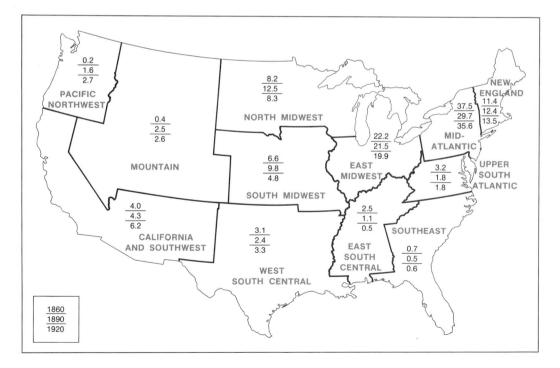

Figure 13.2   Regional Distribution of Foreign-Born Immigrants: 1860, 1890, and 1920 (by %)

Table 13.5   Regional Representation of Northwest Europeans, 1890 (index of deviation)

	Ire.	Ger.	Eng.	Scot.	Wales	Can.	Nor.	Swe.	Den.	Swit.	Hol.	Boh.[a]
New England	3.0	0.3	2.0	2.2	0.5	5.2	0.1	1.0	0.4	0.1	0.1	0.1
Mid-Atlantic	2.2	1.5	1.7	1.6	2.3	0.5	0.2	0.5	0.4	0.7	1.0	0.5
E. Midwest	0.7	1.5	1.1	1.0	1.0	1.3	0.6	1.3	0.8	1.3	2.6	1.8
N. Midwest	0.7	2.6	0.9	1.2	1.1	2.0	11.8	5.0	4.8	2.0	2.1	3.8
S. Midwest	0.5	1.2	0.8	0.8	0.8	0.5	0.9	1.5	2.3	1.5	1.2	2.5
Mountain	1.0	1.0	3.7	3.3	4.5	1.7	1.2	3.1	6.8	2.6	0.5	0.2
Pacific N.W.	0.7	1.0	1.7	2.4	2.0	2.4	3.4	2.9	3.1	3.3	0.6	0.3
Total in thousands	1,872	2,785	908	242	100	981	323	478	133	104	82	118

[a]Bohemia.

Note: Index of deviation = percent group/percent total population in each region.
See Figure 13.2 for regional boundaries.

construction made extensive use of Chinese labor but, by the mid-1880s, the increasing volume of immigration from East Asia had provoked not only hostility but also exclusionary legislation. In 1890, more than 106,000 Chinese immigrants lived in the United States and more than three-quarters of them were concentrated in the cities and larger towns of northern California and the Pacific Northwest. Although there were only 2,200 newcomers from Japan, they were also concentrated on the west coast, where more than three-quarters of their total were to be found primarily in intensive horticulture (Table 13.6). The Mexican presence in California was, of course, partly a consequence of annexation in 1848, and by 1890 almost 30 percent of the 77,800 people of Mexican birth were recorded there, and almost all the remainder were living along the border in Arizona, New Mexico, and Texas. This period also saw

the final stages of the relocation of American Indians on western reservations. In 1890, fewer than 60,000 Indians were recorded in the Census. About one-quarter of them were concentrated in various parts of the northern Middle West, another third lived in California, and the majority of the remainder were dispersed throughout the Southwest and mountain regions (Table 13.6). Throughout the 19th century, these enforced migrations of Native Americans were accompanied by the continued decline in their numbers, and this trend was not reversed until the present century. The majority of Indians were assigned to reservations where they attempted to maintain their tribal institutions in unfamiliar, isolated, and often distinctly unpromising environments.

Between 1860 and 1890, the black population increased from 4.4 million to 7.5 million, but their proportionate contribution to the total

Table 13.6   Regional Distribution of Selected Minority Groups, 1890 and 1920 (as percentage of total U.S.)

	1890				1920			
	Native America	Mexico	Japan	China	Native America	Mexico	Japan	China
Southwest	36.7	29.8	56.4	68.9	28.6	34.6	65.5	48.9
Pacific N.W.	8.4	0.2	18.9	11.9	5.5	0.2	19.4	8.9
Mountain	9.1	1.1	1.5	9.3	10.0	2.9	9.0	4.9
W. South Central	2.7	66.8	1.0	1.1	24.8	56.6	2.5	56.6
Total in thousands	59[a]	78	2	107	244	486	82	44

[a]Excludes Indians in Indian Territory and on Indian reservations.

See Figure 13.2 for regional boundaries.

population declined from 14.1 to 11.9 percent. Although immigrants continued to avoid the South, blacks were as highly concentrated there in 1890 as they had been in 1860, in spite of the emancipation of slaves in 1863. While the proportion of whites living in the Old South, east of the Mississippi, declined from 22 to 18 percent, that of blacks dropped from 78 to 72 percent (Fig. 13.3). These losses were compensated for by gains in southern states west of the Mississippi and, consequently, more than 90 percent of blacks still resided in the South in 1890. Like the population of the South as a whole, blacks were overwhelmingly rural, but those who lived outside the South were concentrated in Philadelphia, Washington, Cincinnati, St. Louis, Kansas City, and other cities that bordered on the South.

Before 1890, the vast movement of people to the Middle West often deflected attention from the substantial impact of immigration on the industrialization and urbanization of the Northeast. Immigrants from England, Scotland, and Wales joined the native-born in the skilled sectors of the expanding mining, metal working, and textile industries, and in 1890

they were much more strikingly overrepresented in the Northeast than in the Middle West (Table 13.5). The regional distributions of the English and the Scots were quite similar, but the Welsh remained concentrated in the Mid-Atlantic region and were poorly represented in New England. The Irish remained relatively underrepresented in the Middle West and, despite the emergence of a secondary center in California, were more highly concentrated in the Northeast than in 1860 (Table 13.5). The Irish had begun to obtain employment in the semiskilled sectors of several manufacturing industries, but the majority worked as day laborers or domestic servants, or were employed in the workshops of the so-called "sweated" trades. In New England, they shared their regional predominance with the Canadians who had originally come from the English-speaking sections of the Maritime Provinces and Newfoundland, but after the Civil War the French-speaking Québécois also moved there in large numbers. The latter often competed with the Irish for jobs in the textile industry, but English-speaking Canadians were able to enter those skilled trades within

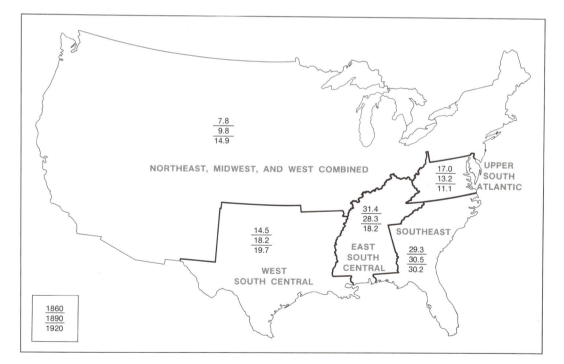

Figure 13.3   Regional Distribution of the Black Population: 1860, 1890, and 1920 (by %)

which advancement to petty proprietorship was still possible. In the Mid-Atlantic region, where the Canadians were not prominent, these small-scale skilled trades were often dominated by German immigrants.

Overall patterns of migration and settlement established before the Civil War, during the first surge of mass immigration, were maintained during those of the early 1870s and mid-1880s. To a much greater degree than in subsequent decades, these immigrants moved directly to the farms and small towns of the agricultural interior. Farther south and especially in the Southwest, native-born migrants were dominant. Substantial numbers of immigrants from the British Isles and to a lesser degree from Germany were concentrated in the industrial centers of the Northeast. On the west coast, where immigrants were also well represented, newcomers from non-European sources had already established a distinctive tone to that region's ethnic pluralism, and in California the Chinese were the largest foreign-born group. Generalizations about the old immigrants exaggerated the assimilative effects of their settlement on the frontier and, in any event, many of them also responded to industrial developments in northeastern cities. Moreover, these same generalizations overlooked the impact of non-European immigration on the West and Southwest. Nevertheless, during the mid-1880s, several new groups made their appearance in the immigrant stream, and their regional destinations were quite different from those of most of their predecessors.

REGIONAL DESTINATIONS: 1890–1920

Immigration from northwestern Europe continued at a relatively high level until the turn of the 19th century, but by the time immigration was restricted in 1924 the proportion arriving from these areas was less than 20 percent (Table 13.2). Nevertheless, considerable numbers of immigrants from these long established sources continued to settle in the regional destinations of their predecessors. The increase in immigration from southern and eastern Europe began slowly in the 1880s, when more than 750,000 people came from these more remote sources and accounted for about 15 percent of the total.

By the first decade of the present century this proportion had increased dramatically to well over two-thirds of total immigration. Foreign arrivals declined slightly in the subsequent decade because of the disruptive effects of World War I. Changes within Europe strongly influenced these shifts in the source areas of immigrants. Diminishing rates of population growth, combined with economic development, had greatly reduced the incentives for emigration from many parts of northwestern Europe. In contrast, the disruptive impact of industrialization on rural societies, which had afflicted northwestern Europe earlier in the century, had finally diffused to many once remote areas of southern and eastern Europe. Quite apart from these economic considerations, political persecution in the form of pogroms greatly accelerated the emigration of Jews from the Russian Empire, while the removal of restraints on movement within the Austro-Hungarian Empire also facilitated emigration from Central Europe.

The changing labor needs of the American economy were also extremely critical in this reorientation of immigrant source areas. The United States was one of the pioneers of the second phase of those technological and organizational innovations that marked the later stages of the industrial revolution and the transition from entrepreneurial to corporate capitalism. Many longer-established immigrants and especially their American-born children were able to move into the growing managerial and clerical strata of the labor force, but an even more voracious demand for semiskilled and unskilled labor could no longer be supplied from northwestern Europe. Moreover, the bulk of this new employment was concentrated in the industrial cities of the Northeast but, just as the agricultural frontier had strongly influenced the destinations of immigrants before 1890, a second, more intensive frontier of manufacturing attracted immigrants as it spread from the Northeast into the eastern sections of the Middle West. Between 1890 and 1920 the earlier decline in the proportion of immigrants living in the Mid-Atlantic region was reversed, and by 1920 almost 36 percent of the foreign-born lived there (Fig. 13.2). The proportions in the eastern Middle West and New England remained relatively stable, and by 1920 well over two-thirds of the total foreign-born lived in the three regions that formed the expanded industrial core of the American economy often described as the American Manufacturing Belt.

These changes in the regional distributions of the foreign-born clearly indicate the predominant destinations of recently arrived immigrants from southern and eastern Europe. Unfortunately, the census tabulations of the diverse immigrants coming from the Russian and Austro-Hungarian empires were rarely consistent and often included several distinct ethnic groups under the same category. As early as 1890 the concentration of southern and eastern European immigrants in the Mid-Atlantic region was especially pronounced and, in addition, the strong representation of Italians in New England and of Poles in the eastern Middle West was also apparent (Table 13.7). Thirty years later, these initial patterns had been maintained but East Europeans and Greeks were now strongly overrepresented in the eastern Middle West. The Italians alone of the new immigrants were weakly represented in the eastern Middle West, while in New England they now shared their prominence with the Russian-born, who were primarily of Jewish background (Table 13.7). Despite their greatly reduced proportionate contribution to the total immigrant stream, northwestern Europeans also concentrated in the industrial core region and, with the exception of the Irish, continued to be well represented in the Middle West and the Far West. The regional distributions of these old immigrants showed few overall changes between 1890 and 1920 (Tables 13.5 and 13.8).

The large cities of the industrial core region were also the primary destinations of black migrants from the South. During the 1870s and 1880s, the net loss of black migrants from the South amounted to about 130,000 but, during the 1890s, when emigration from Europe dropped from the extremely high levels of the previous decade, the South incurred an even greater loss of more than 250,000 blacks. After a slight decline in net migration from the South between 1900 and 1910, the northward flow increased dramatically during World War I, when emigration from Europe was virtually impossible. During this decade the South experienced a net loss of more than 450,000 black migrants, most of whom moved to the cities of the Northeast and the Middle West. With the restriction of foreign immigration in 1924, the migration of blacks became the largest single source of new unskilled labor; in many respects they defined the beginning of a third major era of migration. By 1920 these new patterns of migration were well established, and the decline in the black population of the Old South that had begun before 1890 increased markedly thereafter. By 1920 this region housed just over two-thirds of the total black population, but 10 percent now lived in the Northeast and eastern Middle West (Fig. 13.3). Immigration from both Canada and Mexico also increased substantially after 1890 and especially during World War I. Their long-established regional patterns remained unchanged. More than 70 percent of the French Canadians in the United States were concentrated in New England (Table 13.8), and more than 90 percent of those of Mexican birth were spread along the border states of the Southwest (Table 13.6). In California both the Mexican- and Japanese-born populations had increased, but the Chinese had declined after

Table 13.7   Regional Representation of "New" Immigrants, 1890 and 1920 (index of deviation)

	1890						1920					
	Italy	Rus.	Aus.	Hun.	Greece	Pol.	Italy	Rus.	Aus.	Hun.	Greece	Pol.
New England	1.2	0.9	0.3	0.4	0.6	0.5	2.1	1.7	0.9	0.5	2.9	n.d.
Mid-Atlantic	2.8	2.2	2.4	3.5	1.4	1.4	2.8	2.3	2.1	2.4	1.1	n.d.
East Midwest	0.5	0.7	0.7	0.8	0.9	1.9	0.6	1.1	1.5	1.8	1.3	n.d.
Total in thousands	183	183	123	62	2	147	1,610	3,871	3,130	1,111	176	n.d.

Note: Index of deviation = percent group/percent total population by regions.
See Figure 13.2 for regional boundaries.

Table 13.8   Regional Representation of Northwest Europeans, 1920 (index of deviation)

	Ire.	Ger.	Eng.	Scot.	Wales	Can.	Nor.	Swe.	Den.	Swit.	Hol.	Fr. Can.
New England	3.2	0.3	2.0	2.2	0.4	7.7	0.2	1.4	0.5	0.3	0.2	10.4
Mid-Atlantic	2.0	1.2	1.4	1.4	2.0	0.7	0.2	0.6	0.4	0.9	0.9	0.3
East Midwest	0.8	1.6	1.1	1.1	1.2	1.4	0.5	1.3	0.8	1.3	2.3	0.6
North Midwest	0.6	2.7	0.6	0.6	0.8	1.2	10.0	4.5	4.1	1.8	2.4	1.1
South Midwest	0.6	1.4	0.5	0.5	0.8	0.4	0.9	1.3	2.5	1.2	1.6	0.1
Mountain	0.8	0.6	2.0	1.9	2.8	1.4	1.8	2.7	5.7	2.7	1.3	0.4
Pacific N.W.	0.7	0.9	1.8	2.3	2.0	2.6	4.0	3.1	3.0	2.9	1.4	0.6
Southwest	1.1	0.9	1.8	1.8	1.4	1.9	0.6	1.2	2.1	2.8	0.7	0.1
Total in thousands	1,037	1,686	814	255	67	1,138	364	626	189	119	132	308

Note: Index of deviation = percent group/percent total population in each region.
See Figure 13.2 for regional boundaries.

legislation excluded newcomers. Unlike the Japanese and Mexicans who were closely associated with different aspects of intensive horticulture, the vast majority of the Chinese lived in distinctive ethnic quarters or "Chinatowns" in many of the large metropolitan cities.

THE PREDOMINANCE OF URBAN DESTINATIONS

Throughout the period of mass immigration, cities were the original destinations of most immigrants, and many of the children of those who initially settled in small towns or rural areas eventually moved to larger communities. Between 1890 and 1920, however, almost all the newcomers from southern and eastern Europe moved directly to the cities of the expanding industrial core region. Like the Irish and Germans before them, the proportionate representations of each of the major ethnic groups of the new immigration varied considerably from city to city within the Northeast and Middle West. The percentages of Irish and Germans in the foreign-born populations of American cities declined, but in 1910 they still tended to predominate in different groups of cities (Fig. 13.4). The cities of New England continued to house large proportions of Irish-born and relatively few Germans, but these proportions were reversed in the port cities of the Great Lakes (Milwaukee, Buffalo, Detroit, Toledo, Chicago, and Cleveland) and in Cincinnati, St. Louis, and St.

Paul. In the more than fifty cities with populations greater than 100,000 in 1910, only three—New York City, Jersey City, and San Francisco—had higher than average proportions of both German- and Irish-born, but many cities of the Mid-Atlantic region housed close to the average proportions of both groups (for example, Rochester, Newark, Pittsburgh, Syracuse, Paterson, Albany, and Philadelphia). In contrast, most southern and western cities housed less than average proportions of both groups.

Slavic and Hungarian immigrants from the Russian and Austro-Hungarian empires found their way to major centers of heavy industry in the valleys of Pennsylvania and eastern Ohio and the ports of the Great Lakes. Consequently, the port cities of the Great Lakes, which had for long housed substantial German-born populations, became major centers of eastern European settlement. Other German-dominant cities which did not become centers of heavy industry, such as Cincinnati and St. Louis, housed relatively small proportions of the new immigrants. Few Slavs moved to the Irish-dominated cities of New England, but they did work alongside the Irish in the heavy industrial cities of the Mid-Atlantic region where the Irish and Germans were more evenly represented. Precise measurements of the proportionate representation of different Slavic ethnic groups in various cities are not always possible from the census record. Although immigrants from the Austro-Hungarian Empire included some German-speaking people, the majority were Slavs and Hungarians who were well represented in Pittsburgh and several of the cities of the Great Lakes (Cleveland, Chicago, Milwaukee, and Detroit) but, with the notable exception of Bridgeport, Connecticut, they were sparsely represented in the cities of New England (Fig. 13.5).

In contrast, immigrants from Russia and Italy were only weakly represented in cities with high proportions of people from the Austro-Hungarian and German empires. They were, however, particularly prominent in the larger cities of New England and the Mid-Atlantic coast and especially those with highly diversified and consumer-oriented industries (Boston, Providence, New Haven, New York City, Paterson, Newark, and Philadelphia). Most immigrants from the Russian Empire were of Jewish background who found employment in the rapidly growing clothing industry that had long been associated with the use of "sweated" immigrant labor in small workshops or homes. They were also conspicuous in the rapidly expanding retail sector of not only the large cities of the Northeast, but also of the most major metropolitan centers of the Middle West and the Far West. Southern Italians were especially prominent in cities once dominated by Irish immigrants and, although Italians replaced the Irish in the ubiquitous activities of day laboring, they were also well represented in retailing and other small proprietory activities. In general, new immigrants from southern and eastern Europe were highly represented in fewer of the most populous cities than were those of the old but, with the exception of the South, the ethnic profiles of most large cities included some representation of most nationalities. Moreover, within most large American cities, immigrant settlements followed patterns that were broadly similar from city to city.

THE IMMIGRANT WITHIN THE CITY

For long it was assumed that most immigrants initially clustered in the slums of the inner city and then gradually dispersed into suburbs. The term *ghetto* is often applied to these inner-city concentrations of immigrants, and this American usage has its origins in the settlement of large numbers of East European Jews in Ameri-

can cities during the last two decades of the 19th century. The term rapidly lost its exclusive association with Jewish settlement and was widely used to refer to the residential quarters of other newly arrived European immigrants and eventually to the inner-city concentrations of blacks and Hispanics. Like the term *slum*, the ghetto referred to those parts of the city where congested and unhealthy living quarters and isolation from the remainder of urban society combined to create pathological social conditions. In the ghetto, exotic migrants unfamiliar with American culture exacerbated the problems of the slum.

These negative impressions of the ghetto were part of the more general sense of apprehension at the change in the composition of foreign immigration discussed earlier. These distinctions between the old and the new immigration were perhaps somewhat exaggerated, for immigrants had been closely associated with the slums of large northeastern cities long before the ghetto became a focus of concern. The residential quarters of Irish and German immigrants who settled in American cities during the middle decades of the 19th century were not described as ghettos, but contemporary observers complained of unsanitary living arrangements, social problems, and the immigrant threat to American institutions. Nevertheless, to a greater degree than earlier immigrants from northwestern Europe, the more recent arrivals from southern and eastern Europe were assumed to be less well prepared for residence and employment in the American city and for participation in American society and politics. Deprived of contact with the host society, they would encounter a slower and more painful process of assimilation.

By 1900, the ghetto had become a symbol of the failure of the American dream not only in regard to material advancement, but also because it was associated with pathological social conditions and the "corruption" of American democracy. It was an image that provided justification for efforts to improve the environment of the immigrant and also for campaigns to exclude further immigration from southern and eastern Europe. Following the implementation of immigration restriction, this negative image of the ghetto and its residents was retained to describe the social and living conditions of Hispanic and black migrants from Mex-

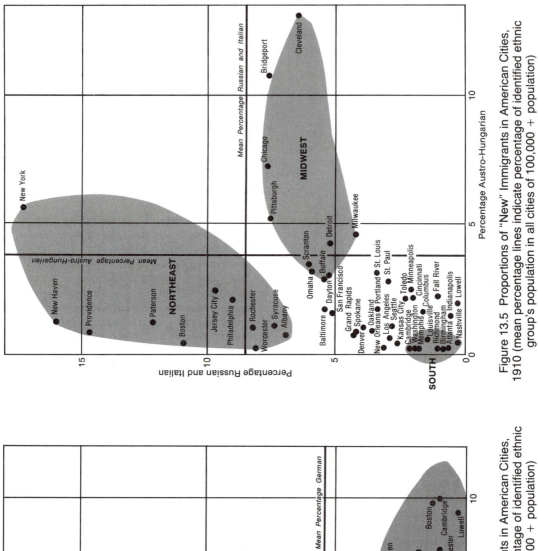

Figure 13.4 Proportions of "Old" Immigrants in American Cities, 1910 (mean percentage lines indicate percentage of identified ethnic group's population in all cities of 100,000 + population)

Figure 13.5 Proportions of "New" Immigrants in American Cities, 1910 (mean percentage lines indicate percentage of identified ethnic group's population in all cities of 100,000 + population)

ico, Puerto Rico, and the American South, who replaced Europeans in the inner sections of American cities. Indeed, these new ghettos became more extensive and more enduring than any of the earlier concentrations of European immigrants. In the extent of their segregation, in the persistence of their poverty, and in the degree of their social disorganization, the black experience in the American city now symbolizes the most extreme manifestation of ghetto conditions. The term *ghetto*, like the term *slum*, projects a negative image of the migrant experience of the American city, but this image is in many respects both simplified and incomplete.

THE ENVIRONMENT OF THE GHETTO

Clearly, the overcrowded and often unsanitary conditions within the ghetto are not a matter of debate. Overcrowded rooms, congested lots, and inadequate utilities contributed to high mortality, the neglect of domestic cleanliness, and the breakdown of family life. These apparent consequences of the adverse environment of the ghetto did, however, differ greatly both between and among immigrant groups. While age-standardized death rates were substantially higher in the inner-city slums than in the growing suburbs, the rates within the congested immigrant quarters were extremely varied. For long, mortality and especially infant mortality among blacks had greatly exceeded that of other minority groups, and during the 19th century Irish death rates were much higher than those of other immigrants from northwestern Europe. Of the diverse immigrants from southern and eastern Europe, the death rates of Russian Jews were generally much lower than those among Italians in adjacent dwellings and also somewhat lower than those of longer established immigrant groups who lived in substantially less crowded conditions. The precise magnitudes of any environmental effects on black and Irish mortality rates were compounded by the degree and longevity of their impoverishment both before and after migration, while low rates among Jewish immigrants were influenced by their prior adaptations to congested and living conditions in the Old World.

The moral life of those who survived in the harsh environment of the ghetto was also pre-

sumed to be in constant danger. Congested quarters with overcrowded rooms threatened the moral fabric of family life, and these environmental pressures were further aggravated by the tendency of migrants to be young, single, or married men without families. They were prepared to work in undesirable jobs and to endure appalling living conditions so that they might save funds sufficient to advance their prospects in their homeland. Moreover, the frequency with which immigrants took lodgers into their already crowded homes was viewed as a serious threat to domestic morality and family stability. Many lodgers however, were relatives or friends, and standards of family privacy were not necessarily any different from those that had long prevailed in the Old World. Many temporary migrants became immigrants and made arrangements for their families to join them. While the prevalence of single-parent households or high proportions of young unmarried men among the early arrivals from southern and eastern Europe was often viewed as an indicator of family disintegration, relatives located in several locations often provided support and resources whenever migration was frequent and sexually selective. These households consisted of dispersed and itinerant individuals and, despite the social costs of separation, families did not necessarily disintegrate, but rather adapted to the consequences of frequent migration.

Originally, these temporary migrants from southern and central Europe were distinguished from northwest Europeans who came to the United States as families with every intention of permanent settlement. In many respects, the Irish migration to the United States was initially an extension of seasonal movements within the British Isles, which could no longer accommodate the impact of famine. Throughout the 19th century, the uneven effects of industrialization on artisans, small farmers, and agricultural laborers had made temporary out-migration an increasingly essential part of rural life in many once remote sections of Europe. This process began as a spasmodic seasonal event over short distances and eventually developed into an intercontinental labor market involving lengthy sojourns in the New World. The rapid growth of labor migration toward the turn of the 19th century was associated with the shift in the source areas of European emigration, but many Irish, like many southern Europeans, viewed migration to the United States as a temporary measure. Only after it became clear that return from a somewhat hostile environment was impossible, did the Irish reluctantly interpret their departure from Ireland as an involuntary eviction.

The Irish quarters of the major northeastern seaports and some of the manufacturing towns of New England aroused great concern even when the vast majority of urban residents lived in cramped and poorly serviced accommodations. Impoverished at the time of their arrival and confined to the most menial occupations in the United States, the Irish were described as intemperate, criminal, disorderly, and immoral. It has been assumed that the Irish were condemned to the slums of their adopted cities for a life term, but it is now clear that they were extremely mobile and moved frequently within the United States in search of employment. Although the movements of the Irish to northeastern cities were more sexually balanced than those of southern Europeans, most females sought employment in resident domestic service and most males were itinerant laborers. These sexually divergent employment patterns often created single-parent households and a critical dependence upon networks of friends and relatives. The initial experience of the Irish in the New World was somewhat exceptional among northwest Europeans, but just as the new immigration included some family emigrants, the old included some labor migrants.

By the turn of the 19th century these anxieties about the Irish had diminished and, consequently, the social problems of the ghetto were associated with southern and eastern Europeans. Similarly, in the more recent past, the prejudicial judgments about southern and eastern Europeans have been obscured as the social problems of blacks and Hispanics have been magnified. Some authorities stress profound differences between the experiences of European immigrants and the more recent migrants to the inner city but, in the organization of their movements around the resources of relatives and friends, blacks and Hispanics have established adaptations to deprivation that have many precedents. Certainly, current concerns about the damaging effects of the sexual division of labor on the family patterns of black migrants resemble early and often insensitive native reactions to Irish immigration. High levels of recorded criminal behavior have also supported negative or defamatory interpretations of the ghetto. And, too, the corrupt administration of public services, institutionalized crime, and the prevalence of adolescent gangs offended dominant legal and moral precepts, but they also revealed a highly organized and elaborateiy regulated pattern of life.

Even those quarters where the environment of the ghetto exacted its mortal toll and which began as colonies of labor migrants eventually established social networks based not only on family and friends, but also on ethnic institutions. Some of these institutions were transplantations of long-established ancestral organizations that were rapidly adapted to meet new demands in an unfamiliar setting. The organizational activities of both secular and religious institutions were not viewed as an appropriate antidote because they tended to delay or obstruct assimilation. These "separatist" developments simply compounded the fears of those who viewed assimilation as conformity to an American Protestant world, but for many immigrants the ghetto served as a "decompression chamber" within which familiar faces and associations mediated the newcomers' encounter with the American city.

The organization of parochial schools, fraternal lodges, and political associations revealed a level of institutional development that was inconsistent with many negative evaluations of the social life of immigrant quarters. The term "urban village" has been coined to describe quarters where economically deprived remnants of these distinctive ethnic subcommunities persisted over several generations. Initially, these positive reports about the social organization of ethnic groups were regarded as exceptions worthy of comment, but as scarcely numerous enough to call into question the negative image of the ghetto. Social disorganization and pathological behavior are no longer regarded as unavoidable outcomes of migration to and prolonged residence in the inner city slums and, increasingly, ghettos have been described in a fashion that is more sensitive to the adaptations of their residents to their deprivation and discomfort.

THE SPATIAL SETTING OF THE GHETTO

Just as negative interpretations of the ghetto assumed that the social isolation of segregated quarters compounded the damaging effects of the environment, some revisionist viewpoints have related the social networks and institutional fabric of the ghetto to high levels of residential concentration. In short, both interpretations share a similar view of the spatial setting of the ghetto. From the negative perspective, residential dispersal would substitute the elevating influences of American society for the contagious moral degradation of the ghetto, but from the opposing viewpoint, this process would undermine ethnic communities. These assumptions about the degree to which immigrants were segregated in ethnically homogeneous inner city quarters have also been qualified. During the period when the term ghetto was first applied to immigrant quarters, the majority of newcomers did live in congested quarters bordering on the central business district or specialized industrial areas. The threatened expansion of business activities into adjacent residential areas had resulted in their abandonment by upwardly mobile families, but the rate of abandonment was quite varied. Accordingly, most immigrant groups settled in several relatively small districts that they shared with at least one other group, while the intervening areas were often dominated by quite different nationalities. Industrial areas were often located on the edge of large cities, or they formed the nucleus of new urban settlements; and under these circumstances, more homogenous ethnic quarters were often established in new, hastily built housing.

At times, the rate of immigration greatly exceeded the supply of available housing and, despite extremely high levels of overcrowding, some immigrants were forced to seek housing in many parts of the city. This problem was especially severe during the middle decades of the 19th century when the first major wave of mass immigration greatly exceeded the available housing in both the northeastern seaports and the newly established cities of the Middle West. Some Irish and German immigrants did concentrate in congested housing near the waterfront and warehouses, but the rate at which established Americans vacated these neighbor-

hoods was much too slow to provide accommodation for newcomers who quickly accounted for a third or more of urban populations. Existing dwellings were hastily converted into multifamily tenements, and their grounds were filled with cheap new structures, but these developments could not meet the rapidly growing demand. Many immigrants were forced to settle in shantytowns on the edge of the city, like migrants to the cities of the less-developed world today. Others clustered on poorly drained, filled land vacated by those who were able to afford more desirable sites.

In mid-19th century cities the small-scale and scattered locations of much urban employment also diminished the degree of immigrant concentration. Many immigrants were involved in the direct service of wealthy families or small proprietors and lived where they worked, in the homes or shops of their employers. German immigrants to mid-19th century cities were on the whole better represented in the petty proprietory artisanal occupations. They moved to newly settled parts of the Middle West and were especially prominent in the ports of the Great Lakes and the river towns of the Ohio valley. Here, in the absence of a large preexisting housing stock, they formed somewhat more extensive ethnic settlements than in the Northeast. In Milwaukee, for example, the Germans were usually more strongly concentrated than were the Irish, but were also scattered in several clusters rather than in one district. Substantial numbers of those in the service and food trades were to be found mixed in with their Irish and native-born clienteles. Only toward the end of the 19th century, when employment was more abundantly available in the adjacent sections of the central business district, did centrally located immigrant quarters house the majority of newcomers who were increasingly drawn from southern and eastern Europe.

Although the expansion of the central business district blighted and diminished the supply of inner-city housing, it was also a major source of employment for new immigrants. Because the growth of the central business district was often spasmodic and different land uses expanded at varying rates, long-lived immigrant settlements were maintained on stable margins. Indeed, some groups were able to settle near to those sections of the business district that provided the bulk of their employment. In most northeastern and midwestern cities, the most striking examples of this relationship were the close proximity of Russian Jews to the clothing workshops and of Italians to the fresh food markets. Immigrant employment was often insecure and seasonal, and usually entailed long and awkward working hours for which neither the schedules nor the routes of the emerging city streetcar systems were appropriate. Despite the housing problem, residence close to the abundant and diverse employment opportunities of the central business district offered advantages unavailable in more desirable residential areas.

The effects of this selective expansion of the central business district and the cumulative consequences of two major waves of immigration were especially striking in Boston (Fig. 13.6). During the middle decades of the 19th century, the Irish had settled in many sections of the city, including the northern and southern margins of the central business district. The

expansion of commercial facilities rapidly displaced the Irish from the southern edge of the business district, but the northward expansion of business was extremely modest and the Irish settlement there persisted to the end of the 19th century. By 1905, the Irish were abandoning the North End and other sections of the inner city of Boston to newly arrived Russian Jews and southern Italians. Italians were rapidly becoming the predominant group in the North End and in East Boston, and Russian Jews had concentrated in the West End and to a lesser degree in the South End (Fig. 13.6). Nevertheless, both the North and West Ends continued to house not only residual Irish populations but also modest proportions of other immigrant groups, while in the South End no one ethnic group predominated.

Moreover, immigrant settlement in the inner city did not form a complete zone around the central business district, because in Beacon Hill and Back Bay an affluent population of native parentage still prevailed. In these districts, immigrants were highly dispersed since they pro-

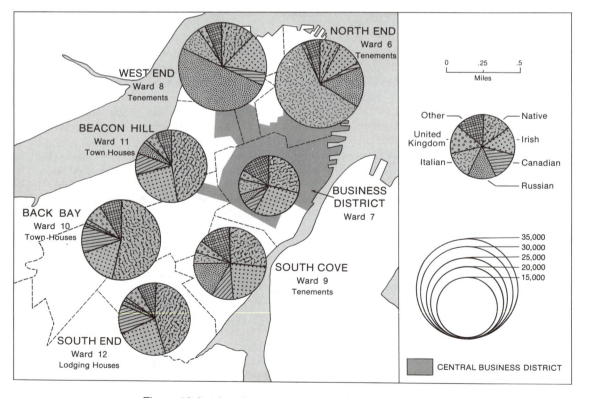

Figure 13.6   Immigrants in the Inner City: Boston, 1905

vided resident domestic service and local services. This mosaic of ethnic residence was not exclusively confined to the inner city. There were also concentrations of newcomers as well as longer-established immigrants in Roxbury, which at that time was considered to be an inner suburb. The leading ethnic institutions and amenities were usually associated with the largest and often earliest concentrations of particular groups and, while these quarters were usually identified as the ghetto, they housed only a minority of each group. These fragmented and complex residential patterns resulted from the uneven availability of cheap housing near appropriate sources of employment at the time of initial settlement.

Although the movement of Puerto Ricans to New York and other northeastern cities did not reach large proportions until after World War II, the settlement of Mexicans in the cities of southern California and the Southwest increased substantially in the 1920s, as did that of southern-born blacks in northeastern and midwestern cities. Mexicans encountered relatively small concentrations of European ethnic groups but, like Orientals, tended to be segregated in small but extremely homogeneous districts. Blacks were initially unable to compete with European immigrants for quarters near to the central business districts of northeastern and midwestern cities; prior to World War I, they had settled in the back alleys and rear lots of substantial dwellings, as they had for generations in southern cities. This somewhat dispersed and decidedly limited supply of housing proved to be inadequate for the increased flow of migrants during World War I. Confronted with a densely occupied inner city and an increasingly racist housing market, blacks were forced to settle in those sections of the inner suburbs where speculative overbuilding had created a supply of vacant middle-income housing suitable for subdivision. New York's Harlem, Boston's Roxbury, and Chicago's South Side all indicate the degree to which the initial foci of black ghettos was established beyond the outer fringer of the inner city settlements of European immigrants.

After World War I, further increases in the cityward movement of southern blacks transformed these small nuclei into ghettos that became more extensive and more enduring than any of the earlier concentrations of Euro-

pean immigrants. Similarly, with the expansion of migration from Mexico, extensive and exclusive Hispanic settlements described as "barrios" developed in cities of the Southwest and southern California. These developments created an extent and level of residential segregation unprecedented among European immigrants, and distinctions among European ethnic groups appeared to be of minor consequence when compared with those between black, Hispanic, and white. These new distinctions were further emphasized by the suburban dispersal of the descendents of European immigrants and their presumed assimilation into an homogenous, but white, American society. In contrast, the most recent minorities of the inner city have encountered many obstructions in their efforts to follow the suburban course of their predecessors. While it is clear that the ghettos formed after 1920 have proved to be more extensive and persistent than earlier concentrations, the presumed relationships between suburbanization, social mobility, and assimilation of the former residents of the inner city have been questioned.

SUBURBANIZATION AND ASSIMILATION

Although the social problems of the slum and the ghetto were often simplified or exaggerated, efforts to alleviate the environmental disabilities of the inner city were facilitated by suburbanization. Despite the modest impact of public intervention on living conditions in the inner city, suburbs by the late 19th century appeared to provide a partial solution to the housing problem for a progressively larger proportion of the urban population. From this perspective, the ghetto could be viewed as the temporary residential quarters of newly arrived immigrants, from which they or their immediate descendants would eventually disperse into the growing suburbs. Since suburban populations were presumed to be defined by social and economic status and stage in the lifecycle rather than by ethnic heritage, social and residential mobility were associated with final assimilation into American society. Certainly, revised interpretations of the social world of the ghetto were more consistent with assumptions about the material advancement and suburbanization of immigrants and their descendants than with one that stressed the pathological social consequences of the ghetto environment.

While levels of residential segregation among most of the descendants of European immigrants were lower than those of their migrant ancestors, these changes do not necessarily record a simple trajectory from inner-city ghetto to integrated suburb. Modest proportions of some groups have retained some sections of their original ethnic quarters, and the dispersed larger community continues to patronize the long-established ethnic institutions and amenities there. Suburban movements did not always take the form of dispersal from an inner city concentration, but occurred in the form of a contiguous wedgelike expansion in one or two well-defined directions. Eventually the inner margins of this wedge were abandoned, and among highly mobile groups a completely suburban residential pattern was established. Under these circumstances, new suburban foci of ethnic institutions were developed, and today they are frequently as closely associated with the ethnic heritage of their clientele as were their original inner-city quarters. Although the original ethnic communities of the inner city were based upon an overlapping mosaic of neighborhoods, the ethnic associations and networks that serve the needs of suburban residents are not necessarily dependent upon high levels of residential concentration. Ethnicity may thus have a diminishing influence upon suburban residential differentiation, but some ethnic identities and associations have persisted despite suburbanization.

If diminished levels of residential segregation have been viewed as measures of suburban dispersal and, by inference, of assimilation, in many cities both the rates and the dimensions of these changes have been quite modest. In contrast, suburbanization did involve dramatic improvements in the quality of the living environment and in access to avenues of occupational mobility. From this perspective the experiences of immigrants and especially their descendants have been envisaged as a set of "escalators" on which the rate of advancement varied from group to group. In general, it was assumed that the course of upward advancement followed an almost natural or inevitable order, in which long-established groups were expected to hold the most remunerative and desirable occupations, and newly arrived migrants the least secure and lowest paid jobs. In short, with each successive wave of immigration, the ethnic division of labor was altered as newcomers entered the lowest strata of the labor force and the descendants of earlier immigrants moved on to more rewarding positions. While many, perhaps the majority, of newcomers initially worked in unpleasant and poorly rewarded jobs, they assumed they would return to their homeland with their accumulated savings or that they or their children would eventually gain access to more remunerative employment. In each phase of immigration there were also some newcomers who were able to avoid the lower floors, while others were condemned to prolonged residence on the ground floor long after the arrival of more recent immigrants.

In many respects, a preoccupation with the environmental deficiencies and social isolation of the ghetto and the slum has obscured the degree to which the fluidity or rigidity of the ethnic division of labor has influenced the material predicament and residential patterns of the most-deprived minority groups. The damaging effects of inner city life have varied considerably among its diverse residents, and both the environmental and spatial attributes of ghettos have been reinterpreted in a fashion that is more sensitive to the positive adaptations of their residents. Nevertheless, these adaptations are strained beyond their limits whenever access to avenues of economic advancement are blocked by deliberate exclusion or depressed economic conditions. Today, levels of residential segregation among blacks and some Hispanics are far higher and more persistent than they were among the migrant generation of European groups and, despite their material advancement and suburbanization, the decline in the levels of residential segregation among the descendants of European migrants has been relatively modest. The inner city today is more isolated from not only the remainder of urban society but also from the increasingly decentralized urban employment opportunities than it was during the era of European immigration. The boundary between the inner city and suburb has for long been the graphic expression of apparently temporary blockages in the process of social mobility. During the 1890s these obstructions presented a more permanent look and aroused anxieties about the impact of the "new" immigration, and today similar concerns about impoverished minorities have provoked questions about the desirability of immigration.

OVERVIEW: REGIONS AND CITIES IN A PLURAL SOCIETY

Despite the proverbial geographical mobility of Americans and the loss of many overt ethnic traits among the children of immigrants, the regional destinations of the immigrant generation have proved to be quite persistent. Certainly, many of the descendants of northwest European immigrants have joined those with a longer American ancestry in the movement to the Pacific coast. By far the most conspicuous change in the distribution of ethnic groups has been the movement of blacks to the cities of the Northeast and Middle West. Overall, however, the regional representations of different ethnic groups have resulted from an incremental process of migration of varying volume and composition. Regional destinations were often established on the basis of new opportunities, or

occasionally they were the unavoidable outcome of pressures to emigrate. Networks of information and family ties often reinforced these initial patterns of settlement. The cities of each major region also displayed variable ethnic profiles, but for each major phase of immigration certain general observations about ethnic residential patterns may be made. The term "ghetto" was developed to describe the common disabilities of immigrant quarters. This negative view, however, has been substantially modified, as have interpretations of the suburban movement as a process of rapid assimilation. Emigration certainly altered the ancestral cultures of most American immigrants profoundly, but these changes were already underway before their departure. Moreover, while these alterations were often in the direction of a single, well-defined national culture, some aspects of ethnic identity were voluntarily redefined or preserved through discrimination. This persistent if changing pluralism of American society is directly derived not only from the complex composition of several major phases of migration, but also from the varied geographic consequences of each migration flow.

ADDITIONAL READING

Books

Barton, J.J. *Peasants and Strangers: Italians, Roumanians, and Slovaks in an American City, 1890–1950.* Cambridge: Harvard University Press, 1975.

Borchert, J. *Alley Life in Washington: Community, Religion and Folklore in the City, 1850–1870.* Urbana: University of Illinois Press, 1980.

Conzen, K.N. *Immigrant Milwaukee, 1836–1860: Accommodation and Community in a Frontier City.* Cambridge: Harvard University Press, 1976.

Glazer, N., and Moynihan, D.P. *Beyond the Melting Pot.* 2nd. edition. Cambridge: M.I.T. Press, 1970.

Golab, C. *Immigrant Destinations.* Philadelphia: Temple University Press, 1977.

Gordon, M.M. *Assimilation in American Life.* New York: Oxford University Press, 1964.

Higham, J. *Strangers in the Land: Patterns of American Nativism, 1860–1925.* New Brunswick: Rutgers University Press, 1955.

Philpott, T. *The Slum and the Ghetto: Neighborhood Deterioration and Middle Class Reform in Chicago,*

1880–1930. New York: Oxford University Press, 1978.

Piore, M.J. *Birds of Passage: Migrant Labor and Industrial Societies.* New York: Cambridge University Press, 1979.

Steinberg, S. *The Ethnic Myth: Race and Ethnicity and Class in America.* New York: Atheneum, 1981.

Taylor, P. *The Distant Magnet: European Emigration to the United States.* New York: Harper & Row, 1971.

Thernstrom, S.B. *The Other Bostonians: Poverty and Progress in the American Metropolis, 1860–1970.* Cambridge: Harvard University Press, 1978.

———., ed. *The Harvard Encyclopedia of American Ethnic Groups.* Cambridge: Belknap Press, 1982.

Ward, D. *Cities and Immigrants: A Geography of Change in Nineteenth Century America.* New York: Oxford University Press, 1971.

Zunz, O. *The Changing Face of Inequality: Urbanization, Industrial Development and Immigrants in Detroit, 1880–1920.* Chicago: University of Chicago Press, 1982.

Periodicals

American Historical Review, journal of the American Historical Association (Smith, 1978).

American Sociological Review, journal of the American Sociological Association (Yancey et al. 1976).

Annals of the American Academy of Political and Social Science (Hershberg, 1979).

Journal of Historical Geography (Groves and Muller, 1975).

Institute of British Geographers Transactions (Ward, 1983).

14

The National Integration of Regional Economies, 1860–1920

DAVID R. MEYER
Brown University

Between 1860 and 1920 the national economy changed from a set of regional economies with low levels of interchange to a continental set of integrated regions. Much of the shift to national integration had occurred by 1890. Improvements in transportation and communication provided the means for producers in agriculture, lumbering, and mining to ship their output long-distance. Regions specialized in resources in which they were well endowed. Manufacturers also benefited from transportation and communication improvements; they acquired inputs cheaply from the natural resource sector or from other manufacturers and efficiently distributed their output to markets outside their region. The growing specialization of regions, in turn, created a demand for additional improvements in transportation and communication. This circular and cumulative relationship between increased specialization and enhanced integration of regions was a principal driving force in the American economy between 1860 and 1920.

The emergence of a nationally integrated set of regional economies was inseparable from the prodigious growth of the American economy between 1860 and 1920. The following economic indexes (beginning with 1870, except for mining, 1880) provide indications of this change. Population grew by 2.7 times, but the economy as a whole (gross national product) expanded by 7.4 times. Per capita gross national product, consequently, increased by 2.5 times, and Americans thus had more resources to purchase a wider array of products. Farm and lumber output increased just 3.0 and 2.7 times, respectively, roughly equal to population growth. More significant, mineral output grew 7.3 times, and manufactures expanded by 7.7 times. The enormous growth of these latter two sectors reflected the economy's structural change from an agricultural to an industrial base. In the following discussion, changes in the integrating mechanisms of transportation

and communication are identified as a foundation for considering the evolution of regional specialization in agriculture, lumbering, mining, and manufacturing. The culmination of these specializations is described as a core-periphery organization of the national economy.

REGIONAL ECONOMIES IN 1860

In 1860 most regional economies were east of the Mississippi River; they had a relatively low level of integration with each other. Each regional economy was headed by a metropolis that dominated a surrounding hinterland. The metropolis controlled and coordinated both intraregional trade and the limited amount of interregional trade. The eastern regions were becoming significant markets for midwestern agriculture, especially meat, wheat, and corn. The East supplied approximately equal volumes of manufactures to the Middle West and South, but the most rapidly growing part of this trade was to the Middle West. The degree to which this trade included foreign manufactures is unknown, although the southern trade probably included significant amounts from foreign producers. The South exported its cotton to northern and to foreign markets.

The orientation of midwestern trade to the East was secure by 1860. Long-distance, efficient connections via one consistent transport mode were not yet available, but combinations of railroad and water (lake, river, and canal) transport linked both regions. By the 1850s, massive quantities of midwestern agricultural produce moved eastward on the Erie Canal, but the railroad emerged simultaneously as a competitor with the eastern canals; it also redirected trade away from the Ohio-Mississippi River route and its New Orleans outlet. Five major railroads were completed from the East to the border of the Middle West by the early 1850s: the Pennsylvania to Pittsburgh; the Baltimore and Ohio to the Ohio River; the New York Central and New York and Erie railroads to Lake Erie; and the Northern Railroad and Vermont Central from Boston to Ogdensburg, New York, at the east end of Lake Ontario. Within the Middle West, extensive networks of railroads were constructed during the 1850s.

They focused on each of the regional metropolises of Cleveland, Detroit, Cincinnati, Milwaukee, Chicago, and St. Louis, but a few lines also linked these metropolises with each other by 1860 (Fig. 14.1).

By 1860 the United States was at an early stage in the emergence of a continental space-economy. Interregional trade within the East and within the Middle West was increasing,

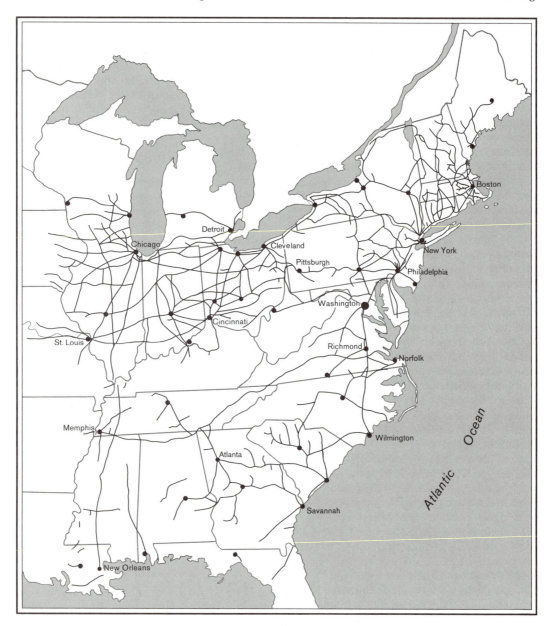

Figure 14.1   Railroads in 1860

and long-distance trade was also growing. A tenuous long-distance bond existed by ocean between eastern metropolises, especially New York, and the burgeoning western metropolis of San Francisco which served the Pacific coast mining communities. Portland and its Oregon hinterland were also linked to the East via San Francisco. Gold mining and fur trading in the Rockies were connected to the Middle West and East through metropolises such as St. Louis, but these links were still on a relatively small scale. For example, Colorado in 1860 had a resident population of only 34,000, and farming and ranching expansion into the Great Plains was just beginning. On this base of growing interregional trade came major changes in transportation (the railroad) and in communications (mail and the telegraph) that were the means of forging a highly integrated national space-economy by the end of the century.

TRANSPORTATION AND COMMUNICATION CHANGES

The railroad has a justly deserved place as the pivotal integrator of the national space-economy between 1860 and 1920 and as a major component of late 19th-century economic growth. Although commodities moved by rail throughout the East and Middle West in 1860, the 30,626 miles of track did not comprise an integrated network (Fig. 14.1). The standard gauge (4 feet 8½ inches) existed on about half the track. Continuous movement occurred between Boston and New York along the tracks of the four railroad companies in southern New England that used the standard gauge. Elsewhere in the East such direct connections were not possible. The networks focusing on New York, Philadelphia, and Baltimore were incompatible. Some individual long-distance lines, such as the New York and Erie Railroad or the Pennsylvania Railroad, had a single gauge throughout their length, but their different gauges prohibited movement between them. Most of the freight carried by major eastern railroads, such as the New York Central, Pennsylvania, and Baltimore and Ohio, therefore did not travel beyond their respective lines. Long-distance, continuous connections between East and Middle West were hindered

both by incompatible gauges and by a lack of bridge crossings at major rivers, such as the Ohio and Mississippi. Within the South, gauges were also different and few north-south lines existed. Continuous movement through some cities such as Montgomery (Alabama), Charleston (South Carolina), and Savannah (Georgia) was impossible because rival railroads failed to connect their tracks. The gauge differences and gaps in the network added significant transshipment costs to railroad use.

This loosely coordinated railroad network was altered significantly within the thirty years following 1860. In a circular and cumulative fashion the increase in through freight and improvements in the network reinforced each other over time. The pressures for improvements were particularly strong during the 1860s, when the difficulties of transporting Civil War troops and supplies focused attention on the lack of a coordinated network and led to federal pressure for change. Congress reinforced its demand that the rail network be integrated by legislating that the standard gauge be used on transcontinental railroads. Moreover, the growth of the grain trade further promoted integration and led to lower costs of moving midwestern grain to eastern markets and to transshipment ports for export. By 1880 almost 81 percent of the railroad mileage was standard gauge. This was a significant increase over the 1861 proportion of 53 percent, especially since railroad mileage in 1880 was triple that of 1861. By 1890 almost all track was standard gauge.

The enormous growth in railroad track mileage effectively bound all parts of the nation by 1890. During the Civil War little new track was added, but within a span of only nine years (1866 to 1875) the rail net doubled from 36,801 to 74,096 miles. A map of railroad lines in 1880 (Fig. 14.2) reveals that the eastern half of the nation was blanketed by railroads, and the west coast had two links, the Union/Central Pacific and the Southern Pacific, to the Middle West. By 1887 the rail net had doubled again to 149,214 miles. In 1920 the rail net had reached 259,941 miles, within 1,000 miles of its maximum mileage in the 20th century.

Three boom periods of construction occurred during the thirty years after the Civil War (Table 14.1). During the first period, 1868–73, the most dramatic development was the comple-

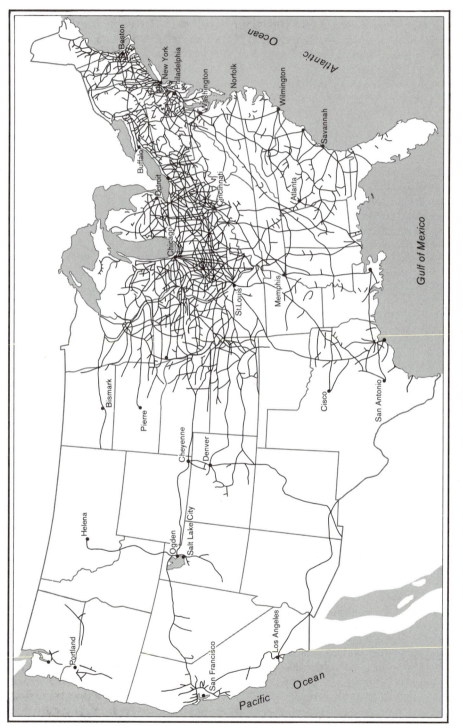

Figure 14.2   Railroads in 1880

tion of the first transcontinental railroad in 1869 when the Central and Union Pacific lines were joined at Ogden, Utah. It is significant that almost half of the new railroad track was laid in the West. This was the first extensive construction of railroads to serve the growing number of farms in the Great Plains. Between 1860 and 1870 the number of farms in North and South Dakota, Nebraska, and Kansas increased from 13,000 to 52,000, and by 1880 there were 220,000 farms on the Plains. The second period, 1879–83, witnessed even greater railroad expansion in the Plains. When the European demand for grain and meat increased significantly beginning in 1879, the railroads provided low-cost transportation from the Plains' farms to the eastern ports, such as New York, Philadelphia, and Baltimore. Between 1873 and 1884 numerous routes were completed that connected the Great Plains and the Pacific Coast. The western expansion of the railroad network was dominant during all periods (Table 14.1), so that by the 1890s the entire West,

Table 14.1   Railroad Mileage Constructed by Region for Selected Periods (percent of total U.S. mileage)

Region	1868–1873	1879–1883	1886–1892
East	21	8	7
Midwest	16	19	15
South	16	13	24
West	47	60	54
Total	100	100	100
Number of miles	24,589	39,553	46,818

including the Pacific Coast, was integrated with the rest of the nation. Equally significant, during all periods the rail net was intensified in the areas of highest population density and of earliest agricultural and industrial development—the East, Middle West, and South, especially the latter. About half of the new mileage was built in this area, which comprised just one-third of the national territory. By 1890 the railroad network thus provided linkages between most places in the nation; the subsequent intensification of the network filled the interstices.

Technological changes and organizational in-

novations also increased the efficiency of railroad transportation. Steel rails replaced iron rails because they were more durable and permitted heavier loads to be carried. More powerful locomotives and larger freight cars increased train capacity, and a host of inventions, such as the automatic coupler and the air brake, improved operation. Organizational innovations became standard during the 1870s and 1880s, and they allowed the railroads effectively to coordinate the growing volume and complexity of traffic. Functional divisions were established within railroads to handle different responsibilities, and accounting was revolutionized to organize the data on the enormous flows of goods. Railroads also devised cooperative arrangements for moving commodities long-distance, such as fast freight and express companies, the bill of lading, and the car accountant office. The bill of lading was a record of the goods, routes, and charges, and each railroad kept a copy. The car accountant office of a railroad monitored its own cars as well as those of competitors on its tracks. Larger railroad systems were created by aggressive financiers such as Jay Gould, who encouraged defensive tactics by other railroads. Two of his competitors, the Pennsylvania Railroad under its president, J. Edgar Thomson, and the New York Central, under the Vanderbilts, were organized as large railroad systems covering the Middle West and the East. Cornelius Vanderbilt piously criticized railroad speculation by financiers such as Gould: "There are a great many worthless railroads started in this country without any means to carry them through. Respectable banking houses in New York, so called, make themselves agents for the sale of the bonds of the railroads in question and give a kind of moral guarantee of their secureness." Vanderbilt, however, was not above stock manipulation when the opportunity arose, as when he inflated the number of shares of the New York Central in 1868. By the 1880s large railroad systems, nevertheless, had become characteristic of railroad organization throughout the nation.

The expansion of the rail network and technological and organizational innovations combined to make the railroads one of the most productive economic sectors in the late 19th century. Between 1870 and 1910, railroad productivity, the change in railroad output (for example, volume of freight moved) relative to railroad input (including locomotives, cars, and track), increased at an average annual rate of 2.0 percent, compared with 1.5 percent for the economy as a whole. This productivity resulted in a decline in freight rates between 1859 and 1910 from 2.6 to 0.75 cents per ton-mile. The vastly expanded railroad network and declining rates stimulated an enormous increase in the amount of goods shipped. The number of ton-miles shipped grew thirtyfold from 2.6 billion in 1859 to 80 billion in 1890 and more than tripled again to 255 billion in 1910. These flows both contributed to and were affected by the increasing specialization of regions.

The communications changes of the late 19th century were inseparable from those in transportation. Communication improvements provided the critical control and coordination functions necessary to move the growing volume of commodities efficiently over the expanding national transport network. The mail and telegraph were the most important long-distance communication media; a national telephone network did not exist until after 1910, twenty years after the national space-economy was effectively integrated. As the railroad network expanded it became the major carrier of long-distance mail. Concurrent with the growing volume of mail from the 1850s to the 1870s, the post office implemented organizational and operational changes that made it capable of handling large volumes of long-distance mail shipments with numerous origins and destinations. The telegraph provided instantaneous nationwide communication for business by the mid-1860s. Telegraph lines were strung along railroad rights-of-way, and the railroad used them to coordinate trains. From its inception in the 1840s the telegraph became a nationwide system along with the railroad. By 1866 Western Union was established as the first national multiunit company in the United States. The first long-distance telephone lines, on the other hand, were not completed until the late 1880s, and an extensive network east of the Mississippi River was not available until at least 1907. The long-distance network did not reach Denver until 1910 and San Francisco until 1915. The telephone, therefore, was not a factor in the rise of a national space-economy. The improvements in mail and the telegraph enabled firms to control and coordinate exchange with each

other and within each firm. The reduction in time to transport commodities and to communicate information reduced the relative amount of goods that were held in-transit and in inventories. Firms gained wider access to information to make informed business decisions and to respond rapidly to business problems. These improvements lowered costs for the entire economy and facilitated greater regional specialization of production.

REGIONAL SPECIALIZATION

Regional specialization in production is the domestic equivalent of the principle of comparative advantage that is used to explain both specialization among nations and the trade that occurs among them. A region specializes in production of those commodities it can produce more cheaply than other regions. Some of the output is usually consumed within the region that produces it, but the export of the commodity to other regions is the basis of specialization. Regional specialization may change as new regions enter production of a commodity, and earlier settled regions may be forced to change specialties. Because new regions entered production of numerous commodities, especially between 1860 and 1890, and because transportation and communication improvements occurred nationally, regional specializations were in a state of flux. The emerging specializations in agriculture, lumbering, mining, and manufacturing thus proceeded at different rates.

Agriculture

Agricultural products are bulky, heavy, and low in value relative to their weight; therefore, transportation cost reductions after 1860 increased shipping distances significantly. The decline of railroad transportation costs in the fifty years following 1860 meant that biophysical conditions, especially soil, slope, and climate, increased in significance. Regions with favorable environmental conditions for a given crop produced it at lower cost than less favorably endowed regions, even if the former were farther from the market than the latter. Of course, a region near the market *and* favorably endowed environmentally had both advantages. Although transportation costs declined, they did not become insignificant. The regional specialization of U.S. agriculture that emerged after 1860 reflected both the role of distance and the increased importance of biophysical conditions.

In 1860 regional specialization in agriculture was limited. Environmental factors were dominant in the location of cotton in the South; cotton requires a long growing season (200 frost-free days or more) and a moist spring and summer, followed by a dry, cool autumn. The increased output of wheat, corn, cattle, and hogs in the Middle West during the 1840s for shipment to the East had some environmental bases. The flat, rich soils of midwestern farms produced crops at lower cost per acre than hilly eastern farms. This regional specialization, however, was limited, and only one-third of the nation's area was as yet included in production. Although corn was somewhat more concentrated in the Middle West, it was also widely grown in the South and East. Wheat was grown extensively in the East as late as 1860, although little was grown in the South. With the exception of a concentration in eastern Texas, cattle were ubiquitous. The Middle West's specialties were chiefly determined by distance from eastern markets. Midwestern wheat farms were competitive with the East's farms because land costs were low and large farms could be assembled. The typical midwestern farm had 140 acres in 1860, 30 percent more than the 108 acres of the average eastern farm. By using machinery, the midwestern farmer produced low-cost wheat. The corn, cattle, and hog products were also a response

to distance from market. The corn was fed to hogs, and a variety of grains were fed to cattle. The meat was then shipped to market in salted form (or driven to market). As meat, it had a higher value per unit weight and withstood long-distance transport. Corn was also converted to high-value whiskey.

By the 1920s regional agricultural specialization had changed dramatically (Fig. 14.3). The entire continental United States was divided into broad regions of specialized agriculture. These regions have remained relatively intact throughout the 20th century; two significant exceptions are the demise of the traditional Cotton Belt in the Piedmont of the Carolinas, Georgia, and Alabama, and the introduction of soybeans especially to midwestern agriculture. This regional specialization was essentially complete as early as the 1890s.

During the 1860s recently settled areas in Illinois, the western half of Indiana, and southern Wisconsin had large increases in improved acreage, while earlier settled areas in northeastern Indiana, southern Michigan, and Ohio also added farmland (Table 14.2). A large expansion of improved farmland occurred in sparsely farmed areas in southeastern Minnesota, eastern Iowa, the northern half of Missouri, the Central valley and selected coastal areas in California, and the Willamette valley in Oregon. In the 1870s the new areas of expansion in the previous decade added substantial amounts of new farmland, while older settled midwestern areas added less. The new lands of the 1870s were in the Great Plains (eastern Nebraska and Kansas) and an area in eastern

Table 14.2 Change in Improved Farmland, 1860–1920

U.S. census region	Number of acres (millions)			Percent change	
	1860	1890	1920	1860–1890	1890–1920
New England	12.2	10.7	6.1	−12.3	−43.0
Middle-Atlantic	26.8	31.6	26.6	17.9	−15.8
East North Central	41.2	78.8	87.9	91.3	11.5
West North Central	11.1	105.5	171.4	850.5	62.5
South Atlantic	34.9	41.7	48.5	19.5	16.3
East South Central	25.9	35.7	44.4	37.8	24.4
West South Central	7.3	30.6	64.2	319.2	109.8
Mountain	0.2	5.5	30.1	2,650.0	447.3
Pacific	3.4	17.6	23.9	417.6	35.8
Total United States	163.1	357.6	503.1	119.3	40.7

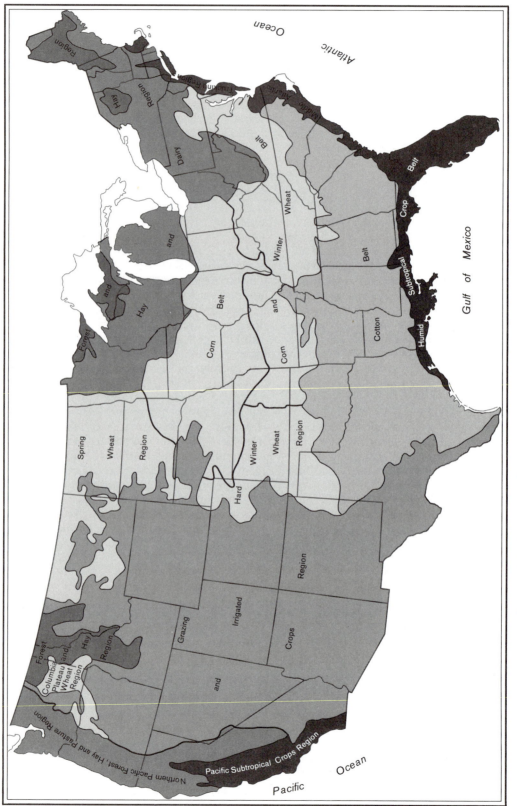

Figure 14.3   Agricultural Regions in 1920. Almost the entire eastern seaboard
is included in the Fruit and Vegetable Belt.

Texas between Dallas and San Antonio. The eastern half of the Great Plains and California's Central Valley continued to add farmland during the 1880s. Large areas also came under cultivation for the first time: the Red River valley of North Dakota and Minnesota; the eastern third of North and South Dakota; western Nebraska and Kansas; eastern Washington and northeastern Oregon; and southern California near Los Angeles. Most increases in farmland during the 1890s occurred in the eastern Great Plains and in eastern Washington. Following 1900 the western Plains added most of the new farmland in the nation. Most agricultural lands that were important to the emerging regional specialization were being farmed by 1890, with the exception of the arid portions of the western Great Plains.

As agricultural lands were added in the Middle West and West after 1860, other lands in the East and South were withdrawn from cultivation; these withdrawals, however, were not large before 1890 (Table 14.2). During the 1860s parts of southern New England exhibited a large decline in cultivated land, a continuation of antebellum trends. The southern Piedmont also declined significantly, but this was probably as a result of Civil War dislocation. In the following decade, the southern Piedmont's declining agricultural lands were roughly balanced by additions to cultivated lands in other areas. In New England a similar balance existed; the northern half declined, while the southern half reversed course and added agricultural land. Beginning in the 1880s declines in agricultural land became more widespread. In the South, only southern Texas had a significant decline, but in the North a broad area from eastern Ohio to New England began to lose agricultural land. In the 1890s, the decline in New England agriculture accelerated and New York continued its decline. This was also the decade when substantial quantities of farmland were withdrawn from production in the arid areas of the Great Plains, especially in Texas. Subsequent decades witnessed a decline in agriculture in those areas of the South, Middle West, and East that were hilly and less favorably endowed with good soils. The declines in improved farmland, nevertheless, were modest in scale compared with the large increases during the 1860–1920 period. The emerging regional specialization of agriculture,

therefore, was accomplished by a shift in types of agriculture in older farming areas and by the addition of previously unexploited areas, rather than by large-scale decline in older areas.

Technological change in agricultural machinery had minimal impact on the emergence of specialized agricultural regions, with the important exception of the wheat regions. The basic principles of most agricultural machinery manufactured in the late 19th century were known by 1860. Iron and steel plows and harrows for tilling the soil, reapers and other harvesters for cutting grain, and threshers for separating grain from the rest of the plant were particularly important in increasing labor productivity. Before 1920 no machinery had been invented for cotton picking. Improved farm machinery permitted the operation of larger farms by a given number of workers, but this had little direct impact on regional specialization in the areas of the Middle West and East settled by 1860. The Middle West already was specialized in corn and wheat. The most important impact of new machinery was to make dry-land wheat farming feasible. Because crop production per acre was low, farms were economical only if they were large, but farming large acreages required machinery.

The most important specialized wheat regions were in production by 1890 (Table 14.3 and Fig. 14.3). They emerged through successive advancing waves, consolidations, and retreats, stimulated both by rising domestic demand and fluctuation in foreign demand. The spring Wheat Belt first emerged in the expansion of 1878–85 in the Red River valley of the eastern Dakotas and western Minnesota. A second wave, 1913–16, expanded the region into the western Dakotas and eastern Montana, displacing cattle ranching. The Kansas portion of the winter Wheat Belt and the Columbia Plateau wheat region were also established by 1890. The Central Valley of California also was a major wheat producer by 1890; it expanded initially in the 1870s and had diversified by 1910. The emergence of these wheat regions was bound inseparably to the expanding railroad network. In addition to the transcontinental railroads, an elaborate network of westward-branching railroads was constructed into the eastern margins of the Great Plains by 1880 (Fig. 14.2). They were connected to the

Table 14.3   Leading Wheat and Corn States, 1860–1900

1860	1870	1880	1890	1900
Leading Wheat States				
Illinois	Illinois	Illinois	Minnesota	Minnesota
Indiana	Iowa	Indiana	California	North Dakota
Wisconsin	Ohio	Ohio	Illinois	Ohio
Ohio	Indiana	Michigan	Indiana	South Dakota
Virginia	Wisconsin	Minnesota	Ohio	Kansas
Pennsylvania	Pennsylvania	Iowa	Kansas	California
56%	56%	53%	50%	49%
Leading Corn States				
Illinois	Illinois	Illinois	Iowa	Illinois
Ohio	Iowa	Iowa	Illinois	Iowa
Missouri	Ohio	Missouri	Kansas	Kansas
Indiana	Missouri	Indiana	Nebraska	Nebraska
Kentucky	Indiana	Ohio	Missouri	Missouri
Tennessee	Kentucky	Kansas	Ohio	Indiana
Iowa	Tennessee	Kentucky	Indiana	Ohio
Virginia	Pennsylvania	Nebraska	Kentucky	Texas
Alabama	Texas	Tennessee	Texas	Kentucky
Georgia	Alabama	Pennsylvania	Tennessee	Oklahoma
71%	72%	79%	81%	76%

Note: Percentages indicate proportion of total production accounted for by the listed states.

termini of Minneapolis, Kansas City, and Chicago, which, in turn, were linked to the east coast metropolises. The railroads vigorously promoted the settlement of the wheat regions through sales of land from their land grants.

Only large-scale wheat farms were profitable in the Plains; by the 1880s typical farms were 150–200 acres in size, and a small number, especially in the Red River valley and California's Central Valley, were termed "bonanza farms." The latter were 1,000 acres or more, and a few in North Dakota were between 25,000 and 100,000 acres in size. They were organized as corporations and financed by external investors, the precursors of 20th-century corporate farms. Their size was not unusual; large cattle ranches existed ten to twenty years earlier. The impressive fact was that the bonanza farms were planted in crops. Such massive wheat farms required large plows, reapers, and threshers. Threshing had to be completed soon after the wheat was cut, before rain could damage the grain; the portable steam-powered thresher was the solution. It was invented before 1860, but the rise of the specialized wheat regions gave the major impetus to its adoption.

By 1880 these threshers were common in all the wheat regions, and the bonanza farms were their principal users. The high fixed cost of the machines also encouraged the emergence of custom threshers, who moved among farms and worked the machines.

The specialized wheat regions that emerged between 1860 and 1890 were unusual in American agriculture because they were so internally homogeneous; other agricultural regions tended to have more diverse agriculture because moister climates permitted a wider variety of crops. Before 1890 older wheat-growing areas in the Middle West and East did not decline in absolute terms, but declined relatively as the new specialized regions supplied the net additions to domestic and foreign demand. As late as 1890 the states of Illinois, Indiana, and Ohio were among the nation's six leading wheat states, but by 1900 only Ohio remained in that group (Table 14.3).

Cattle and sheep raising were also established throughout the West by 1890 (Fig. 14.3). At that time the eastern margin of livestock production was farther east, but it was pushed westward by the expanding wheat frontier between 1890 and 1920. This encroach-ment of wheat on grazing lands was a continu-ation of a process begun in the 1860s. Texas remained the leading cattle state throughout the period, 1860–1920, with its cattle popula-tion increasing from 2.9 million to 6.2 million during that same time span. As a percentage of the national total, however, the Texas cattle population declined from 17 in 1860 to 9 in 1920. Although the Texas cattle drives to termi-nals along westward-extending railroads have remained vivid in western folklore, they actu-ally occurred only during the few years from the late 1860s through the 1870s. The railroad termini such as Abilene, Wichita, and Dodge City successively emerged in Kansas because the wheat-farming frontier eliminated open land for cattle drives. During the 1880s cattle ranching spread throughout the western Plains and the Far West. By 1890 a degree of speciali-zation had arisen; western ranches bred and raised young calves that were shipped by rail for fattening to Corn Belt farms in eastern Nebraska, eastern Kansas, Iowa, and Illinois.

Large-scale cattle ranches were common in the West by the 1870s, and they were a logical adaptation to the need for a large acreage of arid land to support each animal. For a brief period in the 1880s, vast ranches were pur-chased by English and Scottish corporations. Two of the largest were the Arkansas Ranch in southern Colorado and the Cimarron Ranch in northeastern New Mexico with 2.2 million and 2.6 million acres, respectively. Each ranch was more than three times the size of the state of Rhode Island. Irrigated pasturage, which per-mitted intensive grazing, developed between 1870 and 1890 along river valleys draining from the Rocky Mountains. By 1890 total irrigated acreage was 2.7 million, but not all was pasture; the major growth in irrigated land came in the following twenty years, and by 1910 the acre-age totaled 11.6 million. Although cattle are associated typically with the West, sheep in the Mountain and Pacific regions actually outnum-bered cattle in every state in 1890 and in 1920, except in Arizona in 1890 (Table 14.4). In aggre-gate, there were slightly more than twice as many sheep as cattle in 1890 and about 1.7 times as many in 1920. Both sheep and cattle were widely distributed throughout the Moun-tain and Pacific regions; they were mainly ab-sent from the arid areas of Arizona and Nevada

Table 14.4 Number of Cattle and Sheep in the West, 1890 and 1920 (in thousands)

Region	Cattle		Sheep	
	1890	1920	1890	1920
Mountain				
Montana	668	1,269	1,859	2,083
Idaho	192	715	358	2,356
Wyoming	674	875	713	1,860
Colorado	641	1,757	718	1,813
New Mexico	559	1,300	1,249	1,640
Arizona	263	822	102	882
Utah	154	506	1,014	1,692
Nevada	202	356	273	881
Pacific				
Washington	184	573	265	624
Oregon	406	851	1,780	2,002
California	1,050	2,008	2,475	2,400
West total	4,994	11,031	10,807	18,233

and the heavily forested areas of Oregon and Washington. Sheep were profitable between 1860 and 1920 because prices were high and they could tolerate the short grasses, cold weather, and semiarid conditions in the Rocky Mountains and bordering areas.

The rise of the Corn Belt (Fig. 14.3) between 1860 and 1890 was related integrally to the westward expansion of wheat and the growth of western cattle ranching. Corn is a superior feed for cattle and hogs, and the emerging Corn Belt had ideal conditions for growing corn—fertile soil and warm, humid summers. As national demand for meat grew, demand for corn as feed increased. A combination of large output per acre and high price per bushel made corn more valuable per acre than wheat in the evolving Corn Belt, so it became dominant there. Wheat shifted westward to the low-cost, drier lands. Corn's westward expansion halted when it reached the approximately 20–inch-per-year rainfall line in the eastern Dakotas and the western portions of Nebraska and Kansas. The changes in the top ten corn states from 1860 to 1900 document the emergence of this Corn Belt (Table 14.3). In 1860 the four leading states—Illinois, Ohio, Missouri, and Indiana—represented the older core of the region. South-ern states, where corn was a traditional human food and animal feed, also remained important corn producers. During subsequent years Iowa, the core of the Corn Belt, rose to its leading position; Kansas and Nebraska joined the ten largest producers during the 1870s and moved rapidly upward in later years. As well as feeding the corn to locally bred and raised cattle and hogs, the Corn Belt specialized in fattening western-bred cattle. This was feasible only because the railroad provided low-cost transportation from the western ranch country. The Corn Belt, therefore, emerged by 1890 as an intermediate link in providing meat for midwestern and eastern urban markets.

South of the Corn Belt was an east-west band, loosely termed the "corn and winter wheat belt" (Fig. 14.3). The soils were less fertile and the topography quite hilly; agricultural output per acre, consequently, was lower. The Ozarks of southern Missouri typify this region, which also contained the specialty tobacco growing area of Kentucky, an area that accounted for 25 percent of national output in 1860 and, significantly, 45 percent by 1890.

In contrast to the Corn Belt, the Pacific Coast's specialization in fruits and vegetables for national markets was in its infancy in 1890. The base was already in place, however, for enormous expansion in the 1890–1920 period (Fig. 14.3). The isolation of the region hindered its growth as a fruit and vegetable grower. Two thousand miles, two mountain ranges, and deserts separated it from the nearest midwestern markets, and the east coast cities were an additional thousand miles away. It is not surprising that wheat was the first specialty crop grown in the Central Valley of California for nonlocal markets. It moved to export markets by slow ships or followed the one transcontinental railroad link from northern California. During the years 1860 to 1890, the chief market for fresh fruits and vegetables were the Pacific Coast settlements themselves; their economy was spurred by mining, lumbering, cattle ranching, and wheat growing. This was a crucial learning period: farmers grew a wide variety of fruits and vegetables and developed irrigated farms during the 1880s. Two transcontinental railroads were completed by 1880 and, within ten years, an additional two links were available, so all sections between the Canadian and Mexican borders had eastern connections. During the 1870s another crucial requirement was met for marketing the produce outside the Pacific Coast: refrigerated rail cars were perfected sufficiently to handle transcontinental shipments of perishable fruits and vegetables. Coordination of the complex transcontinental production, transportation, and marketing of these perishables required more time, but this problem could not be resolved fully until large shipments were initiated.

Irrigated land in California grew fourfold between 1890 and 1920; by the latter date 4.2 million acres were irrigated. Fruits and vegetables were grown in the Central Valley and in the coastal valleys from San Francisco to San Diego. California became a leading supplier of winter fruits and vegetables to eastern markets and year-round supplier of a wide range of subtropical fruits grown only in southern California. By the 1920s, California was the nation's source for one-third of its winter vegetables, two-thirds of its oranges, three-fourths of its grapes, prunes, and figs, and almost all of its lemons, almonds, and apricots. Oregon and Washington were small-scale producers of fruit prior to the mid-1880s, but their production increased following the completion in 1883 of the Northern Pacific Railroad that linked Puget Sound with Minnesota and the midwestern rail network. By the 1890s apples, pears, peaches, and cherries were specialties in the Pacific Northwest. The irrigated fruit and vegetable agriculture in the Southwest—Arizona and the bordering Imperial Valley of California, and New Mexico—arose after 1890, and was only moderately developed by 1920.

Southern agricultural patterns continued to be based on climatic advantages of a long growing season and ample rainfall. Florida's subtropical location conferred benefits that were analogous to southern California's situation. After 1890 Florida emerged as a leading citrus area and secondarily as a supplier of winter vegetables to northern markets (Fig. 14.3). By 1919 it was second to California in citrus fruit production, and ranked third by value of vegetables grown. The sugarcane area of Louisiana was an old specialized producer dating from the 1820s. Following a slow period of recovery after the Civil War, it regained large-volume production between 1890 and 1920. Sugarcane production was always a highly capitalized enterprise consisting of large farms (1,000–3,000 acres), small railroads for moving cane to the sugar mills, and large steam-powered refineries on the farms. Rice growing emerged later along the Gulf Coast. Before 1860 rice had been a specialty crop in the Carolina-Georgia tidewater that dated back to the 18th century. In the 1880s settlers from the Middle West began irrigated rice farming in a 250–mile band along the southwestern Louisiana and southeastern Texas Gulf Coast. Extensive use of agricultural machinery, combined with ideal soil and climatic conditions, resulted in highly productive rice farms that competed in Asian markets, even though the latter had lower-cost labor. And the Cotton Belt had been a well-established agricultural region since the 1840s. By 1860 it extended from the Carolinas to eastern Texas and southeastern Arkansas. After 1860 it expanded progressively westward in Texas and northward in Arkansas and, after 1890, into southern Oklahoma (Fig. 14.3). These new areas had richer soils than the older cotton-producing areas in the east. After 1890 the northward and westward movement of cotton was further encouraged as a way of avoiding the advance of the boll weevil. About two-thirds of the steadily growing cotton output was exported in the late 19th century. It remained a heavy labor-intensive crop during the 1860–1920 period primarily because of the lack of a suitable mechanical cotton-picker.

The crystallization of the corn and wheat regions, including their dominance of cattle and hog production, forced adjustment both in older eastern agriculture and in the area from Michigan to eastern Minnesota that had developed between 1840 and 1870. This latter area had a variable combination of cool, humid climate, poor soils, and hilly topography that often precluded efficient use of farm machinery. The East lost its competitiveness in corn, wheat, cattle, and hogs before 1860, and the upper midwestern band of farm counties lost their competitiveness during the next several decades. The adjustments took two forms that had begun in the East before 1860: a Dairy Belt emerged across the northern tier of states, and an intensive "truck gardening" region emerged in the East (Fig. 14.3). Throughout both areas large urban demand for milk, vegetables, and dairy products influenced the form of these newer agricultural regions.

The Dairy Belt comprised two sets of products with different location patterns based on transportation cost and value. Liquid milk for human consumption is valuable but expensive to transport, whereas butter and cheese have high value per unit weight and transportation cost is less important in their location. Following 1860, improvements in milk handling and refrigeration made consumption of fluid milk safer, and the perfection of refrigerated rail cars after 1870 permitted long-distance transportation of dairy products. Fluid milksheds, the hinterlands from which cities acquire their fresh milk, emerged around the large metropolises and industrial cities in the East and Middle West during the thirty years following 1860. The growing efficiency and density of the railroad network surrounding the largest cities permitted the milksheds to expand beyond their cities' immediate environs. Dairy farms near cities produced fluid milk, while cheese and butter became a specialty of the dairy farms across the northern tier of states that were more distant from large cities. An area between central New York State and northeast Ohio specialized in cheese before 1860, and by the 1870s southern Wisconsin produced cheese for export to eastern markets in refrigerated rail cars. Butter production for distant markets lagged somewhat behind cheese because the manufacture of butter was simpler and not amenable to specialization by type, as was cheese. By 1890 the Dairy Belt had completed its formation and had developed its typical crop pattern of about half of the arable land in hay and pasture for feeding the dairy cattle. Pockets of specialized fruit production also arose in the region along the east and south shores of the Great Lakes, in locations that provided protection from frost and low winter temperatures. Smaller-scale dairy specialization also occurred around all the nation's large cities; for example, even the rapidly growing Pacific Coast cities had small adjacent dairy areas.

The term "truck gardening," which signifies vegetable production for nearby city markets, evolved as a short-hand phrase after motor-powered wagons were introduced early in the 20th century, but the east coast vegetable region grew much earlier in response to demand from the burgeoning populations in the metropolises of Boston, New York, Philadelphia, and Baltimore, and in the numerous small industrial cities surrounding them. The post-1860 growth of the east coast urban belt, coupled with gradually rising incomes, stimulated demand for vegetables. Improvements in canning during the Civil War spurred output of summer vegetables beyond the immediate needs of summer consumption; the canned vegetables could be consumed all year. When large shipments of fresh vegetables from California and Florida began after 1890, a specialization in fresh vegetables between the east coast and these other states occurred. California and Florida supplied fresh vegetables to the east coast markets in the winter and spring, and the east coast supplied the summer vegetables. Subtropical fruits and vegetables, of course, were supplied from California and Florida all year. On the East Coast, vegetable production tended to be specialized by area; for example, potatoes in Maine and Long Island, New York; onions in Massachusetts and Connecticut; and tomatoes from New Jersey to Maryland. Some fruits were also grown, such as cranberries in eastern Massachusetts and peaches in southern New Jersey. At a smaller scale all metropolises and large cities in the rest of the nation developed fresh vegetable zones surrounding them, but none has ever equaled the east coast region.

Most of the broad pattern of 20th-century regional specialization in agriculture existed by the 1890s; it was based on an 87 percent increase in farm output between 1870 and 1890. During the thirty years following 1890, farm output grew by 63 percent, but this somewhat smaller percentage rise consisted of an enormous absolute increase because the 1890 base was much larger than the 1870 base. The transportation and communications improvements following 1860 facilitated an emerging regional specialization simultaneously with new lands entering production. Settlers moved to western agricultural frontiers either because significant local markets for agriculture existed, such as mining or lumbering areas, or because opportunity existed to produce for the national market. The emergence of new agricultural regions required, in turn, that older regions adjust their agriculture to remain competitive in national markets.

Lumbering

The widespread distribution of forests in the United States, excluding the lightly populated arid areas of the West, precluded the lumber industry from becoming as regionally specialized an industry as other sectors of agriculture throughout most of the 1860–1920 period. Specialized lumber districts emerged, but before 1880 their dominant markets were either within the region or in nearby regions. In subsequent years, flows became more prevalent from the Pacific Northwest and the South to deficit areas in the East and Middle West. Because trees take twenty to thirty years or more to grow to commercial size, lumbering inevitably depleted this resource. The rise and decline of lumber areas, therefore, is a consistent theme of the period (Table 14.5).

Maine, New York, and Pennsylvania were major suppliers of eastern lumber prior to 1860, but between 1860 and 1890, with the exception of a few short periods of recovery, they remained stagnant. From the 1870s to the mid-1890s the Great Lakes states of Michigan and Wisconsin were the largest lumber producers; in 1880 they accounted for 29.3 percent of national employment (Table 14.5). Their lumber firms were larger and more heavily capitalized than eastern firms. They first supplied markets in their states, other Great Lakes states, and along the Mississippi River, then supplied an increasing volume of lumber to the East and to the Great Plains. Ten years or more before the decline following the mid-1890s, Michigan and Wisconsin lumberers purchased timberland on the Pacific Coast and in the South to assure future production.

The Pacific Coast achieved national prominence after 1890. Throughout the period between 1860 and 1920, its heavily capitalized lumber industry served markets on the west coast and export markets around the Pacific basin. California was the leading lumber state before 1890, spurred by its rapidly growing local markets. In 1880, California, with 10.2 percent of national employment, was second in the nation to Michigan and far ahead of the other two Pacific Coast states of Oregon and Washington. Humboldt Bay and its city of Eureka in northern California was the center of the redwood lumber industry. After 1880 Oregon and Washington grew rapidly as lumber states. Local markets contributed to their growth, as well as the increased demand from the California and Pacific basin markets. The completion of the Northern Pacific railroad in 1883 was not an immediate boon to export to the East. Eastward shipments were not large until the late 1890s, when the Great Lakes

Table 14.5   Leading Forestry Employment States, 1880–1920

	Percent of Total Employment	
1880	1900	1920
20.5 Michigan	9.3 Pennsylvania	11.7 Washington
10.2 California	8.8 Michigan	7.6 Michigan
9.4 Pennsylvania	7.7 Washington	6.8 Minnesota
8.8 Wisconsin	6.1 California	6.5 Wisconsin
5.0 Minnesota	5.5 Wisconsin	5.8 Maine
4.0 New York	4.9 Minnesota	5.1 Oregon
3.0 Maine	4.1 Arkansas	4.0 California
2.6 Missouri	3.9 Louisiana	3.8 Louisiana
2.5 Georgia	3.6 Georgia	3.3 Pennsylvania
2.4 Alabama	3.3 North Carolina	3.1 New York
31.6 all other states	42.8 all other states	42.3 all other states
100.0 total	100.0 total	100.0 total
55,931 employed	140,599 employed	217,378 employed

lumber industry finally began its decline. By 1900 California had slipped to fourth rank nationally in forestry employment while Washington had surged to third rank; Oregon was not yet in the top ten in employment (Table 14.5). Within twenty years Washington was the nation's leading lumber state and Oregon had moved up to sixth place.

The southern lumber industry's large expansion began in the 1880s; before 1880 markets were located locally within the South. In 1880 Georgia and Alabama were ranked ninth and tenth nationally, with 2.5 and 2.4 percent of total forestry employment. Growing markets in the East, which could not be served by eastern lumber mills, and the decline of competition from the Great Lakes states after the mid-1890s, provided the basis for a steady growth of southern lumbering that served local, midwestern, and eastern markets. By 1900 Arkansas, Louisiana, Georgia, and North Carolina occupied the seventh through tenth places in forestry employment, and together they accounted for 14.9 percent of the nation's lumber employment (Table 14.5). By 1920, lumbering had emerged as regionally important in the Great Lakes, Pacific Coast, and the South; older lumber areas in the East—Maine, Pennsylvania, and New York—also had revived. Even so, imports from Canada began to increase because U.S. lumbering could not keep up with demand. Although specialization in lumbering was not equivalent to that in agriculture, some

locations were heavily reliant on the lumber industry—especially Washington, Oregon, Maine, and numerous scattered sites throughout the southeastern states.

Mining

In the latter part of the 19th century mining output grew twice as fast as manufacturing output as metals replaced most wood in manufacturing, and energy resources were required in larger quantities to power the expanding national economy. Except for coal for heating and steam power, which was relatively widespread in the nation, most mining districts were specialized producers for a national market. The localization of the key coal-producing areas during the 1860–1920 period was tied to the development of the iron and steel industry. The eastern Pennsylvania anthracite coalfields continued to supply fuel for heating and steam power and for the eastern iron and steel mills, as they had done prior to 1860. After 1860, bituminous coal from the western side of the Appalachians became the principal fuel for the rapidly growing iron and steel industry. The coal was transformed into coke and, by 1890, the Connellsville region of western Pennsylvania and northern West Virginia produced half of the nation's coke.

As late as 1879 more than half of the iron ore needed by industry was mined in the East in New York, New Jersey, and Pennsylvania, but the shift to other richer deposits occurred rapidly after 1879 (Table 14.6). The Lake Superior mines in Michigan and Wisconsin expanded after the Sault Ste. Marie Canal, connecting Lake Superior and Lake Huron, was finished in 1855; it provided a clear passage to the lower Great Lakes. By 1890 the eastern mines' share had fallen below 20 percent, and half of the iron ore now came from the Lake Superior district. During the 1880s two other important iron ore districts commenced significant production. The area around Birmingham, Alabama, reached 11.8 percent of national production by 1890; over the next thirty years its percentage declined slightly. The Mesabi range of northern Minnesota, the nation's richest iron ore area, developed slowly; by 1890 it accounted for only 5.6 percent. Within ten years, however, its output surged to more than one-third of the nation's and by 1910 had climbed to more than 50 percent; the Lake Superior district declined simultaneously to about one-quarter. These changes in iron ore mining were relative; the absolute output in all districts expanded to serve the burgeoning iron and steel industry in the East and Middle West. The expansion of the Lake Superior mines in the 1860s initiated the pattern of input linkages for the industry that persisted well into the 20th century. Ore freighters linked the Lake Superior–Mesabi mines to the iron and steel mills along the lower Great Lakes, or to rail connections at ports for transporting ore to inland mills in eastern Ohio and western Pennsylvania. Connellsville coke was transported by barge and rail to the mills.

Michigan was also a major supplier of copper before 1880. The depletion of the best ore deposits, however, required the development of distant mines in the West that could not enter production until the completion of the transcontinental railroads and feeders to them. Butte, Montana, was the first district to develop, followed by several Arizona districts. By 1889 Butte and Arizona accounted for 43 and 14 percent, respectively, of national production, while Michigan accounted for 39 percent. Further relative shifts occurred during the subsequent thirty years. In 1919 Arizona had become the nation's chief producer with 47 percent, while the Butte and Michigan districts had declined to 16 and 19 percent, respectively. New districts had emerged in Utah, Nevada, and New Mexico; their combined production increased from less than 2 percent in 1889 to 17 percent in 1919. By 1920, therefore, 80 percent of the nation's copper came from western districts that were distant from the Manufacturing Belt in the East and Middle West.

Copper, coal, and iron ore mining were all heavily capitalized businesses throughout the period from 1860 to 1920. Although gold and silver miners are immortalized in folklore as rugged individuals who braved all odds to mine their precious minerals, large heavily capitalized firms in fact took over mining after the easily reached veins had been exhausted

Table 14.6   Iron Ore Production, 1879–1920

	Percent of Total Iron Ore Mined				
	1879	1890	1900	1910	1920
Minnesota	0.0	5.6	35.7	56.1	58.4
Michigan	23.0	44.5	36.0	23.3	25.9
Wisconsin	0.5	5.9	2.7	2.0	1.5
Alabama	2.4	11.8	10.0	8.4	8.7
Tennessee	1.3	2.9	2.2	1.3	0.6
New York	15.8	7.8	1.6	2.3	1.4
Pennsylvania	27.4	8.5	3.2	1.3	1.1
New Jersey	9.5	3.1	1.2	0.9	0.6
All other states	20.0	9.8	7.4	4.4	1.9
Total U.S. (%)	99.9	99.9	100.0	100.0	100.1
Total U.S. (in thousands of long tons)	7,120	16,036	27,553	57,015	67,604

within the first few years of a mine's existence. The 1860s witnessed the start of numerous gold and silver mining districts. Following the California gold rush of the preceding decade, Nevada became prominent with the discovery of the Comstock Lode near Reno. The Butte, Montana, gold and silver mines also opened in the 1860s. Colorado experienced several successive mining booms, including the Central City district in the 1860s, the Leadville district in the late 1870s, and the Cripple Creek district in the 1890s. Because refined gold and silver were valuable per unit weight, railroads were not essential; therefore, this mining could begin in the West earlier than other mineral mining. Lead, for example, was not mined in the West until the 1880s when railroad feeder lines were connected to the transcontinental trunk lines. In 1870, 60 percent of the nation's lead still came from mines in the Great Lakes states. During the 1870s, the famous Tri-State District in southwestern Missouri and bordering parts of Oklahoma and Kansas commenced production. This district, which also had zinc, accounted for one-third of all lead mined by 1920. In the 1880s the lead districts in Colorado and Nevada emerged; they followed earlier Utah lead mines near the transcontinental railroad. Leadville, Colorado, was one of the most famous districts. These western districts accounted for about two-thirds of production during the 1880s. Mining in the Coeur d'Alene district of Idaho, to become the nation's most productive, did not begin until the 1890s.

Oil was the latest of the major minerals to be developed during the late 19th century, but its role in regional development was more significant and long-lasting. The first important oil production began in the 1860s near Titusville in northwestern Pennsylvania. Through most of the 19th century oil was used chiefly for lighting and as a lubricant for machinery. Fuel oil and gasoline did not become important until about 1910, after the appearance of the automobile. Transportation quickly became a crucial factor in oil development because oil was bulky, difficult to handle, and of low value. Short branch railroads were soon employed to link oil fields to the nearest trunk rail lines. In the 1870s short pipelines were linked to the main railroads and, within a decade, networks of long-distance pipelines were established. John D. Rockefeller early recognized the value of forming large, integrated oil companies that combined acquisition, refining, and distribution of oil. In reference to Standard Oil's takeover of much of Cleveland's oil-refining capacity in the early 1870s, he is reputed to have responded to a refusal to sell a refinery: "You can never make money, in my judgment. You can't compete with Standard. We have all the large refineries now. If you refuse to sell, it will end in your being crushed."

Pennsylvania and other portions of Appalachia remained the leading oil producers until 1900 (Table 14.7). The Ohio-Indiana field became a major producer in the mid-1890s and continued for about a decade. During the first

Table 14.7   Crude Petroleum Output by Region, 1900–1919

Field	Percent of total crude petroleum output				
	1900	1905	1910	1915	1919
Appalachian	57	22	13	8	8
Ohio-Indiana	34	17	3	2	1
Illinois	—	—	16	7	3
Kansas-Oklahoma	1	9	28	44	51
Gulf Coast	—	27	5	7	6
California	7	25	35	31	27
Others	1	—	—	1	4
Total %	100	100	100	100	100
Total production in millions of barrels	64	135	210	281	378

few years after 1900 new discoveries in the Gulf Coast (Texas) and in southern California saw these fields grow rapidly. The last major fields to develop were in Kansas-Oklahoma and Illinois after 1905. Two fields were dominant by 1919: Kansas-Oklahoma and California. Because the newer oil fields were distant from major consuming areas, the oil industry was forced to devise an elaborate system of production, transportation, refining, and distribution that spanned the nation by the first two decades of the 20th century. Many of the nation's largest oil corporations were in existence by 1910, including Standard, Gulf, Texaco, Union, and Sun. Mining districts were highly integrated into the national space-economy by 1890 and, as new resources such as oil emerged, they also quickly became part of a national market. Given the close tie between mining and manufacturing, it is not surprising that manufacturing also made significant strides toward national market integration before 1890.

Manufacturing

The choice of manufacturing location is influenced by a variety of factors, especially transportation cost, labor cost, and agglomeration economies. Raw material processing manufactures such as sawmills, flour mills, and smelting have large weight loss of waste material, or convert material to a more suitable form for transportation; they locate near raw material sites. Other manufactures for which transportation cost is important locate near the market; examples are bread and bricks. These manufactures have high transportation costs for the final products because they are perishable, delicate, or low value relative to their weight. Some manufactures do not need such close proximity and are termed "regional-market" manufactures. They are produced in each region and are transported throughout it, but they cannot be shipped outside the region because the cost is too high. During the mid-19th century, examples of this were furniture, paper, and iron foundry products (heavy metal components and machines). Another category of market-oriented manufactures is termed "multiregional" or "national market" manufactures. Their transportation costs are not factors in location because they comprise such small proportions of the final sale prices, such as

textiles, drugs, and gloves. Other industrial location factors like special labor advantages (for example, low wages) or agglomeration economies also may be important. Agglomerations of industries linked in production sequences may occur because of savings in transportation cost between plants or because of the need for access to information about production requirements. Examples are carriage parts manufacturers located near carriage factories, or auto parts producers near auto factories.

Between 1860 and 1880 the relative importance of these location factors changed, and the result was a concentration of most industry in what has been termed the American Manufacturing Belt (Fig. 14.4). This great industrial region persisted as the nation's industrial core through much of the 20th century. Its emergence was inseparable from the westward-expanding natural resource sectors of agriculture, lumbering, and mining. The outline of the belt was determined by the 1860–80 period, as a set of regional industrial systems emerged. In each region a metropolis provided financial, wholesaling, warehousing, and transportation service for manufacturers who located in the metropolis or in an industrial city in the hinterland. Examples of the provision of metropolitan services are: Boston for cotton textile manufacturers in New England; Philadelphia for iron manufacturers in southeastern Pennsylvania; and Chicago for agricultural machinery firms in northern Illinois.

Prior to 1860, and especially before 1840, most industrialists served demands originating in their own region. Four sources of demand were significant: household consumers, urban infrastructure, the natural resource sector, and intraregional and interregional trade. Households demanded a diverse set of manufactured products that included clothes, furniture, stoves, houses (lumber, doors, and windows), and food (flour, sugar, spices, and meat). The growth of cities stimulated demand for construction materials such as bricks, lumber, pipes, glass, nails, and hinges. Two important components of the natural resource sector, agriculture and extraction/processing, demanded manufactures. Commercial agriculture required construction materials such as lumber, nails, and hinges to build fences and barns. Farmers also needed implements such as axes, hoes, and rakes, and machinery such as plows,

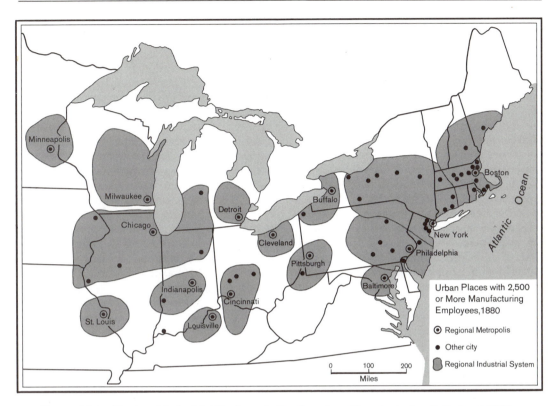

Figure 14.4   Regional Industrial Systems in the American Manufacturing Belt about 1880

harrows, mowers, reapers, and threshers. The extraction/processing sectors required extensive manufactures. Mining employed hand tools and machinery for crushing and smelting, and lumbering used saws and sawmill machinery. Food processing such as flour milling used water- and steam-powered machinery, and meatpacking used hand tools. Intraregional and interregional trade stimulated diverse manufactures. Containers such as boxes and barrels were needed in large quantities. Steamboats ran with steam engines, and railroads used locomotives and cars (rails were supplied mostly from foreign producers). These four diverse sources of demands for manufactures stimulated a crucial set of manufactures that are called the "pivotal producer durables." They included iron foundries, machine shops, and machinery firms. Because their products were used in a wide variety of industrial processes, they emerged simultaneously with other manufactures. They equipped factories for production and supplied on-going needs for parts and machinery. Many products such as steam en-

gines and locomotives were themselves machines. Each regional industrial system developed a producer durables sector.

As each new region was settled before 1860, a regional system of manufacturing emerged. The east coast industrial systems, developed in the 1790–1830 period, were centered on Boston, New York, Philadelphia, and Baltimore. These industrial systems also produced the first national market manufactures such as textiles in Boston's hinterland, hardware in New York's hinterland, and drugs and chemicals in Philadelphia. In a successive manner the industrial systems of Pittsburgh and Cincinnati emerged in the 1810–40 period, and those of St. Louis, Detroit, Cleveland, Chicago, and Milwaukee in the 1840–60 period. By 1860, therefore, the key regional industrial systems of the Manufacturing Belt were already established.

Comparable industrial systems did not emerge in the South before 1860, even though it was experiencing westward settlement, as was the Middle West. The reasons for limited manufacturing in the South are complex and disputed. Individual southern factories were comparable in size and profitability to northern factories, and the broad types of manufactures were similar in both areas. The aggregate demand for many manufactures produced for markets in a region, however, was substantially lower in the South. White population size and density were lower in regions surrounding metropolises such as Charleston, Mobile, and New Orleans than around midwestern metropolises such as Cincinnati or Cleveland. Slaves contributed little to demand because their consumption patterns were restricted by their owners. Large plantations were relatively self-sufficient in many everyday items. Overall urban population was small, and urban infrastructure manufactures were limited. Agricultural machinery was not used to grow the major commercial crop, cotton, and it did not require processing. The small southern railroad network needed few locomotives and cars. Because this wide variety of manufactures was demanded in small volume, the producer durables sector was equally small. Before 1860 the South's demand for these diverse regional manufactures was less than both the Middle West, which grew simultaneously, and the East, which had emerged earlier.

The expanding volume of manufactures shipped between regions during the 1840–60 period was an omen of the sweeping changes in industry that took place after 1860. Intraregional markets declined in relative importance for many manufactures as they increasingly produced for markets in other regions; new manufactures were produced for multiregional and national markets. Because regional markets ceased being the foundation of a region's manufactures, later settled or lagging regions had difficulty acquiring manufactures. The technological knowledge, efficient factories, and marketing networks were solidly established in the industrial systems of the Manufacturing Belt, so it eventually stopped expanding westward. After 1860 the Manufacturing Belt's industrial systems grew enormously as each developed specialities for multiregional and national markets. This specialization was supported by the increased efficiency of transportation and communication.

The Manufacturing Belt's industrial systems were nationally dominant by 1860, and they maintained their position in 1900. The percentage of interstate trade in manufacturing value-added that each section (several industrial systems) contributes measures the relative importance of a section in interstate (interregional) trade. The Manufacturing Belt accounted for the overwhelmingly majority of the interregional trade in manufacturing in both 1860 and 1900. In 1860 southern New England was a leading national manufacturer of textiles, paper, leather products, fabricated metals, non-electrical machinery, and instruments. The Mid-Atlantic section was a leader in food, apparel, furniture, printing and publishing, rubber, leather, primary metals, non-electrical machinery, transportation equipment, and instruments. In contrast, the Middle West was only moderately important in food, lumber and wood products, and furniture. By 1900 southern New England remained a leader in textiles and leather products, but had declined relatively in numerous other manufactures. The one exception was its rise to dominance in rubber production. The Mid-Atlantic section remained a leader in apparel, printing and publishing, leather, primary metals, non-electrical machinery, and instruments; it declined significantly in food and rubber. In contrast, the Middle West made substantial gains in food, lumber and wood products, furniture, fabricated metals, non-electrical machinery, and transportation equipment.

A rich texture of specialization among both metropolises and small industrial cities existed as early as 1880 (Tables 14.8 and 14.9). Some metropolises had almost 20 percent or more of their manufacturing employment in a single manufacture. Such high percentages occurred, for example, in men's clothing and fruit and vegetable canning in Baltimore, men's clothing in Milwaukee, miscellaneous textiles in Philadelphia, and iron and steel in Pittsburgh. The location quotient, which measures the percentage of a city's employment in a manufacture relative to the national percentage employed in that manufacture, is a better measure of specialization. Large location quotients indicate a high degree of specialization. Metropolises that were highly specialized in manufactures included Baltimore with fruit and vegetable canning, Boston with musical instruments, Chicago and Indianapolis with slaughtering and meatpacking, Milwaukee with malt liquor (beer), Philadelphia with miscellaneous tex-

Table 14.8 Manufacturing Specialization in Regional Metropolises, 1880

	Persons employed in manufacturing	Percent of total manufacturing employment and location quotient[a]		
		Foundry and machine-shop products	Selected other industries	
New York City (inc. Brooklyn)	274,939	5.0 (0.9)	17.8 (3.0)	Clothing, men's
			4.7 (5.2)	Clothing, women's
			3.9 (1.9)	Printing & publishing
Philadelphia (inc. Camden, N.J.)	189,897	5.7 (1.1)	25.6 (17.8)	Misc. textiles
Chicago	79,414	6.2 (1.2)	1.3 (0.9)	Agricultural implements
			10.7 (1.8)	Clothing, men's
			6.2 (2.8)	Furniture
			9.4 (9.4)	Slaughtering & meat packing
Boston (inc. Cambridge, Chelsea, & Somerville)	68,403	6.4 (1.2)	13.6 (2.3)	Clothing, men's
			3.4 (8.5)	Musical instruments
			5.4 (2.6)	Printing & publishing
Cincinnati, Ohio (inc. Covington & Newport, Ky.)	59,190	6.6 (1.2)	6.0 (3.2)	Carriages & wagons
			15.7 (2.7)	Clothing, men's
			6.2 (2.8)	Furniture
			1.9 (1.9)	Slaughtering & meat packing
Baltimore	56,338	4.7 (0.9)	19.8 (3.4)	Clothing, men's
			19.4 (17.6)	Fruits & vegetables, canned & preserved
Pittsburgh (inc. Allegheny)	43,401	8.1 (1.5)	13.4 (14.9)	Glass
			39.6 (7.6)	Iron & steel
St. Louis, Mo.	41,825	8.3 (1.6)	6.8 (1.2)	Clothing, men's
			3.2 (3.2)	Liquors, malt
			5.4 (2.6)	Printing & publishing
Cleveland	21,724	11.7 (2.2)	1.7 (5.4)	Brooms & brushes
			13.8 (2.7)	Iron & steel
Milwaukee	20,886	7.0 (1.3)	20.6 (3.5)	Clothing, men's
			5.0 (5.0)	Liquors, malt
Buffalo	18,021	12.0 (2.3)	4.4 (101.4)	Glucose
			1.4 (36.0)	Refrigerators
Louisville	17,448	9.0 (1.7)	4.7 (2.1)	Furniture
			7.9 (6.6)	Tobacco, chewing, smoking & snuff
Detroit	16,110	6.4 (1.2)	5.0 (2.4)	Printing & publishing
Minneapolis–St. Paul	10,574	5.6 (1.1)	7.2 (3.4)	Flour
Indianapolis	10,000	13.1 (2.5)	6.4 (3.0)	Printing & publishing
			8.9 (8.9)	Slaughtering & meat packing

[a]Location quotient (in parentheses) is computed as $(CM_i/CM_t)/(NM_i/NM_t)$ where CM_i and CM_t are respectively a city's employment in industry i and total manufacturing employment, and NM_i and NM_t are respectively the national employment in industry i and total manufacturing employment.

tiles, Pittsburgh with glass and iron and steel, Cleveland with brooms and brushes, Buffalo with glucose and refrigerators, and Louisville with tobacco (Table 14.8). Foundry and machine-shop products, which are indicative of the pivotal producer durables sector, were well represented in all metropolises.

Similarly, small industrial cities in the hinterlands of metropolises had high percentages of their industrial labor force in some manufactures, and they were highly specialized relative to the nation (Table 14.9). A high percentage of industrial workers were employed in furniture in Grand Rapids, miscellaneous textiles in Paterson, distilled liquors (whiskey) in Peoria, agricultural implements in Springfield, Ohio, and cotton goods in Taunton. Compared with national employment (location quotients), the most specialized cities were Columbus with carriages and wagons, Grand Rapids with furniture, Peoria with distilled liquors, and Springfield with agricultural implements. Some of the small industrial cities were even specialized in foundry and machine-shop products; for example, Fort Wayne and Taunton. This degree of specialization in both metropolises and small industrial cities suggests that some of their manufactures were being sold in multiregional and national markets by 1880.

Three manufactures—iron and steel, cotton textiles, and electrical machinery—exemplify various kinds of changes in manufacturing between 1860 and 1920. The first two were old, while the third was a new manufacture. The iron and steel industry is sometimes considered the epitome of the changes in late 19th-century manufacturing. This is not entirely accurate because iron and steel firms were always atypically large, compared with firms in other industries. In 1860 the iron industry already had acquired some characteristics that anticipated changes over the next 60 years. East of the Appalachian Mountains many large iron firms were using anthracite coal from the fields of northeastern Pennsylvania long before 1860. The blast furnaces that produced pig iron, and the rolling mills that transformed pig iron into rails and bar iron, were clustered in the river valleys and other areas near the large metropolises of Boston, New York, and Philadelphia. Most iron firms on the west side of the Appalachians still employed charcoal as fuel for the blast furnaces, but the use of coke had begun.

Charcoal blast furnaces were scattered throughout rural areas for easy access to timber supplies for making the charcoal. In contrast, the rolling mills, which used coal to power steam engines, were located in Pittsburgh and at numerous sites along the Ohio River, as well as in other midwestern metropolises such as Buffalo, Cleveland, Detroit, and Chicago.

A trend of increasing integration and rising scale of firm began in the 1860s with the start of Bessemer steel manufacture. To manufacture steel efficiently, close integration was necessary between the blast furnaces, which produced pig iron, and the Bessemer converter, which made steel from the pig iron. At the same time Connellsville coke was adopted increasingly by blast furnaces; this freed them from rural locations, because coke was transported more easily than charcoal. Blast furnaces, therefore, could be located near Bessemer converters. Finally, the large output of Bessemer converters encouraged rolling mills to be part of Bessemer steel works. Efficiencies were achieved by close integration of the sequences of steel manufacturing. Large integrated steel works appeared in some locations, but the parts remained separate at other places. The open-hearth iron and steel process became important after the 1880s. It operated at a smaller scale than the Bessemer process, but by 1890 the trend toward large, integrated iron and steel mills was firmly established. The open-hearth process was slower than the Bessemer process, but the former permitted greater quality control over the characteristics of the steel. In addition, the open-hearth process used scrap metal to supplement iron ore, which further lowered costs. A negative characteristic of the Bessemer process was that it required non-phosphorous iron ore, and this ore was not widely available. As demand for steel shifted from rails to higher-quality steels, the open-hearth process increasingly became the preferred method of production.

Midwestern and western railroad expansion were important sources of demand for steel after 1860. This was met by the large Bessemer rail mills in Pittsburgh and Chicago. Midwestern demand for bridges, structural parts, and machinery also undergirded the iron and steel industry expansion. The industry, therefore, gradually shifted to the Middle West, although the eastern mills still remained important suppliers for eastern demand. The growing use of

Table 14.9   Manufacturing Specialization in Small Industrial Cities, 1880

	Persons employed in manufacturing	Percent of total manufacturing employment and location quotient[a]		
		Foundry and machine-shop products	Selected other industries	
Albany–Troy	34,219	13.5 (2.5)	12.7 (2.4)	Iron and steel
Columbus, Ohio	5,490	7.0 (1.3)	13.8 (7.3)	Carriages and wagons
			9.7 (1.9)	Iron and steel
Fort Wayne	2,735	34.6 (6.5)	11.4 (2.1)	Lumber, sawed
Grand Rapids	5,172	5.3 (1.0)	34.9 (15.9)	Furniture
Paterson	19,799	14.2 (2.7)	59.2 (6.2)	Misc. textiles
Peoria	4,067	5.2 (1.0)	26.5 (132.5)	Liquors, distilled
Springfield, Ohio	3,970	6.8 (1.3)	59.9 (42.8)	Agricultural implements
Taunton	5,154	23.9 (4.5)	28.9 (4.3)	Cotton goods
Worcester	16,559	14.4 (2.7)	14.6 (2.9)	Boots and shoes
			14.4 (2.8)	Iron and steel

[a]Location quotient (in parentheses) follows the percent of total manufacturing employment for the given industry. For computation see footnote in Table 14.8.

Lake Superior iron ore and Connellsville coke, along with the demand of midwestern markets, resulted in the location of iron and steel mills at points that were minimum transport sites to acquire inputs and distribute outputs to markets. Between 1890 and 1920 major concentrations of blast furnaces and integrated mills occurred in Pittsburgh and along the river valleys surrounding it, including the Ohio, the Mahoning (Youngstown, Ohio, vicinity), and Shenango (Sharon, Pennsylvania, vicinity); and in Buffalo, Cleveland, Detroit, and Chicago. In the East the iron and steel industry concentrated at fewer sites as the scale of firms increased. By the early 20th century, New England's iron and steel industry had declined, and the larger mills were located in eastern Pennsylvania and Baltimore. Birmingham, Alabama, which had local deposits of iron ore and coal, became the leading southern center for steel after 1888.

Organizational changes also occurred with the increasing size of iron and steel plants and their concentration at fewer locations. Andrew Carnegie, the foremost innovator in implementing organizational changes in the industry, applied experience gained as one of the managers of the Pennsylvania Railroad, the pioneering business organization that introduced modern management techniques to large-scale firms. The crux of Carnegie's approach in his firm, Carnegie Steel, was a fanatical attention to cost control. He claimed that, "One of the chief sources of success in manufacturing is the introduction and strict maintenance of a perfect system of accounting so that responsibility for money or materials can be brought home to every man." Through the organizational structure and cost-reporting system that he implemented, all facets of Carnegie Steel were under his control. By the 1880s, some large individual firms such as Carnegie Steel were multifunctional, multilocational enterprises that combined mills, iron ore, and coal mines in one enterprise. When U.S. Steel was organized in 1901 as a "combination of combinations," large integrated firms had been in existence for more than a decade. Throughout most of the period between 1860 and 1920, iron and steel firms tended to serve regional and multiregional markets from individual plants. Transportation costs were sufficiently important that it was not feasible to serve a national market from one region.

The cotton textile industry had a somewhat different pattern of development after 1860. Its input, cotton, was valuable per unit weight and had little weight loss in manufacture. The products—thread and cloth—were also valuable per unit weight. The cotton textile industry, therefore, has never been constrained in its location by transportation costs. Although it was widely scattered initially, once economies of scale in manufacture were achieved and marketing channels established, the industry, as early as 1840, was heavily concentrated in New England, with some smaller concentrations in eastern New York and in Philadelphia and its vicinity. New England's dominance in cotton textiles persisted as late as 1890 when it accounted for about three-fourths of the nation's spindles, a figure unchanged from twenty years earlier. The exploitation of most waterpower sites by 1870 forced the industry to expand with steam power. Coastal locations and other non-waterpower sites were used. By the early 1870s, Fall River had surpassed the old center of Lowell, Massachusetts, and New Bedford, near Fall River, was a major center by the 1880s. The other older textile centers along the Merrimac River from Lawrence, Massachusetts, to Manchester, New Hampshire, and along the Maine coast continued to expand up to 1890. Future changes were signaled, however, by the rapid growth of cotton textiles in the southern Piedmont from North Carolina to Georgia between 1870 and 1890; textile cities, such as Augusta and Columbus in Georgia, began to emerge. In 1900 the South had about 25 percent of the nation's spindles and by 1914 about 40 percent. The northern industry did not decline absolutely during these years; rather, the southern industry grew faster. Most southern expansion was based on locally owned firms, not from relocation of northern mills. Southern Piedmont capital was more profitably employed in cotton textiles than in cotton growing, and the low-wage labor of the Piedmont provided a competitive labor supply.

Although electricity had been used in the telegraph beginning in the 1840s, the electrical machinery industry and its closely allied parts of lighting and traction first developed in the late 1870s. Electrical machinery quickly became a national market industry dominated by two firms, General Electric and Westinghouse. In the late 1870s, arc lighting was perfected for street lights and, during the 1880s, numerous companies emerged to build the dynamos for the lighting companies that appeared in many cities. The equipment firms often started the lighting companies. Already in the late 1880s consolidation occurred as capital requirements rose. One of the leading firms was Thomas-Houston, headquartered in Boston and with its main plant in nearby Lynn. Arc lighting was not practical in homes because it was too bright and it flickered. In the late 1870s, Thomas Edison invented the incandescent lamp, and by 1882 the first power station to light the lamps was built on Manhattan in New York. The Edison Electric Light Company was formed in 1878 to build machinery, encourage development of power stations, and produce lamps. In 1886 the Schenectady works of Edison's company was started, and the Edison General Electric Company was founded in 1889 as a combination of eight companies. Westinghouse Electric Company in Pittsburgh became a vigorous competitor of the Edison firm beginning in the mid-1880s. Further combination occurred in 1892 when Edison's firm was merged with Thomas-Houston to form General Electric. By the mid-1890s, therefore, the electrical machinery industry was dominated by Westinghouse and General Electric. They built locomotives, electric rail cars, and power station machinery. Three of their modern plant locations were the dominant centers in the 1890s: General Electric's Lynn and Schenectady works, and Westinghouse's Pittsburgh works. The electrical machinery industry took only 10 to 15 years to move from inception to national market stature. Because the industry required skills that were closely related to nonelectrical machinery, the leading firms of this "new" industry were located in the Manufacturing Belt.

Late-developing regions in the 19th century had limited opportunities to acquire manufactures, except for residual local and regional market types. Many of these latter shifted to multiregional market scale (for example, iron and steel), and new manufactures quickly became national market in orientation (for example, electrical machinery). Entrepreneurs outside the Manufacturing Belt did not have the skills to compete successfully for new national market manufactures. Given the outline of the belt (Fig. 14.4) and the changes in transportation, communication, and manufacturing, it is plausible to suggest that the belt was established no later than the 1860–1880 period.

Much of the 1860–1920 period, therefore, was characterized by increasing specialization of industrial systems within the belt, and growing interchange both among them, and between them and areas outside the belt. The South missed joining the belt by 1860; its acquisition of cotton textiles during this period was an exception and was based on its low labor cost advantage. The Great Plains, Rocky Mountains, Pacific Coast, and Southwest were settled too late and at too low population density to acquire manufactures. The exceptions were resource processing such as canning, lumber milling, and smelting, that were raw material oriented and followed the exploitation of natural resources.

CONCLUSIONS

Between 1860 and 1920 the United States expanded to a continental set of integrated regional economies. Transportation and communication improvements, along with organizational changes in business, made possible the national integration of regions. This nationalization of the economy progressed at varying paces in different economic sectors. Most agricultural regions were integrated by 1890, but some late specializations occurred in the Southwest (Arizona and New Mexico) and the western part of the northern plains (Montana, western Dakotas). Lumbering lagged somewhat behind agriculture in terms of a continental scale of integrated regions. Specialization for multiregional lumber markets within the East, Middle West, and on the Pacific Coast was prevalent before 1890, and some long-distance shipments between them occurred before 1890, such as from the Middle West to the East. Mining was highly specialized among regions by 1890. Some minerals were more widespread than others and moved chiefly within regional or multiregional markets; coal

is a prominent example. Yet industrial minerals and precious metals were shipped long distances before 1890. Even oil, which was moderately distributed at least among several regions, quickly evolved into a complex network of national production and distribution when output increased significantly between 1890 and 1910. Industrial specialization among regions occurred earliest. Some regions served multiregional and national markets before 1860, especially New England, and others produced for markets outside the region by 1880. Some manufactures were still evolving into national market manufactures and many new national market manufactures arose after 1880, but only the regional industrial systems in existence by 1860 could become specialized at a national scale. At a broader level of generalization a large core, the Manufacturing Belt, emerged between 1860 and 1880, and a vast periphery of resource regions developed to provide specialties such as agricultural products, lumber, and minerals to this core in exchange for manufactures. This core-periphery organization of the national economy persisted from about 1880 until the mid-20th century.

These internal patterns of expansion, growth, and reorganization in the American economy between 1860 and 1920 had significance within a larger geographical context. From an international perspective, the United States had gained new stature in the north Atlantic industrial world as a result of its enormous internal development. Even before 1860, American agricultural output had surpassed that of western Europe. By 1871, America's population of more than 42 million and its coal production of over 50 million tons had passed the dimensions of the new, united state of Germany. By the late 1890s, it had surpassed the United Kingdom, the original "workshop of the world," in coal and steel production and in total manufacturing output. The United States thus entered the 20th century as the leading industrial nation in the world.

ADDITIONAL READING

Books

Anderson O.E. *Refrigeration in America: A History of a New Technology and Its Impact*. Princeton: Princeton University Press, 1953.

Armstrong, J.B. *Factory Under the Elms: A History of Harrisville, New Hampshire, 1774–1969*. Cambridge: M.I.T. Press, 1969.

Chandler, A.D. *The Visible Hand: The Managerial Revolution in American Business*. Cambridge: Belknap Press, 1977.

Cox, T.R. *Mills and Markets: A History of the Pacific Coast Lumber Industry to 1900*. Seattle: University of Washington Press, 1974.

Greever, W.S. *The Bonanza West: The Story of the Western Mining Rushes, 1848–1900*. Norman: University of Oklahoma Press, 1963.

Johnson, E.R.; Van Metre, T.W.; Huebner, G.G.; and Hanchett, D.S. *History of Domestic and Foreign Commerce of the United States*. 2 vols. Washington, D.C.: Carnegie Institute of Washington, 1915.

Kirkland, E.C. *Industry Comes of Age: Business, Labor, and Public Policy 1860–1897*. New York: Holt, Rinehart & Winston, 1962.

Modelski, A.M. *Railroad Maps of North America: The First Hundred Years*. Washington, D.C.: Government Printing Office, 1984.

Perloff, H.S.; Dunn, E.S.; Lampard, E.E.; and Muth, R.F. *Regions, Resources, and Economic Growth*. Baltimore: Johns Hopkins University Press, 1960.

Pred, A. *The Spatial Dynamics of U.S. Urban-Industrial Growth, 1800–1914*. Cambridge: M.I.T. Press, 1966.

Schlebecker, J.T. *Whereby We Thrive: A History of American Farming, 1607–1972*. Ames: Iowa State University Press, 1975.

Schwartz, S.I., and Ehrenberg, R.E. *The Mapping of North America*. New York: H.N. Abrams, 1980.

Shannon, F.A. *The Farmer's Last Frontier: Agriculture, 1860–1897*. New York: Holt, Rinehart & Winston, 1945.

Sitterson, J.C. *Sugar Country: The Cane Sugar Industry in the South, 1753–1950*. Lexington: University of Kentucky Press, 1953.

Taylor, G.R., and Neu, I.D. *The American Railroad Network, 1861–1890*. Cambridge: Harvard University Press, 1956.

Temin, P. *Iron and Steel in Nineteenth-Century America: An Economic Inquiry*. Cambridge: M.I.T. Press, 1964.

Ward, D. *Cities and Immigrants: A Geography of Change in Nineteenth-Century America*. New York: Oxford University Press, 1971.

Warren, K. *The American Steel Industry, 1850–1970: A Geographical Interpretation*. Oxford: Clarendon Press, 1973.

Williamson, H.F., and Daum, A.R. *The American Petroleum Industry: The Age of Illumination, 1859–1899*. Evanston: Northwestern University Press, 1959.

Williamson, H.F.; Andreano, R.L.; Daum, A.R.; and Klose, G.C. *The American Petroleum Industry: The Age of Energy 1899–1959*. Evanston: Northwestern University Press, 1963.

15

The Progress of American Urbanism, 1860–1930

MICHAEL P. CONZEN
University of Chicago

American urban life in the 19th century, if viewed as progressing en masse toward a new condition, passed sometime after the Civil War a distinct threshold of material quality, scale, and quickened pace, compared with what had gone before. The war was not the critical factor in this change, although the unprecedented dislocations of supply and demand, as well as the warping of interregional contacts and physical disturbance of settlements in the war zones, were certainly powerful events. They precipitated an energetic reformulation of the country's production and distribution system and simultaneously retarded or boosted the fortunes of a large number of individual towns within or beyond the theaters of war. But the changes that occurred in the 1870s and 1880s mostly had their origins in the panoply of experiment and innovation that suffused the nation's cities, particularly those in the North, during the two decades preceding that traumatic conflict.

These changes reflected the extension of the national network of cities to exploit the western portions of the continent and the onset of major industrialization, particularly in the developed Northeast. The resulting economic growth and social adjustment recalibrated the human use of time and space within the larger cities. This altered pace trickled down through the urban hierarchy, especially after the war, affecting even the smaller regional centers, so that "city" life became even more sharply distinct from the rural and small-town existence that the majority of Americans understood and took to be the "norm." To the extent that the altered quality and timbre of urban life were the product of changing urban scale and economic functions, such trends need to be placed in the context of the evolving national system of cities.

GROWTH OF THE NATIONAL CITY SYSTEM

The American economy has always required cities as articulation points in the interregional flow of investments, commodities, labor, and services. What changed remarkably in this period (1860–1930) was the proportion of national production emanating from urban places and consequently the proportion of the national population concentrated in cities to achieve this. As late as 1860 four out of five Americans still lived in completely rural surroundings (that is, in settlements with less than 2,500 inhabitants), whereas by 1920 the number of urbanites in aggregate finally outnumbered those in rural areas. While these particular benchmark dates exhibit clear and simple ratios, the thrust of deep change in the settlement fabric of America was longer lived and more variable than these figures suggest.

The American city system has always been tied to broad trans-Atlantic and worldwide patterns of trade and economic control. During the colonial period strong links to metropolitan centers in Europe ensured that individual members of the city "system" shared rather low levels of economic and social interdependence, while exhibiting low "closure" as a system because of the strong individual ties beyond it to overseas. During the 19th century this changed to one of high interdependence and somewhat increased "closure" with greater American autonomy in general economic relations. Within this broad context, the sweep of American urbanization during the 19th and early 20th centuries falls into three broad phases that hinge upon the pivotal census years of 1840, 1880, and 1930, as reflected in certain fundamental measures (Table 15.1). The 1840s and 1850s initiated a mid-century period

Table 15.1   Measures of American Urban Growth, 1840–1930

	Pre–1840	1840–1880	1880–1930
Number of urban places (over 2,500)	131	939	3,165
Average number new towns per annum	2	20	45
Urban population as % of total population	10.8	28.2	56.2
Rate of increase in urban share	1.1	4.4	5.6
Average decadal % change in urban population	56.4	67.3	37.7
Non-agricultural labor force as % of total	36.9	48.7	78.4
Average decadal % change in non-agricultural labor force	2.6	2.9	5.9

Note: Figures apply to the end date in each period.

of unprecedentedly rapid urban growth, a period in which the Civil War failed to slow or reverse any index of national urban growth and in structural terms only complicated but did not redefine the course of urban change. Between 1840 and 1930, the census year 1880 marks a major turning point after which the shift away from agricultural occupations doubled, and the urban proportion climbed more vigorously. It was to take the Great Depression of the 1930s to puncture this long record of urban florescence.

Considering the dramatic developments in the nation's economy during the later 19th and early 20th centuries—expansion of the agricultural, pastoral, and timber domains, major mineral discoveries, transport innovations on a continental scale, immigration, regional specialization, massive but regionally selective industrialization, and the burgeoning of commerce that wove these elements together—it is appropriate to explore how the national system of cities functioned to mold, and be molded by, the regional structure of this economic transformation. Change in the city system can be separated into three major components that describe distinct but interrelated processes: spatial expansion, functional differentiation in

city roles, and economic integration. These processes operated simultaneously, but with greater or lesser power in any given period or region.

Expansion, 1840–1930

The Period 1840–1880. The urbanization that occurred between 1840 and 1880 is well expressed by the numerical increase in "urban places" from 131 to 939. Many villages and towns in the established regions along the northeastern seaboard benefited from rural migration and foreign immigration and blossomed into small towns and cities, thickening the urban settlement cover. Much more dramatic was the geographical reach of the expansion with the rise of towns beyond the Appalachian Mountains.

The Ohio valley as recipient of early migration streams over the mountains had already achieved a significant level of urbanization by 1840, anchored by Cincinnati—testimony to the agricultural wealth of the region and the utility of the river as an avenue of commerce. To this was added the healthy growth of Louisville and the emergence of places like Covington and Evansville (for evidence of the expansion of the upper levels of the city system, see Fig. 15.1). The South in 1880 was deep in the throes of recovery from the economic dislocations of the Civil War, and the urban pattern there was changing. Earlier the region had been structured to depend upon peripheral entrepôt towns such as Savannah, Mobile, and New Orleans, but now some inland centers— Atlanta and Memphis, in particular—were emerging as nationally significant urban places.

Meanwhile, the upper Middle West had developed a yeoman economy of mixed grains and livestock, the huge trade surpluses of which spawned a well-spaced network of large and medium-sized cities centered upon Chicago and reaching as far as St. Paul and Minneapolis. Beyond that, agricultural settlement, aided by the railroads, spread across the eastern Great Plains, giving new business to rising places like Kansas City and Omaha. By 1869, the year of the "golden spike," the iron rails linked up the old goldfield supply base of San Francisco with the nation's core, with such new nodes as Denver serving intermediate territory, including the mines of Colorado.

The Period 1880–1930. The pattern of expan-

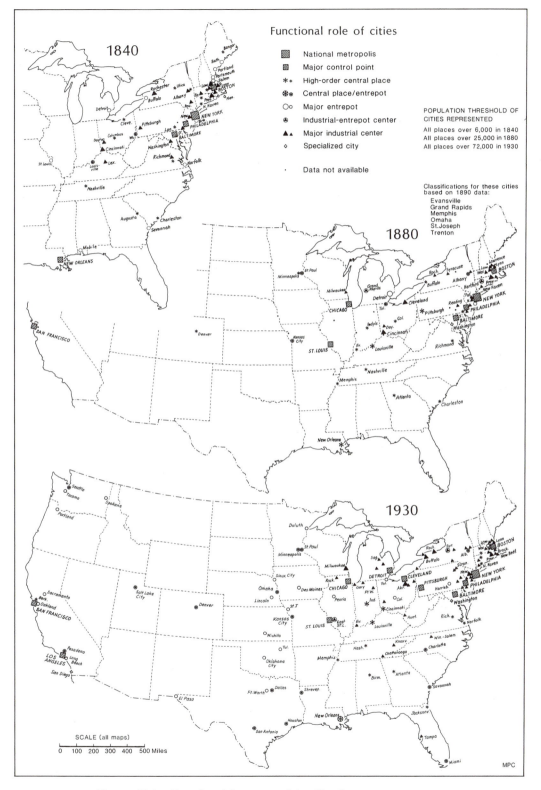

Figure 15.1   Functional Structure of the City-System, 1840–1930

sion to 1930 was to add to the upper levels of the national urban system practically all the remaining cities that today constitute the apex of the hierarchy (Fig. 15.1). In all, "urban places" expanded from 939 to 3,165, although the telling change occurred among towns in the 50,000–100,000 population range, of which there had been 15 in 1880 and 98 by the onset of the Depression.

Colonization of the Far West proceeded apace, although discontinuously, and belied the declaration of the Census Bureau in 1890 that the American frontier was closed. Settlements grew in the Northwest based on timber exploitation and agriculture, and in California through agricultural and, later, limited industrial development. In addition to San Francisco the major cities of Salt Lake City, Seattle, and Portland arose, and Los Angeles quadrupled in population from 319,000 to 1.2 million in the twenty years from 1910 to 1930. These centers developed truncated regional town networks around them, serving a dispersed population clustered in often isolated pockets of fertile, or not so fertile, settlement zones separated by vast distances (usually 400 miles or more) and rather extreme biophysical environments. These urban subsystems of the West varied considerably by the 1920s in historical development, resource base, and commercial articulation. Their archipelago-like network structure differed from the kinds of urban hierarchies evident in eastern zones of continuous settlement, and certain levels of local autonomy within the national system were much higher than elsewhere. As an example, manufacturing was often very balanced and diverse in the cities of the Far West, including Los Angeles, because the intense division of labor that was developing among Manufacturing Belt cities could not be upheld in the West, where alternative sources of supply that would give competition were so distant.

In the eastern third of the country much infilling of the urban pattern occurred throughout the South, now including Florida, and around the margins of the Appalachian Mountains. Less dramatic but equally significant was the rise of new and enlarged cities in the Northeast and Middle West as a result of processes of economic specialization. In between, there were similarly important developments in the Great Plains states, where agricultural settle-ment pushed the Wheat Belt up against the ranching territory of the high Plains, and stimulated urban development in a broad north-south band from Minnesota and the Dakotas to Texas.

A Case Study of Assigned Urban Systems. Railroads became the heart, and perhaps the soul, of town development on the western margins of continuous agricultural settlement. As they penetrated the Plains in the 1880s and 1890s, the railroads not only stimulated cattle shipments from the vast ranches of the region, but also provided the framework that enabled farmers to colonize the northern Plains and ranchers to move farther west. For their part, the railroads applied corporate lessons learned in more easterly settings (beginning with the Illinois Central Railroad in 1850) in matters of advertising, selling, and colonizing land, locating railroad lines and stations, and stimulating traffic and related commercial development. In effect the railroad companies coordinated the laying out not only of numerous townsites along their tracks, but the very network structure of the urban system that would serve the regions they plied. In South Dakota, for example, of the 278 towns founded by 1889, 140 were railroad-developed.

The spread of farming settlement west of the Missouri River in northern South Dakota was delayed by the opening of Indian reservations to white land purchase, but was spurred by the transcontinental ambitions of the Chicago, Milwaukee, St. Paul and Pacific Railway (the "Milwaukee Road"). By 1910, the railroad had constructed a careful dendritic network of lines west of Mobridge with well-spaced towns along them (Fig. 15.2a). What distinguished these new urban networks from those in the settled East was the fluidity of townsite locations and the railroads' tactics in determining them, as well as their ability to influence subsequent growth. On the Great Plains, the railroads were present at, or shortly after, the birth of most nucleated places, and often would bypass young townsites by a mile or two to establish their own "town" and control what urban development took place in that vicinity. In one stroke, the railroads could make or break new small towns, causing people and businesses to migrate to the rail connection, and eliminating the investments of precocious townsite speculators not in their "confidence." Furthermore,

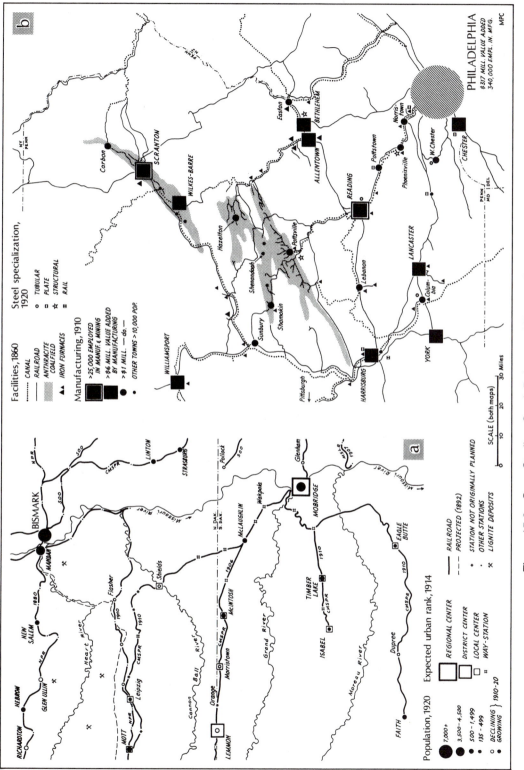

Figure 15.2 Case Studies: South Dakota and Eastern Pennsylvania

the railroads had clear ideas about the appropriate spacing of towns along the tracks and even tried to set the level in the urban hierarchy that each new town should attain. They could do this through actively seeking colonists in eastern cities, advertising widely to encourage the establishment of specific businesses in particular places, netting would-be local bankers, and controlling through exclusive contracts which major shipping and supply firms (often those headquartered in Minneapolis) would set up facilities—elevators, lumber yards, and the like—in each town along the railroad.

The Milwaukee Road's town-founding in the Mobridge district provides a case in point. As an inducement to western settlement, the company published an annual directory to the "New Towns and Business Opportunities Along the Lines of the Chicago, Milwaukee, and St. Paul Railway," which embraced all new stations from Iowa to the Pacific. The directory gave brief descriptions and current population figures for towns mentioned (generally inflated) and, more significantly, mentioned large numbers of individual types of business as either "well represented" or having desirable "openings" at each place. The pattern revealed in the referrals for the Mobridge district indicate a rough hierarchy of towns in the minds of the corporate compilers, composed of regional centers, district centers, local centers, and waystations. Wakpala, for example, regarded as a typical waystation in 1914, was advertised as needing a drugstore, a blacksmith, and a dentist. Higher on the prospective urban scale, Lemmon was declared in need of an implement house, brickyard, flour mill, hospital, foundry, and machine shop. At the top of this regional town system, Mobridge was considered well endowed with varied retail businesses and services in 1914, but the railroad saw fit to tout the need for a 150-room hotel and for wholesalers (in a community of approximately 2,000 souls).

The urban networks of the Plains were largely creatures of corporate strategy as the railroads became experienced "central place" planners in the West. It is ironic that these early 20th-century town systems, although strongly adjusted to a finely tuned collection and distribution machine—the railroad network—proved highly sensitive to external conditions.

With the spread of the automobile and the rise of direct mail-order houses with free rural postal delivery, business and shopping patterns changed at the expense of the small-town merchant, and many trade centers declined or even withered away after the World War I. This was somewhat of a national pattern, but its effects were especially felt in areas of monoculture and extensive agriculture such as the Great Plains.

Differentiation: Increasing Complementarity

The expansion of the urban network was accompanied by, and indeed made possible largely through, changes in the spatial distribution of urban functions among cities in the national system, aided by improvements in transportation, marketing, and manufactures. In earlier times the urban network could consist of a wide array of small central places tied to a few major seaboard entrepôts which shared the coast with small ports and fishing towns. By the mid-19th century, this "Atlantic" pattern changed to accommodate the tide of continental expansion and industrialization.

Commercial penetration of the interior required chains of *wholesaling centers* to concentrate and forward agricultural surpluses and other resources to the dense markets on the East Coast. These new zones of exploitation attracted settlers who stimulated the development of local *central places* to provide administrative and retail services in the new areas. Such growth encouraged the concentration of high-order control functions—banking, investments, transport, export-import trade—in a few of the large cities, increasing their size and making them *major control points*. Industrial capacity emerged to substitute for manufactured imports; while it flowered in districts of ready energy and raw materials, it accrued increasingly to the eastern mercantile centers, reinforcing their dominant positions in the national urban system. With the dispersal of the national market, manufacturing emerged in smaller and more concentrated *industrial centers* that could provide locational advantages with respect to one or more factors of production and distribution. Finally, other functions could develop so singularly as to create *specialized cities*, such as seats of government. All these major functions—wholesaling, retailing, financial and legal services, transportation, industry, government, and social services—were likely present to some degree in most large and medium-sized cities across the country, but their proportions varied so widely as to create distinctly different "urban roles" that formed marked and changing spatial patterns over time. The logic of this pattern and process becomes somewhat clearer when viewed in terms of complementarity at the national scale.

In 1840 the spatial differentiation of the city system was well under way. Still an Atlantic-oriented system, the major control centers continued to be the early established "gateway" cities—New York (by then the undisputed economic capital), Philadelphia, Boston, and Baltimore—which benefited from immediate, fertile, mixed-farming, and industrious hinterlands with access to the continental interior (Fig. 15.1). More stunted gateways to the planter South included, first and most important, New Orleans, but also Mobile, Savannah, Charleston, and Norfolk. The penetration of the continental interior by chains of wholesaling towns—the "spearheads of the frontier"—from New York to Albany, Buffalo, and Detroit; or Philadelphia to Pittsburgh, Cincinnati, and St. Louis—was what helped northeastern ports perpetuate their trading primacy. In the immediate hinterlands around these large Atlantic ports many towns had grown into major regional service centers, creating local "central place" networks that filled in the territory between the great entrepôts. Also, numerous towns were emerging as small industrial centers. In the west, this pattern was being replicated, although St. Louis and Detroit acted very much as large outposts of the commercial system. New Orleans's occupational profile was clearly that of a large wholesaling center (64 percent of all occupations were in commerce and navigation, compared with 44 percent for St. Louis), but its position controlling the Mississippi trade outflow was so central to the development of the national urban system as to warrant being considered a major control point up to the Civil War.

In the following forty years, the rivers, canals, and then railroads of the upper Mississippi and Great Lakes region articulated a transport system that initially balanced the trade outlets south to New Orleans and east to New York, making St. Louis a national control point after 1850. But the increasing attraction of shipping via the Great Lakes route and the availability of direct rail linkage to the East, together with the blockages created by the Civil War, tipped the Middle West's commerce substantially eastward and subordinated St. Louis's growth to that of Chicago, so that in a mere thirty years Chicago developed into a major national control point (Fig. 15.1). New Orleans never recovered from this fundamental reorientation of long-distance trade, and slipped to the more modest level of a "high-order," or regional-level, central place. Southern towns that grew large did so on the basis of predominantly central-place functions, such as Atlanta or Memphis, a regionally homogeneous trend that reached as far north as Evansville and Indianapolis in Indiana.

The progress of the "mercantile" urban frontier was heralded by the emergence of a distinct wholesale alignment running south from St. Paul through Omaha and St. Joseph to Kansas City, representing a new chain of "gateways" to the prairie Wheat Belt. Farther west, San Francisco surpassed 230,000 inhabitants by 1880; what New Orleans had been to the Mississippi basin before the Civil War, San Francisco became for the entire Pacific coast region—a great entrepôt and regional capital.

Within the nation's expanded "core" region—now including the Great Lakes margin—the press of industrialization affected many old market towns well placed within the market-rich zone. Worcester, Lawrence, New Haven, Syracuse, Scranton, and Reading, among others, grew through greatly increased concentration on industrial pursuits. At the same time, the spread of commerce in the Middle West created larger markets for industrial products that combined with nearby resources and capital to foster a diversified pattern of industrial growth that benefited both small towns and large cities. Erstwhile mercantile centers, such as Milwaukee and Cleveland, underwent heavy industrialization. Poised at the neck of this emerging "hourglass" manufacturing belt was Pittsburgh, industrializing strongly but gaining even more rapidly the diversified employment of a large regional metropolis (in 1880 the city had 21,204 people employed in mineral industries and manufacturing and 21,358 in the service sector). More specialized yet, of course, was Washington, D.C., with a population of

178,000 (1880), in which almost two-thirds of those employed worked in service occupations.

Between 1880 and 1930, the complementarity of urban roles during this half century of strong general urbanization came to be very clearly regionalized, while wholesaling and industry gained ascendancy over purely central-place functions. At the apex of the system, major new national control points emerged on the West Coast and in the heart of the Manufacturing Belt. Los Angeles profited from its climate, scenery, movie industry, and proximity to oil to claim economic control of southern California. Pittsburgh broke into the ranks of the nation's largest business centers, soon followed by Detroit and Cleveland—evidence of the power of the steel and automobile industries to concentrate allied corporate activities. Notwithstanding these shifts, including Chicago's success in becoming the nation's second city, the ability of the four old eastern ports to remain at the top of the urban hierarchy underscores their continued entrepreneurial dynamism and the geographical inertia it represents.

The most striking development of all was the rise in importance and diffusion of commercial functions among American cities by 1930. A thick belt of wholesaling towns along the eastern margin of the Great Plains enlarged upon the base evident in 1880 and stretched from Duluth to San Antonio, while the remainder of the West was crisscrossed with mercantile chains (Fig. 15.1). Furthermore, new wholesaling chains were emerging in the highly developed East along new axes, involving smaller-sized cities that represented "bypass" routes through the industrial heartland. The clearest of these axes included Jersey City, Harrisburg, (Pittsburgh), Columbus, and East St. Louis.

The high-order central place was more widespread. Many of the large cities that embraced rather specialized wholesale or industrial functions also acted as regional metropolises offering superior retail, professional, and other services for their surrounding regions. As these functions historically could disperse over broad territories according to hierarchical principles of supply, many of America's regional central places in this period were not large enough to appear in the scheme presented here. The upper portions of the service hierarchy, however, may be seen in 1930 in such cases as Cincinnati, Indianapolis, Louisville, Nashville, and Mem-

phis, as well as in more mixed cases such as Minneapolis–St. Paul, Kansas City, Houston, Denver, Salt Lake City, and Seattle. The South, in fact, experienced an urban renaissance during this period with the rise of a number of regional centers such as Birmingham, Jacksonville, and Miami, based largely upon diversified service functions.

National industrial capacity between 1880 and 1930 became overwhelmingly urban in location, with many enterprises failing in small towns and rural areas, as economies of scale and agglomeration concentrated production. This aided the established industrial towns, but it also helped medium-sized centers rise in the ranks of the national system. Examples include Waterbury, Schenectady, Erie, Youngstown, Lansing, South Bend, and Rockford. In addition, a new form of industrialization based on cheaper, nonunionized labor and greater proximity to raw materials was causing various industries to concentrate in the border South, favoring such towns as Knoxville, Chattanooga, and Winston-Salem.

A Case Study of Maturing Industrialism. The effect that industrialization had on urban systems in long-settled regions is well illustrated in eastern Pennsylvania. The rich farmland between the Delaware and the front range of the Allegheny Mountains had matured as the Philadelphia hinterland during the colonial and early 19th-century periods. This territory was dotted with comfortable county towns such as Easton, Reading, Lancaster, and York, with smaller service centers and numerous hamlets filling out the settlement hierarchy, copiously linked by turnpikes and, as early as 1840, by four railroad lines radiating from Philadelphia. The remoter country behind the front range, long settled by mid-century, had also developed a dense pattern of small towns serving local needs, likewise bound to Philadelphia by rapidly expanding rail and canal networks snaking along the deeply etched valleys and basins of the middle Susquehanna and Lehigh rivers. This pattern was already set before the Civil War; comparatively few railroads and no canals were added later (Fig. 15.2b). As in New England and New York State, capital from mercantile pursuits began to be attracted into the development of local manufactures, which diversified in type and dispersed in locational pattern. By 1850, Philadelphia itself was well launched upon an industrial path, combining port functions with light and heavy industry of all types, and supported in no small measure by the proximity of rich deposits of anthracite coal and iron ore in the hills to the north. The iron industry grew in the hinterland, and its products fed newly industrializing towns such as Lancaster, which rose from 12,000 to 20,000 people between 1850 and 1870, largely on the strength of the 278 manufacturing firms the city had acquired in the interval.

The industrialization of the region in the later 19th century depended not on transport innovation, but rather on the agglomerating effects of proximity to raw materials and final markets. From 1860 to 1910, the region industrialized through coal and steel production supplying a national market. Numerous mining towns sprang up, sprawling across mountainsides or tucked into narrow valleys. The largest—Scranton, Wilkes-Barre, Hazleton, Pottsville, and Shamokin—grew larger than their neighbors mainly because of the additional manufacturing they attracted, enterprises that came to the coal and thus saved the expense of haulage. Other towns concentrated on mining, and places like Shenandoah and Mount Carmel developed one-sided industrial profiles that oscillated widely with the fortunes of the Pennsylvania anthracite industry.

The ready availability of coal and limestone encouraged steel production near the mines, and over time the trend toward larger and more integrated facilities encouraged the growth of a few urban places within the region (Pottsville, Scranton, and Harrisburg, in particular), as well as towns with better access to Philadelphia and ocean outlets (Reading, South Bethlehem, Allentown, Columbia, Pottstown, Phoenixville, and Norristown). Tied to this heavy base of coal and steel came "next-stage, resource-using" industries such as foundry products and machinery, textile factories run on steam power, and construction materials (wire, nails, and the like). Here, location within the general region was sufficient to reap economies of agglomeration and scale, and of equal importance were factors such as transport, labor, and facility siting. Many industries of this type supported the growth of the largest cities in the area and of medium-sized towns like Williamsport, Sunbury, York, Lebanon, and West Chester.

The hierarchy of industrial production eventually gave substantial shape to the hierarchy of urban places by century's end, which had not been true in 1860. Presiding over the region's transformation, and molding much of the early decision-making through capital flows, the merchants and manufacturers of Philadelphia ensured that the port city remain the region's dominant economic focus. By 1910, the metropolis had 1.5 million inhabitants and contributed 70 percent ($317 million) of the value-added by manufacture in eastern Pennsylvania. Highly diversified though Philadelphia's manufacturing was, its leading industrial sectors were represented by woolen goods, iron and steel, and foundry and machinery products (for example, the famous Baldwin Locomotive Works). Far behind Philadelphia in industrial might was Reading in second place, with $21.3 million value-added, based largely on iron and steel, hosiery and knit goods, and foundry and machine goods. Reading had not yet surpassed 100,000 population in 1910, yet its well-rounded industrial base pushed it ahead of Scranton which, with a population of 129,000, was second in overall population size to Philadelphia. While Scranton had attracted much industrial capacity, especially in silk goods, liquors, and machinery products, the manufacturing mix added less overall value, and the city's size owed as much to coal as to manufacturing.

These patterns of industrial urbanization are not typical of all parts of the developing Manufacturing Belt, but do represent some key geographical circumstances. In this regional example the basic occupation of territory had been accomplished long before industrial growth became the dominant engine driving urban development. Thus, a town network was already in place and transport networks largely established. What industrialism brought was a resifting of the urban hierarchy for those locations that would yield the best combination of least costs for the factors of production in a variety of industries. Eastern Pennsylvania possessed superior natural resources close to the most highly developed rural and urban markets and industrialized massively late in the second half of 19th century. This benefited Philadelphia greatly and brought the whole region to a level of urban expansion and specialization similar to that achieved in New England and in upstate New York.

Summary. The increasing differentiation in economic roles among the cities of the national system during the period was not accidental. It reflected a reasonably efficient spatial division of labor, considering that the country they served stretched across 3,500 miles of longitude and 1,800 miles of latitude and by 1930 harbored a population of 122.7 million, of whom 68.9 million lived in these urban environments. The Northeast contained the oldest metropolises that served a dense regional population, that many of whose towns had industrialized on the basis of initial advantage and cumulative economies of scale. This urban-industrial "core" spread to the Middle West because it contained rich farmlands, minerals, high accessibility, and a dense population. The long-settled South remained less industrialized, but cities there prospered on central-place functions. A band of medium-sized cities arose as classic "gateways" at the margins of the Great Plains, while the mountain and far west regions developed networks of long-distance entrepôts, of which the larger ones provided regional capital functions as well.

Integration:
Intercity Links and Urban Hinterlands

The expansion and differentiation of the urban system could not have progressed so far in the ninety years from 1840 to 1930 without parallel developments in the technology and management of communications that would keep the individual settlements in the far-flung system interacting, because division of labor assumes interdependence. Urban interdependence grew as new ways were devised to conquer distance. Sheer physical communication improved dramatically during this period through sequential connection by river, turnpike, canal, railroad, automobile, and air and through revolutions in electronic transmission of information. The effect of these changes was to redefine distance in terms of reduced cost and time, thus bringing urban places economically and psychologically closer together. Geographically, however, these improvements were severely biased in favor of some city and regional links rather than others, and even with the ultimate diffusion of some communication innovations throughout the city system, patterns

of use were not uniform. The reasons lay not just in the variable routes used to reach resources and markets, but also in the distinction between urban functions that controlled the physical movement of people and goods (*transport control*) as distinct from functions that controlled the terms of exchange (*exchange control*). The former could be shared among many nodal centers in the extended chains of communication; the latter required fewer hubs because of the greater scale economies realized, given information transfer that could eliminate intermediate processing points.

It is axiomatic that these improvements in exchange and movement tended to occur earliest between already favored places—favored, that is, with superior information and market potential—and that such initial advantage produced urban integration on terms favorable to established centers. The system expanded on such a scale, nevertheless, that new urban competitors with locational advantages could arise (and did, especially in the Middle and Far Wests), and territorial competition for hinterland trade and manufacturing capacity led to new forms of interdependence and spatial orderliness.

Within this matrix, various levels of autonomy existed as young settlements matured. In a city system context, partial autonomy means the degree of control a center could exercise in effecting changes in the system that rebounded to its benefit. From this perspective the most successful city throughout the period was New York, which managed to coordinate so much of the nation's trade as to remain the country's economic capital. While it became eccentric to the westward gravitational shift of the domestic market (a shift that heavily favored Chicago after the Civil War), New York's entrepôt position facing the vital trans-Atlantic markets in Europe assured its national mercantile dominance in the control of exchange, even after it had yielded much of its earlier control over physical movement. Other cities enjoyed much smaller measures of autonomy based on their regional location and "bridge" positions within the system.

An overview of national urban integration during the period can be gained from two sources. Neither is ideal, since no single index captures the complexity of the process, and systematic empirical evidence is hard to find on this topic. Nevertheless, the skeletal pattern of advancing urban interdependence with respect to the control of movement within the system can be glimpsed from the sequence by which cities that were engaged in long-distance commerce surpassed various thresholds of employment in transport and communications (Fig. 15.3a). Not all such employment represented long-distance transport functions, to be sure, but large absolute numbers in these occupations did isolate places with coastal or inland entrepôt activities. Clearly, there is an expectable association with the interregional expansion of the city system as a whole, particularly in the West. But many towns and cities in the Northeast, Middle West, and South gained significance only in later periods as transport nodes of major proportions, particularly those cases where other functions such as manufacturing or retail servicing provided the main impetus to growth.

A view of the more discriminating patterns of the control of exchange can be gleaned from banking relations among large cities and between them and their trade hinterlands between 1880 and 1910. The "correspondent" system then used by America's individual banks to create a smoothly flowing financial exchange network allows a reconstruction of its evolving geographical structure. Since early in the 19th century, the large eastern seaports had been active in developing financial ties with the interior, with New York in the lead. By 1880 a well-articulated pattern of high-level banking interdependency existed in which New York had strong reciprocal banking relations with Boston and Chicago and dominant influence over all other cities among the top 24 banking centers in the country (Fig. 15.3b). Chicago appeared the next most integrated center on the basis of mutual banking exchange with New York, Boston, and Philadelphia, and links with twenty out of this group of cities. High-level integration was far less developed at the next lower stage, for Philadelphia and St. Louis could each boast major correspondent links with only three other places.

Thirty years later, however, banking integration had evolved considerably. The major lines of connectivity in this same set of cities had not changed substantially, but the pattern of cross-linkages based on regional groupings and hierarchial relations had intensified markedly. Boston, Philadelphia, and St. Louis had been particularly successful in winning additional channels of interaction from both larger and smaller centers. In the Northeast, small banking centers branched out with strong direct ties to cities other than just New York and Chicago, and all three west coast metropolises broadened their direct banking connections within the system.

The new spatial order showed also in the patterns of hinterland organization that emerged around large cities, and the "nesting" of hinterlands that resulted from hierarchical or nonhierarchical relationships among places. Eastern cities had long contended with their close-in neighbors for the limited backcountry each could claim as its own; their mercantile interests were active throughout the 19th century in reaching out to the west for additional "tributary" territory, even if it had to be shared. In banking, antebellum New York had enjoyed virtual monopoly throughout the country regardless of distance or the remoteness of small-town banks. As late as 1876, New York banks had ties to 96 percent of all banks, but other centers began to give it competition in the 1880s. By 1910, patterns of territorial "partition" among the major centers were anything but regular (Fig. 15.3b), reflecting in part the inability of New York's correspondent network, with links to only 64 percent of all banks, to keep pace with bank proliferation nationwide. Except for Boston and Philadelphia, New York controlled much of the East outright, including all the Old South, keeping banking centers such as Cincinnati and Pittsburgh in very subordinate roles. Chicago, however, had "organized" practically the whole West except for a slender region of influence oriented to St. Louis. These patterns suggest the major strides made, particularly in the later 19th century, in forging the business integration of the urban system.

Implications

Several inferences can be drawn from an urban network view of American cities during the period from 1860 to 1930. The constant expansion of the system meant that economic opportunity was always present, even if it meant

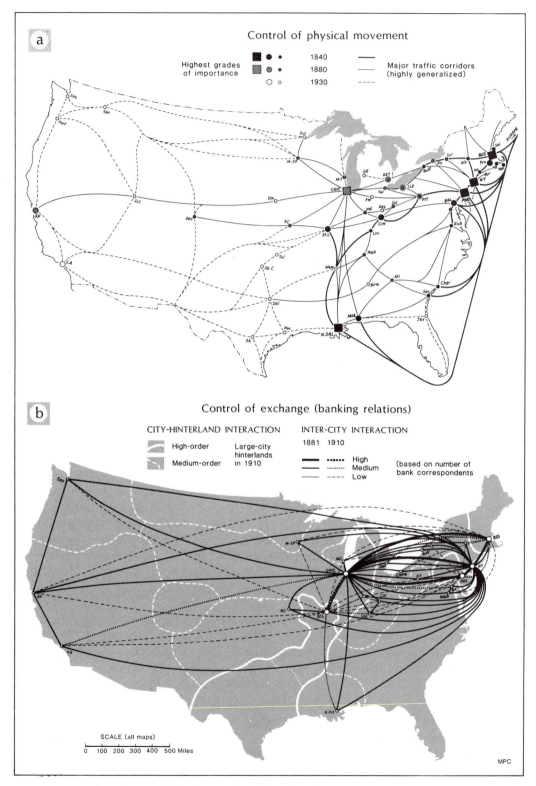

Figure 15.3   Integration of the City-System, 1840–1930

migration elsewhere and trying one's luck in a new place. The founding of new communities offered exceptional opportunities to those able to apply entrepreneurial or craft skills in fluid situations. Thus, social mobility often meant geographic mobility and the urban network became a complex stage on which to test this principle. Western cities were generally newer, less formed, and more open to new entrants. Specialization among cities meant new sources of growth and wealth, and this was not confined spatially. The mobility of capital ensured that geography could be put to work to concentrate resources at optimum locations for various purposes. In general, smaller towns had fewer economic functions and a narrower range of occupational classes, but such distinctions varied by region. Indeed, the regional differences in the timing and means of urbanization during this period were so distinct that one can only emphasize how greatly they matter in approaching questions about the general nature of urban change, both between and within cities.

EVOLVING CITY PATTERNS

The evolving functional role of a particular city in the urban system during the later 19th century strongly influenced the changing numbers of people, types of jobs, and nature of buildings and other facilities that concentrated at that location. Changes in the needs and opportunities of the expanding urban system, and each city's response to them, largely regulated the amount, periodicity, and kind of new investments, particularly whether established patterns would be simply extended or radically changed. Such changes translated into social and physical requirements that put variable pressure on the existing spatial structure and physical construction of the city. Because built forms are in themselves inert, the city's shifting needs led unceasingly to selective alteration of the built environment to keep up with new preferences. Yet while the city's morphology was changing, it was doing more than just passively catching up. The existing layout of landholdings, streets, and buildings powerfully influenced—and often controlled—the framework within which decisions about ac-commodating new buildings and land use were taken.

The Dynamics of Physical Expansion

America's large cities faced immense problems in accommodating their exploding populations between the Civil War and the 1920s. They grew by extending the boundaries of their built-up areas far into the countryside and by increasing the density of the building stock within these areas, notably in and near the urban core. Citywide densities varied greatly among cities: in 1880 New York averaged 46 people per acre, whereas Philadelphia then had a density of 10 (figures for other major cities were Chicago 22, Boston 15, St. Louis 9, Baltimore 39, Cincinnati 16, and San Francisco 9 people per acre).

Chicago provides a good example of the changing connection between people, land, and buildings during the period. Chicago in 1890 contained a population of 1,112,575 within a city composed of an estimated 171,000 buildings distributed over 53,117 acres of subdivided land. It is notable that in the thirty years before 1890 population rose at a steeper rate than subdivision activity and overall building construction (Table 15.2). Building lots and housing had been in such supply that the ratio of people to land and buildings was very favorable through the 1880s. After 1890, subdividing slowed down relative to population and building construction because of the large surfeit of house-lots. For example, the 3,827 single houses built in 1912 were exceeded by the 4,341 apartment buildings constructed that year, a trend sustained well into World War I. The high proportion of new buildings to new lots reflected the prior spatial dispersion of urban platting in the 19th century, the decline in the total number of new lots coming on the market, and the pressure—for locational reasons—to occupy available lots within the existing city area.

Urban growth through the outward extension of cities involved several processes. Landowners in the path of expansion responded sooner or later to increasing market prices and converted their land to urban, generally residential, use by subdividing it into streets, blocks, and lots for individual sale. Characteristically, American urban land development in

Table 15.2   Indices of Chicago's Physical Growth, 1860–1930

Period	Population index	Subdivision index (1890 = 100)	Construc- tion index	Population per subdivided acre	Population per building	Number of new buildings per newly subdivided acre[a]
Before 1860	11	27	24	8.2	2.9	2.9
1860–1870	28	45	57	12.9	3.2	5.8
1870–1880	50	75	75	13.9	4.3	1.9
1880–1890	100	100	100	20.9	6.5	3.3
1890–1900	153	119	149	26.8	6.7	8.1
1900–1910	196	125	195	32.8	6.6	24.8
1910–1920	243	144	247	35.4	6.4	9.1
1920–1930	303	158	314	40.2	6.3	14.8

[a]Last column applies to buildings erected during the indicated time period. All other columns apply to end date in each period.

the mid-19th century largely separated the functions of selling house-lots and actually building houses. Numerous entrepreneurs did build up whole streets at a time, but the scale of physical land planning was small, and in most cases new lot owners were expected to find their own means to erect their residences. Rectilinear street grids were near-universal, lot densities varied widely in close proximity, street systems did not always coordinate, and no inevitable logic applied to the sequence and timing by which the old land parcels of an area would be developed. As a result, many urban extensions were rigid in their microgeometry but haphazard in their gross patterns within the cityscape, although the extreme effects could be mitigated by either the informality of individually designed houses or the coherence of uniform buildings, particularly rowhouses. By the turn of the century some changes were afoot, notably the growing popularity of curvilinear street layouts for better-class subdivisions, the rise of many integrated realtor-builder firms, and the advent of city planning, which introduced some rules concerning urban design.

Urban extension took many residents farther from their places of employment, and the growth of residential districts away from the urban core would have been inconceivable without new transport facilities. The advent of mass transit in the mid-19th century signaled the end of the completely "walking" city. Transport extension spanned several eras of

technological innovation, from the horse-drawn omnibus introduced in New York in 1827, to the short-haul steam train, the horse-car and, by the late 1880s, the cablecar and electric streetcar. Each improvement saved time for the commuter and allowed ever more remote neighborhoods to enter the commuting field, while increased carrying capacity created operating efficiencies that resulted in lower travel costs as a proportion of income. This sequence of changes in intraurban travel permitted not only a greatly accelerated spatial expansion of the city, but also the enhanced use of space as a means of separating formerly mixed urban activities of all kinds.

The role of streetcars in urban extension has been well explored in Boston (Fig. 15.4). Boston in the late 19th century illustrated some of the more extreme problems of urban modernization that beset mature, densely built-up east coast cities. For long constrained by a peninsular site, Boston spilled over the surrounding tidal flats, and by the 1880s development was rapidly absorbing the territory of recently annexed Roxbury. Between 1870 and 1900 the countryside character of much of Roxbury and the neighboring Dorchester district was transformed by the building up of what have been referred to as "streetcar suburbs." The streetcar helped create residential districts of great physical variety, constructed mostly by small builders and businessmen, that offered a range of housing types and physical settings, all representative for their price levels of the new subur-

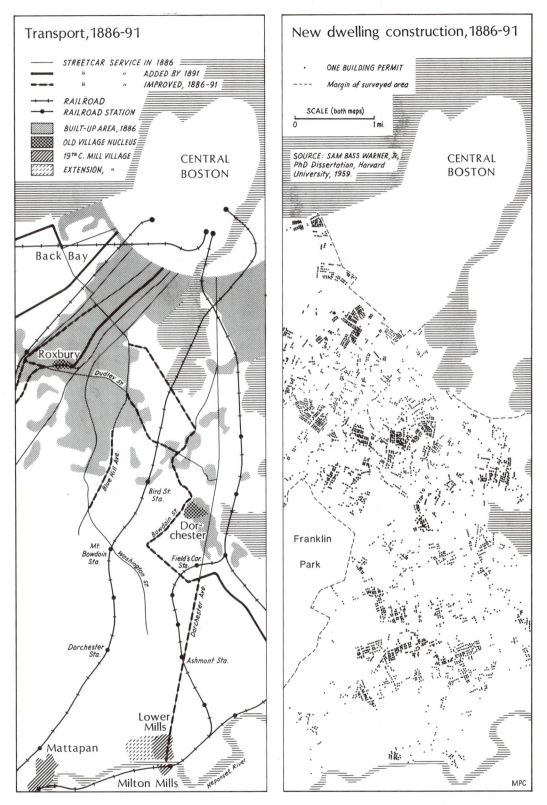

Transport, 1886-91

STREETCAR SERVICE IN 1886
" " " ADDED BY 1891
" " " IMPROVED, 1886-91
RAILROAD
RAILROAD STATION
BUILT-UP AREA, 1886
OLD VILLAGE NUCLEUS
19TH C. MILL VILLAGE
EXTENSION, "

CENTRAL BOSTON

Back Bay

Roxbury

Dudley St.

Blue Hill Ave.

Bird St. Sta.

Bowdoin St.

Dor-chester

Mt. Bowdoin Sta.

Washington St.

Field's Cor. Sta.

Dorchester Ave.

Dorchester Sta.

Ashmont Sta.

Lower Mills

Mattapan

Milton Mills

Neponset River

New dwelling construction, 1886-91

ONE BUILDING PERMIT
Margin of surveyed area

SCALE (both maps)
0   1 mi.

SOURCE: SAM BASS WARNER, JR., PhD Dissertation, Harvard University, 1959.

CENTRAL BOSTON

Franklin

Park

MPC

Figure 15.4   The Urban Extension of Boston, 1886–1891

ban ideal for superior living. On tree-shaded streets on sloping sites, new Queen Anne frame houses shared the quietude with late Italianate, Gothic Revival, or Richardsonian Romanesque detached homes, often of brick or stone. There were also Boston "bowfronts," reproduced from the South End or Beacon Hill, and street after street of clapboard triple-deckers—a three-story, three-unit housetype that was a marvelous stepladder to immigrant residential success.

Streetcars were not the only influence in the growth of these districts. The "suburban" movement was played out upon a landscape of colonial origin, fitting into a fairly dense network of existing roads connecting old village centers via established crossroads settlements, each road being more-or-less lined with former farmhouses, exurban residences, hotels, and taverns. To this settlement matrix was added, first, the steam railroad which, in connecting the old village nodes with Boston, also contributed small knots of villas and occasional businesses in the vicinity of the railroad depots (Fig. 15.4, left). These developments began at about three miles from downtown Boston, and by the 1880s a railroad-based suburban culture and landscape were well established.

As the infilling of the residential territory proceeded in Roxbury and Dorchester, the streetcar at first supplemented and only slowly superceded the train as the major means of journeying to work in central Boston. From a previously unpublished map by Sam Bass Warner, Jr., it is clear that the detailed locational pattern of new home construction in the area between 1886 and 1891 bore only a partial relation to either the extension, or increased frequency, of streetcar service (Fig. 15.4, right). The Washington Street line had been running since at least 1872, and the housing development along its southerly reaches had been modest to 1891. While the energetic housing construction in the Ashmont Station vicinity was well able to benefit from the upgraded service of the Dorchester Avenue line (from half-hourly to quarter-hourly), such development and that to the west of it capitalized on the proximity of the railroad depots nearby. Most striking was the geographical distribution of new construction as a whole in relation to the substantially built-up zone as it was in 1886 (Fig. 15.4, left). New buildings were going up

in as much profusion within this zone as they were in the far suburban reaches approaching the Lower Mills area. In no way can this be described as a "wave" phenomenon. In this respect, Boston does reflect general American processes of urban land development of the period, for the element of urban anticipation ensured that development would be scattered and thus, in an established region like Boston's, the streetcars responded to development as much as stimulated it. In the Los Angeles region, across the continent and in a slightly later period, the stimulative role of the streetcar, as Warner has noted, was far more the dominant one.

House-lots and streetcars were not the only prerequisites to urban extension. Utilities such as piped water, sewage drains, domestic gas and electric service, street lighting and paving were all developed in time to be included on any list of necessary or desirable accoutrements of urban—and suburban—living. Major expenditures were required to supply most utilities to individual households because they involved installing extensive networks of pipes or cable above and below ground throughout the urban area. Patterns of wavelike service extension gradually moved outward from the business district, with master facilities sweeping along the major arterial streets to areas where the highest development densities would justify early connection. The issue of urban utilities often underlay the other concomitant process of urban extension—change in governmental jurisdiction. Spectacular physical expansion of urban areas became commonplace in America only after mid-century, and extension of cities' governmental authority followed almost naturally in the wake of significant numbers of urban workers' pioneering residence in the suburbs. By 1869, sufficient sentiment existed in Roxbury and Dorchester to win a vote for annexation to Boston. There was opposition from traditional quarters in these towns, but the central city was perceived as a great provider of modern urban services and an an appropriate governmental form for the changing character of these formerly fringe towns.

Emerging Land Use Stratification

The term *metropolis* came into increasing favor during the middle of the 19th century to describe America's largest cities as a singular type of phenomenon, and it had gained common currency by the 1920s. This shift in nomenclature denoted both an altered size and scale to the city as well as a greater social and physical complexity. Geographically, it was expressed in the spatial separation of economic and social activities that had formerly coexisted in the same buildings and on the same streets. Although New York, Boston, and Philadelphia had some specialized land-use districts even in the late colonial period, the degree of functional separation, and indeed segregation, of activities in urban space was to emerge quite clearly after the 1850s and become an immediate feature of newer cities.

The most striking developments were the rise of the central business district (CBD) as a highly specialized land use zone within the city; the gradual separation of industrial activity from the business core and its decentralization to industrial corridors and fringe belt zones that excluded most other land uses; the filtering of social and economic classes throughout the residential territory of the city so that particular districts and neighborhoods became socially, ethnically, and occupationally homogeneous; and the emergence of a hierarchically arranged network of subsidiary business centers in step with urban expansion. American cities before 1850 without doubt contained people and activities that varied in their concentration from one part to another, but urban size and changing social and economic forces combined after that date to reformulate spatially the large American city into clearly recognizable and often sharply bounded functional areas by the outbreak of World War I. Growing size and complexity encouraged a certain degree of spatial order for reasons of efficiency.

The business core of most large cities in the 1850s contained a great mixture of wholesale and retail traders, financiers, professionals, craftsmen and industrial concerns, haulers and handlers, messengers and cabbies, some government offices, and a motley array of residences of various types, all competing for decent locations within what was already a very high rent district. Between 1860 and 1920 the power of capital operated to sort out the winners and losers in this "bidding" contest: the economic growth of the metropolis demanded constant enlargement of the business district in terms of employment and space needs and

pumped in the financial resources continuously to update and modernize the physical fabric of the business district. With each new business building, a nudge was given to land uses no longer in need of, or capable of retaining, central locations. With time, business not only came to dominate the downtown, to the virtual exclusion of residential functions, but it also modernized its own pattern to the extent of evolving distinct subdistricts within the CBD in which types of business concentrated heavily together for the convenience of interaction and efficient supply. By the end of the period most major cities had separate downtown sectors for produce markets, wholesaling, retail shopping, finance, and government administration.

In the era of the walking city, the business core catered to practically the whole urban population; but as urban expansion progressed many retail functions were replicated in newly developing neighborhoods at some distance from the center. Bakers, butchers, boot and shoe dealers, dry goods merchants, and the like spread across the city, clustering along major arteries and at key traffic nodes, to form subsidiary business centers. Over time, specialized retailers such as book and furniture stores, men's clothiers, and jewelers proliferated in the more important of these, representing a diffusion of more and more specialized retail services from the CBD down the hierarchy of shopping districts. As small operators were replaced in the CBD by large concerns, including after 1870 the new department stores and luxury goods merchants who sought trade among the commuters and hotel visitors, a great resorting of retail trade occurred whereby mundane and middle-level functions were increasingly offered by non-central shopping districts at strategic locations within the expanded city.

Industry likewise began in the urban core in craft workshops located near commercial facilities such as waterpower sites, harbors, railroad stations, and other businesses. As the urban core became congested, land values rose, and many industrial processes became mechanized and larger-scale, a dualism developed in industrial location patterns within large cities. Those industries that needed access to water or rail transport, such as the building trades or machinery production, or depended on the business of the CBD, such as job printing or garment making, tended to stay within or near the margins of the business core. As that core expanded, such industry moved again but stayed within range of the downtown market. The development of Printer's Row at the south end of Chicago's Loop in the 1880s illustrates this pattern. Other manufacturing that needed larger and cheaper space more than proximity to clients moved farther away, such as the Union Stockyards. By the 1890s, railroad companies and land developers were creating specialized areas like the Central Manufacturing District in Chicago at some distance from the city center with integrated transport and power facilities and convenient labor pools in the ethnic neighborhoods that quickly grew up around them.

In some cases these industrial belts encircled the city's growth rings of previous periods; in others they simply colonized the major waterway sites and railroad axes. Detroit's pattern was established early by the riverfront manufacturing belt and extended around the old city by belt railroads as the automotive and allied industries became established (Fig. 15.5a).

Social Processes and Residential Consequences

The social space of the mid-century walking city was comparatively heterogeneous. People of greatly differing income and social status often lived side by side in residential districts. Well-to-do neighborhoods, such as Society Hill in Philadelphia and Beacon Hill in Boston, were in close proximity to the bustling urban core, remnants of a passing era when the wealthy lived at the heart of the urban scene. Such areas were also close to districts of very different character, such as the backside of Beacon Hill in Boston where a small community of blacks lived, or the North End with its artisans, shopkeepers, and longshoremen.

Immigrants arriving to live in eastern port cities after mid-century had little choice but to occupy cramped, run-down housing close to the work opportunities in and around the business core or wherever temporary jobs and squatting possibilities existed. In general, they formed a human wedge between the expanding commercial building stock and the traditional residents, who withdrew to better housing away from the CBD. This removal of the established social classes had begun earlier with the mounting commercial congestion of the inner city, the pioneering of more spacious residences at the edge of the city, and the appearance of public transport on major streets, but it unquestionably gained momentum with accelerated immigration.

Unprecedented urban growth created much new housing, which increasingly acclimatized people to change residential ownership more frequently and thus to quicken the pace of residential "filtering." By this process the well-off gained the latest in housing styles, generally at the urban fringe, the middle classes took over the vacated homes of the former, and the working classes moved into houses disposed of by their former middle-class owners. Urban growth was generally so strong, however, that filtering needs to be seen in context: the supply of homes at particular prices rarely satisfied demand, so filtering was only a small part of the overall process by which housing was provided, new areas built up, and the city's social geography defined.

The social structure of American cities in the later 19th century grew at the extremes with consequences for residential patterns. Status differentials, whether denoted by occupation, income, or other measures, continued to rise as the propertied classes benefited from industrialization and general business growth and gained in wealth and numbers. This wealth was used to find residential seclusion from the "teeming masses," employing space to maintain social distinctions on a scale rarely seen before. The middle classes attempted a similar strategy, and the social mobility possible in late 19th-century urban America found supreme expression in residential mobility, with its concomitant geographical mobility as a widespread familial experience. The poorer classes, full of immigrants, were consigned by low income to rent in slum and near-slum conditions, and to frequent moves within confined districts; when family savings allowed escape, it was to areas remarkably uniform in general social composition. When substantial numbers of blacks began migrating to industrial cities in the Northeast and Middle West after the turn of the century, they found themselves at the very bottom of the social hierarchy, with residential options reminiscent of the earliest immigrant groups.

The consequence of these social cleavages for residential patterns in most large cities was that

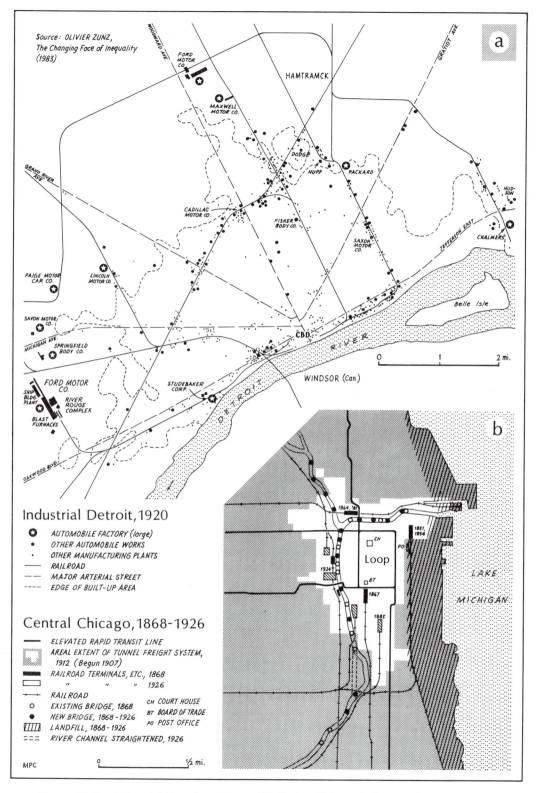

Figure 15.5   Industrial Detroit, 1920, and Relieving Chicago's Congestion, 1868–1926

social geography became spatially explicit. More and more, the wealthy disengaged residentially from the heart of the city and withdrew into secluded precincts, the increasing homogeneity of which was protected by the financial barriers to ownership. This class, numerically small but financially significant as agents in the formation of the cityscape, generally created thin sectors of costly residential fabric, oriented to amenities such as lakeshores (Chicago's Gold Coast) or scenic hilly terrain (Washington's Mount Pleasant). The much larger middle class also moved centrifugally, although with less exclusivity, absorbing genteel housing districts within the city where available but, and more important, colonizing many new suburban areas. This opened the way for the even larger working class (including most immigrants) to expand into what existing housing opened up, often to double up in buildings converted for higher-density occupation (generally in the urban core), and also to absorb cheap housing in less desirable settings, such as floodplains, tidal flats, and awkward land parcels in the interstices between industrial plants and railroad facilities. Middle- and working-class districts proliferated widely, often arranged in sectors or discontinuous rings radiating from the urban core, depending on topographical barriers, timing of business cycles, and the location of industry. In the older eastern cities, the old neighborhoods of the urban core suffered various fates. Depending on location, they either succumbed to CBD expansion and were replaced by commercial buildings, or became rooming house districts or tenement quarters (in which, say, two-story housing was replaced by five- and six-story tenement blocks, as in Boston's North End), or they simply deteriorated into slum conditions through overpopulation and financial disinvestment.

Social stratification by class, defined largely by income, may have determined the broad outlines of the large city's social geography, but that pattern was powerfully rewoven with ethnic thread. Immigrants who settled in cities often came to form ethnic "ghettos," districts overwhelmingly inhabited by non-native people, either almost exclusively of one origin or of several in varying degrees. Common bonds and a common predicament held immigrants together in these usually dense neighborhoods

until younger generations, more Americanized, would convert better incomes into residential relocation, perhaps even suburbanization. The "ghetto" model of ethnic enclaves, developed to describe the residential experience of some groups in some east coast port cities such as New York and Boston, by no means fits all large American cities during the later 19th century. In Milwaukee, for example, Germans were proportionately numerous enough to have settled districts of the city so extensive as to accommodate rich and poor alike within occupationally diverse neighborhoods that eased adjustment to American urban life far removed from the ghetto experience. Recent work in Detroit has suggested that for that late-industrializing city, the period from 1880 to 1920 represented a major transformation from a social geography defined primarily by ethnic differences to one stratified clearly by class, and in which ethnic differences, although not absent, were not the guiding force in neighborhood reformation.

PROBLEMS OF URBANISM

The rapid growth, changing roles, and sharp internal transformations of large American cities from 1860 to 1930 placed enormous stress on their social and physical functions. Economic developments occurred in a generally laissez-faire ideological environment that enlarged the problems of providing adequate amenities such as infrastructure, housing, health, and governance. Responses to these problems took varied forms, ranging from franchises for private provision of public services, to metropolitan jurisdictions for certain assets and, after the turn of the century, to the advent of comprehensive planning principles in a formal framework, signaled by the introduction in 1916 of land-use "zoning" in New York City. Some problems had very clear geographical dimensions.

Upgrading the Infrastructure

Commercial Improvements. The critical needs of commerce and industry in an urban context were (a) to keep abreast of technical improvements in transport facilities, and (b) to persuade the civic authorities whenever possible to subsidize their introduction, particularly where this involved costly rearrangement of the layout and fabric of the urban core. Improving harbors to accommodate ever-larger ships, bridging waterways for better downtown access, and rationalizing freight interchange among railroad terminals were the key issues. Harbor commissioners demarcated new wharf lines, landfilling occurred and bridges were built at public and private expense, and rights-of-way were easily granted for belt railways and terminal consolidations. The changes these wrought in one burgeoning city can be seen in the case of Chicago (Fig. 15.5b).

Building fabric and landfill. Most American cities were founded on flat, low-lying sites, and many encountered physical limits as building proceeded. Boston almost doubled its core area between 1860 and 1917 through extensive landfill on the surrounding tidal flats. Beginning in 1885, Chicago found it necessary to elevate its street system four feet above original grade to ensure drainage and functioning sewers. This enterprise required that all buildings in the city be built to the new level or raised up over fill to meet it. In working-class districts with little surplus cash for such modernization, many individual owners failed to comply, or raised their cottages over a new basement and left the yards unfilled, creating undulating streetscapes with footbridges to some front doors that survive to this day. The urban fires that ravaged many cities mostly affected downtown areas. Chicago's 1871 fire was so extensive that building in wood was forbidden within subsequently established "fire limits," a requirement also disregarded and loosely policed in many localities, but which did result in the CBD's overnight conversion to brick and stone construction.

Congestion. By far the most-common large-city problem was chronic downtown congestion, arising from the sharp rise in traffic within a business core that became denser year by year as ever-taller buildings covered larger percentages of their ground lots. Hardest hit were northeastern cities like Boston and New York with narrow colonial streets. Street widening became common in Boston in the 1850s, sometimes robbing owners of the front 10 to 15 feet of their buildings when they could not be moved. By the 1890s, pedestrians, horse-drawn traffic, and electric streetcars confined to their

tracks often created "gridlock," and cities sought solutions in separating some of the traffic. *Rapid* transit made its appearance in New York with an elevated steam train in the 1870s, but electrification was to provide the real key to elevated and subway service. Boston's subway system began in 1897, New York's in 1904, and elevated systems became popular in several cities, notably with the construction of Chicago's Loop in 1897 (Fig. 15.5b).

Amenities. The rising congestion of large cities after mid-century in both business and residential areas led to major movements to install urban parks as vital breathing spaces. Boston Common had long provided a model, but it was the application of new rural cemetery designs to New York's Central Park (begun in 1857) that started a trend, one which quickly became metropolitan in scale and systemic in concept (for example, the South and West Park system in Chicago, 1865–71). Provision for open space in really central locations did not fare well, as evidenced by the short life of the six-block public park set aside in Omaha's first plat in 1856, which succumbed to encroachment within a decade.

The difficulties encountered in developing a wide range of urban amenities in this period is reflected in what emerged through commercial enterprise, public initiative, and philanthropic gesture. Dance halls were common and taverns ubiquitous but complex in their contribution to public well-being. More gracious were the beer gardens and private concert parks, often established by German interests, but they fell afoul of prohibition sentiment by the 1920s for their support of family drinking. Private amusement parks, race tracks, small museums, and exhibition halls proliferated, generally catering to popular taste. It was left to public effort and large-scale philanthropy to add major city libraries, museums, opera houses, and symphony orchestras to give leadership to the arts in the city. Occasional extravaganzas, like the 1876 Philadelphia Cenntennial Exposition or the World's Columbian Exposition in Chicago in 1893, played significant roles in spreading ideas and interest in new forms of living, technology, and urban design.

Housing, Health, and Social Adjustment

The free market in housing was unable to deflect the rise of urban slums in late 19th-century

America. The tides of foreign immigration and rural influx propelled urban housing markets based on profitmaking to rely upon "filtering" to cope with redistribution. No profit could be made by housing the very poor in new housing, as opposed to cramped quarters in inner city locations in rundown buildings or in purpose-built tenement structures. The problems spurred "five-percent philanthropists" to experiment with subsidized housing for the poor, but generally such efforts were short-lived and foundered through mismanagement. Native-born capitalists have often been blamed for slumlordism in this period; Boston's North End, for example, while belonging to Yankee owners in the 1860s and 1870s during its Irish occupation, had passed largely into Jewish and Italian ownership by 1917, when its residents were largely Italian.

Overcrowding in districts with primitive household and street sanitation naturally encouraged epidemic outbreaks of disease, particularly cholera, that eventually led to reforms in water supply and public health services. In New York by the turn of the century, however, high mortality did not always coincide with the heaviest overcrowding and was sometimes variable among immigrant groups, with the Irish and Poles experiencing higher rates than Jews or Italians.

The concatenation of urban ills that built up over the decades after the Civil War in the largest cities drew forth a major effort at reform—of everything from housing and health to crime, pollution, politics, and private morals. Reformers were convinced that the appalling state of the inner urban environment, and in particular the delapidated and overcrowded housing, was the source of social deviance, and that improving this environment would eliminate poverty and criminal and immoral behavior. Model tenements were constructed, model educational programs were instituted, and "settlement houses," like Jane Addams's Hull House begun in Chicago in 1889, sought to improve the circumstances and conduct of the poor family and to clean up the neighborhoods.

Such efforts were not ineffective, for infant mortality was reduced, vocational training helped ghetto youths, kindergartens eased working mothers' daily problems and, above all, these initiatives focused a powerful spotlight on slum conditions. In failing to eradicate urban poverty they raised the question whether the causes of poverty lay elsewhere than in the quality of the physical environment. The moral crusades to banish specific vice districts provided a clear lesson of this kind, since they were more successful in relocating than in eliminating prostitution and gambling, although the lessons were not always understood at the time.

Jurisdictional Conflicts: Annexation, Suburban Incorporation, and Metropolitanism

The period between 1870 and 1920 witnessed major shifts in urban governance. Cities modernized their charters and developed bureaucracies commensurate with their growing street-level workforces in an attempt to keep up with the increasing complexity of urban life. That mounting complexity was in some measure the result of enlarged scale, and cities, like corporations dedicated to self-perpetuation, generally attempted to expand their bounds through annexation. Boston's absorption of Roxbury and Dorchester in 1869 has been noted, Chicago's annexation of Lake and Hyde Park Townships in 1889 more than doubled the city's area in a single year, and New York expanded in 1898 through consolidation of Manhattan, the Bronx, Brooklyn, Queens, and Staten Island to form a metropolis of 3 million people. During most of the 19th century, the city was viewed as a harbinger of urban services and efficient government.

As the century came to a close, however, that view changed among the suburbs. Outlying municipalities became disenchanted as city size bred inefficiency, indifference to local interests, higher taxes, and increasingly corrupt government. In most large metropolitan regions, annexations dwindled in size and frequency as suburban incorporations rose. Cambridge and Brookline refused union with Boston, but these entities had a long history of local government. More impressive was the wave of incorporations around cities such as Chicago as comparatively new railroad commuter suburbs sought their own destiny, even at the price of initially small-scale and limited development. Before 1920, Chicago's expansion had run up against an almost continuous encircling wall of incorporated "villages" and "cities."

Finally, large cities with major immigrant

populations were experiencing a change in the distribution of power as ethnic leaders flexed their political muscle and "boss" government became a reality. The traditional leaders sought, often with considerable success, to delay and dilute some of this transition by metropolitanizing urban governance. In Boston, the traditionally established Brahmins transferred as many functions as possible to the state legislature, the governor, and metropolitan commissions (for water, parks, and the like), and changed city councillors from ward to at-large representation, simply diversifying power "to spread it around in little indistinct piles so the Irish would find it hard to gather."

VARIATIONS ON THE THEME: REGIONALISM AND SMALL TOWNS

No overview of this size can hope to do justice to the regional variations in American urban structure and form that emerged between the Civil War and the 1920s. Broad differences not considered here distinguished cities that were ethnically plural from those with few immigrants. What held in terms of class formation, residential accommodation, and industrialization for New York, Worcester, or Cincinnati, would not have applied to Portland or Salt Lake City. The effects of race on southern cities in this period must also be acknowledged, for the cleavages in ethnic relations in northern

cities remained qualitatively different from the experience of a racial caste system that no Civil War would immediately eradicate. Regions separated cities in terms of the channels of urban innovation they were a part of, whether by the diffusion and timing of street railways or of building types. Further, regional variations reflected differences—whether of economic development or social character—between urbanization in so-called "instant" or "shock" cities of the West and those more easterly that arose more slowly through organic evolution.

Equally important is the caveat concerning urban scale. Much of the concern has been with large cities, because in them new trends perhaps emerged earliest or with greatest impact because of their size. But there are valid questions to pose about urban thresholds for any and all urban phenomena: did urban traits diffuse regionally, by proximal visitation as it were, or rather hierarchically, because towns reached a size when a characteristic would naturally emerge? Was the small town in late 19th- and early 20th-century America merely an incipient metropolis, or was it a distinct type needing, in view of stunted or stagnant growth history, its own analysis? Certainly, small towns past their own booms and locked in at low levels of the urban hierarchy possessed a resignation to smallness that contrasted with a generally expansionist cultural milieu which, considering the significance of the small town in American life, calls for separate but deserving treatment.

ADDITIONAL READING

Books

Herbert, D.T., and Johnston, R.J., eds. *Geography and the Urban Environment: Progress in Research and Applications, Vol. 4.* New York: Wiley & Sons, 1981. See chapters by Radford and Conzen.

Hershberg, T., ed. *Philadelphia. Work, Space, Family and Group Experience in the 19th Century.* New York: Oxford University Press, 1981.

Hudson, J.C. *Plains Country Towns.* Minneapolis: University of Minnesota Press, 1985.

LeBlanc, R.G. *Location of Manufacturing in New England in the Nineteenth Century.* Dartmouth: Dartmouth College Publications in Geography, 1969.

Lewis, P.F. *New Orleans: The Making of an Urban Landscape.* Cambridge: Ballinger, 1976.

Mayer, H.M., and Wade, R.C. *Chicago: Growth of a Metropolis.* Chicago: University of Chicago Press, 1969.

Miller, R.B. *City and Hinterland: A Case Study of Urban Growth and Regional Development.* Westport: Greenwood Press, 1979.

Olson, S.H. *Baltimore: The Building of an American City.* Baltimore: Johns Hopkins University Press, 1981.

Pred, A. *The Spatial Dynamics of U.S. Urban Industrial Growth, 1800–1914.* Cambridge: Harvard University Press, 1966.

———. *Urban Growth and City Systems in the United*

States, 1840–1860. Cambridge: Harvard University Press, 1980.

Schneider, J.C. *Detroit and the Problem of Order, 1830–1880: A Geography of Crime, Riots, and Policing.* Lincoln: University of Nebraska Press, 1980.

Vance, J.E., Jr. *The Merchant's World: The Geography of Wholesaling.* Englewood Cliffs: Prentice-Hall, 1970.

Ward, D. *Cities and Immigrants: A Geography of Change in Nineteenth Century America.* New York: Oxford University Press, 1971.

Ward, D., and Radford, J.P. *North American Cities in the Victorian Age.* Norwich, England: Geo Books Historical Geography Research Series, 1983.

Warner, S.B., Jr. *Streetcar Suburbs: The Process of Growth in Boston 1870–1900.* Cambridge: Harvard University Press, 1962.

Zunz, O. *The Changing Face of Inequality: Urbanization, Industrial Development, and Immigrants in Detroit, 1880–1920.* Chicago: University of Chicago Press, 1982.

Periodicals

Annals, Association of American Geographers (Meinig, 1972; Lewis, 1972).

Economic Geography (Meyer, 1980).

Geographical Review, journal of the American Geographical Society (Borchert, 1967).

Journal of Historical Geography (Conzen, 1975; Groves and Muller, 1975; Conzen and Conzen, 1979; Pred, 1981; Vill, 1986).

PART V

REORGANIZATION

TWENTIETH CENTURY

Canada could have enjoyed:
English government,
French culture,
and American know-how.
Instead it ended up with:
English know-how,
French government,
and American culture.

J.R. Colombo, *Oh Canada*, 1965

This monster of a land, this mightiest of nations, this spawn of the future, turns out to be the macrocosm of microcosm me . . . For all our enormous geographic range, for all our sectionalism, for all our interwoven breeds drawn from every part of the ethnic world, we are a nation, a new breed . . . California Chinese, Boston Irish, Wisconsin German, yes, and Alabama Negroes, have more in common than they have apart. And this is the more remarkable because it has happened so quickly.

John Steinbeck, *Travels with Charley*, 1962

The remarkable thing is not that government costs so much, but that so many people of wealth have left. It's outrageous that the development of the metropolitan community has been organized with escape hatches that allow people to enjoy the proximity of the city while not paying their share of taxes . . . Fiscal funkholes are what the suburbs are.

John Kenneth Galbraith, *The New York Times*, 1975

16

Forging a Canadian Nation

GRAEME WYNN

University of
British Columbia

"Whoever wishes to know what Canada is . . . should begin by turning from the political to the natural map," wrote Goldwin Smith in 1891. The first portrayed a vast territory, with Atlantic and Pacific shores, that ran unbroken from the United States to the North Pole; the second revealed "four separate projections of the cultivable and habitable part of the Continent into arctic waste." These projections not only differed in size. Their productive areas were set apart by "great barriers of nature, wide and irreclaimable wildernesses or manifold chains of mountains," and each was more closely linked with adjoining parts of the United States than with adjacent Canadian areas. The continent was a physical and economic whole and its grain was north-south; to divide it, argued Smith, was "to wage a desperate war against nature." In this view, Canada was "artificial"; the country was no more than a cluster of partly integrated regions. The physiographic map exposed the essential weakness of an attenuated dominion; as one contemporary expressed it, God and nature never designed a trade between Ontario and the Maritime Provinces.

But science and sentiment did. The political map of Canada in 1891 reflected the integrative capacity of industrial technology and the conviction that a distinctive future lay before the amorphous, extensive, northern realm that it portrayed. By 1891, the railway linking the Atlantic and Pacific and running where some had said railways would not go, was the spine of the country. Without it the political framework created by the British North America Act of 1867 must have crumbled. Confederation was predicated on territorial integration. The creation of a national market was implicit in the 1867 act, and the vision of a northern empire was inseparable from the railroad's power to reduce the friction of overland distance. Yet incredible toil and expense and faith had gone into the making of the railway. Ultimately the

country existed, reflected the Reverend George Grant in response to Goldwin Smith's claims, because its people had said, "let us rise up and build."

Smith and Grant could hardly have been further apart. For Smith, the formal topographic regions of North America were the building blocks of an argument for continental integration. In his view, the union of Canada with the American Commonwealth would bring "a great increase in prosperity." In contrast, George Grant made the continental coexistence of two nations (defined as functional, administrative, and economic regions) the foundation of his nationalist position. Faced with arguments for the fragmentation of Canada—"as if," he said, "the putting of it together had been merely a bit of child's play on the part of grown babies"—Grant was incredulous. He maintained that the economic underpinnings of Smith's position were essentially trivial. Surely, he urged, "every nation must be ready to pay a price." At base, Smith threw the hard facts of profit and topography against the intangibles of Grant's patriotism. The two disagreed on the viability of Canada and, in disputing the likelihood that a separate northern nation could survive in North America, they raised a question of fundamental and recurring importance to the existence of modern Canada (Fig. 16.1).

The country began, quite simply, as an idea. Colonial union had been mooted, without wide enthusiasm, for years before 1866. Then it seemed to offer the means of economic survival after the removal of imperial preferences in the 1840s and the ending of free trade agreements with the United States formalized in the Reciprocity Treaty of 1854. Confederation also raised hopes for the development of a "new nationality." But Canada remained "a geographical expression." Scattered territories were united by political fiat; there was little complementarity in their economies. The prob-

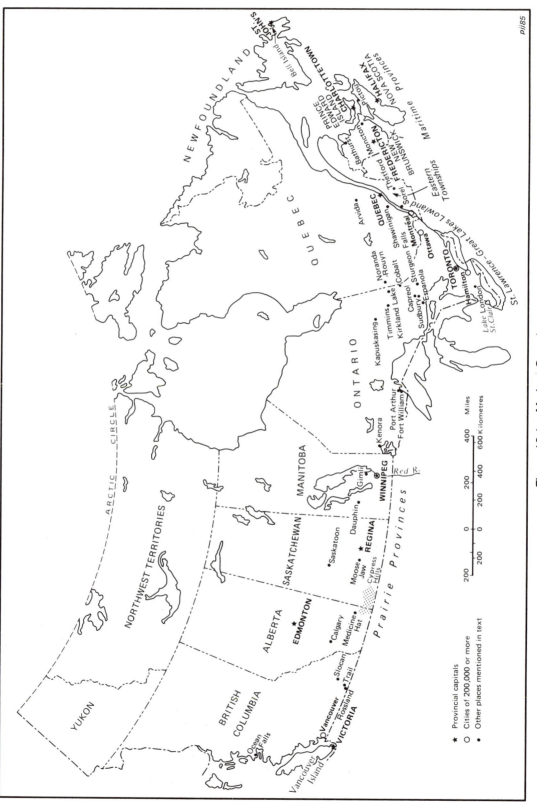

Figure 16.1   Modern Canada

lems of financing and building the railroads had yet to be faced, and means of territorial administration had yet to be found. Diverse communities had been drawn together by the promise of railways, but improved communications threatened their cultural variety and heightened the prospects of conflict—between lifeways, economic interests, and ethnic groups —previously minimized by isolation.

From the outset, Canada was a mix of hopes and contradictions. Unlike earlier nations that grew by accretion and the gradual extension of authority across space, it was created by decree, and the challenge of its cohesive development was hugely intensified by the success and vigor of its southern neighbor. The country was an amalgam of disparate elements. Its citizens, united by necessity as much as by desire, faced the enormous task of realizing a transcontinental state and securing for themselves the separate future implicit in the very idea of their country. Yet new and delicate as the nation was in 1867, its essential lineaments had been adumbrated through earlier decades of European trade and settlement in the northern part of the continent.

In 1866, British North America's population of approximately 3 million was scattered across an enormous area. Other than the 2.5 million settlers of the St. Lawrence–Great Lakes lowland, these people occupied tiny, ill-connected fragments of territory. In the east, settlement clung to the shores and penetrated inland only along a few fertile river valleys. A thousand miles of wild, rugged country separated the St. Lawrence settlements from a small enclave of Europeans at the Red River. Beyond were a few thousand Métis (descendants of indigenous women and early fur traders) and the aboriginal inhabitants of the eastern prairie. Most of the interior was fur-trading country, the domain of the Hudson's Bay Company. Across the Rocky Mountains, aboriginal peoples outnumbered approximately 10,000 newcomers by perhaps three to one. Even the Canadas East and West, which later historians would unite in the "commercial empire of the St. Lawrence," were divided by language, religion, and experience. Nowhere was the wilderness very distant in space or time.

The fundamental pattern of European colonization in this northern realm was clear, and time would reveal its resilience. Primary re-

source industries were the basis of settlement. The fur trade, the fishery, the timber trade, agriculture and (in the far west) the lure of gold had brought people to the wilderness and sustained them there. Each industry had generated its own distinctive settlement patterns and landscapes, but all depended on lines of communication that facilitated trade, that focused on towns, and that connected local economies to others beyond North America. To a greater or lesser extent each had also generated markets for imported and locally produced foodstuffs and consumer goods. By 1860, small industrial foci were emerging in parts of Canada West and in Montreal, but British North America was an overwhelmingly pre-industrial, staple-producing cluster of predominantly rural and artisan-based communities linked through a handful of urban commercial centers to a transatlantic hearth. Its political and economic consolidation would extend and ultimately transform this structure, but would not quite obliterate it. The idea with which the nation began and that was articulated after 1867 by the development of a territorial base, the integration of space, the expansion of settlement, and the creation of a national economy, both reflected and refracted economic alignments and settlement patterns rooted in the configuration and endowment of Canadian space.

BUILDING THE NATION'S HOUSE

The essential territorial foundation of the new nation was established in less than a decade. The British North America Act, which created the Dominion of Canada on July 1, 1867, united Canada West (Ontario) and Canada East (Québec) with New Brunswick and Nova Scotia. Three years later, Rupert's Land and the far northwest were transferred to the federal government (Fig. 16.2). Together they amounted to more than six times the area of the original provinces. The province of Manitoba was created from a small part of this extensive domain in 1870. In 1871, the Crown colony of British Columbia entered Confederation, and Prince Edward Island became the seventh province in 1873. With the transfer of the Arctic islands from Britain to Canada in 1880, the late 19th- and early 20th-century limits of the Dominion

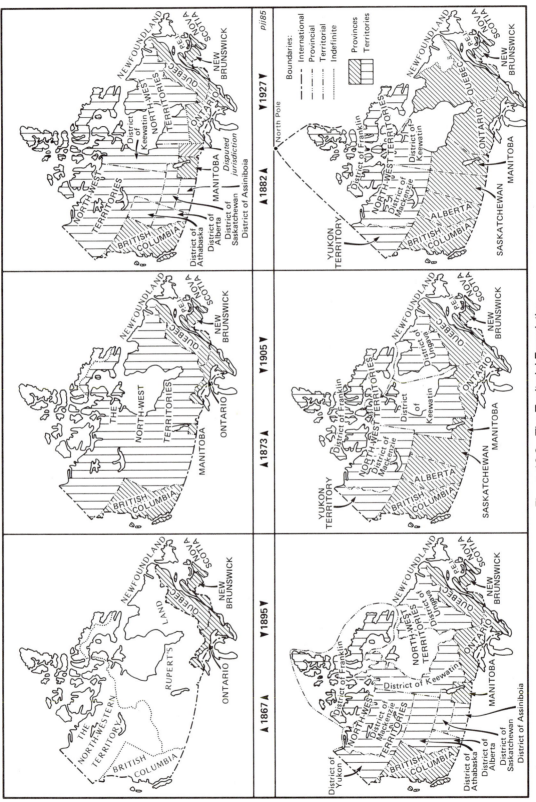

Figure 16.2   The Territorial Foundation

were established. Although the country's territorial claims extended to the North Pole by 1931, it was not until 1949, with the addition of Newfoundland, that Canada assumed its present territorial form.

Within this matrix, internal boundary changes and shifting political jurisdictions reflected, variously, administrative requirements, the advance of settlement, and competing territorial ambitions. The district of Keewatin was created from the vast unorganized Northwest Territories and placed under the jurisdiction of Manitoba in 1876. In 1881 the boundaries of Manitoba were enlarged, and a year later the provisional districts of Alberta, Assiniboia, Athabaska, and Saskatchewan were set off from the Northwest Territories under their own lieutenant-governor. Renewing a long-standing claim to land north and west of its existing boundary, Ontario disputed the eastward extension of Manitoba; in 1889 resolution of the issue extended Ontario's territory to James Bay and contracted that of Manitoba. By 1898, Québec's northern boundary was realigned to correspond with that of Ontario; the Yukon was a separate territory (reflecting the discovery of gold in the Klondike); and three new districts had been erected in the remaining Northwest Territories (Fig. 16.2). A growing population on the Prairies brought provincial status to Saskatchewan and Alberta in 1905, and in 1912 the boundaries of Québec, Ontario, and Manitoba were extended to their present limits. There were minor changes in the district boundaries of the Northwest Territories in 1920, and in 1927 the coast of Labrador was deemed to extend to the drainage divide between Ungava Bay and the North Atlantic.

As the country expanded into the Prairies and the northwest, a series of "treaties" (dated between 1871 and 1921) documented the surrender of aboriginal claims to the land in return for reservations (of at least 160 acres per family), initial payments, and annuities. In British Columbia, where land appropriation had proceeded since 1864 without "reference to the consent or wishes of the original occupants," the aboriginal peoples were treated even more illiberally. Confined, for the most part, to rural ghettos, the indigenous peoples of the west were regarded as awkward and generally unwelcome elements of the new nation. Displaced and disorientated by the pace of change,

many of them became defensive and discouraged. With their needs largely ignored, new diseases spreading among them, and their traditional cultures eroding, their numbers generally declined through the first decades of the 20th century. Constituting more than half the population of British Columbia in 1881, they accounted for less than one-eighth of the total by 1901.

By its acquisition of the Northwest Territories in 1870, the federal government both established the basis for a transcontinental nation and transformed the nature of Confederation. The original Dominion was a federation of equal provinces, each responsible for the administration of its Crown (or public) lands, and entitled to revenues derived from them. In this, Canadian practice adhered to a British precedent quite distinct from the arrangements that made unappropriated lands in the United States the property of the federal government and established national jurisdiction over the public domain. Mindful of their nation-building task, however, the Canadian government retained direct control of Crown land in the Western Interior. All ungranted or waste lands in the Northwest Territories and the new province of Manitoba were defined, by statute, as a national endowment to be used "for the purposes of the Dominion," and this provision was subsequently applied to Crown lands in the provinces of Alberta and Saskatchewan. With British Columbia entering Confederation on the same basis as the original provinces, the separate treatment accorded the Prairie provinces has been a continuing source of grievance. Although control of their Crown lands and natural resources was transferred from the federal to the provincial governments in 1930, and the magnitude of the public purposes for which they were first retained has rarely been denied, the legacy of the "Dominion lands" policy will likely be felt for years to come by Prairie dwellers.

With "one great country before it," the Dominion government implemented "one vast system of survey" across the Western Interior. Following the American pattern, the prairie region was divided into a rigid grid of farm holdings based on the 640-acre section and the 36-section township that marks the landscape from the Rio Grande to the Arctic Circle. Deviations from this pattern were rare. By the terms of the transfer of Rupert's Land, blocks of 50,000 acres or less were allowed the Hudson's Bay Company in the vicinity of their trading posts. River lots granted by the company were recognized, and the river lot system was continued until 1884 for those (mostly Métis) who wanted it. In all, some 1.4 million acres were set aside by the Manitoba Act for Métis families. Special surveys were also implemented on certain irrigation lands in Alberta. Two sections of every surveyed township in the Dominion lands were set aside as an endowment for public schools; and south of the North Saskatchewan River the Hudson's Bay Company received one-twentieth of the surveyed land, a total of 6.6 million acres. By an Act of 1872, provisions for the settlement of Dominion land were established. Homestead entries on quarter sections (160 acres) were registered for a $10 fee. Title to the property was granted after three years' residence and the completion of specified improvements.

Railroads were the frame of the new national structure. The transcontinental domain presupposed their construction; the integration and development of the nation depended on it. The British North America Act provided for the construction of an intercolonial line from the St. Lawrence to Halifax; British Columbia entered

Confederation on terms that included the completion of a transcontinental railway; Prince Edward Island had joined Canada on the promise of better links with the mainland. Railway building was a sustaining focus of early Canadian politics; the results, in terms of track miles, were impressive. In 1867, Canada had 2,278 miles of operating track, most of it in Ontario. By 1875, 4,331 miles of first main track were in use; a decade later the figure topped 10,000; and by 1891 it was almost 14,000 miles. The Intercolonial (I.C.R.) reached Halifax in 1876, and in November 1886 the Canadian Pacific (C.P.R.) line linked Vancouver to the St. Lawrence (Fig. 16.3). Each followed routes more influenced by politics than by economics. Tracing a circuitous path intended to reduce its vulnerability to American attack, the I.C.R. ran through wilderness for much of its length and was built and operated by the Dominion government. It failed to provide a return on capital invested.

For the C.P.R. a southern route was favored over one through the fertile dark brown soils of the aspen parkland, to reinforce Canadian interests in the border country. Construction of an all-Canadian line also meant construction through the unproductive Canadian (Precambrian) Shield north of Lakes Huron and Supe-

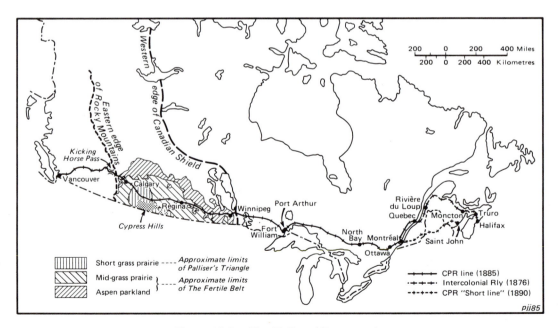

Figure 16.3   The Railroad Framework

rior. Because the immediate prospects of private return on costs were far lower than the social benefits of the railroad, the line was heavily subsidized by Dominion, provincial, and municipal governments. In all, the C.P.R. received $25 million and 25 million acres of land from the Dominion government as well as tax and right-of-way concessions. Sizable sections of line built by government contractors west of Thunder Bay and in British Columbia were handed over to the company. After surrendering some 6.8 million acres to retire debts in 1886, the company held alternate sections totaling approximately 18 million acres in three large blocks of the more fertile prairie. In broad terms, its holdings amounted to 2 million acres in Manitoba, 6 million in Saskatchewan, and 10 million in Alberta (Fig. 16.4). Here, especially, C.P.R. development policies, and the checkerboard pattern of its holdings, would retard the introduction of irrigation, disperse settlement, reduce the local tax base, and contribute to resentment of the company, not only for its monopoly power and rate structure but also for its "land-lock."

Nor was the C.P.R. the sole corporate recipient of prairie land. Shorter "colonization railroads" proliferated during the 1880s. Ultimately, almost 3,000 miles of land-subsidized track were laid on the Prairies, and the C.P.R. main line accounted for barely one-third of this total. In the 1890s, almost half the agricultural land in the western interior was in railway hands. In all, railway land grants in the region amounted to some 32 million acres.

Vigorous efforts to encourage occupation of the western interior began with the annexation of the northwest. Suddenly, an area once considered an extension of the Great American Desert, with soils dismissed as "sand and gravel with a slight intermixture of earth," offered the promise of Eden. Productive land seemed as boundless as the promoters' hopes, the climate as equable as their prose. Laudatory pamphlets appeared in enormous numbers from the pens of government, C.P.R., and local authors. Many of them were widely distributed. More than 1 million copies of the government's *Information for Intending Emigrants* were in circulation by 1873. In the scramble to boost the region, enthusiasm sometimes overwhelmed accuracy. But optimism was more characteristic than deliberate misrepresenta-

tion. Manitoba was sunny and fruitful. Farms were "free" and land was of the best. How alluring were advertisements for 2.75 million acres in the "Park Lands of the Fertile Belt." One Hudson's Bay Company advertisement of 1880 pointed out: "The Land is Prairie, not Bush Land." Who could deny the force of this simple assertion after viewing John Macoun's suggestive juxtaposition of sketches depicting the first years of pioneering in the eastern forest and the landscape after two years of settlement on the prairie (Figs. 16.5 and 16.6)?

On the eastern flank of the prairies, migrants from Ontario settled in small but increasing numbers after 1870 to practice wheat cultivation on a scale no longer practicable in their home counties. Several group settlements stemmed more directly from government encouragement. In the mid-1870s, 6,000 Mennonites from the Ukraine were given religious freedom, exemption from military service, and exclusive use of sizable blocks of land in southeastern Manitoba. Between 1874 and 1886 some 5,000 French Canadians from New England and Québec established a dozen or so communities along the Red River and its tributaries. Icelanders and others also received group settlement lands in these years. Although many of the settlements were ethnically and linguistically distinct, traditional agricultural practices and settlement patterns rarely continued unaffected by the economic and environmental circumstances of the prairies. By 1886, the agglomerated farm villages ("strassendorfer") of the Mennonites were giving way to dispersed homesteads, and many Icelanders had left the Gimli region in search of better land.

Development also proceeded in the far western interior. Here pastoralism dominated. As the "beef bonanza" swept western North America, the small cattlemen who had begun ranching in the Alberta district during the 1870s were challenged by a growing number of large cattle companies. By 1886 there were 12,000 people, 100,000 cattle, and 25,000 sheep between the Cypress Hills and the Rockies; perhaps 80 percent of the beef stock was in herds of 400 or more. Four years later, with railroad connection to the St. Lawrence assured, beef from the Canadian cattle kingdom was firmly established in the British market. In technique and economic character this industry

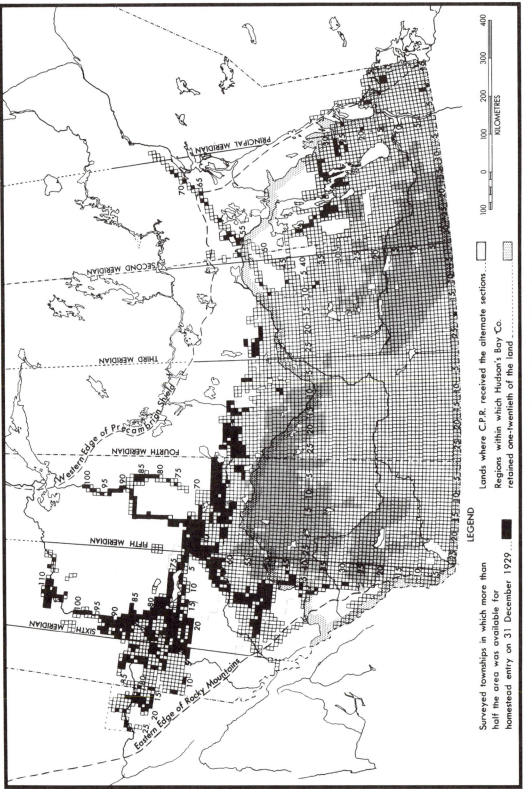

LEGEND

☐ Lands where C.P.R. received the alternate sections....

▨ Regions within which Hudson's Bay Co.
retained one-twentieth of the land ......

▨ Surveyed townships in which more than
half the area was available for
homestead entry on 31 December 1929 ....

Figure 16.4   The Prairie Land Survey (after Kerr)

Figure 16.5 First Year in the Bush. A Pioneer Landscape of the Eastern Forest (from John Macoun, *Manitoba and the Great Northwest,* 1882)

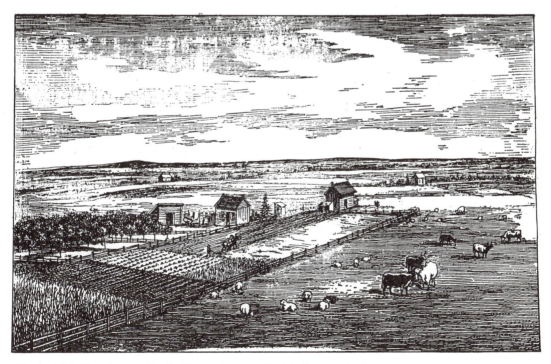

Figure 16.6 Two Years after Settlement on the Prairie (from John Macoun, *Manitoba and the Great Northwest,* 1882)

bore many resemblances to its American counterpart, but those engaged in it—largely drawn from the Central Canadian middle class and the lesser landed gentry of Britain—were socially distinct from their American neighbors. The control of range access after 1881 by a leasing system borrowed from Australian experience further set the Canadian ranching frontier apart from the American tradition of squatter sovereignty on "free grass" land. By offering as much as 100,000 acres for periods of up to 21 years at a rental of 1 cent per acre, the Canadian government exercised more direct control over western development than did its American counterpart; and perhaps, this tended to prevent the violence and overstocking that marked the American rangelands.

Yet these were small gains from a frenzy of promotion. In 1886 the western interior had only 163,000 inhabitants, of whom some 60,000 were concentrated in the Manitoba lowlands, within 75 miles of Winnipeg, a city of 20,000. Most of the remainder were scattered across southwestern Manitoba and along the railroad in the Qu'Appelle Valley. Few had penetrated the semiarid area known as Palliser's Triangle, between Moose Jaw and Medicine Hat. The years between 1872 and 1885 accounted for only 8.8 percent of all prairie homestead entries recorded before 1930. On average there were fewer than 3,000 entries a year between 1876 and 1896. If the western interior was no longer the "Great Lone Land" of the 1860s, it remained for much of the 19th century a region of few people and vast, undeveloped extent.

Faced with the need to develop the west, the effects of worldwide recession, the dumping of excess American industrial production in the Canadian market, and the emigration of unemployed Canadian workers to the United States, the Dominion government erected tariff walls to create a strong, relatively self-sufficient economy built on an expanded domestic manufacturing base and the promotion of interregional trade. Between 1879 (when the protective system, cleverly designated the National Policy, was first implemented) and 1887, a complex set of new duties was imposed on imported commodities. The general impost on unspecified items was set at 20 percent. Rates on other specified commodities were set to make domestic products competitive with imports. In broad terms, finished consumer goods incurred the

heaviest tariffs: furniture and clothing bore *ad valorem* charges of approximately 35 percent, while pig iron and rolled steel were levied duties of 10 to 20 percent. Together these fiscal policies offered something to every important economic interest in the country. By raising the cost of imports and thus allowing Cape Breton coal into Montreal furnaces, Ontario flour into Maritime ovens, and central Canadian reapers onto Prairie farms, they were to integrate the regions of the new nation. According to John A. Macdonald, who led the Conservative Party to electoral victory on the tariff's promise, protection was a vital part of a wider national policy, resting upon territorial expansion, railway construction, and immigration that would "make this union a union in interest, a union in trade, and a union in feeling." Twenty-five years later another prime minister spoke of the need to "consolidate Confederation" and to "bring our people . . . gradually to become a nation." Behind such rhetoric lay the fact that, in 1900, Canada still bore the mark of 19th-century settlement more clearly than it reflected the vision embodied in Confederation and the national policy.

REALIZING A DISTINCTIVE FUTURE

By 1930 a great transformation had been wrought in the northern half of the continent. Some 10 million people called Canada home (Fig. 16.7). Ontario had almost as many residents as the country of 1867. Growth, the leitmotif of the period, was evident on almost every front. New railroads, symbols of the national achievement, split the northern forest, wound through the cordillera, and crisscrossed the plains. There was a mile of main track for every 237 Canadians. Wheat production was up almost 25-fold from its 1871 level. Prairie sod was still being broken and, deep in the Canadian Shield, new mines yielded gold and silver and nickel. Hydroelectric power, clean and inexhaustible, was being generated at scores of remote dams. Pulp and paper mills turned northern trees into commercial products. Scientific surveys, transport improvements, and oil and mineral discoveries made the north a focus of commercial interest. In the south, cities had grown at an astonishing rate. Montreal, a place of 100,000 people at Confed-

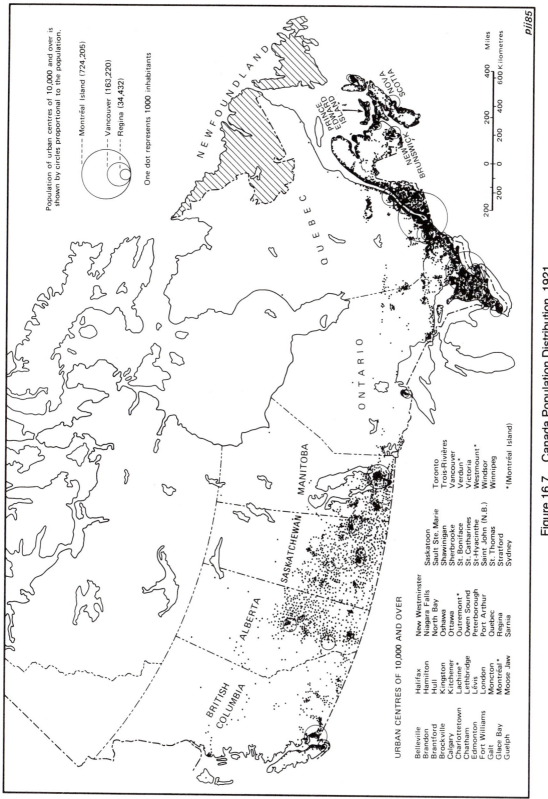

Figure 16.7   Canada Population Distribution, 1921

Population of urban centres of 10,000 and over is shown by circles proportional to the population.

--- Montréal Island (724,205)
--- Vancouver (163,220)
--- Regina (34,432)

One dot represents 1000 inhabitants

URBAN CENTRES OF 10,000 AND OVER

Belleville	Halifax	New Westminster	Saskatoon
Brandon	Hamilton	Niagara Falls	Sault Ste. Marie
Brantford	Hull	North Bay	Shawinigan
Brockville	Kingston	Oshawa	Sherbrooke
Calgary	Kitchener	Ottawa	St. Boniface
Charlottetown	Lachine*	Outremont*	St. Catharines
Chatham	Lethbridge	Owen Sound	St-Hyacinthe
Edmonton	Lévis	Peterborough	Saint John (N.B.)
Fort Williams	London	Port Arthur	St. Thomas
Galt	Moncton	Quebec	Stratford
Glace Bay	Montréal*	Regina	Sydney
Guelph	Moose Jaw	Sarnia	

Toronto	
Trois-Rivières	
Vancouver	
Verdun*	
Victoria	
Westmount*	
Windsor	
Winnipeg	
*(Montréal Island)	

pjj85

eration, exceeded 750,000 in the 1920s. Toronto grew almost tenfold in fifty years from its 1871 total of 56,000. By 1921, four other cities—Vancouver, Winnipeg, Ottawa, and Hamilton—had populations in excess of 100,000. An integrated network of urban places, linked by rail and, increasingly, by telephone, formed a national system, and midway through the decade a majority of Canadians became urban dwellers. The number of Canadians employed in manufacturing had more than tripled (from 182,000 to 595,000) between 1870 and 1927, and value-added had soared from $96 million to $1.4 billion in the same period.

Population patterns provide the best single measure of geographical change during these years. Most striking was the sheer increase in numbers. The total rose by 24 percent between 1881 and 1901 and by 64 percent in the twenty years that followed. In numerical terms this was an advance from 4.3 million to 5.3 million to 8.8 million, a doubling in forty years. Equally significant was the westward shift in the distribution of Canadians. Some 6.15 million immigrants arrived in Canada between 1870 and 1930. Before 1900 they came primarily from Britain and northwestern Europe; thereafter their number included an increasing proportion of central and eastern European peoples. Equally significantly, the average annual inflow for the first half of the period (56,265) stood far below that for the second (152,886), when the Prairies attracted a greater proportion of immigrants than any other region of the country. Taken together, the original provinces accounted for a shrinking fraction of the nation's people between 1871 and 1931 (Table 16.1). Their growth, in the last decades of the 19th century, was less than the natural increase of their populations, and only Ontario among them recorded a net in-migration in the 20th century. Prince Edward Island and Nova Scotia each lost population over at least one decade before 1931. At the local scale these tendencies were even more evident: some 70 counties in unproductive parts of the Maritimes, in the Eastern Townships of Québec, and on the morainic soils of Ontario lost more than 300,000 people between 1881 and 1931. Some estimates suggest that immigration exceeded emigration by a mere 500,000 in the century after 1851. Yet there was also a considerable westward migration of native-born Canadians. In 1931, approximately 780,000 Canadians lived outside the province of their birth. Among them were 112,000 Maritimers, 154,000 Québecers, and 315,000 Ontarians; together these regions included only some 266,000 native-born, interprovincial migrants. Manitoba, Saskatchewan, Alberta, and British Columbia counted some 515,000 Canadians born beyond their borders. In all, the four western provinces had

Table 16.1   Percentage Distribution of the Canadian Population by Province, 1871–1931

	1871		1881		1891		1901		1911		1921		1931	
Prince Edward Island	—		2.5		2.3		1.9		1.3		1.0		0.8	
Nova Scotia	10.8		10.2		9.3		8.6		6.8		6.0		4.9	
New Brunswick	7.9	96.8	7.4	96.0	6.6	92.7	6.2	87.9	4.8	75.7	4.4	71.7	3.9	70.3
Québec	33.1		31.4		30.8		30.6		27.8		26.9		27.7	
Ontario	45.0		44.6		43.7		40.6		35.0		33.4		33.0	
Manitoba	0.7		1.4		3.1		4.8		6.4		6.9		6.7	
Saskatchewan							1.7	7.9	6.8	18.4	8.6	22.2	8.9	22.6
Alberta							1.4		5.2		6.7		7.0	
		2.0		2.7		5.1									
Northwest Territories	1.3		1.3		2.0		0.4		0.1					
Yukon							0.5	0.9	0.1	0.2		0.1		0.1
British Columbia		1.0		1.1		2.0		3.3		5.4		6.0		6.7
Canada Total			3,595,236		4,324,810		4,833,239		5,371,315		7,206,643		8,787,949		10,376,786

more than 3 million people in 1931, five times their population of thirty years earlier. In proportional terms their share of the national total had risen from 11 percent to almost 30 percent in three decades.

By 1931, Canadians were far more heterogenous than ever before. Those of British origin were still the most numerous, but their proportion of the total fell from 61 percent to 52 percent between 1871 and 1931 (Table 16.2). Canadians of French origin, accounting for 31 percent of the total and 82 percent of those from continental Europe in 1871, had fallen to 28 and 62 percent of those categories sixty years later. Seven other European origins were enumerated in 1871; of these only "German" (202,991) and "Netherlander" (29,662) numbered more than 2,000. In 1931, twenty European origins other than Britain and France were specified in the census; none counted fewer than 5,000 people, and only Greeks and Lithuanians numbered fewer than 10,000. Germany accounted for 473,000, the Ukraine for

225,000; there were approximately 150,000 each of Polish, of Jewish, and of Dutch origin. Italians, Norwegians, Russians, and Swedes were each 80,000 to 100,000 strong. And there were 46,500 Chinese and 23,000 Japanese among the 84,548 Canadians of Asiatic origin.

This polyglot population was also more heavily urban than that enumerated in earlier Canadian censuses. In broad terms, the country's population urbanized at a rate of 6 percent a decade between 1871 and 1901; in the first decade of the new century the rate increased by a third; in 1911–21 and 1921–31 it was back to approximately 4 percent. In sum, the proportion of urban Canadians rose from 19.6 percent to 53.7 percent in sixty years, and an increasing fraction of this urban population lived in large centers. In 1881 Montreal, with 140,000 people, was the only city of 100,000 or more. By 1931, 2.3 million Canadians, a fifth of the total and fully 45 percent of those living in incorporated centers, resided in seven such places. Conversely, the relative significance of small towns

Table 16.2 Origins of the Canadian Population, 1871–1931 (all population figures in thousands)ᵃ

	1871 #	1871 %	1881 #	1881 %	1901 #	1901 %	1911 #	1911 %	1921 #	1921 %	1931 #	1931 %
British	2,111	61	2,549	59	3,063	57	3,999	55	4,869	55	5,381	52
English	706	(33)ᶜ	881	(35)	1,261	(41)	1,871	(47)	2,545	(52)	2,741	(51)
Irish	846	(40)	957	(38)	989	(32)	1,075	(27)	1,108	(23)	1,231	(23)
Scottish	550	(26)	700	(27)	800	(26)	1,027	(26)	1,174	(24)	1,346	(25)
All other European	1,323	38	1,598	37	2,107	39	3,007	42	3,700	42	4,753	46
French	1,083	(82)	1,299	(81)	1,649	(78)	2,062	(69)	2,453	(66)	2,928	(62)
Other N.W.ᵈ	234	(18)	290	(18)	378	(18)	582	(19)	600	(16)	878	(18)
E & Centralᵉ	2	—	4	—	71	(3)	341	(11)	608	(16)	894	(19)
Asiatic	—	—	4	—	24	—	43	—	66	—	85	—
Otherᶠ	52	1	174	4	177	3	158	2	153	2	158	2
Total	3,486ᵇ	100	4,325	100	5,371	100	7,207	100	8,788	100	10,377	100

ᵃAs a census category "origin" has embodied a mix of biological, cultural and geographic attributes. In cases of mixed derivation, origin is determined by paternal reference for those of European descent, and by reference to either parent for children of those of Indian, Asiatic or black origin.

ᵇ1871 data are for the four original provinces of Canada only.

ᶜPercentages in parentheses relate the subgroup to the group, i.e. English were 33 percent of those of British origin.

ᵈOther N.W. European includes Belgian, German, Netherlander, Scandinavian.

ᵉEast & Central European includes Austrian, Czech and Slovak, Greek, Hungarian, Italian, Jewish, Lithuanian, Polish, Romanian, Russian, Ukrainian, Yugoslavic.

ᶠIncludes native Indian and Inuit and Negro.

Note: In 1891 Origin data were collected on a different basis.

declined. In 1871 almost two-thirds of the population of incorporated places lived in centers with fewer than 30,000 residents. By 1901 the proportion had fallen to 56 percent; in 1931 it was down to 41 percent. Regional variations in this pattern were considerable, although all areas of the country counted an increasing proportion of urban residents. The Maritimes (40% urban) and the Prairies (31%) were the only predominantly rural regions of Canada in 1931, when almost two-thirds of Ontarians and 60 percent of Québecers lived in urban places. British Columbia, the least urbanized of jurisdictions in 1871 (9%), was second only to Ontario in its proportion of urban residents by 1931. In Saskatchewan and Prince Edward Island only one in five inhabitants was urban in 1931; all other provinces but Alberta (in 1904) had crossed this threshold in 1891 or earlier.

Together these changes reflected the economic transformation of Canada. Before 1850, growth in the British North American economy depended heavily upon the extension of settlement and the exploitation of resources. Despite commercial expansion, there was little structural change in the economy. After 1850, primary activity (agriculture and natural resource extraction) accounted for a shrinking proportion of national income. Real output per capita also grew more quickly than before. Although contemporaries compared Canada's growth unfavorably with that of the United States in the last third of the 19th century, per capita growth rates during these years of limited immigration were above the 1867–1967 average. During the "wheat boom" of the early 20th century, Canada's gross national product soared: in real terms it increased 3.7-fold in the four decades after 1890. Rapid growth in the primary sector, and rising exports of wheat, flour, minerals, and pulp and paper accounted for a substantial part of this quickening. But export expansion was paralleled by an increase in the specialization, diversification, and integration of the Canadian economy predicated upon a massive extension of the country's transportation infrastructure and the development of its energy sources. The effects were immense and manifest in all sectors of economic life.

When the editors of the *Manitoba Free Press* expressed their wish in 1899 for "all the railways we can get," they echoed the sentiments of promoters, politicians, boosters, and settlers across the country. Prairie farmers were reluctant to take up land more than ten miles from the railroad, and a network of branch lines, rarely more than twenty miles apart, was built across the western interior. Advocates of colonization in northern Ontario and Québec saw railroads as the means to realize their ambitions. They were built. Mines in the shield and the cordillera required railroads to get their ore to markets. They were built. In 1901 and 1902 two new transcontinental railroads were initiated. The Grand Trunk Pacific (between Prince Rupert and Winnipeg) operated in conjunction with the National Transcontinental (built by the federal government from Winnipeg to Moncton) that cut through the heart of the Canadian Shield. The Canadian Northern, from Vancouver to Montreal via Edmonton, Dauphin (Manitoba), Capreol, and Ottawa, grew initially by the amalgamation of local lines. Both systems received huge subsidies in cash and land from federal, provincial, and municipal governments. Although neither of the new transcontinentals was complete in 1914, railway mileage in operation had all but doubled since 1900. By 1915, 48,000 track miles were in service; of the 20,000 miles or so of first main track added since 1896, approximately one-half was in the Prairie provinces (Fig. 16.8). By this surge of development, new areas were opened up for settlement and exploitation, and new territory was integrated into the expanding Canadian economy. But the impact of recession, war, and inflation upon an overbuilt railway network was disastrous. Between 1917 and 1923, the Grand Trunk Pacific, the Grand Trunk, and the Canadian Northern were taken over by the federal government and consolidated with the Intercolonial, the National Transcontinental, and the railways of Prince Edward Island to form the government-owned Canadian National Railway system. Several miles of duplicate track were dismantled, a potential C.P.R. monopoly was avoided, and the state deepened its commitment to maintaining the framework of east-west integration.

Before 1929, Canadian energy requirements were largely met by coal and hydroelectricity, and production of both increased enormously as the economy expanded. Coal was the fuel of the 19th century, and Canadian reserves were large; output rose steadily from 2 million tons

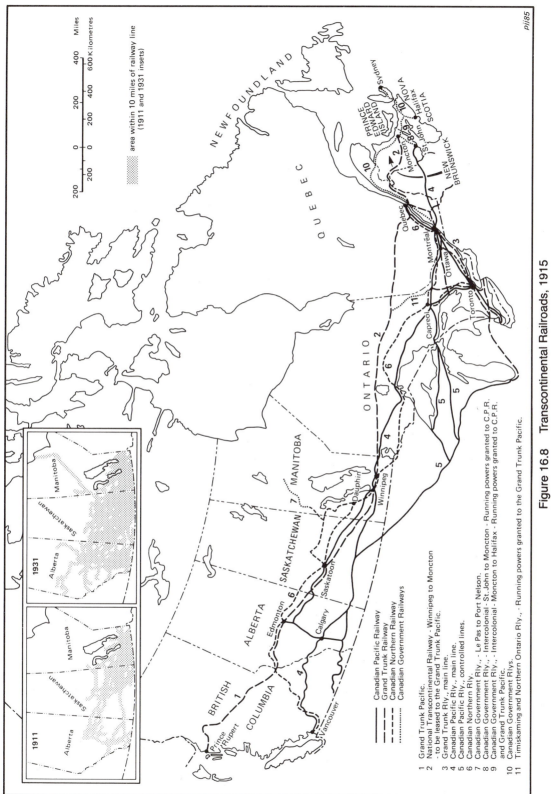

Figure 16.8 Transcontinental Railroads, 1915

Canadian Pacific Railway
Grand Trunk Railway
Canadian Northern Railway
Canadian Government Railways

1 Grand Trunk Pacific.
2 National Transcontinental Railway - Winnipeg to Moncton
  - to be leased to the Grand Trunk Pacific.
3 Grand Trunk Rly., main line.
4 Canadian Pacific Rly., main line.
5 Canadian Pacific Rly., controlled lines.
6 Canadian Northern Rly.
7 Canadian Government Rly., - Le Pas to Port Nelson.
8 Canadian Government Rly., - Intercolonial - St. John to Moncton - Running powers granted to C.P.R.
9 Canadian Government Rly., - Intercolonial - Moncton to Halifax - Running powers granted to C.P.R.
  and Grand Trunk Pacific.
10 Canadian Government Rlys.
11 Timiskaming and Northern Ontario Rly., - Running powers granted to the Grand Trunk Pacific.

area within 10 miles of railway line
(1911 and 1931 insets)

pii85

in 1886 to 15 million in 1913 and continued at this level, on average, through 1929. But Canada's coal lay on the flanks of the country, in Nova Scotia, around the Crowsnest Pass in the Rocky Mountains, and on Vancouver Island. Coastal British Columbia was a major supplier of coal to San Francisco. Crowsnest coal heated homes, drove trains, and fired British Columbian smelters, but was remote from the country's major centers of consumption. The National Policy tariff was never sufficient to exclude American competitors of Cape Breton producers from the Ontario market, and the little protection it did afford declined as the price of coal doubled in the first quarter of the 20th century. Although mines in Nova Scotia shipped 2.4 million tons of coal to Québec in 1914 and accounted for more than half of Canadian production, their main market was local. Canada—essentially central Canada—imported some 15 million tons of coal; national exports were a small fraction of this total. Thus the United States supplied some 50 to 60 percent of Canadian coal requirements before World War I. Competition, distant markets, and inadequate capitalization plagued the industry from the first. Several Nova Scotian mines were forced to close in the 1880s. Here, if not in the mines opened slightly later in Alberta and southeastern British Columbia, the tentacles of metropolitan integration were felt in a series of mergers that left Montreal interests in control of many mines in Pictou and Cumberland counties. By 1893, the Dominion Coal Company had integrated most Cape Breton mines into a network of external financial control, and this pattern was emphasized in the early twentieth century. With the sale of surplus American coal production in the Canadian market after 1918, the rising importance of gas and oil as alternative energy sources in the 1920s, and an internal decline in Canadian iron and steel production, the Canadian coal industry endured a decade of financial and industrial turmoil after World War I. Attempts to reduce labor costs by cutting wages generated bitter strikes in mining towns, but the industry could not stave off decline. The preeminence of coal as an industrial energy source had suffered serious challenge from the rapid increase of hydroelectric power generation after 1900. In approximate terms, waterpower accounted for

60 percent of the energy produced by coal consumption in 1921.

The importance of hydroelectricity to Canadian development in the early 20th century far exceeded its relative share of the Canadian energy budget. Late 19th-century solutions to the problems of long-distance transmission made possible the large-scale generation of power at sites distant from consumers and gave Central Canada its own indigenous energy source. Contemporaries celebrated the potential of Canada's "white coal" and, although much of this optimism was tempered by time, hydroelectricity development did allow the introduction of new industries and hastened the economic diversification of Canada. By 1904, the Shawnigan Power Company was transmitting electricity some 90 miles to Montreal and had encouraged power-intensive industries (aluminum processing, pulp and paper, and chemical manufacturing) to locate near its plant on the St. Maurice River. Ten years later transmission lines ran from Shawnigan to Québec City and under the St. Lawrence to Sorel and Thetford Mines.

In Ontario, early development of hydroelectricity centered on the Niagara escarpment, which had the largest power plant in the world in the 1920s. Scale economies and public control of the resource (by the Ontario Hydro Electric Power Commission) brought Canadian energy costs below those in the United States, and considerable quantities of power (fully a third of domestic production in 1910) were purchased by American firms before 1914. With Ontario Hydro's vigorous promotion of electricity for use in domestic manufacturing, exports accounted for a shrinking share of production, at least until 1929. Electro-chemical firms crossed the border to take advantage of Canadian rates. Elsewhere, pulp and paper mills and ore-refining plants were closely dependent on the production of hydroelectricity. Dams marked the edge of the Shield in the mill towns of Kenora and Sturgeon Falls; they supplied the pulp towns of the Clay Belt; and they powered smelters in Arvida, Québec, Sudbury, Ontario, and the Kootenay District of British Columbia. In addition, electric power drove the tramways and lit the streets of Canadian cities from Victoria to Saint John. Well might contemporaries have felt that hydroelectric development was the key to Canada's century, the harbinger of a new industrialization that would reduce the country's dependence on American coal and free it from its "hewer of wood" relationship to American industry.

After years of modest growth, agricultural settlement of the prairies forged ahead after 1896; massive investment was drawn into the region and the country, and the rate of capital formation in Canada quickened as each new homestead generated demand for buildings, farm machinery, and equipment. New farms stimulated railroad expansion and spawned hundreds of new grain-handling centers, each with its sidings, elevators, and loading platforms. New families required consumer goods, ranging from clothing to hardware and home furnishings, and stores and warehouses sprang up to meet the demand. With the tariffs securing this market for Canadian producers, the occupation of the western interior was a vital stimulus to national economic growth in the early 20th century.

The pace of prairie settlement during these years was astonishing. Almost two-thirds of all homestead entries made between 1872 and 1930 occurred in the fifteen years before World War I. There were more entries between 1900 and 1904 than in the previous quarter-century; between 1909 and 1912 new homesteads were created at a rate of more than 40,000 a year. The population of the three Prairie provinces quadrupled between 1901 and 1916. Between 1901 and 1911 the number of farms in the region rose from 55,200 to almost 200,000. Some 73 million acres of farmland were taken up, and the area of improved land increased more than fourfold. Well over 40 percent of this improved land was in wheat by 1911; a decade later the figure was approximately 50 percent. Wheat was an even more significant fraction of the area under field crops (56 percent in 1911 and 69 percent in 1921). Coarse grains for livestock feed took up much of the remaining cropland in this pre-tractor age. Beef, dairy cattle, and hogs were of local importance in some areas but had little effect upon crop patterns. Between 1901 and 1911 Canadian wheat production rose from 55 million to 230 million bushels, with the Prairie provinces accounting for 90 percent of the total. Ten years later Manitoba, Saskatchewan, and Alberta accounted for 93

percent of Canada's 300 million bushel output; in 1929 the country's wheat exports averaged 1 million bushels a day. As wheat went out through the Lake Superior ports of Port Arthur and Fort William, or through the mountains to the west coast, so in a massive counterflow, lumber, machinery, and people entered the Prairies from British Columbia, Central Canada, and beyond. The east-west articulation of trade that the National Policy sought had begun to be realized.

To Clifford Sifton, Minister of the Interior between 1896 and 1905 and vigorous advocate of prairie settlement, has gone much of the credit for these developments. He streamlined his department, required railroads to choose their grant lands so that settlement could proceed without ambiguity, and encouraged the recruitment of agricultural immigrants from new, especially Slavic, areas of Europe. But exogenous structural factors—rising wheat prices in industrializing Europe and the United States, falling transport costs, declining interest rates, improvements in milling machinery, farm equipment and grain varieties, and the closing of the American frontier—were much more important determinants of change than Sifton's personality. But neither singly nor together are these factors sufficient to account for the timing of agricultural expansion in the Prairies.

It must be recognized that western Canadian settlement was part of a wider North American process and that much of the prairie was at the margins of 19th-century cultivation. Only the Red River area had a sufficiently long growing season (170 days) to allow maturation of wheat varieties available in the 19th century, and agricultural settlement was largely confined to this area before 1890. Beyond the core of Palliser's Triangle, where there is usually insufficient rainfall to provide a crop, wheat yields in the semiarid zone were extremely variable under conventional cropping techniques. Given the farmers' aversion to risk on this scale, encroachments on this area were sustained only as long as rainfall remained above the norm. With subhumid land still available in the United States, as it was in the 1880s, settlement would gravitate to those areas. After the development in 1889 of summer fallowing techniques that reduced the variability of yields in the semiarid zone, there was a sudden shift in the extensive margin of cultivation. As wheat prices began to rise in the 1890s and the availability of subhumid land declined, farmers moved into the semiarid regions of both Canada and the United States. By the first years of the 20th century there was a considerable northward migration from the American plains into the Canadian prairies, fostered by the expansive optimism of these boom years in the "last best west" (Fig. 16.9). Many of those who came north were likely earlier emigrants from eastern Canada, but perhaps one-third of Saskatchewan's 1931 population was American-born.

Beyond the Prairies, agriculture responded to new circumstances created by mechanization, market shifts, and the growing integration of the Canadian economy. In the Great Lakes–St. Lawrence lowland, the transformation began early. Increasing population densities and the devastating impact of midge and rust on Québec wheat production in the 1830s had diversified farming in that province and disconnected it from the market until the 1850s. Then dairying and the cultivation of oats ex-

panded in response to local and American urban demand. With the depression of the 1870s, technical improvements and the specialization of production were encouraged. Overall, dairying came to dominate a mixed farming economy. By 1900 there were almost 2,000 butter and cheese factories in Québec. Subsidiary patterns of regional specialization also emerged: market gardening in the vicinity of Montreal; livestock in the Eastern Townships and along the south shore of the St. Lawrence below Québec City; hay for lumber camps and for New England in the Beauce, the St. Maurice, and the Ottawa valleys; horses in Chambly County east of Montreal; and tobacco in the Joliette area. In the 20th century, the number of Québec farms decreased as their average size increased. Dairy production expanded to account for some 28 percent of agricultural income in 1929, but problems of quality control and New Zealand competition in the British market were already evident obstacles to the continuing vitality of this sector. Hay remained important. It accounted for half the value of Québec field crops before 1930 and, until cars

Figure 16.9   Attractions of the "Last Best West" (*Laurier Does Things*, 1904)

and tractors replaced horses on prairie farms, there was a substantial market for Québec hay in the west.

In Ontario, new machinery and new markets recast agricultural patterns in the late 19th century. New machinery (reapers, binders, cream separators) reduced the effort required by particular tasks and allowed farmers to improve production. The average farm expanded its improved area from 51 to 65 acres between 1871 and 1901. Its occupant, said the *Farmers' Advocate* in 1907, had gone "from the rank of a strenuous toiler to the more complex status of a business proprietor." As urban growth generated a demand for meat, dairy, and truck products, and British markets for butter, cheese, and stock expanded, mixed farming with an emphasis on livestock came to dominate much of old settled Ontario. The wheat-fallow-wheat rotation characteristic of the pioneering period remained important on the northern fringes of the settled province, but wheat, the leading crop occupying some 18 percent of Ontario farmland in 1880, accounted for only 5 percent of the total twenty years later. Between 1885 and World War I, as prairie farming expanded, Ontario's contribution to the national wheat crop fell from 85 to 15 percent. Barley, the other large cash crop of the Confederation years, was all but excluded from its American market by the McKinley tariffs of 1890, and the acreage devoted to it fell by one-half in three years. Other field crops, eggs, and poultry were also largely shut out of the American market by rising duties in the 1890s. They were replaced by feed grains, hay, and root crops. By 1910, the province's production of oats was four times that of 1870; corn was of increasing importance. Over the same period the number of milch cows rose by 70 percent, and other cattle and swine numbers doubled. The quality of stock was improved, and dual-purpose cattle (Ayrshires, Shorthorns) gave way to more specialized breeds (Jerseys for cream; Holsteins for milk) as farming became more differentiated. Agricultural production was gradually adjusted to take advantage of regional differences in soil and climatic conditions.

Broadly similar circumstances affected agriculture in the Maritime provinces, but in this marginal environment their impact was more detrimental. With the opening of the West, local production of cereal grains declined considerably. Competition from imported meat led to a decline in cattle (other than milch cows) and sheep numbers after 1881. In consequence of an 1874 American impost on potatoes, the area in that important crop fell by 50 percent in thirty years; yields declined by 3 million bushels between 1881 and 1921. At the same time regional production of oats and roots, and butter output, increased considerably. To a significant degree these gains were attributable to improved farming practice. A 50 percent increase in acreage yielded a 250 percent increase in root crops between 1881 and 1911; the number of milch cows declined by 14 percent while butter output rose by 25 percent between 1891 and 1921. Substitution of apples (sold on the British market) for potatoes alleviated the consequences of exclusion from the American market in the fertile Annapolis-Cornwallis valley area; the organization of butter, egg, and bacon marketing cooperatives gave some farmers access to the expanding urban markets of New England; and a short-lived fox-ranching industry made fortunes for a few Prince Edward Island families. But increasingly, Maritime farmers concentrated on those crops least susceptible to outside competition, or ran their holdings to provide the bulk of their own needs. Many left the land. Others joined the "harvest excursions" late each summer to bring in the Prairie wheat crop and, perhaps, to remain in the West.

Change was equally sweeping in other fields of primary production. On both east and west coasts, concentration and consolidation marked the fishery. In the Maritime provinces, new expensive Banks trawlers challenged the viability of the traditional dispersed inshore fishery by catching more fish with fewer men and serving a handful of large processing plants. At an intermediate scale, gasoline-powered boats allowed those who could afford them to range more widely in search of fish. Rail links gave certain harbors a great advantage as cold storage facilities opened new central Canadian markets early in the 20th century. Taken together with a falling market for salt cod, these developments spelled hardship in the traditional economy. Despite diversification into lobster, salmon, haddock, and sardine fisheries, overall employment in the industry declined substantially between 1900 and 1930; yet capitalization and productivity were up. On the Pacific coast, similar trends marked a very different fishery. Many of the canneries built at the mouths of almost all British Columbia's major rivers during the expansion of commercial salmon fishing in the late 19th century were closed, as larger motor-driven boats brought their catches considerable distances to centralized processing plants located on the Fraser and Skeena rivers. Here, too, there was consolidation of financial control, as numerous independent canneries either banded together under common leadership or were acquired by limited liability companies with economic roots in Britain and the United States.

Patterns of forest exploitation were transformed between Confederation and the Great Depression. The traditional square-timber trade of eastern Canada declined rapidly in the late 19th century and had almost disappeared by 1912. Sawn lumber accounted for an increasing proportion of Canadian wood production after 1830, and American markets absorbed a considerable fraction of the nation's output in the late 19th century. By 1905, the United States took more than half of Canadian exports. In the east, new supply areas were opened up by railroads that broke the industry's dependence on water courses for the movement of wood to markets. By 1886, the north shore produced a third of the total cut of Georgian Bay and there were a number of sawmills to the west where the C.P.R. crossed south-flowing rivers. Integrated systems of wood production, transportation, and marketing replaced the diffuse patterns and informal organization of the earlier timber trade; mills grew in size and in capital cost as new saws, new machinery, and new power sources allowed a clear tenfold increase in daily output between 1850 and 1900.

In the west, the impact of modern technology was even more decisive. Hand logging, by which the enormous trees of the Pacific coast were felled directly into the sea using only axes, jacks, and human effort, gave way to larger operations dependent upon steam engines in the 1890s and logging railroads early in the new century. With these developments came locational concentration and the preeminence of a relatively small number of firms whose mills drew logs from sizable camps scattered over considerable distances. With the settlement of the Prairies, the major market for British Columbian lumber turned from the sea-

borne cargo trade to the Western Interior. By World War I, prefabricated buildings of British Columbian lumber, carried east on the C.P.R., dotted the landscape from the foothills of Alberta to the clay belt of Ontario.

Canada's forest resource was further exploited as a consequence of technological advances in paper manufacturing that gave rise to a wood pulp and paper industry in the late 19th century. From modest beginnings (there were five small mills in 1881), pulpwood production rivaled lumber output in value during the 1920s and exceeded it in the next decade. By 1923 almost $400 million dollars were invested in the pulp industry. Some 25,000 people worked in approximately 100 mills, most of them in Québec, Ontario, New Brunswick, and British Columbia. Woodpulp output exceeded 2 million tons in 1922 and was valued at $85 million; paper production (mainly newsprint) was worth more than $100 million. It is significant that American capital and American corporate enterprise lay behind many of these new mills. With their strong ties to American markets, and their often remote peripheral locations (for example, Bathurst, Kapuskasing, Espanola, Ocean Falls) chosen for access to the resource, they profoundly influenced patterns of trade and settlement in the country by 1929.

For much of the 19th century, Canadian mining was an essentially haphazard, frequently ephemeral enterprise. Most mines were locally organized, small in scale, and poorly capitalized. Production was largely for domestic markets, although the United States took some coal from Cape Breton and Vancouver Island and asbestos from Québec. Nonmetallic minerals and fuels dominated production. With the exception of gold (which stimulated population rushes into the remote interior of British Columbia), most mining activity occurred in, or on the fringes of, already settled regions. This pattern was radically transformed at the turn of the century. With the exception of the placer gold operations in the Yukon that fired hopes of an Eldorado for small-scale, individual prospector-miners in 1897–98, Canadian mining since 1890 has been capital-intensive and largely dependent upon costly facilities for ore extraction, reduction, and smelting. A revolution in metallurgical technology generated enormous new demands for metallic minerals (which accounted for over a third of Canadian output by 1910). Railway and geological surveys through distant wildernesses revealed new sources of supply. Cordilleran British Columbia and the Canadian Shield were quickly opened for exploitation. By 1900 British Columbia claimed the title of "Mineral Province of Canada"; it accounted for more than a quarter of Canadian mineral production by value. Only a few years later, however, it yielded preeminence to Ontario.

New mining towns dotted the landscape after 1890. In British Columbia many of these places were little more than temporary camps. They grew almost overnight, provided work for a decade or two, then declined. The Slocan valley in southeastern British Columbia illustrates the pattern. Virtually unknown in 1890, it was connected to two transcontinental railways (one in the U.S.) by 1895, and was once again a relative backwater by 1912. In the interim its mountainside mines had yielded almost $30 million of silver and lead. Sandon, the focus of mining activity and a boisterous place of 2,000 (with 17 hotels and 50 stores) in 1897, slipped into insignificance; by the late 1920s it was a ghost town. Of course, not all places were as short-lived. Trail, developed initially for the treatment of gold-bearing ore from Rossland, evolved into a regional center of silver-lead smelting, and subsequently expanded to produce zinc. It remains an important processing center today. Similarly, several mining centers in the Shield—Copper Cliff, Timmins, Cobalt—developed around costly chemical processing plants that operated for decades and became sizable towns with a variety of functions.

Technological advances, transport improvements, and reciprocity with the United States had "set agoing an industrial revolution" in the Canadas in the 1860s; by 1870, manufacturing contributed 19 percent to the country's gross national product. But this industry was heavily concentrated in the Montreal and Toronto-Hamilton regions. Perhaps three-quarters of Canadian manufacturing output came from Montreal in the 1870s; here both capital investment and productivity far exceeded Ontario levels, where traditional workplaces were the norm. Even in 1871, 88 percent of Toronto's industrial establishments had fewer than 30 workers; in Hamilton, the average firm had 17 employees although here, as in Toronto, more

than one-half of the city's workers toiled in establishments employing 50 or more. Commercial functions remained significant in all three cities; beyond them, manufacturing was overwhelmingly small in scale and oriented to local or regional markets.

This base was transformed during the half-century after 1879. Decade by decade (with the exception of the 1890s), Canadian manufacturing expanded at a rate in advance of those achieved by most other industrializing countries. Between 1870 and 1915, the value of output rose at a compound annual average rate of 4.2 percent. During this period, the ratio of primary to secondary manufacturing changed little, but the leading industries of the 1870s—secondary iron and steel products, primary wood products, secondary leather products, and food and beverages (primary and secondary)—accounted for a shrinking fraction of value-added as the range of Canadian manufacturing broadened.

Expansion and diversification were accompanied by an increasing concentration of capital and control. Industrial growth in the 1880s was led by a few hundred entrepreneurs, men of relatively small means who parlayed limited assets and their local market positions into considerable fortunes during the depression of the 1870s and the buoyant years that followed. Individualistic and aggressive, many of these individuals found themselves in vigorous competition as transport improvements broke down "natural" (local) monopolies and their businesses expanded into regional or national markets. Partnerships, mergers, and combines were the result. Early in the 1890s the creation of Massey-Harris from two agricultural implement producers based originally in separate small towns in Ontario, and the organization of the Dominion Cotton Mills, which sought to bring all gray cotton producers in Canada into a single company, marked the drift toward oligopoly in Canadian manufacturing. The pace of the movement increased enormously in the early 20th century. As expansion and integration proceeded, as new power sources and new production techniques were introduced, as new products were developed, and as competition intensified, personal and joint-ownership of manufacturing plants gave way to "public" financing generated by the issue of stocks and bonds. Only through corporate mergers and the floating of joint-stock companies could the costs of big business be borne. Between 1900 and 1913 there were 56 major industrial consolidations in Canada. Almost 3,500 joint-stock companies were chartered during this period; their capitalization stood at a staggering $2.23 billion. The consequences were dramatic. In 1870, some 39,000 Canadian manufacturing establishments employed 18,200 people; in 1890, 70,000 firms employed 351,000. Fifteen years later, an additional 31,000 Canadians worked in manufacturing, but they did so in a mere 15,200 plants. Although the number of establishments increased thereafter, the trend to larger enterprises continued. In 1929, 22,000 plants employed 666,000 Canadians.

The regional impact of these developments was far from even. Under the shelter of the National Policy, countless small towns in eastern Canada expanded their manufacturing sectors. Villages turned into "hives of industry." In the Maritimes, cotton mills, sugar refineries, rope works, steel mills, and iron and steel manufacturing plants were established or expanded in a string of towns along the Intercolonial Railway and in a scatter of coastal centers. Most of them were the co-operative ventures of groups of local entrepreneurs; the Nova Scotia Steel and Coal company, for example, developed from a modest partnership of two blacksmiths with the support of New Glasgow's leading merchant families in the 1880s. In Ontario during the 1880s, more than half of all manufacturing occurred in places with populations that have never exceeded 10,000. There were dramatic increases, of 66 percent in Nova Scotia and 51 percent in each of Ontario and Québec, in the value of manufacturing output during the 1880s. But growth was most evident in the larger centers of these provinces. In Toronto, the major indices of manufacturing activity (output, value-added, capital invested, and numbers employed) more than doubled between 1881 and 1891; expansion in the production of food, beverages, and transport equipment gave Montreal almost 40 percent of national output in each of those sectors by 1891; if growth was less marked in Halifax, the value of industrial capital invested there more than doubled between 1880 and 1890. Despite a slight decline in population, Saint John, New Brunswick, grew more rapidly in industrial capital and output than Hamilton, Ontario, a

rising center of textile production and metal fabrication. Winnipeg, alone on the Prairies, also showed the beginnings of railroad-related industry.

As industrial growth gained momentum, so the centralizing tendencies of modern technology worked their effects on the geography of Canadian manufacturing. The growth of scale economies, the advantage of industrial linkages, and the capacity for spatial integration offered by the railroad all hastened change. In the late 19th century the consequences were perhaps most marked at the provincial scale and most evident in Ontario. At Confederation, manufacturing was widely dispersed; Toronto and Hamilton led the province in manufacturing employment, but there were significant concentrations in most of the older settled counties west and along the north shore of Lake Ontario. Twenty-five years later, most places had more manufacturing, but many of them had lost ground in relative terms. Secondary industry had concentrated in a narrow triangle with its apex near Lake St. Clair and its base on the western end of Lake Ontario. Six counties in this area accounted for half of the secondary manufacturing in Ontario and, in comparison with their population, had a disproportionately high share of the province's total. Three of the four fastest-growing secondary manufacturing counties encompassed Toronto, Hamilton, and the Grand River valley; the other centered on the town of London. Much primary manufacturing, tied to the location of its raw materials, remained scattered. Sawmilling, for example, was dispersed across the province in 1891, but the most important production centers were on the northern periphery of settled Ontario, bordering the Canadian Shield. Brick and tilemaking, with near ubiquitous inputs, followed the pattern of secondary manufacturing as growth consolidated the slight concentration of mid-century.

Industry by industry and community by community, this trend implied significant change. Brewing illustrates the case (Fig. 16.10). Demand for its product was virtually ubiquitous, and breweries were widely distributed; 78 places accounted for the hundred or so establishments in the province in the late 1860s. In the 1890s there were fewer than eighty establishments in perhaps 45 centers, although employment in brewing doubled and the value of

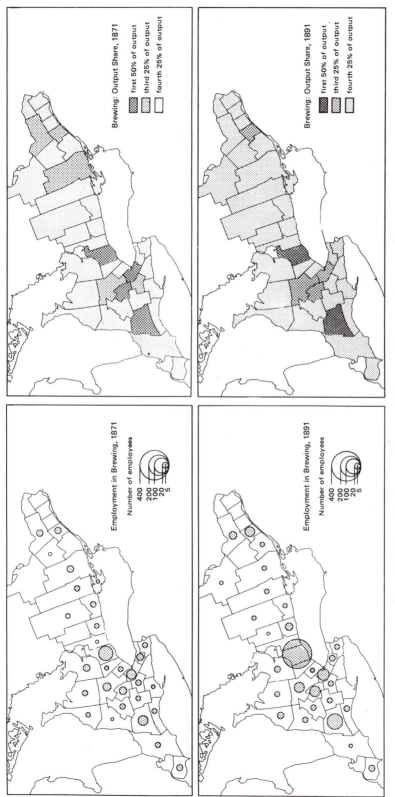

Figure 16.10   The Ontario Brewing Industry, 1871 and 1891 (after Gilmour)

its output tripled between 1871 and 1891. During these years an increasing share of production came from a few centers. By 1891, Toronto and London had fourteen breweries and accounted for more than half of southern Ontario's beer production. Plants distant from these centers continued to produce draft beer for local markets, but they were small and many of them eventually succumbed to the competition of large breweries in the bottled market. Fully indicative of the returns to scale and the market reach that were causing the deindustrialization of small towns across the country was the Toronto-based Dominion Brewing Company, which produced well over 1 million gallons annually and sold its product from Vancouver to Québec during the 1890s.

By 1900, the sting of the developing central Canadian metropolis was being felt well beyond the St. Lawrence. In the Maritimes, a large number of the community-based, locally financed manufacturing concerns developed after 1879 were taken over by central Canadian companies. By 1895, only confectionery production, and manufacturing tied to the iron and steel and staple industries, remained in the control of local entrepreneurs. Several of the region's textile, rope, sugar, glass, and paint manufacturing plants were closed in the "rationalization" that followed consolidation. With local supplies of coal and ready access to the rich Bell Island iron ore deposits of Newfoundland, the region's iron and steel and related plants remained competitive with their central Canadian counterparts through the early 20th century. Indeed, demand for the industries' rails, bridges, railcars, wire, nails, and stoves soared with the spread of western settlement. Nova Scotia pig iron production increased some 13-fold between 1896 and 1912. By World War I, the Scotian Steel Company of Pictou County had some 6,000 employees engaged in mining coal and ore, producing pig iron and steel, and manufacturing a wide range of secondary metal products. But elimination of the government bounty on iron and steel production in 1912, changing product demands, and distance from the growing concentration of industry in Ontario began to undermine Nova Scotia's importance as an iron and steel producer. Its share of Canadian pig iron production fell from 43 to 30 percent in 16 years after 1913. The impact of these changes was com-

pounded by draconian adjustments to the rate structure along the Intercolonial Railway after its incorporation into the Canadian National system. In essence, freight rates that had allowed Maritime commodities into central Canadian markets were raised between 140 and 216 percent. With the recession and price collapse that terminated spiraling postwar inflation in 1920–21, this was a crippling blow to the region's manufacturing sector. Despite efforts to realize scale economies by mergers and consolidations—one of which saw Scotia Steel subsumed within the Montreal-based British Empire Steel Corporation that controlled the Cape Breton industry—the industrial base of the Maritimes was severely damaged. In 1925, the net value of regional manufacturing output was less than half that of 1919. Although tariff and freight-rate adjustments subsequently ameliorated the worst problems of manufacturing in the Maritimes, the rise in manufacturing employment in 1928 and 1929 reflected a reorientation rather than a recovery. Growth was largely confined to the new staples of pulp and paper.

The steady decline in the Maritime's share of Canadian consumer goods manufacturing was mirrored in the tertiary sector as upper-echelon financial and service functions concentrated in central Canada. Early in the 20th century, Maritime banks moved to, or were absorbed by, financial houses in Montreal and Toronto. After 1910, Toronto-based manufacturers (among them Maple Leaf Milling, Massey-Harris, and Canadian General Electric) established wholesale outlets in the major cities of the region. In the 1920s, local retailers felt the competition of brand-name goods offered by branches of metropolitan-based, national retail chains such as Tip Top Tailors and the T. Eaton Company. Overall, branch businesses based outside the Maritimes accounted for less than 10 percent of all business in 1881 but more than 55 percent by 1931. In fifty years a high degree of regional autonomy in resource extraction, manufacturing, construction, transportation, trade, and services had given way to a considerable measure of dependence and the hegemony of Toronto and Montreal.

By 1929, 82 percent of Canadian manufacturing output came from central Canada; Ontario alone accounted for 51 percent of the total. Production of the durable consumer goods that would lead manufacturing growth in the new age of electricity and the internal combustion engine was even more concentrated: at least 95 percent of Canadian automobiles, rubber tires, and agricultural implements came from Ontario; the province also dominated in electrical goods (77 percent), machinery (72 percent), and hardware and tools (68 percent). Québec's leadership was most evident in pulp and paper (54 percent of the national total), the manufacture of railway rolling stock (53 percent), and in traditional slow-growth nondurable consumer goods such as cigars and cigarettes (86 percent), cotton (75 percent), boots and shoes, rubber footwear, and men's clothing (each 60–62 percent). It is significant that the only areas in which the rest of Canada counted more than its 18 percent share of national manufacturing was in Central Electric Stations, railway rolling stock, and nonferrous metal smelting (22–25 percent). Similar patterns were evident in the financial and commercial sectors of the economy. In the 1880s the country had some 44 chartered banks based in eighteen centers with approximately 300 branches; in the 1920s there were 11 banks with more than 4,000 branches, all but one of them headquartered in Montreal or Toronto. Developing insurance, trust, and loan activities, and an important mining stock exchange added further to the financial and managerial significance of Toronto. With more than half of Canada's population concentrated in the St. Lawrence–Great Lakes lowland, Montreal and Toronto were also hubs of wholesale and retail trade. In 1929, Ontario and Québec accounted for 63 percent of retail sales in the country. Sales in Ontario alone exceeded those of the Maritimes, the Prairies, and British Columbia combined, and the country's leading chain and department stores made their headquarters in Canada's two largest cities.

National integration had yielded a clear pattern of regional specialization in Canada. In agriculture as in manufacturing, in commerce as in finance, the centralizing, consolidating tendencies of quicker and cheaper communication, improved industrial technology, modern marketing systems, and modern managerial practices had undermined characteristic early 19th-century patterns of land use and economic organization. Relatively unspecialized regional economies and relatively high levels of local self-sufficiency in foodstuffs, goods, and

services gave way between 1850 and 1930 to a considerable degree of regional specialization in particular resource subsectors, and a corresponding dependence upon long-distance exchange. On the eve of the Great Depression, a central Canadian heartland provided capital, manufactures, and services to an extensive hinterland that contributed resources (minerals, energy, wheat, food and, in the case of the Maritime provinces and the rural fringes of Ontario and Québec, labor) to the developing Canadian economy. The national policy had created the east-west trade that its proponents considered essential to the existence of a national economy, but economic integration failed to generate sentimental or emotional unity among Canadians. Rather, it fostered a strong drift toward regional inequality that emphasized the historical and geographical divisions of the country.

Canada's growing cities were likewise transformed between 1850 and 1930. At the beginning of this period, even the largest urban places were relatively undifferentiated spatially. Wharf and warehouse districts, retail zones, and fashionable streets might be distinguished, but none was entirely homogeneous. If rich and poor, merchant and laborer occupied different streets, they did so in most sections of the city. Segregation was at the level of the block rather than the neighborhood. Thus the urban fabric was an intricate tapestry of heterogeneous land-use patterns, contrasting occupations, and different housing types. Smaller places, down to the busy commercial villages with a handful of mills and workshops that were scattered across the settled countryside, were even more strikingly unsegregated. Income and status differences set families and individuals apart, but in these pedestrian cities and towns proximity reinforced perceptions of the community as a whole.

Seventy-five years later, with improvements in intraurban transport, the growth of urban populations, the rise of industry, and the expansion of commerce, both large and small places bore the specialized, differentiated stamp of the modern urban center. To be sure, broad differences set heartland cities apart from those in the hinterland. Financial, managerial, and manufacturing activity concentrated disproportionately in the former; trading and resource processing tended to be more dominant in the latter. Such differences, however, were not always clear-cut. In Montreal and Toronto, as in such middle-order places as Hamilton and Saint John, sizable areas were devoted to manufacturing. In the dynamic western cities of Winnipeg and Vancouver, commercial uses dominated downtown areas, and there were growing manufacturing zones centered on resource-processing plants (abattoirs, flourmills, sawmills) but including enterprises producing construction materials and consumer goods. In each of these cities, there was also a clear pattern of residential segregation. The rich occupied peripheral areas, their large dwellings remote from the bustle and dirt of the commercial and manufacturing sections of the city; the middle ranks of society (white-collar workers and some skilled tradesmen) concentrated in less grandiose inner suburbs; and the poor occupied deteriorating houses on the fringes of the factory and commercial districts, or built modest dwellings on small lots in newly developed, workingmen's suburbs. Now, as they could not have a half-century earlier, such expressions as "the working-class part of town" and "the other side of the tracks" had meaningful currency. The divisions they reflected were as marked in the landscapes of the cities as they were in the consciousness of their inhabitants.

The case of Vancouver is revealing (Fig. 16.11). When the Canadian Pacific Railway opened a portion of its massive land grant on a hill overlooking the city to development in 1908, its position as a prestigious suburb was secured by a covenant which required that all houses built in the area cost no less than $6,000. Most of them far exceeded this threshold. Abandoning the city's first elite residential area to the more modest dwellings and walk-up apartments that came with streetcar service, lumber barons, real estate lawyers, property speculators, railway executives, and other leaders of Vancouver society erected large, ornate mansions along the curving streets and around the twin greens of Shaughnessy. They had already created a social world, symbolized by the exclusive Vancouver and Terminal City Clubs and the recreational enclaves of tennis and rowing clubs, that affirmed their power and privilege. Downslope from this haven of conspicuous consumption, sawmill hands and their families occupied pairs of 10-by-12-feet

rooms in wooden tenements close to workplaces on the banks of False Creek. On the eastern fringe of the city's warehouse district, more than 5,000 people occupied housing that was crowded and inferior. Even in this new city the social distance between the elite and the laboring population was vast. Blurred to some extent by the pervasive rhetoric of opportunity, the development of comfortable white-collar residential areas to the west of the city core, and the construction of modest cabins by the working class, graphically defined the new order of urban society.

Two novels illustrate the consequences of this transformation. Set in Winnipeg, *The Magpie* (1923) by Douglas Durkin lays bare the tensions generated by marked disparities in the circumstances of urban dwellers. Spacious riverside mansions and "little green and white shack[s]" in straggling suburbs betoken the social composition of the city. Guests at both an "almost majestic" three-storey house with "a roof of red tile . . . a [flanking] wing composed mostly of windows . . . and a stone porch which served as a shelter for visitors entering from automobiles," and at its owner's huge log "cottage" on a nearby lake, were treated to cocktails (despite prohibition), fine dinners, and cigars. A visitor to the modest home of a returned World War I veteran noticed how sparsely it was furnished, with "linoleum on the pine board floor," cheap, cretonne-covered wicker chairs in the living room, and dime-store prints of "The Angelus" and "The Age of Innocence" on the walls; he noticed, too, that the "old sadness" of the soldier's wife mirrored the expressions of lower-class English and French women even as they had celebrated the end of the war in 1918. In these settings, working men lamented the power of the "big fellows" for whom they had fought, for whom they had worked, and by whom the Mounted Police had been called out "to clear the streets with bullets" when labor had gone out on strike. And the rich grew anxious about the "Bolsheviki business" that seemed to threaten the order in which they had prospered.

Writing of Montreal some years later, Gabrielle Roy revealed an even more severely divided city. Although pioneer municipal reformer H.B. Ames had documented the crowded, insanitary housing, the insufficient employment, and the high death rates of the

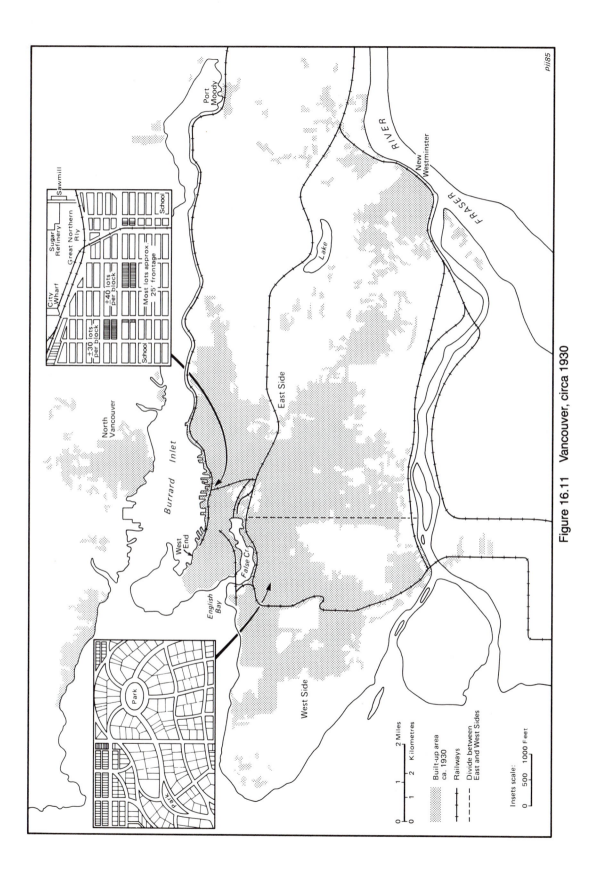

Figure 16.11 Vancouver, circa 1930

City Wharf

Sugar Refinery

Great Northern Rly

Sawmill

School

±30 lots per block

±40 lots per block

Most lots approx 25' frontage

School

North Vancouver

Burrard Inlet

West End

English Bay

False Cr

Park

PARK

West Side

East Side

Lake

Port Moody

New Westminster

RIVER

FRASER

0   1   2 Miles
0   1   2 Kilometres

Built-up area ca. 1930

Railways

Divide between East and West Sides

Insets scale:
0   500   1000 Feet

pij85

French-Canadian, English, and Irish population of Montreal's old industrial quarter in *The City Below the Hill* (1897), little but the ethnic composition of these neighborhoods had changed forty years later. If residents of the wealthy English hill suburb of Westmount were unmoved by the existence of urban poverty as they gazed across the picturesque lights below, *The Tin Flute* (1947) makes clear that the inhabitants of Saint Henri knew little of the city beyond their quarter. French, Catholic, on the margins of relief, and trapped in a run-down neighborhood of factories, railroad crossings, uncertain employment, and rented houses "forbidding in their ugliness and indifference," they rarely crossed its bounds. In this "antheap with the soul of a village" the attitude of a generation "could be summed up by internal torment, outward railery and enforced indolence." To those of Saint Henri, neighboring Mount Royal, with its captivating Olmsted-designed park, was unknown but for the Saint-Joseph oratory and—in ironic reflection of the rift of language, culture, and wealth that divided Montreal society—"the cemetery where the people from down below laid their dead beside those who lived on the hill."

UNCERTAINTY AND THE IDEA OF CANADA

Sharp tensions stretched the fabric of social and economic life in Canada during the early 20th century. In countless, often subtle ways, the traditional ethos—rural, conservative, individualistic, and optimistic—was challenged by urbanization, the rise of socialism, labor organization, and the stark reality of urban poverty. New organizations appeared to represent emerging middle-class professions. Agriculture and industry struggled to secure their respective interests. French-Canadian nationalism stirred by Métis resistance to Protestant settlement in Manitoba in 1870, given a symbol by the execution of Métis leader Louis Riel in 1885, and sharpened by resentment at the Imperial fervor with which English Canadians sent troops to the Boer War, gained momentum with the restriction of French instruction in Ontario schools after 1912 and the introduction of military conscription in 1917. Reflecting the sectionalism of interest, occupation, and lan-

guage that divided the country, the election of 1921 returned a divided House: the Progressives (representing rural Canada) carried the Prairies and several Ontario constituencies; the Conservatives (who had introduced the National Policy) gained most of their seats in industrial Ontario; and the Liberals (opponents of conscription) were the party of Québec. The Canadians might well have concluded, with their wartime prime minister, that the storms of 1914–18 had moved the world from its accustomed anchorage. Looking forward with the disquieting sense that the past had not been assimilated, that Canada had failed to develop an indigenous tradition, they wondered (to paraphrase literary critic Northrop Frye) "where here was."

The question owed something to the pattern of Canadian settlement. The country had been occupied piecemeal. Between New England, the Great Lakes, and the Canadian Shield or, farther west, between the 49th parallel and the climatic limits of agriculture, discrete pockets of land had been occupied over several centuries by successive waves of predominantly European migrants. In each, particular European backgrounds, different technologies, and peculiar economic and environmental circumstances had combined to yield a distinctive mix of people and place. As pockets filled, so people left them, but their destinations lay to the south more often than they did to the west. In the 19th century, most Maritimers and French-Canadians who migrated in search of opportunity ventured to New England; their counterparts in Ontario entered Michigan, the farther Middle West, and the northern Plains. Thus there was little spatial continuity to Canadian settlement. The broken ribbon of towns and farms and camps that marked the northern ecumene was an attenuated archipelago; networks of administration and communication linked its islands, but their people shared too little history to feel strong emotional bonds. Even in 1900 the essence of common experience was local. For all their economic importance, the railroad and the telegraph had hardly had time to create a spiritual community out of disparate settlements scattered across Canada's great east-west distances.

Here the contrast between Canadian and American experience was profound. Lacking the continuously unfolding agricultural frontier that sustained American economic growth for three centuries, Canada barely knew the westward replication of established cultural patterns that gave the appearance of New England, for example, to landscapes across the northern Middle West, and that, north and south, imparted a sense of spatial continuity to the American experience. Nor was there much opportunity in Canada for the western blending of different eastern traditions to produce a distinctive, relatively homogeneous, national culture. And lacking these things, Canada also lacked the mythology associated with the ongoing American occupation of a bountiful land. Try as they might, Canadians would have difficulty seeing themselves in the way Frederick Jackson Turner envisaged his fellow Americans as similar products of the frontier crucible; metaphorically, their country was a mosaic rather than a melting pot. Where good land ran back so quickly into forest, swamp, and muskeg, where the prospects of independent survival were so often circumscribed by thin soils, an intractable climate, or resources that required large capital for their extraction, the pervasive belief in individual opportunity that underlay American liberalism could not flourish. Americans also possessed a firmer sense of North American roots than did Canadians. The *Mayflower*, the "city upon a hill," Lexington, Manifest Destiny, and Reconstruction spoke, symbolically, to the foundation and continuous expansion of the American idea. The Declaration of Independence severed colonial ties to the mother country. By contrast, the Canadian past was short and fragmented, and the country's autonomy uncertain. Canada's longest-established European populations looked back to their subjugation. French Canadians remembered the English conquest, the loss of a vast North American domain, and the financial dominance of an English and Scottish bourgeoisie. Acadians recalled their brutal expulsion from the Bay of Fundy as Nova Scotians developed a tourist trade on the popularity of *Evangeline*, H.W. Longfellow's epic poem about these events. The development of an English-speaking "Canada" was essentially a 19th-century phenomenon, but for much of this period the term "Canadian" (whether Upper, Lower, Western, or Eastern) referred only to a fraction of the people who entered Confederation. Then the Dominion retained its imperial allegiance. Moreover, the achievement of a larger Canada came so suddenly, and so hard on the heels of the pioneer experience that, as Northrop Frye has it, "to feel 'Canadian' was to feel part of a no-man's-land with huge rivers, lakes and islands that very few Canadians had ever seen."

West and east across the country, landscapes reflected these tensions and uncertainties. Newly rich British Columbians demonstrated their material success by the houses they built, but their sources of stylistic inspiration, all external, were curiously diverse. Variants on the Tudor theme—archetypically English with a fashionable suggestion of medievalism and a touch of the Arts and Crafts movement—were common. Symmetrical clapboarded homes suggested the landscapes of colonial New England; massive classicism evoked southern plantations; fretwork, finials, and gables embellished mansions that would not have been out of place in the prosperous milltowns of late 19th-century Maine or Michigan. Versions of the Queen Anne and shingle styles appeared; some found their antecedents in the Spanish missions of California; and a few bore no clear allegiance to any single model but mirrored in their eclecticism the shallow-rooted character of this society.

On the Prairies, past, present, and future often seemed to coalesce. The thatched houses and barns of Galician immigrants, replicas of traditional, fondly remembered Ukrainian structures, stood within sight of the railroad and alongside prefabricated wooden dwellings carried east from British Columbia's large modern mills. Self-sufficient Hutterite colonies followed the communal practices of their 17th-century European predecessors, while in camps and resource towns "blanketstiffs" and bunkhousemen lived hard, transient lives far from home and kin, near the untempered edge of the capitalist labor market. Across the three provinces, civic boosters proclaimed the inevitability of expansion and, whatever the harsh realities of rural life, many viewed the region's farms as stepping-stones to the boundless future envisioned in countless travelers' accounts and immigration pamphlets.

In contrast, eastern landscapes prompted nostalgia and gloom as readily as they inspired optimism. Here, where cities and industry continued to expand, where rundown farms reflected the urban drift of population, and where many a small town felt the erosion of prosperity through the competition of department store catalogues and distant manufacturers, prominent commentators questioned the direction in which Canadian society was developing. Most outspoken among them, perhaps, was Andrew MacPhail, a medical doctor and McGill University professor who railed against the ruinous consequences of continued urbanization. For him, modern cities were a blight on man and nature, their inhabitants necessarily middle-class drones or oppressed factory hands, every one of whom was "more miserable than a Macedonian shepherd and less efficient than a Chinese peasant." There was no society more suited to human fulfillment than that centered on family and farm; together these provided "a world in miniature." Here, as in MacPhail's own Prince Edward Island boyhood (the inspiration of his 1939 novel *The Master's Wife*) families were self-sufficient, women understood their place, existence had more meaning than it did in the city, and people would find inner peace. No matter that such ideas had a long history; Jeffersonian physiocracy flourished as Canada urbanized. The old arguments of some Québec clergy (who saw rural settlement as the savior of traditional spiritual values) were fleshed out and popularized in Louis Hemon's *Maria Chapdelaine* (1921), a bucolic novel with the message that agrarian life was morally and socially superior to the temptations of the city. And several turn-of-the-century analyses of rural-urban migration transcended their statistical bases to make the same point.

If country folk seemed naive to big city slickers, were not their lives rooted in values that mattered, and lived at a pace and a scale that made sense? This was a central question of Stephen Leacock's *Sunshine Sketches* (1912), a bittersweet commentary on the fate of countless small towns, and their people, in an urban age. In population and plan, Leacock's little town of Mariposa was surely familiar to his readers. Dozens of places exhibited its physical characteristics: a broad Main Street; three hotels, two banks, a Post Office; a Fire Hall, an Oddfellows Hall, and a Y.M.C.A.; a newspaper office, a professional block, a hardware store; and side streets of maple trees, wide sidewalks, trim gardens, and houses with verandahs. In

most of them, Main Street presented a scene "of deep and unbroken peace"—to careless observers and visitors from New York whose "standard of vision . . . [was] all astray." Those who lived in such places, and understood them, knew better. Behind the quiet facades, dentists and lawyers sat with their coats off ready to work at any moment. Mariposa was even on the transcontinental railway, and that elevated it above its neighbors, gave it a cosmopolitan air, put it in touch with the larger life—though most trains went through at night and did not stop. Nor were Mariposans ignorant of modern means of getting ahead. Humble Jefferson Thorpe, the barber, realized a fortune by investing in mining stock, after all, and in local eyes he seemed bound to join the ranks of Carnegie and Rockefeller, until the collapse of a bogus, New York-based land company in which he had speculated left him penniless and a barber once more. There is much to amuse in the gullibility of Thorpe, the puffery associated with a local steamboat excursion, and the character of the Rev. Mr. Drone. But for all their foibles the people of Mariposa are kind-hearted and well-intentioned; there are satisfactions, Leacock suggests, in shaving one's townsfolk or otherwise earning a living in such places as Mariposa, satisfactions still grudgingly admitted by rich men sitting in the dull quiet of the city's Mausoleum Club and talking of "the little town in the sunshine that they once knew."

Anxiety about Canada's large urban centers reflected more than a yearning for lost rural innocence. Many felt that the country faced an urban crisis. In their view, Montreal, Toronto, even Winnipeg and Vancouver, were sorely crowded with immigrants. Social and moral degradation seemed endemic; saloons, brothels, squalor, and vice existed in every city of the country. The urban environment had been despoiled by monopolies and the quest for profit; once-pleasant waterfronts were now thick with warehouses and railroad tracks; utility poles and telegraph wires gave downtown streets the appearance of "a Chinese harbor after a typhoon." Civic government was ineffective if not corrupt. Much urban development was dreary, with too many drab buildings and too few parks and trees. Motivated by such perceptions and recognizing that cities were a part of the new order, reformers exposed an assortment of evils in the hope of improving urban circumstances. This did little, however, to allay the concerns of most Canadians. For all its progressive inspiration and its focus on the promise of "Tomorrow's Metropolis," the reform movement emphasized the extent of past improvidence and the problems of urban life. Deeply critical of the individualistic spirit that seemed to have spawned the urban crisis, reformers articulated an organic conception of the city and a collectivist ethos that were both unfamiliar and threatening to many of their compatriots.

As automobile ownership increased during the 1920s, the emerging pattern of urban life seemed to downplay communal involvement and enhance personal freedom. Improved intraurban mobility changed the nature of urban space by setting work and resident farther apart and generalized residential patterns to the extent that urbanites could choose the location of their dwelling more freely than the rigid routes and schedules of streetcars had allowed. It also helped to change the nature of society. New forms of recreational behavior gained popularity as periodic communal outings by wagon or railroad gave way to more spontaneous, family-centered activities. At the same time, movies brought a wider world to the local theater, and new professional sports, increasingly broadcast by radio, began to undermine local allegiances to neighborhood or workplace teams. In a paradoxical way, the rise of mass culture began to fragment experience and emphasize the autonomy of the nuclear family.

In the last analysis, all these developments reflected the Canadian impact of a revolution that had built momentum across North America since 1850. Its progress had been uneven and its ramifications were complex. Hindsight suggests that it was underway in central Canada at Confederation but that parts of the Maritime Provinces escaped its full keen impact until the 1930s. Yet everywhere, at some time, older localized patterns of community life were eroded by the spread of metropolitan influence, the rise of national economic, religious, and political institutions that accompanied improvements in communication, and the wider organization of society that they allowed. Territory ceased to define community. The dense web of social relations that had enveloped, and provided context for, the existence of town dwellers was torn by activities that connected

families and individuals to a larger, more impersonal world. The mesh of personal familiarity that structured local trade was unraveled by the spread and growing dominance of the market economy. Small places lost much of their political and cultural autonomy.

Of course, the extent of this transformation must not be exaggerated. No pre-Confederation settlement was an entirely self-contained and harmonious community, and proximity continues to shape patterns of daily interaction. In the 1920s, many families still lived close to kin. Certain groups, such as the coal miners of Cape Breton, clung doggedly to traditional notions of the moral economy despite their employers' insistence that costs and profits alone defined workplace relationships. And in Canada as in the United States, the Knights of Labor dreamed, for a few brief years at the end of the nineteenth century, of arresting the segmentation of society by fostering community (rather than craft) solidarity among producers in their district assemblies. But as society grew larger and more complex, the public and private dimensions of life grew more distinct, people developed allegiances that transcended locality, the affective community of any individual was more likely to be a part than the whole of local life, and the pattern of shared experience and interdependence that had bound inhabitants of early 19th-century settlements was diluted. "Community" did not collapse, but it was redefined. Older patterns of communal behavior persisted among friends and family. They were blended with new forms of impersonal interaction in the economic and institutional spheres. In this dualistic society, the demands of work, family, ethnicity, religion, politics, and locale often pulled in conflicting directions. Family life was intensified— even eulogized (MacPhail, Hemon)—as a buffer against or perhaps a haven from the impersonality of public life. Because measures of status and identity were blurred as individuals filled different roles in different contexts, ostentatious display became a symbol of worldly success (as in Vancouver). As the informal obligations of small-town life were eroded, the morality of the marketplace was questioned. And reform efforts attempted to ameliorate some of the consequences of the transformation.

Thus Canadians confronted one of the central dilemmas of modernity: the tension between efficiency (reflected in the rationalization, specialization, and centralization of production in technological society) and community (representing traditional human and social values). At the local level the issue was rarely perceived in quite these terms. In many a country town it was a question of survival. Lacking the population to provide efficient services, small places had limited futures in the developing national urban system. Without expansion, decline threatened. But the railroad, population growth, and industry brought change as well as the hope of prosperity in their collective wake and transformed the familiar fabric of town life they promised to save. For individuals, the alternatives were often shrouded by other emotions: parental disappointment at a son's refusal to continue on the family farm because the labor it demanded far exceeded that required for material comfort in a distant town; regret that life's possibilities had been shackled by family obligations; guilt at the denial of ethnic traditions in quest of worldly success. Such themes recur in novels and short stories set in early 20th-century Canada; their authors remain our most sensitive chroniclers of the impact of this tension on ordinary lives.

In the hinterlands of the country, the community/efficiency dialectic was reflected in regional efforts to resist the centralizing monopolistic imperatives of the national policy. Thus Prairie farmers developed grain handling and marketing cooperatives to escape the domination of eastern businesses, bankers, and middlemen. Out of these emerged, in 1917, a regional joint stock company (the United Grain Growers Limited); cooperative wheat pools followed in the 1920s; and in the 1930s came populist political organizations defending regional interests. In the Maritimes, where miners' cooperative stores had developed in response to the growing corporate dominance of coalfield life, deteriorating economic conditions in the 1920s spawned the Maritime Rights movement. Among its diverse platforms was the argument that national economic strategies should be sensitive to the needs of all the country's constituent communities.

Especially in those areas where familiar scales and patterns of local life were threatened by the integration of space, so the region came into focus as a more concrete and comprehensible locality than the abstract nation. So, too, the homogenizing tendencies of modern metropolitan culture were resisted, at least temporarily, by the invigoration of regional identities defined at a scale approximately congruent with that of the islands of Canadian settlement. In Québec, for example, the espousal of economic development and the doctrine of progress by provincial entrepreneurs and industrial leaders precipitated a significant backlash among a considerable group of educated French Canadians. They sought to conserve the traditional values of their society through the publication of a nationalist journal, *L'Action Française*, the editorials of a Catholic press (led by *Le Devoir* of Montreal), and such organizations as the Association Catholique de la Jeunesse Canadienne-française. In the 1920s, some among them dreamed of Quebec as a separate Laurentian republic, sheltered from the disrupting spirit of modern life, a society devoted to "things of the Spirit and scornful of wealth and economic development." To the east, there were similar cries for self-determination from the Maritimes. Significantly, residents of the three provinces were reminded of their distinctiveness and enjoined to "bring the great fact of Maritime Candianism home to . . . [their] hearths and bosoms as it never came before." Early in the 20th century there was a remarkable outpouring of prairie fiction, much of which portrayed the distinctiveness of regional land and life while exploring the conflicting values of traditional community and materialistic society.

Similarly, nationalist concerns reflected the tension between efficiency and community in the 1920s. Subject to the insistent northward spread of the goods, attitudes, and values of technological America, the very existence of a distinctive Canada appeared in question. Much of the new mass culture emanated from the United States. It seemed certain to color Canadian attitudes with what the Vancouver *Star* described as "a reeking cloud of lower Americanisms." According to a contemporary source the trickle had already become a flood by 1920: Canada was a vassal state; its economy, its society, even its universities bore the strong imprint of the United States. Most would have considered such claims exaggerated, but there were more than 300 American firms in southern Ontario by 1914. By 1926, American investment in Canada exceeded British, and with

American capital had come American union organizations. André Siegfried's conviction (developed just before World War I) that the Canadian dilemma was framed in the phrase "moeurs américaines, loyalisme britannique" was amply confirmed in the 1920s. Even in government, it was observed at the end of the decade, "most of what is superimposed is British, but most of what works its way in from the bottom is American." Without resistance to the standardizing tendencies of modern American life, only time seemed to stand between Canadians and the erosion of their cultural and national autonomy.

Old arguments affirming Canadian individuality by contrasting Canadian and American attitudes and institutions were advanced again in the 1920s. Their proponents generally made tradition and heritage the cornerstones of their position by emphasizing the significance of Canada's British connection, the "Norman blood" of its English and French populations, the tory tinge of its society, and so on. Others built their nationalist claims on "geographical" factors, especially land and location. These also seemed to set the country apart from the United States. Canada was the "true north" whose people were, in the environmentalist views of the time, necessarily strong and free. Travel accounts, explorers' reports, novels, painting, and poetry developed northern imagery. In the "folk geography" of the late 1920s, concluded a contemporary, "Canada means the North." In 1930, Harold Innis remarked that Canada existed not in defiance of geography (as Goldwin Smith had claimed), but because of it.

Those who defended local, regional, and national communities often found their interests in conflict. Developing regional sentiment diluted the importance of local identities, just as a vigorous provincial press undermined small-town newspapers. In the same way, economic strategies pursued in defense of the national community often seemed detrimental to regional interests when viewed from the hinterlands, but the communities defined at each of these scales were integral parts of the Canadian experience. In some sense, therefore, the Canadian challenge has been to resolve the multifaceted tension between efficiency and community while reconciling the competing interests of the country's several constituencies. It has

meant a continuing struggle to establish (according to the dictates of scale and context) a viable and satisfying *modus vivendi*, and compromise and adjustment have necessarily been central to this process.

"Deep underlying differences cannot be permanently settled by coercion" observed the Royal Commission on Dominion-Provincial Relations, appointed in 1937 in response to the financial strains of the Great Depression. Yet the poverty and distress of the "dirty thirties" and "the creaking of the federal system" in the extraordinary circumstances of those years demanded decisive action. Provinces and municipalities were quite unable to meet their constitutional responsibilities to provide relief; year by year, between 1930 and 1937, the Dominion government passed emergency legislation to assist local bodies until it met some 40 percent of relief costs across the country. Longer-term changes in the structure of Canadian economic and social life had also undermined the effectiveness of the division of powers between federal and provincial authorities established in 1867. By 1930, education could no longer be administered efficiently as a purely local concern. Providing roads for the rising number of Canadian automobiles had imposed a severe, and unforeseen, burden on provincial budgets. The responsibility for the old and the unemployed vested in the provinces was clearly more appropriately handled at the national scale. Thus the federal government perceived a growing need to deal with social welfare matters, to reorganize the system of public finance and, in the wake of the Depression, to improve management of the money supply. Within a decade of the establishment of the Bank of Canada in 1935, responsibility for economic and social conditions in Canada was heavily concentrated in Ottawa.

Implicit in this centralization was a new conception of Canadian federalism that reflected the growing industrial base of the Canadian economy. Essentially responsible under the British North America Act for national defense and economic development, and with ultimate authority in those matters (such as agriculture and immigration) that it shared with the provinces, the Dominion government played a large role in the growth of Canada through the half-century after 1867. But with the west largely settled, the federal purpose was less evident after 1918 than it had been earlier. Moreover, the great postwar expansion of hydroelectricity generation, pulp and paper production, and mineral extraction (returning resource revenues to all but the Prairie provinces) steadily increased the importance of provincial governments in the 1920s. In this context, recognizing the frictions generated by the differential costs and benefits incurred in various parts of the country through national economic policies, and following the pattern of income transfers between regions necessitated by the uneven incidence of destitution during the Depression, the federal government assumed the role of national broker, collecting most of the money required to provide services in the "national self-interest" and redistributing much of it to the provinces according to need.

This strategy did not win universal approval. When transfer payments were first mooted, the premier of Ontario dismissed them as "an unashamed raid by the orphans of Confederation on the pockets of Central Canada." Some residents of the country's "cadillac" zones have objected, ever since, to the redirection of their taxes to Canada's "cart" regions. But times change, and in recent years once-prosperous and occasionally resentful Ontarians and British Columbians have quietly accepted the revenues that have come with their own economic downturns. Far more important than the sporadic voice of prosperous self-interest has been the firm national commitment, since World War II, to maintain "at least minimal . . . standards for education, public health and care of the indigent" across the country. By the early 1970s this meant, for example, that Nova Scotia and New Brunswick received transfer payments amounting to approximately 80 percent of their provincial revenues, and that equalization grants and specific-purpose transfers more than doubled the funds available to the government of Prince Edward Island. In addition, transfers to individuals (in the form of old age security, guaranteed income supplements, unemployment insurance payments, and family and training allowances, and the like) have tended to be higher in "have not" regions; in the mid-1970s they amounted to almost $540 per capita across the Atlantic region, compared with an average of $410 nationally. Such payments have undoubtedly alleviated the worst consequences of economic

decline and limited the deterioration of living standards for many Canadians.

Recognizing that, in general, transfer payments moderate the symptoms of regional disparity without addressing their causes, the federal government also moved to encourage structural changes and economic expansion in the lagging regions. In the 1960s, in particular, this spawned a succession of federal-provincial programs once familiar by their acronyms: ARDA (the Agricultural Rehabilitation and Development Act of 1961) and the Agricultural and Rural Development Act (1965) were directed at rural farm and non-farm poverty; FRED (the Fund for Rural Economic Development of 1966) offered assistance to primary industry, tourism, and manufacturing in designated parts of the country; they were rationalized, with other development programs, under the auspices of DREE (Department of Regional Economic Expansion) in 1969. The success of these and allied initiatives is probably beyond final determination. Each has had its critics and its defenders, not least because most of them have been seen as political instruments, capable of bringing investment and jobs to particular constituencies as well as to recognizably depressed regions. But they did produce a high level of government participation in the planning and management of many facets of Canadian economic life.

Federal initiatives in other realms expanded concurrently. Since the 1950s, government involvement in amateur athletics, the arts, and letters has grown alongside its commitment to hospitalization, public health services, and welfare. These programs have also generated controversy, because they impinge on the patterns and quality of cultural life within the diverse nation. Yet for all the regional objections and east-west stresses that such government policies have created, they have had their staunch defenders and a clear purpose, at the national scale, as the pressures of continental rationalization have increased.

The Americanization of Canada has been a constant threat and a growing reality since 1930. American capital has surged into the country. By 1950, it accounted for 39 percent of all investment in Canadian manufacturing and 37 percent in mining and smelting; twenty years later it stood at 47 percent and 59 percent in these sectors, respectively, and topped 60 percent in petroleum and natural gas industries. A clear and more general pattern of convergence was apparent in the human landscapes of the two countries. Canada lagged where the United States led, but in both, automobiles, telephones, radios, and television shaped new urban morphologies, continued the transformation of the countryside, and encouraged continent-wide patterns of consumer consumption. The banners of Safeway, McDonalds, and the Kentucky Colonel adorn many a Canadian commercial strip and, in the 1970s, the editor of *Macleans*, Canada's weekly newsmagazine, berated his countrymen for acting like "facsimile Americans."

Yet the border between the countries is not simply a porous political relict. Just as Canadians abroad acknowledge their national sentiment while reinforcing the idea of their country by correcting the common European tendency to describe them as Americans, so Canadians at home—and their elected representatives—have shown a continuing commitment to the east-west alignment and autonomy of their country. Periodic arguments for freer North-South trade have led some Canadians to a rhetorical demand for closure of the 49th parallel; the country has had an agency to review, and influence, patterns of foreign investment in the national economy; the state still operates transcontinental railroad and airline services; and it largely underwrote the construction of a trans-Canada highway. The defeats of two 20th-century governments—one Liberal and one Conservative—have been attributed, in part, to their excessively accommodating stance toward the United States. There have been concerted efforts both to link the country culturally (through the radio and television networks of the Canadian Broadcasting Corporation) and to resist the deluge of American mass culture (by various Canadian content regulations relating to broadcasting, for example).

Together, these events and initiatives suggest that Canadians have felt, and valued, the distinction between their country and the United States. Beneath the surface of continental patterns of consumption built on mass production, there are fundamental differences in the conception and composition of the two countries. Canada is not a monolithic nation. Built on the union of British North America's French- and English-speaking populations—populations with different values and traditions as well as different languages—it has grappled with pluralism from the beginning. The debate has been long and sometimes tortuous, but it has been marked, in the end, by a toleration of differences. Historian W.L. Morton pointed out long ago that this was possible because the country is a society of allegiance (to the monarchy) rather than a society of compact (such as the United States). By giving the law and the state of Canada an objective reality, this has allowed the country to accommodate "a thousand diversities," whereas the government of the United States, resting upon common assent, requires a consensus on fundamentals and depends on conformity. Arguably, too, tolerance was necessary because the patterns of Canadian experience created such distinct cultural and regional interests within the country. In the long run the accommodation of diversity has given Canadian nationalism a broad and inclusive cast. There has been no single set of values to which newcomers could be expected to subscribe; and thus there has been neither a Canadian equivalent of Crèvecoeur's new American man, nor a clearly identifiable "Canadian way of life."

From Canadian experience, in short, has come a Canadian commitment to the development and refinement of an organic society the constituent parts of which are linked by mutual interest, interdependence, and a concern for the common weal. Far from believing themselves a single community, Canadians characteristically admit a tangle of allegiances at local, regional (or provincial), and national scales. On many an issue their community of relevance is smaller than the nation. Yet they confirm the nation by legitimizing its institutions. And the nation maintains its part by implementing social welfare policies, fostering regional development, and attempting income redistribution among the provinces. Provincial governments also contribute to the pattern. Several of them operate essential utilities, some have established a degree of public control in natural resource development, and two have used large resource revenues to create Heritage Funds for the common good. Such arrangements both reflect and bolster an underlying Canadian conception of individual and community as mutually reinforcing, rather than competing, interests.

Canada, in consequence, is a society at once more communitarian than the United States and less collectivistic than the world's social democracies. It is also a society whose constituents have been buffered to some degree against the impact of both increasingly powerful technologies and increasingly anonymous bureaucracies by its underlying commitment to communitarian principles. Yet there can be no doubt that nationhood has exacted its price, as George Grant believed it would. The levy can be measured in part (as Goldwin Smith suggested) in lower material standards of Canadian, vis-à-vis American, living. It has also included the struggle and dissent necessary to secure the middle ground. But the price has had its return in the creation of a distinctive North American nation, a community of communities forged from the particular historical and geographical circumstances of time and place, in which groups as well as individuals share a consensus based on diversity and freedom. To sustain this achievement through the current technological revolution will be a challenge of the utmost magnitude. Not to meet it in the ideological climate of the late 20th century may well be to see diversity eroded and community submerged by the further advance of a monolithic liberal individualism.

ADDITIONAL READING

Books

Aitken, H.G.J., ed. *The State and Economic Growth*. New York: Social Science Research Council, 1959.

Armour, L. *The Idea of Canada and the Crisis of Community*. Ottawa: Steel Rail, 1981.

Artibise, A.F.J., and Stelter, G.A., eds. *The Usable Urban Past: Planning and Politics in the Modern Canadian City*. Toronto: Macmillan of Canada, 1979.

Bender, T. *Community and Social Change in America*. New Brunswick: Rutgers University Press, 1978.

Bercuson, D.J., ed. *Canada and the Burden of Unity*. Toronto: Macmillan of Canada, 1977.

Breen, D.H. *The Canadian Prairie West and the Ranching Frontier, 1874–1924*. Toronto: University of Toronto Press, 1983.

Brown, R.C. and Cook, R. *Canada 1896–1921. A Nation Transformed*. Toronto: McClelland & Stewart, 1971.

Canada. Department of Interior. *Atlas of Canada*. Ottawa: Department of Interior, 1915.

Careless, J.M.S., ed. *The Canadians 1867–1967, Part 1*. Toronto: Macmillan of Canada, 1968.

Dales, J.H. *The Protective Tariff in Canada's Economic Development*. Toronto: University of Toronto Press, 1966.

Easterbrook, W.T., and Watkins, M.H., eds. *Approaches to Canadian Economic History*. Toronto: McClelland & Stewart, 1967.

Fisher, R. *Contact and Conflict*. Vancouver: University of British Columbia Press, 1977.

Forbes, E. *The Maritime Rights Movement, 1919–1927: A Study in Canadian Regionalism*. Montreal: McGill—Queen's University Press, 1979.

Fowke, V.C. *The National Policy and the Wheat Economy*. Toronto: University of Toronto Press, 1957.

Friesen, G. *The Canadian Prairies. A History*. Toronto: University of Toronto Press, 1984.

Gentilcore, R.L., ed. *Canada's Changing Geography*. Scarborough: Prentice-Hall of Canada, 1967.

Gilmour, J.M. *Spatial Evolution of Manufacturing: Southern Ontario, 1851–1891*. Toronto: University of Toronto Press, 1972.

Grant, G. *Technology and Empire*. Toronto: Anansi Press, 1969.

Grant, G.M. *Canada and the Canadian Question*. Toronto: C.B. Robinson, 1893.

Kerr, D.G.G. *Historical Atlas of Canada*. Don Mills: T. Nelson & Sons Ltd., 1975.

Klinck, C.F., ed. *Literary History of Canada: Canadian Literature in English*. Toronto: University of Toronto Press, 1965.

Linteau, P-A.; Durocher, R.; and Robert, J.C. *Québec. A History, 1867–1929*. Toronto: J. Lorimer, 1983.

Marr, W.L., and Patterson, D.G. *Canada: An Economic History*. Toronto: Macmillan of Canada, 1980.

Martin, C.B. *Dominion Lands Policy*. Toronto: McClelland & Stewart, 1973.

McCann, L.D., ed. *Heartland and Hinterland: A Geography of Canada*. Scarborough: Prentice-Hall of Canada, 1982.

Morton, W.L. *The Canadian Identity*. Madison: University of Wisconsin Press, 1965.

National Atlas of Canada. Toronto: Macmillan of Canada, 1974.

Nelles, H.V. *The Politics of Development. Forests, Mines and Hydro-electric Power, Ontario, 1849–1941* Toronto: Macmillan of Canada, 1974.

Owram, D. *Promise of Eden: The Canadian Expan-*

sionist Movement and the Idea of the West. Toronto: University of Toronto Press, 1980.

Palmer, B.D. *Working Class Experience*. Toronto: Butterworth, 1983.

Rasporich, A.W., and Klassen, H.C., eds. *Prairie Perspectives*. Toronto: Holt, Rinehart & Winston of Canada, 1973.

Smith, G. *Canada and the Canadian Question*. Toronto: Hunter, Rose, 1891.

Stelter, G.A., and Artibise, A.F.J., eds. *The Canadian City. Essays in Urban History*. Toronto: McClelland & Stewart, 1977.

Tyman, J.L. *By Section, Township and Range: Studies in Prairie Settlement*. Brandon: Assiniboine Historical Society, 1972.

Urquart, M.C., and Buckley, K.A.H., eds. *Historical Statistics of Canada*. Toronto: Macmillan of Canada, 1965.

Ward, W.P., and McDonald, R.A.J., eds. *British Columbia: Historical Readings*. Vancouver: Douglas & McIntyre, 1981.

Warkentin, J., ed. *Canada. A Geographical Interpretation*. Toronto: Methuen, 1968.

Weaver, J.C. *Hamilton, an Illustrated History*. Toronto: J. Lorimer, 1982.

Zaslow, M. *The Opening of the Canadian North, 1870–1914*. Toronto: McClelland & Stewart, 1971.

Periodicals

Acadiensis: Journal of the History of the Atlantic Region (Acheson, 1972; McCann, 1981; McCann, 1983).

Agricultural History, journal of the Agricultural History Society (Norrie, 1973).

Canadian Geographer, journal of the Canadian Association of Geographers (Rees, 1976; Lehr, 1985).

Canadian Historical Review (Smith, 1970; Harris, 1985).

Canadian Issues/Thèmes Canadiens, journal of the Association for Canadian Studies (Westfall, 1983).

Historical Reflections/Réflexions Historique (Cook, 1974).

Journal of Canadian Studies/Revues d'Etudes Canadiens (Bercuson, 1977; Norrie, 1979; Heintzman, 1979).

Journal of Economic History, journal of the Economic History Association (Norrie, 1975).

17

America Between the Wars:
The Engineering of a New Geography

PEIRCE LEWIS
Pennsylvania State University

THE MELODRAMATIC YEARS

As the United States entered the 20th century, it was approaching a culminating moment in its national career. Ever since the beginning of the 1800s, the country had been converting itself from a collection of small rural settlements on the western margins of the Atlantic into an urban industrial power of continental scale. The momentum of change had been increasing rapidly, especially since the Civil War. By the time the United States entered World War I in 1917, America had become a fast-growing but still half-rural country, seen by many foreigners (and by some Americans) as a kind of political and economic adolescent—a country to be viewed warily but not altogether seriously by the world's great powers. Two years later, in the Hall of Mirrors at Versailles, America took its seat as a rather uneasy equal among those great powers. By 1945, at the end of World War II, there could be no further doubt; the United States had come of age economically, and it was unquestionably the most powerful nation on earth. Looking back across the whole long period, America seemed to resemble a very large machine, driven by an enthusiastic but inexperienced driver, that had been accelerating erratically in second gear for a long time. In the period between World Wars I and II, amid great lurchings and grindings, that machine shifted into high gear.

Throughout the whole chaotic period, America's geography was undergoing profound and irreversible change but that fact was far from obvious at the time. To be sure, some of the changes were subtle, and most people were too close to them to see overall patterns clearly. But it was also easy to be diverted by the procession of epic events between 1917 and 1945: World War I, the economic boom of the 1920s, the Great Depression of the 1930s, and finally a second World War. They were events of high drama, but that very drama tended to obscure basic changes that were already underway, quite independent of wars and economic convulsions.

The two wars were dreadful enough—ghastly international blood-lettings that left both winners and losers exhausted, impoverished, and embittered. But for many Americans, the wars were more exciting than terrible. The United States was a latecomer to both wars, and most of the fighting took place overseas, so that American territory largely escaped physical damage. In both wars, however, the power of American factories and armies ultimately tipped the balance of victory. By the end of World War II, historians had begun to call the 1900s "the American Century."

The two decades between the wars were just as dramatic, although at times they simply seemed demented. For many Americans (though by no means all) the Roaring Twenties were times of unprecedented prosperity, while at the same time, the whole national libido seemed to be spilling over in an orgy of hedonistic excess. To Americans of traditional mind, the country seemed to have come unhinged. Newspapers painted lurid pictures of sexual license and gang warfare, of bomb-throwing anarchists, and of courtroom trials to determine whether men had descended from monkeys. Bizarre creatures appeared from nowhere: flappers, Bolsheviks, rumrunners, hoodlums. And then, as a fitting climax to a crazy decade, the economy ballooned, then burst and crashed with paralyzing finality on Wall Street in October 1929, leaving the nation prostrate and sending shock waves around the world. Yet the crash was only the curtain-raiser for another epic drama, equally amenable to vivid caricature: a ruined nation, led by a charismatic president, struggling to reform its institutions and ultimately emerging chastened from the worst economic disaster in its history.

Then, just as things seemed to be getting better, a new and more frightful war broke out, and America was dragged once more into the fighting. Altogether, it is hard to find three decades of American history as lurid and as packed with melodrama.

But the parade of colorful events obscures more subtle long-term happenings. During the interwar period, three major changes were taking place that would alter fundamentally the geography of the United States and with it the whole character of the country. One change was *technological*, involving nothing less than a total overhaul of the nation's system of transportation and communications, the whole machinery that held the country together. A second was *political*, as the federal government began to assume a much more active role in what had previously been regarded as private matters—the migration of people, and the management of land and water. The third was *demographic*: the American people were migrating in unexpected numbers and in unexpected directions, leaving some parts of the country desolated and propelling others into positions of new importance.

BUILDING A NEW SYSTEM OF TRANSPORTATION AND COMMUNICATIONS

Revolutions are hard to recognize by those involved in them. So it was with the generation of young Americans who were growing up at the turn of the 20th century. Very few realized that they were about to participate in a social and geographic upheaval, caused by the almost simultaneous adoption of four machines of transportation and communications. These were the automobile (and the road system the automobile would require), the telephone, motion pictures, and the wireless radio. Any one of these devices by itself would have provoked major change. Arriving in combination, they brought on a cataclysm.

It was not the *invention* of the machines that made such an enormous difference in the fabric of American life. Actually, no single person "invented" any one of them. Each was a complicated device that had been evolving through a sequence of major and minor inventions, spread over the last quarter of the 19th century.

As of 1900, none had yet made any important impact on the fabric of American life; all were crude and expensive playthings for inventors or for rich people in big cities, but not taken seriously in most of the country. What converted these gadgets into instruments of revolutionary change was *engineering*—the ingenious combination of machinery and corporate organization that would transform these curiosities into cheap, reliable, mass-produced necessities. That happened almost simultaneously in the short period between 1910 and 1925, when all four abruptly reached critical mass and were enthusiastically adopted by millions of Americans. By the end of the 1930s, almost nothing in America would be the same, including some of the country's most basic maps.

(The airplane arrived at about the same time, of course, invented in 1903, and employed with spectacular effect in both World Wars. Unlike the automobile, however, the airplane never came into common public use, partly because of cost, partly because it required great technical proficiency to fly an airplane. It was not until after World War II that airplanes came into widespread commercial use and began to affect the nation's transportation system on a grand scale.)

The Coming of the Automobile

The automobile made the biggest difference. For the last half of the 19th century, the railroads had been the single dominant fact of America's transportation system—a centerpiece in the life of all Americans. If goods or people were moved any significant distance, they moved by railroad—or they did not move. Even ideas traveled by railroad, which handled most bulk deliveries of newspapers, magazines, and nearly all the nation's mail. To be located at any distance from a railroad was to be removed from the mainstream of the country—America's equivalent of Siberia. Altogether, it is hard to imagine a large country so totally dependent on a single technology.

By their very success, however, railroads had smothered competing modes of transportation. The nation's excellent system of inland waterways had been allowed to fall into disrepair. It was even worse with rural roads; most of them were miserable tracks of mud and rubble, used mainly for short hauls of goods and mail between farms and the nearest railroad siding—and then only in good weather. There was nothing remotely approximating a national or even a state highway system.

While railroads provided mobility on a national scale, they were irksome things to many ordinary Americans. Privacy during travel was impossible; unless one owned a private railroad car, one traveled in the intimate company of strangers. Travelers were forced to conform to fixed rails and fixed schedules and, if they had a long wait for a connecting train or simply had to stop overnight away from home, they had to stay in hotels near the railroad station, often disagreeable places in the noisiest and most crowded part of town.

The automobile promised freedom from all that—the promise of its name, *auto*-mobility. With a privately owned automobile, individuals could travel where and when they wanted, rapidly and cheaply over long distances. Such a thing had never happened before in human history, and the prospect was exhilarating. But two things were needed first. The price of automobiles had to drop to the point where ordinary people could afford them. And the country needed a system of decent long-distance roads. Both would require enormous expenditures of money and effort, but the rewards were too alluring to postpone. By 1910, both things had begun to happen; by 1920, America was in the process of retooling its whole basic transportation system. An elemental part of that process was the Model-T Ford, the most popular car ever built and, along with the cotton gin, the most influential machine ever manufactured in America.

Before the Model-T, most automobiles were toys for rich folk—expensive finely machined racing cars that would operate properly only on the smooth surfaces of race tracks or city streets. Henry Ford changed that, not by any single invention, but by engineering a combination of previous inventions into a new form of industrial institution. In effect, he did three things that nobody had ever done before. First, he designed a car that was durable enough to stand up under the pounding of country roads, yet simple enough to be repaired by any ingenious farm boy with reasonable access to spare parts and a bit of scrap metal or piano wire. Second, Ford designed a production line that reduced the act of assembling a complex ma-

chine to a large number of very simple steps. By so doing, he could hire factory workers with little mechanical experience, Americans fresh from the hills of Appalachia or European immigrants who could barely speak English, but who could turn out high-quality machines that would keep running for a long time. Third, and equally important, he designed and put into place the first large-scale system of automobile agencies. By 1927 there were 7,000 Ford agencies, ready to supply Ford owners with spare parts or to sell a new Ford to people who had never driven a car before, and had never imagined they could own one. Now, at unbelievably low prices, the Model-T was within the reach of Everyman.

Ford introduced the Model-T in 1909, and it was an instant success. In 1915, his factories in Detroit turned out a million cars—the first time that ever happened. Ford continued building Model-Ts until 1929, when competition from Chevrolet finally forced him to go into production of the more sophisticated and comfortable closed sedan, the Model-A. By that time, however, he had produced some 29 million Model-Ts. It averaged out to an amazing figure: one Model-T for every four Americans.

The biggest change was in the lives of farmers. Before the Model-T, the word "farmer" was insultingly (but often correctly) used to describe a person who was isolated, ignorant, and crude. The Model-T started a process that would eventually make that definition obsolete in America. Ford's cheap little machine may not have looked like much, but it brought to a sudden end the mind-numbing rural isolation that had afflicted farmers since the beginning of history.

Like any huge complicated enterprise, the auto industry soon came to be dominated by a few, large, powerful companies. At the beginning of the century, a host of competitors had struggled to seize a corner of the mass market, or at least to carve out new niches in that market. Most of the new companies promptly went out of business—some because they were mismanaged, some because they misjudged the product or the market, but most because they were undersized and undercapitalized. The most successful of Ford's competitors imitated Ford's own techniques of mass manufacturing and mass marketing, and operated at the same gigantic scale. By the 1930s, the automobile industry had swelled to become the largest consumer of industrial raw materials in the United States, and its labor force was enormous. It was no place for corporate pygmies.

The immediate result was geographic concentration, as the biggest companies settled in a small number of urban places, focused on southern Michigan. Detroit was the acknowledged capital, the location of Ford's main plants and the headquarters of Ford's chief competitors, the gigantic General Motors Corporation and the Chrysler Corporation. The city of Detroit exploded in consequence, from a modest Great Lakes port to the nation's fourth largest city. But similar things were happening throughout the manufacturing belt from southern Wisconsin to northern Ohio, and town after town became a booming city when the automobile industry moved in. The result was a region of large company towns, utterly dependent on one specific auto company and utterly dominated by that company. South Bend, Indiana, for example, became the creature of the Studebaker Corporation. Flint, Lansing, and Pontiac, Michigan, meant, respectively, Buick, Oldsmobile, and Pontiac. Furthermore, the scale of the automobile industry was so huge that mere suppliers of auto parts became industrial giants in their own right, and they too were concentrated in a few highly specialized places. Akron, Ohio, became a city of 250,000 people by supplying tires for the auto industry; Saginaw, Michigan, supplied General Motors with spark plugs and cast-iron motor blocks. All these places took on much the same character: a boom-or-bust economy, depending on corporate whimsy or public taste for a particular model or brand—huge bursts of prosperity and immigration when plants were in production, equal bursts of unemployment and out-migration when the plants were shut down for retooling, as most of them were each summer. Even worse, the auto industry was notoriously sensitive to economic fluctuations; if money was in short supply, cars were the first thing Americans stopped buying. As a result, the Depression struck the auto industry's undiversified towns with paralyzing force. It was no coincidence that those same cities saw the organization of America's biggest and most militant industrial labor unions during the 1930s, and some of the country's bitterest and most violent strikes.

The explosive growth of the automobile industry during the 1910s and 1920s sent ripples, then tidal waves, across the face of the American economy. Nowhere was the effect felt more immediately than in the petroleum industry. Before the automobile, most of America's oil was refined into kerosene for use in oil lamps. Most of that oil had come from relatively small fields, like those of western Pennsylvania (where the world's first successful oil well had been drilled in 1859) and southern California, and a few in Texas. In 1901, however, wildcatters brought in the most spectacular gusher the world had ever seen—at Spindletop, near Beaumont in east Texas. The resulting oil rush ·revealed that Texas and Louisiana were sitting on top of not just one, but several of the world's biggest oil and gas fields. Texas promptly became the nation's leading producer of oil and gas; and when subsequent discoveries were made in Oklahoma, they were more than matched by still newer discoveries in west Texas. By 1941, the American economy was so dependent on Texas, Oklahoma, and Louisiana oil that the federal government built a network of pipelines to the Northeast to carry the oil and gas and bypass the Nazi submarines that had been torpedoing tankers in the Atlantic.

The oil boom, in turn, produced its own effects, both immediate and distant. In the vicinity of the oil fields, byproducts from refineries formed the basis for a sizable chemical industry along the Gulf Coast and lower Mississippi River. That industry was greatly stimulated by the discovery of ways to make synthetic rubber to replace natural rubber supplies from southeast Asia, which had been seized by the Japanese during World War II. The boom in postwar plastics was another result of that episode.

Even more important, however, was the simultaneous production of natural gas and cheap fuel oil for domestic heating. Most 19th-century Americans had heated their houses with wood- or coal-burning stoves. In most parts of the country, there was no shortage of either. By the turn of the 20th century, however, central heating had become a common fixture in most new houses, especially in the growing cities, and the fuel was almost always coal. Clean-burning anthracite was much favored over the oily and sulferous bituminous, and northeastern Pennsylvania prospered mightily because it produced the bulk of the world's anthracite.

The discovery of Texas oil and gas, and the building of a national pipeline system, gave middle-income Americans the option of heating their houses with cheap, clean fuels that burned in furnaces that needed almost no tending. The conversion from coal to gas or oil was swift and joyful, as men and boys from coast to coast were freed from the daily chore of shoveling coal, hauling ashes, and breaking clinkers, and women were liberated from cleaning soot and coal dust from clothes, curtains, and furniture. By the end of World War II, coal furnaces were converted as fast as American families could afford to do so. As they did, the Pennsylvania anthracite fields started to shut down, and thousands of miners were put out of work. It was not long before northeastern Pennsylvania would be in a state of acute permanent depression. Nor was it an isolated instance. The automobile and the machinery that went along with it set in motion chain reactions that reverberated back and forth across the economic map of the United States.

The huge new oil discoveries, furthermore, guaranteed America an unlimited supply of cheap gasoline at precisely the time that middle-class Americans were first beginning to use cars in large numbers. The increase in gasoline consumption, therefore, reflects not only the growth of a rich new industry in Texas, but also serves as an excellent measure of how much Americans were using their cars. During the 1920s that increase was meteoric. In 1919 Americans consumed about 2.7 billion gallons of gasoline; by 1922, consumption had doubled. By 1926, it had doubled again and was on its way to doubling once more when the New York Stock Exchange collapsed in 1929. Thereafter, the data are curious and revealing. Even during the worst days of the Depression, gasoline consumption declined only once (1931–32) and then only very slightly. From 1933 onward, consumption continued to increase, albeit not quite at the same frantic rate. The figures show that Americans had stopped buying many new automobiles, but had not stopped driving the ones they already owned. And by 1941 there were almost 30 million cars and about 99 million people of driving age—one car for every 3.3 people. The automobile had become an entrenched institution in American life. Even an economic cataclysm could not dislodge it.

New Roads
for New Cars

The explosion in auto production set off a simultaneous explosion in road building. Good roads, of course, made the ownership of automobiles increasingly attractive and symbiotically stimulated the sale of cars. Car owners, furthermore, tended to be fairly affluent and quickly came to constitute one of the most vocal and powerful voting blocs in the country. Politicians were not slow to recognize that road-building was a popular task for any government, irrespective of political party or ideological coloration.

It was one thing to build a good road here or there, but quite another to build a national road system. The main question was how to pay for such a system; it was an expensive business to build highways that would stand up under heavy traffic and bad weather. A few experiments with toll roads in the New York metropolitan area were successful because New York was affluent and densely populated. But in most parts of the country, few roads could pay for themselves on a mile-by-mile basis. If a road system was to service the whole country, it would have to be a government enterprise—rather like running the post office or maintaining an army or navy. As early as the 1890s, several states had created highway departments, charged with the job of designing roads to proper standards and letting bids to competent contractors. In 1916, Congress passed the Federal Aid Road Act, committing the federal government to support a national program of road improvement, but leaving ultimate control of highway systems in the hands of individual states.

Meanwhile, engineers had been devising techniques of building cheaper roads that would stand up under heavy use. The greatest breakthrough came in 1920 with the discovery that eight inches of reinforced concrete, laid on a proper base of crushed rock, could withstand very heavy loads. Although concrete roads were initially costly, they required little maintenance. Before the end of the 1920s, concrete had become the material of choice in building any important road in the United States. More than incidentally, those concrete roads made possible the use of increasingly heavy trucks. Within thirty years, trucks had taken over the haulage of most general cargo in the United

States and had driven many of the nation's railroads to the brink of bankruptcy.

Leaving control of roads in the hands of individual states had two unintended effects. First, since political support for road-building came largely from farmers, states put a high priority on building light-weight macadamized "farm-to-market" roads, in preference to heavy-duty interstate highways. In its initial stages, then, the building of good roads did not encourage long-distance traffic either of people or goods; the railroads retained that business until the end of World War II. Instead, the new roads greatly stimulated short and medium-distance traveling—weekend excursions to grandmother's house a hundred miles away or a few days of camping alongside the road. Thus, while Americans were not yet in the habit of using cars for long-distance vacations, they were developing the institutions that would grow into a full-blown roadside tourist industry after World War II. What began as whimsical adventures in roadside tenting quickly produced new institutions: first, free, municipally financed campgrounds evolved into more elaborate campgrounds where a small fee was required, then to campgrounds with rude shelters, then to more permanent structures with running water and mattresses, then to "kozy kabins" with bedding and heating and running water, and ultimately a "motel," a term reportedly used for the first time in San Luis Obispo, California, in 1927. Although nationwide motel chains would not emerge until after World War II, a New England restaurateur named Howard Johnson had discovered in the 1930s that travelers could be taught to stop at a roadside establishment if it looked familiar and if it held out the promise of quick service and clean, unsurprising victuals. Howard Johnson's became the first of many fast-food chains to array their interchangeable logos and interchangeable food along the sides of America's newly democratic highways.

The second effect of state financing of roads was that only the richest states were able or willing to pay for elaborate road networks. Poor areas like the South were conspicuously lacking in good roads, and so was much of the West, where it was prohibitively expensive to build long-distance roads through sparsely populated areas.

Despite the gaps, a genuine national road system had begun to develop. By 1925, the network had grown so complicated that the American Association of State Highway Officials was impelled to devise a national highway numbering system, replacing the colorful but undependable practice of naming arterial highways. By that time, it had become possible to drive on uninterrupted paved roads to all the main population centers in the Northeast, and along most of the well-traveled vacation routes between New York and Miami (Fig. 17.1, top).

The 1930s saw rapid completion of the basic system, largely the result of the Depression. The New Deal undertook road-building on an unprecedented scale, part of a massive public works program for relief of the unemployed. In the highly political business of road-building, it is not surprising that special favor was bestowed on regions of the country that returned Democratic majorities, and on the home districts of powerful congressmen. In effect, that meant the "Solid South," the 11 states of the old Confederacy that had been voting against Republicans since Reconstruction. During Franklin D. Roosevelt's first two terms of office, an area that had been almost roadless at the beginning of the Depression gained an excellent system of concrete highways. By the end of the Depression, it was possible to drive from coast to coast entirely on paved roads. Except in sparsely populated areas of the dry or mountainous West, most of America's rural country lay within easy reach of a paved road. All in all, it amounted to a national transformation (Fig. 17.1, bottom).

Roads would not be used routinely for long-distance travel in most parts of the United States until well after World War II; driving was simply too slow. Highway engineers had not yet gotten into the habit of building bypasses around cities and towns, so that long-distance drivers inevitably confronted a procession of urban traffic jams. In the country, a plethora of crossroads and driveways made driving both frustrating and dangerous. Commercial clutter alongside major highways made things even worse.

There was an obvious but expensive solution: to build special arterial roads, where access was limited to a few carefully engineered intersections, and where commercial development was banned completely from the roadside. Typically, New York City provided the leadership in trying out the idea on a large scale. Even before World War I, a few limited-

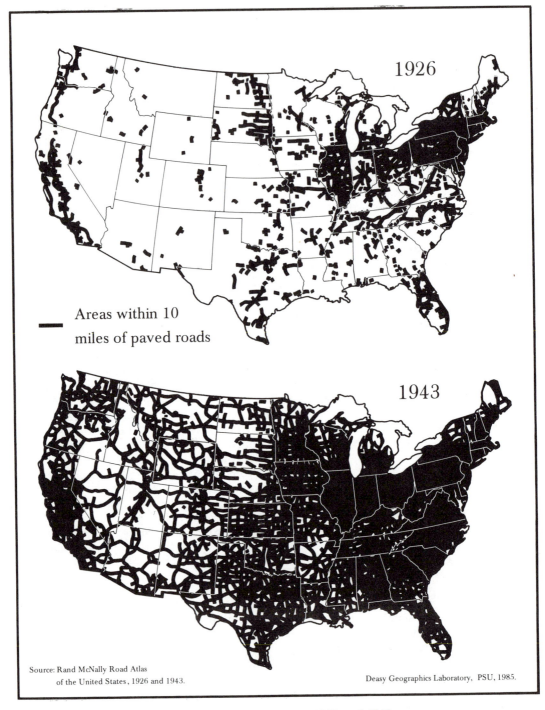

Areas within 10
miles of paved roads

Source: Rand McNally Road Atlas
    of the United States, 1926 and 1943.

Deasy Geographics Laboratory, PSU, 1985.

Figure 17.1   Paved Roads, 1926 and 1943

access tollways had been built around New York to serve affluent suburbanites (the Bronx River Parkway, finished in 1923, was the first). But it was Robert Moses, in the 1920s and the 1930s, who used his extraordinary powers as director of the Port of New York Authority to finance and build an elaborate system of expressways and bridges that would shortly tie the huge New York metropolitan area together, and that would ultimately extend its tentacles far into the surrounding countryside.

Long-distance driving, however, was still unusual. When it happened, as when New Yorkers drove to Miami on vacation, or when Okies migrated to California on Route 66, it was a cause for comment. During the late 1930s, two roads were built that would lay the groundwork for a massive change in American driving habits after World War II. One was the Pennsylvania Turnpike, a limited access tollway that sliced smoothly across the Appalachian Mountains and reduced travel time between Pittsburgh and Harrisburg from two grueling days to an easy (and scenic) five hours. (It is ironic that the turnpike was built atop the unfinished roadbed of a bankrupt railroad.) The other was the Arroyo Seco Parkway (now the Pasadena Freeway), a multilane, limited-access free highway between downtown Pasadena and Los Angeles. Each road proved an important point. The turnpike demonstrated that low-gradient, limited-access highways could be built for long distances, even over very difficult terrain, and still generate enough traffic to pay for themselves. The Arroyo Seco proved that Americans were willing to pay for extremely expensive roads by use of taxes, not by collecting special tolls. Both ideas were fundamental to democratizing American highways and to the thinking that created the interstate highway system of the 1950s and 1960s.

A NEW COMMUNICATIONS SYSTEM: TELEPHONES, MOVIES, AND RADIOS

Automobiles and roads were revolutionary devices because they made it easy and attractive to move goods and people in all sorts of directions in which they had never moved before. But there was a simultaneous revolution in the movement of *ideas*, sparked by powerful machines of communication: telephones, motion pictures, and wireless radios.

All these technologies did essentially the same thing: they allowed Americans in almost any part of the country to be plugged into the same national circuitry of ideas and tastes, to see faces and hear voices from the farthest corners of the earth. It was a highly democratic technology, cheaply available to huge numbers of people over vast expanses of territory. Before long, that technology had begun to blur some of America's sharpest geographic distinctions, the regional differences between North and South, between East and West, between city and country.

The effect of the telephone was felt first. At the turn of the century the telephone had been in commercial use for about two decades, but there were only about 1 million instruments in the whole country—primitive devices used mostly for short-distance intraurban business conversations. The invention of the vacuum tube in 1906 made it possible to amplify telephone signals over long distances, and the first transcontinental commercial service was put in place by 1915, using only three relay stations. Still, long-distance calling was expensive; a three-minute call from New York to San Francisco cost $20.70. Short-distance service was much cheaper, however, and from 1900 to 1930, telephones were installed at an almost steady rate of about 600,000 instruments per year. By the time of the Wall Street crash in 1929, 40 percent of American households possessed a telephone, about 20 million in all.

The Depression halted the telephone boom for a short time, but it did little to dampen American enthusiasm for the telephone. Just as with automobiles, few people had enough money to install a new instrument, but those who already had one continued to use it at an increasing rate. In 1930, Americans held 80 million phone conversations per day, and they kept talking throughout the Depression. In 1940, with almost the same number of instruments, the number of conversations was up to 95 million a day. Well before the beginning of World War II, Americans had obviously acquired the telephone habit. They would never lose it.

To be sure, telephone service did not spread

uniformly across the country. Cities received telephones first, just as later they acquired dial instruments and automatic switching equipment; the rough-and-ready quality of rural telephone exchanges served as the butt of bad jokes until well after World War II. Poor parts of the country had very few phones, conspicuously in black areas of the South. But the cost of service continued to go down. The Bell Telephone Company, owner and operator of most American telephones, was applying the same principles of high-quality technology at very low prices that Henry Ford had used to democratize the Model-T. By 1945, the cost of that three-minute transcontinental call had dropped to $2.50, and local service was even cheaper by comparison. By the same time, an enormous proportion of the nation's social and commercial business was being transacted by telephone, and the majority of Americans had come to view telephone service as a kind of basic human necessity. To be without phone service was to be stranded in limbo.

Still, telephones were mainly instruments of two-way communication between individual persons. Radio and motion pictures stimulated a different kind of communication, for they operated en masse, and they operated one-way, from producer to consumer, spreading mass culture almost instantaneously across the entire nation. Nothing like that had ever happened before in a large modern country, and it is hardly surprising that the intelligentsia from Europe's heterogeneous cultures were highly critical of American mass communications—especially movies, which were popular not only in America, but all over the world. It did them little good. Once movies and radio came to town, nothing would ever be the same again.

The movies came first. Although they were widely available early in the century, they were hard to take seriously—flickering five-minute reels, designed for nickelodeons, showed simple-minded dramas, crudely staged and crudely acted. All that changed rapidly in the first decades of the 20th century. By 1912 D.W. Griffith had produced "The Birth of a Nation," sometimes described as the first full-length feature film. It was instantly popular and hugely profitable; other such films were quickly produced in such numbers that any American

town of any consequence possessed at least one movie house by the end of the decade. By 1927, Warner Brothers released Al Jolson's "The Jazz Singer," the first commercial film with coordinated sound track; by 1929, silent pictures were things of the past, as Hollywood went over to making "talkies." Meanwhile, box office receipts were booming. In 1922, the first year when data were available, American movie theaters were selling 40 million tickets per week. By 1930, the figure had risen to 90 million, and annual receipts totaled almost three-quarters of a *billion* dollars. Considering the scarcity of money at the time, this was an enormous sum.

American movie-making had become big business, and it soon began to act like one. Just as automobile producers had achieved economies of scale by concentrating production in one small region, the movie industry settled down in southern California, taking advantage of the region's enormous environmental variety and year-round good weather for outdoor filming. And just as auto production put the horse and buggy out of business, the movie industry fairly well destroyed small-scale local entertainment in the United States—and a good deal of local color in the process. Whether the critics liked it or not (and many did not), the movies opened a whole new world to millions of Americans. And it was the *same* world for everybody: people from farms and small towns saw exactly the same features and the same newsreels that big-city people were seeing; they laughed at the same jokes, wept at the same bathos, and thrilled to the same deeds of heroism. As a force of cultural convergence, there had never been anything like it.

But there shortly would be. In 1920, radio arrived like a thunderclap on the American scene and promptly began to do the same thing to the the nation's culture that movies had been doing. As with telephone and the movies, basic radio theory had been known since the late 19th century, and long-distance radio transmission by Morse code had become common before World War I. But not until 1915 had the technology accumulated to permit transmission of voice signals without gross distortion over long distances. Once that happened, commercial radio simply exploded. The first commercial radio station, KDKA in Pittsburgh, went on the air in November 1920, broadcasting the returns of the Harding-Cox presidential election. Three years later, there were 556 licensed stations in the United States, and a brand new industry was manufacturing half a million radio sets per year. By 1929, more than 10 million American households were equipped with radios, and by the end of World War II they were virtually ubiquitous.

Unlike the movie and automobile industries, unrestrained competition in the radio industry was intolerable; there were, after all, a finite number of usable wavelengths, and the scramble to control those wavelengths threatened to reduce the airwaves to babbling chaos. In 1927, the government stepped in with the Federal Radio Act, creating what eventually became the Federal Communications Commission, armed with authority to grant licenses and to restrict the range and frequency of transmissions. Public control for radio waves, however, emphatically did not mean public broadcasting. Despite pleas from David Sarnoff of R.C.A., the United States rejected the European model, where license fees were used to support publicly owned networks. American radio would be a commercial venture, supported by advertising revenues, and those revenues soon grew very large indeed. As a result, there was a scramble to gain control of available wavelengths and, after considerable litigation, 1926 saw the creation of the National Broadcasting Company, the first of several nationwide radio networks. It is hardly surprising that those networks came to be based in New York and Hollywood, where the nation's main entertainment industries were already well entrenched. There was, in consequence, much overlap in the ownership of radio networks and motion picture studios, with the result that radio broadcasts quickly grew increasingly homogeneous in content. By 1945, only a tiny fraction of the American population was beyond the range of a radio station, affiliated with one of the four or five major national networks, all broadcasting essentially the same mix of news, drama, and popular music. Very few instruments in the history of technology have done so much so quickly to knock down the boundaries of geographic regionalism in the United States—and so much to promote the acceptance of homogeneous national culture, values, and tastes.

GOVERNMENT AS AGENT OF GEOGRAPHIC CHANGE

Few Americans at the turn of the century could have foreseen the profound impact of the new technology, but another change was coming that was just as difficult to predict, and geographically just as portentous. For the first time on a large scale, the federal government would undertake a permanent, active role in what had previously been regarded as private affairs—especially the movement of immigrants and the use of land and water. It represented a major shift in political philosophy, and it cut raggedly across party lines.

Strong central government had been anathema to Americans since long before the Revolution. Most Americans agreed enthusiastically with Ralph Waldo Emerson's maxim: "The less government we have, the better—the fewer laws, and the less confided power." The Bill of Rights had been written to enforce that idea and had spelled out basic limits to federal power. But Americans held two other geographic rights to be equally fundamental: that people should be allowed to move when and where they pleased, and to do what they pleased with private property.

Toward the end of the 19th century, those attitudes had begun to change, especially as they affected private property rights. Populist farmers of the West and South had agitated successfully for government control over rates charged by private railroad companies. Theodore Roosevelt and his Progressive Republicans had extended that control by arguing that property rights were not absolute, and that state and federal government possessed the power and moral authority to counterbalance the growing might of irresponsible corporations. Woodrow Wilson promoted similar arguments under Democratic auspices. The passage of the Income Tax Amendment to the U.S. Constitution in 1913 laid the financial foundation for an enormous increase in federal power, but it was the logical culmination of a multipartisan process that had been gathering strength for several decades.

The federal intervention came in two sharply different areas, and from quite different political directions. The first occurred during the 1920s under the auspices of conservative Republican administrations, and resulted in stringent controls over immigration. The second came in the 1930s under the New Deal in response to the Depression, floods, and dust storms, and resulted in massive new federal regulation of land and water. In both cases, the federal government took action that would have seemed outrageous at the turn of the century. And in both cases that government action changed the fundamental human and physical geography of the United States.

Immigration Controls

World War I greatly stimulated the growth of government activism and unprecedented interventions in what had traditionally been regarded as sacrosanct private affairs. Some of the wartime interventions were temporary; government seizure of the railroads, for example, came to a speedy end after the Armistice. But other "emergency" measures became permanent. Two in particular would quickly change the complexion of American life. One was national prohibition; the other was the first set of comprehensive laws to limit foreign immigration. Within a very short time, Americans decided that Prohibition had been a mistake, and it was repealed by passage of the 21st Amendment in 1933. Stringent immigration controls, however, became a permanent institution.

Those immigration laws represented a fundamental change in American policy and in American attitudes. Throughout national history, free immigration had been an unquestioned cornerstone of national policy, and the idea of limiting the movement of European people into the country was generally viewed as un-American. (Excluding non-whites was something else again. Immigrants from China had been completely barred since 1882, under provisions of the Chinese Exclusion Act, passed under pressure from Knights of Labor and a coalition of frightened white Californians.) Two forces came together in 1918, however, to bring about a change in those basic attitudes. One was short-run disillusionment with the war—and by extension, with Europeans and other foreigners, in general. The other was a growing fear that the country would be swamped with unasssimilated immigrants.

That fear was shared by a wide variety of Americans. Some of the opposition to immigration came from nativists who simply did not like foreigners—and what they considered foreign ideas. Some came from political reformers, progressives who had begun to doubt that immigrants from European tyrannies could be taught to understand America's democratic institutions. And labor unions almost unanimously feared and resented competition from immigrants who were willing to work for sweatshop wages.

Given the statistics, however, the fears were not ungrounded. As late as the 1890s, when immigration had averaged about 370,000 per year, the volume seemed tolerable. After all, America was a big country with a big population, and most people saw it as a kind of geographic sponge with infinite capacity. But then, in 1902, the numbers suddenly shot upward. In 1905, for the first time, the Commissioner General of Immigration counted more than a million new arrivals in a single year. That figure was coming to be normal, and there was no telling where it would go from there. Furthermore, a vast majority of immigrants had lately been coming from southern and eastern Europe, bringing languages and religions and customs that were unfamiliar and threatening to the native Americans of northwestern European ancestry who mainly owned and ran the country. Even more menacing to the old-line Americans, the area of immigrant origin was spreading eastward and southward into yet stranger parts of the world—deep inside Russia, and into the mountains and deserts of Asia Minor.

German submarines brought transatlantic passenger traffic to a temporary halt, but World War I also brought the first comprehensive legal restriction on immigration—a 1917 act, passed over Wilson's veto, to impose literacy tests for new immigrants, a transparent effort to reduce the flow of people from southern and eastern Europe. Thereafter, legislation came thick and fast. In 1921, Congress established the first comprehensive quota system; in 1924, the law was tightened; and finally, in the National Origins Act of 1929, a law that stayed on the books until 1952, the total number of immigrants was reduced to a mere 150,000 per year, to be apportioned according to national origins of the U.S. population in 1920—that is, overwhelmingly northwestern European. Almost gratuitously, Congress also created a "barred zone" stretching across Asia from Japan to Persia, from which no immigrants of any kind would be admitted. (It is curious that no limits were imposed on immigration from Latin America.)

The geographic effect of the immigration laws was far-reaching, but nowhere more immediately felt than in the nation's big industrial cities, and especially the gateway city of New York. Until World War I, non-English-speaking immigrants had sought refuge among their fellow-nationals in large urban ghettos, which served as waystations between the old and new worlds and cushioned immigrants against the shock of immersion in a foreign environment. More than incidentally, those urban ghettos had furnished urban America with a large pool of very cheap labor—for dirty work in heavy industry, marginal piecework in semilegal sweatshops, and as domestic "help." Indeed, cheap foreign labor had proved so useful that some of the large steel and auto companies routinely sent recruiters to Europe to collect men to work in the factories of Detroit, Buffalo, or Pittsburgh—a practice that naturally outraged both organized and nonorganized labor. The sudden stoppage of immigration forced employers to look elsewhere. From 1914 onward, after German submarines had put an abrupt end to transatlantic passenger traffic, recruiters headed south to seek out workers in the hills of Appalachia and the wornout lands of the old Cotton Belt. The new migrants to the cities were no longer Poles, Italians, and Slovenes, but instead poor rural Americans, at first mainly white, but increasingly black as well.

Controlling the Use of Land and Water

Support for new immigration laws was widespread and had cut broadly across party and ideological lines. That was not true, however, when it came to a second major area of government activism—the array of issues loosely grouped under the heading of "conservation." Few issues so sharply divided "conservatives" from "progressives" as the question of the government's role in managing natural resources and in controlling the use of land and water.

The philosophical division was basic and strongly felt. Conservatives from both parties (but mostly Republican) held that private property was sacrosanct—that government had an obligation to stand aside when private citizens or companies wished to use the resources of land and water: grazing, mining, timbering, or hydroelectric development. Most progressives took the view that land and water were no longer inexhaustible, and that public interest demanded that government take action to conserve, allocate and, if necessary, develop natural resources. While conservatives feared the tyranny of government power, progressives feared and resented the growing power of corporate wealth which, they believed, was bent on plundering the public domain for private profit.

To progressives, government support of conservation was an urgent necessity; to conservatives, government supervision of land and water was a first step toward despotism. The conservation movement had won major successes under the progressive administrations of Theodore Roosevelt and Woodrow Wilson, but it had been hamstrung under the conservative presidencies of Harding, Coolidge, and Hoover. The election of 1932 changed all that, as Franklin D. Roosevelt's New Deal embarked on the most comprehensive and vigorous program of land-use and water control in American history. If the 1920s were bad times for American conservation, the 1930s were correspondingly good, and permanently entrenched the conservation movement in the seats of national power.

The bitterest battle was fought over the generation and distribution of electric power. That fight had lasted several decades and had come to epitomize the political chasm between conservatives and progressives over land and water policy, as well as a wide range of economic, social, and even aesthetic issues. As recently as the turn of the 20th century, electricity was not a major issue in the United States; total national production was only about 6 billion kilowatt hours—a paltry 60 kilowatt hours per capita per year—with much of the power used to run municipal streetcars. By 1929, however, production had risen to 117 billion kilowatt hours, and in much of the country electricity had become a basic domestic necessity. Most farms, however, were still without electricity and the comforts that went with it: lighting and proper refrigeration, not to mention the well-pumps, washing machines, and milking machines that could have reduced the back-breaking work of running a farm. Nor was there much chance for a farmer to obtain electric power as long as it was generated and distributed by privately owned utilities, which saw little profit (and therefore little reason) for extending power lines into sparsely populated rural country. Progressive senators from farm states, led by George Norris of Nebraska, repeatedly denounced the private power trusts and urged the use of public funds to create public power companies and to build hydroelectric dams, but the Republican administrations of the 1920s pronounced such enterprises to be "sheer socialism" (in Herbert Hoover's words), and therefore anathema. Indeed, the Coolidge adminstration almost succeeded in selling the government's Wilson Dam at Muscle Shoals on the Tennessee River to a private holding company. The dam had been authorized during World War I to generate power to make nitrates for munitions, but the conservatives wanted no truck with such schemes in peacetime.

Occasionally, conservatives agreed to use federal funds for large public works projects, but only when they were seen as necessary to protect or enhance private property. Thus, after the Mississippi River went on an epic rampage in 1927, the U.S. Army Corps of Engineers was given permanent authority over flood control throughout the whole Mississippi basin. In 1928, Congress had authorized the building of Boulder (later Hoover) Dam on the lower Colorado River. But power generation was only part of the dam's purpose; the project was also designed to furnish irrigation water to corporate agriculture in the Coachella and Imperial valleys of southern California. It was clearly understood that the power generated at Boulder Dam would be sold to private utilities.

The New Deal changed all that. Roosevelt, elected with a clear mandate to reverse the conservative policies of the 1920s, had a special (and personal) commitment to conservation of land and water, and to federal support for such efforts. Many of his policy advisors were social activists, eager to prove that a democratic government could do more than simply react to emergencies, and could act as a positive force for regional economic and social reform—in sharp contrast with what they saw as the selfish and scandal-ridden record of their conservative predecessors.

An early augury of Roosevelt's ambitions came less than a month after the inauguration, as the President sent to Congress a proposal to establish the Tennessee Valley Authority (TVA). At first blush, TVA seemed merely an expensive scheme to build dams on the Tennessee and Cumberland rivers to produce fertilizer and public power. In fact, it was much more than that. TVA was aimed at nothing less than changing the basic geography of a huge, poverty-stricken region that sprawled over much of the southwestern Appalachians and upper South. It would be a showcase, demonstrating what comprehensive planning by a benevolent democratic government could do.

The backbone of TVA was a system of more than twenty large dams (Fig. 17.2), which would generate power cheap enough for mountain people to afford, and aimed to entice industry and employment to the remote rural area. In addition, the dams would control floods on the evil-tempered rivers and create 652 miles of nine-foot channel, navigable for heavy barges from Knoxville in eastern Tennessee to Paducah on the Ohio River. As an added attraction, the convoluted shores of TVA's many lakes would become available for recreation and an attraction for tourists.

But that was only the beginning. A small army of government planners was dispatched to the valley to teach farmers how to control soil erosion and reforest denuded slopes. Others arrived to help local people create self-supporting, home-owned industries and build new model towns. In all, TVA was designed to help people of the Tennessee Valley build a self-reliant society, free of privation and domination by outsiders—a utopian dream come true. Ultimately, TVA lost much of its luster through administrative and ideological wrangling and, as things turned out, none of its utopian social goals came close to realization. But its physical results were genuinely impressive; much of the valley's most damaged land was restored to productive use, and the abundance of cheap power did attract new industry to the region. It became known all over the world as one of the New Deal's most visible and glamorous achievements.

The New Deal undertook other large hydroelectric projects, although none with quite the panache and sweeping social ambitions of TVA. Boulder Dam was finished by the mid-1930s, and its cheap power and water quickly

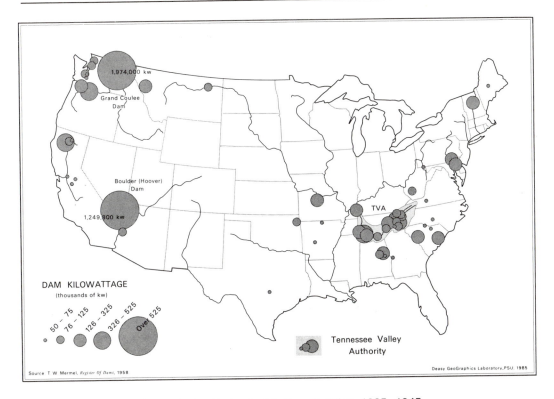

Figure 17.2   Hydroelectric Dam Building, 1925–1945

stimulated economic growth in the desert oases of Arizona, Nevada, and southern California (Fig. 17.2). Even more ambitious was a system of extremely large dams on the Columbia River which, because of its large volume, steady flow, and deep dammable canyons, possessed the largest hydroelectric potential of any American river. The lynchpin of the Columbia system was the colossal Grand Coulee Dam— when it was finished, the largest man-made structure on earth. Before the end of the 1940s, the Columbia was converted from a wild river into a staircase of placid lakes, and Washington, Oregon, and Idaho were wallowing in an abundance of cheap electric power and irrigation water. The Columbia dam system received much less publicity than TVA, but it stimulated vigorous agricultural development in the middle Columbia valley. Even more important in the long run, hydroelectric power from the Columbia became the basis for a major concentration of power-consumptive industries during World War II, notably aluminum, aircraft, and plutonium refining. Only much later would there be questions raised about the envi-·

ronmental consequences of these enormous dams.

The New Deal also undertook a massive program to provide farmers with electric power. Under the aegis of the 1935 Rural Electrification Administration (REA), low-interest loans were made available to string power lines into remote rural areas. By 1941, four out of ten American farms had electric service; by 1950, nine out of ten. The combination of electricity with new rural roads made a quiet revolution in the countryside, for it brought a sudden end to the numbing isolation of American farmers and to the drudgery that had made farm life burdensome since time immemorial. Arthur Schlesinger, Jr., remarked: "No single event, save perhaps for the invention of the automobile, so effectively diminished the aching resentment of the farmers and so swiftly closed the gap between country and city. No single public agency [as REA] ever so enriched and brightened the quality of rural living."

No amount of rural electrification, however, would cure the general economic misery that had plagued American farmers since the end of

World War I. Two facts lay at the root of the matter. First, low and undependable prices of farm products kept many farmers in a state of chronic debt and prevented many from making a decent living. Second, many farmers were trying to eke a living from marginal land. The problem of credit was nationwide, but the land problem was especially grievous in two sorely afflicted regions: the old Cotton Belt of the Deep South, and the wheat and rangeland of the western Great Plains.

Conditions in the rural South were bad at

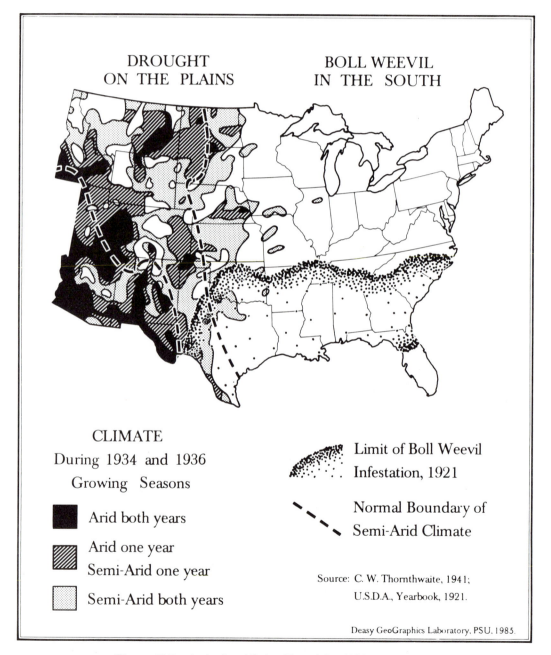

DROUGHT
ON THE PLAINS

BOLL WEEVIL
IN THE SOUTH

CLIMATE
During 1934 and 1936
Growing Seasons

Arid both years

Arid one year
Semi-Arid one year

Semi-Arid both years

Limit of Boll Weevil
Infestation, 1921

Normal Boundary of
Semi-Arid Climate

Source: C. W. Thornthwaite, 1941;
U.S.D.A., Yearbook, 1921.

Deasy GeoGraphics Laboratory, PSU, 1985.

Figure 17.3   Agricultural Calamities of the 1920s and 1930s

best, especially in the old cotton country where the infamous share-cropping system kept millions of blacks and whites in the semifeudal servitude of poverty, malnutrition, and ignorance that was in some ways worse than pre-Civil War slavery. Decades of single-crop farming had completely destroyed the best soils in the South, but the ultimate catastrophe was the boll weevil, an insect that had entered the United States from Mexico in the 1890s and, by the 1920s, had become epidemic throughout the whole Cotton Belt, where it regularly destroyed a large part of the cotton crop (Fig. 17.3). The agricultural depression of the 1920s was the straw that broke the camel's back, and by the 1930s much of the traditional Cotton Belt was in process of disappearing, as huge areas of cropland were abandoned to grow back into piney woods.

In the western Plains, nature had visited a different kind of calamity. In a broad swath of territory from Montana and the Dakotas south to west Texas, farmers and ranchers had incautiously settled on land with highly unpredictable rainfall. Much of the settlement had occurred in years when farm prices and rainfall both were abnormally high, notably during World War I. But after the war, disaster struck. Prices failed in the 1920s and brought economic depression. In the early 1930s rainfall failed, bringing massive crop failures, blinding dust storms, and economic ruin (Fig. 17.3). Unlike the South, where depression was endemic and easy to overlook or take for granted, disaster on the Plains struck suddenly and visibly. In 1934, winds blew topsoil off the dry, plowed fields in vast dramatic clouds, and farmers by the thousands began to abandon the devastated land for greener pastures, most conspicuously California (Figs. 17.4 and 17.5). Even doctrinaire conservatives admitted that something had to be done.

With customary energy, the New Dealers attacked the agricultural crisis on a broad front, passing laws that would become permanent fixtures in American agriculture. After decades of squabbling over range rights, Congress passed the Taylor Grazing Act in 1934, sharply curtailing the density of grazing on government-owned land. In 1935, during the worst of the Dust Bowl times, a permanent Soil Conservation Service (SCS) was created as an agency of the Department of Agriculture. The SCS left permanent marks on the landscape by promoting contour plowing and techniques of dry farming, where strips of land were left fallow in alternate years to conserve and gather moisture. Just as far-reaching, the government undertook to raise farm prices by regulating both supply and demand. As for demand, the government set about to create it when necessary by guaranteeing to purchase and store a variety of basic (and not so basic) commodities at fixed prices. In return for guaranteed prices, farmers were required to curtail production by a complicated system of limits on planting and harvesting. The system eventually turned the federal government into a major force in determining who would grow what, where, and how much. By the end of the 1930s, the invisible hand of the free market no longer designed the nation's agricultural landscape, but rather the federal government.

In addition, the New Deal undertook massive programs aimed to repair and restore damaged land. Government land acquisitions were hugely increased so that in the first three years of the New Deal alone, the government purchased twice as much forest land as had been bought in the entire previous history of the national forest system. One of Roosevelt's favorite programs was the Civilian Conservation Corps (CCC), in which unemployed young men could submit to quasi-military discipline and go out into the wilds to plant trees, fight fires, and build campgrounds, trails, and firetowers, in return for food, shelter, and nominal pay. By the time of World War II, some 2.5 million young men had served in CCC. Although its lifespan was short, the impact of CCC was profound, especially in reforestation. It has been calculated that of all the trees ever planted in the United States, CCC was responsible for planting more than half of them.

But the main problems of marginal land could not be solved by public works projects or congressional legislation. In much of the United States, the only really satisfactory answer was to reduce agricultural population on those lands. Throughout the interwar period, a steady stream of defeated farmers packed their families and possessions into automobiles and departed permanently. As Will Rogers remarked, America was the only nation in the world to go to the poorhouse in an automobile. Ironically, very little land was actually retired

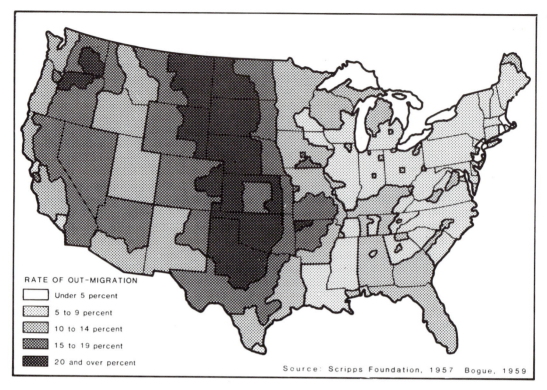

Figure 17.4   Outmigration: 1935–1940

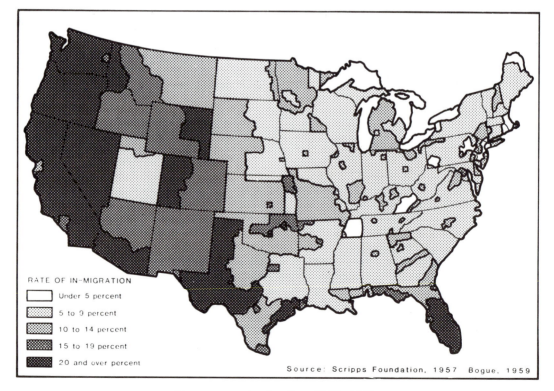

Figure 17.5   Inmigration: 1935–1940

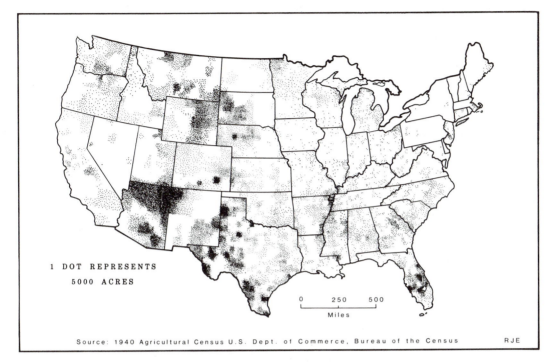

1 DOT REPRESENTS
5000 ACRES

Source: 1940 Agricultural Census U.S. Dept. of Commerce, Bureau of the Census   RJE

Figure 17.6   U.S. Farmland Acreage Increase, 1930–1940

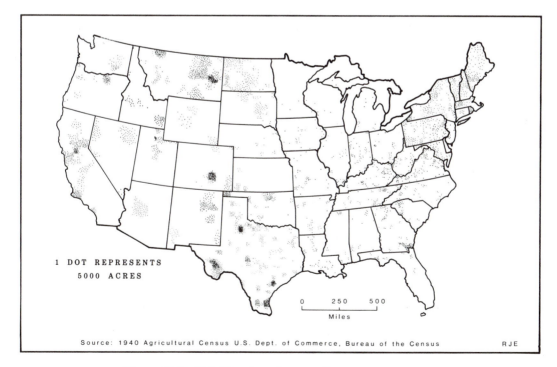

1 DOT REPRESENTS
5000 ACRES

Source: 1940 Agricultural Census U.S. Dept. of Commerce, Bureau of the Census   RJE

Figure 17.7   U.S. Farmland Acreage Decrease, 1930–1940

from agriculture during the 1930s, and in the stricken regions of the western Plains, farm acreage actually increased (Figs. 17.6 and 17.7). The net effect was to increase the *size* of individual farms and ranches, which in turn reduced pressure on the land and eventually encouraged conservation. That long-run benefit, however, was of little comfort to the stricken farmers who continued to flee. As the decade of the 1930s wore on, the whole nation seemed to be moving.

PEOPLE MOVING

Mobility has always seemed an especially American trait: mobile people settled the country in the first place, and geographic mobility had always served as the key to economic and social betterment. In some ways, then, the mobility of the interwar period was merely a continuation of something that had been going on for a long time. But in other ways, the incessant movement of whole populations seemed more feverish than anything that had gone before. For one thing, the wild fluctuations of the economy—the boom of the 1920s, the depression of the 1930s—alternately pulled and pushed people from place to place with unprecedented force, often under dramatic and heart-rending circumstances. For another, increasing numbers of people were moving to new places not so much for traditional economic reasons, but simply for pleasure. For yet another, the newly democratized automobile allowed people to move to places that would have been unreachable by railroad in previous time, with the result that utterly new patterns of population began to emerge on the American map. But, just as important, movements of people to and fro across the country had begun to attract attention from the radio and motion picture industries and from popular novelists, so that internal migration was now taking place in the glare of unremitting publicity.

Although the movement of people during the 1920s and the 1930s sometimes seemed frantic and confused, rather as if someone had kicked over an anthill, in fact most of the migration fell into one of three major streams: from rural to urban areas, from central cities to the suburbs, or from cold climates toward sunshine and balmy temperatures.

Rural Losses, Urban Gains

Rural-urban migration, of course, was nothing new to the United States; urbanization had long been one of the basic demographic hallmarks of industrializing nations throughout the world. But 1920 marked a tip-point in the shifting balance of population: for the first time in American history, the Census reported that more people were living in urban areas than in rural areas.

That aggregate statistic, however, tells only part of the story. There was no absolute decline in rural population, at least as the Census defined the word "rural." Indeed, during the worst years of the early depression, rural areas reported a sharp surge in population, as people who had moved to the city to find jobs in the 1920s went home again to escape urban breadlines. But despite boom and bust, national population was increasing, and the increase was almost entirely urban. That urban growth was greatly stimulated by World War II and the explosive growth of defense industries, especially in the Northeast and on the west coast. But unlike World War I, which had been followed by a sharp depression, the boom of World War II continued unabated through the 1940s and 1950s, and so did migration to urban areas.

Within the rural areas, moreover, enormous changes were afoot. The population on farms, and in the villages and towns that depended on farms, had been dropping by fits and starts. Meanwhile, other areas were growing rapidly, especially the unincorporated fringes of large cities—suburban territory that the Census defined as "rural" but in fact was rural in name only.

Although farm population varied only slightly between 1910 and 1940, hovering between 32.5 million and 30.5 million, World War II brought a sudden change, and between 1940 and 1945 the nation's farm population dropped by more than 6 million people. Taken as a proportion of the national total, the decline was even more dramatic. At the beginning of World War I, about one-third of the American population lived on farms. At the end of World War II, it had declined to about one-sixth. That age-old institution, the family farm, was in the process of evaporating.

Strong national and regional forces were at

work to dislodge farmers from the land. Part of the trouble went back to World War I, when the United States had taken on the job of feeding, clothing, and supplying both its own armies and those of its Allies—not to mention a sizable part of the Allied civilian population as well. The price of food shot up dramatically as a result: staples like meat and milk roughly doubled in price from 1914 to 1920, and the price of potatoes and flour tripled. Farmers rushed out to buy new land and machinery at inflated prices, but could not pay for them when the boom ended after the Armistice when prices dropped as European farmers reentered the international market. The 1920s therefore saw not only a depression in American farm prices, but a terrible episode of mortgage foreclosures and farm abandonment that was especially cruel in poor and marginal parts of the countryside. If farm conditions seemed to improve slightly after the Wall Street crash, it was only because the depression in the cities was so grim. Even without cash income, most farmers could at least feed their families from local produce, which was more than could be said for the men selling pencils on the streets of Akron or Chicago or Sacramento.

Against the background of general depression, the added burden of crop failure was more than many farmers could take, especially in the Dust Bowl and in the weevil-ravaged country of the Deep South. In both areas, farmers fled the land that once had been among the most productive in the United States (Fig. 17.4). The exodus from the Dust Bowl received especially wide publicity and shocked the national conscience. The dust itself was dismayingly visible; in March 1934 dust clouds blackened the skies over much of the Middle West, and then drifted eastward to deposit a layer of grit as far away as New York and Washington. The dust eventually settled, but the human tragedy went on and on, and the whole episode seemed a cosmic indictment of ecological carelessness and indifference to human pain. Epochal films were made about the subject, notably *The Plow That Broke the Plains* (1936), a documentary made by the federal government to warn against the tragic consequences of thoughtless agricultural practices, but which also won widespread acclaim as a chronicle of human tragedy and waste, and its companion piece, *The River*, which re-

counted the destruction wrought by uncontrolled floods on the Mississippi. The two films were powerful propaganda for federal conservation efforts—and not-so-subtle attacks on laissez-faire economics. The best-known and most influential account of the Dust Bowl exodus, however, was John Steinbeck's *The Grapes of Wrath* (1939), which recounted the tragic flight of the Okies from their ravaged farms on the High Plains, westward across the deserts to a hostile reception in the not-so-green Eden of southern California. Few American migrations had ever received such unfavorable publicity.

In the long run, however, it was the movement of people from the old rural South to the new urban North that would make the greatest difference to the future of America. Northward migration had been going on ever since the Civil War, but it was greatly stimulated by World War I, which created a large number of industrial jobs in northeastern cities, where most of America's armaments were being made. Before the war, many of the jobs (especially menial ones) had been filled by newly arrived immigrants. But the war halted European emigration, and to make up the slack employers began to fill the jobs with refugees from rural poverty—and in 1917, that meant southerners. Some were whites from the Appalachian hills and there was nothing unusual about that. But others were black, and that was something new; racism in the United States was deeply embedded in law and custom, and blacks were routinely barred from most industrial jobs. Now with the wartime shortage of labor, some northern employers began to hire a few blacks—not many, and seldom in skilled jobs. But it was a start, especially important in the gigantic auto plants of Michigan and the steel mills of Ohio and Illinois. New jobs did not mean new social attitudes, however, and blacks were excluded from desirable housing and were greeted with hostility by white workers who perceived blacks as menacing to their jobs. But despite wretched housing and threats of violence, the ghettos of Detroit and Chicago provided blacks with better housing and a better living (not to mention better health and education) than the guarantee of poverty, illiteracy, and malnutrition as a share-cropper in Alabama or Mississippi. Thus, while blacks continued to be the last hired and the first fired in the steel mills of Baltimore and the automobile factories of Flint and Lansing, they continued to come.

Except during the depression, nearly all black migration was from country to city, but certain cities were much favored over others. A few blacks drifted into southern cities, if only because they were nearby, but they were rarely seen as havens of opportunity, much less tolerance. The typical black migrant headed north—usually as directly as possible by way of main-line railroads (Fig. 17.8). Thus, blacks from the Carolinas and Florida mainly ended up in east coast cities; those from Alabama and the middle South usually went to Ohio or Michigan; those from the Mississippi valley headed due north, straight up the Illinois Central Railroad's main line from New Orleans to Chicago. The favored destinations were the largest cities—New York, Philadelphia, Chicago, and Detroit; medium-sized cities like Fort Wayne and Syracuse much less so. Genuine small towns, such as the typical Iowa county seat, were almost completely shunned. Sheer distance evidently had a considerable influence on the destination of migrants, and many blacks simply stopped in the first big non-southern city they came to: the "border" cities of St. Louis, Louisville, Cin-

cinnati, Baltimore, and Washington. Conversely, very few went beyond the broad belt of favored cities between Chicago and New York. Distant places like Boston, Minneapolis, Seattle, and Portland (Oregon) received only small numbers of blacks. Starting around World War II, that rule would be broken too as sizable numbers of blacks joined the general westward migration to Los Angeles and the San Francisco Bay area. Few American blacks went to Canada, however, despite the ease of border-crossing and Canada's long-standing reputation for racial tolerance.

For many blacks, the move from unsophisticated regions of the rural South, with abundant supplies of personal space, to the bowels of crowded cosmopolitan cities was shocking and unsettling, damaging to individuals, and destructive of family life. The ghettos of northern cities, it turned out, were functioning quite differently for blacks than they previously had for immigrant whites. That difference was crucial in the history of American race relations. In earlier times, white immigrant ghettos had acted as waystations from Europe to America, as buffers against culture shock in a new land. Thus, in spite of poor, expensive, and crowded

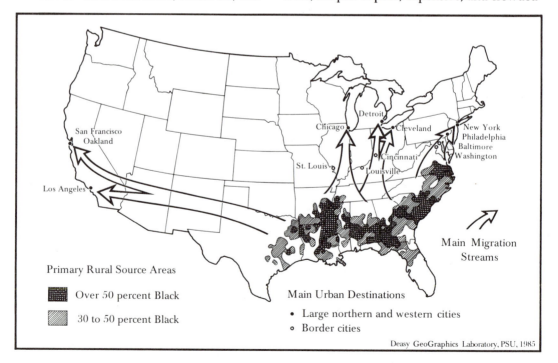

Figure 17.8   Black Migration: World War I through World War II

housing, the ghettos had performed a useful function, and besides, their residents knew that eventually they could move out geographically and up socially. The black ghetto was different. Surrounded by hostile whites, the black person, however talented, had no easy way to escape. To make matters worse, the perpetual shortage of ghetto housing raised rents to extortionate rates, a fact that was especially galling in decrepit buildings owned by absentee white landlords. Meanwhile, ghetto schools and infrastructure deteriorated with the departure of politically influential whites, while young blacks found themselves caught between two cultures—no longer rural South, and not yet urban North. The arbitrary confines of the ghetto created pressure-cookers for acute social frustration.

In spite of white hostility, the black ghettos continued to grow inexorably, commonly forming wedge-shaped sectors that fanned out from the oldest black neighborhoods near downtown railroad stations. Chicago's huge South Side ghetto was typical, spreading from an apex on the edge of the Loop to include the 63rd Street Station (the main Illinois Central Railroad's port-of-entry for blacks from the Mississippi valley), thence southward to the Indiana state line and beyond. Similar patterns emerged on Chicago's west side and in several sectors of Detroit, Philadelphia, Cleveland, and elsewhere. In most instances, those wedges of black population advanced most rapidly into areas of low-value housing that had previously been the homes of older white immigrant groups, and racial angers erupted into open violence—between blacks on the one hand, and Jews, Poles, and Appalachian whites on the other. Chicago saw a major race riot in 1919, as did Detroit in 1943.

Flight to the Suburbs

Despite the volume of black migration to northern cities, the total growth of those cities slackened significantly during the 1920s and 1930s. Although the depression was immediately responsible for the slow-down in the early 1930s, there was a second, more permanent reason: the quickening movement of middle- and upper-income whites to the suburbs. Census enumerations showed that many of the new suburbanites had moved out from the inner city, and that was no surprise. But the Census also revealed that an equal number were new migrants from distant places who moved *directly* to the suburbs—newcomers who wanted the economic benefits of living in a metropolitan area but had no wish to live in the crowded city. From the 1920s onward, suburbs would be the fastest growing segment of America's human landscape.

Suburbs were nothing new in the American experience. Even in the late 18th century, affluent New Yorkers lived on the bosky bluffs of Brooklyn Heights and commuted by ferryboat to Manhattan. But the great suburban revolution erupted only in the late 19th century, with the building of electric streetcar systems. By 1910, on the eve of the automotive age, all American cities of any consequence had attracted a spattering of suburbs beyond their city limits, strung like beads along commuter railroads and electric trolley lines. In very large cities—Chicago's North Shore and Philadelphia's Main Line, for example—those strings of affluent suburbs had begun to develop clear and powerful regional identities, based on the rail lines that fed them.

From 1910 onward, however, suburbs were increasingly being designed for people with automobiles. And just as the automobile changed almost everything it touched, it changed the shape and behavior of suburbs too. It allowed suburbs to grow faster than they ever had before, made their shapes more amorphous, and encouraged sparser densities than were usual in the relatively compact streetcar suburbs.

The geographic pattern of these new suburbs would have important political consequences. By the 1930s, most big northeastern cities had discovered to their dismay that further territorial expansion had been choked off by a noose of incorporated suburbs, each of which made its own laws, collected its own taxes, and defied annexation by the city that had spawned it. A kind of siege mentality resulted, with the city pitted against its encircling suburbs in a state of permanent political hostility, which made comprehensive metropolitan planning extremely difficult. In addition, the duplication of municipal services turned out to be very expensive, especially to the parent city which had to maintain aging infrastructures with a diminishing tax base. The arrangement was racially ominous, too, because many suburbs had learned to use a combination of zoning ordinances and real estate covenants to bar settlement by blacks. Although such restrictions were declared to be unconstitutional and thus unenforceable in the 1950s, they had been deeply entrenched during the 1920s, when the inner rings of automobile suburbs were taking on permanent form. Thus, the inner city grew blacker and poorer, while the suburbs remained almost lily white and, inevitably, much more affluent than the city. So while the law ultimately changed, the geographic patterns scarcely changed at all. As in so many ways, human geography turned out to be a very conservative thing.

As often happens in geographic matters, west coast suburbs looked different than those of the East—and the difference led to widespread misunderstanding about what was happening to American cities. In the Northeast, most big cities had grown up during the 19th century around clearly defined nucleated cores focused on railroad junctions. In the West, however, notably on the Los Angeles Plain and around the fringes of San Francisco Bay, the automobile had begun to produce a host of scattered settlements that looked like suburbs but failed to cluster tightly around any single dominant core. As those settlements grew inexorably together in the 1910s and 1920s, a new kind of urban fabric began to emerge—not a ring of suburbs around a city, but instead a conurbation of nuclei that together *was* the city. Supercilious northeasterners described Los Angeles as "fifty suburbs in search of a city" and persuaded themselves that Los Angeles's urban morphology was somehow peculiar to California, and therefore perverse. They failed to comprehend that the use of automobiles discouraged the creation of *any* new cities with nucleated cores. So, while eastern cities retained such centers from earlier times and would continue to use them, it was different in the new cities of the South and West where clearly defined nuclei were small or nonexistent. As factories and shopping centers moved out gradually to the country in pursuit of the affluent residents, suburbanites increasingly found it unnecessary to commute downtown for shopping and work, but found jobs and did their shopping nearby. On a map, this new urban morphology looked like a galaxy of stars and planets, held together by mutual gravita-

tional attraction, but with large empty spaces between. This "galactic city," it turned out, was not some Californian peculiarity, but an altogether new kind of city that would burst into full bloom after World War II wherever new cities were under construction. It happened first and most conspicuously in the South and West, and was increasingly visible on the extended fringes of the old northeastern cities. From 1940 onward, the process was epidemic, but it was not new. The skeletal structure of that galactic city was already in place in Los Angeles by the end of the 1920s.

Downtown decay would reach crisis proportions in most of the Northeast by the 1950s or 1960s, but that had not yet happened in the 1920s and 1930s. Commercial development in the suburbs was still small-time stuff, and the best jobs were still found in downtown offices and in factories surrounding downtown. Furthermore, "going downtown to shop" was a deeply ingrained habit in America, so that while the 1920s saw a huge increase in suburban building, the decade also produced some of America's grandest skyscrapers. Although the skyscrapers were modern, there was nothing modern about most of their architecture, which usually evoked various kinds of historic European styles—classical, Gothic, Romanesque, or the elegant melange of Beaux-Arts ornaments that had become popular for public buildings after the 1893 Columbian Exposition in Chicago. Even today, a casual observer can identify the 1920s core of an American city simply by looking for the highest ornamented skyscrapers in the skyline. The boxy buildings of the international style would not appear in any numbers on the American skyline until well after World War II.

The suburbs of the interwar period were architecturally distinctive as well, and today are easy to recognize because they contrast so sharply with the look of what came before and after. Through the 19th century and well into the 20th, fashions in American domestic architecture had been changing with some regularity, so that whole neighborhoods were often dominated by whatever style happened to be in vogue at the time: neo-Gothic, neo-Italianate, neo-Romanesque, all culminating with the decorated enthusiasms of the Queen Anne mode of the 1880s and 1890s, which combined a variety of styles *tutti frutti* on the same building. By World War I, fashions had become calmer but no less eclectic. Settlers in the new suburbs could choose from a large fixed menu of styles, collectively termed "period houses of the 1920s."

All period houses did not look alike, but all of them evoked the supposed architectural spirit of some far-off place or far-off time from the vaguely historic but always picturesque past. One set of styles came putatively from American tradition, bearing such names as "colonial," "federal," "Cape Cod," or "Williamsburg." Another set of styles evoked picturesque Europe: neo-Tudor with imitation half-timbering and imitation leaded windows, Dutch Colonial with gambrel roofs, and a variety of "Hispanic" or Mission style houses whose popularity was stimulated by America's sudden discovery of Florida's and California's supposed Iberian roots. Of greatest long-run significance, however, was the California bungalow, the first vernacular American house to come from the west coast and not the East.

Since period houses and bungalows both came in various forms, they could be set down next to one another in any of innumerable combinations. The result was no single style, but rather a special mixture of styles that distinguished the automobile suburb of the 1920s. But as with so many other things, the Depression ended it all. After the Wall Street crash, very few people had money to build houses of any kind, and the moratorium continued through World War II, with shortages of labor and building material. When building resumed after the war almost twenty years had elapsed, and it was as if the country had emerged from a period of architectural amnesia. All that remained of the rich pre-depression variety was a small selection of neo-colonial styles, much beloved of postwar real-estate developers, and built by the square mile for returning veterans. That hiatus between the period eclecticism of the 1920s and the homogeneous neo-colonialism of the later 1940s remains as perhaps the most conspicuous relict of the Depression in the contemporary landscape of urban America.

Migration to the Sun

Of all the migration streams of the interwar period, the migration to the sun seems best to capture the *zeitgeist* of the 1920s and 1930s. The migration itself was not new; people had been moving to Florida and California in significant numbers since the mid-19th century, so that each had grown consistently at rates well in excess of the national average. Nor was the motivation new. Migrants to both states had been lured by hyperbolic advertising, descriptions of lotus lands where ordinary people could escape from the corrupted environments of the North and East, where human cares would evaporate under sunny skies and balmy breezes, and where easy fortunes were made on every side—in gold mining, in real estate, or in cultivating exotic fruit. Moving to California or Florida was a promise of better health, greater wealth, and a plenitude of happiness, in an environment that was distant and exotic enough to be interesting, but not so exotic as to be uncomfortable. In the American experience it was a new kind of migration, where people moved less for economic improvement or religious principle than for reasons that were largely hedonistic. While hedonism had not yet become quite respectable, the migration was receiving enormous national publicity from radio and motion pictures. There was good reason for the publicity. Between 1920 and 1940, Florida and California were far and away the fastest-growing states in the Union, and the population of both states doubled (Fig. 17.5).

Ever since the gold rush, California had enjoyed a special niche in America's geographic imagination. Among other things, the state had been promoted as a place of great agricultural opportunity, where a host of environments would permit almost anything to grow, and where failed farmers from the East could not help but succeed. The facts, alas, were otherwise, and few of the migrants ended up as farmers. The reasons were simple and powerful. Most of California's best land was owned by a few large corporations, notoriously the Southern Pacific Railroad, the state's largest private landowner, which had run much of southern California like a feudal fiefdom. Furthermore, for most of California to yield up its promised bounty, irrigation was necessary with water brought in from great depths or great distances—and that was expensive, far beyond the means of the ordinary dirt farmer. Then too, California's most profitable agricultural products were not ordinary marketables like wheat or cattle (although California raised plenty of both), but exotics that could be grown nowhere else in the United States, and thus enjoyed a national monopoly. But national distribution of exotic high-priced crops like winter lettuce or artichokes was not a job for small-time amateurs, even when cooperatives like Sunkist (oranges) and Calavo (avocados) were formed to help keep quality and prices high. Most of the market was halfway across the continent, and that market could be reached only with mass planning and major capital investment. California agriculture, in short, was big business—*Factories in the Field*, to borrow the title from Carey McWilliams's (1939) book on the subject. Except for migrant farm laborers, most newcomers to California therefore ended up living in cities, rarely on farms or in small towns. The small market town of the midwestern sort was a rare species in most of California. For most migrants, a new beginning meant the San Francisco Bay area or the Los Angeles Plain.

Meanwhile, California had gradually ceased to act merely as a receptacle for people and ideas from the East and was rapidly becoming an innovator and arbiter of national fashions. During the 19th century, Californians had done everything possible to escape the stigma of being a frontier outpost. Cultural artifacts of every kind were slavishly and self-consciously designed to look "eastern." Buildings and monuments were copied from eastern architects; eastern biota were planted in gardens and arboreta; towns were laid out to look as much like Missouri or Ohio as possible. By the turn of the century the trend had begun to reverse, and a few Californian innovations began to flow eastward. The watershed date was 1915, when the state held two major world's fairs simultaneously: the Panama-Pacific Exposition in San Francisco, and the California-Pacific Exposition in San Diego. The San Francisco fair was the more dignified, partly a celebration of the city's recovery from the 1906 earthquake, partly a reminder that "America's Mediterranean" was an important place in its own right. The San Diego exposition was far more eye-catching, designed as a monument to California's Hispanic heritage, and notifying the world that California was now mature enough to possess its own history. Within a short time California architecture had suddenly become a national vogue, with California bungalows and

"mission style" cosmetics erupting all across the country.

Thus, for all the snide remarks by easterners that California was becoming a kind of Cloud-Cuckoo-Land, where exotic plants and exotic people grew in the eternal glare of Hollywood klieg lights, California was in fact becoming a super-American place. If America was affluent and mobile, urban and comfortable, California was all of those things, and more so. (It seemed only natural that Californians would own more cars per capita than the people of any other state.) If America's cities were growing bigger and spreading over larger areas, California would have some of the biggest and most sprawling cities in the country. And despite the sniping from eastern highbrows, many foot-loose people seemed enchanted by California's combination of super-Americanism and benevolent environment, and migrants continued to go west. When, in World War II, California served as America's main port of embarkation for the Pacific theater of war, thousands of young servicemen saw California for the first time and liked what they saw. When they returned from the war, many of them returned not to Keokuk or Schenectady, but to the suburbs of San Francisco and Los Angeles, there to raise families and live happily ever after. Twenty years later California had become the most populous state in the Union.

Florida, however, was a different matter, although at first glance it seemed to have a good deal in common with California, at least as seen from a distance by potential migrants. Both states were insular places, made attractive by their climate, but removed from the main centers of American population to be reached only by long journeys across uninviting territory—the driest parts of the arid West, the poorest parts of the poverty-stricken South. Both were exotic to their respective regions; if California was the least western of western states, Florida was the least southern state in the South. And both states boomed in the 1920s and the 1930s, growing at similar rates and for many of the same reasons. Nevertheless, there were crucial differences, largely explained by Florida's eccentric history and geography.

Until the 1890s, most Floridians lived in a ragged fringe of isolated rural country just south of the Alabama and Georgia state line.

That concentration had dictated the location of the state capital in Tallahassee, sited in limbo at the midpoint between the two old Spanish settlements of St. Augustine on the Atlantic coast and Pensacola on the Gulf of Mexico. Elsewhere, the state's population was scattered in a desultory array of small fishing villages and nascent fruit and vegetable farms along the Indian River. The slave economy of the deep South had never penetrated much of Florida, which remained largely empty—off-sides to the southern mainstream and to the national mainstream as well.

The change began in 1883 when Henry Flagler, a major shareholder in Standard Oil, brought his ailing wife to an isolated health resort on the lower St. Johns River. He concluded that Florida's climatic charms were salable to northerners if only there were hotels to house the visitors and a railroad to bring them there. Flagler built his Florida headquarters at the palatial Ponce de Leon Hotel in St. Augustine and, by the early 1900s, his Florida East Coast Railroad was finished to Key West, with hotels strung along the rail line at several intermediate locations. Almost at the same time another Yankee tycoon, Henry Plant, built a similar system to attract tourists to the Gulf coast, anchored by a rail line to Tampa, where he built the flamboyantly Moorish style Tampa Bay Hotel. Flagler and Plant promptly started to advertise the virtues of Florida, in a crescendo of ballyhoo that set the tone for much of Florida's later growth.

There was a permanent quality of impermanence to that growth, in sharp contrast with that of California. Florida was very poor in natural resources which, in combination with the state's eccentric location, had discouraged the growth of permanent manufacturing industries. Even Florida agriculture tended to be a chancy kind of thing. Its chief products were citrus fruit and winter vegetables, both highly sensitive to winter frosts and to perturbations in northern commodity prices. Florida's growth, therefore, tended to come in flashes and to depend inordinately on sandy beaches and balmy winters. Even climate was a mixed blessing. Florida summers were hot, steamy, and seemingly eternal. Until the arrival of air conditioning, a tourist might come to enjoy the winter weather; but summer was a time to sit in the shade and do as little as possible or, better yet, flee the state entirely. Many people came to Florida, therefore, as seasonal visitors, with no intention of remaining as permanent residents. (The main exception was St. Petersburg which, by the 1920s, had become a retirement place for the elderly, and America's largest geriatric city.) All this was in sharp contrast with California, where sheer distance made temporary visits from the Northeast and Middle West both difficult and expensive. Thus, Florida clearly won over California in attracting the rich trade in winter tourists. People went to California to put down roots; Florida was a place to escape the cares of the world, to unwind, relax, and enjoy oneself.

The difference profoundly affected the kinds of places that California and Florida would ultimately become. Migrants to California, knowing themselves to be permanent settlers, took fierce interest in purifying the state's political apparatus, in creating a first-class public university system, and in protecting California's handsome mountains and coasts from commercial despoliation. It was natural that California would give birth to institutions like the Sierra Club, and that much of its coastline and wildland would be reserved for public enjoyment. Environmentalists found hard going in Florida, where state parks were virtually unknown. There most land was simply viewed as real estate; state parks seemed a waste of private land and the chance to make a profit. Much of the state was up for sale to the highest bidder.

By the early 1920s, the bidding had grown very shrill indeed, as the greatest of all Florida real-estate booms rolled into high gear. Frederick Lewis Allen called it "the most delicious fever of real-estate speculation which had attacked the United States in ninety years." Suddenly towns and cities were springing up where Flagler had built lonely hotels. Land was subdivided, sold, bought, and resold; bridges and roads were thrown across sand dunes and mangrove swamps; residential streets were carved into the quivering muck. Prices went up and up again, in a dizzying spiral of speculation, profit-taking, and fraud. The most frenzied speculation and the most extravagant swindles occurred in Miami, whose population leaped from 30,000 in 1920 to 75,000 at the peak of the boom in 1925, but nearly all of east coast Florida was caught up in the rampage. Subdivisions, hotels, and new cities were springing up from Jacksonville to Key West, and if the Gulf coast was spared the worst excesses, it was only because much of that coast remained inaccessible.

The bubble had to burst, and it did. In early 1926, the bottom dropped out of the real-estate market, and Florida investors received a financial preview of what the whole nation would behold on Wall Street three years later. Then in September, as if nature itself had been waiting to administer the *coup de grâce*, the most ferocious hurricane in living memory struck Miami and the adjacent "Gold Coast." The storm killed 400 people outright, injured 6,300, and left 50,000 people without homes. It ruined the city of Miami and its promising suburb of Miami Beach, and it left the real-estate market prostrate.

But only for a while. Despite human frailty and natural disaster, people still came to Florida, and they kept coming even during the depression. By 1940 it was obvious that Florida was a state that would have to be taken seriously. No longer was it an outpost on the tattered fringe of the nation's poorest region, but was rapidly becoming one of America's most populous and influential states. As retirement ages dropped and Americans were finding more leisure time at their disposal, Florida would receive more winter tourists and more elderly retirees as permanent residents. And as America grew more affluent and more demanding, Florida's subtropical agriculture would become very big business, greatly encouraged by new methods of freezing vegetables and (of all things) concentrated orange juice. In a way, Florida's growth was a metaphor for America at large. Only a very large and very affluent country could afford to create and support a whole state whose main income derived from orange juice, sunbathing, and profits from the sale of real estate. Florida had

become big and exotic because America had become big and rich.

ENGINEERING A NEW AMERICAN GEOGRAPHY

The first half of the 20th century was a pageant of dramatic events and colorful personalities. But if we look beyond the details and the dazzle, it becomes clear that the period was a watershed between an older geographic order of the late 19th century, and a new streamlined order of the late 20th. While few Americans suspected it at the time, for better or for worse, they were engineering a new world.

The full shape of that new world would not become evident until well after World War II, but the basic structure was clearly visible by the late 1930s. The structure had been set in place with the greatest innocence. The business of technology was typical. In the forty years between 1900 and 1940 the United States installed a whole new basic network of transportation and communications, but it would not dawn on most Americans until the 1950s and 1960s that automobiles, telephones, movies, and radios were more than simple devices that would bring them more comfortable lives, but were like Hindu gods, capable of destroying and creating worlds. With similar unconcern about long-term consequences, Americans had invoked the power of government to regulate the flow of immigrants and to control the use of water and land; only much later would they discover that such things as immigration controls, crop subsidies, and flood-control projects would take on lives of their own and create whole new landscapes. In much the same way, migrant Americans had begun to move in new directions and for unfamiliar reasons, but it would not become apparent until after World War II that the sum of these migrations would yield an entirely new geography. And, whether Americans liked it or not, they would have to live with that new geography. There would be no turning back.

ADDITIONAL READING

Books

Allen, F.L. *Only Yesterday: An Informal History of the 1920s.* New York: Harper & Bros., 1931.

———. *Since Yesterday: The 1930s in America.* New York: Harper & Bros., 1939.

———. *The Big Change: America Transforms Itself, 1900–1950.* New York: Harper & Bros., 1952.

Belasco, W.J. *Americans on the Road: From Autocamp to Motel, 1910–1945.* Cambridge: M.I.T. Press, 1980.

Bogue, D.J. *The Population of the United States.* Glencoe: The Free Press, 1959.

Caro, R. *The Power Broker: Robert Moses and the Fall of New York.* New York: Alfred A. Knopf, 1974.

Furnas, J.C. *The Americans: A Social History, 1587–1914.* New York: G.P. Putnam's Sons, 1969.

Goldman, E. *Rendezvous with Destiny: A History of Modern American Reform.* New York: Alfred A. Knopf, 1953.

Leuchtenburg, W.E. *Franklin D. Roosevelt and the New Deal: 1932–1940.* New York: Harper & Row, 1963.

Schlesinger, A., Jr. *The Crisis of the Old Order: 1919–1933.* Boston: Houghton Mifflin, 1957.

———. *The Coming of the New Deal.* Boston: Houghton Mifflin, 1958.

———. *The Politics of Upheaval.* Boston: Houghton Mifflin, 1960.

U.S. Census Bureau. *Historical Statistics of the United States, Colonial Times to 1970.* Washington, D.C.: Government Printing Office, 1975.

Periodicals

Annals, Association of American Geographers (Nelson, 1959).

Economic Geography (Manners, 1974).

Geographical Review, journal of the American Geographical Society (Hugill, 1982).

18

Revolution in American Space Since 1945, and a Canadian Contrast

JAMES E. VANCE, JR.
University of California, Berkeley

Canada and the United States as we know them today were shaped by mobile Europeans in the first three centuries of our national existence, and by Asians and Latin Americans during the more recent decades. Landing on the coasts of a vast continent thinly populated by native peoples, those in-migrants moved with continuing vigor to occupy a landmass of more than 7 million square miles within a period of four centuries, with more than half that geographical occupation taking place during only the last 100 years. Today few traditional frontiers remain—Ungava and Labrador, the Yukon, the Northwest Territories of Canada, and much of Alaska will probably never support a continuous spread of fixed settlement—so it might seem that the era of mobility has closed. Yet the decades since the end of World War II have shown that the spirit and practice of mobility do not require the traditional frontiers that North Americans occupied for more than four centuries; our culture, so imbued, has found new, nontraditional frontiers to challenge and continuing productive uses for its birthright to mobility. The area of the North American democracies has not changed since 1945, but the nature and use of continental space has been fundamentally transformed. The conception of space, specifically its treatment by North Americans, lies within a continuingly evolving historical geography.

The rise of the mercantilist economy in northwestern Europe during the 16th and 17th centuries sent the continent's first migrants here. Mobility might have motivated the voyagers, but a search for economic domination of more space drove the European merchant class to outfit the ships and pay the crews that brought them to our shores. A process was introduced early in the 17th century that differed from conditions at home: the persons who were "planted" in North America were characterized by a much greater practice of mobility than were the European peasantry and urban proletariat from which their greater numbers were drawn, and they were taking up residence in a demonstrably dependent section of an enlarged national realm. Mobility and dependence were, thus, part of America's birth.

Once free of English control, the coastal 13 colonies and their merchant communities quickly adopted the economic practices of their recent masters and established a "dominated area," at first extending from the front of the Appalachians to the farthest cabin of the now-unleashed frontiersmen. In time the ecumene of America, the region with the power and manufacturing production to dominate its own vast market area of primary staple harvest, did spread west of the Appalachians into a Middle West that was as rich in industry as in agriculture. Even as late as the outbreak of World War II it was still common among geographers to designate a "Manufacturing Belt," distinguishable from the larger body of the nation and exercising a marked economic domination of the space beyond its boundary. National space was of two sorts—the ecumene and the dominated area—each enlarged by national mobility but still quite geographically coherent and distinct one from the other.

The transformation of national space during the last forty years has stemmed from basic shifts in mobility and regional domination. The tendency throughout American experience has been for mobility to be most pervasive in the direction of the frontier, lending power to the view that the frontier has been central to American life, however distant it lay from the ecumene. Since 1945 mobility has become so geographically complex that a new conception of American frontiers is necessary if we are to find any historical continuity for its influence. Since World War II regional domination has virtually disappeared in the United States, while maintaining itself more fully in Canada. This contrast in dependency is probably the greatest human geographical distinction between the two countries today. In the Dominion, the view that "central Canada"—Ontario and Québec—holds both the Atlantic provinces and the Canadian West in economic and political thralldom has dominated politics since 1945, experiencing modest questioning only in the election of 1984 that brought the Progressive Conservative government to power.

THE NEW AMERICAN FRONTIER: ECONOMIC BALANCE

During the 19th century the pattern of settlement spread to enclose all the conterminous territory that became, by 1912, the 48 states. The speed of that expansion was not matched by the spread of the area exercising economic domination over the national space. The Northeast, from Baltimore northward to Bos-

ton, was joined with the eastern Middle West, from Cleveland westward to St. Louis and Chicago and Milwaukee, in holding the financial and corporate reins that shaped the American economy well up to the time of World War I (Fig. 18.1). As the automobile industry grew, late in that period, it contracted geographically into the northeastern Middle West. And as "the aviations" and radio manufacturing became the growth industries of the interwar years, they also were concentrated within this dominating ecumene. Even the petroleum industry began there, with the first oil "centers" being Pittsburgh and Cleveland, where the control tended to remain even after the producing area had spread westward across the Mississippi. There was geographical truth, as well as populist politics, in the cry that the interior and the South and the West were being held in bondage to the investment, commerce, and industry of the East. Most presidents came from the area north of the Potomac and Ohio and east of the Mississippi, and they seemed to

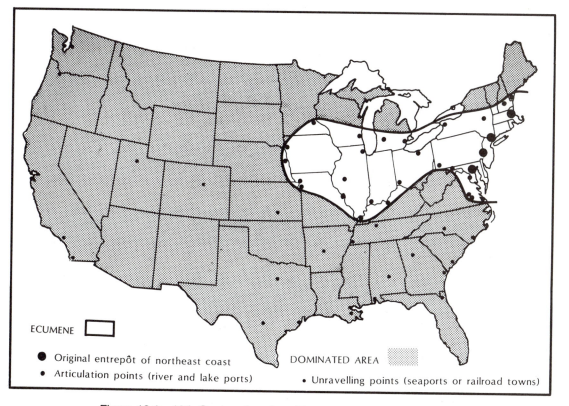

ECUMENE ☐

● Original entrepôt of northeast coast
• Articulation points (river and lake ports)

DOMINATED AREA ▓

• Unravelling points (seaports or railroad towns)

Figure 18.1   19th-Century American Ecumene and Dominated Area serve most obviously the interests resident in that region.

The first hints of change came when one of the most ostensibly typical of those presidents, Theodore Roosevelt, by accident became chief executive, bringing with him a quite uncharacteristic geographical experience. As a young man, Roosevelt had seen himself as maddeningly weak and ailing, a state so unwelcome that he headed west to North Dakota. There he learned the geographical facts about the semiarid interior and its domination not only by a stingy nature, but also by an investing-corporate East. When Roosevelt replaced the assassinated McKinley in 1901, he began a reform movement that is seen in historical terms as "trust-busting" against the domineering corporations, but which should, as well, be acknowledged in geographical terms as an initial attack on regional domination, both by nature and mercantile and manufacturing capital. His new Bureau of Reclamation fought nature just as Roosevelt's economic legislation fought the perpetuation of established regional privilege. A return to that practice came with William H. Taft, in 1908, and was left largely unquestioned when war in Europe diverted Woodrow Wilson from its constraint. The Republican resurgence of the 1920s placed typical conservative and regionally traditional presidents in power.

Not until the 1932 election of Franklin D. Roosevelt was this political-geographical status quo disturbed. As had his distant cousin, Franklin Roosevelt temporarily had left the ecumene to regain his health. Stricken with polio in the 1920s, he had gone to Warm Springs, in the Appalachians of northern Georgia, to seek to regain the use of his legs. In this he was not particularly successful, but his education in the geographical facts of the South and its impoverished country population was startling. When inaugurated in 1933, F.D.R. faced the depression and widespread suffering that the complacent administrations of the 1920s had helped to shape, but he had sufficient wit and energy to renew Teddy Roosevelt's attack on regional domination. In a series of laws, the Soil Conservation Service was organized, the Tennessee Valley Authority was begun (as the first American experiment in regional planning), and many New Deal measures were adopted that sought the blunting of class and geographical domination. Again a war cut short the more active phase of this Rooseveltian crusade for balance. But by F.D.R.'s time, enough had been accomplished so that the postwar period, our time concern, did come to see the full accomplishment of that balance.

A LAND WITH A COURAGE FOR WIDE HORIZONS

The common practice of dividing history into blocks of time separated by wars may seem no more than an arbitrary convenience, yet when we compare the American scene after 1945 with that in the 1930s a critical distinction can easily be shown. Some of this was merely a coming of age of developments underway before 1940, the maturity of which were more evident after a five-year period of necessary inactivity. But much of the transformation grew out of the exigencies of the war and their impact on the mobility and regional balance that particularly concern us here. The 1939 war was the first truly global conflict and the first in which American activity in the Pacific and in Asia was equivalent to that in Europe. On the world scene this brought a much greater American awareness of the Far East, while on the domestic scene it made many Americans conscious for the first time of their own Far West. The observed "westward tilt" during the postwar decades stemmed in considerable measure from the expansion of individual horizons experienced by men from the American ecumene who shipped across country to fight in the Pacific War. The two-front war also encouraged the growth of industry in the central and western parts of the country, a new tilt reinforced by the much-enlarged role of air warfare and its demand for thousands of planes, many of which could be built more easily in the dry and sunny areas of the American Southwest and southern California. At the time this was seen as a dispersal of industry, but from our perspective we can see that that notion rectified a myopic view as to the use of American space, a view constrained by a historical geography of regional domination. Regardless of whether regional balance in industry was inevitable given sufficient time, there is no doubt that World War II brought that reapportionment more quickly than seemed possible in 1939. (This was far less the case in Canada.)

The war limited most road construction, but not entirely so within the emerging band of industrial deconcentration in metropolitan areas. Large factories built for war production, such as the Willow Run plant outside metropolitan Detroit, had to be tied to that traditional housing area by a new freeway. In other metropolises where shipyards, armament factories, steel and aluminum plants, and other mass employers for war production tended to occupy large peripheral sites, industrial arteries were built, enlarging the incipient pattern of metropolitan super-highways begun in the 1930s within the larger urban areas. When the war ended, this transportation infrastructure was available for general use, once civilian auto production was resumed and wartime gas rationing ended. With the beginnings of such a commutation network in place, the wartime experience with the mass-production of houses for defense workers proved the seedbed for the vast, postwar, outer-suburban housing tract.

Other aspects of World War II did encourage a fundamental transformation of American space once the conflict was won. Here it is sufficient to make it clear that the use of 1945 as a historical-geographical divide is far from arbitrary. Although constrained during the actual war, individual mobility was much enlarged once peacetime conditions returned. The automobile had become firmly established as the normal way to get about metropolitan areas. With the high level of earnings enjoyed by railroads during the war, the immediately following years witnessed a major reequipment of rolling stock. The streamlined passenger train, drawn by diesel-electric locomotives, became the standard for long-distance service, bringing a level of luxury and comfort now all but forgotten, and speeds of operation now long reduced. At the same time that American trains were setting world standards for speed and comfort, there occurred the rapid expansion of civil aviation, known in America since the late 1920s but not widely used until after World War II, when the dominance of America in aircraft construction made mass transport in the air practicable. The great success of the new, cheap, mass movement by car, train, and plane joined with the expanded geographical horizons caused by the war to keep Americans among the most mobile of populations. That desire and practice of movement was joined

with a potentially more regionally balanced economy to create a search for wider horizons in economic, cultural, and social terms to match those that had always existed in the United States for generational mobility.

THE TRANSFORMED GEOGRAPHY
OF THE NINETEEN-FIFTIES

The first postwar decade witnessed a quickening of migration within the United States that served to create a new geography of cities and of regions. The fifteen years after the war were a time of suburban revolution when the greatest growth came in the residential band outside the traditional core cities. The Federal Housing Administration policies introduced by the New Deal, the adoption in most metropolitan areas of automotive travel as the nearly exclusive means of movement, and the rapid decentralizaton of employment all contributed to this change. By 1960 only 11 states were more rural than urban, and 20 states were more than two-thirds urban in their population, 10 of those more than three-quarters urban (including Texas and Utah). Just fifty years before, only 13 states had been dominantly urban, with only 4 of those twice as urban as rural. While central cities in Standard Metropolitan Statistical Areas in the decade of the 1950s had grown at a rate of 10.8 percent, less than the nation as a whole, the suburban parts of these metropolises had grown by nearly a half (48.5 percent), almost three times the national rate of increase of 18.5 percent. Using the far better geographical measure of "urbanized-area population" (those living in the truly urban area measured in terms of city morphology), by 1960 the suburban band was the fastest growing American settlement component. As a result, by 1980 the suburban band was the largest settlement type in population in North America (Fig. 18.2).

At the same time that the urban areas were generating population to the point that by 1980 only one out of four Americans lived in rural areas, the cities no longer had the form that tradition assigned them. Daily mobility had led the adequately supported to move to the suburbs, bringing about some dramatic declines in central-city populations. Cities that had approached a million in population in 1950— Cleveland with 914,808, St. Louis with 856,796,

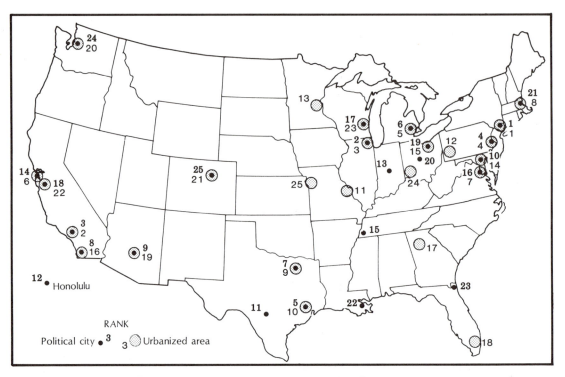

Figure 18.2   Ranking of First Twenty-five Cities, 1980

Boston with 801,444, Pittsburgh with 676,806, and Baltimore with 949,708—began to diminish sharply during the succeeding three decades. Growth was coming about well away from the area that had prospered during the period before 1940, leading to the sporadic rise of suburban challenges to central business district functions, as in the array of shopping centers that grew up in suburban Boston or the outlying office district built at Clayton in St. Louis County. Many predicted the early demise of the city core, causing some nervous planners to accomplish that end even more rapidly through radical redevelopment, as in St. Louis where clearing proved simple in comparison with reconstruction. Even in the stronger central cities, such as Manhattan, Chicago, and San Francisco, the downtown shopping district suffered great relative decline, which tended in the long run to be reflected in serious absolute contraction. John Wanamaker's was just one of the department stores in New York to abandon the central city, while San Francisco lost half its department stores. Where before the war each city of 100,000 or more tended to have at least one local, independent department store, by

the 1970s cities of several hundred thousand people might have no local store, but instead have branches of the few distant large-city department stores that had survived. The impact on taste and merchandising can readily be foreseen.

Within the national space, mobility was equally enhanced and with somewhat similar dispersive results. There is present in current economic thinking a clean and clever model that contrasts geographical cores with their peripheries, with the argument advanced that the periphery is losing out to concentration in the core. Whether this model is widely applicable may be an open question; that it explains American economic activity has already been shown to be far too simplistic. Our postwar American scene has demonstrated a vigorous victory of the edge over the former middle, with each of those standing as a location founded on spatial relatives rather than on absolutes. If one were to designate a "national frame of states," that is, those forming the border of the conterminous 48 states, and thus our national "periphery," it would be found that growth not only in population but also in economic, social, and cultural influence in the country as a whole has appeared disproportionately within the peripheral states. Some of this abstract area was already located in the ecumene from which dominance radiated throughout most of our history—Massachusetts, New York, Pennsylvania, and Maryland—but most lay, as recently as the outbreak of World War II, within the dominated regions (Fig. 18.1). Today there seems to be a skew toward this frame that belies any notion of a disadvantaged periphery.

The population of our national frame has grown at a rate far above that of the entire nation it encloses. In 1950 some 111 million people, two-thirds of the national total, lived in the frame of states enclosing the conterminous United States. In 1980 that population had risen to 174 million, but by then more than three-quarters of the national population lived in the national frame of states, hardly an example of the decline of the periphery. This rise was even

more striking than those figures suggest because the greatest growth took place in the frame states most distant from the former ecumene—that is, those bounding the nation from Virginia southward to Florida, westward to California, and northward to Washington and Idaho. Even in New England, the proportionate growth was greatest in peripheral New Hampshire and Vermont. Where the frame states lay within the ecumene, Maryland to Massachusetts, the greater growth came in states that had previously lain outside the ambit of the larger cities: New Jersey, on the potential suburban band for both Philadelphia and New York, and Connecticut, outside the latter. In a country where there seemed to be a strong national push for continuing personal mobility, daily as well as generational, and for regional balance, the economist's notion of peripheral decline did not work out in practice during the postwar decades (Fig. 18.3).

The contrast between Canada and the United

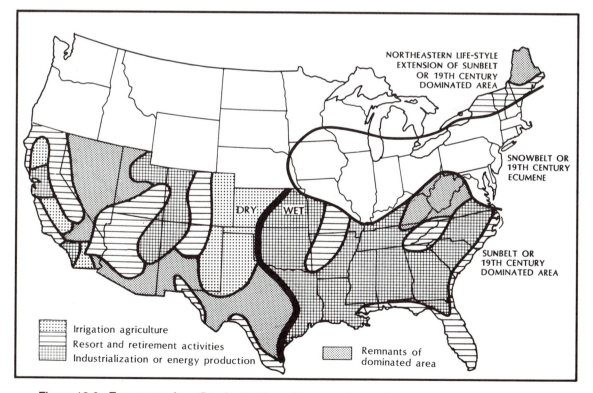

Figure 18.3 Emergence from Dominated Area. The map shows the 19th-century ecumene of the United States (the present-day "Snowbelt" and "Rustbelt") and its "dominated area." For the "Sunbelt" the source of an emancipating infusion of capital is indicated.

States in the matter of the emergence of the national frame to a more equal economic and political situation is rather strongly marked. Atlantic Canada has failed to keep pace with the national growth of the Dominion, while the North has remained the land of future promise as yet to be fulfilled. The development of the vast hydroelectric projects at Churchill Falls in Labrador and adjacent to James Bay in Québec has represented more the outward spread of the Canadian ecumene than the development of the national frame. Only in the Canadian Far West, in British Columbia and Alberta, has there been an experience suggestive of the rise of the American Sunbelt.

To understand the American historical geography of those decades, we must look at mobility and migration in two geographical frames: that within metropolitan areas and their peripheries, and that within the nation as a whole. The thesis is that national policy sought the perpetuation of mobility and the creation of regional balance, and that these efforts reflected a strongly held set of values ingrained in our culture. The national policy was tied tightly to individual practice.

To examine the pursuit of these goals, it is useful to examine events and evolutions categorically under a general heading of the abolition of geographical imbalance, a notion that must be carefully distinguished from the persistence of geographical distinction. Imbalance implies regional enslavement, such as many in Canada's periphery still complain of, whereas distinction implies specialization without domi-

nation. There is now a generational geography of the United States, with residence specialized by age rather than by particular economic, educational, or social class, as was the case before 1945. There are probably more geographical distinctions in the United States today than there were in the past, but there is far less variation by stage of development, cultural practice, income, and occupation. People seek clear geographical differentiation without geographical discrimination.

With both a consciousness of regional imbalance and the adoption in the postwar years of abolitionary programs, the spread of employment opportunities of a broadened scope was less a national policy than the realization of a general geographical shift. As persons moved widely and over considerable distance, the peripheral spread of population (already noted) encouraged a shift in industrial and other employments, further encouraging regional balance. If we compare most simple measures, such as the ranking of states in manufacturing employment, we can observe sharp changes. If we take 1947 as the first characteristic postwar year for manufacturing employment, the dominance of the Manufacturing Belt is evident, with 10 of the first 11 states lying within its boundaries (Table 18.1). Only California, standing eighth, broke that ranking, while the remaining nine states were all in the industrializing Southeast, save for Texas and Missouri (part of the Manufacturing Belt). For comparison we may look at the same simple ranking for 1982 (Table 18.2). Again all the former Manu-

Table 18.1   Manufacturing Employment by Leading States, 1947

Rank	State	Manufacturing employment (in thousands)	Rank	State	Manufacturing employment (in thousands)
1	New York	1,904	11	Connecticut	416
2	Pennsylvania	1,525	12	North Carolina	412
3	Illinois	1,248	13	Missouri	349
4	Ohio	1,245	14	Texas	324
5	Michigan	1,042	15	Georgia	274
6	New Jersey	775	16	Tennessee	254
7	Massachusetts	722	17	Virginia	235
8	California	719	18	Maryland	230
9	Indiana	562	19	Alabama	224
10	Wisconsin	433	20	South Carolina	202
				Total	15,247

Table 18.2   Manufacturing Employment by Leading States, 1982

Rank	State	Manufacturing employment (in thousands)	Rank	State	Manufacturing employment (in thousands)
1	California	1,928	11	Indiana	583
2	New York	1,362	12	Georgia	501
3	Pennsylvania	1,167	13	Wisconsin	496
4	Ohio	1,104	14	Tennessee	468
5	Texas	1,060	15	Florida	460
6	Illinois	1,020	16	Connecticut	416
7	Michigan	874	17	Virginia	398
8	North Carolina	781	18	South Carolina	362
9	New Jersey	728	19	Minnesota	346
10	Massachusetts	637	20	Alabama	337
				Total	18,853

facturing Belt states are included, although all fell in ranking except Ohio. California became first, Texas rose nine ranks, Florida and Minnesota joined the more important manufacturing states, while Maryland and Missouri fell out of the first twenty.

The South Atlantic and East South Central states had, by the 1980s, become as firmly a part of the major manufacturing structure of the United States as was the ecumene that had come to dominate in the 19th century. Texas and California stood as full, but dispersed, participants in American manufacturing. In the West, Arizona, Washington, and Oregon gained significant amounts of manufacturing employment, Arizona growing tenfold in the 35-year period, when total manufacturing employment increased only about 23 percent. These figures justify the notion that the most-concentrated of economic activities during the last century, manufacturing, had become broadly national by the 1980s. Trading employment is so strongly tied to population distribution that major interregional movements of people lead directly and promptly to shifts in wholesale and retail trade.

In the postwar period, Americans for the first time had reasonable geographical choice open to them within most occupations. Just as industry and trade decentralized, so did a wide array of other activities (Fig. 18.3). The rise of the state university to dominance in American higher education assured that a wide geographical spread of teaching and learning took place. The research and development activities associated with universities no longer showed the pre–World War II excessive concentration in the Northeast. In turn, innovation in American production, particularly with respect to the introduction of new products such as computers, other electronics, pharmaceuticals, and other high-technology products, became less a matter of the chance of invention by workmen engaged in an existing industry and more an outgrowth of organized and oriented research, admittedly centered on scientific institutions, but not nearly so much on the location of working industry. By the 1970s, certain areas—the environs of Boston, the North Carolina Piedmont, the Santa Clara valley of California (Silicon Valley), and the Austin area in Texas—demonstrated the direct tie between universities and organized research and development. These university-engendered industrial districts came to be the hope for the future within American manufacturing, as they were the site of a high level of technology not yet dispersed to areas of cheap labor. But by the 1980s, it was clear that inventiveness and production no longer experienced much geographical association. As new products have been advanced to mass production, maintaining a competitive position has led to the dispersal of routine production to external sources of cheap labor. The borderlands of northern Mexico have become tied to American production in electronics, clothing, and other labor-intensive operations that depend upon American ingenuity and design and cheap Mexican labor. So-called "overseas" production has become an integral part of the dispersal of "American" employment.

As we examine the question of an "economically dominated" area, a distinction must be made between the current, surprisingly balanced nature of regional economies *within* the United States and the increasing "domination" of foreign economies by American demands. In the postwar period, American companies have become quite international in their operations, a practice introduced in the interwar years when the mass-production of cars was a great American strength. Ford, Chrysler, and General Motors established "overseas" production for domestic markets in Canada, Britain, on the European continent, and in South Africa and Australia, depending upon advanced manufacturing technology. Since 1945, however, this foreign production by American companies has become increasingly oriented toward a world market, but one that includes the domestic market of the United States in that world. Once American industry learned the advantages of domestic geographical shifts in production, it was quick to apply those lessons on a global scale. The gains in corporate profits were considerable. But as Americans have learned with the decline of the American ecumene as a manufacturing region, for social health this regional balancing must be tied to the freedom to move widely within the enlarged integrated economy. In the United States workers could follow production to California and Texas; in the world at large that is socially and politically impossible. The creation of balance within America can include such arrangements as the common market between Canada and the United States in the manufacture and sale of automobiles and their parts, which will work in a mobile and relatively uniform society. It seems not to work as well with the perpetuation of a *dominated area*, now overseas and isolated from the practicable mobility of American workers. The analysis of this "new economic geography" needs to be as fully a social and cultural study as an economic one.

In the years between the two world wars and immediately after 1945, a large number of American firms sought to avoid Canadian tariff barriers by opening branch plants in the Dominion. The concern this engendered among economic nationalists in the northern democracy was at first quite justified, and the long-

serving Trudeau Liberal Party governments played on the fear of American domination to shape controls on foreign—that is, American—investment. Unfortunately, events overtook the policies: just as dispersal of the actual production carried out by American companies moved to cheap-labor areas beyond our borders, guided by the creation of "multinational companies," so did significant amounts of manufacturing that had previously taken place in Canada. The Dominion has lost the same sorts of factory employment that the United States has, and to the same distant lands. In terms of trade within North America, Canada has become extremely dependent upon the American market, selling therein nearly three-quarters of her exported products, and in 1984 running a nearly $20 billion trade surplus in this largest of all bilateral exchanges. It seems now established that Canada gains the vast market she needs for prosperity from the almost tariff-free exchange with the United States. If any concern is raised by the "American branch plant," it comes from the conduct of research in the United States, suggesting that Canada will not participate in innovation. But the capital resources of the United States and the scale of her markets may be essential to effective research, much of which leads to production in those Canadian branches.

STRIKING A CULTURAL BALANCE

The matter of regional balance extends far beyond simplistic economic measures, even though those tests tend to be the ones best understood and most frequently applied. The aggressively non-feudal attitudes that grew quickly in the newly cleared areas where the 17th- and 18th-century Europeans settled on the eastern seaboard of North America assured that a novel contrast would emerge between the culture of the countryside and that of the city. In Britain, as elsewhere in western Europe, the long practice of feudalism during the Middle Ages had conferred on the countryside a political, social, and cultural power that is hard for Americans to understand. Because power during the medieval period resided in the rural aristocracy, cities and their mercantile patriciate were held in a subservient state. Establishment of refined culture, highly regarded social practice, and political power was based on large rural landownerships. The earlier settlers of the Chesapeake Bay country sought to perpetuate this "rural dominance," with disastrous effects on city formation in the area. But in New England a very different balance between the city and the countryside took place. The Puritans settling in and around Boston under the Massachusetts Bay Company grant came from those classes elevated in status by economic success and enterprise more than by landownership. This was a mercantile, basically capitalist society wherein economic, social, and political power tended to be concentrated in ports, and later in manufacturing cities.

The hearth of a polite culture thus stood in the plantation society of the Chesapeake tidewater country, in the Middle Colonies, and in the ports of New England. Beyond the limits of each of these culturally dominating settlement components lay a distinctly American component, the self-sufficient pioneer farms occupied and worked by their owners and their families. The outlying, regionally dispersed family farmstead, a distinctive American original in terms of its numbers and local significance, stood in many ways as a competing power on the American scene. Although most farms sought through sales to increase the commercial over the self-sufficient in their production, the general nature of their cultivation was such that the family farmer's interest was quite distinct from that of the "mercantilists" of the coast. The coastal people were by occupation outward-looking and greatly influenced by the polite culture of Europe; the backcountry farmers were by necessity much more local and "American" in their cultural horizons. Even in colonial times this contrast was apparent; with independence in 1783 the distinction remained but was transformed politically. Where before independence the "coastal culture" had been far more powerful, because it possessed the weight of the culture of the mother country, after liberation that borrowed authority was missing, and the weight of population numbers in a democracy was added to the "country culture."

Independence brought a trying time for culture in America. Those adhering to the coastal culture, which continued to remain greatly influenced by outside practices, particularly those of Britain, could not accept the narrow horizons and chauvinism of the emerging country culture. Those in the countryside found the culture of the coast effete, artificial, and largely unrelated to the reality of life *within* America. While this cultural conflict was becoming stronger, there was a political contest underway that pitted the mercantile federalism of the coast against the agrarian republicanism of the interior, leading within a generation to the shift of state capitals away from the coast, with the significant exception of those in southern New England, where rapid rural industrialization was maintaining a coincidence of interest between the coast and the industrializing interior.

Even as late as 1945 the coast-country split was still strong. It ranged from the choice of strong drink—the coast drank Scotch whisky whereas, where such indulgence existed in the country, bourbon whiskey was preferred—through preferences in meat—the coast ate lamb, which the country generally found inedible in a world possessed of beef—to a great variety of attitudes and interests that divided along geographical lines.

Formal culture and education in the United States had contributed to this split. Puritan New England and the Tidewater Chesapeake had organized colleges well before the Revolution, as had the mercantile communities of the Middle Colonies. These were, like the English colleges on which they were modeled, privately endowed and classically focused. They stood in or adjacent to the mercantile ports and were tied strongly to coastal culture, receiving it and perpetuating it. When country political power rose continuously during our first century of independence, a number of states, even those on the coast, set up what were culturally rival institutions supported by the state, and later by federal land grants, and located well away from the cosmopolitanism of the coast. There is little question that qualitative differences were perceived between the two sets of educational institutions. The private, more classically oriented coastal colleges, with a few peers later established somewhat inland, viewed themselves as cultural in a way no "state college" could ever hope to be. In turn, the state institutions tended to view themselves as the centers of "practical education" largely lacking in the classical and gender-separated colleges of the coastal states.

In the postwar years the split remains, but its qualitative validity has largely disappeared. Increasingly over the last forty years, the state institutions have gained relative importance. Even in the areas of strongest coastal culture—Massachusetts and New York, for example—where state universities were absent or weak, as in most of New England, state universities have been founded handsomely or expanded impressively. And in the country, where the state university has always been strong, the private colleges, which formerly saw themselves as modest but culturally elevated peers of the eastern private colleges, often have been hard-pressed to survive. Rankings of universities, always a bit suspect, have nevertheless shown such a steady elevation of state institutions that the arrival of a formal cultural balance in the United States seems established. No doubt this rise in the quality, along with a vast expansion of the quantity of education in state universitities, has contributed to the sounder geographical balance that we shall see growing in a number of cultural activities.

The geographical experience in literature and in art has shown the two sides of this shifting balance. At the close of World War II American society contained a youthful group who had experienced a level of geographical mobility beyond that of even the traditionally high American standard. Millions of men, and in its early years it was mainly a masculine cultural movement, had been shipped overseas between 1941 and 1945, after common, parochial, youthful experiences dictated by the severe depression starting in the Hoover years. When those millions returned to America in 1945 and 1946, their realm of geographical perception had been changed in a fundamental way. It can be argued that they wished to use space differently from their fathers; they wanted to gain a level of generational mobility that was national rather than local, as it had been within metropolitan areas since the introduction of the trolley in the 1880s. Movement became a measure of youth with its ample curiosity, already activated by the enforced travel of wartime. Along with that enlarged geographical curiosity went the rediscovery of America in an innocently patriotic context. Never before, or since, has the United States been so highly regarded by the rest of the world; it did not seem chauvinistic to be intrigued by the American space and

by American culture, its country aspects as well as its coastal. To see it all and to experience its variety meant getting about.

Mobility and the exercise of geographical curiosity had become integral to American life by the early 1950s. Writers saw this clearly and shaped the *inter*regional novel and the topological lifestyle that was to gain over the parochial. In these years the regional novel and the "interregional" novel both gained great strength. At the same time, painters and many other artists failed to perceive the importance of space to Americans, logically enough gaining more international acclaim than American appreciation for their work. Painters substituted introspection for observation, personalization for national culture, abstraction for representation, and immobilization and enclosure for the American goal of mobility and the sensual enjoyment of space. The regional novel flowered while regional painting withered. While writing spread throughout the land, painting crowded into the citadel of coastal culture that New York had become in the 19th century. The "Beats" stand for the ascendency of geographical curiosity and its balancing role, whereas the "Abstract Expressionists" became the leaders of an art that lost both space and geographical perception. Painting could be done anywhere, it just was commonly done in New York where talk and psychology fed the artist rather than the observation and experience that fed the writers.

The geographical significance of the Beats of the 1950s came not merely from their early gathering in San Francisco, although that settlement shifted the focus of American literature away from its traditional locale within the ecumene. The geographical significance was caused by the way the Beats viewed *space*. For them the United States had come to fill the full frame of states that shaped its borders; it had become a mobile society to match the kinesis that was growing into the geographical process operative for those who were young in these postwar years. A fairly direct psychological background to that mobility stemmed from wartime experiences, but a major evolution in thinking about transportation also played a role. By 1916 a constitutional basis had been established for federal involvement in road-building within the states, but the arguments seemed at first to support only localized construction. By the end of World War II a much broader constitutional interpretation was accepted, so in the climate of mobility of the 1950s an interstate highway network was begun in 1954. The Interstate Highway System of more than 40,000 miles was intended particularly for interregional connection, and when completed the craving for national mobility was increasingly being satisfied.

In the decade of the 1950s the automobile became fundamental to American youth. For the first time in our history, high-school age males commonly had access to cars and built their use into everyday life. The drive-in theater, the "fast-food" or drive-in restaurant, "cruising" by car down the Main Streets of small-town America on Saturday night, and the evening dash by car into the surrounding countryside were parts of life all across the country, making the young far more mobile than their parents.

As this generation, whose ownership of carefully revivified cars started at a young age, grew older, mobility was being quickly enlarged through the construction of a national highway network and by changes in aircraft technology. In the interwar years air travel was uncommon and costly and was embraced only by a small number of Americans. After 1945 usage began to grow, encouraged by the introduction of four-engine planes (such as the DC-4 and the *Constellation*), a relative decrease in fares, and a much diminished fear of flying owing, in part, to experience and, in general, to a search for more mobility. Flying was largely domestic, as the planes of the 1950s were costly to operate over the long hops across the oceans. When civil aviation began, in the 1950s, to overtake train travel as the way to move about North America, the result was a revolution in the conception and use of American space. The combination of a much improved highway system in the emerging network of interstate highways, and of a rapidly enlarging flow of airline passengers commenced the correspondingly rapid decline of passenger rail services.

The rise of interstate highway usage and of air travel brought about a significant change in conception, and thereby use, of American space. The older local roads that had been strung together to provide a passable form of long-distance route maintained the intimate ex- perience of the countryside through which they passed. The interstate highway's limitation of access and frequent relocation of the prior routes greatly reduced the geographical intimacy of the past. The three- to five-day transcontinental car journey became possible, but with a considerable simplification of geographical experience, largely because the diverse regional restaurants and overnight lodgings came to be replaced by vast chain operations, such as Howard Johnson's, Holiday Inn, and Denny's. The clam chowder might still be made in Quincy, Massachusetts, but its consumption in Barstow, California, was the result of at least a metaphorical tanker operation.

The increasing use of air transport further narrowed geographical experience, especially after the more advanced four-engine planes, the DC-6, the DC-7 and *Super-Constellation*, permitted one-stop or even non-stop flying across North America. In the latter case association with the population of the country disappeared: on a flight from San Francisco to New York, one might expect to meet only the people from those two areas. It is not surprising that such coastal parochials began, in the late 1960s and in the 1970s, to divide American space between the home of the cognoscenti, which they placed on either coast, and Middle America, what we have here termed the "country," where, it was assumed, much was benighted and all was provincial.

Political conflict has taken on clear geographical associations. It is certainly much too simplistic to argue that the evolving split between an increasingly conservative Middle America and the increasingly questioning and activist centers located within coastal America grew out of the narrowing geographical experience gained from interstate highway and air travel within the United States, but certainly that change played a part. Its impact may have been greatest on the very group that was seeking change, "liberalization" as they saw it. The free-speech movement that began in Berkeley in the fall of 1964 spread to other college campuses, apparently using the topological network first suggested for youth by Jack Kerouac and the Beats. Eventually each region, even most states, had universities that were centers of questioning of "established" American values. These nuclei had increasing impact as the war in Vietnam proved to be unwinnable, even to its strongest supporters. By the early 1970s that failure to effect a victory, combined with the questioning of the accomplishments of the effort, led the conservative president, Richard Nixon, to leave Vietnam without a "victory." The spread of questioning seemed to have become national, suggesting that the new, sharp political distinction between coast and country had had a short life. That notion seemed proven when the moral corruption of the Nixon administration brought it down. The country was united in decrying that corruption and in finding the Vietnam experience ultimately ill advised, but that particular union of national cohesiveness merely hid what were still national divisions and regional differences.

In the late 1970s a new cultural and political regionalization of the United States came into view. The shift of industry away from the ecumene could be noted in a sharply lower level in the membership of trade and industrial unions in those plants being built in the emerging Sunbelt, particularly in the South and Southwest but also in most parts of southern California. Those who urged factory location in these areas cited the existence of "right-to-work" laws, thereby weakening the power of unions and of a populace only recently entered into factory employment who were thus unaware of the historical role of unionism. Industrialization here did not seem to lead to a proletarianization of society; rather it sapped the strength of industry, and thereby of unions, in the former ecumene, which shifted the political complexion of America to the right. This decline in the power of trade unions was undoubtedly encouraged by the rise of tertiary employment (in services) as the dominant opening for American job seekers.

Added to the rise in economic activity in the Sunbelt, which caused increased interregional migration, was the regional shift of older persons to this band of country with its relatively mild winters. The older members of most societies tend to be more conservative than their children and grandchildren, so an increasing conservatism arose in what had previously been politically a more liberal, or at least a populist, region. During the strong changes in regional balance at the time of the New Deal, most of the South and the future Sunbelt was staunchly committed to Franklin Roosevelt.

These were the areas where a sense of domination, and desire to end it, were most clearly perceived and where the liberal policies of the New Deal had their greatest impact on geography—physical, social, and economic. From 1952, when Dwight Eisenhower was first elected, until the present, the historic divide between a Republican North and Middle West (the ecumene) and a Democratic South and Far West (the dominated area) has progressively closed. Only great shocks, such as the missile gap argument of John Kennedy in 1960, the radical shift to the right by Republicans in nominating Barry Goldwater in 1964, and the moral collapse of the Nixon administration in 1972, have returned the Democrats to power. Democratic electoral margins have been smaller, leading to the conclusion that the shaping of a more uniform American has meant the creation of a generally more conservative one.

POLITICAL CONSERVATISM HARNESSED TO SOCIAL LIBERALISM

If regional balancing has worked toward a politically more conservative majority within the United States, its parallel process—mobility—has tended to make Americans less traditional and parochial socially and culturally, mainly by greatly increasing their national and foreign experience. Whereas foreign travel (beyond going to a Canada that was sufficiently similar to the United States not to seem truly "foreign") was quite uncommon before World War II, in the postwar decades it has become a part of the experience of probably a majority of middle- and upper-class Americans. The travel of the servicemen during the war may have sparked this increased curiosity about more distant areas, but the force that brought its satisfaction was the introduction of the jet plane in 1958.

The wider travel of Americans, and the spread of American business and culture to other parts of the world, is blamed by many Europeans, Japanese, and others for working an Americanization of their countries; and is stated commonly in the anguished cries of their more left-wing politicans and intellectuals. What seems less widely noted is the transformation of those Americans who returned from these distant trips. Although not all brought

back favorable memories of their travel, a sufficient number did to work an even further mixing of culture within the United States, and in
Canada. In the 19th and early 20th centuries
most of the cosmopolitanism in America came
from the flood of immigrants reaching our
shores each year. Even now those newcomers
arrive in considerable numbers, but their impact seems less because returning Americans
introduce so many other forces of cultural mixing. The eating of raw fish has spread not by
great Japanese or Swedish immigration, but at
the hands of Japan Airlines– and S.A.S.–transported Americans. These changes have been
highly incremental, which means that we can
perceive some of them only by contrasting the
American culture of the late 1940s with that of
the present. In food, clothing, furniture, auto
purchases, popular music, drinking habits,
camera and small-appliance buying, and a
great variety of other elements of our material
life we have been Germanized, Gallicized, and
Niponized. Who in 1947 would have predicted
that within 35 years more than half the cars
sold in our most auto-dominated state, California, would not be of American manufacture?

The search for balance has gone far toward
destroying the sharper cultural contrasts
among regions, while the practice of a growing
international mobility for Americans and Canadians has worked against chauvinism and its
nationalization of culture. By the 1970s these
forces had shaped a new North American cultural geography, *sensu strictu*, paired with the
transformed economic geography that has
moved America's dominated area outside her
borders (a situation not fully true of Canada,
where Ontario and Québec still are perceived
as economic overlords). It is impossible here to
trace more than the more graphic aspects of the
new cultural geography, some of which have
already been mentioned.

A NEW CULTURAL GEOGRAPHY

Literary America has spread throughout the
full American space with the creation of both a
national orientation for postwar American writing and the shaping of a very healthy regional
literature. The Northeast still has important
authors centering their interests there—the late
John Cheever in Boston's outer suburbs, Peter

DeVries in New York's exurbia, Phillip Roth in
the vast Jewish homeland of New York City,
and William Kennedy in Albany—but these are
no longer areas that stand as the sole purlieus
of our cultural existence. Thomas Burger has
brought Cincinnati and the Great Plains into
that realm, as have Joyce Carol Oates (Detroit),
Saul Bellow (Chicago), Robert Lewis Taylor (the
Mississippi valley), a number of southerners
(the modern rural South), and Joan Didion and
many other Californians (that kinetic society).
And the regional murder mystery has covered
the seamier side of life from the Framingham
Barracks to lowlife San Francisco. Whereas the
regional novel of earlier times tended to be
quaint and somewhat saccharine, heavy on
local color and weak on literary significance,
that does not remain the case. The Kansas of
Truman Capote's *In Cold Blood* is a frightening
part of mainstream America and its writing; the
life of Marin County portrayed in Cyra Mac-
Fadden's *The Serial* is as trendy and shallow as
anything to be found in the Hamptons on Long
Island.

More mundane elements such as trends and
styles have also become nationalized, even in-
ternationalized; the clearest example of that
larger geographical spread is not a product of
New York's Garment District, but rather of San
Francisco's needle trades. In the 1970s, Levi's
jeans spread eastward across America, and
then onward to the fashionable quarters of
Paris, where they became acceptable dress
even in the best restaurants. Dallas and Los
Angeles rival New York for stylish women's
clothing; Berkeley, Portland, and Seattle challenge New York's dominance in serious sports
clothing; and Florida and California are New
York's rivals for resort wear.

Equally as important in creating a shared
national culture were the influences of the general popular culture of movies, television, and
popular music. Television increased the impact
of rapidly changing fashions to a daily dosage,
and in all parts of the country. Popular music in
the postwar years was at first merely an American contribution, as it always had been; but in
one of those unexpected shifts that affect popular culture, in the mid-1950s British popular
music began a startling secular rise to international acceptance after decades of only parochial importance. This spread of rock music
occurred in the television era, so it was accom-

panied by the visual depiction of the extreme fashions of the largely British working-class performers. The first 1960s wave of British working-class youth clothing styles failed to take hold for long in America, but in the 1970s a second wave, now the garb of punk rockers, made a successful jump to our shores, both north and south of the 49th parallel.

The geographical signficance of this transplant is to be found in the fact that, for the first time, an international spread of "style" came not at the hands of the middle class and within polite society, but from the youth culture and its sometimes deliberately impolite models. The creation of pervasive and rapidly shifting, truly national fashions for the young, and for some of their elders, has transformed the geography of fashion. The rise of the "urban cowboy," in New York City as well as in Houston, showed that fashion spreads widely from rural areas to the cities and from the country to the coasts, bringing wealth to bootmakers from Marlborough, Massachusetts, through Texas, to Santa Rosa, California.

Before World War II the United States was less strongly centered in its cultural activities than Britain or France. Symphony orchestras made their homes in the larger cities of the ecumene—Boston, New York, Philadelphia, Pittsburgh, Cleveland, Chicago, St. Louis, and Minneapolis—as well as in some of the smaller places there and in some major centers in the dominated area, such as San Francisco and Los Angeles. But the "Big Five" orchestras (Boston, New York, Philadelphia, Cleveland, and Chicago) were in the traditional dominant areas. Since World War II the theater and music have become national, with some critics holding that the vitality in the former lies more in Louisville, Minneapolis, Los Angeles, and on college campuses than in New York. Orchestras have taken on a level of professionalism in Los Angeles and Oakland and in a dozen other regional centers; the ballet and modern dance are strong in San Francisco, and again on a number of campuses from Hanover, New Hampshire, all the way to the Pacific, as much in Canada as in the United States.

In commercial sport the rise of professional football in the years since the war has led a trend that is clearly national, with a strong showing in the South and West that was missing from the first generations of major-league baseball. Even Canada has joined the big leagues of America's national pastime, while ice hockey has spread from Canada to a number of metropolitan cities in the United States. The bidding among those cities is fierce when a franchise for a professional baseball, football, basketball, or hockey team is available. Past and prospective expansions in various sports leagues have come in response to an enlarged market, but the geography of sport has responded to two postwar geographical facts: the search to end a real discrimination such that a regional balance is sought, and the advent of commercial aviation by jet planes, which makes tight schedules throughout settled North America possible.

A GEOGRAPHY OF SPECIALIZED SOCIAL AREAS

Geographical analysis of the United States has traditionally been regionalized along economic and physical lines, with distinctions drawn among areas in terms of climate, the nature of the earth's surface, and major regional economic activities. For example, New England was seen as severely glaciated and heavily transformed into a manufacturing area in the 19th century, whereas the Southeast was viewed as errosively well-watered and yet only importantly industrialized in this century. Deeply embedded in this basic physical-economic analysis of American geography was some notion that the history of European settlement played a role, although seldom was that suggestion used at all synoptically. With the passage of time and the rather considerable changes in the human geography of the United States, it is now evident that economies are subject to considerable transformation, and even the significance of what seems to be immutable physical geography can be greatly transformed.

Teddy Roosevelt demonstrated the latter point with his Bureau of Reclamation that "made the desert bloom." In the postwar years we have continued the fundamental transformation of arid environments, which is in no way "reclaiming" the past, but instead "creating" a present. We have also created a second climatic transformation, not one oriented toward agriculture but rather one aimed at "completing" the European settlement of the United States. Within a nation of persons whose ancestors came mostly from Europe, the hot-wet and hotter-dry climates in the American Southeast and Southwest seemed daunting to many European settlers. In agriculture these regions were ultimately taken into the economic realm of the United States for the production of subtropical crops and the open-range production of cattle and sheep. But for the practice of trade, finance, and manufacturing, these areas were avoided except for what was a basic minimum of population. New Orleans, the largest city of the South for more than a century, was considered highly unhealthy; Charleston, its nearest rival for much of that time, was routinely abandoned in summer as its elite moved to "resorts" in the North and the Appalachians. The South and Southwest were seen as basically unhealthy until (in a limited way) they were taken up as winter resorts with the coming of railroads in the 1880s, in the first application of what was then called "medical climatology." Hot regions in the United States could make only a rather constrained seasonal appeal until the years after 1945, when air conditioning changed not the climate itself but rather human perception of it. Absolute physical geography was the same as it had always been, but the human geography was transformed by the technical ability to transform sensate climate. In Canada a similar "amelioration" was sought in her season of trial, the winter, through the creation of underground cities, shopping centers, and university campuses. This experience suggests that in place of a simplistic analysis of American regions in terms of an "immutable" physical geography and an "unchanging" economic geography, it is better to view American space as broken into regions with a historical geography that is always changing and a social geography that must be evolutionary.

Any study of human migration has always been about people rather than about physical geography or economic activity. Both those influences affect mobility, but in the end human will rather than physical determinism guides the geographical course of any movement. What we need, then, is to understand *the human geography of American space*, viewed in an evolutionary sense, if we seek to understand the present-day historical geography of the

United States. Working so close to the present faces us with peculiar analytical problems since events are not finished, even by episode let alone by the full course of change. The solution to this problem lies in the establishment of processes that work over both space and time. We have considered at length two of these—mobility and regional balance—to which may be added a third that has become both operational and powerful in the postwar years that here concern us. This force has been the widespread adoption by Americans of age-specific residence, leading to the process of generational shift in geographical residence, viewed both in local (metropolis and its exurban penumbra) and national terms.

The enhanced mobility of youthful America after World War II rapidly enlarged the balancing forces within American regions. The immediate post-1945 migration to California allowed that state to grow by more than 50 percent in the decade of the 1940s, a rate basically continued in the next decade despite the much higher base in 1950. The works of young writers in this period seemed to make such interregional shifts a common aspect of youth. Those who could not move to California demonstrated their awareness of the transformed nature of American life by moving to the suburbs, making a metropolitan tilt in this period to match the national one. And among southern blacks migration "out" was seen as a way to gain greater freedom and equality than could then be found in their traditional home. Hispanics were widely attracted to cities throughout the country during the postwar years, in search of a prosperity they had never been able to secure in the countryside in their Latin America homelands or as initial immigrants as agricultural workers in the United States. In both these flows of "non-whites," it was the young who picked up stakes to seek a better world beyond their birthplace. That generational shift began in absolute terms well before 1945, but there can be no question that this was the time when its practice became a national characteristic for all groups. It was the young who made it so.

California, an area where elderly New Englanders had gone to spend their declining years in the 1870s and where Iowans seeking to retire in the 1930s found a year-round warmth, became more youthful. In 1940 the median age in California was 33 years, the oldest of all the then-48 states and four years older than the median for the country as a whole. By 1970, after the full impact of the postwar migration, California and the United States had identical median ages of 28 years, and 19 states had older average populations, with Florida being the oldest, on the average. In metropolitan areas there was a similar enhancement of the youth of the suburban band when compared with the population of the central cities. The two settlement frontiers had become the residence of the young.

The cultural impact of such shifts can easily be imagined. Whereas California had been perceived before the war as a valetudinarian haunt, it became after that conflict the citadel of a newly important youth culture. Particularly with the advent of the Beats in the 1950s, the appeal of the Golden State became greener. By the end of that decade the next maturing generation looked upon San Francisco and the West in general, as the land of change and freedom, as opposed to the traditional practices and values commonly associated with the Northeast and Middle West. These followers of the Beats, soon to be called Beatniks, flooded San Francisco and its environs, hoping to find there a radically different culture, only to discover that the Beats had been few in number and had now gone off to the countryside at Big Sur or to wilderness in the Cascade Mountains. They left behind a youthful and cosmopolitan society, but one not disaffected from a broader national culture. After a year or so of increasing disillusionment in San Francisco, the Beatniks began a national wandering. A diaspora of these disaffected youths settled widely, if not for long, encouraging the growth of pockets of "cultural opposition" in a number of cities, particularly those possessed of the more cosmopolitan universities.

Within cities there came to be *oppositional areas* in the core city, which significantly avoided the youthful destinations of the 1950s in the suburbs. Abandonment by striving youth and some older components of the population had left the central area largely to an underclass of recent immigrants—blacks from the South, Hispanics, and Asians. Native whites seeking to oppose American culture, which the Vietnam war had made them see as highly faulted, were not in any way tainted by neighboring with the underclass, whom they

perceived as victims of that same majority culture.

All this social and political ferment, certainly a major force in determining the human geography of the United States in the 1960s and 1970s, served to shape American social geography independent of economy and physical geography. It is hard to consider human geography during the postwar decades without being struck by the dominating role that age has played. Those who were young at the close of the war began geographical shifts that defined much of the use of American, and to a lesser degree Canadian, space during this period. The westward tilt of settlement, the adoption of a topological conception and usage of the national space, the move to the suburbs and the creation there of what came to be seen as the most typical expression of American life, and the expansion of vacation travel from intraregional to national and intercontinental all had youthful pioneers.

Once age divisions had arisen, those of advancing years were encouraged, if not forced, to create their own transformation of what before the war had tended to be a more familial pattern of mobility. Within metropolitan areas the "adult community" was created by developers in a deliberate isolation of older people from the daily familial life that had been the traditional environment of advancing age. This change was aided by the introduction during the New Deal of Social Security payments that permitted the old to be economically self-sufficient, and thereby to live in separate households. The generational split, first internal to the metropolis, soon took on a national importance, since it was only a short step from the age-divided residence within the city to a geographical separation of residence on a national scale.

Even before 1945 there was a geography of seasonal resort. With the age-separation introduced by the hypermobility of the young after 1945 and the pensioning of the old, conditions had been set by the mid-1950s for the transformation of a geography of seasonal resort into one of permanent retirement residence. The greatest appeal existed for retirement to areas of warm, or at least mild, winters; that is, to the former areas of winter resort. Because such resorts had been affordable to only a relatively small component of the population and for no more than a short season, the introduction of retirement populations to these areas worked a radical transformation in the scale of in-migration and in the actual life-style. Florida was the objective for retirement from the most populous part of the country and took the brunt of this brand-new flood. The Sunshine State grew in population from the twenty-seventh state in 1940 to the seventh in 1980, experiencing a 78.7 percent growth in the first great retirement decade (1950–59) and even a 43.5 percent growth in the most recent decade (1970–79) (Table 18.3). It is predicted to become our fourth-most-populous state by 1990. For comparison, California grew from fifth in population to first in that interval, having a proportionately more-rapid growth in the 1940s (43.9 percent) and a more-modest 18.5 percent increase in the last decade.

It is commonly argued that recent movement has been a shift to the Sunbelt, but careful analysis shows that term to be less than adequate to explain the geographical pattern of full migration, much of which has been of the young as well as of the old. The young have continued to move widely (in search of various opportunities), whereas the elderly have shown a proclivity to retire in more narrowly defined areas, often moving only to their previous areas of resort, summer as well as winter. All the previously dominated area has experi-enced an above-average growth in population except for the central and northern Great Plains area (Table 18.3). Even northern New England, previously part of the dominated area, has grown faster than the nation, probably because of migration there of retirees seeking the same physical and social factors that had made this one of our earliest resort areas. In the South and even in the border states, the Appalachian region as well as the coast grew, as did Arkansas in the Ozarks-Ouachitas, which grew faster than California. Economic activities attracting the young apparently drew new workers to the southern Great Plains, Wyoming, and Montana, whereas migration of retired persons enhanced the growth of all the Rocky Mountain states and parts of the Great Basin, particularly Nevada and Arizona. A similar correspondence of more-moderate economic growth joined with now-reduced flows of retirees to continue the expansion of the Pacific Coast populations. Thus, it is possible to explain the postwar shifts in American population in terms of age-specific geographical objectives within each group, but it is more than just a shift toward the sun. It is also the filling out and balancing of economy, society, and culture within what was, until 1940, the American dominated area.

In our time, push factors seem to have gained on those that pull us to specific locales. Since the 1930s, events in Europe such as the

Table 18.3 Percentage Increase of Population by States, 1970–1979

Rank	State	Percent increase (1970–1979)	Rank	State	Percent increase (1970–1979)
1	Nevada	63.8	16	Georgia	19.1
2	Arizona	53.1	17	Arkansas	18.9
3	Florida	43.5	18	California	18.5
4	Wyoming	41.3	19	Tennessee	16.9
5	Utah	37.9	20	North Carolina	15.7
6	Alaska	32.8	21	Louisiana	15.4
7	Idaho	32.4	22	Vermont	15.0
8	Colorado	30.8	23	Virginia	14.9
9	New Mexico	28.1	24	Mississippi	13.7
10	Texas	27.1	25	Kentucky	13.7
11	Oregon	25.9	26	Montana	13.3
12	Hawaii	25.3	27	Maine	13.2
13	New Hampshire	24.8	28	Alabama	13.1
14	Washington	21.1	29	W. Virginia	11.8
15	South Carolina	20.5		U.S. average	11.4

Nazi practice of genocide against the Jews and others created a new diaspora that eventually led heavily to the United States. Since that time smaller conflicts have driven Arabs to America to escape Middle Eastern strife, great numbers of people from former Indo-China to follow in the wake of the departing American troops, and uncounted people from Latin America and the Caribbean to flee the cancerous growth of population and poverty there. So much of this movement has been close to panicked flight that great numbers of somewhat reluctant and ill-equipped immigrants have arrived to tax the strength of the American reception areas where immigrants were traditionally acculturated, namely the cities.

Those cities have lost relative strength as the younger and more aspiring left for other regions, or at least for the suburbs. In the 19th century, cities receiving immigrants had great need for massive amounts of simple labor, but today the cities' needs can be met with far fewer people than have arrived. Poverty, hopelessness, and a seeming breakdown in the processes of upward social and economic mobility have affected many of these recent arrivals, of Hispanics in most large American cities, of blacks who left the South immediately after World War II, and more recently of Asians. Urban unemployment sometimes seems to be the result of racial discrimination, when often it is merely the result of a change in an occupational structure that once used a long-continuing in-migration of persons with little to offer beyond their physical strength. Blacks who have made their way in the present-day occupational structure have achieved social and economic mobility, and have become part of the geographical mobility. Because the reception area for newcomers remains in the cities (although cities with major international airports have now supplanted cities with ports, none of which handles any significant passenger-steamship service today), the social acculturation and the economic-assimilation processes still must take place there. With the decreased real economic need for unskilled immigrants, there have been numerous failures in the assimilation process, resulting in a growth of crime and antisocial behavior in the hearts of the larger cities. This behavior has been intensified by the use of such cities as the site of the social opposition areas created not by those coming in from outside who seek to become part of America, but rather by those from inside who seek to detach themselves from socialized American life, often through the use of drugs. In either instance antisocial behavior is likely to occur.

This collection within cities of those not admitted to, or voluntarily departing from, the normal aspects of American life has created yet another push factor, one that encourages the departure of the socially and economically integrated population from the traditional city. As public safety has become a particular issue, many older persons have departed to seek safety in the suburbs or even in more distant regions. Before 1945 cities were perceived by many in the country as morally corrupting; now they are perceived even by their own older citizens as unsafe, thus adding to the generational shift begun by the young.

THE CONTINUOUS SHAPING OF NORTH AMERICA

In 1920 Americans could expect to live 54 years, on the average. Today that figure is twenty years longer, although men and women have diverged by seven years of life expectation (in 1982 men could expect 71 years but women 78) where they were just a year apart at the beginning of the century. In this same period, which remains fully within the historical experience of more than 16 million Americans, our national population has more than doubled, from 106 million in 1920 to 239 million in 1985. This scale of population change would be expected to create a major transformation of the American landscape, but that metamorphosis has been enlarged even further by the scale of interregional migration. In only the most recent period for which data are available, 1975 to 1980, more than 11 million persons engaged in internal migration: the greatest single group left the Middle West (3.5 million), with the Northeast only slightly behind (3.1 million); the greatest objective of movement was the South (4.7 million), followed by the West (3.1 million); the more narrowly defined South Atlantic areal division gained a net in-migration of more than 1 million, and the Middle Atlantic and East North Central divisions lost more than 1 million each. These figures suffice to show the origins of the regional balancing that has re-shaped America in our lifetime—not from externally based immigration, although it remains relatively high. Since 1820 more than 50 million persons have been immigrants to the United States, and even in the last decade (1970–79) nearly a tenth of that 160-year total has arrived, so that the role of our cities as the reception areas for acculturation has persisted in full measure. When we add the historical proclivity of Americans to move restlessly about to this continuation of what stands as one of the world's great folk movements, it is not surprising that mobility is the essence of American life and that balance has become the salient characteristic of American space.

It is possible here to examine only a few of the more striking features in the geography of a vast nation of 3.5 million square miles, a nation that is twice as populous as it was in the youth of millions of still active Americans. Sufficient notice has been taken of mobility and regional balance, but in conclusion greater emphasis should be placed on the emergence of two related features of America's present-day human geography.

The first in time was the onset of the age-specific geography of residence, certainly present in the past but made a national norm in the period we have considered here. The post-war suburb and the creation by a youth culture of a topological conception of the use of national space divided the spatial perception of the generations. The "greening" of California came as the first of a number of interregional migrations of note, employing the longer stride of the young to show the way by which this generational separation of residence could create a new American geography. In time other areas came more into use; much space within the South Atlantic states became the objective of the elderly persons less vigorous than the hypermobile of the late 1940s. The rise of retirement, signaled by the increment of twenty years on our average lifespan and supported by the introduction of Social Security, involved a previously parochialized element of our population in this expanding generational separation.

The second feature of this new human geography, a logical outgrowth of the first, appeared as the elevation of shared "life-style" to the level of a new determinant of social loca-tion, an ultimate component of our historical geography. Age separation led the way, and a greater choice of livable locations has made further clustering of people by cultural attitudes and practices a possibility. The kinesis that came into American life during the war in Vietnam served as a catalyst for a further geographical separation in America's cultural geography. Marital and sexual orientation led groups to different areas, as did recreational desires, wishes in the raising of a family's children, broadening occupational choices, and a number of basically aesthetic and cultural preferences.

American space has gained a social complexity that was previously unknown. It has also lost the previously strong distinction between rural and urban life and residence, encouraged by the cultural aspects of regional balance here noted. Geographical domination has declined because of a wider spreading of the broad range of economic activities and the contemporaneous shaping of a complex national culture, one accepting the validity of diverse life-styles. The average American today is more traveled, less chauvinistic, and more receptive of other cultural practices, both within the nation and in the world at large, than were his parents or are the citizens of most other countries today. The frontiers of America have always been expansive spatially, but now they are increasingly so culturally, creating the elements of a historical geography that is as complex socially as our space has always been physically.

The postwar years were times of change in Canada as well as the United States, but there conditions were sufficiently different to make a joint consideration difficult and excessively comparative. We must settle instead for a few general remarks relating to the different working of the significant spatial processes to the north of the 49th parallel. To understand the relationship we should note that in the early decades, French settlement in Canada and English settlement in what became the United States were quite similar, with economic domination by France as strong as was England's. The fundamental contrast came in the matter of mobility, wherein the French Canadian was often more footloose than his American neighbors.

With Britain's capture of Canada in 1763, a new and strange frontier was introduced to surround the French, reaching from Britain's oldest colony in Newfoundland, through the non-revolting British colonies of Nova Scotia and New Brunswick and the Eastern Townships of Lower Canada, to the barrier of an Upper Canada peopled from the British Isles. The only open French frontier lay toward Ungava, where nature soon drew a harsh line against peasant settlement. The French Canadian, driven from his own settlement frontiers to the west and even from much of the life of his cities at home, became the first immobilized North American. What migration he could undertake in the 19th century was mainly southward into the more economically open and dynamic society of the New England mill towns.

With the French thus largely barred from the spread across the vast continental interior of North America, the area from the Arctic Ocean to the Rio Grande became the realm for economic domination by the assortment of transferred European mercantilists commonly thought of in Canada as "British," but existing as a group mainly united by language rather than by ethnic origin.

Most of what can be said about the dominated area of the United States before 1945 can also be said about Canada west of Sault Ste. Marie, but with the qualification that emancipation from domination has been slower and harder to achieve in the Canadian West. Only quite recently has the manumission of the Prairies and British Columbia seemed at all possible, even if not yet so clearly accomplished as the balancing that now exists within American regionalism. Economic domination by Ontario and the English-speaking business component of Montreal is still strongly perceived by western Canadians. The Liberal Party, which controlled the Canadian Parliament for most of the postwar period, has been at best a regional party, with most of its support in Ontario and Québec. Only the startling 1984 Progressive Conservative Party sweep, which saw Québec drop heavily away from the Liberal narrow-regional alliance and when even Ontario shifted its majority, created a nationwide political consensus similar to the one the New Deal provided in working toward regional balance a generation earlier in the United States. The immobility of the French remains a distinction that sets Canadian geographical experience

apart from American. The rise of the Parti Québécois, with its call for a "sovereignty association" that could be used to enforce cultural pluralism on all of Canada, has come partially from that geographical immurement. As long as another language and its culture are seen as dominant by French Canadians, the Francophone will be perceived as a geographically inhibited North American, afflicted by an English domination of mercantile trade and barred from mobility even within Canada.

In this geographically constraining situation the French Canadians began a "quiet revolution" in 1960, when they started to abandon the retreat to the countryside that their ancestors had used as a defense of their language, religion, and culture after the British capture of 1763. For two centuries the cities and the urban Canadian economy and culture were left almost wholly to those mercantilist "English." But in the 1960s the French began to flood into the cities, particularly Montreal, where vigorous efforts were made to limit and turn back the use of the English language. In this provincial context the Canadian started to implement the age-specific residential choice found among Americans but only in metropolitan terms. The creation of life-style distinctions still increased in both major sections of Canadian society, although on parallel rather than on coincidental courses. In any consideration of the historical geography of Canada since 1945, this cultural separation presents a striking contrast to the evolution found in the United States. One North American experience, however, is shared by all. Ethnicity and language do form internal cleavages, but the broadest aspects of culture and the use of space are continental. Although based on a provincial land area that is vast by European standards, Québec must still feel immured within a North American context of free and widely practiced mobility.

As in so many aspects of modern life, Canada seems to partake of American evolution, but a time lag there leaves some problems yet unresolved that might have become less urgent in the United States. At the same time, Canada through that lag avoids some recent problems for Americans. With that fact partly in mind the nationalistic Trudeau governments of the Liberal Party sought increasingly to insulate Canada from the full culture of the United States. Between two neighbors who share the largest bilateral trade in the world, the most open and frequently crossed border between major nations, and the closest common historical and geographical inheritance of any two vast countries, such an artificial segregation is likely to be quite ineffectual. The possession of a common historical geography of necessity leads to a shared evolution toward a North American use of space. The rejection of the Liberal Party's narrow regionalism in the 1984 election came in

considerable part because Québec turned away from the notion of special status in a special region and risked its future on the creation of an ultimate regional balance in Canada. In the same way the Dominion turned away from economic nationalism to hazard its future in closer economic ties with the United States and in a North American context wherein distinction decreasingly led to discrimination and dominance.

ADDITIONAL READING

Books

Adams, J.S., ed. *Contemporary Metropolitan America*. 4 vols. Cambridge: Ballinger, 1976.

Blouet, B.W., and Lawson, M.P., eds. *Images of the Plains: The Role of Human Nature in Settlement*. Lincoln: University of Nebraska Press, 1975.

Firey, W.I. *Land Use in Central Boston*. New York: Greenwood Press, 1947.

Gottmann, J. *Megalopolis: The Urbanized Northeastern Seaboard of the United States*. New York: The Twentieth Century Fund, 1961.

Hart, J.F., ed. *Regions of the United States*. New York: Harper & Row, 1972.

Hudson, J.C. *Plains Country Towns*. Minneapolis: University of Minnesota Press, 1985.

Issel, W. *Social Change in the U.S. 1945–83*. Boston: Schocken Books, 1985.

Jackson, J.B. *American Space. The Centennial Years: 1865–1876*. New York: W.W. Norton, 1972.

McCann, L.D., ed. *Heartland and Hinterland: A Geography of Canada*. Scarborough: Prentice-Hall of Canada, 1982.

McWilliams, C. *Southern California Country: An Island on the Land*. New York: Duell, Sloan & Pierce, 1946.

Meinig, D.W. *Southwest. Three Peoples in Geographical Change*. New York: Oxford University Press, 1971.

Muller, P.O. *Contemporary Suburban America*. Englewood Cliffs: Prentice-Hall, 1981.

Rose, H.W. *The Black Ghetto: A Spatial Perspective*. New York: McGraw-Hill, 1971.

Spectorsky, A.C. *The Exurbanites*. Philadelphia: J.B. Lippincott, 1955.

Ullman, E. *Geography as Spatial Interaction*. Seattle: University of Washington Press, 1980.

Vance, J.E., Jr. *The Merchant's World: The Geography of Wholesaling*. Englewood Cliffs: Prentice-Hall, 1972.

———. *Location in a System of Global Extent: A Social Geographical Model of Settlement*. Reading: University of Reading Geographical Papers, 1982.

Warkentin, J., ed. *Canada: A Geographical Interpretation*. Toronto: Methuen, 1968.

Yeates, M. *Main Street: Windsor to Quebec City*. Toronto: Macmillan of Canada, 1975.

Zelinsky, W. *The Cultural Geography of the United States*. Englewood Cliffs: Prentice-Hall, 1973.

Index

Acadia, 227, 232; changes in, 8; deportation of Acadians, 90–91; French settlement, 72, 74, 78, 80, 83, 85–86, 89
L'Action Française, 404
Adams-Onis treaty, 284–85
Agriculture: barley, 78, 137; beans, 70, 106; bees and honey production, 139; British North American, 220, 225, 232–33; Canada, 375, 377, 399, 382, 386, 389–91, 397, 399; Chesapeake colony, 106, 109; commercialization of, 199–200, 204–6; cotton and weather frontier, 424; dairy products, 206–7, 333; dry farming, 276–77, 420; economic readjustment and reorganization, 204–7; in Far West, 287–90, 293–97; fruit orchards, 137, 294; grains, 18, 172–74, 178; interregional ties, 136–44; milk production, 137–38; northeast America, 65, 67, 69–70, 74, 83; oats, 78, 137, 259, 268, 275; Québec Province, 240–43; regional specializations, technological changes, 326–34; squash, 70, 106; sun belt and environment, 433–34; trans-Appalachian development, 172–94; *see also* Corn; Cotton; Rice; Sugar; Tobacco; Wheat
Aircraft, life styles changed by, 411, 441, 449
Alabama, 82; frontier economy, 170–71; Spanish exploration, 44, 51; westward movement and land claims, 150, 154
Alaska, frontier expansion, 17
America, naming of, 39–40
Amerian Indians: 50, 52–54, 66–68, 70–72, 74, 79, 82, 90, 99, 126, 149, 163, 223, 225–26, 256, 261, 264–66, 271; aboriginal landscape, 25–26; Creek Treaty of 1790, 167; cultural regions, 16, 26–29; Curtis Act, 1898, 254; Dawes Act, 1887, 265; disease affecting, 126; and explorers, 45; Far Western tribes, 279–82, 297; fire, use by Indians, 29; Fort Peck Reservation, 265; Great Plains, 264–66; land cessions, 162–65, 167, 256–57, 264; reservations and organizations of society, 18–20; as slave owners, 165; and social origins of settlers, 97, 99, 112; trade and westward movement, 149; U.S. Peace Policy, 264–65; Wounded Knee massacre, 264–65
American Rectangular Land Survey System, 130, 155–62
Amish, rural settlement and property, 127, 130
Appalachia: settlement, 149; Spanish exploration, 44
Arizona, early Spanish settlement, 53–54, 62
Arkansas, Spanish exploration, 44
Assimilation: Canada, 400; frontier movement, 200; Great Plains, 256, 265; migrants and suburbanization, 317–19
Aztec-Maya culture, 3, 50

Baltimore and Ohio Railroad, 175, 202, 214, 322–33
Bison, buffalo, 18
Black Hills, 264, 266–68
Blacks: population growth, 122–23, 125–27; urban housing, 429–31
Breweries, 79, 394, 396

Bridger, Jim, 284
Britain: Anglo-American settlers, 93–120; eastern seaboard settlement, 45–47; Far West movement, 148, 282–85
British Columbia, 223, 226
British North America: cultural landscape, 220–53; Loyalists in, 220–53
British North America Act of 1867, 373, 375, 378, 405
Brown, Ralph H., 6–7
Burlington Railroad, 272

Cabot, John, 37–38
California: early Spanish settlement, 50, 55–56, 60, 62; gold, 288, 290–91; settlement, 287–88, 290
Calvinism, in Colonial America, 126–27
Canada: Agricultural Rehabilitation and Development Act, 406; Agricultural and Rural Development Act, 406; agriculture, 69, 382, 386, 389–91, 397; bilingual education, 400, 404; breweries, 394, 396; British and French in, 220–53; coal production, 386, 388; commerce and trade, 396–98; economic policies, 382–400; energy requirements, 386, 388–89; fishing, 66, 68, 391–92; fox-ranching, 381; France in northeast America, 65–92; French settlement, 75, 78–80, 82–83, 85–89, 91; Fund for Rural Economic Development, 406; gold, 375, 377, 382, 392–93; growth, 248–49, 382–400; homesteading, 378–79, 382, 389–90; hydroelectric power, 382, 386, 388–89, 406; industrial expansion, 373, 393–94, 396–98; iron and steel, 393–94, 396; labor movement, 400, 403; livestock production, 379, 382, 389–91; manufacturing, 393–94, 396–98; Métis, 225, 375, 378, 400; mineral deposits, 382, 386, 392, 406; Montreal settlement and influence, 220, 225, 234, 248–49; nationalization, 373–409; organization of society, 16–19; petroleum production, 382; public lands and government policy, 377–78; pulp and paper mills, 382, 386, 392, 397, 406; railroads and nationalization, 373, 375, 378–79, 382; settlement along St. Lawrence, 70, 73–74; 78, 82–83, 85–86, 89, 220, 223, 227, 236, 372–82; silver and nickel, 243, 382, 393; tariff, national policy, 388–89, 391, 394; textiles, 393–94; timberlands, 375, 392–93; 20th-century tensions, 400–408; urbanization and anxieties concerning, 384–86, 397, 400, 402–4; westward movement, 384–85; wheat production, 382, 386, 389–91, 404; *see also* Northeast American
Canadian National Railway, 386
Canadian Northern Railroad, 386
Canadian Pacific Railroad, 378–79, 382, 386, 392, 398
Canals, 240–45; northeastern regional integration, 201–2; promoting economic growth, 173, 175–76, 181–84, 236, 242–43, 321–26; use of, for regional trading, 201, 203, 205–6, 211, 213
Cape Breton Island, 232–33; fish and fisheries, 66, 68, 90; French settlement, 83, 86
Capital and capitalism, in colonial settlements, 13, 17